MW01174759

International Handbook of E-learning, Volume 1

The *International Handbook of E-learning, Volume 1* provides a comprehensive compendium of research and theory in all aspects of e-learning, one of the most significant ongoing global developments in the entire field of education. Covering history, design models, instructional strategies, best practices, competencies, evaluation, assessment, and more, these twenty-seven contributions tackle the tremendous potential and flexibility inherent in this rapidly growing new paradigm. Past and present empirical research frames each chapter, while future research needs are discussed in relation to both confirmed practice and recent changes in the field. The book will be of interest to anyone seeking to create and sustain meaningful, supportive learning environments within today's anytime, anywhere framework, from teachers, administrators, and policy makers to corporate and government trainers.

Dr. Badrul H. Khan is the founder of McWeadon Education, a professional development institution. He previously served as Founding Director of the Educational Technology Leadership (ETL) graduate cohort program at The George Washington University, Founding Director of the Educational Technology (ET) graduate program at the University of Texas, Brownsville, and Instructional Designer and Evaluation Specialist in the School of Medicine at Indiana University, Indianapolis. Professor Khan has the credit of first coining the phrase "web-based instruction" and popularizing the concept through his bestselling 1997 book *Web-Based Instruction*, which paved the way for the new field of e-learning.

Dr. Mohamed Ally is Professor in the Centre for Distance Education and Researcher in the Technology Enhanced Knowledge Research Institute (TEKRI) at Athabasca University, Canada. He previously served as Director of the Centre of Distance Education at Athabasca University, Canada's Open University. He is Past President of the International Federation of Training and Development Organizations (IFTDO) and a Founding Director of the International Association of Mobile Learning (IamLearn).

The Routledge International Handbook Series

The Routledge International Handbook of the Arts and Education
Edited by Mike Fleming, John O'Toole and Loira Bresler

The Routledge International Handbook of English, Language and Literacy Teaching
Edited by Dominic Wyse, Richard Andrews and James Hoffman

The Routledge International Handbook of the Sociology of Education
Edited by Michael W. Apple, Stephen J. Ball and Luis Armand Gandin

The Routledge International Handbook of Higher Education
Edited by Malcolm Tight, Ka Ho Mok, Jeroen Huisman and Christopher C. Morpew

The Routledge International Companion to Multicultural Education
Edited by James A. Banks

The Routledge International Handbook of Creative Learning
Edited by Julian Sefton Green, Pat Thomson, Ken Jones and Liora Bresler

The Routledge International Handbook of Critical Education
Edited by Michael W. Apple, Wayne Au, and Luis Armando Gandin

The Routledge International Handbook of Lifelong Learning
Edited by Peter Jarvis

The Routledge International Handbook of Early Childhood Education
Edited by Tony Bertram, John Bennett, Philip Gammage and Christine Pascal

The Routledge International Handbook of Lifelong Learning
Edited by Peter Jarvis

The Routledge International Handbook of Teacher and School Development
Edited by Christopher Day

The Routledge International Handbook of Education, Religion and Values
Edited by James Arthur and Terence Lovat

The Routledge International Handbook of Young Children's Thinking and Understanding
Edited by Sue Robson and Suzanne Flannery Quinn

Routledge International Handbook of Educational Effectiveness
Edited by Chris Chapman, Daniel Muijs, David Reynolds, Pam Sammons, Charles Teddlie

The Routledge International Handbook of Dyscalculia and Mathematical Learning Difficulties
Edited by Steve Chinn

International Handbook of E-learning, Volume 1: Theoretical Perspectives and Research
Edited by Badrul H. Khan and Mohamed Ally

International Handbook of E-learning, Volume 2: Implementation and Case Studies
Edited by Mohamed Ally and Badrul H. Khan

International Handbook of E-learning, Volume 1

Theoretical Perspectives and Research

Edited by Badrul H. Khan and Mohamed Ally

NEW YORK AND LONDON

First published 2015
by Routledge
711 Third Avenue, New York, NY 10017

and by Routledge
2 Park Square, Milton Park, Abingdon, Oxon OX14 4RN

Routledge is an imprint of the Taylor & Francis Group, an informa business

Library of Congress Cataloging-in-Publication Data

International handbook of E-learning / edited by Badrul H. Khan, Mohamed Ally.
volumes cm. — (The Routledge international handbook series)
Includes bibliographical references and index.
Contents: v. 1. Theoretical perspectives and research — v. 2. Implementation and case studies.
1. Internet in education. 2. Internet in education—Case studies. 3. Web-based instruction. 4. Web-based instruction—Case studies. 5. Distance education—Computer-assisted instruction. 6. Distance education—Computer-assisted instruction—Case studies. I. Khan, Badrul H. (Badrul Huda), 1958- editor of compilation. II. Ally, Mohamed, editor of compilation.
LB1044.87.I5564 2015
371.33'44678—dc23 2014033703

ISBN: 978-1-138-79368-2 (hbk)
ISBN: 978-1-315-76093-3 (ebk)

Typeset in Bembo, ITC Stone Sans
by Apex CoVantage, LLC

Printed and bound in the United States of America by Edwards Brothers Malloy on sustainably sourced paper

Contents

Preface ix
Foreword xi
Acknowledgments xiii
About the Editors xv
Contributing Authors xvii

1 Introduction to E-learning 1
Badrul H. Khan

2 Historical Perspectives on E-learning 41
Michael Moore

3 E-Learning: Past, Present, and Future 51
Joseph Rene Corbeil and Maria Elena Corbeil

4 The Quality of Massive Open Online Courses 65
Stephen Downes

5 Instructional Theory and Technology for the New Paradigm of Education 79
Charles M. Reigeluth

6 Pedagogical Development, E-learning and Teaching in Higher Education 93
Marti Cleveland-Innes, Stefan Hrastinski, O. Bälter and Colin Wiseman

7 Towards Effective and Less Stressful Online Collaborative Learning: Strategies to Promote Engagement While Minimizing Unnecessary Cognitive Load and Stress 115
Insung Jung, Masayuki Kudo, and Sook-Kyoung Choi

8 Formulating Best Practices and Guidelines for Emerging E-learning Technologies 127
Robert A. Wisher, Robert C. Brusso, Christina K. Curnow, Josh Hatfield, Arthur Paddock, and Randall D. Spain

9 Revisiting the Need for Strategic Planning for E-learning in Higher Education 139
Mark Bullen

10 E-learning Design—From Instructional Events to Elements 153
Florence Martin

11 Competences for Teaching and Learning in an E-learning Setting 171
Guillermo Bautista and Anna Escofet

12 Creating Online Courses Step-by-Step 181
Peter S. Cookson

13 The Role of the Online Learner: A Competential Model for Students When Learning Online 197
Federico Borges and Anna Forés

14 Collaborative Design Models for Blended, Online, and Traditional Courses: Five Approaches That Empower Students and Educators in the Twenty-first Century 207
Craig Perrier

15 Learner Interaction in E-learning 217
Cynthia D. Cummings, Diane R. Mason, Sheryl R. Abshire, and Daryl Ann Borel

16 VISCAL: A Practical Guide for Adapting Face-to-Face Course Materials for Effective Online Delivery 227
Emily A. Moore

17 Practical Strategies for Motivating and Retaining E-learners 247
Andrea Henne

18 Accessibility and Instructional Design in E-learning 257
Cindy Poore-Pariseau

19 An Overview of Accessible E-learning 269
Aina G. Irbe and Jonathan Avila

20 E-learning Evaluation 279
John G. Hedberg and Thomas C. Reeves

21 Designing and Evaluating E-learning Interactions 295
João Mattar

22 A Theory of Mobile Learning 309
Helen Crompton

23 Developing Instructional Materials and Assessments for Mobile Learning 319
Jack A. Hyman

24 Emerging Learning Ecologies as a New Challenge and Essence for E-learning 331
Antonella Esposito, Albert Sangrà and Marcelo Fabián Maina

25 The Leadership Imperative for Higher Education in the Twenty-first Century 343
Narimane Hadj-Hamou

26 Leadership Challenges in Online Distance Education 357
John Nworie

27 Beyond E-learning: Rethinking Purpose and Design 375
Yoany Beldarrain

Glossary *385*
Index *389*

Preface

The field of e-learning has matured significantly since I first started to work on the *Web-Based Instruction* book in 1995 (Educational Technology Publications). Its enormous acceptance worldwide has resulted in invitations to speak in different parts of the world. Through these experiences, I have learned about online learning initiatives globally, have had the privilege of meeting many researchers and practitioners, and can say that, in my humble opinion, among all emerging and new disciplines, e-learning is the fastest and the most recognized internationally. I always felt that there was a tremendous need for someone to compile the diversity of experiences, applications, and practices of e-learning from different parts of the world. This endeavor of putting together the two volumes of the *International Handbook of E-learning* is the result. After developing the proposal for the handbook, I realized that by myself I could not accomplish the huge task of putting together the handbook. The first individual I thought of who could greatly contribute to the handbook is none other than Professor Mohamed Ally, an expert in mobile learning with whom I worked on several global e-learning projects, including "ICT and E-Learning in the Middle East," a special May/June 2010 issue of *Educational Technology*. I am very pleased to have him as my partner in this endeavor.

Badrul H. Khan

In both volumes of the international handbook, we tried to include e-learning theoretical practices, research, and case studies from different parts of the world. Some authors are not native speakers of English; therefore their presentation of materials in their respective chapters may appear different. We tried to keep their original expression and did not attempt to modify them. This allows the reader to get the essence of what is happening in different parts of the world. Diversity is an integral part of e learning, and this handbook is not any different in that sense. I am delighted to be co-editing both volumes of the international handbook with Dr. Badrul H. Khan, who is a world leader in the field of e-learning. He has published many book and papers in the field of e-learning and his books have been translated into many languages.

Mohamed Ally

Foreword

This compendium of 57 chapters in the two volumes is presented as an international handbook of e-learning even though a majority of the authors are from Canada and the USA. Does this matter? When I served as a senior official of UNESCO, which brings together nearly 200 member states, we required a greater diversity and spread of country participation before calling a project 'international'.

The essential point, however, is not the variety of national flags on the papers, but whether, taken as a whole, the contributions in these volumes give a genuinely international perspective on e-learning. I give credit to the editors for even attempting to pull together a global picture of such a fast-moving field. The effort is worthwhile because, in their long journey into e-learning, most institutions have only reached the foothills, so any hints about how to surmount the challenges of the climb ahead are useful. In his annual surveys of e-learning in North America, for example, Tony Bates judged that it was only in 2013 that most institutions engaging in e-learning began to do so with an acceptable degree of competence. This means that the enterprise is now ready for lift-off, which makes this book timely.

As is all too common in writing on educational technology, most of the authors implicitly assume that e-learning began with the Internet and focus on comparing e-learning with classroom instruction. While classroom teaching will indeed be the more familiar environment for most readers, it is also important to situate e-learning within the long tradition of distance education that goes back decades, centuries, or even millennia, depending on one's reading of history.

Those who forget the past can be condemned to relive it, which explains why Bates found that institutions were taking so long to get up to speed in e-learning. In his book *Harmonizing Global Education: From Genghis Khan to Facebook*, Jon Baggeley opines that Asia does e-learning better than the West. This is because traditional distance education coexists alongside e-learning in Asian countries and the lessons from the older body of research on distance learning have not yet been forgotten.

Whether e-learning has made the techniques of distance learning converge on a common approach is an important question. Thirty years ago, the US interpreted distance education rather differently from most of the rest of the world, including, interestingly, Canada. In the US, simultaneous remote classroom instruction through video links was all the rage, whereas in other countries distance learning usually meant independent study through multimedia with tutorial support. This in turn reflected much older differences in approaches to teaching: an emphasis on tutorials and seminars in Europe and a focus on classroom teaching in America.

The Internet unquestionably brought these approaches together and, for a time in the 1990s, the virtues of 'asynchronous' communication were lauded everywhere. Although the continuing advance of technology now makes it possible to blend synchronous and asynchronous learning in a great variety of ways, it is fascinating to see how differences in approach persist. MOOCs are a striking example, as the chapter by Stephen Downes illustrates. The early Canadian MOOCs, circa 2008, were based on multidirectional discussions and multiple exchanges of open educational resources among learners, whereas the later US MOOCs, circa 2012, used unidirectional video for what was essentially a remote-classroom approach, although it was delivered asynchronously. MOOCs have diversified greatly since those 'early' days. Like many other innovations, they began in universities but may find their major application in professional training and at other levels of education.

The main conclusion that I take from the frenzy that greeted MOOCs is the (very old) lesson that purpose and process are more important than technology. As they breathlessly proclaimed MOOCs to be a revolution in higher education, the news media forgot two facts. First, history shows that higher education develops by evolution, not revolution. Second, and more importantly, the most important power that societies give to their universities is the authority to award degrees and credentials.

Open Educational Resources and MOOCs are important contributions to the e-learning space, but it is vital for the future that e-learning focus on the more challenging task of creating courses and programmes that include serious student assessment leading to credible credentials. The criticism that too much assessment in e-learning uses trivial multiple choice questions is equally valid for much traditional campus instruction, but that is not a sufficient excuse. Fortunately, groundbreaking work is being done in various places, such as the UK Open University's Knowledge Media Institute, to harness technology to the development of assessments that are both relevant and academically challenging.

This is the dynamic and exciting world that is the focus of this handbook, an enormous endeavor compiled by Badrul H. Khan and Mohamed Ally, two eminent scholars and practitioners of e-learning. I am sure that, by dipping into the variety of articles that it contains, all those who are charged with improving the quality and impact of e-learning in their institutions will find much to inspire and guide them.

Sir John Daniel
2014-08-16

Acknowledgments

We would like to thank the following reviewers of the chapters:

Abed Salem, Adolfo Tanzi Neto, Ahmed Ali, Alex Sergay, Alice Stefaniak, Amanda Funk, Amy Scott, Andrea Bosshard, Antonia Jokelova, Arifa Garman, Barbara Smith, Carlos R. Morales, Carmen Winter, Chetan Bhatt, Chris Heizer, Cindy Poore-Pariseau, Dale Mueller, Daniel Strozzi, Dave Hallmon, Dave Hildebrandt, Deyu Hu, Didem Tufan, Dustin Summey, Ellen Taricani, Emre Sezgin, Glen Gatin, Harold Jeffrey Rosen, Ida L. Rodgers, James Braman, Jennifer B. Staley, Jeremy Schwehm, Jerry Pon, Jill P. Viers, Jillian Wojcik, Kathy Jackson, Kim A. Hosler, Kim Jamison, Konstantinos Kalemis, Lisette Reyes-Paulino, Ludwika Goodson, Manuela Rodrigues, Margaret Wherry, Martin Addison, Mary Ann Remnet, Mauri Collins, Mike Menchaca, Muhammad Sabri bin Sahrir, Nicola Ritter, Nicole Dalton, Nirupama Akella, Noam Ebner, Nor Aziah Alias, Norma Ortiz Rodriguez, Pam Jimison, Patrick Devey, Patrizia Maria Margherita Ghislandi, Peter Young, Robyn Defelice, Rosemary Talab, Sabrina Leone, Shaira Ali, Shelagh McGrath, Sheri Anderson, Vrinda, William Diehl, and Zoaib Mirza.

We also want to thank Alex and colleagues of Routledge who worked with us to publish this handbook.

About the Editors

Dr. Badrul H. Khan is a world-renowned educator, author, speaker, and consultant in the field of distance education. He has 20 years of experience in developing and managing distance education programs. Professor Khan has the credit of first coining the phrase "Web-based instruction" and popularizing the concept through his 1997 best-selling *Web-Based Instruction* book, which paved the way for the new field of e-learning. In recognition of his unique contribution to the field of e-learning coupled with his services to worldwide e-learning communities, Egyptian E-Learning University Council on August 13, 2012, appointed Dr. Badrul Khan as an honorary distinguished professor of e-learning.

His *Managing E-Learning* book has been translated into 14 languages. He contributed to the development of US virtual education policies organized by the White House Office of Science and Technology Policy and the Naval Postgraduate School, the National Educational Technology Plan by the US Department of Education, and the Review of Joint Professional Military Education organized by the Joint Chiefs of Staff. He served as contributing and consulting editor of nine prestigious international learning journals and magazines. He is a past president of the International Division of the Association for Educational and Communication Technology (AECT). He authored and coauthored 11 books/manuals and over 100 papers in the field of e-learning and distance learning. He delivered keynote speeches in more than 50 international e-learning and distance learning conferences.

He is the founder of McWeadon Education (a professional development institution). He previously served as the founding Director of the Educational Technology Leadership (ETL) graduate cohort program at The George Washington University, the founding Director of the Educational Technology (ET) graduate program at the University of Texas, Brownsville and an Instructional Designer and Evaluation Specialist in the School of Medicine at Indiana University, Indianapolis. Dr. Khan has served as a consultant to distance education, learning development and human resource development projects at: (a) the World Bank, (b) the US Federal Government, (c) the Asian Development Bank, and (d) various academic institutions and corporations in the US and throughout the world. For more information, please visit his personal website: http://BadrulKhan.com/

Dr. Mohamed Ally is Professor in the Centre for Distance Education and Researcher in the Technology Enhanced Knowledge Research Institute (TEKRI) at Athabasca University in Canada. He was Director of the Centre of Distance Education at Athabasca University, Canada's Open University. He obtained his Ph.D. from the University of Alberta, Canada. His current areas of research include mobile learning, e-learning, distance education, and use of emerging learning technologies in education and training. Dr. Ally is Past President of the International Federation of Training and Development Organizations (IFTDO) and is one of the Founding Directors of the International Association of Mobile Learning (IamLearn). He recently edited seven books on the use of emerging technologies in education. His book *Mobile Learning: Transforming the Delivery of Education and Training* won the Charles A. Wedemeyer Award for significant contribution to distance education. Dr. Ally has presented keynote speeches, workshops, and papers in many countries.

Contributing Authors

Sheryl R. Abshire, Ph.D., is an Assistant Professor at Lamar University in Beaumont, Texas, U.S.A. teaching in a fully online master's program for educational leadership and technology leadership candidates. She received her Ph.D. in Educational Leadership through the University of New Orleans in New Orleans, LA, U.S.A. Dr. Abshire has served as a catalyst to initiate the integration of technology throughout the nation and internationally by providing leadership on numerous national, state, and district committees focusing on the role of technology and curriculum in changing educational practice. She is currently involved in an international electronic portfolio research initiative for the Coalition for Inter/National Electronic Portfolio Research with universities in the U.S.A., Australia, and the U.K. Her professional experience includes chief technology officer, school principal, K-5 teacher, and library/media specialist. She is the past chair of the Board for the Consortium for School Networking (CoSN), is on the K-12 Advisory Board for Blackboard, Dell's Platinum Advisory Committee, Promethean National K-12 Advisory Committee, and ISTE Standards and Accreditation Committee, and is Co-Chair of the ISTE/CoSN Policy Committee. Sheryl is past President of LACUE and serves on the FCC Universal Services Administrative Corporation (USAC) Board representing America's K-12 schools and libraries. She has received numerous awards for her work, most recently the National Coalition for Technology in Education and Training (NCTET) Community Builder Award and the ISTE Public Policy Advocate of the Year Award for her decades of work promoting educational technology.

Jonathan Avila is the Chief Accessibility Officer of SSB BART Group (SSB), a company that specializes in accessibility of information and communication technology (ICT). Jonathan has been in the field of accessibility for 15 years and has worked to implement accessibility into various frameworks, websites, and organizations. He has worked with users of assistive technology, programming screen readers to work with varied environments including call centers, office applications, and proprietary applications. He maintains best practices for accessibility of varied technology platforms including mobile, PDF, Flash, web, and Windows native software through SSB's Accessibility Management Platform (AMP).

O. Bälter is an Associate Professor at the department of Media Technology and Interaction Design at KTH—Royal Institute of Technology in Stockholm, Sweden. He teaches programming, presentation techniques and human–computer interaction. In 2009, when he was Vice Dean of Education of one of KTH's ten schools, the school was appointed Centre of Excellence in Higher Education by the Swedish National Agency for Higher Education. He has also been awarded personally for his teaching skills and was elected Teacher of the Year by the students at the School of Surveying, KTH in 1987 and was Awarded KTH's price for prominent achievements in undergraduate education in 1989. In 2008 he was STINT Fellow at Williams College, Williamstown, MA, USA through the STINT Excellence in Teaching program. Current research interests are online course design, web-based data collection and technology enhanced learning.

Guillermo Bautista is a Doctor of Pedagogy. He is a Professor on the Faculty of Psychology and Educational Sciences at the Open University of Catalonia (UOC) and researcher at the UOC eLearn Center. His areas of research are related to the integration of ICT into teaching and learning processes, teacher training in the didactic use of ICT and Smart Classrooms.

Yoany Beldarrain is Professor of Business Communication at ESB School of Business, Reutlingen University in Germany. She is an international speaker, author and consultant with over 18 years of experience in curriculum and instruction, e-learning, and administrative educational leadership. Her experiences include evaluation and assessment of e-learning initiatives, integrating multicultural approaches in the decision-making process, entrepreneurship, improving business communication and developing international management strategies. Dr. Beldarrain previously worked at Florida Virtual School as instructor and administrator, and adjunct professor at La Salle University in Philadelphia, USA. She is the coauthor of *Anonymity and Learning in Digitally Mediated Communications: Authenticity and trust in cyber education* (Hershey, PA; USA: IGI Global) and author of other book chapters and internationally peer-reviewed articles on the topic of distance learning and communication. She earned an MS degree in Educational Leadership from Nova Southeastern University, Florida, and a doctoral degree in Instructional Design for Online Learning from Capella University, Minnesota. Her research interests include best practices in e-learning, and how technology innovations influence interaction and communication, especially across cultures.

Daryl Ann Borel received a B.S. in Mathematics and an M.Ed. in Supervision specializing in Computer Science. She will complete her doctorate in Educational Leadership in 2013. She began her professional career in corporate America by working at a national insurance company. After a successful career, she left the industry to enter the education field. Ms. Borel's educational experience includes serving as Chief Information Office in the seventh largest school district in the nation, director of technology, middle and high school teacher and adjunct professor. Ms. Borel is an Adjunct Professor in the Educational Leadership Department at Lamar University in Beaumont, Texas, where she helped develop the online curriculum for the Technology Leadership Master's program, helps faculty incorporate e-learning activities into their teaching, and teaches administrative leadership and technology coursework for students enrolled in the online master's programs. Recently she has been engaged in an international research initiative regarding the use of e-Portfolios in higher education and K-12 and a research project involving the use of synchronous web conferencing in online classrooms. Ms. Borel also serves as the Executive Director of Grant Administration for the Beaumont Foundation. Her work involves awarding technology, grants and scholarships to nonprofit organizations, schools and underserved individuals across the U.S.

Federico Borges is a doctoral candidate at the Doctoral Programme in Education and E-Learning of Universitat Oberta de Catalunya (UOC), an online university based in Barcelona, Spain. His Ph.D. dissertation is about the role of the online learner. He was an online lecturer of English at UOC for over 12 years, where he also trained novice online instructors. He has authored a number of articles and book chapters on online learning and the online learner.

Robert C. Brusso, M.S., is an Associate at ICF International. He is currently working on his dissertation en route to a Ph.D. in Industrial/Organizational Psychology at Old Dominion University. His previous work is related to the employment of emerging technologies in the workplace with publications focusing on interactions between individual differences and training design elements for e-learning and videogame-based training environments. At ICF, Mr. Brusso has assisted with numerous projects related, but not limited, to technology in the workplace, selection, and training and development.

Mark Bullen, Ph.D., is the Education Specialist for e-learning at the Commonwealth of Learning in Vancouver, Canada. From 2005 to 2012 he served as the Dean and Associate Dean of the Learning & Teaching Centre at the British Columbia Institute of Technology (BCIT). Before moving to BCIT he served as Associate and Acting Director of Distance Education & Technology at the University of British Columbia (UBC) and Director of the UBC Centre for Managing and Planning e-learning.

Sook-Kyoung Choi is a doctoral candidate at the International Christian University in Japan and researches on mobile learning and online collaboration.

Marti Cleveland-Innes is Professor and Chair in the Center for Distance Education at Athabasca University in Alberta, Canada. She teaches Research Methods and Leadership in the graduate programs of this department. Martha has received awards for her work on the student experience in online environments and holds a major research grant through the Canadian Social Sciences and Humanities Research Council. In 2011 she received the Craig Cunningham Memorial Award for Teaching Excellence and in 2009 she received the President's Award for Research and Scholarly Excellence from Athabasca University. She is currently Guest Professor of Education Media Technology at The Royal Institute of Technology in Stockholm, Sweden. Her work is published in academic journals in North America and Europe. Current research interests are in the areas of leadership in open and distance higher education, online teaching and learning and the effects of emotion on learning.

Peter S. Cookson is currently a professor in the Department of Educational Technology at the Universidad DaVinci in Tamaulipas, Mexico. He has held administrative and/or graduate teaching appointments at Delaware State University (USA), Consorcio Clavijero (Veracruz, Mexico), University for Peace (Costa Rica), Athabasca University (Canada), and the Pennsylvania State University (USA). At Athabasca University he was the founding editor of International Review of Research in Open and Distance Education (www.irrodl.org). He obtained his B.S. and M.S. degrees in Sociology and Latin American Studies from Brigham Young University and his Ph.D. in Adult Education from the University of Chicago.

Joseph Rene Corbeil, Ed.D., is an associate professor at The University of Texas-Brownsville with over 15 years' experience in designing, developing, and teaching courses via e-learning. He earned his doctorate in Curriculum and Instruction with an emphasis on Instructional Technology from the University of Houston, and a Master of Education in Educational Technology from The University of Texas at Brownsville. Research interests include best practices in distance learning design, development, facilitation, and assessment; enhancing communication through synchronous and asynchronous channels; and developing and maintaining learning team collaborations in computer-mediated environments. He is currently researching effectiveness of Web 2.0 and social networking tools including wikis, blogs, instant messaging, and microblogs for enhancing social presence and teacher immediacy in e-learning environments. Other research interests include exploring the potential of 3D virtual environments for formal and informal collaborative learning. He has published articles in numerous journals and contributed chapters to books on innovations in e-learning and distance education. He has earned several awards, including the 2007 EDUCAUSE Quarterly Contribution of the Year, as well as the IACIS Best Pedagogy Paper (2007) and Best Technology Paper (2010). For his contributions to teaching he was recognized with the 2012 UT System Regents' Outstanding Teaching Award.

Maria Elena Corbeil, Ed.D., assistant professor at The University of Texas at Brownsville, earned a postgraduate certificate in Online Teaching and Learning from the University of Florida and a doctoral degree in Education in Curriculum and Instruction from the University of Houston. For twelve years, she has developed and taught fully online undergraduate and graduate educational technology courses. She has also focused on maintaining teaching excellence and program quality through the mentoring and training of online adjunct faculty. She currently has publications in national and international journals, book chapters, and conference proceedings in the areas of best practices and innovations in the design, development, and implementation of web-based distance education courses. Articles she has published received awards, including, the 2007 and 2011 Selected Papers from the International Conference on College Teaching and Learning, the 2007 IACIS Best Pedagogy Paper Award, and the 2007 EDUCAUSE Quarterly Contribution of the Year. In 2011, in recognition of her outstanding teaching, scholarship, and service, she was honored with the IACIS Ben Bauman Teaching Excellence Award.

Helen Crompton received her Ph.D. in technology and mathematics education from the University of North Carolina in Chapel Hill. Crompton is currently an Assistant Professor in the Department of Teaching and Learning at Old Dominion University, Virginia. Crompton studies the field of mobile learning, with a particular emphasis on context-aware ubiquitous learning, which is a subcategory of mobile learning. Crompton is also an Instructional Consultant and a member of faculty for the International Society for Technology in Education (ISTE).

Cynthia D. Cummings, Ed. D., earned her doctorate in Educational Leadership from Lamar University. She is an Assistant Professor in the Educational Leadership and Technology Department, Lamar University in Beaumont, Texas, U.S.A. where she teaches master's and doctoral level educational leadership and technology courses in a fully online program. Dr. Cummings' professional experience also includes elementary and secondary classroom teacher, central office administrator, and consultant. She recently developed the American Education Reaches Out (AERO) English Language Arts framework for the US State Department's Office of Overseas Schools. In addition to her expertise in English Language Arts, Dr. Cummings is recognized for her expertise in technology and its integration in content areas. In 2010–11 she served on a Texas Education Agency committee to revise technology curriculum standards. Her research interests include school improvement, technology, global leadership, online learning, and professional learning. She is currently involved in an international electronic portfolio research initiative for the Coalition for Inter/National Electronic Portfolio Research with universities in the U.S.A., Australia, and the U.K.

Christina K. Curnow is the Director of the Center for Workforce Research and Performance and a Vice President at ICF International. She has over 18 years of experience conducting research and evaluations related to training, leadership and e-learning. She has worked with clients across the full spectrum of federal and state governments. Dr. Curnow holds a Ph.D. in Industrial and Organizational Psychology from The George Washington University.

Stephen Downes A researcher for the National Research Council of Canada since 2001, Stephen Downes brings 20 years of education technology and new instructional media design expertise to the development of new online learning environments. Downes is widely known for his online newsletter, OLDaily, in addition to publications in such fields as learning objects, learning management systems, personal learning environments, and open educational resources. Downes is a pioneer in the field of learning networks and learning content syndication, and built the world's first MOOC software, gRSShopper. Today Downes manahes the NRC's Learning and Performance Support Systems research program, a federally funded initiative linking learners with learning opportunities and personal professional development and support.

Anna Escofet, 1996, is Doctor of Pedagogy, Professor at the Faculty of Pedagogy at the University of Barcelona. Her areas of research are related to the educational uses of ICT, distance learning and empowerment and the digital gap.

Antonella Esposito is currently a Ph.D. candidate in the Education and ICT (E-learning) doctoral program at the Universitat Oberta de Catalunya (UOC). Her doctoral dissertation investigates the emerging learning ecologies of Ph.D. students in the digital age, using the Bakhtinian notion of choronotope to highlight the capacity of the newer researchers of acting upon or being acted upon via the open web. She has been working at the University of Milan, where she was director of the local e-learning center for seven years. In 2011 she obtained a Master's of Research in Educational and Social Research from the Institute of Education, London. Her current research interests focus on the impact of Web 2.0 ecologies on the changing academic practices and on research ethics in online settings.

Anna Forés is Ph.D. in Education and B.A. in Pedagogy from Universitat de Barcelona. Her main working fields are Pedagogy, Social education, Resilience and E-learning. At present she is doctoral Vice-dean of the Education Science Department at Universitat de Barcelona, and Coordinator of the "Education and Society" project. She is professor of the Department of Teaching and Educational Organization at Universitat de Barcelona, where she has been academic Secretary. For sixteen years she was professor of Education and Social Assistance at Universitat Ramon Llull, Barcelona, where she held various management and leading posts. She is a member of the recognized research group GR-EMA (Settings and Materials for Learning) of the ICE (Educational Sciences Institute) at Universitat de Barcelona, and a member of the recognized innovation group INDAGA'T. She has authored a number of books and articles on Higher Education and online learning. She has also been part-time online lecturer at the Universitat Oberta de Catalunya (UOC).

Narimane Hadj-Hamou is currently the CEO of the Center of Learning Innovations and Customized Knowledge Solutions (CLICKS) based in Dubai, UAE. Previously she has assumed the role of the Assistant Chancellor for Learning and Academic Development (Provost) at the Hamdan Bin Mohammed e-University (HBMeU), in Dubai where she has established and led the academic, research and e-learning vision of the first online University to be recognized and accredited by the Ministry of Higher Education and Scientific Research in the UAE. Dr. Hadj-Hamou has been a driving force in the promotion of online education and blended learning within the MENA Region by leading many pioneering projects and initiatives including creating awareness campaigns on e-learning, encouraging and engaging in regional and international research communities in the field, developing strategies and frameworks for implementing different forms of technology-enabled education and establishing associations and networking platforms that are dedicated to the promotion of open, innovative and flexible education and promote the principles of knowledge transfer and sharing best practice thinking. She was the founder and first elected President of the Middle East eLearning Association (MEeA), the first Arab regional association addressing e-learning in the North African and Middle Eastern area. Over the years, she has delivered numerous local, regional and international keynote addresses and workshops and led several roundtables and panel discussions. She was also the founder and editor of the *International Journal of Excellence in eLearning* for several years and acted as a chair for numerous conferences and forums. Today, Dr. Hadj-Hamou is pursuing her passion for advocating excellence and innovative thinking in higher education by leading the Center for Learning Innovations and Customized Knowledge Solutions (CLICKS) as a partner for learning institutions that support the development of academic excellence, innovative thinking, capacity building and knowledge solutions transfer for the twenty-first century.

Josh Hatfield is a Senior Associate in ICF International's Center for Workforce Research and Performance. He has ten years of experience providing workforce solutions in the areas of organizational assessments, employee performance, and training. He received his Master's of Science from Kansas State University.

John G. Hedberg holds the Millennium Innovations Chair of ICT and Education in the School of Education at Macquarie University in Sydney, NSW, Australia. A graduate of Syracuse University, he has taught postgraduate courses on cognitive strategies, interface design for learning, and implementation and evaluation of technology-based learning. He has also taught strategic planning for technology implementation in schools and has also written on policy aspects of new technologies in education. He has designed training needs assessments and evaluation systems and has conducted workshops on the instructional design and evaluation of e-learning environments. He has been keynote speaker at numerous conferences on the educational technologies in Canada, United States, Singapore, Malaysia, China, Europe, and many states in Australia. Professor Hedberg currently serves on the Editorial Advisory Boards of the Journal of Interactive Learning Research, ALT-J, Distance Education and the program committee for Asia-Pacific e-Learning Conference. From 2000–2006, he was the Editor-in-Chief of Educational Media International, a refereed journal for those interested in the application of media and technology in learning contexts throughout the world, and he served as the President of the International Council for Educational Media, a UNESCO affiliate between 2006 and 2008.

Andrea Henne is Assistant Professor in the College of Liberal Arts and Sciences at DeVry University. Previously she was the Dean of Online and Distributed Learning at a multicampus community college district in California, enrolling 12,000 students each semester in online courses. She has extensive experience at the community college and university levels in creating accessible online learning environments that meet best practices in technology-based teaching, faculty development, student learning outcomes, and quality standards. Her online teaching experience includes teaching Instructional Technology at National University, undergraduate courses in Critical Thinking and Problem Solving, and graduate courses in the Master's in Education Program at DeVry. Educated at UCLA in Higher Education Leadership (doctorate) and Business-Economic Education (master's), she is a frequent presenter at conferences, workshops, and webinars on the topics of best practices in technology-based teaching, faculty development, student success, course assessment, and quality standards.

Stefan Hrastinski received his PhD from Lund University in 2007 and is Associate Professor (docent) since 2011 at KTH Royal Institute of Technology. He has published nearly 100 journal articles, books, book chapters and other publications on IT-supported learning and collaboration. Stefan's book *Nätbaserad utbildning: en introduktion* (2009) is the most widely used book on online education in Sweden.

Jack A. Hyman, Ph.D., is an adjunct faculty member at The George Washington University, Educational Technology Leadership Program and works for IBM Corporation as an industry product strategist. Jack's research interests include Human Computer Interaction, Satisfaction Measurement, Mobile Computing, and Enterprise 2.0. He holds a Ph.D. in Information Systems from Nova Southeastern University, an M.A. in Education & Human Development, Educational Technology Leadership from The George Washington University, and a B.S. in Computer Information Systems from American University.

Aina G. Irbe has 20 years of experience in the training and e-learning field as a Senior Training and e-learning Project Manager and Senior Instructional Designer. She is fluent in the technologies and techniques for accessible e-learning development in small to large training initiatives and experienced in managing and applying the full life cycle of the instructional design process and principles of adult learning. Her primary expertise lies in developing accessible training and e-learning programs. She has worked for over a decade as an e-learning consultant to U.S. federal agencies, established and successfully managed the first training department at EYT, Inc., served as Adjunct Faculty at The George Washington University where she taught Master's degree level online classes in the Educational Technology Leadership M.Ed. Program, and has developed the first web-based language training course for the Foreign Service Institute's (FSI) School of Language Studies (SLS). Currently, Ms. Irbe is a doctoral learner at Capella University, specializing in Education, as well as the Senior Director of Learning Technologies at ACDI/VOCA (acdivoca.org).

Insung Jung is currently Professor of Education at the International Christian University in Tokyo, Japan and has a long record of professional practice and publication in e-learning designs and policies. She is coauthor and coeditor of recent publications, 'Distance and blended learning in Asia'; 'Quality assurance and accreditation in distance education and e-learning: Models, policies and research'; and 'Quality assurance in distance education and e-learning: Challenges and solutions from Asia'.

Masayuki Kudo is an associate professor of Hokkaido Institute of Technology and researches on online collaborative EFL learning design.

Marcelo Fabián Maina is Professor in Technology Enhanced Learning at the Department of Psychology and Education of the Universitat Oberta de Catalunya (UOC). He coordinates courses in the Education and ICT Program and lectures in courses in the Master in Education and ICT (e-learning). He obtained a BA in Communications and Education from the Universidad Nacional de Entre Ríos (Argentina), a Master's in Communication Sciences from the Université de Montreal, and his Ph.D. in the Information and Knowledge Society Programme at UOC. His research encompasses such topics as learning ecologies, learning design methods and tools, emerging digital pedagogies, personalized learning, and open educational practices. He is currently a member of the eLearn Center of UOC and the Edul@ab Research Group, where he develops his research interests.

Florence Martin is an Associate Professor in the Instructional Systems Technology program at the University of North Carolina, Charlotte. She received her doctorate and master's in Educational Technology from Arizona State University. Previous to her current position, she taught at University of North Carolina Wilmington for seven years. She also worked on instructional design projects for Maricopa Community College, University of Phoenix, Intel, Cisco Learning Institute, and Arizona State University. She worked as a co-principal investigator on the Digital Visual Literacy NSF grant working with Maricopa Community College District in Arizona. She researches technology tools that improve learning and performance (synchronous virtual classrooms, mobile technologies, learning technologies, etc.). She served as the President of the Multimedia Production Division at AECT from 2012 to 2013. She can be reached at fmartin3@uncc.edu

Diane R. Mason, Ph.D., is Assistant Professor in the Educational Leadership and Technology Department, Lamar University in Beaumont, Texas, U.S.A. where she teaches administrative leadership and technology coursework for master's and doctoral candidates enrolled in fully online programs. She obtained a Ph.D. in Educational Leadership through the University of New Orleans in New Orleans, LA, U.S.A. Prior to becoming a full-time faculty member at Lamar University in 2010, Dr. Mason was employed in the Calcasieu Parish School System in Lake Charles, LA, U.S.A. for 30 years. Her professional experiences included Technology Training Center Coordinator, elementary principal, middle school assistant principal, K-8 classroom, and eight years as an adjunct professor. Dr. Mason is the immediate past president of the ISTE-LACUE Affiliate, volunteers with ISTE Special Interest Groups, peer reviews articles for NCPEA, First Monday, IRRODL, and conducts presentations/research studies for ISTE, NCPEA, AERA, and CoSN. Dr. Mason is also Co-Editor of Lamar University's Center for Action Research and School Improvement resource. Research interests include technology, administrative, and global leadership, online learning, Web 2.0 tools, and professional development. Most recently she has been involved in an international electronic portfolio research initiative for the Coalition for Inter/National Electronic Portfolio Research with universities in the U.S.A, Australia, and the U.K.

João Mattar has a graduate certificate in teaching and learning in higher education (Laureate International Universities), a master's in educational technology (Boise State University), and was a postdoctoral visiting scholar at Stanford University. Author of several articles, chapters, and books on educational technology and distance education, he teaches at University Anhembi Morumbi/Laureate International Universities (Brazil) and TIDD—Interdisciplinary Graduate

Program in Technologies of Intelligence and Digital Design (PUC-SP, Brazil), where he is also advisor and researcher in the line of interaction and learning in virtual environments.

Emily A. Moore holds an M.Ed. in Educational Technology and has worked as an Instructional Designer in higher education for several years. She has also taught online graduate-level courses addressing the use of multimedia in education. Under her maiden name (Vander Veer), Ms. Moore wrote over a dozen books on Internet-related topics for adult learners, including several . . . For Dummies titles. Prior to entering the field of education, Ms. Moore worked in software design and marketing.

Michael Moore Since first defining distance education in a 1972 article, Michael Grahame Moore's career has been dedicated to the development of distance education as a pedagogical theory and as a field of scholarship. Milestones include founding *The American Journal of Distance Education* in 1987, and the 1996 textbook, *Distance Education, a Systems View*, which appears in five languages and three editions; a third edition of *The Handbook of Distance Education* was published in 2012. As practitioner, achievements include one of the world's first international e-learning courses, taught at Penn State university from 1987 to 1995, using audio, video and computer conferencing, with groups of students in USA, Europe and Mexico. Consulting includes work for Ministries of Education in Brazil, Mexico, South Africa, Russia, Romania, and Egypt, and in several international agencies, including a full time appointment at the World Bank. Achievements have been recognized by Penn State University with a Distinguished Professorship and a Lifetime Achievement Award, by a Fellowship at University of Cambridge, UK, Visiting Professorship at UK Open University, Honorary professorships in China and Argentina, an Honorary Doctorate at the University of Guadalajara, Mexico, and Senior Fellowship of European Distance Education Network.

John Nworie is currently an independent researcher and consultant. He has previously held positions in higher education including Director of the Center for Innovation in Teaching and Learning, Executive Director of Instructional Technology, Curricular and Course Development Consultant, Academic Technology Consultant, Coordinator of Media and Technology Services, and other similar positions. He completed his Ph.D. program in Instructional Systems at Pennsylvania State University, and a graduate certificate in Distance Education. Dr. Nworie has published in various journals and presented at national and international conferences.

Arthur Paddock is a Senior Associate with ICF International in the Center for Workforce Research and Performance, and has over nine years of experience in research and consulting. He has worked on projects related to training research and development; competency development; personnel assessment research and development; and those addressing topics of leadership, organizational development and change management. Mr. Paddock received his M.S. in Industrial-Organizational Psychology from the University of Baltimore.

Craig Perrier is the High School Social Studies Specialist for Fairfax County Public Schools in Fairfax, VA. Previously, he taught at American Schools in Brazil for six years and for six years in public schools in Massachusetts. After leaving the classroom, Perrier was the Coordinator for Curriculum and Instruction for Social Studies and History at Virtual High School and then the PK-12 Social Studies Coordinator for the Department of Defense Dependent Schools. He has a MA in Global History from Northeastern University and is pursuing his Ph.D. in Educational Leadership and Social Studies education at George Mason University. Perrier is also an online adjunct professor of history at Northeastern University and SNHU, and maintains a blog, "The Global, History Educator."

Cindy Poore-Pariseau has worked in higher education for over 20 years, assisting students from all walks of life as they pursue their education beyond high school. Cindy is currently a Coordinator for Disability Services for a Massachusetts community college. She is also an adjunct instructor, teaching students in the online environment.

Thomas C. Reeves is Professor Emeritus of Learning, Design, and Technology in the College of Education, The University of Georgia. He earned his Ph.D. at Syracuse University with a focus on program evaluation. He is former Fulbright Lecturer in Peru and he has been an invited speaker in the USA and 30 other countries. In 1995, he was selected as one of the "Top 100" people in multimedia by *Multimedia Producer* magazine, and from 1997 to 2000, he was the editor of the *Journal of Interactive Learning Research*. In 2003, he received the inaugural AACE Fellowship Award from the Association for the Advancement of Computing in Education, and in 2010 he was made a Fellow of the Australasian Society for Computers in Learning in Tertiary Education (ASCILITE). His *Interactive Learning Systems Evaluation* book (coauthored with John Hedberg) was published in 2003 and his *Guide to Authentic E-Learning* book (coauthored with Jan Herrington and Ron Oliver) was published in 2010. His latest book, *Conducting Educational Design Research* (co-authored with Susan McKenney), was published in 2012. His current research interests include educational technology evaluation, authentic tasks for online learning, educational design research, and educational technology in developing countries.

Charles M. Reigeluth Dr. Charles Reigeluth has a B.A. in Economics from Harvard University and a Ph.D. in Instructional Psychology from Brigham Young University. He taught high school science for three years, was a Professor in the Instructional Systems Technology Department at Indiana University for 25 years, and was chairman of the department for three years. His research focuses on paradigm change in public education, the design of high quality instruction, and the design of technology systems for the learner-centered paradigm of education. He facilitated a paradigm change process in the Decatur Township Schools in Indianapolis for 12 years to develop more knowledge about how to help school systems to transform. He is internationally known for his work on instructional methods and theories. His most recent research includes advancing knowledge about personalized, integrated, technology systems that support the learner-centered paradigm of education. He has published ten books and over 160 journal articles and chapters on those subjects, and four of his books received an "outstanding book of the year" award from the Association for Educational Communications and Technology (AECT). He has received the "Distinguished Service" award from AECT and the "Honored Alumnus" award from Brigham Young University's School of Education. His most recent book is Reinventing Schools: It's Time to Break the Mold, which is the culmination of much of his work on paradigm change and instructional theory. Web: www.reigeluth.net, www.reinventingschools.net

Albert Sangrà, Ph.D., is Academic Director of the UNESCO Chair in Education & Technology for Social Change at the Universitat Oberta de Catalunya. He is also a Professor in the Psychology and Education Department and a researcher in the Edula@b research group. At the UOC, he has served as Director of the eLearn Center, the research, innovation and training centre for online education, and as Director, Methodology and Educational Innovation until 2014, being in charge of the educational model of the university. He formerly served as Director of the M.Sc. in Education & ICT (e-learning) (2006–2012). His main research interests are ICT uses in education and training and, particularly, the policies, organization, management, and leadership of e-learning implementation, and its quality assurance. He has played the role of consultant in several online education and training projects in Europe, America, and Asia, and he has also served as a consultant for the World Bank Institute. He currently is Vice-President for the European Foundation for Quality in E-Learning (EFQUEL), and advisor for the Italian Agency for the Evaluation of Quality in Higher Education (ANVUR). He has been a member of the Executive Committee of the European Distance and E-learning Network (EDEN), and served on the Advisory Board of Portugal's Universidade Aberta.

Randall D. Spain is a Research Psychologist at the U.S. Army Research Institute (ARI), where he conducts behavioral science research that aims to improve Army readiness and performance through the use of technology-based training. His current research interests include using maturing training technologies such as mobile devices, virtual environments, and simulation-based platforms to deliver tailored training and assessments to Soldiers and Leaders. Dr. Spain received his Ph.D. in human factors psychology from Old Dominion University.

Colin Wiseman, M.A., is a native of Hornby Island, BC and completed his M.A. in Sociology at the University of Calgary in 2007 with a focus on Venezuelan oil policy as it relates to theories of institutional change. His academic work has appeared in the *Canadian Journal of Latin American and Caribbean Studies* and the *Journal of Distance Education*, and he is an editorial contributor to numerous consumer titles worldwide. Colin has served as a Research Assistant on multiple projects in the Centre for Distance Education at Athabasca University.

Robert A. Wisher is an independent consultant to the training industry. Previously, he was a Research Professor at the Naval Postgraduate School, Monterey, California; Director of the Advanced Distributed Learning Initiative at the Pentagon, Arlington, Virginia; and a research psychologist at Defense Laboratories in the areas of learning, memory, and training evaluation. Bob is a member of the U.S. Distance Learning Association Hall of Fame. He holds a doctorate degree in cognitive psychology from the University of California, San Diego.

1

Introduction to E-learning

Badrul H. Khan

Significant development in e-learning over the past decade has tremendous implications for educational and training practices in the information society (Khan, in press). With the advent of the Internet and online learning methodologies and emerging technologies, e-learning has become more and more accepted in the workplace. Academic institutions, corporations, and government agencies worldwide have been increasingly using the Internet and digital technologies to deliver instruction and training. Moreover, the need to address the training and learning requirements of a globally dispersed workforce is also driving the demand for e-learning programs. At all levels of these organizations, individuals are being encouraged to participate in e-learning activities. Since 1990, the field of e-learning has enjoyed exponential growth and recognition. According to a new report by Global Industry Analysts, Inc., "The global e-learning market is projected to reach $107.3 billion by the year 2015, driven by its benefits in the form of reduction in operational costs, flexibility in learning activities, and simplified training programs."[1] The e-learning market is one of the most rapidly growing sectors in the global education industry.[2]

The emerging field of e-learning has a tremendous impact on our educational and training systems and hence created a new paradigm of education and training. Participants in this new paradigm require rich learning environments supported by well-designed resources (Reigeluth & Khan, 1994). They expect on-demand, anytime/anywhere high-quality learning environments with good support services. In other words, they want increased *flexibility* in learning—they want to have more say in what they learn, when they learn, and where and how they learn.

They may choose a mix of traditional and new learning approaches and technology; they may want to study at their chosen time and location and at their own pace. To stay viable in this global competitive market, providers of education and training must develop efficient and effective learning systems to meet society's needs. Therefore, there is a tremendous demand for *affordable, efficient, easily accessible, open, flexible, well-designed, learner-centered, distributed and facilitated* learning environments.

Can we do what learners want? Nunan (1996) stated,

> Teaching and learning may be created through exploring different ways of delivering education. When 'delivery' or 'learning' is coupled with the word flexible, the intention to

> increase for learners both their access to, and their control over, particular teaching and learning environments is implied.
>
> (Nunan, T. (1996). Flexible delivery - what is it and why is it a part of current educational debate?. *Different Approaches: Theory and Practice in Higher Education.*)

New developments in learning science and technology provide opportunities to develop learning environments that suit students' needs and interests by offering them the choice of increased flexibility. A mix of traditional and new learning approaches and technologies is instrumental in creating innovative learning environments with increased flexibility.

However, many communities around the world are still in the process of implementing e-learning with varying results. Many instructors and trainers are being asked by their institutions to convert their traditional instructor-led face-to-face (f2f) classroom courses to e-learning. However, individuals involved in designing e-learning or converting f2f courses to online environments are faced with many challenges, which raises these questions: *What is e-learning and how is it different from face-to-face (f2f) learning? What does and does not work for e-learning? How does one define and measure e-learning success?*

In this section, e-learning is discussed from the perspective of an open and distributed learning environment; and how its various learning features can be designed to create meaningful e-learning environment. The following is an outline:

- What Is E-learning?
- Open and Distributed Learning Environment
- Traditional Instruction and E-learning
- Learner Focused E-learning System
- Components and Features of E-learning

What Is E-learning?

With the rapid growth of Internet and digital technologies, the Web has become a powerful, global, interactive, dynamic, economic, and democratic medium of learning and teaching at a distance (Khan, 1997; Taylor, 2014). The Internet provides an opportunity to develop learning-on-demand as well as learner-centered instruction and training. There are numerous names for online learning activities, including Massive Open Online Course (MOOC), Web-Based Learning (WBL), Web-Based Instruction (WBI), Web-Based Training (WBT), Internet-Based Training (IBT), Distributed Learning (DL), Advanced Distributed Learning (ADL), Distance Learning, Online Learning (OL), Mobile Learning (or m-Learning) or Nomadic Learning, Remote Learning, Offsite Learning, a-Learning (anytime, anyplace, anywhere learning), etc. In this book, the term ***e-learning*** is used to represent all open and distributed learning activities.

Designing and delivering instruction and training on the Internet requires thoughtful analysis and investigation, combined with an understanding of both the Internet's capabilities and resources and the ways in which instructional design principles can be applied to tap the Internet potential (Ritchie & Hoffman, 1997). Designing e-learning for open and distributed learning environments is new to many of us. After reflection on the factors that must be weighed in creating effective open and distributed learning environments for learners worldwide, the following definition of e-learning is formulated in this book.

> *E-learning can be viewed as an innovative approach for delivering well-designed, learner-centered, interactive, and facilitated learning environments to anyone, anyplace, anytime by utilizing the attributes*

and resources of various digital technologies along with other forms of learning materials suited for the open and distributed learning environment.

The above definition of e-learning raises the question of how various attributes of e-learning methods and technologies can be utilized to create learning features appropriate for diverse learners in an open and distributed environment.

Open and Distributed Learning Environment

What is an open and distributed learning environment? A clear understanding of the *open* and *distributed* nature of the online learning environment will help us create meaningful flexible e-learning (Khan, 2012). According to Calder & McCollum (1998), "The common definition of open learning is learning at your own time, pace and place" (p. 13). Ellington (1995) notes that open and flexible learning allows learners to have some say in how, where, and when learning takes place. Saltzbert and Polyson (1995) noted that distributed learning is not synonymous with distance learning, but they stress its close relationship with the idea of distributed resources:

> Distributed learning is an instructional model that allows instructor, students, and content to be located in different, non-centralized locations so that instruction and learning occur independent of time and place. . . . The distributed learning model can be used in combination with traditional classroom-based courses, with traditional distance learning courses, or it can be used to create wholly virtual classrooms.
>
> (p. 10)

Janis Taylor of Clarke College in Iowa, who teaches students coming from different places in the Midwest, commented on open and distributed learning:

> Consider a student user who described her online education as open because she can sit out on her back deck supervising her children in the swimming pool while doing her homework. Now that's open-air and *open* learning. One of my preservice teachers works in a chemical lab in Cleveland, another is a court reporter three hours drive from me and another is a nurse in rural western Iowa. I, their teacher, am sitting in a small liberal arts college in eastern Iowa, a state badly needing to tap new people to come into the teaching profession. How could I get them all here to my campus if e-learning weren't *distributed?* This open and distributed learning environment made learning flexible for a young traveling business woman who says "I take my college course, my instructor, and all of my fellow students with me on every business trip. With my laptop in my hotel room, I can view my teacher's demonstration, discuss it with my classmates in the Chat Room, and turn in my assignment by email." Now that's a *flexible* college program.
>
> (J. Taylor, personal communication, June 22, 2004)

Flexibility in learning is, therefore, dependent on the openness of the system and the availability of learning resources distributed in various locations. A clear understanding of the *open and distributed* nature of learning environments will help us create meaningful learning environments with increased flexibility. Figure 1.1 graphically shows how an open philosophy of education, when combined with distributed educational systems and technology, results in flexibility for student learning.

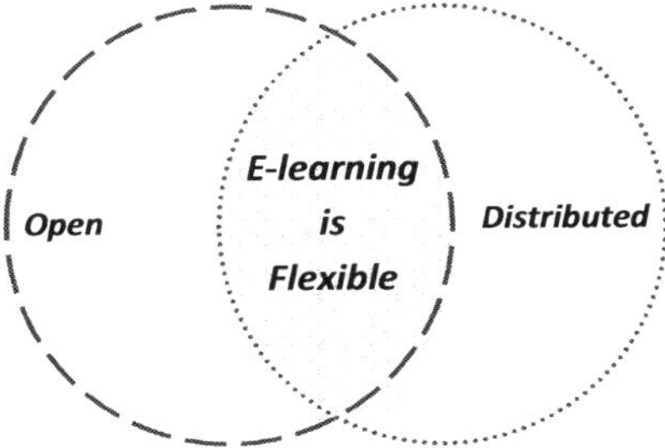

Figure 1.1 Open and Distributed Learning Yields Flexibility

Traditional Instruction and E-learning

The design and format of open and distributed e-learning can be quite different from traditional classroom instruction. Traditional classrooms are space bound. Traditional instruction treats learning pretty much as a *closed system*, taking place within the confines of a given classroom, school, textbook, field trip, etc. (Greg Kearsley, personal communication, January 27, 2000). The traditional classroom-taught courses are not necessarily closed systems; many teachers assign students to do library-based research papers, interview members of a professional community, engage in service-learning activities, and extend their learning initiatives far beyond the classroom itself. Unfortunately many classes are bound by their four walls, involving only the thoughts of the instructor, the textbook writer, and occasional student comments. Classroom courses are also closed in the sense that they are limited to only those students who can physically come to the location (Janis Taylor, personal communication, May 24, 2004).

On the other hand, e-learning extends the boundaries of learning, so that learning can occur in the classrooms, from home and in the workplace (Relan & Gillani, 1997). It is a flexible form of education because it creates options for learners in terms of where and when they can learn (Krauth, 1998). A well-designed e-learning course allows learners to become actively involved in their learning processes. However, a poorly designed e-learning course can be just as rigid, dogmatic and noninteractive as a poorly taught face-to-face course. The scope of openness and flexibility in e-learning is dependent on how it is designed. "While having an open system has its appeal, it can make designing for it extremely difficult, because in an open system, the designer agrees to give up a certain amount of control to the user" (Jones & Farquhar, 1997, p. 240). The more open the learning environment, the more complex is the planning, management, and evaluation of it (Land & Hannafin, 1997). For example, the instructor cannot monitor who helps the student on tests unless the tests are proctored.

Learner-Focused E-learning System

A leading theorist of educational systems, B. H. Banathy (1991), makes a strong case for learning-focused educational and training systems where "the learner is the key entity and occupies the nucleus of the systems complex of education" (p. 96). For Banathy, "*when learning is in focus*, arrangements are made in the environment of the learner that communicate the learning task, and learning resources are made available to learners so that they can explore and master learning tasks" (p. 101). A distributed learning environment that can effectively support learning-on-demand must be designed by placing the learners at the center of the focus. In support of learner-centered approach, Moore (1998) states:

> Our aim as faculty should be to focus our attention on making courses and other learning experiences that will best empower our students to learn, to learn fully, effectively, efficiently, and with rewarding satisfaction. It is the responsibility of our profession to study ways of maximizing the potential of our environments to support their learning and to minimize those elements in their environments that may impede it.
>
> (p. 4)

***Success** in an e-learning system* involves a systematic process of planning, designing, evaluating, and implementing online learning environments where learning is actively fostered and supported. An e-learning system should be meaningful not only to learners, but it should also be meaningful to all stakeholder groups, including instructors, support services staff, and the institution. For example, an e-learning system is more likely to be meaningful to *learners* when it is easily accessible, clearly organized, concise and well written, authoritatively presented, learner centered, affordable, efficient, and flexible, and has a facilitated learning environment. When learners display a high level of participation and success in meeting a course's goals and objectives, this can make e-learning meaningful to *instructors*. In turn, when learners enjoy all available support services provided in the course without any interruptions, it makes *support services staff* happy as they strive to provide easy-to-use, reliable services. Finally, an e-learning system is meaningful to *institutions* when it has a sound return-on-investment (ROI), a moderate to high level of learners' satisfaction with both the quality of instruction and all support services, and a low drop-out rate (Morrison & Khan, 2003).

Now, the question is what kind of e-learning environment should one expect? Obviously, a good one! The one that would provide various features that support online learning including: *interactivity, authenticity, learner-control, convenience, self-containment, ease of use, online support, course security, cost effectiveness, collaborative learning, formal and informal environments, multiple expertise, online evaluation, online search, global accessibility, cross-cultural interaction, nondiscriminatory*, etc. The more features conducive to learning are integrated meaningfully into an e-learning course, the richer the learning environment becomes. The challenge is to make sure each of these learning features is created by addressing (a) issues critical for all stakeholders groups, including learners, facilitators and support staff; (b) types of learning contents; and (c) capabilities of digital technologies to support learning (Romiszowski, 2004).

In the next section, various attributes of the Internet and other digital technologies are discussed in terms of how they can be used to create meaningful learning environments.

Components and Features of E-learning

An e-learning program is discussed here in terms of various components and features that can be conducive to learning. *Components* are integral parts of an e-learning system. *Features* are characteristics of an e-learning program contributed by those components. Components, individually and jointly, can contribute to one or more features (Khan, 2001b; see Figure 1.2). For example, *e-mail* is an asynchronous communication tool (component) that can be used by both students and instructors to interact on learning activities. Therefore, with appropriate instructional design strategies, e-mail can be integrated into an e-learning program to create

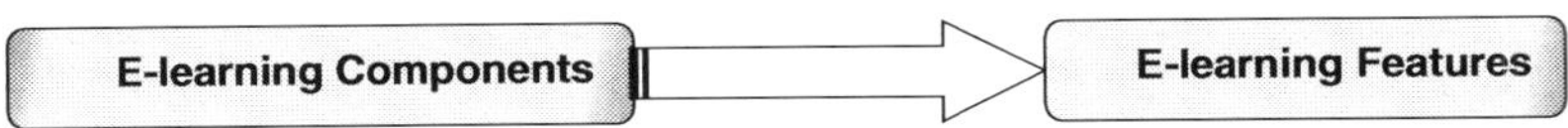

Figure 1.2 Components Contribute Features

an *interactive feature* between students and the instructors. Think about it this way. While traveling on an airplane, passengers can use Airfone to communicate with others on the ground. In this case, *Airfone* is a component of the airplane system that allows passengers to establish a *synchronous communication* (feature). Likewise, *e-mail, mailing lists, newsgroups, conferencing tools* (components) along with appropriate *instructional design principles and strategies* can contribute to a *collaborative* feature for students working on a group project. The website http://BooksToRead.com/wbt/component-featur.ppt hosts a PowerPoint slide presentation emphasizing the point made above.

E-learning Components

I have organized e-learning components into seven groups. As the e-learning methodologies and technologies continue to improve, components within the seven categories may need to be modified and new components may be available to be added. Components updates can be found at http://BooksToRead.com/wbt/component.htm. Please note that none of these components can create meaningful e-learning features without the proper integration of *instructional design*, which is included in the list below as one of the most important part of e-learning components. [Note: Jane Hart compiled a resourceful list of "Top 100 Tools for Learning" (http://c4lpt.co.uk/top100tools/)].

E-learning Features

A well-designed e-learning program can provide numerous features that are conducive to learning. However, these features should be meaningfully integrated into an e-learning program to achieve its learning goals. The more components an e-learning program meaningfully integrates, the more learning features it is able to offer. However, the effectiveness of e-learning features largely depends on how well they are incorporated into the design of the programs. The quality and effectiveness of an e-learning feature can be improved by addressing critical issues within the various dimensions of an open and distributed learning environment (discussed later in the "E-Learning Framework" section). The following are examples of some e-learning features: Interactivity, authenticity (authentic learning), learner-control, convenience, self-containment, ease of use, online support, course security, cost effectiveness, collaborative learning, formal and informal environments, multiple expertise, online evaluation, online search, global accessibility, cross-cultural interaction, nondiscriminatory unbiased materials and content. As components of e-learning improve as a result of the advent of the Internet and online learning methods and technologies, existing e-learning features will improve and new features may be available to us. Several features that are contributed by e-learning components are presented in Table 1.2.

It is critical to make sure each of these features (Table 1.2) is designed appropriately to create meaningful e-learning environments. Various e-learning issues (in the form of questions) are discussed with a global e-learning framework. These questions serve as the review criteria for use while creating meaningful e-learning.

Table 1.1 E-learning Components

1. Instructional Design (ID)
   - Learning and Instructional Theories
   - Instructional Strategies and Techniques
2. Multimedia Component
   - Text and Graphics
   - Audio Streaming (e.g., Real Audio)
   - Video Streaming (e.g., QuickTime)
   - Links (e.g., Hypertext links, Hypermedia links, 3-D links, imagemaps, etc.)
3. Internet Tools
   - Communications Tools
     - Asynchronous: E-mail, Listservs, Newsgroups, Social Networking (i.e., LinkedIn, Facebook, Twitter, Google Plus+, Instagram), Video-sharing site (YouTube), etc.
     - Synchronous: Text-based (e.g., Chat, IRC, MUDs, messaging, etc.) and audio-video conferencing tools.
   - Web 2.0 Tools (Blog, Wiki, Social Networking, Social Bookmarking, etc.)
   - Remote Access Tools (log in to and transferring files from remote computers)
     - Telnet, File Transfer Protocol (ftp), etc.
   - Internet Navigation Tools (access to databases and Web documents)
     - Text-based browser, Graphical browser, VRML browser, etc.
     - Plug-ins
   - Search Tools
     - Search Engines
     - Collaborative encyclopedia
     - Wikipedia
   - Other Tools
     - Counter Tool
4. Computers and Storage Devices
   - Computer platforms running Graphical User Interface (GUI) based operating systems such as Unix, Windows, Macintosh, Linux (i.e., Android) and non-GUI based operating systems such as DOS.
   - Mobile devices such as smart phones (http://en.wikipedia.org/wiki/Smartphone), handheld personal digital assistants (PDAs), Pocket PC Windows and other platforms. The mobile operating systems (OS) used by modern smartphones include Google's Android, Apple's iOS, Microsoft's Windows Phone, etc.
   - Hard drives, flash drives, CD ROMs, DVDs, Google Drive/Docs, etc.
5. Connections and Service Providers
   - Dial-in (e.g., standard telephone line, ISDN, etc.) and dedicated (e.g., 56kbps, DSL, digital cable modem, T1, E1 lines, etc.) services
   - Mobile technology (e.g., connected wireless, wireless LAN, wireless WAN, wireless PAN or personal area network) http://www.webopedia.com/quick_ref/internet_connection_types.asp
   - Application Service Providers (ASPs), Hosting Services Providers (HSPs), Gateway Service Providers, Internet Service Providers (ISPs), etc.
6. Authoring/Management Programs, Enterprise Resource Planning (ERP) Software, and Standards
   - Scripting Languages (e.g., HTML—Hypertext Markup Language, VRML—Virtual Reality Modeling Language, XML—Extensible Markup Language, RSS—Rich Site Summary, is a text-based format, a type of XML http://www.faganfinder.com/search/rss.shtml#what, XSL—Extensible Style Sheet language, XHTML—Extensible Hypertext Markup Language, CSS—Cascading Style Sheets, WML-Wireless Markup language, Java, Java scripting, etc.).

(Continued)

Table 1.1 Continued

- 3D virtual world platform
- Learning Management System (LMS) and Learning Content Management System (LCMS)
- HTML Converters and Editors, etc.
- Rapid Development Tools (http://www.commlabindia.com/elearning-solutions/rapid-development.php)
- Presentation software
- Authoring Tools and Systems (easier to use than programming languages)
- Enterprise Application or Enterprise Resource Planning (ERP) software in which e-learning solutions are integrated. (An article entitled "Integrating your Learning Management System with your Enterprise Resource Planning System" provides valuable information: http://www.llmagazine.com/e_learn/resources/pdfs/Integration.pdf)
- Interoperability, Accessibility and Reusability Standards (http://www.adlnet.org/)

7. Server and Related Applications
   - HTTP servers, HTTPD software, etc.
   - Server Side Scripting Languages—JavaServer Pages (JSP), Active Server Pages (ASP), ColdFusion, Hypertext Preprocessor (PHP), Common Gateway Interface (CGI)—a way of interacting with the http or Web servers. CGI enables such things as image maps and fill-out forms to be run.
   - Wireless Application Protocol (WAP) gateway—changes the binary coded request into an HTTP request and sends it to the Web server.

Table 1.2 Features and Components Associated with E-learning Environments

E-learning Features	*E-learning Components*	*Relationship to Open and Distributed Learning Environment*
Ease of Use	A standard point and click navigation system.Common User Interface, Search Engines, Browsers, Hyperlinks, etc.	A well-designed e-learning course with intuitive interfaces can anticipate learners' needs and satisfy the learners' natural curiosity to explore the unknown. This capability can greatly reduce students' frustration levels and facilitate a user-friendly learning environment. However, delays between a learner's mouse click and the response of the system can contribute to the frustration level of users. The hypermedia environment in an e-learning course allows learners to explore and discover resources that best suit their individual needs. While this type of environment facilitates learning, it should be noted that learners may lose focus on a topic due to the wide variety of sources that may be available on an e-learning course. Also, information may not always

(*Continued*)

Table 1.2 Continued

E-learning Features	*E-learning Components*	*Relationship to Open and Distributed Learning Environment*
		be accessed because of common problems related to servers such as connection refusal, no DNS entry, or broken links (Khan, 2001a, 2001b).
Interactivity	Internet tools, hyperlinks, browsers, servers, authoring programs, instructional design, etc.	Interactivity in e-learning is one of the most important features of instructional activities. Engagement theory based on online learning emphasizes that students must be meaningfully engaged in learning activities through interaction with others and worthwhile tasks (Kearsley & Shneiderman, 1999). E-learning students can interact with each other, with instructors, and with online resources. Instructors and experts may act as facilitators. They can provide support, feedback and guidance via both synchronous and asynchronous communications. Asynchronous communication (i.e., e-mail, listservs, social media, etc.) allows for time-independent interaction whereas synchronous communication (i.e., conferencing tools) allows for live interaction (Khan, 2001a, 2001b).
Multiple Expertise	Internet and WWW	E-learning courses can use outside experts from fields around the world to act as guest lecturers. Experiences and instruction that come directly from the sources and experts represented on the Internet can tremendously benefit learners.
Collaborative Learning	Internet tools,instructional design, etc.	E-learning creates a medium of collaboration, conversation, discussions, exchange, and communication of ideas (Relan & Gillani, 1997). *Collaboration* allows learners to work and learn together to accomplish a common learning goal. In a collaborative environment, learners develop social, communication, critical thinking, leadership, negotiation, and interpersonal and cooperative

(*Continued*)

Table 1.2 Continued

E-learning Features	*E-learning Components*	*Relationship to Open and Distributed Learning Environment*
		skills by experiencing multiple perspectives of members of collaborative groups on any problems or issues.
Authenticity	Internet and WWW, instructional design, etc.	The conferencing and collaboration technologies of the Web bring learners into contact with authentic learning and apprenticing situations (Bonk & Reynolds, 1997). E-learning courses can be designed to promote authentic learning environments by addressing real-world problems and issues relevant to the learner. The most significant aspect of the Web for education at all levels is that it dissolves the artificial wall between the classroom and the "real world" (Kearsley, 1996).
Learner-Control	Internet tools, authoring programs, hyperlinks, instructional design, etc.	The filtered environment of the Web allows students the option to actively participate in discussion or simply observe in the background. E-learning puts students in control so they have a choice of content, time, and feedback and a wide range of media for expressing their understandings (Relan & Gillani, 1997). This facilitates student responsibility and initiative by promoting ownership of learning. The learner-control offered by e-learning is beneficial for the inquisitive student, but the risk of becoming lost in the Web and not fulfilling learner expectations can be a problem and will require strong instructional support (Duchastel & Spahn, 1996).

People, Process, and Product Continuum in E-learning

In e-learning, *people* are involved in the *process* of creating e-learning materials, or *products* and making them available to its target audience. The People-Process-Product or the P3 continuum can be used to map a comprehensive picture of e-learning (Figure 1.3).

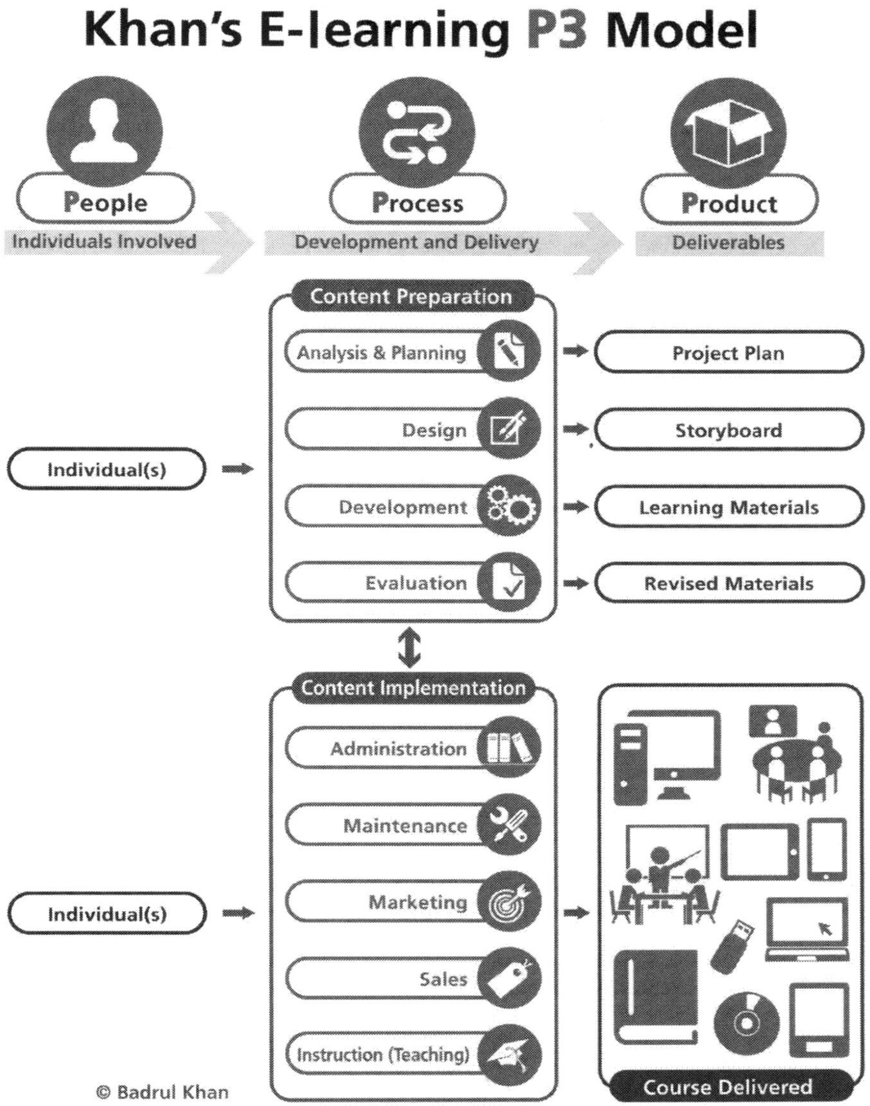

Figure 1.3 E-learning People-Process-Product Continuum
Copyright © Badrul Khan

People

Based on the size and scope of the project, the number of individuals involved in various stages of an e-learning project may vary.

Roles and Responsibilities

Some roles and responsibilities may overlap as many e-learning tasks are interrelated and inter-dependent. A large-sized e-learning project may require the involvement of various individuals with unique roles for each. In a small or medium-sized e-learning project, some individuals may well be able to perform multiple roles. Please note that each e-learning initiative is unique. It can either be a *one-person* project, or one person may even play multiple roles, with differing responsibilities required for each role. However many of us in academia and business single-handedly develop online courses, with only intermittent help from others. When an e-learning course is completely designed, developed, taught, and managed by a single individual, it is clear that the same individual fills the role of a content expert (or subject matter expert), instructional designer, programmer, graphic artist, project manager, etc.

Table 1.3 lists roles and responsibilities of individuals involved in e-learning. This list is by no means exhaustive. The purpose of the list is to showcase the required tasks involved in e-learning initiatives, depending on the person's role and the particular stage in the process.

Table 1.3 Roles and Responsibilities Involved in E-learning

Role of Individual	*Responsibilities*
Director	Directs e-learning initiatives. Develops e-learning plans and strategies.
Project Manager	Supervises the overall e-learning process, including design, production, delivery, evaluation, budgeting, staffing, and scheduling. Works with coordinators of various e-learning teams.
Business Developer	Develops business plan, marketing plan, and promotion plan. Coordinates internal and external strategic partnerships.
Consultant/Advisor	Provides independent, expert advice and services during various stages of e-learning.
Content Preparation Phase	
Research and Design Coordinator	Coordinates e-learning research and design processes. Informs management and design teams about the latest data pertaining to online learning activities and research.
Content or Subject Matter Expert (SME)	Writes course contents and reviews existing course materials (if any) for accuracy and currency.
Instructional Designer	Provides consultation on instructional strategies and techniques for e-learning contents and resources. Helps select delivery format and assessment strategies for e-learning.
Interface Designer	Responsible for site design, navigation, accessibility and usability testing. Responsible for reviewing interface design and content materials to be compliant with the accessibility guidelines (e.g., section 508 of American disability Act—ADA, Web Content Accessibility Guidelines (WCAG) Overview).
Copyright Coordinator	Provides advisement on intellectual property issues relevant to e-learning. Responsible for negotiating permission to use copyrighted materials including

(*Continued*)

Table 1.3 Continued

Role of Individual	*Responsibilities*
	articles, book chapters, videos, music, animations, graphics, Web pages, etc. from copyright holders.
Evaluation Specialist	Responsible for evaluation and assessment design and methodology. Conducts and manages student assessment and evaluation of e-learning environments.
Production Coordinator	Coordinates e-learning production process.
Course Integrator	Responsible for getting all pieces of e-learning (e.g., Web pages, chat rooms, Java applets, e-commerce, etc.) working together under a learning management system.
Programmer	Programs e-learning lessons following the storyboard created in the design process.
Editor	Reviews e-learning materials for clarity, consistency of style, grammar, spelling, appropriate references and copyright information.
Graphic Artist	Uses creativity and style to design graphical images for e-learning lessons.
Script Writer	Responsible for writing audio and video scripts.
Narrator	Responsible for audio and video narrations, voice-over for e-learning modules.
Multimedia Developer	Responsible for creating multimedia learning objects such as audio, video, 2D/3D animations, simulations, etc.
Photographer/Videographer (cameraman)	Responsible for photography and video related to e-learning contents.
Learning Objects Specialist	Guides the design, production and meaningful storage of learning objects by following internationally recognized standards (e.g., Tin Can API—Application Programming Interface or Experience API, SCORM—Sharable Courseware Object Reference Model, AICC—Aviation Industry CBT Committee, IEEE—Institute of Electrical and Electronics Engineers, etc.).
Quality Assurance	Responsible for quality control in e-learning.
Pilot Subjects	Participants in e-learning pilot testing.
Content Implementation Phase	
Delivery Coordinator	Coordinates the implementation of e-learning courses and resources.
Systems Administrator	Administers LMS/LCMS servers, user accounts and network security.
Server/Database Programmer	Responsible for server and database-related programming especially for tracking and recording learners' activities.

(Continued)

Table 1.3 Continued

Role of Individual	*Responsibilities*
Online Course Coordinator	Coordinates the instructional and support staff for online courses.
Instructor (or Trainer)	Teaches/facilitates online courses.
Instructor Assistant	Assists the instructor or trainer in instruction.
Tutor	Assists learners in learning tasks.
Discussion Facilitator or Moderator	Moderates and facilitates online discussions.
Customer Service	Provides generic help and points to appropriate support services based on specific needs of customers (i.e., learners).
Technical Support Specialist	Provides both hardware- and software-related technical help.
Library Services	Interactive library services for learners who can ask questions of librarians about their research, both asynchronous and real time, via the Internet.
Counseling Services	Provides guidance on study skills, self-discipline, responsibility for own learning, time management and stress management, etc.
Administrative Services	Responsible for admissions, schedules, etc.
Registration Services	Responsible for efficient and secure registration process for e-learning.
Marketing	Responsible for marketing e-learning offerings.
Sales	Responsible for sales e-learning products.
Other (specify)	

Question to Consider

Can you think of any additional roles and responsibilities of e-learning not listed in Table 1.3?

Process

The process of creating quality e-learning products begins with a comprehensive analysis of learners, learning content and context, and ends with performing a quality check. The final product is then ready for delivery to the client. The entire process of creating e-learning products brings together a group of people with different competencies but this process can be also performed by fewer people—or by one person working alone (Khan & Joshi, 2006).

The process for creating an e-learning product is much like a building a custom-built house. We wouldn't begin constructing a house without a plan and giving thought to some other considerations. For example, we would discuss the number and size of rooms needed and funding needed to complete the project. We may even want to get an idea of how long this project will take. Once these decisions are made, an architect puts together an effective blueprint (or design floor plan) for the house by employing architectural design principles and techniques. The contractors (i.e., builders) follow the specifications in the blueprint to build the house with necessary raw materials (steel, wood, cement, bricks, sand, etc.). Throughout construction, the architect, owner, and others, like state or local building inspectors, check to see that the builders are following the design plan and that the plan works. At the end of the process, the house is built and we move in.

Similarly, we don't begin creating e-learning course without analysis and a design plan. We decide what we want the outcome of the course to be—what students will be able to do when they have completed the course and the knowledge and skills we will need to teach to get them to that outcome. We also need to consider what the students already know, and any constraints for the course in both resources and time. Then, the instructional designer works much like an architect. He or she uses appropriate instructional design principles and techniques appropriate for e-learning to develop a course design guide ("blueprint") for the course that includes a detailed outline and specific information needed to develop the course. The course developers (i.e., writers, programmers, graphic artist, etc.) follow the specifications in the course design guide to develop the course. Throughout development the Instructional Designer and the Subject Matter Experts (SMEs) review/evaluate the course to ensure it has the correct content presented in the right order for effective learning, and the application exercises reflect performance objectives. When a course is delivered via distance learning method, in the classroom or in a blended learning format, the Instructional Designer collects learners' evaluations for course improvement.

The e-learning process includes several stages: analysis, planning, design, development, delivery, and evaluation (see Figure 1.4). The process is iterative, taking corrective feedback and incorporating it into the various stages. Individuals involved in the e-learning process should be in contact with each other on a regular basis and revise materials whenever necessary. It is important to note that although different people may use different terms for the e-learning stages (i.e., planning, analysis, etc.), each stage of the process must be followed to completion. Ongoing evaluation for improvement (i.e., revision) should always be embedded within each stage of the e-learning process (please note that "evaluation" is shown in both phases of the process in Figure 1.5). In e-learning, *people* are involved in the *process* of creating e-learning *products* and making them available to a specified audience. The People–Process–Product Continuum or P3 Model (Figure 1.3) can be used to map a comprehensive picture of e-learning content preparation and implementation.

The e-learning process can be divided into two major phases: (1) Content Preparation and (2) Content Implementation (see Figure 1.5).

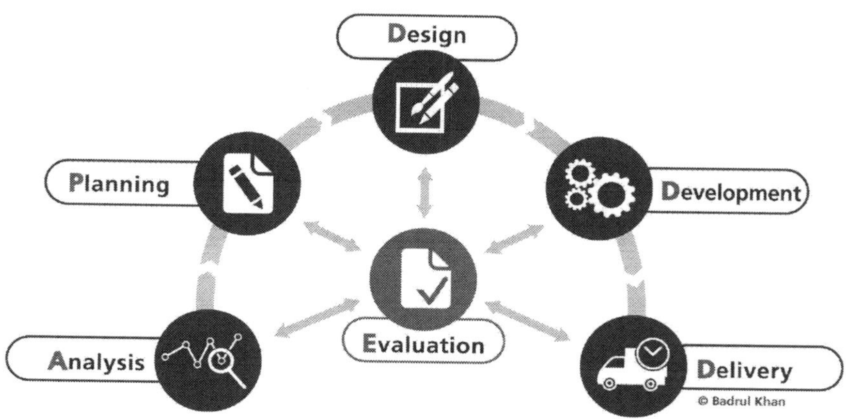

Figure 1.4 E-learning Process Model
Copyright © Badrul Khan

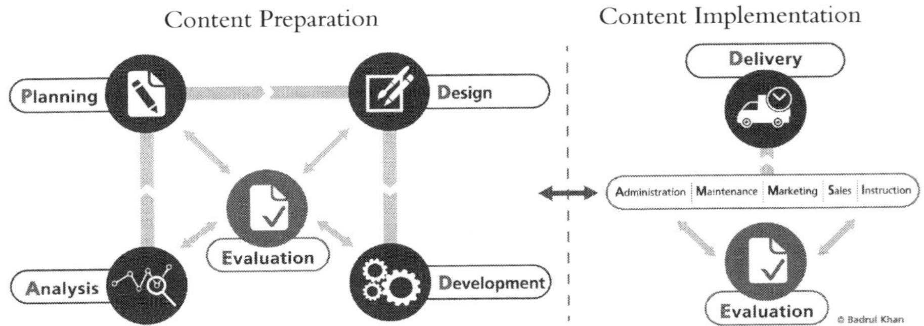

Figure 1.5 E-learning Content Preparation and Implementation Phases

Phase I: Content Preparation

During the content preparation phase all e-learning materials are designed based on instructional design principles and produced following a plan that implements those principles to create meaningful learning activities. The content preparation phase consists of activities including analysis, planning, design, development, and evaluation.

Analysis

The analysis stage consists of analyzing the *who, what, where, why*, and *by whom* of e-learning. This is when learning goals and objectives are established with the identification of attributes of existing learning context and learners' knowledge and skills. It is therefore broad and contains many diverse activities including:

Needs analysis helps to identify if e-learning is the best solution to deliver the instruction and training. The needs analysis allows the identification of general, high-level course goals (Ghirardini, 2011).

Learner or target audience analysis helps to identify key characteristics of the learners (e.g. their previous knowledge, skills and capabilities, geographical origin, learning context and access to technology).

Context analysis helps to identify the setting/environment where the actual learning will take place.

Task analysis helps to identify the specific skills that are involved in the task or job (Moore & Kearsley, 2011) that learners should learn.

Content analysis helps to identify and classify the course content. Typical content analysis process includes breaking down large bodies of subject matter or tasks into smaller and instructionally useful units. These instructionally useful units may include facts, concepts, processes, procedures, or principles. This analysis becomes the basis for writing objectives, test items, sequencing instruction and other design decisions.[3]

Media selection analysis helps to determine the appropriate e-learning delivery solution for either synchronous or asynchronous learning environments, and will aid the instructional designer or subject matter expert (SME) in determining the most appropriate medium to be selected. The instructional designer may choose a combination of media to meet the desired learning objectives.[4]

Planning

Planning is a very critical stage of the whole e-learning process, and success and failures of the entire project depends on how well it is planned. Based on results and information from the analysis stage, a comprehensive e-learning plan can be developed that should serve as a "road map" that shows the practical steps to develop the learning materials needed to achieve organizational e-learning goals. Typical questions during the planning stage may include, but are not limited to: Where do we begin? What kind of personnel will we need? What providers and resources are available to us? How do we create accessible e-learning? How do we hire and train instructors? What are the costs involved? (Clark & Berge, 2005). What is the timeline for project completion?

Design

Design of e-learning follows a logical and orderly method of organizing course contents with learning objectives, relevant learning strategies, assessment instruments, exercises, and delivery media. The following steps are outlined for design activities.[5]

- Aligns learning objectives to tests, quizzes, interactivities, etc.
- Reviews any existing source material for the given subject and performs analysis on this content. The objective is to create a lesson plan and identify existing media, or gaps in the media. These include things such as graphics, animations, illustrations, audio/video files, and other "digital assets." Document the project's instructional, visual and technical design strategy by taking into account the existing content and the target audience, and select the most appropriate technologies and audio/visual layout for the project.
- Establish the course flow by creating a course outline that includes a lesson plan, table of contents, learning objectives, interactivity points, and so on.
- Select and apply the most appropriate instructional design strategies according to the intended behavioral outcomes by domain (cognitive, affective, and psychomotor).
- Create a mockup of the player interface (pause, play, table of contents, etc.) and the content area (on-screen text, images, etc.) for use in the production of a prototype.
- Create a prototype, which is a rough-draft version of the proposed content format. For e-learning, this may include outputting a course using the selected course authoring tool and covering each of the various page types including introduction, lesson, quiz, interactivity, etc.

Development

This is the production stage of e-learning. Following the details in the course storyboard constructed during the design stage, relevant learning materials for each objective of the course are created.

Evaluation

E-learning requires an ongoing review throughout the e-learning process. Therefore, "evaluation" (see Figure 1.5) is included in both *content preparation* and *content implementation* phases to remind ourselves that we can improve e-learning products and services based on ongoing review and feedback from our stakeholders. By conducting ongoing evaluation, we can improve the e-learning product as it is being developed. By reviewing ongoing customers' comments and feedback, we can improve the e-learning design and delivery mechanisms. Therefore, ongoing evaluation is inherent in both content development and delivery phases.

Phase II: Content Implementation

During the implementation phase all e-content is distributed to or is accessible by its stakeholder groups at anytime from anywhere in the world. In this phase, all e-learning content is uploaded to the server (usually all e-content is hosted on LMSs—Learning Management Systems or LCMSs—Learning Content Management Systems). All supplemental course materials (e.g., CD, DVD, audio and video cassette, book, course pack, etc.) are also delivered to its stakeholder groups. Before offering an e-learning course to its target population, an institution should have an efficient administrative system to register students, experienced technical support system to maintain/update e-learning content, and effective market strategies to attract customers and generate sales with great return on investment. The content implementation phase consists of activities including administration, maintenance, marketing, and sales of learning products and instructional/learning environment (see Figure 1.5).

Administration of Learning Environment

Institution should have a procedure for training instructors and facilitators on course curriculum, learning outcomes, method of delivery, and testing procedures. Similar procedures should be in place for technical and other support staff (e.g., library staff, counselor, etc.) and students. Course enrollment and registration are major administrative tasks for e-learning.

Maintenance of Learning Environment

Institution must employ a robust system of updating and monitoring of all e-learning materials on a regular basis. During this stage it is critical that all internal and external links and resources are active, and all security measures are in place.

Marketing of Learning Offerings

Like any new and innovative products or services, e-learning also needs marketing to let potential customers know what's available to attract both inside and outside customers, and keep them satisfied and enthusiastic for coming back for more. There are two types of marketing involved in e-learning: *internal marketing* for inside customers and *external marketing* for outside customers.

Inside customers are individuals within the organization who have stakes in e-learning (e.g., instructors, trainers, training sponsors, and other support staff). They need to buy into the idea that e-learning is flexible, efficient, high quality, and meaningful, and provides great return-on-investment (ROI) for both its stakeholders and the organization. That's internal marketing! When the stakeholders see the value of e-learning and ROI, they become the promoters—both internally for their own training and to their external customers. With greater buy-in from internal people, institutions are better able to spread the word across the organization and get the work out to their consumers. Therefore, it is necessary to fire up the insiders and utilize internal networks to create a viral campaign. Individuals in e-learning may not be trained in marketing, but even good ideas will need promotion to get the word out. It is like latent talent that must be expressed in order to have an impact. Selling a good innovation just helps to diffuse the innovation across the organization and its customer base.

On the other hand, outside customers are consumers of education and training services (i.e., students) who must be well-informed about what they receive being truly high quality and meaningful products, and they must also realize their investments are worthwhile. Educational and training providers should market vigorously to their consumers as the market is very competitive. That's external marketing! Ongoing surveys on the utility of e-learning products that collect feedback from all stakeholders should be used for the development of improved products and services.

Institutions should conduct ongoing market research to identify the best practices in e-learning and develop new or modify existing e-learning materials. Talent management of an organization is important for effective marketing. Various social media (LinkedIn, Facebook, Twitter, blogs) and other marketing approaches should be in place to recruit qualified full-time and part-time adjunct instructors and staff. The field of education and training is changing a great deal. Institutions should come up with increasingly innovative marketing strategies to cope with the demand and the evolving communication vehicles.

Sales of Learning Products

Sales can be of two types in e-learning: *internal sales* and *external sales*. The term *Sales* in e-learning may be confusing to some organizations when it comes to training within their own organizations. In reality, e-learning products and services that are used to train individuals within an organization are paid by a specific fund in the organization such as Human Resources (HR) Office. HR sells training to other branches in an organization. At the end of the fiscal year, HR may calculate how much spent and how much earned! That's internal sales. On the other hand, when an academic institution (e.g., higher education institutions) sells e-learning courses, certificates and programs to its consumers (i.e., students), that's external sales.

The education and training market has been extremely competitive. With the advent of MOOCs (Mass Online Open Courses), consumers have more options. They look for high quality products from brand name institutions that they can afford. One prominent technology school is offering a three-year master's degree in computer science that can be earned entirely online—and that will cost less than $7,000. According to research by GetEducated.com, the average cost of an online computer science master's degree program is just under $25,000. Georgia Tech undercuts that average by more than two-thirds (http://business.time.com/2013/05/21/the-7000-computer-science-degree-and-the-future-of-higher-education/#ixzz2XMTt31e8).

How do other institutions cope with this new threat? Both marketing and sales groups should work together to provide as much information about the institution's product and services—including its ranking, accreditation, quality control, instructors' ranking (i.e., RateYourProfessor.com), competitive prices, etc.—as possible.

Engagement with the Instructional (Teaching/Learning) Environment

Engagement occurs when students are actually receiving instruction and facilitation. At the course instruction stage, instructional (e.g., instructor, tutor, course facilitator, discussion moderator, trainers, etc.) and support services staff (e.g., technical support, librarian, counselor, etc.) are involved.

When a course is offered, the instructional and support staff (ISS) is on the front line. Students deal with them directly based on their specific needs. They expect uninterrupted and meaningful learning environments. The institution should make sure that registered students receive orientation for the course, know what help support is available to them, and understand how to access it, and that ISS support is available as promised.

Question to Consider

Is one stage of the e-learning process more important than another?

Activity

1. Using Internet search engines, locate at least one article that discusses the e-learning process.
2. List any barriers one may encounter during any stages of the e-learning process.
3. List ways that your organization could market its e-learning content internally and/or externally.

Product

In the previous sections, roles and responsibilities of people involved in the step-by-step process of e-learning activities were discussed. In this section, we will focus on what they produce (see Figure 1.6).

Project Plan

At the *analysis and planning* stages, individual(s) involved should develop a *project plan* by analyzing various aspects of e-learning issues. The plan must be pedagogically and financially sound and should guide each individual involved in various stages of e-learning process (e.g., production, evaluation, delivery, maintenance, instructional, support services, marketing and sales) to help him or her engage in his or her respectively assigned activities. The project plan should clearly identify the people, process, and product for each stage of the e-learning. In addition, the plan should indicate the estimated completion time for each task.

Storyboard

At the design stage, instructional designers or individuals involved in e-learning develop a *storyboard* that outlines the visuals, text and audio, video elements, interactions, navigation and content sequencing in the e-learning course. Storyboards serve as the course blueprint or design guide and give direction to the course development.

During the development of the course storyboard, the instructional designer communicates with individual(s) involved in production and delivery regarding any technical and production-related issues. Instructional designers are knowledgeable about how to use various attributes and resources of the Internet and digital technologies to design e-learning activities. Based on the content types, they can incorporate instructional strategies and techniques best suited for the target audience. However, it is important to note that instructional design services may not be adequately available in some institutions. With knowledge of the instructional design process, instructors can design their own online courses.

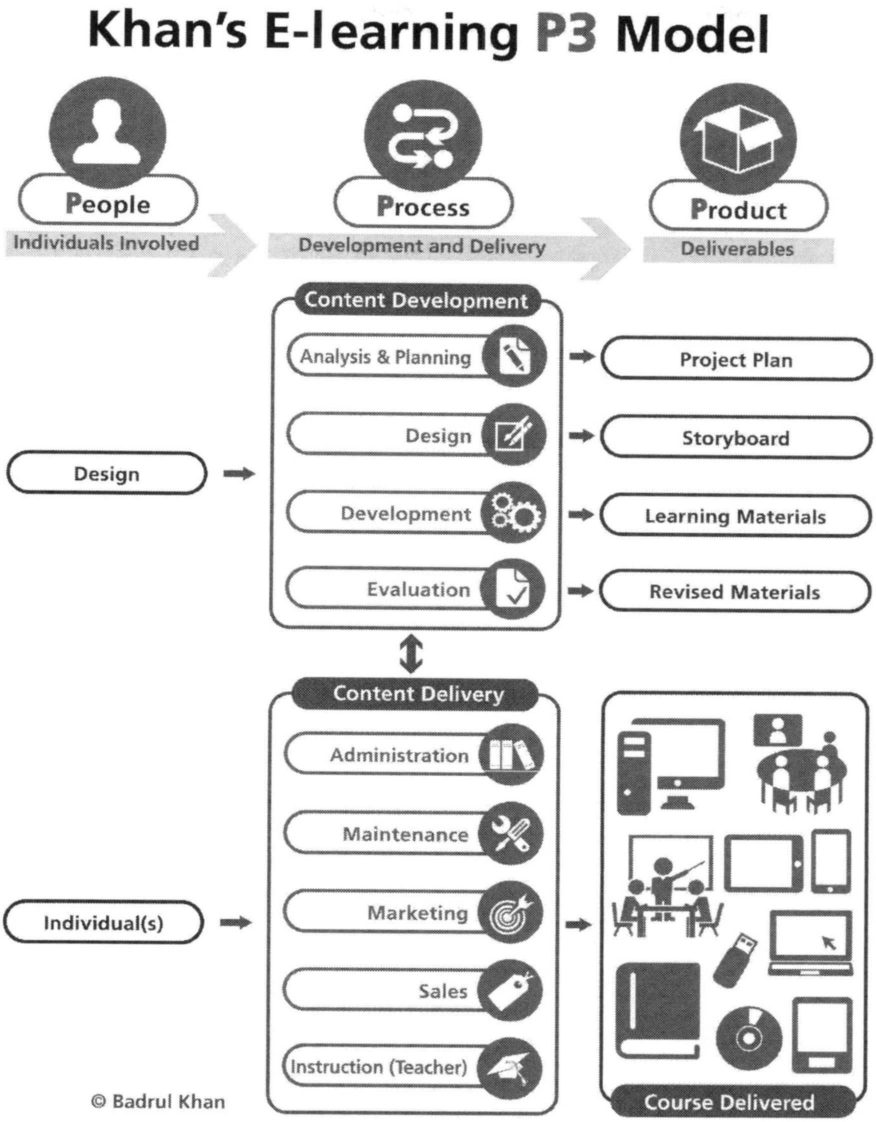

Figure 1.6 E-learning People Process Product Continuum
Copyright © Badrul Khan

Learning Materials

At the course production stage, the production team creates the online course from the course storyboard developed during the design phase. The production coordinator leads e-learning production process. Team members include, but are not limited to: course integrator, programmer, graphic artist, multimedia developer, photographer/videographer (cameraman), editor, learning objects specialist, script writer, narrator, and quality assurance (see Table 1.3 for Roles and Responsibilities).

The production coordinator should make sure the timeline is maintained for all deliverables. The e-learning production process is time consuming. It is a collaborative process in which each member does his or her own specific tasks for a course. For example, the course integrator cannot put all parts of a lesson together if each member does not provide his or her part of the task on time.

In e-learning, members of the development team can be remotely located. The production coordinator should make sure members are in good communication with each other and in compliance with due dates for their respective tasks. Members should put their works in designated areas on a centralized server (which we can call a *development server*). The development server becomes a collaborative work space for the e-learning members. I served as a consultant for an e-learning project development at the World Bank where I worked with the project manager, instructional designers, graphic artists and programmers, all of whom were remotely located.

It is always wise to create two resource sites during the content development process: (1) a project support site (PSS) and (2) a knowledge management (KM) site. The PSS can be discontinued after the project is completed whereas the KM site is an ongoing knowledge sharing site for an organization.

Once the course is created, it is important to do a pilot test with a representative group of diverse learners. For the pilot testing, learners can access the course at the development server with a password. These learners can be remotely located. For an efficient evaluation of the pilot project, the course should be designed to receive learners' comments on a specific page. For an example, if a learner finds a symbol is culturally offensive on a page, he or she can attach his or her comments with that specific graphic or the page. The production coordinator can make these comments available to responsible team members. Data from the pilot testing will provide valuable information about what works and what does not work. The instructional designer and the interface designers can work with the production team and revise the course whenever appropriate.

The *product* of the production process is *course materials* ready for pilot testing (see Figure 1.6).

Revised Materials

By conducting ongoing formative evaluation, we can improve the e-learning product as it is being developed. Summative evaluation is usually conducted to do the final assessment of e-learning products. However, e-learning projects undergo ongoing evaluation for improvement. Therefore, formative evaluation is inherent in the e-learning development process. Learners' feedback from the pilot testing can be analyzed to revise the course materials.

The *product* of the evaluation process is *revised course materials* which are ready to be offered to learners.

Course Delivered

All online course materials should be accessible by the learners at anytime from anywhere in the world. All supplemental course materials (e.g., CD, DVD, audio and video cassette, book, course pack, etc.) should be delivered to learners. Individuals such as the systems administrator, server/database programmer, Webmaster, etc., are responsible for maintaining an effective and efficient learning environment; providing technical support to students, instructors, and support staff; and managing Learning Management System (LMS) user accounts and network security. They also provide technical assistance.

The *product* of the implementation phase is *course delivered*, a set of well-maintained learning materials available for registration.

A Global Framework for E-learning

The design of open and distributed e-learning environments requires a comprehensive understanding of the question: *What does it take to provide virtual learning environments for learners worldwide?* Since 1997, I have communicated with learners, instructors, administrators, and technical and other support services staff involved in virtual learning (in both academic and corporate settings) all over the world. I have researched virtual learning issues discussed in professional discussion forums, and I have designed and taught online and blended learning courses. I have surveyed online educators and students (Khan & Vega, 1997; Khan & Smith, 2007; Khan, Cataldo, & Bennett, 2007). Also, as the editor of *Web-Based Instruction* (1997), *Web-Based Training* (2001), *Flexible Learning in an Information Society* (2007), *Learning on Demand: ADL and the Future of E-learning* (2010), *User Interface Design for Virtual Environments: Challenges and Advances* (2012), *International Handbook of E-learning* (in press), and *The MOOC Case Book: Case Studies in MOOC Design, Development and Implementation* (in press), I have had the opportunity to work closely on critical virtual learning issues with more than 500 authors worldwide, many of whom have contributed chapters to these books.

Through these activities, I have learned that e-learning represents a paradigm shift, not only for learners, but also for instructors, administrators, technical, and other support services staff, and the institution. Just as we are accustomed to teaching and learning in a closed system like a physical classroom, the openness of virtual learning is new to us. To create effective virtual learning environments for diverse learners, we need to jump out of our closed system mentality and change our mindset. We need to be more attentive to a variety of new and emerging issues of e-learning, and address them in the design stages of learning environments. That's the paradigm shift! In order to facilitate such a shift, and in response to the range of issues I saw in my research, I created a *Framework for E-learning* (Figure 1.7).

Through my research I found that numerous factors help to create a meaningful virtual learning environment, and many of these factors are systemically interrelated and interdependent.

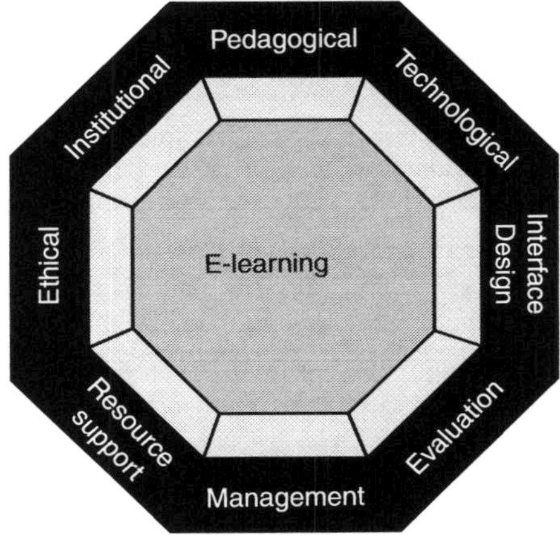

Figure 1.7 Framework for E-learning
Copyright © Badrul Khan

A systemic understanding of these factors can help us create meaningful virtual learning environments. I have clustered these factors into eight dimensions: *institutional, management, technological, pedagogical, ethical, interface design, resource support,* and *evaluation*. Each dimension has subdimensions or factors, and each factor can generate one or more issues or checklist questions.

> **D**imensions (e.g., *1. INSTITUTIONAL*) (Table 4)
> **F**actors (e.g., *1.3.2. Orientation*) (Table 5)
> **I**ssues (e.g., a checklist item or a QAC such as *Are instructor/tutor/technical staff available during online orientation?*) (tables 6–11)

The purpose of this Framework is to help us think through every aspect of what we are doing during the steps of the e-learning design process. Therefore we should look at each of the eight dimensions or categories of this Framework (Table 1.4 and Table 1.5), and show what questions (see checklist section) we should ask about each dimension as we design a flexible learning segment, whether a lesson, a course or an entire program.

Eight Dimensions of the E-learning Environment

Table 1.4 Eight Dimensions of the E-learning Environment

Dimensions	*Descriptions*
Institutional	The institutional category is concerned with issues of administrative affairs, academic affairs and student services related to e-learning.
Management	The management of e-learning refers to the maintenance of the learning environment and distribution of information.
Technological	The technological category examines issues of technology infrastructure in e-learning environments. This includes infrastructure planning, hardware and software.
Pedagogical	The pedagogical category refers to teaching and learning. This category addresses issues concerning content analysis, audience analysis, goal analysis, medium analysis, design approach, organization, and learning strategies.
Ethical	The ethical considerations of e-learning relate to social and political influences, cultural diversity, bias, geographical diversity, learner diversity, the digital divide, etiquette, and legal issues.
Interface design	Interface design refers to the overall look and feel of e-learning programs. Interface design categories encompass page and site design, content design, navigation, accessibility, and usability testing.
Resource support	The resource support category examines the online support and resources required to foster meaningful learning.
Evaluation	The evaluation of e-learning includes both assessment of learners and evaluation of the instruction and the learning environment.

Each dimension of the framework is composed of a number of factors. Table 1.5 lists several factors under each dimension. It is important to note that the factors identified here are by no means exhaustive. As we learn more about e-learning environments, more and more factors may be added to the list.

Factors of E-learning Environments

Table 1.5 Factors of E-learning Environments

1. INSTITUTIONAL
   - 1.1 Administrative Affairs
     - 1.1.1 Needs Assessment
     - 1.1.2 Readiness Assessment (Financial, Infrastructure, Cultural and Content readiness)
     - 1.1.3 Organization and Change (Diffusion, Adoption and Implementation of Innovation)
     - 1.1.4 Implementation
     - 1.1.5 Budgeting and Return on Investment
     - 1.1.6 Partnerships with Other Institutions and Stakeholders
     - 1.1.7 Program and Course information Catalog (Academic Calendar, Course Schedule, Tuition, Fees, & Graduation)
     - 1.1.8 Marketing and Recruitment
     - 1.1.9 Admissions
     - 1.1.10 Financial Aid
     - 1.1.11 Registration and Payment
     - 1.1.12 Information Technology Services
     - 1.1.13 Instructional Design and Media Services
     - 1.1.14 Graduation Transcripts and Grades
   - 1.2 Academic Affairs
     - 1.2.1 Accreditation
     - 1.2.2 Policy
     - 1.2.3 Instructional Quality
     - 1.2.4 Faculty and Staff Support
     - 1.2.5 Class Size, Workload and Compensation and Intellectual Property Rights
   - 1.3 Student Services
     - 1.3.1 Pre-enrollment Services
     - 1.3.2 Orientation
     - 1.3.3 Faculty and Staff Directories
     - 1.3.4 Advising
     - 1.3.5 Counseling
     - 1.3.6 Learning Skills Development
     - 1.3.7 Services for Students with Disabilities
     - 1.3.8 Library Support
     - 1.3.9 Bookstore
     - 1.3.10 Tutorial Services
     - 1.3.11 Mediation and Conflict Resolution
     - 1.3.12 Social Support Network
     - 1.3.13 Students Newsletter
     - 1.3.14 Internship and Employment Services
     - 1.3.15 Alumni Affairs
     - 1.3.16 Other Services

(*Continued*)

Table 1.5 Continued

2. PEDAGOGICAL
   - 2.1 Content Analysis
   - 2.2 Audience Analysis
   - 2.3 Goal Analysis
   - 2.4 Medium Analysis
   - 2.5 Design Approach
   - 2.6 Organization
   - 2.7 Learning Strategies
     - 2.7.01 Presentation
     - 2.7.02 Exhibits
     - 2.7.03 Demonstration
     - 2.7.04 Drill and Practice
     - 2.7.05 Tutorials
     - 2.7.06 Games
     - 2.7.07 Storytelling
     - 2.7.08 Simulations
     - 2.7.09 Role-playing
     - 2.7.10 Discussion
     - 2.7.11 Interaction
     - 2.7.12 Modeling
     - 2.7.13 Facilitation
     - 2.7.14 Collaboration
     - 2.7.15 Debate
     - 2.7.16 Field Trips
     - 2.7.17 Apprenticeship
     - 2.7.18 Case Studies
     - 2.7.19 Generative Development
     - 2.7.20 Motivation
3. TECHNOLOGICAL
   - 3.1 Infrastructure Planning (Technology Plan, Standards, Metadata, Learning Objects)
   - 3.2 Hardware
   - 3.3 Software (LMS, LCMS, Enterprise Application)
4. INTERFACE DESIGN
   - 4.1 Page and Site Design
   - 4.2 Content Design
   - 4.3 Navigation
   - 4.4 Accessibility
   - 4.5 Usability Testing
5. EVALUATION
   - 5.1 Assessment of Learners
   - 5.2 Evaluation of Instruction & Learning Environment
   - 5.3 Evaluation of the Program
6. MANAGEMENT
   - 6.1 Maintenance of Learning Environment
   - 6.2 Distribution of Information
7. RESOURCE SUPPORT
   - 7.1 Online Support
     - 7.1.1 Instructional/Counseling Support

(*Continued*)

Table 1.5 Continued

7.1.2 Technical Support
7.1.3 Career Counseling Services
7.1.4 Other Online Support Services
7.2 Resources
7.1.1 Online Resources
7.1.2 Offline Resources
8. ETHICAL CONSIDERATIONS
8.1 Social and Political Influence
8.2 Cultural Diversity
8.3 Bias
8.4 Geographical Diversity
8.5 Learner Diversity
8.6 Digital Divide
8.7 Etiquette
8.8 Legal Issues
8.8.1 Privacy
8.8.2 Plagiarism
8.8.3 Copyright

Issues of E-learning Environments

Each factor in Table 1.5 focuses on a specific aspect of an e-learning environment. One could ask, *What are the critical issues associated with many of these factors that can help in the design of meaningful e-learning environments?*

There may be numerous issues within each factor of each e-learning environment. These issues can be explored as *questions* that designers can ask themselves when planning an e-learning environment. Each e-learning project is unique. It is important to identify as many issues (in the form of questions) as possible for your own project by using the octagon framework. One way to identify critical issues is by putting each stakeholder group (such as learner, instructor, support staff, etc.) at the center of the framework and raising issues along the eight dimensions of e-learning. This way you can identify many critical issues and answer questions that can help create a meaningful e-learning experience for your particular group. By repeating the same process for other stakeholder groups, you can generate a comprehensive list of issues for your project.

As indicated previously, the purpose of this Framework is to help us think through every aspect of what we are doing during the steps of the e-learning design process. Therefore, it is important to review each of the eight dimensions of this Framework and explore what questions we should ask about each dimension as we design an e-learning environment segment, which can be a *learning feature, a lesson, a course* or an *entire program.*

Review of E-learning with the Framework

The Framework can serve as a diagnostic tool for a holistic evaluation of an e-learning environment. In this section, an e-learning *feature* and e-learning *products* from various stages of e-learning process are reviewed from the perspectives of quality assurance criteria and assessment rating.

Quality Assurance Criteria and Assessment Rating

Quality Assurance Criteria items (QACs) are specific questions assessing the quality and utility of e-learning features and products. QAC items represent the key issues within each dimension of the e-learning environment (i.e., pedagogical checklist items, technological checklist items, etc.). It may be challenging to come up with questions for some dimensions of the Framework for some specific stages of the e-learning phases given the interrelationship among the characteristics of the eight dimensions. In such situations, I recommend not worrying about those particular dimensions and continuing with other dimensions. Some questions may appear to be a good fit for more than one dimension. You may come up with or find some QAC questions not fitting into any of the eight dimensions of the framework—that's ok—we can use them as long they are critical and relevant for evaluating e-learning.

In addition to structured questions (i.e., quantitative or hard data) in the QAC, for a comprehensive program evaluation of e-learning, it is necessary to gather qualitative or "soft data" such as constructive comments/feedback from stakeholders, reviews of documents and site visits.

Assessment Rating is used as Score Card for the evaluation of e-learning features and products. The QAC questions support the assessment of a program's progress in completing the critical e-learning activities and an *Excellent-Sufficient-Deficient* rating is used as Assessment Rating (Score Card).

- **Excellent—**Yes, the issue(s) discussed in the question is/are well addressed.
- **Sufficient—**Yes, the issue(s) discussed in the question is/are partially addressed.
- **Deficient—**No, the issue(s) discussed in the question is/are not addressed.

How do you go about selecting a rating of *excellent, sufficient* or *deficient*? Is there a benchmark to use? In some instances, there is. If there is an existing benchmark, I contend that you should use it. The ultimate intention is to judge the status of a product using the best possible information available. Some benchmark criteria may not always be fully applicable to some institutional contexts. Even so, judgment will always be subjective. The Framework-guided review encourages the most transparent, unbiased and reasonable judgment in the review of a product.

Review of E-Learning Features with the Framework

As indicated earlier, all e-learning features must be designed to help students achieve their learning goals. Comprising an e-learning program of well-designed instructional features can lead to its success. The eight dimensions of the E-learning Framework can identify the critical issues of an e-learning environment and provide guidance on addressing them. We can improve the effectiveness of an e-learning feature by answering the questions raised in the framework. For example, *ease of use* is one of most important features in an e-learning environment. Within the scope of this book, in Table 1.6, only one e-learning feature (i.e., *ease of use*) is reviewed for its effectiveness in a course from the perspective of each of the eight dimensions for one of the stakeholder groups (i.e., students). Using Table 1.6, similar reviews can be conducted for other stakeholder groups (i.e., instructors, technical staff, etc.).

There are questions similar to those in Table 1.6 that can be used to review how a feature such as *ease of use* can be made a part of an e-learning program. All these questions in Table 6 covering the eight e-learning dimensions point to one critical element: *Is it really easy to use*?

Table 1.6 E-learning Feature Review

E-learning Feature	*E-learning Dimension*	*Quality Assurance Criteria (QAs)*	*Assessment Rating (Score Card)*		
			Excellent	*Sufficient*	*Deficient*
Ease of Use	*Institutional*	Are instructor/tutor and technical staff available during online orientation?			
	Management	Does the course notify students about any changes in due dates or other course-relevant matters such as server down?			
	Technological	Are students taught how to join, participate in, and leave a mailing list?			
	Pedagogical	Does the course provide a clear description of what learners should do at every stage of the course?			
	Ethical	Does the course provide any guidance to learners on how to behave and post messages in online discussions so that their postings do not hurt others' feelings?			
	Interface design	How quickly can users find answers to the most frequently asked questions on the course site?			
	Resource support	Does the course provide clear guidelines to the learners on what support can and cannot be expected from a help line?			
	Evaluation	If learners are disconnected during an online test, can they log back in and start from where they left off?			

Therefore, for each feature we should explore as many issues as possible within the eight dimensions of the e-learning environment.

Review of E-learning Products with the Framework

Why review only the products? What about the other two parts of the P3 (i.e., people and process)? A product is the result of people being involved in a process. By examining the quality of the product, we are comprehensively evaluating the performance of the people involved in producing that product.

In order to gain a comprehensive, accurate assessment of any e-learning environment, we must examine all final products through various e-learning stages based on *eight* evaluation criteria methods.

Table 1.7 Product Review: E-learning **Analysis** and **Planning** Stage

Product	*E-learning Dimension*	*Quality Assurance Criteria (QAs)*	*Assessment Rating (Score Card)*		
			Excellent	*Sufficient*	*Deficient*
Project Plan	*Pedagogical*	How well does the plan map course goals into course outcomes (corresponding course goals to its outcomes)?			
	Technological	How well are the selection criteria for Learning Management System (i.e., licensing arrangements, instructor, staff and students experience with, advantages over other systems) considered?			
	Interface Design	Has the plan addressed accessibility concerns (such as Americans with Disabilities Act's Section 508 compliance) for e-learning materials?			
	Evaluation	How well is learner/user assessment addressed?			
	Management	Has the plan identified the roles and responsibilities of individuals? Or how has the project team planned for e-learning?			

(*Continued*)

Table 1.7 Continued

Product	*E-learning Dimension*	*Quality Assurance Criteria (QAs)*	*Assessment Rating (Score Card)*		
			Excellent	*Sufficient*	*Deficient*
	Resource Support	Has the plan identified the number of hours for online technical and other support services?			
	Ethical	Has the plan addressed the geographical diversity of time zones affecting synchronous learning activities and technical/administrative support services?			
	Institutional	Has the plan addressed any specialist training required to accompany the implementation?			
	Feedback and Comments from Stakeholders:				
	Notes from Site Visit(s) and Document Reviews:				

Table 1.8 Product Review: E-learning **Design** Stage

Product	*E-Learning Dimension*	*Quality Assurance Criteria (QAs)*	*Assessment Rating (Score Card)*		
			Excellent	*Sufficient*	*Deficient*
Storyboard	*Pedagogical*	How well is the instructional strategy being used for each objective?			
	Technological	How well are e-learning standards for interchangeability of learning objects (i.e., Sharable Content Object Reference Model- SCORM) used throughout the course?			

(*Continued*)

Table 1.8 Continued

Product	*E-Learning Dimension*	*Quality Assurance Criteria (QAs)*	*Assessment Rating (Score Card)*		
			Excellent	*Sufficient*	*Deficient*
	Interface Design	If different delivery formats (i.e., online, face-to-face lecture) are used in the course, how well are content structure, navigation and multimedia in each format integrated so that learners can switch between different types without confusion or interruption?			
	Evaluation	How well is Subject Matter Expert (SME) feedback regarding the storyboard incorporated?			
	Management	How well does the storyboard use existing learning materials?			
	Resource Support	Has the plan identified the number of hours for online technical and other support services?			
	Ethical	Is the content requiring copyright permission identified?			
	Institutional	Can the organization offer the course independently as well as in a blended program?			
	Feedback and Comments from Stakeholders:				
	Notes from Site Visit(s) and Document Reviews:				

Table 1.9 Product Review: E-learning **Development** Stage

Product	*E-learning Dimension*	*Quality Assurance Criteria (QAs)*	*Assessment Rating (Score Card)*		
			Excellent	*Sufficient*	*Deficient*
Learning Materials	*Pedagogical*	How good is the content? How well do learners interact with it?			

(*Continued*)

Table 1.9 Continued

Product	*E-learning Dimension*	*Quality Assurance Criteria (QAs)*	*Assessment Rating (Score Card)*		
			Excellent	*Sufficient*	*Deficient*
	Technological	How do the course materials fare with the existing technology infrastructure for the learners?			
	Interface Design	Are online course contents easy to use?			
	Evaluation	How relevant is the content in regard to course objectives?			
	Management	Are the external links used in the course still active?			
	Resource Support	How well does the online help (if any) function?			
	Ethical	Are course materials designed with good cross-cultural sensitivity?			
	Institutional	How well are course materials developed from the perspective of the academic or training standards of the institution?			
	Feedback and Comments from Stakeholders:				
	Notes from Site Visit(s) and Document Reviews:				

Table 1.10 Product Review: E-learning **Evaluation** Stage

Product	*E-learning Dimension*	*Quality Assurance Criteria (QAs)*	*Assessment Rating (Score Card)*		
			Excellent	*Sufficient*	*Deficient*
Revised Materials	*Pedagogical*	How well are course contents presented for meaningful learning activities?			
	Technological	How well does the Learning Management System (LMS) manage and deliver the online content?			
	Interface Design	How satisfied are the learners with the look and feel of online content?			

(Continued)

Table 1.10 Continued

Product	*E-learning Dimension*	*Quality Assurance Criteria (QAs)*	*Assessment Rating (Score Card)*		
			Excellent	*Sufficient*	*Deficient*
	Evaluation	From a real-world perspective, how do learners feel about what they learned?			
	Management	How well are various learning materials maintained and managed?			
	Resource Support	How well are various support services provided?			
	Ethical	How well are various ethical issues addressed in the learning materials?			
	Institutional	How well do the course contents maintain the academic quality of the institution?			
	Feedback and Comments from Stakeholders:				
	Notes from Site Visit(s) and Document Reviews:				

Table 1.11 Product Review: E-learning **Delivery** Stages

Product	*E-learning Dimension*	*Quality Assurance Criteria (QAs)*	*Assessment Rating (Score Card)*		
			Excellent	*Sufficient*	*Deficient*
Course Delivered	*Pedagogical*	How well does/do the instructor(s) facilitate learning?			
		How instructionally sound is the course?			
		Are learning materials easily accessible by learners?			
		How well does the course design contribute to an interactive and flexible learning environment?			
	Technological	How well are technology tools (Webinar, etc.) used by instructor(s)?			
		How well does the Learning Management System (LMS)			

(*Continued*)

Table 1.11 Continued

Product	*E-learning Dimension*	*Quality Assurance Criteria (QAs)*	*Assessment Rating (Score Card)*		
			Excellent	*Sufficient*	*Deficient*
		manage and deliver the online content?			
		How well does the technology integration improve the effectiveness of the course?			
	Interface Design	How well are online and offline activities seamlessly integrated during the instruction period of the course?			
		How easily can learners navigate the learning materials?			
		How well do the look and feel of the course content contribute to efficiency and effectiveness?			
	Evaluation	How well are students' assessments done in the course?			
		How well are the assessments of students and evaluations of instructional/support staff supported?			
		How well is learners' assessment integrated into the course for academic performance measures?			
	Management	How well are course contents updated?			
		Are learning materials delivered and updated efficiently?			
		Are resource support services well maintained?			
	Resource Support	How well are resource support services provided during the instruction period?			
		Are course materials accessible 24/7?			
		Do the course resource support services improve the efficiency and effectiveness of the courses?			

(*Continued*)

Table 1.11 Continued

Product	*E-learning Dimension*	*Quality Assurance Criteria (QAs)*	*Assessment Rating (Score Card)*		
			Excellent	*Sufficient*	*Deficient*
	Ethical	How well are ethical issues (such as copyright, learner and geographical diversities) honored during the instruction period?			
		How well are legal issues handled?			
		Are ethical considerations included in the course to improve diversity, cross-cultural and legal issues?			
	Institutional	How well are institutional academic standards and regulations followed during the instruction period?			
		How well are course materials received by students?			
		How much does the course improve the return on investment?			
	Feedback and Comments from Stakeholders:				
	Notes from Site Visit(s) and Document Reviews:				

Table 1.12 Quality Assurance Summary: Products of E-learning Process

Performance Criteria	*E-learning Course/Program*							
	Pedagogical	*Technological*	*Interface Design*	*Evaluation*	*Management*	*Resource Support*	*Ethical*	*Institutional*
Excellent								
Sufficient								
Deficient								
Feedback and Comments from Stakeholders:								
Notes from Site Visit(s) and Document Reviews:								

Framework Applicable to Massive Open Online Courses (MOOCs)

With the emergence of new communication and computing technologies, we are becoming increasingly accustomed to new buzzwords to describe technology-based learning. One of the latest buzzwords is *MOOC*, short for "Massive Open Online Course" (Corbeil, Corbeil, & Khan, in press).

With the introduction of a new wave of online delivery methods, you may wonder, whatever happened to the term *e-learning?* To reassure you, e-learning is still alive and will be with us, in one form or another, for all time. If the *e* in e-learning is short for *electronic* then, as long as media is delivered electronically, e-learning will continue to exist in technology-based education. Just as Electronic Performance Support Systems (EPSS), first coined in 1991, are still in active use today, e-learning is also alive and well; but with extended capabilities and identities. One of its most recent manifestations is the MOOC, the massive open online course designed to offer large-scale free education courses to the masses (Milheim, 2013).

Although they offer benefits, MOOCs currently face several challenges. Milheim (2013) cites four major problems associated with MOOCs: (a) high dropout rates, (b) lack of a financial model, (c) credentialing, and (d) academic integrity. However, failure in e-learning courses is more often associated with poor execution of some aspects of the initial project design and dissemination/implementation (Romiszowski, 2004).

By their definition, MOOCs are delivered through an open and distributed e-learning environment. The design, development, implementation, and evaluation of open and distributed learning systems, such as MOOCs, require a thoughtful analysis and investigation of how to use the attributes and resources of the Internet and digital technologies in concert with instructional design principles and issues important to various dimensions of online learning environments (Khan, 2012). The e-learning framework (http://BadrulKhan.com/framework) that was developed back in 1997 for Web-Based Instruction is applicable to MOOCs, as a form of WBI. Various factors discussed in the eight dimensions of the framework can provide guidance in the design, development, delivery, and evaluation of open and distributed learning environments such as MOOCs (see Figure 1.8).

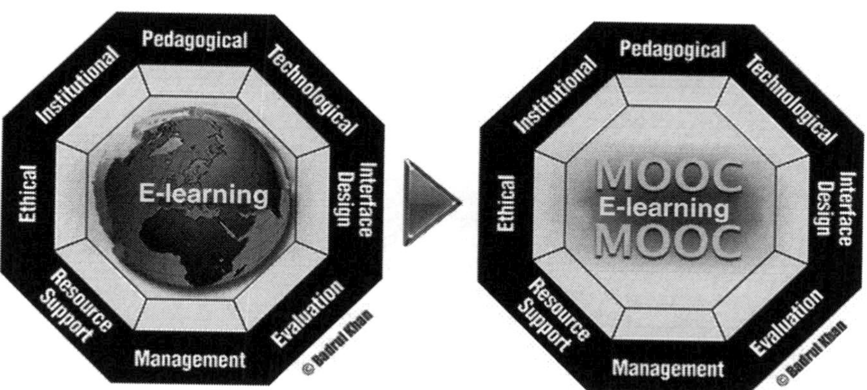

Figure 1.8 E-learning Framework Applicable to MOOC
Copyright © Badrul Khan

Conclusion

With the emergence of new communication and computing technologies, e-learning is growing globally. One of its most recent manifestations is the MOOC, the massive open online course designed to offer large-scale free education courses to the masses (Milheim, 2013).

Designing open and distributed learning systems for globally diverse learners is challenging; however, as more and more institutions offer flexible learning to students worldwide, we will become more knowledgeable about what works and what does not work. We should try to accommodate the needs of diverse learners by asking critical questions along the lines of the eight categories of the Framework. The questions may vary based on each flexible learning system. The more issues (in the form of checklist questions) within the eight categories of the Framework we explore, the more meaningful and supportive is the learning environment we can create. Given our specific contexts, we may not be able to address all issues within the eight categories of the Framework, but we should address as many as we can in order to provide increased flexibility for learners.

Additional Resources

7 Ways to Market E-Learning, http://www.kineo.com/elearning-reports/7-ways-to-market-e-learning.html

Three Tips for Selling More E-learning, http://www.tagoras.com/docs/3-Tips-for-Selling-More-E-learning.pdf

Notes

This chapter is a modified version of the introductory chapter of *Khan's E-learning Tips*, Linus Books, 2015.

1 http://www.prweb.com/releases/elearning/corporate_elearning/prweb4531974.htm
2 http://www.prnewswire.com/news-releases/global-market-for-elearning-to-reach-169-billion-by-2018-private-tutoring-nears-103-billion-in-market-value-180027521.html
3 http://www.nrcs.usda.gov/wps/portal/nrcs/detail/national/nedc/?cid=nrcs143_024073
4 http://www.ien.idaho.gov/media/Best_Practices/USDLAReport.pdf
5 https://sites.google.com/site/instructionaldesignandtraining/e-learning/addie-for-elearning

References and Recommended Readings

Ally, M. (2012). Designing mobile learning for the user. In B.H. Khan (Ed.), *User interface design for virtual environments: Challenges and advances* (pp. 226–235). Hershey, PA: IGI Global.

Banathy, B.H. (1991). *Systems designs of education: A journey to create the future*. Englewood Cliffs, NJ: Educational Technology.

Banathy, B.H. (1995). Developing a systems view of education. *Educational Technology, 35*(3), 53–57.

Barry, B. (2002). ISD and the e-learning framework. Retrieved January 24, 2003, from http://www.wit.ie/library/webct/isd.html

Bedard-Voorhees, A., & Dawley, L. (2008). *Evaluating SL course experience: A learner's evaluation and faculty response*. Retrieved November 12, 2008, from http://www.aect.org/SecondLife/08-archives.asp

Berge, Z., & Clark, T. (Eds.). (2005). *Virtual schools: planning for success*. New York: Teachers College Press.

Bonk, C.J., & Reynolds, T.H. (1997). Learner-centered Web instruction for higher-order thinking, teamwork and apprenticeship. In B.H. Khan (Ed.), *Web-based instruction* (pp. 167–178). Englewood Cliffs, NJ: Educational Technology.

Boshier, R., Mohapi, M., Moulton, G., Qayyum, A., Sadownik, L., & Wilson, M. (1997). Best and worst dressed Web courses: Strutting into the 21st century in comfort and style. *Distance Education, 18*(2), 327–348.

Calder, J., & McCollum, A. (1998). *Open and flexible learning in vocational education and training*. London: Kogan Page.

Cheon, J., & Grant, M. M. (2009). Are pretty interfaces worth the time? The effects of user interface types on web-based instruction. *Journal of Interactive Learning Research, 20*(1), 5–33. Chesapeake, VA: AACE.

Chin, K.L., & Kon, P.N. (2003). Key factors for a fully online e-learning mode: A Delphi study. In G. Crisp, D. Thiele, I. Scholten, S. Barker, & J. Baron (Eds.), *Interact, integrate, impact: Proceedings of the 20th annual conference of the Australasian Society for Computers in Learning in Tertiary Education*. Adelaide, Australia, 7–10 December 2003.

Corbeil, J.R., Corbeil, M.E., & Khan, B.H. (in press). *The MOOC case book: Case studies in MOOC design, development and implementation*. Ronkonkoma, NY: Linus Books.

Dabbagh, N.H., Bannan-Ritland, B., & Silc, K. (2000). Pedagogy and Web-based course authoring tools: Issues and implications. In B.H. Khan (Ed.), *Web-based training* (pp. 343–354). Englewood Cliffs, NJ: Educational Technology.

Davies, A., & Dalgarno, B. (2008). Learning fire investigation the clean way: The virtual experience. In *Hello! Where are you in the landscape of educational technology?* Proceedings ascilite Melbourne 2008. Retrieved Jan 26, 2015 from http://www.ascilite.org.au/conferences/melbourne08/procs/davies.pdf

del Galdo, E. M., & Nielsen, J. (Eds.) (1996). *International user interfaces*. New York: John Wiley & Sons.

Dillenbourg, P., Schneider, D.K., & Synteta, P. (2002). Virtual learning environments. In A. Dimitracopoulou (Ed.), *Proceedings of the 3rd Hellenic Conference on Information & Communication Technologies in Education* (pp. 3–18). Greece: Kastaniotis Editions.

Duchastel, P., & Spahn, S. (1996). Design for web-based learning. *Proceedings of the WebNet-96 World Conference of the Web Society*. San Francisco, CA. October 15–19, 1996.

Duggan, L. (2012). *Teaching Android application development in a collaborative online environment*. Retrieved March 3, 2014, from http://files.eric.ed.gov/fulltext/ED533664.pdf

Ellington, H. (1995). Flexible learning, your flexible friend. In C. Bell, M. Bowden, & A. Trott (Eds.), *Implementing flexible learning* (pp. 3–13). London: Kogan Page.

El-Tigi, M.A., & Khan, B.H. (2001). Web-based learning resources. In B.H. Khan (Ed.), *Web-based training* (pp. 59–72). Englewood Cliffs, NJ: Educational Technology.

Gilbert, P.K. (2002). *The virtual university an analysis of three advanced distributed leaning systems*. Retrieved February 24, 2004, from http://gseacademic.harvard.edu/~gilberpa/homepage/portfolio/research/pdf/edit611.pdf

Global eLearning market to reach $107.3 billion by 2015. (n.d.). *PRWeb*. Retrieved from http://www.prweb.com/releases/elearning/corporate_elearning/prweb4531974.htm

Goodear, L. (2001). *Cultural diversity and flexible learning*. Presentation of Findings 2001 Flexible Learning Leaders Professional Development Activity. South West Institute of TAFE, Australia. Retrieved February 24, 2004, from http://www.flexiblelearning.net.au/leaders/events/pastevents/2001/statepres/papers/lyn-handout.pdf

Hall, B. (2001). *ELearning: Building competitive advantage through people and technology*. A special section on elearning by *Forbes* Magazine. Retrieved January 24, 2003, from http://www.forbes.com/specialsections/elearning/

Jones, M.G., & Farquhar, J.D. (1997). User interface design for Web-based instruction. In B.H. Khan (Ed.), *Web-based instruction* (pp. 239–244). Englewood Cliffs, NJ: Educational Technology.

Kao, D., Tousignant, W., & Wiebe, N. (2000). A paradigm for selecting an institutional software. In D. Colton, J. Caouette, & B. Raggad (Eds.), *Proceedings ISECON 2000* (Vol. 17) Philadelphia: AITP Foundation for Information Technology Education.

Khan, B.H. (in press). Introduction to e-learning. In B.H. Khan & M. Ally (Eds.), *The international handbook of e-learning*. New York: Routledge.

Khan, B.H. (1997). Web-based instruction: What is it and why is it? In B.H. Khan (Ed.), *Web-based instruction* (pp. 5–18). Englewood Cliffs, NJ: Educational Technology.

Khan, B.H. (2001a). Virtual U: A hub for excellence in education, training and learning resources. In B.H. Khan (Ed.), *Web-based training* (pp. 491–506). Englewood Cliffs, NJ: Educational Technology.

Khan, B.H. (2001b). Web-based training: An introduction. In B.H. Khan (Ed.), *Web-based training* (pp. 5–12). Englewood Cliffs, NJ: Educational Technology.

Khan, B.H. (Ed.). (2007). *Flexible learning in an information society*. Hershey, PA: Information Science.

Khan, B.H. (Ed.). (2012). *User interface design for virtual environments: Challenges and advances*. Hershey, PA: IGI Global.

Khan, B.H. (2014). *Continuum in e-learning: People, process and product (P3)*. Retrieved April 7, 2014, from http://elearningindustry.com/continuum-in-e-learning-people-process-and-product-p3

Khan, B.H., & Ealy, D. (2001). A framework for web-based authoring systems. In B.H. Khan (Ed.), *Web-based training* (pp. 355–364). Englewood Cliffs, NJ: Educational Technology.

Khan, B.H., & Joshi, V. (2006). E-learning who, what and how? *Journal of Creative Communications, 1*(1), 61–74.

Khan, B.H., Waddill, D., & McDonald, J. (2001). Review of Web-based training sites. In B.H. Khan (Ed.), *Web-based training* (pp. 367–374). Englewood Cliffs, NJ: Educational Technology.

Kearsley, G. (1996). The World Wide Web: Global access to education. *Educational Technology Review, Winter* (5), 26–30.

Kearsley, G., & Shneiderman, B. (1999). Engagement theory: A framework for technology-based teaching and learning. Retrieved March 3, 2014, from http://home.sprynet.com/ gkearsley/engage.htm

Krauth, B. (1998). Distance learning: The instructional strategy of the decade. In G.P. Connick (Ed.), *The distance learner's guide* (Chapter 1). Upper Saddle River, NJ: Prentice Hall.

Kuchi, R., Gardner, R., & Tipton, R. (2003). *A learning framework for information literacy and library instruction programs at Rutgers University Libraries*. Recommendations of the Learning Framework Study Group. Rutgers University Libraries.

Land, S.M., & Hannafin, M.J. (1997). Patterns of understanding with open-ended learning environments: A qualitative study. *Educational Technology Research and Development, 45*(2), 47–73.

Martin, F.G. (2012). Will massive open online courses change how we teach? *Communications of the ACM, 55*(8), 26–28.

Mello, R. (2002, June). 100 pounds of potatoes in a 25-pound sack: Stress frustration, and learning in the virtual classroom. *Teaching With Technology Today, 8*(9). Retrieved February, 2004, from *http://www.elearningmag.com/elearning/article/articleDetail.jsp?id=2031*

Milheim, W.D. (2013). Massive Open Online Courses (MOOCs): Current applications and future potential. *Educational Technology, May-June*, 38–42.

Moore, M.G. (1998). Introduction. In C.C. Gibson (Ed.), *Distance learners in higher education*. Madison, WI: Atwood.

Moore, M.G., & Kearsley, G. (2011). *Distance education: A systems view of online learning*. Boston: Wadsworth.

Morrison, J.L., & Khan, B.H. (2003). The global e-learning framework: An interview with Badrul Khan. *The Technology Source*. A Publication of the Michigan Virtual University. Retrieved May 18, 2003, from http://ts.mivu.org/default.asp?show=article&id=1019#options

Reigeluth, C.M., & Khan, B.H. (1994, February). *Do instructional systems design (ISD) and educational systems design (ESD) really need each other?* Paper presented at the Annual Meeting of the Association for Educational Communications and Technology (AECT), Nashville, TN.

Relan, A., & Gillani, B.B. (1997). Web-based instruction and traditional classroom: Similarities and differences. In B.H. Khan (Ed.), *Web-based instruction* (pp. 41–46). Englewood Cliffs, NJ: Educational Technology.

Ritchie, D. C., & Hoffman, B. (1997). Incorporating instructional design principles with the World Wide Web. In B.H. Khan (Ed.), *Web-based instruction* (pp. 135–138). Englewood Cliffs, NJ: Educational Technology.

Romiszowski, A.J. (2004). How's the elearning baby? Factors leading to success or failure of an educational technology innovation. *Educational Technology, 44*(1), 5–27.

Rosenberg, M.J. (2001). *E-learning: Strategies for delivering knowledge in the digital age*. New York: McGraw-Hill.

Saltzbert, S., & Polyson, S. (1995, September). Distributed learning on the World Wide Web. *Syllabus, 9*(1), 10–12.

Singh, H. (2003). Building effective blended learning programs. *Educational Technology, 44*(1), 5–27.

Smith, H.L., & Khan, B.H. (2007). Program satisfaction survey instrument for online students. In B.H. Khan (Ed.), *Flexible learning* (pp. 320–337). Englewood Cliffs, NJ: Educational Technology.

Taylor, A. (2014). A look at Web-based instruction today: An interview with Badrul Khan, Part 1. *eLearn Magazine. A Publication of ACM*. Retrieved March 19, 2014, from http://elearnmag.acm.org/archive.cfm?aid=2590180

Wisher, R., & Khan, B.H. (Eds.). (2010). *Learning on demand: ADL and the future of elearning*. Alexandria, VA: Advanced Distributed Learning.

Zhang, J., Khan, B.H., Gibbons, A.S., & Ni, Y. (2001). Review of web-based assessment tools. In B.H. Khan (Ed.), *Web-based training* (pp. 137–146). Englewood Cliffs, NJ: Educational Technology.

2

Historical Perspectives on E-learning

Michael Moore

Historical Foundations of E-learning

Introduction

As each new electronic communication technology has entered common usage, educators have looked for ways of integrating it into their teaching and their students' learning, both in classrooms and beyond. Modern e-learning pedagogy has evolved from these experiences extending back almost a century. Three phases of this evolution can be identified. For the first half-century the technology was one-way broadcasting. Next, from the 1970s to the 1990s came the teleconferencing technologies, first audio, then video and finally computer based, allowing interactivity between instructors and students. Finally this was superseded by the internet, browser and World Wide Web. This chapter will further describe each of these phases, including brief reference to how educational institutions responded to each of these developments.

Broadcasting. The first generally available e-learning technology was the radio, or "wireless" as it was popularly known, with the first for-credit courses broadcast in 1925 at the State University of Iowa. Several "schools of the air" were also established in the late 1920s to broadcast to K-12 classrooms. Examples include the Ohio School of the Air founded in 1929, the RCA Educational Hour established in 1928 with sponsorship from the National Broadcasting Company (NBC), and the American School of the Air in 1930, sponsored by CBS.

E-learning by television began in the 1930s. Between 1934 and 1939, the State University of Iowa broadcast some 400 programs, and in 1939 in Los Angeles, television was introduced into the high school. After World War II, when broadcast frequencies were allocated, 242 of the 2,053 channels were given to noncommercial use. In addition to programs broadcast on these public channels, some of the best educational television was pioneered by commercial stations. NBC aired Johns Hopkins University's *Continental Classroom* and CBS broadcast their *Sunrise Semester*, both used by colleges in their credit programs. Chicago TV College pioneered television teaching in the community colleges. In 1956 closed circuit television was introduced in the public schools of Washington County, Maryland. In 1961 programs were broadcast from airplanes over six states in the Midwest Program on Airborne Television. According to Unwin and McAleese (1988), this project, which lasted six years, helped break down resistance to the idea of teaching across state borders, as well as setting a precedent for future e-learning by satellite. In 1967, Congress set up the Corporation for Public Broadcasting (CPB), which promoted educational broadcasting for decades ahead. By the end of the 1970s, there were about 150 educational stations, broadcasting programs for students from K-12 through postsecondary education.

ITFS and cable television. Instructional Television Fixed Services (ITFS) was a closed circuit distribution system that delivered television pictures within a radius of about 25 miles, and was greatly valued as a way of sharing specialist teachers and covering low enrolment subjects. The first licence was issued by the FCC in 1961 to the Plainedge School System, New York. Another pioneering effort in this was the Stanford Instructional Television Network (SITN), which in 1969 began broadcasting 120 engineering courses to 900 engineers at sixteen partner companies (DiPaolo, 1992).

With the spread of cable television (CATV) in the 1970s, the Federal Communications Commission (FCC) required all operators to provide an educational channel. Among the early leaders in this form of e-learning were the Appalachian Community Service Network based at the University of Kentucky, the Pennsylvania State University's Pennarama Network, the privately funded Mind Extension University, the Electronic University Network, and the International University Consortium (Wright, 1991, pp. 55–63). By the mid-1980s, there were around 200 college-level "tele-courses", delivered to more than 1,000 colleges and 600,000 adult students. Starting in 1981, the Annenberg Foundation supported the CPB on a project that provided funds typically in the 2–3 million dollar range for the production of university-level tele-courses with world-class production values. For example, a Californian consortium led by Coastline Community College was awarded $5 million to produce a telecourse called *The Mechanical Universe*.

New technology-based institutions. The late 1960s and early 1970s was a time of epic change in the emergence of e-learning, as educators looked to capitalize on new technology through changes in how their institutions operated, leading in turn to new instructional techniques and new theorizing about teaching and learning itself. The two most important such experiments were the University of Wisconsin's AIM Project and Great Britain's Open University. The purpose of the Articulated Instructional Media Project (AIM) was to test the idea of linking (i.e., "articulating") a variety of technologies to maximize the effectiveness of each, so that not only could content be better presented than through any one medium alone, but also individual learners could choose the combination most suited to their learning styles. To produce such multimedia programs, AIM invented the idea of the course design team, formed of specialist instructional designers, technologists, and content experts (Wedemeyer & Najem, 1969). AIM's director, Charles Wedemeyer, went on to advise a British project aimed at opening access to higher education to every adult in a new, campus-less "university of the air". What emerged, the Open University, was the world's first national university based primarily on electronic communications, using design and teaching methods first tested in the AIM project. Seen as successful and excellent beyond the most optimistic hopes at the time, the open university model has been widely emulated in other countries. (For a list, see Moore & Kearsley, 1996, p. 43.)

No such national university was set up in the United States, though several smaller innovations shared some of its characteristics. One example was Nova University of Advanced Technology, inaugurated in 1964, later changing its name to Nova University, and finally Nova Southeastern University. Another, the Empire State College, was created in 1971 in the State University of New York to deliver bachelor's and associate degree programs exclusively at a distance. Other open degree programs started in the 1970s included those of Goddard College,

Syracuse University, Regents College of New York and Thomas Edison College. A few U.S. universities, notably Rutgers, the University of Houston and the University of Maryland, adapted courses from the OU-UK itself. By the early 1990s most major universities were developing policies and procedures for transforming their correspondence and extension courses into e-learning distance education systems. At Penn State University a policy statement asserted, "distance education will become a substantial part of the University's future"; it recommended "the assignment of substantial resources" and setting up a special university-wide unit, which later became known as its World Campus (See Moore & Kearsley, 1996, p. 194). Although a trend-setter, this university was not alone in consciously shifting distance education from the periphery to the mainstream of its operations. At the same time, faced with the costs of investment in new technology and program specialists, many institutions turned to a different type of organizational structure, the *consortium*. This was a voluntary collaboration between several otherwise independent institutions, one of the first being the University of Mid-America (UMA), established by nine Midwestern universities, based at the University of Nebraska. The idea was that some of the advantages of the UKOU—scale, technology and high production values—could be achieved if each member university produced a limited number of courses to be distributed throughout the consortium (McNeil, 1993). Other early consortia included the National Technological University (NTU), a network of 50 institutions established in 1984, and the National University Telecommunications Network (NUTN), established in 1982 with about 60 member institutions.

Interactive audio technologies. The first synchronous interactive e-learning technology, quite widely used during the 1970s and into the 1980s, was *audio-conferencing*. Unlike one-way broadcast lessons, audio-conferencing allowed instructors and students to interact in real time and from different locations. Individual students could join an audio-conference from their homes or offices using regular telephones, although the more successful format was interaction by groups of students connected by telephone but using specially designed microphones and speakers. Almost any number of sites could be joined together by an operator or by means of a bridge—a device that links any number of callers automatically and simultaneously. The first major educational audio-conference system was set up at the University of Wisconsin in 1965 as part of the AIM project, at first to provide continuing education for physicians. The system grew to 200 locations in university campuses, county courthouses, libraries, hospitals, and schools with over 35,000 users and more than 100 programs every week, mostly for continuing professional education (Moore & Kearsley, 1996, pp. 90–91).

Satellites and teleconference networks. The first communications satellite was launched in 1965, and barely ten years later, the ATS-6 satellite was dedicated to education. Among pioneers in this technology were the University of Alaska, and the University of Hawaii's Pan-Pacific Education and Communications Experiments by Satellite (PEACESAT), distributing programs over some 20 Pacific Islands. Programs were usually transmitted to receiving stations and then distributed locally by ITFS or cable networks. Typically the program had one or more speakers on a video screen, with questions from the audience by telephone or other audio feed. One of the first consortia to support programs by satellite was the National University Teleconferencing Network (NUTN), transmitting primarily from its base at Oklahoma State University. Over the next 10 years, the network grew to more than 250 organizations, either providing or receiving a range of over 100 programs, delivered to as many as 6,000 people at a time, located at some 200 receive sites (see Oberle, 1990 for a fuller account). Another consortium, The National Technological University, founded in 1984 with support from Hewlett-Packard, IBM, Lockheed Martin and Motorola, and based in Fort Collins, Colorado, became an accredited university offering graduate and continuing education courses in engineering, and awarding its own degrees. Courses were provided from some 50 participating institutions, uplinked to NTU and redistributed to downlinks in some 500 locations.

Other consortia created in the 1980s to use satellites for teleconferencing included the following:

> The Agricultural Satellite Network, with 32 institutional members provided courses primarily on agricultural topics.
>
> The Satellite Communications for Learning consortium distributed foreign language news broadcasts from 35 countries to be used in language and current affairs courses.
>
> The Community College Satellite Network was for members of the American Association of Community and Junior Colleges.
>
> The Black College Satellite Network (BCSN), based at Howard University, distributed programs to 105 colleges located in 23 states and the District of Columbia.
>
> Various state consortia, such as the Indiana Higher Education Telecommunications System and the Oklahoma Telecommunications Network, distributed programs at the state level.
>
> Several international collaborative experiments in the 1980s included, notably, the Global Pacific University, one of several innovations in satellite applications inspired by Takeshi Utsumi.
>
> (See Utsumi, Rossman, & Rosen, 1990 for a full account.)

Business TV. In 1987 half of Fortune 500 companies and most professional associations used e-learning by satellite, often called "Business TV", for delivery of training and continuing education programs. IBM had its own Interactive Satellite Education Network with studios in four cities and receiving sites in thirteen. Federal Express had daily programs to 800 downlinks; Kodak Corporation twice weekly, two-hour-long training programs; Domino's Pizza sent a mobile uplink to any store where an employee had something to teach. For organizations not having their own satellite networks, time could be bought from one of several vendors. An example was AREN, the American Rehabilitation Educational Network, delivering continuing education for health care professionals at nearly 100 sites. In 1987 an AREN program, Management Vision, was broadcast to 650 sites with subscribers from corporations, hospitals, and colleges. The Public Service Satellite Consortium delivered programs for the American Hospital Association, the American Law Institute, the American Bar Association, the National Education Association, the AFL–CIO, and the U.S. Chamber of Commerce. The Health Education Network had over 300 hospital members, focusing on in-service training of medical personnel and patient education with approximately 40 programs monthly.

Satellite programs in K-12 schools. In 1987 Congress passed the federal Star Schools Program Assistance Act, authorizing a five-year budget of $100 million to promote the use of telecommunications for instruction in math, science, and foreign languages at the K–12 level. The first awards were to: The Midlands Consortium, consisting of five universities in four states; the Texas based TI-In network included three state agencies, four universities, and a private corporation, Ti-in Inc. A third consortium of state education agencies and state television authorities, SERC, provided high school courses in 19 states. Together the Star Schools consortia covered 45 states and almost 3,000 schools; 32,037 students participated in science programs. In 1990 four new grants, totaling $14,813,000, were awarded to consortia located in the northeastern and northwestern United States. The Star Schools program had tremendous impact on growing the idea of e-learning in K–12 classrooms, particularly in getting equipment installed and programs developed, and providing teachers with training. (For a list of Star Schools projects see Moore & Kearsley, 1996, p. 52.)

Two-way video-conferencing. Communication in the Star Schools, university and business TV systems was invariably two-way in sound, but one-way in video. Thus participants at all sites could see and hear presenters from the originating site, but they could respond only by audio. As the 1990s wore on, two-way video-conferencing became more widely available. The first technology provided pictures from one studio to another transmitted at "T1" (1.5 megabits per second), the signals compressed by a device called a *codec*. The earliest codecs were as large as a refrigerator, but by the mid-1990s they could be fitted inside a personal computer so that two-way video-conferencing became feasible at transmission rates as low as 56 kbps (kilobits per second). Using a T1 network, Michael G. Moore at Penn State University initiated the first full for-credit graduate courses delivered by two-way video teleconference in January 1986, linking students in a studio on the campus at University Park with groups in Erie, Pennsylvania. Because they need studio facilities and camera operators, these programs were complex to organize and facilitate, and soon, with the evolution of personal and desktop computers, were replaced by simpler forms of video-conferencing.

Computer networks. The idea of using a network of computers to deliver e-learning programs was initiated in the 1970s at the University of Illinois in its PLATO (Programmed Logic for Automatic Teaching) project, which allowed students at several sites to dial in using telephone lines to a mainframe computer. In 1975 when the first personal computer, the Altair 8800, came onto the market, the potential of e-learning through computer networks increased dramatically. Pioneering experiments included those at Duke University, whose students developed a system called USENET in 1980, and work by Ira Fuchs at the City University of New York (CUNY) and Greydon Freeman at Yale University who invented BITNET ("Because It's Time Network"). This first extended network of computers dedicated solely to education grew quickly to almost 500 educational institutions by 1991. At the same time, in the mid-1980s, the National Sciences Foundation developed NFSNet, a network of five supercomputer centers connected to universities and research organizations. Like BITNET, it could be used for exchanging e-mail and data files, and accessing bulletin boards and library facilities.

Audio-graphics. BITNET and other emerging networks had very limited bandwidth, and it was necessary to deliver speech independently of text and images. Referred to as audio-graphics, text and images were transmitted to a computer on one telephone line to enhance the audio presentation on another line. Peripherals attached to the computers included tablets and light pens, cameras to transmit slow-scan pictures, and scanners for transmitting documents. When linked through a bridge, the computers at a number of sites allowed students and teachers to interact in real time with the graphic and visual images as well as with the audio messages. Experiments at the Pennsylvania State University in the mid 1989s aimed to use computer conferencing (using the BITNET network) to internationalize e-learning, teaching cohorts of about 100 students in groups in different cities in Mexico, Finland and Estonia, as well as in the United States (Collins & Berge, 1994). Another major experiment in computer conferencing was the Electronic University Network, an undergraduate degree program of courses delivered from 19 universities with accreditation awarded by Thomas Edison College in New Jersey. Course materials were delivered on computer disk and in print; interaction with instructors occurred through computer, telephone, and mail. Similar programs were developed by Buena Vista, The University of Wisconsin, The UK Open University and the CoSy system at the University of Guelph, among others. A list of early computer networks for K-12 students is given in Moore and Kearsley (1996: 56).

Arrival of the Internet and Web-based education. A leap forward in the transformation of distance education into modern e-learning began with the emergence of the World Wide Web, and, in 1993, the first Web browser, called Mosaic. It has been estimated that in 1992 the Web contained only 50 pages, but in less than a decade had risen to over a billion (Maddux, 2001). In the new century, high-speed networks developed rapidly. With the emergence of the Internet's Web, many organizations increasingly started to use the Web as Web-Based Information systems for their product and services. Badrul Khan recognized the potential of the World Wide Web for education early in 1996 and coined the phrase "Web-Based Instruction" (Khan, 1997), which paved the way for the new field of e-learning. The use of the Web for educational purposes continues to grow, and works of many global researchers and practitioners in online learning inundated publications with different names: Web-based training, e-learning, flexible learning, mobile learning, blended-learning, distributed learning, massive open online course (MOOC), etc. In 2001, Internet 2 was a consortium of 180 U.S. universities, 78 corporate partners and sponsors, 10 U.S. government agencies and over 30 foreign organizations, building a new data pipeline to link the institutions at speeds 45,000 times faster than that provided by the best telephone modems previously in use (http://www.internet2.edu).

In this new generation of Web-based e-learning, another factor was at work, as significant as the technology itself, and that was reinvention of the basic concept of education, as a growing number of scholars came to realize that education is more than a single process that can occur only in a single geographic location. As early as 1993 *The American Journal of Distance Education* could assert:

> The Virtual University is now technically viable. Such an organization could make instructors anywhere available to students anywhere, and could make courses prepared by any institution available to students anywhere. A student's faculty need no longer be limited to those who assemble in any one place any more than a teacher's students would have to assemble in one place. Students could learn wherever they are located from instructional resources wherever they are located. No student would need to take instruction from exactly the same teacher as any other; students could have access to teachers from any state or country at any time and in any combination; they could have access to information resources from any state or country at any time and in any combination. Students also could have universal access to advice and guidance.
>
> (Moore, 1993, p. 4)

Stimulated by the new technology, as well as cost pressures and competition for students, more and more universities set up new programs or administrative units to design and deliver e-learning courses on the Web. An early provider of e-learning degree programs was the Online Campus of the New York Institute of Technology, and another was Jones International University, claiming to be "the first fully online, accredited university" (http://www.jiu.edu/). By the end of the decade, 84.1% of public universities and 83.3% of four-year public colleges and 74% of community colleges offered Web-based courses (Green, 2001). Some traditional universities attempted to spin-off for-profit online enterprises; Temple University established Virtual Temple, New York University created NYU Online and Cornell University developed its e-Cornell initiative. Among the more successful new e-learning universities were for-profits Jones International University, University of Phoenix Online, and Capella University and Western Governors University. Important in early public sector e-learning was the eArmyU, enabling soldiers to enroll in courses from 24 higher education institutions. Several other early enterprises passed away. California Virtual University was abandoned in 1999; Fathom, a consortium of arts and educational institutions, closed in 2003.

To sell e-learning services, new companies were established at the end of the 1990s, examples being Digital Think, Element K, eMind, Netg, and SmartForce. SmartForce claimed to be the world's largest e-learning company, with over 2,500 corporate customers. Other companies sold e-learning tools for higher education, notably Blackboard.com, WebCT and eCollege. A related phenomenon in the 1990s was the emergence of companies that specialized in testing, with the market dominated by three companies related to the publishing industry: Prometric (acquired from Sylvan Learning Systems by Thomson Corp. of Canada for $775 million), CatGlobal (a division of Houghton-Mifflin) and Virtual University Enterprises (a division of NCS Pearson). The abundance of such resources and online courses led to the development of Web portals and a variety of information organizing sites, examples being Hungry Minds, Learn2.com and SmartPlanet.com.

Virtual reality and multiusers domains. Virtual reality (VR) began with experiments at the Massachusetts Institute of Technology with Head-Mounted Displays that gave the illusion of seeing objects in three dimensions. Over the next 20 years techniques were developed for computer-generating scenes in which participants could be immersed and navigate. In 1988, the National Aeronautics and Space Administration (NASA) created a virtual reality laboratory, and in 1990 a VR replica of the city of Seattle was shown at the conference of the Association for Computing Machinery (Rheingold, 1991). The first online multiusers environment, established by the Quantum Computer Service (later America Online) allowed about 500 participants to interact through graphical representations of bodies and objects called avatars. Interaction in these early Multi-Users Domains (MUDs) and Multi-Object Oriented MUDs (MOOs) was by text. An experimental educational VR environment called the CyberCampus developed by the NTT Software Corporation included videos and live sound. Other influential virtual learning environments introduced in the mid-1990s included the Virtual Reality Multi-User Dungeon (VRMUD) and the Virtual European School Project (Bouras et al., 2001).

Theory and Scholarship

It would be disastrously incorrect to view e-learning or any other form of distance education as nothing more than the adding of technology to otherwise standard classroom teaching. The added technology, to be successfully used for learning, must be integrated into new and different methods of designing course work and facilitating the interaction of students with that content, as well as with an instructor and each other. Such fundamental insights into the curricular and instructional characteristics of all forms of distance education first began to infiltrate the educational literature and discourse in the 1970s, initiated by a small, international group of scholars. The leading figures in this movement were Charles Wedemeyer with his assistant, Michael G. Moore, at University of Wisconsin-Madison; Borje Holmberg in Sweden; and Otto Peters in Germany (for an introduction to these theorists see Diehl (2012) and Black (2004). Although Moore published the first version of his transactional distance theory in 1972, (see Moore, 2012), by the end of the decade research was still atheoretical, descriptive institutional evaluation research. Nevertheless, throughout the 1980s a steady trickle of such articles built awareness of the potential of e-learning by computer networks as a new form of distance learning. One of the first was an evaluation report by Hiltz and Turoff (1981) of students' attitudes and experiences in the Electronic Information Exchange system. Early studies of social interaction included the work of Siegel and colleagues (1986), who described the effects of computer-mediated communication on communication efficiency, user participation, interpersonal behavior and group choice. The state of the art in 1986 can be seen in an ERIC Clearinghouse document in which the author (Tucker, 1986) discussed various aspects of electronic networking.

Research and scholarship at this time were hampered by the paucity of journals, a situation that changed in 1987 with the founding of the *American Journal of Distance Education*. This was soon followed by what proved to be a significant turning point, in July 1988, that set the stage for American research activity in the 1990s. This was the First American Symposium on Research in Distance Education, the first time that academics and practitioners had met specifically to plan an agenda of e-learning research (Black, 2012, p. 5). A book of chapters authored by participants at the symposium constitutes the first collection of North American research on distance education (Moore, 1990). Evolving from the symposium, and others that followed, to keep scholars in contact, one of the first social networks was set up: an electronic bulletin board and e-mail network called DEOS—the Distance Education Online Symposium, meeting on one of the first public computer networks, Compuserve. Such growth of interest in research and scholarship in the 1990s led to the setting up of programs of study and professional development. Among these were certificate programs offered by Penn State University's adult education program and by the University of Wisconsin-Madison. Soon several major institutions were offering master's degrees, including Athabasca University, Canada, the UK Open University and University of Maryland University College in collaboration with the University of Oldenburg in Germany. The number of doctoral dissertations tripled in the first decade of the twenty-first century compared with the previous decade (Black, 2012, pp. 7–8, 16).

References

Black, L. M. (2004). *A living story of the origins and development of scholarship in the field of distance education* (Doctoral dissertation). The Pennsylvania State University, University Park.

Black, L.M. (2012). A history of scholarship. In M. G. Moore (Ed.), *The handbook of distance education* (3rd ed., pp. 3–20). New York, NY: Routledge.

Collins, M., & Berge, Z. (1994). Student evaluation of computer conferencing in a (primarily) audio-conferencing distance education course. In M. M. Thompson & M. G. Moore (Eds.), *Internationalism in distance education: A vision for higher education* (pp. 115–129). Research Monograph Number 10. University Park, PA: The American Center for the Study of Distance Education.

Bouras, C., Philopoulos, A., & Tsiatsos, T. (2001). e-Learning through distributed virtual environments. *Journal of Network and Computer Applications, 24*, 175–199.

Diehl, W. C. (2012). Charles Wedemeyer: Visionary pioneer of distance education. In M. G. Moore (Ed.), *The handbook of distance education* (3rd ed., pp. 38–48). New York, NY: Routledge.

DiPaolo, A. (1992). The Stanford instructional television network: A partnership with industry. *European Journal of Engineering Education, 6*(7), 243–246.

Green, K.C. (2001). *The 2001 national survey of information technology in US higher education*. Encino, CA: Campus Computing Project.

Hiltz, S.R., & Turoff, M. (1981). The evolution of user behavior in a computerized conferencing system. In R. Kling (Ed.), *Social impacts of computing*. Communications of the ACM, 24(11).

Khan, B.H. (Ed.). (1997). *Web-based instruction*. Englewood Cliffs, NJ: Educational Technology.

Maddux, C.D. (2001). *Educational computing: Learning with tomorrow's technologies*. Needham Heights, MA: Allyn & Bacon.

McNeil, D.R. (1993). The rise and fall of a consortium. The story of the University of Mid-America. In L. Moran & I. Mugridge (Eds.), *Collaboration in distance education* (pp. 123–131). London, UK: Routledge.

Moore, M. G. (Ed.). (1990). *Contemporary issues in American distance education*. Oxford, UK: Pergamon Press.

Moore, M.G. (1993). Editorial: Free trade in higher education. *American Journal of Distance Education, 7*(3).

Moore, M. G. (2012). The theory of transactional distance. In D. Keegan (Ed.), *Theoretical principles of distance education* (pp. 22–38). London, UK: Routledge.

Moore, M.G., & Kearsley, G. (1996). *Distance education: A systems view*. Belmont, CA: Wadsworth.

Oberle, M. (1990). The National University Teleconference Network: A living laboratory for distance learning. In M. G. Moore (Ed.), *Contemporary issues in American distance education* (pp. 81–95). Oxford, UK: Pergamon Press.

Rheingold, H. (1991). *Virtual reality*. New York, NY: Simon and Schuster.

Siegel, J., Dubrovsky, V., Kiesler, S., & McGuire, T. (1986). Group processes in computer-mediated communication. *Organizational Behavior and Human Decision Processes, 37*, 157–187.

Tucker, S. (1986). *Electronic networking*. ERIC Digest. ERIC Clearinghouse on Information Resources, Syracuse, NY. (ERIC Document Reproduction Service No. ED 278 417).

Unwin, D., & McAleese, R. (Eds.). (1988). The encyclopedia of educational media communications and technology. New York, NY: Greenwood Press.

Utsumi, T., Rossman, P., & Rosen, S. (1990). The global electronic university. In M. G. Moore (Ed.), Contemporary issues in American distance education (pp. 96–110). Oxford, UK: Pergamon Press.

Wedemeyer, C., & Najem, C. (1969). *AIM: From concept to reality*. The Articulated Instructional Media Program at Wisconsin. Syracuse University: Center for the Study of Liberal Education for Adults.

Wright, S.J. (1991). Opportunity lost, opportunity regained: University independent study in the Modern Era. In B.L. Watkins & S.J. Wright (Eds.), *The foundations of American distance education: A century of collegiate correspondence study* (pp. 37–66). Dubuque, IA: Kendall/Hunt.

3

E-learning

Past, Present, and Future

Joseph Rene Corbeil and Maria Elena Corbeil

Introduction

> *Throughout the history of human communication, advances in technology have powered paradigmatic shifts in education.*
>
> —Frick (1991)

Predicting the future is a risky business, but the advantages make the risks worthwhile (Gentry & Csete, 1995). For e-learning practitioners, studying the history of distance education provides a sense of identity and belonging, as they become modern-day explorers, imagining new and better ways to deliver instruction through emerging practices and communication technologies.

While we may live in the present, we plan for and dream about the future. History enables us to understand ourselves, as well as the hopes and aspirations of our predecessors. If we were to consider the motivations of those who contributed to the early development of distance learning, we would recognize the same motivation in them that we hold today—making education accessible to a broader audience of learners who strive to advance their education and professional development while juggling family and work responsibilities.

This chapter will present a timeline, by decade, of the most influential people, events, and trends, impacting the development of e-learning from its origins to the present. Studying the history of e-learning enables us to forecast future directions for short-term and far-term trends.

E-learning Defined

In 1997, Khan laid the groundwork for e-learning through his book *Web-Based Instruction*, which focused international attention on web-based learning and "paved the way for the new field of e-learning" (Khan, 2013, para. 1). He defined e-learning as "an innovative approach for delivering electronically mediated, well-designed, learner-centered, and interactive learning environments to anyone, anyplace, anytime by utilizing the Internet and digital technologies in concert with instructional design principles" (Morrison & Khan, 2003, para. 3). His work on web-based instruction led to the development of *A Framework for E-learning* (Khan, 2012), whose eight dimensions "provide guidance in the design, development, delivery and evaluation of flexible, open and distance learning environments" (Khan, 2012, para. 3).

As advancements in technology developed at a seemingly lightning speed in the late 1990s, access to information became readily available to exponentially larger audiences and changed the landscape for training and workplace learning. One of the first definitions of the evolving forms of learning via the Internet is attributed to Elliott Masie, who in 1997 observed, "Online learning is the use of network technology to design, deliver, select, administer, and extend learning" (as quoted in Cross, 1999, p. 104). It was then that Jay Cross began making the case for the need to redefine learning in order to meet the fast-paced, changing global needs of business. In doing so, he coined the term *e-learning* in 1998 (Cross, 2004). Since then, e-learning definitions have continued to evolve.

Cross (2004) emphasized that e-learning had less to do with formal learning in academic realms and more to do with learner control and workplace performance. He defined e-learning as "learning on Internet Time, the convergence of learning and networks" (p. 104). Noting its potential, he added, "e-learning is a vision of what corporate training can become" (p. 104). A year later, researchers at Cisco Systems built upon previous definitions, noting, "eLearning is Internet-enabled learning. Components can include content delivery in multiple formats, management of the learning experience, and a networked community of learners, content developers and experts" (Cross, 2004, p. 104). In 2004, Jeurissen (as cited in Moeng, 2004, para. 4) further defined e-learning as "the use of innovative technologies and learning models to transform the way individuals and organisations acquire new skills and access knowledge." Different from the first conceptualizations in the late 1990s, Jeurissen's definition no longer referenced the Internet. Instead of becoming more specific, subsequent definitions became broader to include both a wider range of technologies (some not even developed at the time) and the impact the technologies have had on learning itself.

Even today, 16 years after the debut of e-learning, its definitions are as varied as its applications. Each stakeholder (e.g. business, education, communications technologies, computer information systems) assigns the technologies, as well as the magnitude of their reach and intentions, differently. Consequently, in their 2012 study, Sangrà, Vlachopoulos, and Cabrera sought to build an all-inclusive definition of e-learning by conducting a comprehensive review of literature and a Delphi survey of experts in e-learning from different specializations. The results of their study revealed four categories by which e-learning definitions are classified: "(1) technology-driven; (2) delivery-system-oriented; (3) communication-oriented; and (4) educational-paradigm-oriented" (Literature Review, para. 4). The definition developed from these categories and the survey of experts from their study is used to define e-learning in this chapter:

> E-learning is an approach to teaching and learning, representing all or part of the educational model applied, that is based on the use of electronic media and devices as tools for improving access to training, communication and interaction and that facilitates the adoption of new ways of understanding and developing learning.
>
> (Sangrà et al., 2012, Survey of Expert Opinions, para. 12)

Since Khan, Masie, Cross, and other visionaries first made their marks in history over 15 years ago, e-learning has taken a foothold, making learning truly time and place independent. The following section delineates the history of e-learning by decade from the 1980s to today. It is an exciting time for learning, both in workplace and academic settings, as new technologies and global marketplace demands drive innovations in learning and workplace performance.

The History of E-learning

E-learning in the 1980s

Although the term *e-learning* was not coined until the late 1990s, Internet-based distance learning was being developed in universities and organizations around the world as early as the 1960s. Prior to the invention of the Internet, distance learning was offered through a variety of formats, including correspondence, telephone, video and audio tapes, radio, and television.

Rooted in behaviorist theory of the 1920s and programmed instruction of the 1960s, the predecessor to Internet-based distance learning was computer-based training (CBT) of the early 1960s and 1970s. Through programmed instruction, learners worked through lessons by themselves and at their own pace. At the end of each lesson, they were tested for comprehension and immediate automated feedback was given. Programmed instruction made the leap from paper-based to computer-based instruction with the introduction of the computer.

PLATO (Programmed Logic for Automated Teaching Operations), originally developed at the University of Illinois through the 1950s and 1960s, and later transferred to Control Data Corporation (CDC), was one of the first computer-based training programs (K Alliance, n.d.). Developed six years before the launch of the Internet, it offered instruction to university students and local school children. The PLATO system used a "drill-based approach to training and allowed students to skip lessons they already knew" (K Alliance, n.d., para. 2). Although the program ended in 2006, its contribution to computer and web-based instruction is significant for its pioneering use of a host of online communication tools, including message boards, discussion forums, chat rooms, instant messaging, and remote screen sharing. These tools are now standard features in most of today's learning management systems.

As far as institutions of higher education leading the development of distance learning models, in the 1960s, the University of Wisconsin-Madison built a system, that others later modeled worldwide, that incorporated a myriad of communication technologies to increase access to off-campus students. The program "provided much more rapid and modern way to share information and education with students who could not attend traditional courses" (Distance Learning Net, n.d., para. 4).

One of the first documented online programs, however, was not until twenty years later, when CYCLOPS was developed in the early 1980s at Britain's Open University. The CYCLOPS system enhanced the teleconferencing method of distance education delivery through the use of a shared whiteboard that allowed for real-time annotation of downloaded graphics. Supplemental instructional resources to support the live discussions were distributed to learners through cassettes tapes (McConnell & Sharples, 1983).

With the birth of the modern Internet in 1982, and the development of the World Wide Web in 1989, web-based distance learning was set to explode. Acceptance of web-based distance education was accelerated with the introduction of Mosaic, the world's first Web browser, in 1993. Using a mouse to point-and-click on hyperlinked text and graphics enabled users to navigate the Web effortlessly, making it user-friendly and accessible to the average person.

Yet, e-learning, as we know it today, would not have been feasible without the availability of affordable and portable computers users could set up and use from home. While computers were available on university campuses and in schools in the early 1970s, it was not until the microcomputer, also known as the personal computer or PC, became widely adopted by consumers, that e-learning took off.

Although Hewlett-Packard is credited with inventing the first programmable microcomputer in the early 1970s, the Xerox Alto was the first desktop computer to include a monitor, keyboard, and mouse. The Alto also had a simple graphical user interface that became the inspiration for Microsoft and Apple's graphical operating systems. In 1977, the Commodore PET was the first computer adopted for personal use, proceeded by the Apple II and TRS-80 (PC World, 2006).

Since their introduction, personal computers have increased in power and speed, while becoming smaller and lighter. By 1975, laptop computers made the personal computer portable. Since then, laptops have assumed different form factors, also becoming thinner, lighter, and more powerful. Today, high-end sub-notebooks, called Ultrabooks, pack the processing power of full size PCs into devices that are less than an inch thick and weigh less than three pounds, enabling e-learners to become mobile learners.

The rapid commercialization of the Internet, coupled by the speedy advancements in computer technology and the rapid decline of computer prices of the 1980s, made the Internet and web-based distance education accessible to the masses. As the 1980s came to a close, the stage was set for the emergence of web-based instruction.

E-learning in the 1990s

Throughout the 1980s, the publishing, electronics, television, computer, information services and telecommunications industries developed in isolation of one another. In the 1990s, these industries converged and became almost indistinguishable (McGreal, 1994). If the 1980s were the decade of the Internet and the personal computer, the 1990s could easily be recognized as the era of the learning management system.

One of the first distance education networks to employ a learning management system was the TeleEducation network of the Province of New Brunswick (TeleEducation NB). Established in 1993, its open distributed network was implemented through a primitive DOS-based learning management system that included an electronic blackboard, audio conferencing, and screen and software sharing. By 1995, it had more than 100 public and private sites throughout the province (McGreal, 1994).

Jerrold Maddox (1997), a professor of art at Penn State University, is credited with teaching the world's first fully web-based course in the spring of 1995 (Maddox, n.d.). The course, titled *Commentary on Art*, consisted of a series of web pages, including: Syllabus, Tools, Class Members, and FAQs, linked together through a common menu located at the top of each page. Also included in the menu was a link to the Penn State Library Catalog, Yahoo search tool, and the online Encyclopedia Britannica. Communication was facilitated through e-mail, a live chat client, a listserv, and a bulletin board (Maddox, 1997).

Also in 1995, Murray Goldberg, a Computer Science professor at the University of British Columbia, began working on a new platform for constructing web-based learning environments (The Ernest C. Manning Awards Foundation, 2004). Through prior experience, he discovered that building online courses from scratch was very expensive and time consuming. This experience provided the inspiration for Web Course Tools, or WebCT, a user-friendly program to facilitate the rapid development of online courses. Goldberg launched WebCT in early 1996.

Shortly after the release of WebCT, Daniel Cane, an undergraduate student at Cornell University, began writing automated scripts for instructors who wanted to integrate technology into their classes (Bradford, Porciello, & Backus, 2006). In August 1997, he and Stephen Gilfus founded CourseInfo LLC and released the Teachers Toolbox. Among the programs included in the toolbox were tools to generate course sites, announcements, quizzes, and surveys (Nagler, 1997). In June 1998, CourseInfo LLC merged with Blackboard Inc., a consulting firm founded by Michael Chasen and Matthew Pittinsky. Their learning management system, dubbed

Blackboard CourseInfo LLC, was released in 1998 (Bradford et al., 2006). Within a year, over 100 educational institutions were using his course management system (The Ernest C. Manning Awards Foundation, 2004).

While Goldberg and Cane were developing their learning management systems, University of Texas at Brownsville professor Badrul H. Khan set out to write the definitive text on web-based distance education. His groundbreaking book, titled *Web-Based Instruction*, included discussions from nearly 100 authors on the most significant aspects of web-based instruction. Published in 1997, it was translated into multiple languages and quickly became a worldwide best seller. In response to the book's immediate success, working with his Educational Technology graduate students, Khan developed the university's first fully online course. Although beta versions of various learning managements systems were available to universities for testing, they did not become commercially available for at least two years. Therefore, Khan's online course consisted of content pages coded in HTML, a third-party web-based discussion forum and an online quiz generator. The user interface, which resembled a modern-day LMS, was divided into three sections: a horizontal title bar, a vertical menu located in the left frame, and a main content frame where the individual pages of the course appeared. The course was developed to serve as a model of effective web-based instruction as described in the book. It became a template for additional courses in the program, and positioned the Master of Education in Educational Technology to become one of the first fully online programs for the fledgling University of Texas TeleCampus, established in 1998.

Toward the end of the 1990s, universities across the United States and abroad started to experiment with web-based distance education. Founded in 1993, Jones International University became the first fully online university, with the first courses for a Master of Arts in Business Communications offered in 1995 (Jones International University, n.d.). On March 5, 1999, Jones International University made history again by becoming the first fully accredited, fully online university in the United States (Jones International University, n.d.).

Another development of the 1990s that paralleled the growth of the Internet was the advancement of audio and video as an instructional medium. With the introduction of the MPEG audio and video compression standard in 1993, full motion video could be recorded onto compact discs, also known as CDs, and distributed to students (Tudor, 1995). In the early days of dial-up Internet service, audio and video took a long time to download. Therefore, some university programs supplied CDs to students to supplement digital content of their online courses.

As Internet speeds increased, so too did the proliferation of web-based multimedia for instruction. With the development of video streaming in 1995, short audio and video broadcasts could be added to e-learning content, making audio and video streaming practical and affordable. While Internet speeds for consumers were gradually increasing throughout the 1990s, video streaming permitted multimedia to begin playing before the download was complete, thus reducing wait time (Hood, 2012). With increased usability, video on demand became a staple of technology-enhanced and web-based classes.

Although e-mail predates the modern Internet by at least a decade, the incredible growth of personal computers and the Internet through the 1980s and 1990s, drove the rapid expansion of e-mail from privately owned governmental and corporate systems to commercially available public services. Invented in 1971 by Ray Tomlinson, a computer engineer working for a company contracted to build ARPANET, the precursor to the Internet, e-mail was conceived as an efficient way for programmers to leave messages for each other (Campbell, 1998). According to Tomlinson, the @ symbol was chosen to designate the location of the sender's mailbox on a particular server. The first official e-mail message was from Tomlinson to other networked users to announce its existence (Campbell, 1998). E-mail became extremely popular and within two years, 75% of all traffic on ARPANET was e-mail (Campbell, 1998). Because of its low cost, availability, and ease of use, e-mail quickly spread across multiple industries and became an essential communication tool in education and web-based instruction.

As the 1990s came to a close, the first generation of digital natives was coming of age (Palfrey & Gasser, 2008). This new generation of learners, immersed in digital technologies from birth, was a major catalyst for a shift in pedagogy in the late 1990s, from teacher-directed to learner-centered instruction (Tapscott, 2009, as cited in Jones, 2010). "In order for schools to adapt to the habits of Digital Natives and how they are processing information, educators need to accept that the mode of learning is changing rapidly in a digital age" (Palfrey & Gasser, 2008, p. 239). One of the biggest changes involved how digital natives conducted research. Instead of making a trip to the library, Palfrey and Gasser opined, "they are more likely to check Wikipedia" (p. 239).

The rapidly changing educational environment brought on by the digital natives, combined with an infusion of new digital communication technologies and the introduction of the learning management system, accelerated the growth of the e-learning movement through the 1990s and positioned it for massive growth in the coming decade. In the closing months of 1999, two new learning management systems appeared on the digital scene, Desire2Learn, an integrated and user-friendly system designed from the ground up, and Moodle, the world's most successful and fastest growing open source LMS. While the 1990s were a period of creativity for emergent learning management systems, the 2000s were a period of intense growth and competition, characterized by Blackboard's growth through acquisitions and an attempt to corner the market by patenting the LMS.

E-learning in the 2000s

Since 2000, the world has witnessed an explosion in e-learning opportunities for learners of all ages. The National Center for Education Statistics (2003) reported that from 2001 to 2002, over 50% of institutions that awarded degrees offered distance education to all levels and types of learners, causing enrollment to skyrocket to over 3 million. In 2007, Allen and Seaman (2008) noted that "the 12.9 percent growth rate for online enrollments far exceeds the 1.2 percent growth of the overall higher education student population" (p. 1). Accessibility, and the tools that allowed for the increased access were the catalysts for this phenomenal growth in e-learning.

The evolution of technical advancements that led to this phenomenon began with the proliferation of web conferencing. Prior to the 2000s, web conferencing was reserved mainly for business users or those who could afford expensive high-speed Internet and costly equipment. Web conferencing, as we know it today, provided e-learning with new capabilities that were not previously possible. According to Roberts (2004), although video conferencing played a role in the history of e-learning, its features were limited. Web conferencing, on the other hand, "is the total package" (para. 1). It provides

> not just the opportunity to chat and communicate via webcam so that you can see each person in your conferencing link, but to exchange documents, share applications, access shared desktops, use PowerPoint, whiteboards and other presentation features and even poll participants.
>
> (Roberts, 2004, para. 1)

Like most technologies, web conferencing evolved over several decades, but did not come into fruition until recent years with the increased affordability of personal computers and the emergence of peer-to-peer (P2) Internet file sharing.

With these advancements, along with the development of Voice Over Internet Protocol (VoIP), distance learning programs began utilizing web conferencing to increase interactivity and real-time collaboration in higher education learning environments (Nefsis, n.d., para. 22). Since then, a wave of free and subscription services, as well as web conferencing-enabled tablets and smartphones, have exploded onto the scene, putting the capability of mobile web conferencing into the hands of millions of users.

The introduction of MP3 players, like the iPod, made possible new ways of easily sharing audio files, known as podcasts. Podcasts are digital audio files that can be easily shared, downloaded, and created. Due to their affordability, accessibility, and flexibility, podcasts, and a few years later, vodcasts (video versions of podcasts) became popular e-learning tools. Rohrer (2006) observed, "One of the exciting features of podcasts and vodcasts is the ability to 'subscribe' to them" (para. 6) using RSS (Really Simple Syndication). The RSS software checks all podcasts a user is subscribed to and automatically downloads them to the designated device. Such was the impact of these developments on e-learning that in 2006, Cebeci and Tekdal noted, "Currently, podcasting is being debated as a new promising e-learning tool that will possibly change mobile learning" (para. 1). These advancements not only facilitated the way people accessed content, but they also freed up learners to review it on their own time and in a location of their choice—even while on the go. It also exponentially increased the availability and variety of content.

In 2005, Chad Hurley, Steve Chen, and Jawed Karim revolutionized the online sharing of videos with the launch of YouTube (Wikipedia, History of YouTube, n.d.). This new service allowed for proprietary videos to be easily published and shared online, thereby reaching worldwide audiences. According to YouTube Statistics (Viewership, n.d.), today, "More than 800 million unique users visit YouTube each month; over 6 billion hours of video are watched each month; 80% of YouTube traffic comes from outside the US." YouTube and the expansion of web-based multimedia spawned a host of educational sites, including Khan Academy, founded by Salman Khan in 2006 (khanacademy.org, n.d.), and TED Talks, launched in 2007 by the Chris Anderson Sapling Foundation (Ted.com, n.d.).

The growth of on-demand audio and video would not have been possible without Wi-Fi (Wireless Fidelity). "Wi-Fi refers to wireless networking technology that allows computers and other devices to communicate over a wireless signal" (TechTerms.com, Wi-Fi, n.d.). For e-learning, Wi-Fi (which caught on with mainstream consumers in 2001) meant access to all of the resources afforded by the Internet on Wi-Fi-enabled devices (desktop computers, tablets, laptops, smartphones, videogame units, digital audio players, e-book readers, etc.) without the need for a physical, wired connection.

Another leap in the advancement of e-learning came with the growth and popularity of online virtual worlds, as they showed potential for exposing learners to a greater diversity of people and experiences, as well as developing problem-based learning opportunities. This was especially relevant for education and training in professions such as teacher education, health, information systems, and criminal justice. Cartelli, Connolly, Jimoyiannis, Magalhaes, Maillet, and Stansfield (2008, para. 1) observed, "The demand for higher education is expanding exponentially throughout the world with the majority of Universities now offering an array of e-learning programs and modules to students from a wide range of different backgrounds and geographical locations." E-learning programs have responded by creating virtual learning environments in popular online services, such as Second Life. It is through these virtual learning environments that "students can gain access to a range of educational experiences and resources" (Cartelli et al., 2008, para. 1). Although the origin of virtual worlds can be traced to early literature and cinematography, when Second Life was launched in 2003, it put virtual reality into the hands of millions of users worldwide.

E-learning Today

Web conferencing, podcasts, VoIP, Wi-Fi, and virtual worlds represent only a segment of the e-learning technologies available today. Perhaps the most notable difference between e-learning in previous decades and today is that e-learning has gone mobile. Partridge (2012) observed that in particular, the touch screen in mobile devices has changed the way learners interact with content. He noted,

> The practical reality here is that touching things makes us feel differently about those things. This is the core idea behind interface differences in mobile. We paint associative pictures in our minds and the things we touch and handle directly.
>
> (para. 4)

This improved way of interacting with learning has spawned an impressive variety of technologies (e-books, augmented reality, social media) that facilitate users' interaction with each other, the content, and now, even their environments and the objects in them.

Interactivity is a staple of today's e-learning menu. For example, millions of e-books flood the market and many of them no longer resemble traditional textbooks. Today's books are digital and integrate a wide variety of multimedia and interactive features, such as augmented reality (AR). Although AR can be traced back to the early 1900s when author Frank L. Baum wrote about a little boy whose goggles allowed him to see people's true intentions (Willans, 2013), current versions of AR date to the 1990s with military developments, and later, in 2000 with the release of ARQuake, the first mobile augmented reality game (Willans, 2013). According to Asai, Kobayashi, and Kondo (2005), "AR enhances real scenes viewed by the user, overlaying virtual objects over the real world, and works to improve the user's performance in and perception of the world" (p. 1). Handheld devices that put augmented reality into the hands of consumers are already available (e.g., smartphone navigation apps, such as Metro Paris Subway and London Bus; Nokia's City Lens app; Yelp's Monocle; Mattel's i-Tag action figures; Wikitude Drive; and Layar's browser for smartphones).

For e-learning, the benefits of augmented reality include interacting with real and virtual objects to obtain information from an authentic environment in several dimensions, including 3D (e.g., viewing the assembly instructions laid over a machine part); and viewing objects and landmarks from a different perspective, even one from the past (e.g., original architecture blueprints superimposed on a building) (Asai et al., 2005). It also brings a gaming quality to learning, putting the learner in control to solve problems in a way that is interactive and engaging. As such, technologies like augmented reality have changed the expectations for e-learning. Never has this been more evident than with the proliferation of social media tools, such as MySpace, Facebook, and Twitter.

Jane Hart (2009), social media and learning consultant, observed that for years, e-learning environments simply automated the traditional sage-on-the-stage learning model, making the learning independent of location, but also of people. She added that contrarily, in social and workplace environments, people seek out new information and develop new skills by relying on a variety of sources-including each other. This has shifted the focus from formal to informal learning, which is facilitated by the numerous social media tools available today (Hart, 2009). Social media help people "search for and access all kinds of resources: videos, podcasts, blogs, etc., whenever they need them; they create their own resources and store them for easy retrieval" (Hart, 2009, slide 9). "They also make connections with like-minded people with whom they can communicate and share ideas, resources, experiences, and so on" (Hart, 2009, slide 10). Hart noted that formal learning environments are also capitalizing on these benefits, making them more "participative, social, and collaborative" (slide 12). Now that e-learning had gone social, it was poised to go massive.

Massive Open Online Courses, also known as MOOCs, hit the scene in 2008. They began as free, noncredit online courses that anyone with Internet access could take. Although most MOOCs have several thousand participants, some have had over 30,000 enrolled at one time. "The shimmery hope is that free courses can bring the best education in the world to the most remote corners of the planet, help people in their careers, and expand intellectual and personal networks" (Pappano, 2012, What Is a MOOC Anyway?, para. 7). The price of access, however, is limited faculty interaction. Participants, then, need to rely on themselves to view the content and interact with others in the course to complete the assignments. Although there are challenges, such as cheating and low completion rates, for e-learning, MOOCs are a game changer.

In a *New York Times* article titled "The Year of the MOOC," Pappano (2012) interviewed several key players in the recent MOOC movement. They all concurred that MOOCs will change many of the ways higher education institutions manage formal learning. MOOCs have already started to change the way formal learning is perceived, as well as the criteria for hiring and promoting faculty. During the interview, Dr. Stavens, owner of Udacity, the first company to host MOOCs, noted, "They pick instructors not because of their academic research, as universities do, but because of how they teach" (Pappano, 2012, The Flavor of the MOOC, para. 6). He foresees "a day when MOOCs will disrupt how faculty are attracted, trained and paid, with the most popular 'compensated like a TV actor or a movie actor' ... students will want to learn from whoever is the best teacher" (Pappano, 2012, The Flavor of the MOOC, para. 6). Similarly, MOOC innovators also predict major changes in the way that formal institutions accept and award academic credits. Are MOOCs here to stay? Only time will tell. However, the impact that they have already had will leave a lasting impression on the e-learning landscape.

The Future of E-learning

This chapter ends as it started, with an admonition and a promise. As Gentry and Csete (1995) cautioned, predicting the future is a risky business, but failure to plan for it is irresponsible. While we live in the present, we are being called to visualize and build the future. Looking to the future of e-learning, several possibilities present themselves based on trends we see unfolding today, including the ascension of mobile learning, the increase of social learning, the improved availability and quality and choice of online programs, the promise of universal translation for global learning, and the growth of personal learning environments. Each of these elements holds great promise over the next five years.

The *New Media Consortium (NMC) Horizon Report*, published every year since 2002, "is dedicated to charting the landscape of emerging technologies for teaching, learning, and creative inquiry in higher education globally" (Johnson, Adams, & Cummins, 2012, p. 9). Each year, the

Table 3.1 Summary of NMC Horizon 2012 Report for Six Technologies to Watch in Higher Education

Adoption Horizon	*Emerging Technology*
Near-term (within the next 12 months)	Mobile Apps Tablet Computing
Mid-term (within 2–3 years)	Game-Based Learning Learning Analytics
Far-term (within 4–5 years)	Gesture-Based Computing The Internet of Things

Johnson et al., 2012

New Media Consortium, through its Emerging Technologies Initiative, interviews hundreds of technology professionals and educational leaders and analyzes news articles, research studies, and white papers from around the world to generate a list of emerging technologies, trends, and challenges impacting higher education, K–12, and technology-related industries.

Each yearly report identifies the six most significant emerging technologies likely to impact education over the next five years. The report categorizes the six trends into three adoption horizons—near-term, mid-term, and far-term—based on their likelihood to experience widespread adoption within the next 12 months, two to three years, or four to five years (Johnson et al., 2012). Table 3.1 represents the six technologies to watch between 2012 and 2017. It is important to note that each of these emerging technologies exerts a significant impact on e-learning.

Near-term adoption horizon. The 2012 *New Media Consortium (NMC) Horizon Report* identified mobile apps and mobile computing as two of the fastest growing trends to impact e-learning and mobile learning in higher education, with the greatest likelihood of being adopted within the next 12 months. Johnson et al. (2012) noted:

> Always-connected Internet devices using 3G and similar cellular networks, imbedded sensors, cameras, and GPS have proved to be the feature set with hundreds of applications. Apps that take advantage of recent developments in these tools, along with advances in electronic publishing and the convergence of search technology and location awareness, made this category of software enormously interesting in the higher education context.
>
> (pp. 6–7)

App stores for IOS and Android smartphones and tablets feature thousands of apps covering a range of subjects, from math and science, to reading and writing, to music and foreign languages, to history and geography, for learners of all ages. Note taking, annotation, and content creation tools enable users to conduct research and gather data from anywhere at any time. Audio, video, and photography apps, combined with social networking and file sharing apps, facilitate the documentation and sharing of live historical events and natural phenomena, to make teaching, learning, and creative inquiry a continuous, lifelong process. Present-day language translation apps also offer great promise for the future of global e-learning.

Pedagogy, curriculum, and even learning environments can be tailored through portable devices to meet individual student needs and promote personalized learning. "Because of their portability, large display, and touchscreen, tablets are ideal devices for one-to-one learning, as well as fieldwork" (Johnson et al., 2012, p. 15). Presently, many institutions around the country are distributing tablet computers to their students, preloaded with course materials, digital textbooks, and supplemental resources. The rapid adoption of tablets and smart phones is also hastening the ascension of mobile learning from proof-of-concept to real-world application.

Mid-term adoption horizon. The 2012 *New Media Consortium (NMC) Horizon Report* identified game-based learning and learning analytics as two technology trends that will see expected widespread adoption within two to three years (Johnson et al., 2012).

While scholars are still studying its effectiveness, game-based learning in higher education and K-12 classrooms has experienced considerable growth in recent years. According to the 2012 report, "The greatest potential of games for learning lies in their ability to foster collaboration and engage students in the process of learning" (Johnson et al., 2012, p. 7). This form of learning is strongly supported by social learning theory, which states that people learn better when working within social contexts. According to the 2010 U.S. Department of Education's *National Education Plan*:

> Interactive technologies, especially games, provide immediate performance feedback so that players always know how they are doing. As a result, they are highly engaging to students and have the potential to motivate students to learn. They also enable educators to assess important competencies and aspects of thinking in contexts and through activities that students care about in everyday life. Because interactive technologies hold this promise, assessment and interactive technology experts should collaborate on research to determine ways to use them effectively for assessment.
>
> (2.0 Assessment: Measure What Matters, para. 6)

Game-based learning teaches students a number of important skills, including how to work in teams to solve common problems, critical thinking and creativity, and communication and digital literacy. Gaming environments also provide safe realms for experimentation, and learning through trial and error, and even failure (Johnson et al., 2012). The type and level of social learning achieved through game-based learning make it a natural for collaborative e-learning.

The 2012 report also identified learning analytics as a significant mid-term technology with considerable potential for education. These data-mining tools provide faculty with the information they need to identify students' learning needs and make instructional decisions for corrective action. According to Johnson et al. (2012), "Learning analytics loosely joins a variety of data gathering tools and analytic techniques to study student engagement, performance, and progress in practice, with the goal of using what is learned to revise curricula, teaching, and assessment in real time" (p. 7). The significance of learning analytics for teaching and learning are obvious, and would make them essential tools for online instructors, who, due to the limitations of classroom interactions, may not have access to all their students' data, especially data normally obtained in traditional classrooms through direct observation. Data obtained through learning analytics could also impact course design, development, and quality.

Far-term adoption horizon. Two technologies identified by the 2012 *New Media Consortium (NMC) Horizon Report* for the far-term horizon, projected for widespread adoption in four to five years, are gesture-based computing and the Internet of Things (Johnson et al., 2012).

Gesture-based computing uses body motion, facial expressions, and voice recognition as input devices in place of the computer keyboard and mouse. With the introduction of touch screens on smart devices, voice recognition technology like Siri, and sensors that translate body movements on gaming systems, gesture-based technologies have already become commonplace. For years, users have been interacting with smartphones, tablets, and computers by tapping or swiping their fingers across touch-sensitive screens, mice, and touchpads. Likewise, while gaming systems have been pioneering the use of motion sensing accessories for years, infrared sensors and accelerometer-based handheld controllers on newer machines have taken interactive video gaming to new levels, enabling players to move, jump, dance, or point to control their on-screen character's movements. Combined with voice recognition, gesture-based computing has the potential to change how we interact with all of our devices, including our TVs, computers, and smart home appliances. These capabilities have implications for teaching and learning, both in our physical environments and in our interactions in virtual worlds. Although present-day examples of gesture-based computing in education are limited, as an assistive technology: "Gesture-sensing techniques are already having profound implications for special needs and disabled individuals. For example, devices with gesture control are already helping blind, dyslexic, or otherwise disabled students, reducing their dependence on keyboards" (Johnson et al., 2012, p. 27). The writers of the 2012 report recognize that while the desire to have a completely natural interaction with our devices has existed for many years, its full potential has yet to be realized (Johnson et al., 2012, p. 29).

According to Johnson et al. (2012), "The Internet of Things has become a sort of shorthand for network-aware smart objects that connect the physical world with the world of information" (p. 30). This concept, promoted by Vinton Cerf, known as "a father of the Internet" (Internet Society, n.d., para. 1), is the next step in the evolution of smart objects where the line between the physical item and digital information becomes blurred. While the Internet of Things is still more of a concept than a reality, some present-day Internet-enabled devices, including webcams, shared printers, telephones, and other office equipment, already exist. "In the classroom, IP-addressable projectors can already stream the slides or videos professors are sharing so that students who could not physically attend class can view the presentations and lecture materials from wherever they are" (Johnson et al., 2012, p. 31). As the Internet of Things technologies evolve into smart objects capable of transmitting digital information, students in e-learning (and traditional) learning environments will have access to real-time data on mobile devices and computers in a way that was never possible.

Summary

In summary, the 2012 *New Media Consortium (NMC) Horizon Report* for higher education has identified six emerging technologies experts and researchers have predicted to exert a significant impact on higher education within the next five years. Each of these technologies is also important for the growth of e-learning within the same time frame. As educators and trainers in e-learning, it will be incumbent upon us to be aware of these technologies and to begin to explore how they can be exploited to improve the quality of the e-learning experience.

To paraphrase Confucius, we study the past to define the future. This chapter presented a timeline, by decade, of the most influential people, events, and trends impacting the evolution of e-learning over the past 40 years. Studying past, present, and future trends in e-learning gives us a historical perspective from which to guide researchers, practitioners, professors, teachers, trainers, and administrators in making informed decisions and planning for the future.

References

Allen, E., & Seaman, J. (2008). Staying the course: Online education in the United States, 2008. *The Sloan Consortium*, 1–28. Retrieved from http://sloanconsortium.org/publications/survey/staying_course

Asai, K., Kobayashi, G., & Kondo, T. (2005). *Augmented instructions—A fusion of augmented reality and printed learning materials*. Retrieved from http://ieeexplore.ieee.org/stamp/stamp.jsp?tp=

Bradford, P., Porciello, M., Balkon, N., & Backus, D. (2006). The Blackboard learning system: The be all and end all in educational instruction? *Journal of Educational Technology Systems, 35*(3), 310–314. Retrieved from http://dx.doi.org/10.2190/X137-X73L-5261-5656

Campbell, T. (1998, March). The first email message: Who sent it and what was said? *Pretext*. http://www.pretext.com/

Cartelli, A., Connolly, T., Jimoyiannis, A., Magalhaes, H., Maillet, K., & Stansfield, M. (2008). Towards the development of a new model for best practice and knowledge construction in virtual campuses. *Journal of Information Technology Education,* 7, 121–134. Retrieved from http://www.jite.org/documents/Vol7/JITEv7p121-134Cartelli397.pdf

Cebeci, Z., & Tekdal, M. (2006). Using podcasts as audio learning objects. *Interdisciplinary Journal of Knowledge and Learning Objects*, 47–57. Retrieved from http://www.ijello.org/Volume2/v2p047-057Cebeci.pdf

Cross, J. (1999). eLearning: Winning approaches to corporate learning on internet time. *Internet Time Group*. Retrieved from http://internettime.com/Learning/articles/eLearning.pdf

Cross, J. (2004). An informal history of eLearning. *On the Horizon*, 103–110. Retrieved from http://www.internettime.com/Learning/articles/xAn%20Informal%20History%20of%20eLearning.pdf

Distance Learning Net. (n.d.). *The history of distance learning*. Retrieved from http://www.distancelearning-net.com/the-history-of-distance-learning/

Frick, T. W. (1991). Restructuring education through technology. *Fastback Series #326*. Bloomington, IN: Phi Delta Kappa Educational Foundation.

Gentry, C., & Csete, J. (1995). Educational technology in the 1990s. In G. Anglin (Ed.), *Instructional technology: Past, present and future* (pp. 20–33). Englewood, Colorado: Libraries Unlimited.

Hart, J. L. (2009, April 24). *Social learning: Part 1—The future of e-learning is social learning*. Retrieved from http://www.slideshare.net/janehart/the-future-of-elearning-is-social-learnng

Hood, N. (2012). Streaming video. In B. Hoffman (Ed.), *Encyclopedia of educational technology*. Retrieved from http://eet.sdsu.edu/eetwiki/index.php/Streaming_video. San Diego, CA: SDSU Department of Educational Technology.

Internet Society. (n.d.). *Internet hall of fame pioneer: Vint Cerf*. Retrieved from http://internethalloffame.org/inductees/vint-cerf

Johnson, L., Adams, S., & Cummins, M. (2012). *The New Media Consortium (NMC) horizon report: 2012 higher education edition*. Austin, Texas: The New Media Consortium.

Jones, C. (2010). Networked learning, the net generation and digital natives. *Proceedings of the 7th International Conference on Networked Learning 2010*, Aalborg, Denmark, 617–618.

Jones International University. (n.d.). *History of Jones International University*. Retrieved from http://www.jiu.edu/about/history/history-jones-international-university

K Alliance. (n.d.). *The history of computer based training*. Retrieved from http://www.kalliance.com/articles/history-of-computer-based-training.htm

KhanAcademy.org. (n.d.). *Khan Academy*. Retrieved from http://www.khanacademy.org

Khan, B. H. (2012). *A framework for e-learning*. Retrieved from http://asianvu.com/bookstoread/framework/

Khan, B. H. (2013). *Badrul Khan*. Retrieved from http://badrulkhan.com

Maddox, J. (n.d.). Jerrold Maddox. *Penn State University School of Visual Arts*. Retrieved from https://sova.psu.edu/profile/jerroldmaddox

Maddox, J. (1997, February 14). *Web-based distance learning*. Retrieved from http://www.personal.psu.edu/faculty/j/x/jxm22/CAA/JMCAApaper.html

McConnell, D., & Sharples, M. (1983, May). Distance teaching by CYCLOPS: An educational evaluation of the Open University's telewriting system. *British Journal of Educational Technology, 14*(2), 109–126.

McGreal, R. (1994). *TeleEducation NB: An open, distributed, bilingual province-wide distance education network*. Retrieved from http://auspace.athabascau.ca/bitstream/2149/244/1/TeleEducationNB.pdf

Moeng, B. (2004). *IBM tackles learning in the workplace. Training and e-learning*. Retrieved from http://www.itweb.co.za/index.php?option=com_content&view=article&id=18381:ibm-tackles-learning-in-the-workplace&catid=

Morrison, J. L., & Khan, B. H. (2003). The global e-learning framework: An interview with Badrul Khan. *The Technology Source, May/June*. Retrieved from http://technologysource.org/article/global_elearning_framework/

Nagler, M. (1997, October 16). Senior's company helps to produce web pages for college courses. *Cornell Chronicle, 29*(9). Retrieved from http://www.news.cornell.edu/chronicle/97/10.16.97/Web_company.html

National Center for Education Statistics. (2003). *Distance education at degree-granting postsecondary institutions: 2001–2002.* 1–95. Retrieved from http://nces.ed.gov/surveys/peqis/publications/2003017/

Nefsis. (n.d.). *Video conferencing history.* Retrieved from http://www.nefsis.com/best-video-conferencing-software/video-conferencing-history.html

Palfrey, J., & Gasser, U. (2008). *Born digital: Understanding the first generation of digital natives.* New York, NY: Basic Books.

Pappano, L. P. (2012, November 02). The year of the MOOC. *New York Times Education Life.* Retrieved from http://www.nytimes.com/2012/11/04/education/edlife/massive-open-online-courses-are-multiplying-at-a-rapid-pace.html?pagewanted=all

Partridge, A. (2012, April 11). Practical mobile elearning today: Real solutions for creating mlearning for your organization right now, Part 1. *Rapid eLearning-Adobe Captivate Blog.* Retrieved from http://blogs.adobe.com/captivate/2012/04/practical-mobile-elearning-today-real-solutions-for-creating-mlearning-for-your-organization-right-now-part-1.html

PC World. (2006, August 11). The 25 greatest PCs of all time. *PC World.* Retrieved from http://www.pcworld.com/article/126692/greatest_pcs_of_all_time.html

Roberts, L. P. (2004). History of web conferencing—Multi-function conferencing comes of age. *Web Conferencing Zone.* Retrieved from http://www.web-conferencing-zone.com/history-of-web-conferencing.htm

Rohrer, E. A. (2006, February 15). Podcasting and vodcasting opportunities in elearning. *Educator's Voice.* Retrieved from http://ecollege.com/Newsletter/EducatorsVoice/EducatorsVoice-Vol7Iss2.learn

Sangrà, A., Vlachopoulos, D., & Cabrera, N. (2012). Building an inclusive definition of e-learning: An approach to the conceptual framework. *International Review of Research in Open and Distance Learning.* Retrieved from http://www.irrodl.org/index.php/irrodl/article/view/1161/2146

TechTerms.com. (n.d.). *Wi-fi.* Retrieved from http://www.techterms.com/definition/wifi

Ted.com. (n.d.). *About Ted: History.* Retrieved from http://www.ted.com/pages/16

The Ernest C. Manning Awards Foundation. (2004). *$100,000 Encana Principal Award, Murray Goldberg, WebCT (World Wide Web Course Tools).* Retrieved from http://www.manningawards.ca/awards/winners/mgoldberg-media.shtml

Tudor, P. N. (1995). MPEG-2 video compression. *Electronics & Communication Engineering Journal,* 7(6), 257–264.

U.S. Department of Education. (2010). *National education plan: Executive summary.* Retrieved from http://www.ed.gov/technology/netp-2010/executive-summary

YouTube. (n.d.). *Statistics.* Retrieved from http://www.youtube.com/t/press_statistics

Wikipedia. (n.d.). *History of YouTube.* Retrieved from http://en.wikipedia.org/wiki/History_of_YouTube

Willans, J. (2013, January 13). *For real! The amazing story of augmented reality.* Retrieved from http://conversations.nokia.com/2013/01/13/for-real-the-amazing-story-of-augmented-reality/

4

The Quality of Massive Open Online Courses

Stephen Downes

In this short contribution I would like to address the question of assessing the *quality* of massive open online courses. The assessment of the quality of anything is fraught with difficulties, depending as it does on some commonly understood account of what would count as a *good* example of the thing, what factors constitute *success*, and how that success against that standard is to be *measured*.

With massive open online courses, it is doubly more difficult, because of the lack of a common definition of the MOOC itself, and because of the implication of external factors in the actual perception and performance of the MOOC. Moreover, it is to my mind far from clear that there is agreement regarding the *purpose* of a MOOC to begin with, and without such agreement discussions of quality are moot.

Let me begin, then, with a statement describing what I take a MOOC to be. I will then address what I believe ought to be the purpose of a MOOC, the success factors involved in serving that purpose, the design features that impact success, and finally, questions regarding the measurement of those features.

What Is a MOOC?

The term MOOC as is commonly known stands for 'Massive Open Online Course'. There have been numerous efforts recently to define each of these four terms, sometimes, as I observe here, in such a way as to result in an interpretation opposite to the common understanding of the term. Thus in some cases a MOOC is being thought of as a smallish closed offline (or hybrid) ongoing activity. This, for example, is what we see in the phenomenon of the 'wrapped' MOOC.

To my own mind, we should be relatively rigid in our definition of a MOOC, if for no other reason than to distinguish a MOOC from the myriad other forms of online learning that have existed before and since, and hence to identify those aspects of quality that are *unique* to MOOCs. Hence, a MOOC is to my mind, defined along the following four dimensions:

Massive—here I attend not to the success of the MOOC in attracting many people, but in the design elements that make educating many people *possible*. And here we need to keep in mind that to *educate* is to do more than merely deliver content, and more than to merely support interaction, for otherwise the movie theatre and the telephone system are, respectively, MOOCs.

My own *theory* of education is minimal (so minimal it hardly qualifies as a theory, and is almost certainly not my own): "to teach is to model and to demonstrate; to learn is to practice and reflect." Thus, minimally, we need an environment that supports all four of these on a massive scale. In *practice*, what this means is a system designed so that bottlenecks are not created in any of the four attributes: modeling, demonstration, practice, and reflection.

To offer a simple example: an important part of reflection is the capacity to perform and then discuss performance with others. If each person must perform and discuss the performance with a specific person, such as the teacher, then a bottleneck is created, because there is not enough time to allow a large number of people to perform. Similarly, if each performance and discussion involves the entire class, the same sort of bottleneck is created. Hence, in order for a course to be massive, performance and reflection must be designed in a way that does *not* require that certain people view all performances.

Open—I have had many arguments with people over the years regarding the meaning of 'open', and these arguments have most always (to my perception) involved the other people attempting to define 'open' in such a way as to make 'open' mean the same as 'closed'. There is, for example, the famous distinction between free as in '*gratis*', and free as in '*libre*'. In education there is in addition a definition of 'open' which is neither *gratis* nor *libre*, but instead refers to 'open admissions', or the removal of any academic barriers to participation in a course or program.

For my own part, the meaning of 'open' has more to do with *access* to a resource, as opposed to having to do with what one can *do* with a resource. The definition of 'free software', for example, assumes that the software is already in your possession, and defines ways you can inspect it, run it, and distribute it, without limitations (Free Software Foundation, 2014). But this definition is meaningless to a person who, for whatever reason, cannot access the software in the first place. The more common and widely understood meanings of 'free' and 'open' are broader in nature, more permissive with regard to access, and more restrictive with regard to the imposition of barriers.

In particular, something (a resource, a course, an education) is *free* and *open* if and only if:

- the resource may be read, run, consumed or played without cost or obligation. This addresses not only direct fee-for-subscription, but also *enclosure*, for example, the bundling of 'free' resources in such a way that only those who pay tuition may access them; and
- there are reasonable ways to *share* the resource or to *reuse* the resource, and especially to translate or format-shift the resource (but not necessarily to be able to sell or modify the resource).

Having said that, as George Siemens and I discussed the development of MOOCs in 2008, we were conscious of and communicated the fact that we were engaged in a progression of increasingly open access to aspects of education:

- first, open access to educational resources, such as texts, guides, exercises, and the like;
- second, open access to curriculum, including course content and learning design;
- third, open access to criteria for success, or rubrics (which could then be used by ourselves or by others to conduct assessments);
- fourth, open assessments (this was something we were not able to provide in our early courses); and
- fifth, open credentials.

It is worth remarking that by 'open' we very clearly intended both the aspects of *access* and *sharing* to be included; what this meant in practice was that we expected course participants not only to *use* course resources, curriculum, etc., but also to be involved in the *design* of these. Hence, for example, before we offered CCK08,[1] we placed the course schedule and curriculum on a wiki, where it could be edited by those who were interested in taking the course (this was a strategy adapted from the 'Bar Camp' school of conference organization and the EduCamp model as employed by Nancy White and Diego Leal).

It is interesting to contrast our approach to 'open' with the "logic model" devised by James C. Taylor (2007) and eventually adopted by OERu[2] which preserved the openness of resources and courses, but kept closed access to assessments and credentials. Such courses are *not* to my mind 'open courses' as a critical part of the course is held back behind a tuition barrier. Exactly the same comment could be made of 'free' courses that entail the purchase of a required textbook. The fact that some part of a course is free or open does not entail that the course as a whole is free or open, and it is a misrepresentation to assert such.

Online—I mentioned above the phenomenon of 'wrapped' MOOCs, which postulate the use of a MOOC within the context of a traditional location-based course; the material offered by the MOOC is hence 'wrapped' with the trappings of a more traditional education. This is the sort of approach to MOOCs which treats them more as modern-day textbooks, rather than as courses in and of themselves.

But insofar as these wrapped MOOCs are *courses*, they are no longer online, and insofar as they are *online*, they are no longer courses. So whatever a 'wrapped MOOC' is, it is not a MOOC. It is (at best) a set of resources misleadingly identified as a 'MOOC' and then offered (or more typically, sold) as a means to supplement traditional courses.

For a MOOC to be 'online' entails that (and I'll be careful with my wording here) no required element of the course is required to take place at any particular physical location.

The 'wrapped MOOCs' are not MOOCs because you cannot attend a wrapped MOOC without attending the in-person course; there will be aspects of the MOOC that are reserved specifically for the people who have (typically) paid tuition and are resident at some college or university, and are physically located at the appropriate campus at the appropriate time. Just as being online is what makes it possible for these courses to be both massive and open, being located at a specific place makes the course small and closed.

But by contrast, this does *not* eliminate MOOCs that include or allow elements of real-world interaction or activity. Our original CCK08 MOOC recommended (but did not require) in-person meet-ups, for example, and these were held at various locations around the world. MOOCs such as ds106 require that a person go out into the world and take photographs (for example). In *any* online course there will be a real-world dimension; what makes it an 'online' course is that it does not specify a *particular* real-world dimension.

Course—before we launched our first MOOC both George Siemens and I were involved in various activities related to free and open online learning. George, for example, had staged a very successful online conference on Connectivism the year before. I had, meanwhile, been running my newsletter service for the educational technology community since 2001. Each of these was in its own way massive, open and online, but they were not courses. There is obviously some overlap between 'course' and 'conference' and 'community', and people have since suggested that there could be (or should be) massive open online communities of practice and of course there could—but they are not MOOCs.

To be clear: I am very supportive of the idea of massive open online communities, but the MOOC is a different entity, with its own properties and role in the environment. And specifically:

- a course is *bounded* by a start date and an end date
- a course is *cohered* by some common theme or domain of discourse
- a course is a *progression* of ordered events related to that domain.

Why insist on these? Aside, that is, from the pedantic observation that if you call something a 'course' then it ought to have the properties of a course?

My own observation (and I was reluctant at first to create a 'course' precisely because of the three limitations just specified above) is that the creation of temporary and bounded events allows for engagement between communities that would not normally associate with each other. Courses are a way of, if you will, stirring the pot. By creating a limited and self-contained event, we lower the barriers to participation—you're not signing up for a lifetime commitment—and hence increase accessibility.

In a sense, the same reason we organize learning into courses is the reason we organize text into books. Yes, simply 'reading' is useful and engaging, and widely recommended, but 'reading a book' is defined and contained. A person can commit to 'reading a book' more easily than to 'reading', especially if by 'reading' we mean something that never ends.

Hence, massive open online learning that is *not* bounded, does not cohere around a subject, and is not a progression of ordered events, is *not* a course, and is outside the domain of discourse.

The Purpose of MOOCs

The first reaction is to suggest that the purpose of MOOCs is to help someone *learn*—they are, after all, courses. But purposes are never so easily transparent, and education is a domain that defines opacity, and the combination does not easily yield to a simple statement of purpose.

Addressing the purpose of a MOOC as 'learning', for example, does not begin to address why some person, organization or association would *offer* a MOOC, beyond at least those early MOOCs that were offered as much to explore the possibilities of the format as much as to attain any educational objective.

The purpose of MOOCs offered by a commercial entity such as Coursera, for example, is to earn revenue (and beyond that, advance the Coursera brand to enable future courses to also make money). Meanwhile, the purpose of an institution offering a MOOC through Coursera may be multifaceted and nuanced. Consider, for example, the statement that "This is truly in the spirit of what we're supposed to do in higher education, which is providing education and experimentation," from Cole Camplese at Penn State (Ingeno, 2013, para. 10). Compare with what Keith Devlin (2012) says: "What I see is the true democratizing of higher education on a global scale. And in today's world—global village, Flat World, call it what you will—I think that is exactly what we (i.e., the entire world, not just the highly privileged US) will need" (response to online comment on *Devlin's Angle* column).

Even a focus on why students subscribe to MOOCs will not be revealing. Consider what the founders of Coursera say about most students who sign up: "'Their intent is to explore, find out something about the content, and move on to something else,' said Ms. Koller" (Kolowich, 2013, para. 7). Adding tuition fees changes the dynamic, as does adding credentials at the end of the course. Coursera has learned it can earn money charging for authentication services, which satisfies both its need to make money and a student's need for a certificate (though at the expense of no longer being free and open).

Doing what he does so well, Curt Bonk (2012) has compiled a list of twenty "types, targets and intents" of MOOCs, including the following:

- high scoring or impressive MOOC participants get admissions privileges, job interviews, or points if they later apply for a particular degree program, certificate, internship, or job;
- loss leader—give away one course in every department or program as a means to attract new students to that major, program, or department;
- religious revival MOOC;
- bait and switch MOOC—use it as a means to sell a product or to turn the audience on to something else.

It becomes clear through reflection that MOOCs serve numerous purposes, to those who offer MOOCs, those who provide services, and those who register for or in some way 'take' a MOOC.

The original MOOC offered by George Siemens and me had a very simple purpose at first: to explain ourselves. The topic of *connectivism* had achieved wide currency, and was the subject of the online conference mentioned earlier, and yet remained the subject of considerable debate. What was it? Was it even a theory? Did it even apply to education? Was it founded on real research, or was it simply made up? We believed we had good answers to those questions, and the curriculum was designed to lead participants (and ourselves!) through a clear and articulate answering of them.

As we began to design the course (and in particular, as I began to use the gRSShopper application I had designed to support my website and newsletter) it became clearer to both of us that the purpose of the course was also to serve as an *example* of connectivism in practice. After several years of describing the theory, we began to feel some obligation to demonstrate it in practice. So the course design gradually began to look less and less like a traditional course, with topics and readings arranged in a nice linear order, and more like a network, with a wide range of resources connected to each other and to participants. And the course became much less about acquiring content or skills, and much more about making these connections, and learning from what emerged as a result of them.

The participants in our MOOCs also demonstrated a similarly wide range of motivations. We had several participants who were in the course for the research opportunities it offered (and people like Jenny Mackness (2014), Frances Bell (2011) and Sui Fai John Mak (2008) have become voices in their own right in the field). Others came with the intent to learn about connectivism, to supplement their existing studies in a master's or PhD program. Others joined in to participate in what they saw as an event, others to make connections and extend their social network (or as it came later to be called, their 'personal learning network'). At least one (and maybe others) came with the specific intent of discrediting connectivism (and in passing, to call George and me "techno-communists").

Even if we limit our focus to what is putatively the primary function of a course, *to teach*, it becomes difficult to identify the purpose of a MOOC. Much has been made of MOOC completion rates, with the (generally implicit) suggestion that completion is in some respects tantamount to learning. However, it could be argued that enabling a person to sample a course and withdraw without having lost thousands of dollars of tuition is a *success*. Moreover, different people want to learn different things: some about what connectivism is, some, how best to criticize it, some, whether it even makes sense given their own experience.

And there are different senses of learning. In one sense, to 'learn' is to acquire some knowledge or skill, and it is this sense of learning that is most often associated with education, and especially formal education. But there is an equally valid sense of learning, where the objective is to achieve some outcome or complete some task, what Rogers (2008) calls "task-conscious learning". This sort of task-focused outcome is much more common in informal learning; it is the sort of learning I do, for example, when I dip into Stack Overflow (2010) to learn how to set the value of a field before submitting an Ajax form.

It becomes clear that we cannot assess the purpose of a MOOC *qua* MOOC by assessing the reasons and motivations of the people taking them, or even by assessing the reasons and motivations of those offering them. What makes a hammer a good hammer isn't whether it fulfills the reasons and motivations of the people using the hammer, because these people use it variously as a screwdriver, bottle opener, doorstop, weapon, wrench, and general-purpose machine repair device, and as an implement for driving nails, screws, tables, pegs and other objects into various-sized holes. A MOOC, similarly, may be a very good or very poor PR device, may transmit content very well or very poorly, may advance research a lot or not at all, all depending on who is using it, how they are using it, and why.

MOOC Success Factors

The primary criticism of what I will address in this chapter is that success is process-defined rather than outcomes-defined. Without outcomes measurement we cannot measure success, we can't focus our efforts toward that success, we can't become more competitive and efficient, we can't plan for change and improvement, and we can't define what you want to accomplish as a result. All this is true, and yet there is no measure of outcome or success that can be derived from designer and user motivations, or even from the uses to which MOOCs are put. The only alternative is to identify what a successful MOOC ought to produce as output, without reference to existing (and frankly, very preliminary and very variable) usage.

These outcomes are a logical consequence of the design of the MOOC. The same is true of a hammer. This tool is defined as a handheld third-class lever with a solid flat surface at the business end. Anything that satisfies these criteria will, as an *outcome*, have the capacity to drive a nail into a piece of wood (whether or not any hammer is ever used in this fashion). It has to be under a certain weight to be handheld, above a certain mass, and of a certain length, to be a lever, and of certain material and design to have a hard flat surface.

When we are evaluating a *tool*, we evaluate it against its design specifications; mathematics and deduction tell us from there that it will produce its intended outcome. It is only when we evaluate the *use* of a tool that we evaluate against the actual outcome. So measuring drop-out rates, counting test scores, and adding up student satisfaction scores will not tell us whether a MOOC was successful, only whether this particular application of this particular MOOC was successful in this particular instance.

The *design* of a MOOC is, in the first instance, as described above: it is a massive open online course, and the design is successful to the extent that it satisfies those four criteria, and unsuccessful to the extent that it doesn't. That said, however, there are many ways to create a massive open online course, and within that domain, some may be more successful than others. So we need to look at *why* we designed and developed the MOOC the way we did—*why* we made it massive, open, online and a course, as described above. Why *this* model, say, and not a traditional online instructor-led class, or an open online community, or any of a dozen other combinations?

What I begin with is the observation that each person has a *different* objective or motivation for taking a course, and has different needs and objectives (it's a lot like dating that way—we think that everyone wants the same thing, but we find in practice that everybody wants something slightly different). We looked at what we called 'sifters' and 'filters' to create learning recommendation systems, resulting in work I presented at MADLat based on collaborative filtering. "Collaborative filtering or recommender systems use a database about user preferences to predict additional topics or products a new user might like," suggest Breese, Heckerman, and Kadie (2013, abstract). There are different ways to approach this problem; I adopted what we called 'resource profiles' to characterize resources and make them accessible within a learning resources network. Since the work of filtering and selecting could now be done by the metadata, I turned to the question of what would constitute a successful *network*, which I addressed in 2005.

Partially influenced by earlier work I had done in networks (and especially the work of Francisco Varela), it was clear to me that the objective wasn't to connect everything to everything, but to achieve an *organization* in such a way as to support cognition. The work of Rumelhart and McClelland (1987) suggested ways this organization could be defined in terms of nodes and connections and learning mechanisms to achieve what Churchland (1986) and others called "plasticity". The structural properties I described in 2005 were drawn in large part from documents describing the design principles behind the internet. Finally, remarks by Charles Vest about the American university system led me to formulate what I now call the Semantic Principle, also in 2005, which crystalized as the 'Groups and Networks' presentation in new Zealand.

At the risk of repeating myself, let me say here that the Semantic Principle consists of four major elements: autonomy, diversity, openness and interactivity.

Before discussing each of these briefly, let me describe the outcome a network design embodying the semantic principle will achieve. Such a system is not static; it is dynamic. It is self-organizing, and creates these organizations in response to (and as a reflection of) environmental input. It can be thought of as a highly nuanced perceptual system. Over time, it acquires a state such that it can (if you will) *recognize* entities and events in the environment as *relevantly similar* to those it experienced in the past, and respond accordingly. This knowledge is characterized as emergent knowledge, and is constituted by the organization of the network, rather than by the content of any individual node in the network. A person working within such a network, on perceiving, being immersed in, or, again, *recognizing*, knowledge in the network, thereby acquires similar (but personal) knowledge in the self.

Or, to put the same point another way, a MOOC is a way of gathering people and having them interact, each from his or her own individual perspective or point of view, in such a way that the structure of the interactions produces new knowledge, that is, knowledge that was not present in any of the individual communications, but is produced as a result of the totality of the communications, in such a way that participants can through participation and immersion in this environment develop in their selves new (and typically unexpected) knowledge relevant to the domain. A MOOC is a vehicle for learning, yes, but it acts this way primarily by being a vehicle for discovery and experience (and not, say, content transmission).

Not every MOOC will produce this outcome, nor will this form of learning be experienced by every participant (particularly those who sample and leave early); but to judge from the commentary, the experience of new and unexpected emergent knowledge is common and widespread (among many others).

Let me now turn to the four success factors that, I argue, tend to produce this result. My purpose here is not to describe each in any detail—I have done that elsewhere—but rather to consider each as a *success factor*, that is, to consider how each design element contributes to this result.

Autonomy—this is essentially the assertion that members of the network (in this case, participants) employ their own goals and objectives, judgments and assessment of success in the process of interaction with others. This is reflected, for example, in Dave Cormier's 2010 assertion that each individual decides for himself or herself what makes a MOOC valuable. A collection of people working in a MOOC should be, for example, thought of as *cooperating*, rather than collaborating, because though they will exchange value and support each other, each will be pursuing his or her own objectives and depending on personal means and resources.

In our MOOC it was important that we *not* tell people what they ought to learn or what lessons they should take home from the presentations we made and the conversations we led. People perceive what they are looking for, and often only what they are looking for, and our well-intentioned attempts to guide their cognition could just as easily lead to participants missing the information most important to *them*. Similarly, we did not attempt to define *how* participants should interact with each other, but instead focused on supporting an environment that would be responsive to whatever means they chose for themselves.

Without autonomy, a MOOC is not able to adapt to the environment. Rather than enable each person to allow his or her unique perspective or point of view of the world to influence the course design or organization, each person would instead reflect the perspective or world view of some organizer telling them what their objectives should be, what they should learn, what counts as success. It is important that each person respond to the phenomena—the communications of others—in his or her own way, positively or negatively, in order to generate a unique structure or organization.

Diversity—this is a natural consequence of autonomy, and in addition a success factor in its own right. While we typically think of diversity in terms of language, ethnicity or culture, for us diversity applied to a broad range of criteria, including location and time zone, technology of choice, pedagogy, learning style, and more. Participants, for example, *could* experience the course as a series of lectures, and some did, but many skipped the experience. Others treated the course as project-based, creating artifacts and tangible products. Others viewed the course as a venue for conversation and community, focusing on interaction with other participants.

The major concern with diversity so broadly construed is that some people might be seen as 'doing it wrong'. We were, for example, criticized for offering lectures, because it did not follow good constructivist pedagogy; our response was that connectivism is not constructivism, and that it was up to those who preferred to learn through constructivist methods to do so, but not appropriate that they would require that all other participants learn in the same way. Additionally, it should be noted that *it did not matter* whether some particular pedagogical choice was in some respects a failure, since the perceptual recognition that it *is* a failure constitutes success in its own right.

Without diversity, it is not possible to contemplate the possibility of a network's having different states, or different types of organization. A collection of entities that is not diverse is inert, or worse, overly reactive, in that a change in one becomes a change in all. In a computer, we expect each bit of memory to contain different values of one or zero over time than others, for otherwise, our computer could do nothing more than blink off and on and off again. Any sort of complexity requires diversity, and any sort of learning requires complexity.

Openness—this is the idea that the boundaries of the network are porous and that the contents of the network are fluid. In practical terms, it means that participants in the course are free to enroll or to leave as they wish, and to move in and out of course activities equally freely (I once remarked to ALT that what made my talk a success was defined not by the fact that they were all here, but by the fact that they could all leave (but hadn't)). Openness also applies to the *content* of the course, and here the idea is that we want to encourage participants not only to share content they received from the course with each other (and outside the course), but also to bring *into* the course content they obtained from elsewhere.

Openness is necessary because—as the saying goes—you cannot see with your eyes closed. An *a priori* condition for the possibility of perception is openness to perceptual input. Learning requires perception, not only of the thing, but also of its opposite. If we were not open to the perception of evil, we would not be able to define good. If we are not open to the possibility of failure, we are not able to achieve success. We obtain these experiences through openness, by being open to other ideas, other cultures, other technologies, other people. The *free flow* of people and information through a MOOC is as important as the organization of the people therein.

An interesting side effect of openness is that there is no clear line dividing those who are in the course and those who are not. The course resembles not a solid sphere but rather a cluster of more of less loosely associated participants (and resources, and ideas). In a connectivist course, for example, lurkers are seen as playing a role equally as important and valuable as that played by active participants. Off-topic discussions are not distractions but are rather seen as valuable outcomes. As members of the Bar Camp and unconference movement would say, the people who are there are the right people, and the outcome of the event was the right outcome.

Interactivity—through the years I have used various terms for this fourth element, including 'connectedness' and 'interactivity' but none of them suits exactly what is meant by this concept. It is not *simply* that members of the network are connected with each other, and that interaction takes places through these connections. It is rather the idea that new learning occurs as a *result* of this connectedness and interactivity, it *emerges* from the network as a whole, rather than being transmitted or distributed by one or a few more powerful members.

Another way to understand this property is to see it as the stipulation that the graph of network interactions or connections is *not* a power law distribution. In a power law distribution, one or a few members receive most of the connections, creating what I've called the 'big spike', and each of the majority has only a few connections, resulting in what many people have called 'the long tail'. This formation commonly occurs in dynamic networks, the result of what Barabasi (2003) identified as selective attraction: newcomers to the network tend to link to those people who are already popular, resulting in their disproportional growth in popularity.

Networks characterized by a big spike and a long tail are not responsive to their environment, and can overreact to small stimuli, resulting in cascade failure and eventual network death. A more balanced (and dare I say, egalitarian) distribution of connectivity gives the network resilience, and the influence from one perspective cannot become disproportional simply because it came from an influential node. Each signal (each idea, each resource) must face not one challenge but many challenges as it is propagated, person to person, through the network.

Measuring Success

To turn, then to the actual measurement of quality in a MOOC: it is necessary in the first instances to point out what ought *not* be taken into account, not because these elements are not important—they are—but because these elements are not relevant to the evaluation of a MOOC *as a MOOC*.

Paramount among these are evaluations consisting of evaluations of the quality of the course materials used in the course, the sort of evaluation that might be provided, say, by a peer review process or a learning resources review process, such as might be undertaken by a project such as MERLOT. These evaluations examine the resources created for the MOOC or (in fewer instances, if any) the materials shared among each other by participants in the MOOC, and assess such criteria as clarity, accuracy, usability or engagement. Similar (or slightly varying) criteria are used to evaluate other aspects of courses, such as the facilities, the instructors, and the students themselves.

Such evaluations miss the point for several reasons:

- An evaluation of the parts isn't the same as an evaluation of the whole. A strong course can be created out of arguably inferior, even defective, materials, if the course is *organized* appropriately (or, as Hemingway might say, the secret to writing is to create a perfect image out of banal and even defective sentences).
- Even in cases where the parts are important, it is not often the case that better quality results in better outcomes; even a resource that is only average will suffice when the alternative is nothing at all, or as I once tweeted, what we usually need is not someone who is an expert, just someone who knows.
- Similarly, what counts as quality in one context will be perceived as a weakness in others; an explanation that is complete and accurate may be incomprehensible to a beginner.
- Most importantly, the learning that happens in a MOOC is not a consequence of the learning materials, or even the instruction; it is a consequence of an immersion in an interactive community and will result from what emerges from that interaction.

Yes, we can evaluate based on some banal criteria—the website was always down, the text was too scrambled to read, the video was in Farsi—but these, insofar as they render the *MOOC* less successful, can be traced as failures of one or more of the success criteria described in the previous section.

The evaluation of each of the four criteria can be mapped against elements of the course, and then checked off like a counter. For example, we could list the 55 resources employed in the course, and count the number of resources that are free and open (in the sense I described above). But this is in a sense misleading; it makes a course that depends on a key closed resource seem to be 98 percent open, while at the same time it makes a course that had one participant post a lot of Amazon links (to books, which you must buy) seem like it was 50 percent closed. Neither estimation would be correct, but numbers know no context.

Properties like autonomy, diversity, openness and interactivity are not properly discerned by being counted, but by being *recognized*. In this way they are a lot like other properties, like freedom, love and obscenity. A variety of factors—not just number, but context, placement, relevance and salience—come into play (that is *why* we need neural networks [aka, people]) to *perceive* them, and can't simply use machines to count them.

That said, there is a purpose to checklists and rubrics, and that is to ensure that nothing has been omitted from consideration. Even experts depend on checklists, and they are critical in environments such as hospitals and airplanes. As mentioned previously, we see what we expect to see, and checklists remind us what to expect to see.

At this point it would be reasonable to countenance a variety of features of MOOCs, and to assess each for autonomy, openness, diversity and interactivity. For example, consider the question as posed to each of the following elements of a MOOC:

- content selected by the instructor (is it open? Is it diverse? etc.)
- the online platform used by participants
- the authoring environment(s) used by participants
- communication of daily news and announcements
- guest speakers and interviews.

The difficulty with such a checklist is that it can easily become endless. And while posing these questions can be useful when *selecting* technology or when *designing* the course, they become less useful as an evaluation rubric after the fact.

So, a suggestion: think of the course as a language, and the course design (in all its aspects) therefore as an expression in that language. This can be applied as broadly or as narrowly as one wishes, and for the present purpose, can be used to frame an assessment of the quality of an entire MOOC in a single pass.

In consideration of the use of digital artifacts *as* language (for example, 'speaking in LOLcats'), we can identify the different *dimensions* of literacy. Based on work in language and linguistics over the last century, I have identified six major dimensions of literacy: syntax, semantics, pragmatics, cognition, context and change.

It is important to understand that these are distinct from different *types* of literacy. For example, there has been a great deal of attention paid recently to 'digital literacy', along with numerical literacy (or 'numeracy') along with traditional language-based literacy. We can imagine many more types of literacy: performance, simulation, appropriation and more, for example. There's emotional literacy, financial literacy and social literacy. Each of these (according to my account) constitutes in its own way the learning of a *language*. Each of these languages has its own literacy, and literacy in that language may be defined across the six dimensions.

Indeed, I have commented in the past, and it is relevant to point out now, that the act of learning a discipline—a trade, for example, or a science or a skill—is more like the learning of a language than it is like learning a set of facts. Yes, there is an element of memory, but the bulk of expertise in a language—or a trade, science or skill—isn't in knowing the parts, but in fluency and recognition, cumulating in the (almost) intuitive understanding ('expertise', as Dreyfus and Dreyfus (1986) would argue). This sort of fluency is *acquired* by immersion in a language-speaking community (of which a MOOC is a characteristic example) and *described* by the six elements of literacy listed above.

An evaluation of the quality of a MOOC, therefore, after we have passed beyond the gross characteristics of being massive, open, online, and a course, is an assessment of the resulting course *as a network* and *from a linguistic perspective*. Now again, this is a *rubric*, not a checklist. It is not intended to define a MOOC as '49% successful' on the basis of that percentage of boxes being checked. It is an *aid*, used to assist a person who is already fluent in MOOC design (or at least, in the domain or discipline being studied) *recognize* the quality (or lack of quality) of a MOOC.

This rubric thus consists of a set of 24 elements: each of the four success criteria, across each of the six dimensions of literacy. Some of these will be more difficult to comprehend than others, and each will have to be considered at some length before anything like a common understanding is achieved; but the checklist serves as a starting point, and the hard empirical work can now begin.

So, for example, when I think back of the CCK08 course, and the other MOOCs we designed, one of the questions I could ask (among the 24) is 'openness-syntax'. Openness is the quality I described above, and the question here is how well it applied to the forms, rules, regularities, patterns and operations in the course. This, in turn, leads to basic questions such as: could URLs be shared? Is the login form accessible? Are there hidden or unstated regulations or criteria? This list, clearly, would be different for each course, because each course consists of a *different* set of forms, rules, regularities, patterns and operations. It's not a question of whether this is the right set of rules or regularities, or whether one set of rules is better than another (that's like asking whether Spanish or Portuguese is the superior language). It's a question of *whether the language of the course can be learned.*

So there are 23 other sets of questions, each equally important, and this is neither the place to describe them in detail nor even to attempt to enumerate them (and they are more productively considered as separate and individual cases, rather than as a set).

To conclude, I will add some *caveats*.

The discipline of education is as a rule overly fond of taxonomies and distinctions. The taxonomies and distinctions offered in this discussion are the least important aspect of the discussion. In all cases, the taxonomies have been developed in order to enable inferential work to be performed. It doesn't matter whether we divide the properties of successful networks into 'autonomy', 'diversity', etc., whether we focus on learning rules (Hebbian, Back-propagation, Boltzmann) or whatever; what matters is that the design principles of MOOCs are those that reliably result in successful networks, where success itself is a matter of empirical observation, convention and use. The same as with respect to the elements of literacy.

And similarly, with respect to this presentation, it is not the *content* of what is asserted here—it is the fact of the assertion and the manner of the investigation, which should be taken to serve as a model or demonstration of thinking about quality in MOOCs, and not a definitive statement of it.

Notes

Reprinted with permission from the National Research Council of Canada.

1 https://archive.org/details/Cck08UstreamSessionChatOctober312008

2 http://oeru.org/

References

Barabasi, A.-L. (2003). *Linked: How Everything Is Connected to Everything Else and What It Means for Business, Science, and Everyday Life*. New York, NY: Plume.

Bell, F. (2011, March). Connectivism: Its Place in Theory-Informed Research and Innovation in Technology-Enabled Learning. *International Review of Research in Open and Distance Learning, 12*(3). Retrieved from http://www.irrodl.org/index.php/irrodl/article/view/902/1664

Bonk, C.J. (2012, June 16). *Twenty Thoughts on the Types, Targets, and Intents of MOOCs*. Retrieved from Travelin Ed Man: http://travelinedman.blogspot.ca/2012/06/twenty-thoughts-on-types-targets-and.html

Breese, J. S., Heckerman, D., & Kadie, C. (2013). *Empirical Analysis of Predictive Algorithms for Collaborative Filtering*. Retrieved from http://arxiv.org/abs/1301.7363

Churchland, P.M. (1986). *Scientific Realism and the Plasticity of Mind*. Cambridge University Press. Retrieved from http://www.amazon.com/Scientific-Realism-Plasticity-Cambridge-Philosophy/dp/0521338271

Cormier, D. (2010, December 1). *Success in a MOOC*. Retrieved from YouTube: www.youtube.com/watch?v=r8avYQ5ZqM0

Devlin, K. (2012, November 12). *MOOC Lessons*. Retrieved from Devlin's Angle: http://devlinsangle.blogspot.ca/2012/11/mooc-lessons.html

Dreyfus, H. L., & Dreyfus, S. E. (1986). *Mind Over Machine: The power of human intuition and expertise in the age of the computer*. Oxford: Basil Blackwell.

Free Software Foundation. (2014, August 5). *What Is Free Software? Version 1.135*. Retrieved from GNU Operating System: http://www.gnu.org/philosophy/free-sw.html

Ingeno, L. (2013, April 19). Penn State Partners With Coursera, Will Offer Five Free, Mass Online Courses. *The Daily Collegian*. Retrieved from The Daily Collegian: http://www.collegian.psu.edu/archives/article_789fc64b-17b8-5065-97e6-562e96c1313e.html?mode=jqm

Kolowich, S. (2013, April 8). Coursera Takes a Nuanced View of MOOC Dropout Rates. *Chronicle of Higher Education*. Retrieved from http://chronicle.com/blogs/wiredcampus/coursera-takes-a-nuanced-view-of-mooc-dropout-rates/43341?cid=wc&utm_source=wc&utm_medium=en

Mackness, J. (2014, August 14). *Jenny Mackness*. Retrieved from Jenny Mackness: http://jennymackness.wordpress.com/

Mak, S.F. (2008, October 24). *What's New in Connectivism?* Retrieved from Learner Weblog: http://suifaijohnmak.wordpress.com/

Rogers, A. (2008). Informal Learning and Literacy. In N.H. Hornberger, *Encyclopedia of Language and Education* (pp. 544–555). Springer US. doi:10.1007/978–0–387–30424–3_41

Rumelhart, D.E., & McClelland, J.L. (1987). *Parallel Distributed Processing, Vol 1: Foundations*. Cambridge, MA: A Bradford Book.

Stack Overflow. (2010, March 8). *jQuery Set Ajax Return Value in Form Field*. Retrieved from Stack Overflow: http://stackoverflow.com/questions/2405190/jquery-set-ajax-return-value-in-form-field

Taylor, J.C. (2007, October). Open Courseware Futures: Creating a parallel universe. *e-Journal of Instructional Science and Technology* (e-JIST), *10*(1). Retrieved from http://www.ascilite.org.au/ajet/e-jist/docs/vol10_no1/papers/full_papers/taylorj.htm

5

Instructional Theory and Technology for the New Paradigm of Education[1]

Charles M. Reigeluth

One of the few things that practically everyone agrees on in both education and training is that people learn at different rates and have different learning needs. Yet our schools and training programs typically teach a predetermined, fixed amount of content in a set amount of time. Inevitably, slower learners are forced to move on before they have mastered the content, and they accumulate deficits in their learning that make it more difficult for them to learn related content in the future. Also, faster learners are bored to the point of frustration and waste much valuable time waiting for the group to move on—a considerable squandering of talent that our communities, companies, and society sorely need. A system that was truly designed to maximize learning would not force learners to move on before they had learned the current material, and it would not force faster learners to wait for the rest of the class (Reigeluth & Karnopp, 2013).

Our current paradigm of education and training was developed during the industrial age. At that time, we could not afford to educate or train everyone to high levels, and we did not need to educate or train everyone to high levels. The predominant form of work was manual labor. In fact, if we educated everyone to high levels, few would be willing to work on assembly lines, doing mindless tasks over and over again. So, what we needed in the industrial age was an educational system that *sorted* students—one that separated the children who should do manual labor from the ones who should be managers or professionals. So the "less bright" students were flunked out, and the brighter ones were promoted to higher levels of education. This is why our schools use norm-referenced assessment systems rather than criterion-referenced assessment—to help sort the students. The same applied to our training systems. We must recognize that the main problem with our education and training systems is not the teachers or the students, it is the system—a system that is designed more for sorting than for learning (see Reigeluth, 1987, 1994, for examples).

Elsewhere, I have presented visions of what a postindustrial education system might be like—a system that is designed to maximize learning (Reigeluth, 1987; Reigeluth & Garfinkle, 1994; Reigeluth & Karnopp, 2013). With minor adaptations, that vision could be applied to our training systems as well. The purpose of this chapter is to describe instructional theory and technology that support such postindustrial education and training systems. In particular, it will:

- Describe *universal methods* of instruction based on Dave Merrill's "first principles".
- Discuss the importance of tailoring methods to particular *situations* and resolve the apparent contradiction with universal methods.
- Describe the *core ideas* of the postindustrial paradigm of instruction.
- Discuss the importance of, and problems with, task-based instruction (TBI).
- Present a *vision* of postindustrial instruction, complete with several major *instructional strategies*.
- Describe the *roles* that should be played by the "teacher," the learner, and technology in the new paradigm.

Universal Methods of Instruction

M. David Merrill has proposed that there is a set of five prescriptive instructional principles ("First Principles") that enhance the quality of instruction across all situations (Merrill, 2007, 2009). Those principles have to do with task-centeredness, activation, demonstration, application, and integration. Briefly, they are as follows:

Task-Centered Principle

- *Instruction should use a task-centered instructional strategy.*
- *Instruction should use a progression of increasingly complex whole tasks.*

Demonstration Principle

- *Instruction should provide a demonstration of the skill consistent with the type of component skill: kinds-of, how-to, and what-happens.*
- *Instruction should provide guidance that relates the demonstration to generalities.*
- *Instruction should engage learners in peer-discussion and peer-demonstration.*
- *Instruction should allow learners to observe the demonstration through media that are appropriate to the content.*

Application Principle

- *Instruction should have the learner apply learning consistent with the type of component skill: kinds-of, how-to, and what-happens.*
- *Instruction should provide intrinsic or corrective feedback.*
- *Instruction should provide coaching, which should be gradually withdrawn to enhance application.*
- *Instruction should engage learners in peer-collaboration.*

Activation Principle

- *Instruction should activate relevant cognitive structures in learners by having them recall, describe, or demonstrate relevant prior knowledge or experience.*
- *Instruction should have learners share previous experience with each other.*
- *Instruction should have learners recall or acquire a structure for organizing new knowledge.*

Integration Principle

- *Instruction should integrate new knowledge into learners' cognitive structures by having them reflect on, discuss, or defend new knowledge or skills.*
- *Instruction should engage learners in peer-critique.*
- *Instruction should have learners create, invent, or explore personal ways to use their new knowledge or skill.*
- *Instruction should have learners publicly demonstrate their new knowledge or skill.*

While these principles might apply universally to all instructional situations (situations involving aided learning), the specific methods by which each principle is implemented must vary from one situation to another for instruction to be of high quality (Reigeluth & Carr-Chellman, 2009a). For example, for "Instruction should use a *task-centered* instructional strategy," the nature of the task-centered strategy may need to vary considerably from one situation to another. Similarly, for "Instruction should provide coaching," the nature of the coaching should vary considerably from one situation to another. So let's explore these variations, or *situationalities*.

Situational Methods of Instruction

Principles and methods of instruction can be described on many levels of precision (Reigeluth & Carr-Chellman, 2009b). For example, on the least precise level, Merrill states that instruction should provide coaching. On a highly precise level, one could state, "when teaching a procedure, if a learner skips a step during a performance of the procedure, the learner should be reminded of the step by asking the learner a question that prompts the learner to recognize the omission." When we provide more precision in a principle or method of instruction, we usually find that it needs to be different for different situations. Reigeluth (1999a) referred to the contextual factors that influence the effects of methods as *situationalities*.

The challenge for instructional agents (and therefore instructional theorists) is to identify which situationalities are important for selecting each method. Furthermore, methods may be combined into a "package deal" that is made up of an interrelated and interdependent set of methods, in which case we need to identify which situationalities are important for selecting each "package" (set of methods).

Reigeluth and Carr-Chellman (2009a) propose that there are two major types of situationalities that call for fundamentally different sets of methods:

Situationalities based on different approaches to instruction (means), such as:

- Role play
- Synectics
- Mastery learning
- Direct instruction
- Discussion
- Conflict resolution
- Peer learning
- Experiential learning
- Problem-based learning
- Simulation-based learning

Situationalities based on different learning outcomes (ends), such as:

- Knowledge
- Comprehension
- Application
- Analysis
- Synthesis
- Evaluation
- Affective development
- Integrated learning (p. 58)

The chapters in Units 2 and 3 in Reigeluth and Carr-Chellman's (2009c) "Green Book 3" (*Instructional-Design Theories and Models, Vol. III: Building a Common Knowledge Base*) describe the "common knowledge base" for nine of those sets of methods.

In the remainder of this chapter, I provide a more holistic vision of what the postindustrial paradigm of instruction might be like. I start with core ideas, followed by one possible vision, and finally roles of key players for this paradigm of instruction.

Core Ideas for the Postindustrial Paradigm of Instruction

The following are some core ideas for the postindustrial paradigm of instruction. They are presented as dichotomies to contrast them with the core ideas that characterize the industrial-age paradigm of instruction, but it should be understood that dichotomies are usually false, and postindustrial thinking is characterized more by "both-and" than "either-or".

Learning-focused vs. sorting-focused. This core idea was discussed earlier in this chapter. All the following core ideas are chosen to support this central idea.

Learner-centered vs. teacher-centered instruction. McCombs and Whisler (1997) define learner-centered as:

> The perspective that couples a focus on individual learners (their heredity, experiences, perspectives, backgrounds, talents, interests, capacities, and needs) with a focus on learning (the best available knowledge about learning and how it occurs and about teaching practices that are most effective in promoting the highest levels of motivation, learning, and achievement for all learners).
>
> (p. 9)

To this I would add that the instructional methods are largely tailored to each learner and carried out by the learner rather than by the teacher. Learners also play a larger role in directing their own learning, including reflection on and in learning.

Learning by doing vs. teacher presenting. Most of a student's time is spent performing authentic tasks, rather than listening to a teacher. Some talk about such task-based instruction in terms of the "student as worker" and the "teacher as manager," rather than the teacher as worker (Schlechty, 2002). Others call this the teacher as "guide on the side" rather than "sage on the stage." Some call it the constructivist approach to learning. The bottom line is that task-based instruction is active, learner-centered, and largely self-directed.

Attainment-based vs. time-based progress. Each student moves on to a new topic or competency when she or he has attained a standard of achievement, rather than when a certain amount of time has passed. A student is not forced to move on before attaining the standard and is allowed to move on as soon as the standard is attained. This avoids the huge waste of student time that exists in the industrial-age paradigm of education. This is a standards-based approach to education in the truest sense of the term. Mastery learning (Block, 1971; Bloom, 1968, 1981) was an early implementation of this core idea.

Customized vs. standardized instruction. The new paradigm offers customized rather than standardized learning experiences. This goes beyond attainment-based progress (which is customized pacing) to include *customized content* and *customized methods*. While there is a core of knowledge, skills, and attitudes that all students learn, there is considerable time for students to cultivate their particular talents, interests, and strengths. Also, Howard Gardner has shown that students differ in their profile of seven major kinds of intelligence and has argued that a student's strongest intelligences can be used most effectively as "entry points" for learning knowledge, skills, and attitudes (Gardner, 1999). Methods are also customized for some other kinds of learner characteristics and preferences. *Personal learning plans* (different in important ways from IEPs) and learning contracts are valuable tools for customizing learning.

Criterion-referenced vs. norm-referenced testing. The two purposes of student assessment in the new paradigm are to guide student learning (formative assessment) and to certify student attainments (summative assessment). Norm-referenced assessment (another form of summative assessment) is no longer used. *Formative assessment* entails providing each student with immediate feedback on performance, with hints or other forms of guidance to help the student learn from mistakes. *Summative assessment* entails certifying when a student has reached the standard for any given attainment.

Collaborative vs. individual. In the workplace, most knowledge work is done in teams. Collaboration is important in work life, civic life, and family life. Therefore, students need experience in collaborating on small teams. Team-based learning on a task provides an excellent opportunity for students to develop their collaboration skills, but it also provides a valuable opportunity for students to learn from each other. Furthermore, it is strongly supported by social constructivism (Palincsar, 1998; Scardemalia & Bereiter, 1996).

Enjoyable vs. unpleasant. In the age of knowledge work, lifelong learning is essential to our citizens' quality of life and to the health of our communities. Lifelong learning is greatly enhanced by love of learning. The industrial-age paradigm of education makes many students dislike learning, and it has turned the culture of our schools into one that devalues and derides students who excel in learning. That mindset and culture works against lifelong learning. Although lifelong learning has, for many years, been a buzzword in education, the industrial-age paradigm inherently impedes it. The postindustrial paradigm changes this by instilling a love of learning in students. This requires switching from extrinsic to *intrinsic motivation*. It also requires learning though authentic, engaging tasks, as is typically done in problem-based and project-based learning.

These core ideas represent essential characteristics of postindustrial educational and training systems—ideas on a level of universality for postindustrial instruction as Merrill's First Principles of instruction are for all paradigms of instruction. However, the ways in which they are implemented are likely to vary considerably from one educational system to another. The following is a vision of instruction for one possible implementation of these core ideas.

Task-Based Instruction

Student engagement or motivation is key to learning. No matter how much work the teacher does, if the student doesn't work, the student doesn't learn. The quality and quantity of learning are directly proportional to the amount of effort the student devotes to learning. The industrial-age paradigm of education and training was based on extrinsic motivation, with grades, study halls, detentions, and in the worst cases repeating a grade or flunking out.

In contrast, for a variety of reasons, intrinsic motivation is emphasized in the information-age paradigm. Reasons include the importance of lifelong learning and therefore of developing a love of learning, the decline of discipline in the home and school, and the lower effectiveness of extrinsic motivators now than 30 years ago.

To enhance intrinsic motivation, instructional methods should be learner-centered rather than teacher-centered. They should involve learning by doing, utilize tasks that are of inherent interest to the learner (which usually means they must be "authentic"), and offer opportunities for collaboration. This makes task-based instruction (TBI) particularly appropriate as a foundational instructional theory for the information-age paradigm of education and training.

Furthermore, given the importance of student progress being based on learning rather than on time, students progress at different rates and learn different things at any given time. This also lends itself well to TBI, because it is more learner-directed than teacher-directed.

It seems clear that TBI should be used prominently in the new paradigm of education and training. But there are problems with TBI. I explore those next.

Problems with Task-Based Instruction

In my own use of TBI, I have encountered four significant problems with it. Most TBI is collaborative or team based, and typically the whole team is assessed on a final product. This makes it difficult to assess and ensure that all students have learned what was intended to be learned. I have found that often one student on the team is a loafer and doesn't learn much at all. I have also found that teammates often work cooperatively rather than collaboratively, meaning they each perform different tasks and therefore learn different things. In my experience, it is rare for any student to have learned all that was intended. For a system in which student progress is based on learning, it is important to assess and ensure the learning of each and every student on the team. Yet it is rare for this to happen in TBI. This may not be as widespread a problem for higher levels of education, but it is a big problem for lower levels, because gaps in learning can make related future learning difficult and frustrating.

Second, the skills and competencies that we teach through TBI are usually ones that our learners will need to transfer to a broad range of situations, especially for complex cognitive tasks. However, in TBI learners typically use a skill only once or twice in the performance of the project. This makes it difficult for them to learn to use the skill in the full range of situations in which they are likely to need it in the future. Many skills require extensive practice to develop them to a proficient or expert level, yet that rarely happens in TBI.

Third, some skills need to be automatized in order to free up the person's conscious cognitive processing for higher-level thinking required during performance of a task. TBI does not address this instructional need.

Finally, much learner time can be wasted during TBI—searching for information, doing busywork, repeating the use of skills that have already been mastered, and struggling to learn without sufficient guidance or support. It is often important, not just in corporate training, but also in K-12 and higher education, to get the most learning in the least amount of time. Such efficiency is not typically a hallmark of TBI.

Given these four problems with TBI—difficulty ensuring mastery, transfer, automaticity, and efficiency—does this mean we should abandon TBI and go with direct instruction, as Kirschner, Sweller, and Clark (2006) propose? To quote a famous advertisement, "Not exactly." I now explore this issue.

A Vision of the Postindustrial Paradigm of Instruction

Task and Instructional Spaces

Imagine a small team of students working on an authentic task in a computer-based simulation (the *task space*). Soon they encounter a learning gap (knowledge, skills, understandings, values, attitudes, dispositions, etc.) that they need to fill to proceed with the task. Imagine that the students can "freeze" time and have a virtual mentor appear and provide customized tutoring "just in time" to develop that skill or understanding individually for each student (the *instructional space*).

Research shows that learning a skill is facilitated to the extent that instruction *tells* the students how to do it, *shows* them how to do it for diverse situations, and gives them *practice* with immediate feedback, again for diverse situations (Merrill, 1983; Merrill, Reigeluth, & Faust, 1979), so the students learn to generalize or transfer the skill to the full range of situations they will encounter in the real world. Each student continues to practice until she or he reaches the standard of mastery for the skill, much as in the Khan Academy (www.khanacademy.com). Upon reaching the standard, the student returns to the task space, where time is unfrozen, to apply what has been learned to the task and continue working on it until the next learning gap is encountered, and this doing–learning–doing cycle is repeated.

Well-validated instructional theories have been developed to offer guidance for the design of both the task space and the instructional space (see Reigeluth, 1999b; Reigeluth & Carr-Chellman, 2009c, for examples). In this way we transcend the either/or thinking so characteristic of industrial-age thinking and move to both/and thinking, which is better suited to the much greater complexity inherent in the information age—we utilize instructional theory that combines the best of behaviorist, cognitivist, and constructivist theories and models. This theory pays attention to mastery of individual competencies, but it also avoids the fragmentation characteristic of many mastery learning programs in the past.

Team and Individual Assessment

One of the problems with TBI as it is often implemented is that students are assessed on the quality of the team "product." This gives you no idea as to who has acquired which competencies. It also does not give you any indication of each student's ability to transfer those competencies to other situations where they may be needed. Team assessment is important, but you also need individual assessment, and the instructional space offers an excellent opportunity to meet this need. Like the task space, the instructional space is performance oriented. The practice opportunities (offered primarily in a computer simulation for immediate, customized feedback and authenticity) continue to be offered to a student until the student reaches the criterion for number of correct performances in a row that is required by the standard. Formative evaluation is provided immediately to the student on each incorrect performance, often in the form of hints that promote deeper cognitive processing and understanding. When automatization of a skill (Anderson, 1996) is important, there is also a criterion for speed of performance that must be met.

In this manner, student assessment is fully integrated into the instruction, and there is no waste of time in conducting a separate assessment. Furthermore, the assessment ensures that each student has attained the standard for the full range of situations in which the competency will be needed.

When a performance cannot be done on a computer (e.g., a ballet performance), an expert has a handheld device with a rubric for assessment; the expert fills in the rubric while observing the performance, provides formative evaluation when appropriate during the performance, and allows the student to retry on a substandard performance when appropriate for further assessment; and the information is automatically fed into the computer system, where it is stored in the student's record and can be accessed by the student and other authorized people.

Instructional Theory for the Task Space

There is much validated guidance for the design of the task space, including universal and situational principles for the task space (see e.g., Barrows, 1986; Barrows & Tamblyn, 1980; Duffy & Raymer, 2010; Jonassen, 1997, 1999; Savery, 2009). They include guidance for selecting a good task at the right level of complexity, forming small groups, self-directed learning, what the teacher should do, how debriefing should be done, and more. Computer-based simulations are often highly effective for creating and supporting the task environment, but the task space could be comprised entirely of places, objects, and people in the real world (place-based learning), or it could be a combination of computer simulation and real-world environments. STAR LEGACY (Schwartz, Lin, Brophy, & Bransford, 1999) is a good example of a computer-based simulation for the project space.

Instructional Theory for the Instructional Space

Selection of instructional strategies in the instructional space is primarily based on the type of learning (ends of instruction) involved (see Unit 3 in Reigeluth & Carr-Chellman, 2009c). For *memorization*, drill and practice is most effective (Salisbury, 1990), including chunking, repetition, prompting, and mnemonics. For *application* (skills), tutorials with generality, examples, practice, and immediate feedback are most effective (Merrill, 1983; Romiszowski, 2009). For *conceptual understanding*, connecting new concepts to existing concepts in students' cognitive structures requires the use of such methods as analogies, context (advance organizers), comparison and contrast, analysis of parts and kinds, and various other techniques based on the dimensions of understanding required (Reigeluth, 1983). For *theoretical understanding*, causal relationships are best learned through exploring causes (explanation), effects (prediction), and solutions (problem solving); and natural processes are best learned through description of the sequence of events in the natural process (Reigeluth & Schwartz, 1989). These sorts of instructional strategies have been well researched for their effectiveness, efficiency, and appeal. And they are often best implemented through computer-based tutorials, simulations, and games.

Again, this is but one vision of the postindustrial paradigm of instruction. I encourage the reader to try to think of additional visions that meet the needs of the postindustrial era: principally intrinsic motivation, customization, attainment-based student progress, collaborative learning, and self-directed learning. To do so, it may be helpful to consider the ways that roles are likely to change in the new paradigm of instruction.

Key Roles in the Post-Industrial Paradigm of Instruction

Roles are likely to change for teachers, students, and technology (Reigeluth & Karnopp, 2013). Each of these roles is briefly described next.

New Roles for Teachers

The teacher's role has changed dramatically in the new paradigm of instruction from the "sage on the stage" to the "guide on the side." I currently see three major roles involved in being a guide. First, the teacher is a *designer of student work* (Schlechty, 2002). The student work includes that which is done in both the task space and the instructional space. Second, the teacher is a *facilitator of the learning process*. This includes helping to develop a personal learning plan, coaching or scaffolding the student's learning when appropriate, facilitating discussion and reflection, and arranging availability of various human and material resources. Third, and perhaps most important in the public education sector, the teacher is a *caring mentor*, a person who is concerned with the full, well-rounded development of the student.

Teacher as designer, facilitator, and mentor are only three of the most important new roles that teachers serve, but not all teachers need to perform all the roles. Different kinds of teachers with different kinds and levels of training and expertise may focus on one or two of these roles (including students as teachers—see next section).

New Roles for Students

First, learning is an active process. The student must exert effort to learn. The teacher cannot do it for the student. This is why Schlechty (2002) characterizes the new paradigm as one in which *the student is the worker*, not the teacher, and in which the teacher is the designer of the student's work.

Second, to prepare the student for lifelong learning, the teacher helps each student to become a *self-directed and self-motivated learner*. Students are self-motivated to learn from when they are born to when they first go to school. The industrial-age paradigm systematically destroys that self-motivation by removing all self-direction and giving students boring work that is not relevant to their lives. In contrast, the postindustrial system is designed to nurture self-motivation through self-direction and active learning in the context of relevant, interesting tasks. Student motivation is key to educational productivity and helping students to realize their potential. It also greatly reduces discipline problems, drug use, and much more.

Third, it is often said that the best way to learn something is to *teach* it. Students are perhaps the most underutilized resource in our school systems. Furthermore, someone who has just learned something is often better at helping someone else learn it than is someone who learned it long ago. In addition to older students teaching slightly younger ones, peers can learn from each other in collaborative projects, and they can also serve as peer tutors.

Therefore, new student roles include student as worker, self-directed learner, and teacher.

New Roles for Technology

I currently see four main roles for technology to make the new paradigm of instruction feasible and cost-effective (Reigeluth & Carr-Chellman, 2009c; Reigeluth et al., 2008). Each of these is described next for the public education sector, but the roles are equally relevant in higher education, corporate training, military training, and education and training in other contexts.

Record keeping for student learning. Attainment-based student progress requires a personal record of attainments for each student. Technology saves teachers huge amounts of time for this. In this role, technology replaces the current report card, and it has three parts. First, it has a *Standards Inventory* that contains both required educational standards (national, state, and local) and optional educational standards for access by the teacher, student, and parents. These standards are broken down to individual attainments and are displayed in a "domain map" format similar to that of the Khan Academy. Domain Theory (Bunderson, Wiley, & McBride, 2009) is highly instrumental for designing this technological tool. It presents a list of attainments that should or can be learned, along with levels or standards or criteria at which each can be learned. Second, it has a *Personal Attainments Inventory* that contains a record of what each student knows. In essence, it maps each student's progress on the attainments listed in the Standards Inventory (and perhaps some that are not yet listed there). It shows when each attainment was reached, which ones are required, and what the next required attainments are in each area; and links to evidence of each attainment (in the form of summary data and/or original artifacts). Third, it has a *Personal Characteristics Inventory* that keeps track of each student's characteristics that influence learning, such as learning styles, profile of multiple intelligences, special needs, student interests and goals, and major life events (Reigeluth & Carr-Chellman, 2009c; Reigeluth et al., 2008).

Planning for student learning. The personal learning plan, or contract, could also be very difficult for teachers to develop for all of their students. Here, again, is a role that technology is ideally suited to play. It helps the student, parents, and teacher to (a) decide on *long-term goals*; (b) identify the full range of *attainment options* that are presently within reach for the student; (c) select from those options the ones that the student wants to pursue now (*short-term goals*), based on requirements, long-term goals, interests, opportunities, etc.; (d) identify or create *tasks* for attaining the short-term goals; (e) identify and match up with *other students* who are interested in doing the same tasks at the same time (if collaboration is desired or needed) and specify all teammates' roles; (f) specify the *roles* that the teacher, parent, and any other mentors might play in supporting the student in learning from the task; and (g) develop a *contract* that specifies goals, tasks, teams, student roles and responsibilities, parent and teacher roles, method of assessment, and the deadline for each task (Reigeluth et al., 2008).

Instruction for student learning. Trying to "instruct" 25 students who are learning different things at any point in time could be very difficult for teachers—if they had to be the instructional agent all the time, as is typical in the industrial-age paradigm. However, technology can introduce the task to a student (or small team) in the task space, provide instructional tools (such as simulations, tutorials, drill and practice, research tools, communication tools, and learning objects) in the instructional space to support learning during the task (as described earlier), provide tools for monitoring and supporting student progress on the task, and even provide tools to help teachers and others develop new tasks and instructional tools. Technology can make all the above functions available to students anytime and anywhere. Instructional theory is extremely important to guide the design of these tools (Reigeluth et al., 2008).

Assessment for (and of) student learning. Once more, conducting formative and summative assessments of students could be a nightmare for teachers, since students are not all taking a given test at the same time. And once again, technology can offer great relief. First, as mentioned earlier, assessment is *integrated with instruction*. The plentiful performance opportunities that are used to cultivate competencies are used for both formative and summative assessments. Second, the assessments present *authentic tasks* on which the students demonstrate their knowledge, understanding, and skill. Third, whether in a simulation or a tutorial or drill and practice, the technology is designed to evaluate whether or not the criterion was met on each performance and to provide *formative feedback* to the student immediately for the greatest impact. When the criteria for successful performance have been met on x out of the last y performances, the *summative assessment* is complete and the corresponding attainment is automatically checked off in the student's personal inventory of attainments. In the few cases where the technology cannot assess the performance, an observer has a handheld device with a rubric for assessment and personally provides the immediate feedback on student performances. The information from the handheld device is uploaded into the computer system, where it is placed in the student's personal inventory. Finally, technology provides tools to help teachers develop assessments and link them to the standards (Reigeluth et al., 2008).

Note that these four roles or functions are seamlessly integrated (Reigeluth & Carr-Chellman, 2009c). The record-keeping tool provides information automatically for the planning tool. The planning tool identifies instructional tools that are available. The assessment tool is integrated into the instructional tool. And the assessment tool feeds information automatically into the record-keeping tool (Reigeluth et al., 2008; Watson, Lee, & Reigeluth, 2007). In our earlier work we used the term "Learning Management System" for this comprehensive, personalized, integrated tool, but that term is often used to describe course management systems that are teacher-centered. Therefore, to avoid confusion, we have decided to call this the Personalized Integrated Educational System (PIES).

Also, please note that there are many other roles for the PIES (Reigeluth et al., 2008). These "secondary" roles include communications (e-mail, blogs, web sites, discussion boards, wikis, whiteboards, instant messaging, podcasts, videocasts, etc.), PIES administration (offering access to information and authority to input information based on role and information type), general student data (student's address, parent/guardian information, mentor–teacher and school, student's location/attendance, health information), school personnel information (address, certifications and awards, location, assigned students, tools authored, student evaluations that they have performed, teacher professional development plan and records, repository of teaching tools, awards their students have received), and more.

It should be apparent that technology will play a crucial role in the success of the postindustrial paradigm of education. It will enable a quantum improvement in student learning, and likely at a lower cost per student per year than in the current industrial-age paradigm. Just as the electronic spreadsheet made the accountant's job quicker, easier, less expensive, and more enjoyable, so the PIES described here will make the teacher's job quicker, easier, less expensive, and more enjoyable. But instructional theory is sorely needed for technology to realize its potential contribution.

Conclusion

In the postindustrial world, we need to transform most of our educational and training systems from ones that are designed for sorting students to ones that are designed to maximize learning—from ones in which student progress is time-based to ones in which it is attainment-based (Reigeluth & Karnopp, 2013). This transformation will require advances in both instructional theory and instructional technology.

Merrill's First Principles (task-centeredness, activation, demonstration, application, and integration) provide a good, albeit general, summary of the most important features for high quality instruction. For more detailed guidance, we must look at the situationalities that determine the ways in which instruction should differ from one situation to another. Research to date indicates that these are based primarily on differing means (different approaches to instruction) and differing ends (different learning outcomes or kinds of learning).

In addition, it is helpful to look at a more holistic vision of what the new paradigm of instruction might be like. I proposed that it will be characterized by the following core ideas: learning-focused, learner-centered, learning by doing, attainment-based progress, customized instruction, criterion-referenced testing, collaborative learning, and enjoyable learning. I then proposed a vision of instruction for one possible implementation of these core ideas. It describes task and instructional spaces, team and individual assessment, instructional strategies for the task space, and instructional strategies for the instructional space.

Finally, I summarized a set of key roles for the new paradigm of instruction. New roles for teachers include designer of student work, facilitator of the learning process, and caring mentor. New roles for students include worker, self-directed learner, and teacher. Four major new roles were described for technology. First, record keeping for student learning includes offering a standards inventory, a personal attainments inventory, and a personal characteristics inventory. Second, planning for student learning includes helping the student, parents, and teacher to identify or decide on long-term goals, attainments currently within the student's reach, attainments to pursue in the next contract, tasks for learning those attainments, other students to work on a team, roles for the teacher and parents, and a contract. Third, instruction for student learning includes a wide variety of tools for both the task space and the instructional space. Finally, assessment for (and of) student learning is integrated with the instruction and uses authentic tasks and performances, certification of attainments, and formative feedback.

While much instructional theory has been generated to guide the design of the new paradigm of instruction, much remains to be learned. We need to learn how to better address the strong emotional basis of learning (Greenspan, 1997), foster emotional and social development, and promote the development of positive attitudes, values, morals, and ethics, among other things. It is my hope that you, the reader, will rise to the challenge and help further advance the knowledge we need to greatly improve our ability to help every student reach his or her potential.

Note

1 This chapter was published online as Reigeluth, C. M. (2012). Instructional theory and technology for the new paradigm of education. *RED, Revista de Educación a Distancia. Number 32.* September 30, 2012. Retrieved on (30/09/2012) at http://www.um.es/ead/red/32. Significant portions of that article were previously published in Reigeluth (2011) and Reigeluth (2012). They are included here with permission of the publishers.

References

Anderson, J.R. (1996). *The architecture of cognition.* Mahwah, NJ: Lawrence Erlbaum.

Barrows, H.S. (1986). A taxonomy of problem-based learning methods. *Medical Education, 20*(6), 481–486. doi:10.1111/j.1365-2923.1986.tb01386.x

Barrows, H.S., & Tamblyn, R.M. (1980). *Problem-based learning: An approach to medical education.* New York: Springer.

Block, J.H. (1971). *Mastery learning: Theory and practice.* New York: Holt, Rinehart and Winston.

Bloom, B.S. (1968). Learning for mastery. *Evaluation Comment, 1*(1), 1–12.

Bloom, B.S. (1981). *All our children learning.* New York: McGraw-Hill.

Bunderson, C.V., Wiley, D.A., & McBride, R. (2009). Domain theory for instruction: Mapping attainments to enable learner-centered education. In C.M. Reigeluth & A.A. Carr-Chellman (Eds.), *Instructional-design theories and models: Building a common knowledge base* (Vol. III, pp. 327–347). New York: Routledge.

Duffy, T.M., & Raymer, P.L. (2010). A practical guide and a constructivist rationale for inquiry based learning. *Educational Technology, 50*(4), 3–15.

Gardner, H.E. (1999). Multiple approaches to understanding. In C.M. Reigeluth (Ed.), *Instructional-design theories and models, vol. II: A new paradigm of instructional theory* (pp. 69–89). Mahwah, NJ: Lawrence Erlbaum.

Greenspan, S.I. (1997). *The growth of the mind and the endangered origins of intelligence.* Reading, MA: Addison-Wesley.

Jonassen, D.H. (1997). Instructional design models for well-structured and ill-structured problem-solving learning outcomes. *Educational Technology Research and Development, 45*(1), 65–94.

Jonassen, D.H. (1999). Designing constructivist learning environments. In C. Reigeluth (Ed.), *Instructional-design theories and models* (Vol. II, pp. 215–239). Mahwah, NJ: Lawrence Erlbaum.

Kirschner, P.A., Sweller, J., & Clark, R.E. (2006). Why minimal guidance during instruction does not work: An analysis of the failure of constructivist, discovery, problem-based, experiential, and inquiry-based teaching. *Educational Psychologist, 41*(2), 75–86.

McCombs, B.L., & Whisler, J.S. (1997). *The learner-centered classroom and school: Strategies for increasing student motivation and achievement.* San Francisco: Jossey-Bass.

Merrill, M.D. (1983). Component display theory. In C.M. Reigeluth (Ed.), *Instructional-design theories and models: An overview of their current status* (Vol. I). Hillsdale, NJ: Lawrence Erlbaum.

Merrill, M.D. (2007). First principles of instruction: A synthesis. In R.A. Reiser & J.V. Dempsey (Eds.), *Trends and issues in instructional design and technology* (2nd ed., pp. 62–71). Upper Saddle River, NJ: Merrill/Prentice-Hall.

Merrill, M.D. (2009). First principles of instruction. In C.M. Reigeluth & A.A. Carr-Chellman (Eds.), *Instructional-design theories and models: Building a common knowledge base* (Vol. III, pp. 41–56). New York: Routledge.

Merrill, M.D., Reigeluth, C.M., & Faust, G.W. (1979). The instructional quality profile: A curriculum evaluation and design tool. In H.F. O'Neil, Jr. (Ed.), *Procedures for instructional systems development* (pp. 165–204). New York: Academic Press.

Palincsar, A.S. (1998). Social constructivist perspectives on teaching and learning. *Annual Review of Psychology, 49*, 345–375.

Reigeluth, C.M. (1983). Meaningfulness and instruction: Relating what is being learned to what a student knows. *Instructional Science, 12*(3), 197–208.

Reigeluth, C.M. (1987). The search for meaningful reform: A third-wave educational system. *Journal of Instructional Development, 10*(4), 3–14.

Reigeluth, C.M. (1994). The imperative for systemic change. In C.M. Reigeluth & R.J. Garfinkle (Eds.), *Systemic change in education* (pp. 3–11). Englewood Cliffs, NJ: Educational Technology.

Reigeluth, C.M. (1999a). What is instructional-design theory and how is it changing? In C.M. Reigeluth (Ed.), *Instructional-design theories and models: A new paradigm of instructional theory* (Vol. II, pp. 5–29). Mahwah, NJ: Lawrence Erlbaum.

Reigeluth, C.M. (Ed.). (1999b). *Instructional-design theories and models: A new paradigm of instructional theory* (Vol. II). Mahwah, NJ: Lawrence Erlbaum.

Reigeluth, C.M. (2011). An instructional theory for the post-industrial age. *Educational Technology, 51*(5), 25–29.

Reigeluth, C.M. (2012). Instructional theory and technology for a post-industrial world. In R.A. Reiser & J.V. Dempsey (Eds.), *Trends and issues in instructional design and technology* (3rd ed., pp. 75–83). Boston: Pearson Education.

Reigeluth, C.M., & Carr-Chellman, A.A. (2009a). Situational principles of instruction. In C.M. Reigeluth & A.A. Carr-Chellman (Eds.), *Instructional-design theories and models: Building a common knowledge base* (Vol. III, pp. 57–68). New York: Routledge.

Reigeluth, C.M., & Carr-Chellman, A.A. (2009b). Understanding instructional theory. In C.M. Reigeluth & A.A. Carr-Chellman (Eds.), *Instructional-design theories and models: Building a common knowledge base* (Vol. III, pp. 3–26). New York: Routledge.

Reigeluth, C.M., & Carr-Chellman, A.A. (Eds.). (2009c). *Instructional-design theories and models: Building a common knowledge base* (Vol. III). New York: Routledge.

Reigeluth, C.M., & Garfinkle, R.J. (1994). Envisioning a new system of education. In C.M. Reigeluth & R.J. Garfinkle (Eds.), *Systemic change in education* (pp. 59–70). Englewood Cliffs, NJ: Educational Technology.

Reigeluth, C.M., & Karnopp, J.R. (2013). *Reinventing schools: It's time to break the mold.* Lanham, MD: Rowman & Littlefield.

Reigeluth, C.M., & Schwartz, E. (1989). An instructional theory for the design of computer-based simulations. *Journal of Computer-Based Instruction, 16*(1), 1–10.

Reigeluth, C.M., Watson, S.L., Watson, W.R., Dutta, P., Chen, Z., & Powell, N. (2008). Roles for technology in the information-age paradigm of education: Learning management systems. *Educational Technology, 48*(6), 32–39.

Romiszowski, A. (2009). Fostering skill development outcomes. In C.M. Reigeluth & A.A. Carr-Chellman (Eds.), *Instructional-design theories and models: Building a common knowledge base* (Vol. III, pp. 199–224). New York: Routledge.

Salisbury, D.F. (1990). Cognitive psychology and its implications for designing drill and practice programs for computers. *Journal of Computer-Based Instruction, 17*(1), 23–30.

Savery, J.R. (2009). Problem-based approach to instruction. In C.M. Reigeluth & A.A. Carr-Chellman (Eds.), *Instructional-design theories and models: Building a common knowledge base* (Vol. III, pp. 143–165). New York: Routledge.

Scardemalia, M., & Bereiter, C. (1996). Computer support for knowledge-building communities. In T. Koschmann (Ed.), *CSCL: Theory and practice of an emerging paradigm* (pp. 249–268). Mahwah, NJ: Lawrence Erlbaum.

Schlechty, P. (2002). *Working on the work*. New York: John Wiley & Sons.
Schwartz, D.L., Lin, X., Brophy, S., & Bransford, J.D. (1999). Toward the development of flexibly adaptive instructional designs. In C.M. Reigeluth (Ed.), *Instructional-design theories and models: A new paradigm of instructional theory* (Vol. II, pp. 183–213). Mahwah, NJ: Lawrence Erlbaum.
Watson, W.R., Lee, S.K., & Reigeluth, C.M. (2007). Learning management systems: An overview and roadmap of the systemic application of computers to education. In F.M. Neto & F.V. Brasileiro (Eds.), *Advances in computer-supported learning* (pp. 66–96). Hershey, PA: Information Science.

6

Pedagogical Development, E-learning and Teaching in Higher Education

Marti Cleveland-Innes, Stefan Hrastinski, O. Bälter and Colin Wiseman

Introduction

This chapter presents an argument which rests on three interrelated premises regarding the transition to e-learning in higher education. The first is that the phenomenon of e-learning (Web-based teaching and learning) is dramatically affecting faculty roles in higher education, whether faculty are engaged in teaching with technology or not. The second is that the role of faculty member is saturated with requirements, and adding a teaching process that requires advanced teaching expertise in relation to technology and additional time commitments will not fit into the current role of faculty; this is so for e-learning. Finally, we suggest that leadership strategy which will resolve this issue, and afford students the benefits of e-learning, will take an embedded, distributed and dispersed approach. In presenting this argument, we will describe current work–life realities for faculty members in higher education institutions, present interview data from faculty at two institutions of higher education and outline why leadership strategies intended to support the role change required for faculty when teaching with technology may not work.

Emerging technology, the major catalyst behind e-learning, offers the opportunity for significant changes to teaching and learning, responsibilities that make up a major portion of the work–life activities of faculty. At the same time that technological advancement is imposing itself, either because of it or in addition to it, we are currently experiencing the most consequential set of changes in society since the late nineteenth century, when nations went from a largely domestic, rural, agrarian mode of living to an industrial, international, and urban economy (Keller, 2008, preface). These ubiquitous changes are having a significant impact on many things, including higher education institutions and the faculty who work in them. Challenges that faculty experience based on these changes and the effect on teaching must be considered by those leading higher education and responsible for its effectiveness. We recommend a new way of positioning the teaching element of faculty roles and discuss the leadership strategies that will support teaching in this new era.

The opportunity for faculty, and their practice as teachers, to remain the same and not change is not available. This imperative to change and other challenges in education have emerged because "neither the purpose, the methods, nor the population for whom education is intended today bear any resemblance to those on which formal education is historically based" (Pond, 2002, n.p.). Such change makes it increasingly difficult for education to operate in insular ways; attention to changing demographics, global economies and new social mores is required (Keller, 2008). The reach of information and communication technology via the Internet is pervasive, and has changed society and education institutions in "the way we organize ourselves, our policies, our culture, what faculty do, the way we work, and those we serve" (Ikenberry, 2001, p. 63). In the midst of these developments, new ways of teaching and learning have emerged.

These changes, then, provide the focus for updating the academy, indicating what changes are on the way or at the doorstep, and what is not or will not work because of these changes. Common institutional challenges fall under the headings of economics issues, changing demographics, the demand for accountability, new teaching and learning models and emerging technology. Net-based educational opportunities, the result of the last two of these institutional challenges listed here, emerged in the early '90s, most often with a promise of ameliorating problems within education, but also as an educational revolution. This revolution is in response to demands for education reform, particularly in reference to teaching and learning (Kanuka & Brooks, 2010). This reform can begin with faculty role change and careful attention to the structure and process of leadership activities to support it.

Background Information

Faculty Role Change in Reference to Teaching

It is unrealistic to expect higher education faculty to have sound, current content expertise, a productive research program, an active service commitment *and* be expert online teachers. The biggest lie in the academy is that the role of faculty, and its rewards and responsibilities, is made up of a seemingly balanced set of activities around teaching, research and service (Atkinson, 2001). With some variation across type of institution, research is the most valued work and most notably rewarded. While this reality has not changed, "classroom teaching and course materials (have become) more sophisticated and complex in ways that translate into new forms of faculty work . . . such new forms are not replacing old ones, but instead are layered on top of them, making for more work" (Rhoades, 2000, p. 38). It is time to clarify this reality and consider how, if at all, changes in teaching are, or may be, integrated into the role of faculty member. The possibility of change in the work–life experience for faculty, already in a complex, challenging context and role, is probable, in light of new technological opportunities. Within the traditional higher education context, change is available for faculty who wish to use current Internet technology to enhance learning (Cleveland-Innes & Garrison, 2010). However, Rhoades (2000) argues that higher education systems are out of balance as a result of technological change and the new economy and offers that higher education must "rebalance" through organized and careful reexamination of its options and choices. The examination and any resulting changes are likely to create, in the first instance, angst for faculty looking at potential restructuring of work–life, and, in the second, significant changes to the work–life to which they are accustomed.

The rebalance suggested above can support improvements in education access and quality learning experiences afforded by online education delivery; the pressure is on (U.S. Department of Education, 2009). This makes it more likely that faculty roles will change. Online learning involves the use of the Internet for interaction and collaborative engagement previously unavailable to teachers and students. What changes are required to the role of faculty member to allow engagement in online teaching? Any effective teacher must be true to the learning objectives of the subject matter at hand while attending to the multitude of characteristics students bring to the experience. Effective teachers bridge content and student needs through appropriate student engagement, a tactic as old as education itself. The role of effective teacher in online learning environments is newer and more complex. Even more complex are the implications of adopting the new teaching requirements into the current role of faculty.

All the teaching development and technology training in the world will not realize significant quantities of teaching change, even for the most motivated, until the context changes to support and reward teaching in ways that it has not in the past and, in addition, support the increased requirements for teaching activity using new technology. Even before the imposition of new technology, both excellent teaching and excellent research records were difficult to achieve. Fairweather's (2002) research suggests that new ways of teaching will make it more difficult for faculty to be exemplars of research and teaching. This study examines the myth of the "complete faculty member"—that is, one who can sustain high levels of productivity in both research and teaching at the same time. Data from the 1992–93 National Survey of Post-secondary Faculty provided a representative sample of 29,764 part-time and full-time faculty in 962 American research universities, doctoral-granting universities, comprehensive colleges and universities and liberal arts colleges. For the purpose of that study, Fairweather identified faculty as highly productive researchers if refereed publications exceeded the median for program and institutional type over a two-year period. Faculty members identified as highly productive teachers were those above the median in student classroom contact hours. In the first instance, 22 percent of faculty in four-year institutions met both criteria. However, adding collaborative instruction to the teaching criterion reduced the percentage of highly productive researchers and teachers to about 6%. Hence, we are now looking at changes to an already complex and challenging work–life situation.

This time-consuming collaborative instruction is central to the benefits of online teaching and learning. The individualization of communications and the role of instructor as a facilitator of student participation and learning add to instructor workload when teaching online (Davidson-Shivers, 2009).

A central advantage of online delivery is the opportunity to better engage learners in more active and collaborative educational experiences. Tomei (2004) proposes that online student expectations for on-demand, continuous feedback necessitates smaller class sizes relative to those in traditional classroom instruction. This is one option available to compensate for the imposition of time online teaching will impose. For Tomei, the 40–40–20 formula for allocating faculty time (40 percent teaching, 40 percent research, and 20 percent service) suggested by the American Association of University Professors (AAUP) is unrealistic for faculty teaching in an online environment.

It is unrealistic then to assume that emerging Internet technologies will transform teaching practices in higher education within the current context shaping faculty roles. It may be necessary to reconfigure and redefine conceptions of research and scholarship for the online environment and the unique needs of its faculty (Yick, Patrick, & Costin, 2005). This means a major shift in the context and the requirements of work for faculty, hence affecting faculty work–life.

Garrison and Kanuka (2004) give us a detailed view of the experience of academic instructors using online learning environments; the transition is no small matter. Changing teaching practice includes supporting the adjustments new online students require—another role adjustment for faculty (Cleveland-Innes & Garrison, 2009). Instructor suggestions that they prefer online teaching in order to take time to think through responses to students identified that what's good for students may be good for instructors as well. This provides new views regarding the role of online teacher, but not enough to help answer the questions regarding changes to work–life for faculty that may occur in the transition to online learning.

This role change can be explained based on sociological principles of role theory. 'Role' is used here as a sociological construct, defined as a collection of behavioral requirements associated with a certain social position in a group, organization or society (Kendall, Murray, & Linden, 2000). At its most general level, role expectations are dictated by the social structure. Individuals who engage in the role are guided, through a process of socialization, to appropriate role performance. Socialization is the "process by which people learn the characteristics of their group . . . (and) the attitudes, values and actions thought appropriate for them" (Kanwar & Swenson, 2000, p. 397).

At the theoretical level, role change must be understood as a rudimentary social process that occurs repeatedly in any social group. Normally part of the social subtext, this process entails individuals continually testing behaviors until they settle into a pattern of individual behavior for which they most often receive a favorable response. This behavioral pattern then becomes the person's role repertoire and the basis for individual role identity. Role change for faculty (at the level of institutional structure) and role identity adjustment (at the level of the individual faculty engaged in a new ways of teaching) may be facilitated through deliberate intervention by those in positions of influence and leadership.

Role change is an iterative process of exchange and change between individuals interacting as part of a structured social environment. Role change occurs in the form of continually shifting role expectations and requirements. The role exists sui generis as a generalized set of requirements. In the case of a complex role (such as faculty member), the generalized role can be difficult to pinpoint, as it continually shifts. This is particularly true for developing roles such as the role of online teacher, for in many ways we are "making it up" as we go. Under different conditions where long-standing roles exist, individuals engage in "role-taking" behavior, where observation and mimicry of role models allow those new to the role to "practice" appropriate role behaviors. "Role making" occurs as individuals construct aspects of the role with their own individual meanings and satisfying behaviors attached. This occurs under social conditions where such individual autonomy is allowed; such is usually the case for faculty. It also occurs where role models are not readily available, and construction of the role is required (Blau & Goodman, 1995).

The additional duties, responsibilities, and changes being asked of faculty can create a high level of dissatisfaction, particularly if they feel they are not well supported (Satterlee, 2010). It is critical that we have a realistic view of teaching in contemporary higher education and what the change to online teaching might look like. This issue needs more attention; in spite of increasing interest in online education, "most studies have focused only on the students' perspective. Merely a handful of studies have attempted to address the teachers' perspectives and little has been published on the online teaching experience itself" (Gudea, 2008, inside cover).

This online teaching experience and its impact on faculty role need to be considered in reference to the leadership needed to accommodate it. Like good teaching, academic leadership is not telling or transmitting information and ideas; it is the engagement of a supportive dialogue and relationships aimed at helping people to change and develop (Ramsden, 1998). Gibbs, Knapper, and Piccinin (2007) confirm that leadership plays an important role in creating teaching excellence.

Leadership Strategies in Reference to Faculty Role Change

The combined need for institutional and faculty role change points to the need for a new conceptualization of leadership, one that is more in keeping with the rapid, pervasive change which characterizes the current context of higher education. One possible approach, more collegial and collaborative than usual top-down, hierarchical structures, is distributed leadership (Harris, 2007; Hartley, 2007). Originally developed by Gronn (Gronn, 2000; Gronn, 2003), distributed leadership is based on the idea that leadership occurs at all levels of an organization and that we must look at current organizational practices to develop a more inclusive conception of leadership given recent changes in the division of labor (Gronn, 2002). While appealing in theory, there is little empirical evidence to back the efficacy of distributed leadership, especially in educational settings (Harris, 2007; Hartley, 2007; Zepke, 2007). Furthermore, concepts of distributed leadership give little weight to the importance of existing organizational structures and organizational cultures in determining leadership patterns in higher education. While distributed leadership is an important concept that promises to adapt to changing economic conditions, and changing economic structures certainly play a role in organizational change, as suggested by scholars of the new institutionalism (Campbell, 1998; DiMaggio & Powell, 1991; Pierson, 1994, 2004), it is important to recognize the role of pre-existing organizational structures and cultures when attempting to understand higher education leadership in the postindustrial context. Considering the importance of both changing social conditions and past organizational legacies, we suggest a theory of leadership for higher education that relates to both a broader discussion of leadership in society and the role of the individual agent in the institution.

Situating a discussion of leadership in the current context of changing technologies and demands on educational leaders requires sociological explanations that account for broader structural variables and institutional character as it applies to the concept of leadership. Then, drawing upon interviews conducted with professors and instructors at two higher education institutions in Canada, we will offer suggestions as to how this may affect the development of leadership in higher education in the changing society in which we live today.

Toward a Theory of Educational Leadership

In recent years, there has been a push to integrate existing theories of leadership (Goethals & Sorenson, 2006) which has experienced mixed success; in "an intellectual journey of nearly five years duration" in which a multidisciplinary group of prominent leadership scholars attempted to create a "general theory of leadership," nothing of use for practitioners was presented (Austin, 2007). Needless to say, after creating a map of existing theories of leadership, Goethals and Sorenson (2006) did not reach a grand theory. Similar attempts at integration have been called for by groups such as the Association for the Study of Higher Education (Kezar, Carducci, & Contreras-McGavin, 2006) as scholars of leadership studies attempt to reconcile the many conceptions of leadership that appear in literature on the topic (Northouse, 2006). However, there are also those who suggest that we must go beyond current conceptions of leadership to account for socioeconomic changes in the postindustrial society (Keller, 2010; Garrison & Kanuka, 2004; Gurr, 2004; Prewitt, 2004), especially when discussing higher education. Traditional concepts of leadership, changing structural conditions in the postindustrial society, and the resulting pressure on higher education all come together to create the need for a new way of leadership.

Defining Leadership: Leaders, Followers and Social Change

Traditional theories of leadership have largely focused on hierarchical relationships in which there is a clearly delineated power structure with a small minority of individuals in leadership roles and a great number of individuals in the follower role. Intrinsic to trait theories of leadership are individual traits as predictors of leadership capacities. Burns's (1978) highly influential concept of transformational and transactional leadership also presents leadership in terms of leaders and followers. Simply put, "the conventional view of leadership is that individual leaders make a significant and even crucial impact on the performance of their organizations" (Gill, 2006, p. 26). In transformational and transactional leadership, for instance, transactional leaders only attempt to maintain efficiency through maintaining the status quo, while transformational leaders better those that they lead by addressing change in beliefs, values, and attitudes (Bass, 1985; Burns, 1978; Rafferty & Griffin, 2004). Indeed, the role of the individual in leader–follower relationships, particularly with regards to transformational leaders, is still the topic of much leadership research (Chemers, 2000; Groves, 2005; Ilies, Morgeson, & Nahrgang, 2005; Judge, Ilies, & Colbert, 2004; Rafferty & Griffin, 2004). However, a growing body of literature suggests that the traditional conception of leadership as a hierarchical relationship in a rationalized organization has been surpassed by changing economic conditions and a change in the division of labor (Uhl-Bien, Marion, & McKelvey, 2007) and wouldn't be appropriate in self-governed higher education institutions (Beaudoin, 2003, 2005). Traditional conceptions of leadership as "a process whereby an individual influences a group of individuals to reach a common goal" (Northouse, 2006), still in use today, have been surpassed by organizations in which leadership is a complex process resulting from the interaction of agents as opposed to a single authority (Uhl-Bien et al., 2007).

A growing number of academics in recent years have situated their conceptualization of leadership in an understanding of current global structures. But for decades scholars have pointed to the importance of historical context and broader social structures rather than the institution in which leadership takes place (Bass, 1999; Berry & Cartwright, 2000; Biggart & Hamilton, 1987; Gardner, 1990; Selznick, 1957). What is new, however, is the emphasis on the change from rationalized, modernist production of material goods to the postindustrial, globalized economy that is based on "dispersed networks" and the rapid production of knowledge as a commodity. Vana Prewitt provides a particularly succinct account of the changing context of leadership, stating that "the basic assumption of modern industrial theory was that the organization was rational—that logic, algorithms, problem solving and planning would create sustainable structures" (2004, p. 85). "In the post modern world", however, "organizations are increasingly recognized as complex, networked, emotional, and chaotic" (Ibid). This organizational change, according to some, is the result of a shift to a "knowledge economy" (Uhl-Bien et al., 2007), in which the "production of physical things is gradually being surpassed by the production of information goods and services in economic importance" (Child & McGrath, 2001). As a result of new demands, organizations are being forced to abandon traditional bureaucratic models that are incapable of meeting the demands for the fluid and rapid transmission of information for dispersed networks.

New technologies, particularly Internet communication, allow for the transmission of massive amounts of information and the creation of complex networks that can interact across time and space. As a result, employees have greater access to information and leadership is trickling down into lower levels of organizations (Avolio & Dodge, 2000; Avolio & Kahai, 2003), allowing for more informed decision making throughout all levels of the organization. Thus, in knowledge-based organizations, "because the knowledge required to solve complex problems is dispersed throughout organizations, all can contribute to the exercise of influence" (Hatcher, 2005, p. 254). And in the knowledge economy, decision making and the transfer of goods is taking place across dispersed networks and at all levels of an organization. Economic changes have led to a fundamental alteration of the structure of organizations operating in postindustrial societies.

The consequences of changing organizational structures for theories of leadership have been catastrophic, resulting in "a widespread sense of a gap between the rapid development of new organizational forms in practice and the capacity of existing perspectives to account for them in theory" (Child & McGrath, 2001). A recent push in concepts of leadership spanning disciplines from management, to social psychology and education, have attempted to close this gap, but much of the theoretical development is still in the formative stage. However, from the multitude of new perspectives one concept has gained popularity ahead of the rest: distributed leadership.

Distributed Leadership

Originally developed by Spillane and colleagues (Spillane, 2006; Spillane, Halverson, & Diamond, 2004, 2006; Gronn, 2000, 2002, 2003), distributed leadership rests on the assertion that the construct of followership, which dominates twentieth-century literature on leadership, is inherently flawed given the current division of labor. Modern leadership does not work in a binary relationship between leaders and followers, but, instead, is distributed throughout organizations. This is a result of a combination of technological advancements and changing organizational needs, brought forth by changing economic and social conditions. By looking at the actual *practices* of modern organizations, we see an inherently different ascription of leadership status than the hierarchical, individualized form which is presented by bureaucratic structures. More than the power of one individual over others in a binary relationship, leadership, to Gronn, is "a status ascribed to one individual, an aggregate of separate individuals, sets of small numbers of individuals acting in concert or larger plural-member organizational units" (Gronn, 2003). Leadership is then defined in its ascription from one individual to another. Instead of emerging from formalized relationships that are rigid and omnipresent, leadership exists in ascription by active agents in the organization in question. Much like in Foucault's concept of power (Foucault, 1982), Gronn separates formal authority from genuine leadership; leadership exists where it is ascribed through consenting agents. As a result, "(t)he individuals or multiperson units to whom influence is attributed, include, potentially, all organizational members not just managerial role incumbents" (Gronn, 2003, p. 344). Thus, beyond the formalized roles attributed to organizational actors based on their status within an organization, leadership task is evident in its attribution by organizational actors to any number of possible actors, or combination thereof, depending on the task at hand.

Since Gronn's initial taxonomy of distributed leadership there has been much discussion of the relevance and implications of the concept. In the field of education, particularly, dispersed leadership has become a "hot topic" and has even begun to dictate policy (Hartley, 2007). The appeal of distributed leadership, as explained by Harris (2007), is that it is adaptable to many different situations and can "accommodate a wide variety of interpretations and positions" (p. 315). This, however, is also a source of one of its shortcomings: dispersed leadership suffers from conceptual ambiguity as it "is an idea so conceptually vast that it is difficult to separate what does and doesn't constitute distributed leadership" (p. 315). Furthermore, while the theoretical construct of distributed leadership has been the topic of much scholarly work, empirical evidence supporting the efficacy of distributed leadership as a strategy for organizational management is limited. Simply put, "policy is ahead of the evidence" when it comes to distributed leadership (Ibid). Lastly, dispersed leadership is limited theoretically: it fails to account for historical and contextual variables that structure the space in which leadership practices take place.

As noted by Hatcher (2005), "the notion that power and leadership can operate independently underpins Gronn's work" (p. 204). Power, however, cannot be separated from influence through leadership activity as structural authority permeates all levels of an organization, especially in the case of the educational institution. Alluding to Bourdieu's (1998) concept of the "field", Hatcher asserts that individuals are situated hierarchically in the fields in which they act and, in the case of the school, this requires that all action be approved by the individual with the privileged position within the field of action. "Leadership 'from below' can only be translated from the sphere of ideas to that of action when it is sanctioned by the (organizational) authority... Thus, officially sanctioned 'distributed leadership' is always delegated, licensed, exercised on behalf of and revocable by authority" (Hatcher, 2005, p. 256). As a result, distributed leadership cannot be separated from pre-existing structural relationships that determine the balance of power in an organization. And, as social institutions like education exist in a broader relationship between hierarchically organized institutions, the distribution of leadership is ultimately subject to the power relationships that exist at a broader, societal level. Concepts of dispersed leadership, then, must account for broader structural relationships when mapping situational relationships of influence within an institution. In order to do so, we must account for broader contextual variables and seek to construct a more integrative theory of leadership (Avolio, 2007; Goethals & Sorenson, 2006).

In addition, to understand the influence of institutional structures on leadership it is necessary to understand the pre-existing structural and cultural relationships that produce current internal organizational structures. Rigid bureaucratic structures still exist in postindustrial societies; higher education institutions are an example of such institutional structures (Garrison & Kanuka, 2004). How do we account for this rigidity in the face of social change? Despite the move to a knowledge economy and dispersed organizational structures, one need only look at government, military, and education systems to realize that there exist many strong, enduring bureaucratic structures in today's postindustrial societies (Urmetzer, 2005). If dispersed leadership is a reaction to socioeconomic changes and organizations must adapt to changing conditions, why, then, do we still see hierarchically organized institutions in today's society? Entrenched cultural and institutional processes in context of rigidity under pressure are maintained by historical routines and rituals.

The Importance of Context

Although distributed leadership delineates an interesting model of leadership that is well suited to the encroaching knowledge economy of current postindustrial societies, there are theorists who remind us that current models of leadership are not only situated in current and future trends. Gardner (1990) suggests that "[l]eaders cannot be thought of apart from the historic context in which they arise, the setting in which they function . . . and the system over which they preside . . . . They are integral parts of the system, subject to the forces that affect the system" (p. 1). While suggesting that leaders must occupy a position at the helm of an organization, Gardner's insight that "leaders suffer from the mistakes of predecessors and leave some of their own misjudgments as time bombs for successors" (p. 8) reflects the fact that leaders operate in a historically bounded social context.

Taking the institutional focus further, there is a group of scholars who promote the importance of organizational culture in educational leadership. Espousing the "new institutionalism", these theorists (Biggart & Hamilton, 2007; Campbell, 1998; Hall & Taylor, 1996; Pierson, 1994, 2004; Powell & Dimaggio, 1991; Skocpol, 1992) assert that "institutions matter" (March & Olsen, 1989) when understanding organizational behavior. That is, individual agents can be seen as part of a broader organizational context which extends beyond social and economic networks to broader organizational culture and entrenched institutional policies. Simply put, institutions influence the actor just as actors influence institutions. And, "because organizational environments are often uncertain, people's interests are ambiguous and thus their actions are motivated more by institutional routines, habits, rituals, cues and scripts than interests" (Campbell, 1998, p. 163). Because institutions, and society at large, are made up of a highly complex network of actors, influential actions, and forces, actors cannot be aware of all the forces that affect their decision making. As a result, they often rely on cognitive schemata, or ideational maps of norms and values, which link actors together within an organization when making decisions on the best course of action to pursue. Thus, more than responding to changing social conditions, institutional actors (and institutional leaders) also rely on embedded normative understandings when making institutional decisions. Furthermore, in order for decisions to be accepted within a broader organizational culture, it must then fit the normative map that is shared by the organizational culture in question. Simply, historically entrenched organizational cultures mediate everyday institutional behavior and mediate what is seen as acceptable action within institutions. When assuming a leadership role, then, leaders will often rely on cognitive schemata when making decisions, and should be aware of the influencing patterns on such schemata. "Strategies for leadership can only be understood—and can only be successful—within the framework of the social structures of norms in which they are embedded" (Biggart & Hamilton, 1987, p. 430). Thus, historically and culturally appropriate leadership, within a given institution, is needed in order to alter institutional structures before distributed leadership can flourish. A system of leadership that is not in line with social norms will not be accepted and institutional structures cannot be ignored when attempting to understand leadership (Hatcher, 2005). Thus, because institutional hierarchies endure, we cannot forget concepts, such as transformational leadership, that rest on the assumption of the individual leader at the helm of institutional change. It is necessary that cultures and norms, those surrounding leadership expectations and beyond, be transformed within institutional hierarchies before new structures are accepted.

As institutional culture matters when considering strategies of leadership, leadership strategies may differ across settings even when the focus is the same—as is the case for the integration of e-learning. Even organizations with the same goals may differ based on the cultural context and institutional legacies that have shaped their way of thinking and operating. For educational leadership, then, it is possible that leadership strategies may vary across postsecondary institutions even when they aim to fulfill the same goal such as the integration of e-learning in instruction. Even though all universities strive toward the same goal, the unique history and culture of each institution should affect the way that a given university operates and, in turn, determine what types of leadership practices are deemed acceptable within a given institutional setting. It should be the case that we will see differing leadership strategies and different levels of adaptation to changing social pressures based on the institutional cultures of each institution. Despite existing in the same social contexts, distributed leadership, as a concept and in practice, will then be more likely to emerge as a viable alternative in certain institutions.

Application to the Educational Context

Institutions of postsecondary education, like any other social institution, are embedded in the broader social context of the historical moment in which they exist. However, as suggested by new institutionalism, institutions also have a unique set of historical conditions that define the development of a particular group of institutions, or group of institutions, within the broader social context. While modern postsecondary institutions are an essential part of the postindustrial workplace and are charged with preparing individuals for the emerging knowledge economy, they also have a unique history and bureaucratic organization that defines the range of acceptable actions within each particular institution.

Moving into the twenty-first century, education institutions have been increasingly integrated into the fabric of postindustrial societies. For instance, Great Britain privatized further education in 1988 while similar movements have occurred in both Canada (Buchbinder & Rajagopal, 1996; Davidson-Harden & Majhanovich, 2004) and the United States (Perelman, 2006; Saltman & Gabbard, 2003), leading to changes in political relationships within educational institutions (Maguire, 2002). As postsecondary institutions are required to compete for scarce resources, the focus of leadership has had to respond to changing structural conditions. For instance, Gleeson (2001) argues that the privatization of further education in Britain led to a redefinition of leadership roles and new managerial values in higher education. While new managers are being inserted into higher education with a mandate to maximize profits for the university and concern emerges regarding the importance of maximizing learning experiences, the cultural values of institutions of higher education are being challenged. Because of the privatization of education, then, institutional leaders are being forced to focus on maximizing profits ahead of the social service of providing education for individuals. This change in the economic realities of educational institutions has thus led to a redefinition and transformation of leadership roles. The new focus on profiteering and corporatization of higher education is not always accepted by the staff, however, and new leaders must act in a strategic way, within existing institutions, to entice faculty to adopt strategies consistent with a system that is continuously pressed for resources (Gleeson, 2001). The consequences of this statement for proponents of distributed leadership are important to note. Because education systems are increasingly occupying a location in the broader social system as an economic rather than a social institution, their goals are being redefined toward maximizing market share (Lafferty & Fleming, 2000; Pick, 2006; Pritchard, 2005). Rather than simply trying to educate individuals, they are pressed with fulfilling consumer needs for accreditation. In order to do so, they must remain economically viable. This is largely achieved through processes of rationalization, by increasing class sizes and placing further constraints on the limited resources available to staff and teachers working within the system, and, in turn, "challenging the values and ethos" of university workers (Pritchard, 2005, p. 434).

While a rationalized model of education may have worked to educate individuals well trained to hierarchical production systems (Dantley, 2005), the postindustrial society requires adaptive and creative individuals who do not emerge from hierarchical instruction systems. New communication technologies, particularly internet communication technologies (ICT) are allowing new forms of instructional delivery and facilitate rapid and fluid exchange of information. For instance, most postsecondary institutions use learning management systems such as WebCT and Blackboard to facilitate instruction, and e-mail/social media is increasingly being used as a method of communication in place of face-to-face meetings (Gurr, 2004). As the postsecondary environment is increasingly mediated by ICT, new ways of leading are required. Avolio and Kahai's (2003) discussion of e-leadership, while focused on the modern workplace, provides significant insight into the need for adaptive forms of leadership. Citing increased access to information at lower levels of organization, greater connectedness at lower levels of organizations, and the more permanent nature of conversations made using ICTs such as e-mail, leads to more communication between levels of an organization and more permanent access to information that was once reserved for privileged meetings. This, in turn, facilitates independent decision making and more rapid decision making within organizations, and, as a result, increased leadership behavior at lower levels of organizations. The implication for higher education is that if new technologies are utilized to facilitate leadership at lower levels of organizations, it is possible to create leadership networks down to the lowest levels of the organizational hierarchy and create networks of information sharing that do not rely on hierarchically defined leaders. The same technologies that are changing the postindustrial society and the education process can be utilized to change patterns of leadership.

It is not surprising, then, that distributed leadership is a popular concept within scholarship on educational leadership. New technologies are allowing individuals at many levels of educational hierarchies to access information that was previously unavailable and providing them with an unprecedented ability to communicate with one another. With shrinking resources promoting the commercialization of postsecondary education, leadership needs to emerge at new organizational levels as an exemplar for those moving through education institutions into today's postindustrial economy. However, the question remains, how may we implement strategies of dispersed leadership and promote e-learning within institutional cultures that are bound by historically entrenched legacies of hierarchical organization?

It may, in fact, be the case that some institutions are more equipped to react to changing demands than others. For instance, institutions that have traditionally provided distance education have supported the individual student to guide his or her own education. At the forefront of the development of ICT for the classroom are institutions such as Great Britain's Open University and Canada's Athabasca University, which, as institutions created to serve students in need of flexible curriculum delivery through distance education, traditionally provide students with more opportunities to pick their own agendas. As a result of their original mandate to provide alternative forms of education and flexible methods of instruction, it is possible that distance education institutions may display more willingness and possess more knowledge in developing networks of distributed leadership as they have always relied on individual students, and, in recent years, heavily on ICT to create learning environments in which individuals in widely dispersed networks work together toward meeting classroom goals. Without a professor lecturing from the head of the class, students are forced to innovate and mediate their own behavior to produce learning outcomes. With this in mind, we will now turn to a discussion of the findings of a recent set of comparative interviews done with two postsecondary institutions. While existing in similar locations and served with the same goal of producing university educated individuals, it is expected that faculty at one school, the distance education school, will display a different approach to leadership styles and may already promote practices of distributed leadership, or at least promote leadership at more levels than in traditional, classroom-based institutions. This leaves us to consider that different strategies for the implementation of distributed leadership may be necessarily dependent upon the institutional context, and that adjustment to new economic needs will not be a natural occurrence. Rather, it may take different strategies based on different organizational cultures. The emergence of distributed leadership cannot be a natural progression but something that needs to be implemented in different ways based on institutional context.

Faculty Views on Teaching with Technology

Although today's society is made up of increasingly complex and dispersed organizations, there are many entrenched social institutions that endure, largely unchanged, over long periods of time (Immergut, 1998; Pierson, 1994; Skocpol, 1992). This is nowhere more apparent than in the case of higher education. While, as discussed above, dispersed leadership is an idea that is well suited to developing the kinds of experience necessary for today's society, many higher education institutions in the postindustrial world rely on a hierarchical command chain when making decisions (Henkel, 2002). Given recent constraints on the resources of education, structural pressures have forced postsecondary institutions to develop structures in which formal authority is concentrated increasingly in the hands of fewer and fewer individuals (Henkel, 2002; Pritchard, 2005). There is a contradiction between the needs of the knowledge era and the reality of centralized power (Uhl-Bien et al., 2007) in higher education. Students increasingly expect to consume units of knowledge in a consumer-driven education system based on rationalized hierarchies; however, what is needed to produce creative and adaptive individuals is a flexible, distributed learning and leadership system.

In order to question whether the emergence of new forms of leadership is a viable solution to confronting the problem of role change required by e-learning, we reviewed interviews conducted with instructors in two postsecondary institutions in Canada. One is a relatively new distance education institution and the other a 50-year-old traditional higher education institution. It is expected that faculty views toward teaching and leadership will vary across groups given significant differences in mandate, pedagogical strategies and instructor roles between distance and open institutions in comparison to traditional institutions. What is similar is the requirement to adjust faculty roles, whether moving into e-learning from primarily lecture-based teaching of traditional institutions or the more subtle role of tutor in print-based distance education. We reviewed the data in reference to perspectives on change in higher education: roles, teaching and leadership.

Twenty faculty, ten from each respective institution, participated in semistructured interviews regarding the role of learners and instructors in contemporary higher education. The faculty were chosen in a snowball sample which began with faculty known to the researchers as interested in pedagogical forms and curriculum development at each institution. The transcripts from semistructured interviews were coded separately by two research assistants and analyzed using qualitative software program Nvivo for emergent themes. Several themes relevant to this discussion emerged from the interview data as discussed below. Synthesized results from interview data from faculty at the traditional institution is referred to as Group T; the open and distance institution is Group D.

Institutional Constraints

A major topic throughout the interviews was the issue of institutional constraints on the ability of professors to implement changes to instructional delivery; the implication was that this was a result of limited institutional resources and preexisting power structures. This was apparent in both groups, but more prevalent in Group T. According to Respondent T1,

> this notion of expanding my role to not only being a content expert in trying to find time to do that, and then also support learner development ah so that they become independent self-managed learners strikes me as ah, an ambitious goal to say the least and I have no idea or the wherewithal for that to come from.

This excerpt is particularly telling: the professor cannot imagine moving from content expert to facilitator based on time and cost constraints. In this case, time constraints maintain the status quo and the traditional hierarchical relationship between student and teacher. Past policy decisions that have limited teacher resources constrain the ability of professors to implement changes.

Another concern of Group T was related to monetary resources. Faculty are pressed for time with research and teaching responsibilities; with growing class sizes it is increasingly difficult to provide individualized attention. The following excerpt from Respondent T8 exemplifies this concern:

> it will require a lot of resources, it will require a lot of time on, on the part of the ah (pause) of the professor, or I guess in this case probably you would say as a facilitator. And um I don't think in our current political economic system this is possible. Except that we don't even do this at, at the PhD level.

Not only is there a lack of resources to provide individualized curriculum, but also in the current classroom setting there is simply an overload of students compared to teachers; as Respondent T10 asked, "what can they possibly learn? In terms of even, learning in classrooms of two to five-hundred and doing multiple choice exams?" Thus, there are shrinking resources that make it increasingly harder to implement new policy pathways.

> In the current climate of cutbacks, um increased tuition for students, it's ah I'm growing disillusioned with the idea of a learner centered curriculum. Given that more students are working more hours because tuition's gone up, given that there'd been so many downsizings that faculty workloads have increased (so) facilitating increased student engagement and interaction is not an option.

Resource constraints are clearly a bigger issue for Group T as they cite tangible increases in numbers and huge class sizes plus lack of institutional and government willingness to allow them the small classes and time that seem necessary to implement learning changes.

Group D continues to develop flexible curriculum and constraints related to institutional control are not as salient. Respondents identified significant concerns around the commercialization of education, and the lack of faculty input into measures to resist such changes. As a unique institution, the funding model draws far less from government grants and a much greater proportion of funding comes from tuition and fund-raising/endowments. Respondent A2 identified this difference and said,

> students aren't students anymore they are customers, they are clients, and that does really damaging things to my notion of education... There has been a role redefinition in education which has to do with what I would call the commercialization of education.

This influences the relationship between faculty and student; it acts as an institutional constraint. However, the open orientation to the reduction of barriers to education may create a general climate of collaboration and engagement unlike that in traditional institutions.

Role of the Professor

When discussing the role of the professor, all respondents still saw themselves in a leadership role. Group D generally viewed the student as an empty vessel to be filled with information before he or she can make informed choices. For Group T, it's up to the students to seek out their own pathways outside of what the professor offers but they also predict a lot of resistance from many of the more traditional faculty members at the university.

Respondent D7 presents the common view quite succinctly.

> When it comes to the means I think it should be as learner-centered as possible, in the sense of relating it to the student as much as possible to learn in whatever way most closely matches whatever he is thinking at the moment. But as a master you have a much better understanding of the journey than the student has.

Another member of Group D (Respondent D8) backs this up, saying,

> ultimately the faculty member, curriculum committee or whatever, decide what those choices are going to be for students . . . you may give students choices and those choices are limited and I don't think we can get around that.

For Group D, then, the professor still assumes a leadership role. This speaks to the implicit assumption that the professor is the expert in charge of the classroom. Despite a willingness to embrace change, the professor still assumes a leadership role and guides the students toward learning outcomes. It is still a model of choice within constraints with faculty at the helm; it is learner centered, not learner led, and, although leadership may be distributed to lower levels, there is still a hierarchical relationship in which the professor and senior administration exercise power.

For Group T, the professor was still the leader but played less of a role in the educational choices of the individual student. Ultimately, it was up to the students to seek out and utilize the resources available. For instance, Respondent T3 said, "I really put a lot of the emphasis in the response and responsibility on the learner to be the taskmaster at insisting that they get the assistance where they need it, to help them clarify that role." However, the structure of the traditional lecture and institutional constraints were not the only things limiting change in the role of the professor: Group T predicted that the socialized role of the professor in the institution would be hard to change. For Respondent T6, getting the faculty to accept that they are not content experts delivering knowledge was a huge barrier to allowing students to take more responsibility for their own learning, critical to successful e-learning:

> In terms of university-based teaching and learning, I think that one of the biggest barriers is ah faculty members' sense that their content delivery is paramount, that, that they're the ones who own the knowledge, they have to convey that to students in a particular fashion that ensures that ALL of the things that they anticipate the students needing to know are presented to the students . . . and that's a BIG barrier ... which is, in a lot of ways letting go of that, parceling out of knowledge and having people find their way to the knowledge.

Relating the traditional role of the professor as a distributor of knowledge, Respondent T6 is also referring to the commercialized nature of education, or the idea that knowledge can be bought and sold, that it is a product to be delivered by the professor to the students. Respondent T6 elaborates on the socialization of professors into the role of content expert in charge of distributing knowledge, saying,

> It's very hard for that tradition to break without people feeling like they're abandoning their responsibility to their students. Like I don't think ego is necessarily the biggest problem, I think it's a sense of responsibility that's built up in people. Because as you become um, a practitioner and an expert in a vary esoteric discipline, which is what most of, most scholars do, when they become professors, they become more and more specifically engaged with knowledge and more and more expert in their own knowledge area such that in order to pass the BAR, you have to be the world's leading expert on something. You know, you have to go to conferences and give papers and have people sit around and say, "Oh yes you know I never thought about that before, you've created a new way of thinking about something" that's all, that's all built up to be that. So when you come back to mere students, you feel like your responsibility is to bring them into that understanding by your own, the power of your own expertise and to relinquish that power to somebody else who's a mere novice, is pretty hard thing to do when you've been schooled to think of yourself as having this exclusive knowledge.

Professors are socialized to expect to be the distributor of knowledge, to pass down their expertise to students in a hierarchical manner in which their role is clearly defined as the expert with a claim to knowledge beyond what the students themselves can claim to hold. Thus, they feel a social responsibility to pass down knowledge that they have built up through years of rigorous study in the same format in similar institutions. The bottom line is that social roles, once ingrained in the individual and institutional culture, are hard to change. This is backed up by Respondent T7 who says, "knowing some of the faculty around this place … it would, this would be a, you'd have to wait for them to retire before they would cooperate." In short, professors have been socialized to expect their role as a content expert and that would be hard to change. Hierarchical models of education have been culturally ingrained into the institution and a managerial model of knowledge acquisition is privileged above creative pedagogies. Reliance on a higher authority is also put ahead of the spontaneous development of flat networks of learning.

Role Adjustment for Faculty

There was ample discussion of role adjustment for faculty in both Group T and Group D. Both groups predominantly see the instructor's role as becoming more of a facilitator than a dispenser of knowledge. However, some doubt the practicality of this approach as it takes individualized attention, particularly members of Group T. Again, the issue of institutional constraints loomed over the ability of Group T to adjust to further student engagement.

For Group T, resistance was rooted in more than the fact that it would mean extra work; the pressures and constraints put upon them by institutionalized power structures and priorities constrained their ability to adjust their roles. For instance, Respondent T3 reported that faculty would be,

> driven back into more prescribed roles because there isn't enough ongoing support for change. And they have to, I mean remember the faculty are assessed for three things: how

> much research they do, how they teach, and, ah what kinds of contributions they make through service. And *all* faculty who want to get promoted, who want to get merit increments must pay attention, it is a competitive situation and you fight harder and harder for smaller percentages of money.

Ability to change was restricted because they operate in an institution that perpetuates the status quo by tightening its purse strings and emphasizing research and service to the university alongside teaching. A policy legacy toward rationalization, combined with an institutional culture of research taking precedence over teaching, made it hard for professors to relinquish a commitment to the standard role of professor.

Institutional politics were also behind a resistance to change for Respondent T10:

> well I think one of the hardest things that faculty have to work with is the politics of the institution. In an institution that I think is worse than the military in hierarchy and rules and regulations and punishments and ah promotions and demotions and stuff like that, it just um, *big* role adjustment. On one hand you're training or you, you hire all these independent thinkers, free spirits, big egos whatever you want to call them and then on the other hand you place them in a *really* constrictive political institution.

The institution is structured in such a way that change is not a priority, and, rather, faculty are conditioned to fight for promotions in areas outside of teaching and independent of learner outcomes. Respondent T4 adds to this discussion, saying,

> What happens is that we're moving, the whole university's moving toward a more of a research university so the new faculty members that are hired, are hired not for their teaching but for their research. And so, a university before might have had colleagues that could help people but now, ah I think the colleagues are going by the wayside and are more the younger faculty members ah, could easily be scrambling for ah, even doing a good job of a standard lecture let alone something which is learner centered, which is even more complex.

For Group T the issue of institutional constraints again appears as a major inhibitor to change. A culture that values individualized research promotes a minimalist approach to students and teaching prowess. While there is some agreement that faculty must take more of a facilitator role versus an authoritative role, role adjustment to improve student engagement, teach with technology and allow student leadership is considered a possibility in Group D but more of a pipe dream given the institutional politics at Group T's institution.

Discussion

It seems likely that the pressures to teach with technology to foster e-learning, along with other demands for change in higher education, will not just disappear; change will occur over time. We identify here the barriers to such change, why leadership change is necessary to support such teaching change, and what may be hindering change in reference to both. Discussion of institutional constraints suggests that professors are limited in their ability to implement change in teaching and leadership. Professors have difficulty seeing themselves in a role other than expert in the classroom and also think any adjustment of leadership practices in or out of the classroom will be met with resistance from many members of their university's faculty. Furthermore, the commercialization of education and incumbent financial pressure was often identified as a factor limiting the professor's ability to change hierarchical relationships and dedicate more time to encouraging teaching-related initiatives.

Judging by the commentary of the group of professors interviewed, it is apparent that internal hierarchies of leadership in postsecondary institutions are far from fluid structures that change in accordance with external pressures. Beyond a structural relationship, we must consider socio-cultural elements, particularly institutional culture, when examining leadership for change in today's educational setting.

What may be offered by a distributed leadership structure? Throughout the interview data there is a trend to refer to the effects of preexisting institutional structures in determining the capacity of professors to exert their influence. For instance, when Respondent T10 refers to the "politics of the institution" as influencing the decisions that professors make with regards to teaching style, it is clear that professors are bounded by institutional policies regarding promotion. Furthermore, Respondent T8 refers to the "current political economic system" as a major factor that mitigates attempts to change the learning environment. Combined with a culture that has, for many years, emphasized the rationalized production of knowledge and a managerialist approach to learning, we find that many professors from both groups feel pressure to conform to a system in which they are the de facto leader, managing students' knowledge acquisition rather than promoting student initiative in their own search for knowledge. In the context of ongoing pressure to change education and increasing demands on professors with limited resources, dominant organizational structures work a culture that emphasizes political structures, structures that emphasize professor performance as measured by research capacity and their ability to provide students as consumers with an educational product with limited resources, work to maintain the status quo. Professors are encouraged to be managerialist leaders and to retain their position as the expert for the student population. Thus, the structure of the education system, created by historical conditions that encourage rationalized institutional structure, promotes top-down, hierarchical leadership.

Beyond formal institutional structures, many professors are socialized to assume a leadership role. That is, judging by the comments that suggest that professors are not willing to retire the role of content expert or leader, even when working in dispersed networks, there is a cultural element linked to historical structural conditions that have existed in the educational context: namely, the assumption that professors act as leaders in a rigid hierarchy of power within educational institutions. Thus, the assertion that culture matters holds true in this case: rather than simply responding to demands for change, institutional culture and structure created major constraints on professors to respond, and, indeed, intrinsic to the beliefs of many professors in our sample is the idea of the professor as the content expert, bestowing knowledge upon students based on a claim to superior knowledge. In an increasingly marketized education system, the professor remains several rungs above students as a structurally and culturally defined leader. The education system values the professor as a leader and it is built into the belief system as well as the structural relationship of participants that the professor acts in a leadership role, even in dispersed networks. Thus, institutional culture and policies matter, regardless of greater structural shifts.

We do, however, see differences across institutions that support the assertion of new institutionalism; varying institutional cultures matter in the ability of implementing new policy directives. For instance, Group D professors, who come from an institution with a goal of providing varying leadership styles and accommodating students from varying situations, were more open to e-learning type initiatives. They supported student leadership and saw it as a far more realistic possibility. Group T, on the other hand, suggests far greater resistance and a lack of empowerment on professors' behalf; respondents do not always see it as a decision they are able to make. Despite the fact that both institutions are expected to provide the same service and exist in the same political and economic setting (Canada), there are significant differences in the way that they approach the idea of change in teaching, learning and leadership. Institutional culture matters in the implementation of new strategies for educational leadership.

As it relates to the changing educational context, it may be that societal pressure on institutions will discourage the development of dispersed leadership. The entrenchment occurs as a way to deal with rapid change. While new technologies, particularly ICTs, allow dispersed networks to develop in which participants in the education system exchange information from remote locations asynchronously, the manipulation of educational resources and changing institutional culture that focuses resources increasingly on research rather than teaching places serious constraints on the abilities of professors to encourage the development of new teaching strategies. As professors are increasingly pushed to compete for resources in an institutional culture that values research over teaching, and institutions are forced to compete in a marketized economy, there is increasingly less time to devote to the development of dispersed leadership. Support for the efficiency provided by a rationalized model, while ill-suited to prepare students for today's workplace, remains predominant due to structural constraints. Spontaneous dispersion of leadership, in and out of the classroom, is unlikely in an educational context. If professors are to encourage the development of dispersed leadership, they need resources to allow them time to structure dispersed leadership and foster a culture of interdependence within the educational institution. Policies that encourage the rationalization of the education system lock teachers into a path that promotes hierarchical relationships and a redistribution of resources. A change in institutional culture that places emphasis on new relationships will be necessary to implement dispersed leadership—it will not occur spontaneously based on changing external demands.

Suggestions for Future Research

Although distributed leadership is an interesting proposition, it is unlikely that it will occur spontaneously. In the current study, previous policy decisions and changing structural conditions in the educational system do not include the time, energy and support needed for change. Instead, in the educational context, the industrialized notion of a rational institutional structure limits the resources available to adapt to changing trends. History matters (Pierson, 2004) and trends that deny current cultures lock higher education into existing models. It will take conscious, path-breaking policy behavior to implement systems of distributed leadership—it will not be an organic process.

This is not to say, however, that the process will be the same for all of higher education. Indeed, as sociological institutionalists would argue, it seems that, at least in the case of the two institutions under scrutiny, there are differences based on specific institutional cultures. A legacy of progressive policies and a culture that is open to flexible networks has provided Group D with a culture that is more open to the redistribution of leadership to new segments of the institutional hierarchy. In contrast, changing hierarchies are seen as much more difficult to implement in the Group T sample. In order to evaluate whether this holds across differing educational contexts, it is necessary that further research on perceptions of leadership and expectations about e-learning be carried out in institutions across Canada and beyond, of all sizes and with different historical backgrounds. To say that this study provides conclusive evidence of the potential for distributed leadership is off the mark. Rather, this is only a starting point for inquiry into the effect of historical policies and institutional culture on the ability of different institutions of higher education to adapt to changing market through systems of distributed leadership.

Last, research into the degree to which students expect e-learning and more contemporary institutional experiences is needed. As discussed above, many students expect to take passive role in a student-teacher relationship. Student culture will be just as important as that of the professor in changing e-learning and leadership structures in the educational system. Leadership that encourages a change in the values and belief structures of the followers is appropriate for those at the bottom of the current educational hierarchy.

Conclusion

Faculty from a traditional campus and a distance and open higher education institution had similar stories to tell of the imperative to move online, and the leadership required to support this change. Leadership plays an important role in creating teaching excellence (Gibbs et al., 2007). As suggested by Ramsden (1998), faculty identify that "like good teaching, academic leadership is not telling or transmitting information and ideas; it is a sort of conversation aimed at helping people to change and develop" (p. 163). These notions are supported in our research. However, we submit that all the right leadership in the world, in combination with resources and training, will not create faculty who are expert in their own fields of study *and* experts in the use of technology for learning. Support for e-learning will involve a team-based approach for developing courses and instructional material appropriate for learners engaging in distributed learning.

Leadership has been a topic of inquiry for centuries. Recent changes to social and economic structures necessitate an adaptation of leadership patterns. And, in higher education in particular, it is necessary to adapt to changing economic systems to prepare workers for the fluid exchange of information across diverse networks. The marketization of education in recent years, however, encourages rationalized leadership structures that are more suited to the industrial managerial relationship than modern, information-based economics that require the fluid dispersal of information across dispersed networks. In order for change to take place, educational policy makers must recognize the effects of historical policy decisions and the unique cultural relationships that exist across varying institutions within the same systems of higher education. And, while e-learning may constitute a technological advancement that is distributing higher education across dispersed networks, this may be matched as a leadership strategy as well. However, traditional hierarchies are still predominant—at least in the case at hand—and cultural changes must occur across a wide range of institutions for dispersed leadership to emerge in higher education. Historical cultural and political legacies matter when discussing educational leadership in the knowledge era and, far from an organic process, the emergence of new patterns of leadership is a distant vision.

References

Atkinson, M. P. (2001). The scholarship of teaching and learning: Reconceptualizing scholarship and transforming the academy. *Social Forces*, *79*(4), 1217–1229.

Austin, A. (2007). Review of the quest for a general theory of leadership. *Leadership & Organization Development Journal*, *28*(8), 786–788.

Avolio, B. J. (2007). Promoting more integrative strategies for leadership theory-building. *American Psychologist*, *61*, 25–33.

Avolio, B. J., & Dodge, G. E. (2000). E-leadership: Implications for theory, research, and practice. *Leadership Quarterly, 11*, 615–668.
Avolio, B. J., & Kahai, S. S. (2003). Adding the "e" to e-leadership: How it may impact your leadership. *Organizational Dynamics, 31*, 325–338.
Bass, B. M. (1985). *Leadership and performance beyond expectations*. New York: The Free Press.
Bass, B. M. (1999). Two decades of research and development in transformational leadership. *European Journal of Work and Organizational Psychology, 8*, 9–32.
Beaudoin, M. F. (2003). Distance education leadership for the new century. *Online Journal of Distance Learning Administration, 6*(2). Retrieved from: http://www.westga.edu/%7Edistance/ojdla/summer62/beaudoin62.html
Beaudoin, M. F. (2005). *Reflections on research, faculty and leadership in distance education*. Bibliotheks-und Informations system der Carl von Ossietzky University, Oldenburg, Germany.
Berry, A. J., & Cartwright, S. (2000). Leadership: A critical construction. *Leadership & Organization Development Journal, 21*, 342–349.
Biggart, N. W., & Hamilton, G. G. (1987). An institutional theory of leadership. *Journal of Applied Behavioral Science, 23*, 429–441.
Blau, J. R., & Goodman, N. (Eds.). (1995). *Social roles & social institutions*. New Brunswick: Transaction.
Bourdieu, P. (1998). *Practical reason*. Stanford: Stanford University Press.
Buchbinder, H., & Rajagopal, P. (1996). Canadian universities: The impact of free trade and globalization. *Higher Education, 31*, 283–299.
Burns, J. (1978). *Leadership*. New York: Harper & Row.
Campbell, J. L. (1998). Institutional analysis and the role of ideas in political economy. *Theory and Society, 27*, 377–409.
Chemers, M. M. (2000). Leadership research and theory: A functional integration. *Group dynamics: Theory, research and practice, 4*, 27–43.
Child, J., & McGrath, R. (2001). Organizations unfettered: Organizational form in an information-intensive economy. *Academy of Management Journal, 44*, 1135–1148.
Cleveland-Innes, M., & Garrison, D. R. (2009). The role of learner in an online community of inquiry: Instructor support for first-time online learners. In N. Karacapilidis (Ed.), *Solutions and innovations in web-based technologies for augmented learning: Improved platforms, tools and applications* (Chapter 1). Hershey, PA, USA: IGI Global.
Cleveland-Innes, M., & Garrison, D.R. (2010). *An introduction to distance education: Understanding teaching and learning in a new era*. New York: Routledge.
Dantley, M. E. (2005). Moral leadership: Shifting the management paradigm. In F. W. English (Ed.), *The SAGE handbook of educational leadership: Advances in theory, research and practice* (Chapter 2). Thousand Oaks: Sage.
Davidson-Harden, A., & Majhanovich, S. (2004). Privatization of education in Canada: A survey of trends. *International Review of Education, 50*(3–4), 263–287.
Davidson-Shivers, G.V. (2009). Frequency and types of instructor-interactions in online instruction. *Journal of Interactive Online Learning, 8*(1). Retrieved January 26, 2015 from 8.1.2.pdf"www.ncolr.org/jiol/issues/PDF/8.1.2.pdf
DiMaggio, P. J., & Powell, W. W. (1991). *The new institutionalism in organizational analysis*. Chicago: University of Chicago Press.
Fairweather, J.S. (2002). The mythologies of faculty productivity: Implications for institutional policy and decision making. *Journal of Higher Education, 73*(1). Retrieved from http://202.198.141.77/upload/soft/0000/73.1fairweather02%5B1%5D.pdf
Foucault, M. (1982). Afterword: The subject and power. In H. L. Dreyfus & P. Rabinow (eds.), *Beyond structuralism and hermeneutics* (pp. 208–226). Chicago: University of Chicago Press.
Gardner, J. W. (1990). *On leadership*. New York: Free Press.
Garrison, D.R., & Kanuka, H. (2004). Blended learning: Uncovering its transformative potential in higher education. *The Internet and Higher Education*, 7(2), 95–105.
Gibbs, G., Knapper, C., & Piccinin S. (2007). The role of departmental leadership in fostering excellent teaching. *In Practice, 13*, 1–4.
Gill, R. (2006). *Theory and practice of leadership*. London: Sage.
Gleeson, D. (2001). Style and substance in education leadership: Further education (FE) as a case in point. *Journal of Education Policy, 16*, 181–196.
Goethals, G. R., & Sorenson, G. L. (2006). *The quest for a general theory of leadership*. London: Edward Elgar.

Gronn, P. (2000). Distributed properties: A new architecture for leadership. *Educational Management & Administration, 28*, 317–338.

Gronn, P. (2002). Distributed leadership as a unit of analysis. *Leadership Quarterly, 13*, 423–451.

Gronn, P. (2003). *The new work of educational leaders: Changing leadership practice in an era of school reform*. London: Paul Chapman.

Groves, K. S. (2005). Linking leader skills, follower attitudes, and contextual variables via an integrated model of charismatic leadership. *Journal of Management, 31*, 255–277.

Gudea, S. R. (2008). *Expectations and demands in online teaching: Practical experiences*. USA: IGI.

Gurr, D. (2004). ICT, leadership in education and E-leadership. *Discourse: Studies in the Cultural Politics of Education, 25*, 113–124.

Hall, P. A., & Taylor, R. C. (1996). Political science and the three institutionalisms. *Political Studies, 44*, 936–957.

Harris, A. (2007). Distributed leadership: Conceptual confusion and empirical reticence. *International Journal of Leadership in Education, 10*, 315–325.

Hartley, D. (2007). The emergence of distributed leadership in education: Why now? *British Journal of Educational Studies, 55*, 202–214.

Hatcher, R. (2005). The distribution of leadership and power in schools. *British Journal of Sociology of Education, 26*, 253–267.

Henkel, M. (2002). Emerging concepts of academic leadership and their implications for intra-institutional roles and relationships in higher education. *European Journal of Education, 37*, 29–41.

Ikenberry, S. (2001). Foreword. In C. Latchem & D. Hanna (Eds.), *Leadership for 21st century learning: Global perspectives from educational innovators*. Sterling, VA: Stylus.

Ilies, R., Morgeson, F. P., & Nahrgang, J. D. (2005). Authentic leadership and eudaemonic well being: Understanding leader-follower relations. *Leadership Quarterly, 16*, 373–394.

Immergut, E. M. (1998). The theoretical core of the new institutionalism. *Politics and Society, 26*(1), 5–34.

Judge, Timothy A., Ilies, R., & Colbert, A. E. (2004). Intelligence and leadership: A quantitative review. *Journal of Applied Psychology, 89*, 542–552.

Kanuka, H., & Brooks, C. (2010). Distance education in a post-Fordist time: Negotiating difference. In M. F. Cleveland-Innes & D. R. Garrison (Eds.), *An introduction to distance education: Understanding teaching and learning in a new era* (pp. 69–90). New York: Routledge.

Kanwar, M., & Swenson, D. (2000). *Canadian sociology*. Iowa: Kendall/Hunt.

Keller, G. (2008). *Higher education and the new society*. Baltimore: John Hopkins University Press.

Kendall, D., Murray, J., & Linden, R. (2000). *Sociology in our times* (2nd ed.). Ontario: Canadian Cataloguing in Publication.

Kezar, A. J., Carducci, R., & Contreras-McGavin, M. (2006). Rethinking the "L" word in higher education: The revolution of research on leadership. *ASHE Higher Education Report, 31*, 1–240.

Lafferty, G., & Fleming, J. (2000). The restructuring of academic work in Australia: Power, management and gender. *British Journal of Sociology of Education, 21*(2), 257–267.

Maguire, M. (2002). Globalisation, education policy and the teacher. *International Studies in Sociology of Education, 12*, 261–276.

March, J., & Olsen, J. (1989). *Rediscovering institutions: The organizational basis of politics*. New York: Free Press.

Northouse, P. G. (2006). *Leadership: Theory and practice*. Thousand Oaks: Sage.

Perelman, M. (2006). Privatizing education. *Monthly Review: An Independent Socialist Magazine, 57*(10), 45–51.

Pick, D. (2006). The re-framing of Australian higher education. *Higher Education Quarterly, 60*, 229–241.

Pierson, P. (1994). *Dismantling the welfare state? Reagan, Thatcher, and the politics of retrenchment*. Cambridge: Cambridge University Press.

Pierson, P. (2004). *Politics in time: History, institutions, and social analysis*. Princeton: Princeton University Press.

Pond, W. K. (2002). Distributed education in the 21st century: Implications for quality assurance. *Online Journal of Distance Learning Administration, 5*(2). Retrieved from http://www.westga.edu/ distance/ojdla/summer52/pond52.html

Powell, W. W., & Dimaggio, P. J. (1991). *The new institutionalism in organizational analysis*. Chicago: University of Chicago Press.

Prewitt, V. (2004). Integral leadership for the 21st century. *World Futures*, 327–333.

Pritchard, R. (2005). The influence of market force culture on British and German academics. *Comparative Education, 41*, 433–454.

Rafferty, A. E., & Griffin, M. A. (2004). Dimensions of transformational leadership: Conceptual and empirical extensions. *Leadership Quarterly, 15*, 329–354.

Ramsden, P. (1998). *Influences on academic work: Learning to lead in higher education*. London: Routledge.

Rhoades, G. (2000). The changing role of faculty. In J. Losco & B. L. Fife (eds.), *Higher education in transition: The challenges of the new millennium* (Chapter 2). Westport, CT: Bergin and Garvey.

Saltman, K., & Gabbard, D. (2003). *Education as enforcement: The militarization and corporatization of schools*. New York: Routledge.

Satterlee, A.G. (2010). *The relationship between faculty satisfaction and online quality enhancement initiatives*. [EABR & ETLC Conference Proceedings]. Retrieved from http://www.cluteinstitute.com/proceedings/2010_Dublin_ETLC_Articles/Article%20313.pdf

Selznick, P. (1957). *Leadership in administration*. New York: Harper & Row.

Skocpol, T. (1992). *Protecting soldiers and mothers: The political origins of social policy in the United States*. Cambridge: Belknap Press.

Spillane, J. P. (2006). *Distributed leadership*. San Francisco: Jossey-Bass.

Spillane, J. P., Halverson, R., & Diamond, J. (2004). Towards a theory of leadership practice: A distributed perspective. *Journal of Curriculum Studies, 36*, 3–34.

Tomei, L. (2004). The impact of online teaching on faculty load: Computing the ideal class size for online courses. *International Journal of Instructional Technology & Distance Learning, 1*(1). Retrieved from http://www.itdl.org/journal/Jan_04/article04.htm

Uhl-Bien, M., Marion, R., & McKelvey, B. (2007). Complexity leadership theory: Shifting leadership from the industrial age to the knowledge era. *Leadership Quarterly, 18*, 298–318.

Urmetzer, P. (2005). *Globalization unplugged: Sovereignty and the Canadian state in the twenty-first century*. Toronto: University of Toronto Press.

U.S. Department of Education. (2009). *Evaluation of evidence-based practices in online learning*. Retrieved from http://www.ed.gov/rschstat/eval/tech/evidence-based-practices/finalreport.pdf

Yick, A., Patrick, P., & Costin, A. (2005). Navigating distance and traditional higher education: Online faculty experiences. *International Review of Research in Open and Distance Learning, 6*(2). Retrieved from http://www.irrodl.org/index.php/irrodl/article/view/235

Zepke, N. (2007). Leadership, power and activity systems in a higher educational context: Will distributive leadership serve in an accountability drive world? *International Journal of Leadership in Education, 10*, 301–314.

7

Towards Effective and Less Stressful Online Collaborative Learning

Strategies to Promote Engagement While Minimizing Unnecessary Cognitive Load and Stress

Insung Jung, Masayuki Kudo, and Sook-Kyoung Choi

Introduction

Time and space constraints in the conventional classroom, where students work independently on learning tasks and take responsibility only for self typically limit the opportunities for collaborative learning and lead to teachers dominating the information transfer (Sawyer, 2006). By contrast, online environments, less constrained by time and space and flexible and asynchronous, allow knowledge to be constructed, discovered and transformed by the students. They have more freedom in exchanging ideas, opinions, facts, experiences and expectations (McConnell, 2000). They can improve the richness and quality of learning experiences (Bernard, Rojo de Rubalcava, & St-Pierre, 2000). They can foster a learning culture wherein participatory and intersubjective meaning making are promoted (Suthers, 2006), promote creative thinking, reflective writing and critical reasoning (So, 2008), and be more democratic, allowing the shy, the hesitant, the slower and the less articulate students to have an equal say (Clark, 2003). As Johnson, Johnson, and Smith (1991) observe, learning is conceived as something the learner does, not something done to the learner.

There is ample empirical evidence of the pedagogical advantages of online collaboration in a wide range of educational contexts. Benbunan-Fich, Hiltz, and Turoff (2003), in a quasiexperimental study into undergraduate students solving computer ethics issues, found that the use of asynchronous groups generated broader ideas, allowed for fuller exploration of more diverse opinions and options, and resulted in far more comprehensive reports than were compiled by similar face-to-face groups. They also noted that whereas face-to-face groups tended to deal with problems sequentially, asynchronous groups tended to work in parallel on different aspects of problems and spend more time on resolving any discrepancies in their views and findings. Examining the effects of online collaboration by small groups of undergraduate students in developing a computer program, McLoughlin (2002a) reported that while the results overall were positive, only the groups engaged in frequent and productive interactions produced the highest quality learning outcomes and felt that they had been involved in 'real world-like working environments'. Jung, Choi, Lim, and Leem (2002) also found that students engaged in task-oriented online collaborative learning with their peers expressed higher levels of satisfaction with the learning process than those who mainly interacted with their instructors. Conducting a four-year design experiment with students involved in four online university courses aimed at shifting from guided to self-organized inquiry in order to foster knowledge building communities in the classroom, Cacciamani (2010) found that students tended to produce more notes in the guided-inquiry approach but read more and demonstrated more even distribution of work as part of self-organized inquiry.

Qualitative data on the strategies that the students reported as new to their learning experience showed that these fell into three categories common to both guided and self-organizing inquiry: elaborating course content for depth of understanding, collaboration in an online environment, and metacognition, with greater reflection on idea development (Cacciamani, 2010). Distinctive aspects of self-organized inquiry, according to student reports, included going beyond given information, linking new understandings and personal experiences, paying attention to the collective works of the community, and learning from instructor's strategies.

However, to fully achieve such pedagogical benefits, the online collaboration must be carefully designed, facilitated, and scaffolded. Topics, materials and assessment must be planned, unnecessary cognitive and psychological burdens must be eliminated, and students must be motivated and enabled to fully comprehend the aims and nature of the learning tasks and materials involved, and encouraged to share and confirm their knowledge and ideas with their peers, and to actively engage in the problem-solving processes.

Several studies (e.g. Akgun & Ciarrochi, 2003; Jung, Kudo, & Choi, 2012) reveal that unless unnecessary cognitive load and stress and other constraints are eliminated, it is difficult to fully achieve the pedagogical potential of online collaborative learning. Failure to do this will result in negative attitudes in the learners towards collaboration. Eryilmaz et al. (2009) and Koschmann (2003) found that this negativity will manifest itself as unwillingness to contribute to interactions or to formulate ideas or solutions, reluctance to present well-elaborated arguments or criticize or evaluate others' postings, a lack of reflection, and poor performance at the integration and resolution stages of problem solving.

This chapter investigates the cognitive and psychological challenges faced by learners, both individually and as a group in online collaborative learning and suggests a number of design and facilitation strategies for effective and less stressful online collaboration. In particular, it examines two salient challenges, cognitive load and stress, and how these issues should be accounted for in designing and facilitating collaborative activities. It concludes with some suggestions for further research.

Cognitive and Psychological Challenges in Online Collaboration

As Kirschner (2001) pointed out, collaborative learning requires learners, albeit with support from the instructor, to take greater responsibility for their own learning, explore various options to solving problems, draw on the experience, expertise and ideas of their peers, and arrive at agreed group outcomes. Assuming greater responsibility for their learning, working to achieve mutual understanding, and reaching a consensus exposes learners to cognitive and psychological challenges which may slow down their progress or restrict their actions.

Cognitive Load in Online Collaboration

Cognitive load may be defined as load imposed on a learner's cognitive system while processing information or engaging in a learning task (Paas & van Merriënboer, 1994). Cognitive load theory identifies three types of cognitive load—intrinsic, extraneous, and germane. As will be shown, all of these apply to the cognitive demands of online collaborative learning.

Managing Intrinsic Cognitive Load

Intrinsic cognitive load is related to the complexity of the to-be-learned task (Sweller, Ayres, & Kalyuga, 2011). It is measured by the interactions of the cognitive elements held simultaneously in the learners' working memory as they are engaged in the learning task (Sweller & Chandler, 1994). It is determined by the interplay between the amount of the so-called "element interactivity" and the learners' level of expertise (Schnotz & Kürschner, 2007).

Comparing the mental effort invested in individual and collaborative learning, Kirschner, Paas, and Kirschner (2009a) found that learners in a collaborative learning group invest significantly lower mental effort and perform better on their learning tasks than their counterparts engaged in individual learning. They found that the former were able to reduce intrinsic cognitive load by sharing and dividing the mental and other workloads to achieve what they termed the "collective working memory effect". However, online collaboration can involve "transactional costs", the costs of sharing, discussing, remembering and negotiating meanings (Kirschner, Paas, & Kirschner, 2009b). While these costs cannot be totally eliminated, they can be so managed or reduced as to achieve the collective working memory effect. For example, studies by Kudo (2007), Moreno (2007), and Pollock, Chandler, and Sweller (2002) show that this can be achieved by segmenting or decomposing the group learning task. The strategies for managing task difficulty and structure will be considered later in the chapter.

Reducing Extraneous Cognitive Load

Extraneous cognitive load is a consequence of poor instructional design. The reduction of extraneous cognitive load is vital for deep and effective learning when intrinsically demanding learning tasks such as online collaboration are being applied. There are several instructional strategies known to reduce extraneous cognitive load in traditional learning contexts which can be applied to online collaborative learning.

One strategy is the use of worked examples rather than problem solving instructions. It is found that providing model answers leads to better comprehension than asking students to offer their own interpretations (the problem-solving approach). Comparing the use of worked examples and problem-solving instructions in individual and collaborative learning in the mathematical domain, Retnowati, Ayres, and Sweller (2010) found that both sets of learners could benefit from worked examples rather than problem solving because the use of these reduced extraneous cognitive load. The benefits of worked examples in terms of reducing unnecessary extraneous cognitive load and improving group performance are verified in several other studies including one conducted by Van Bruggen, Kirschner, and Jochems (2002).

Fostering Germane Cognitive Load

Germane cognitive load is generated during the process of schema construction and automation (van Merriënboer & Ayres, 2005) and helps learners create new knowledge. Fostering germane cognitive load promotes active learning. Ensuring task variability to motivate learners with different interests and expertise (van Merriënboer & Ayres, op. cit.), and prompting learners to self-explain learning materials or reflect on their own learning in order to encourage deeper learning (Atkinson, Renkl, & Merrill, 2003) are found to be effective means of fostering germane cognitive load.

Schnotz and Kürschner (2007) emphasize the importance of metacognition or learners' self-regulation in stimulating germane cognitive load. Because the success of online collaborative learning depends on each member's active and thoughtful engagement in the group activities, the learners' self-regulation, reflection and self-monitoring of their contributions are critical. Some metacognitive scaffolding strategies will be examined later in this chapter.

Stress and Stressors in Online Collaboration

Stress is an emotional response to a certain task, event, or demand. When tasks, events or demands are perceived to be beyond individuals' capabilities, the level of stress increases (Lazarus & Folkman, 1984). While a certain level of stress can stimulate a learner's physical, cognitive and psychological functions and enhance learning performance (Lepine, Lepine, & Jackson, 2004), persistent or excessive stress can lead to such negative outcomes as anxiety, frustration, depression and health problems and the resultant reduction in learning performance (Karatzias et al., 2002). What is stressful for one learner may not be necessarily stressful for another, so levels of stress and the stress factors need to be individually observed.

There have been relatively few studies investigating the stress factors in online collaborative learning. Allan and Lawless (2003) examined the relationship between stress and dependency on, and trust in, each other through a survey of 35 UK Open University students. They found that higher dependency on each other and low trust resulted in higher levels of stress. This finding echoes Graham and Misanchuk's (2004) views that one of challenges in online collaboration is establishing an appropriate level of interdependence between group members since the higher the level of interdependence, the more the students need to communicate on all aspects of the learning task. A study by Lawless and Allan (2004) identified three factors related to stress in online collaboration: technology, organization, and individual. Problems with the technology; insufficient explanations about the aims, rules and protocols for online working; mismatches between the providers' and the learners' expectations of the learning outcomes; the need to work asynchronously; the low participation of other members; and personal time constraints can all be sources of stress in the online learners, and especially those learning in off-campus environments.

Our previous study (Jung et al., 2012) investigated university students' stress in online collaboration. Discounting the fact that this study was carried out in a high-context culture (Japan) and in a setting where a second language, English, was the medium of communication, the results revealed four stressors affecting the students: lack of self-efficacy, poor instructional design, lack of skills in the use of technology, and the entire experience of online collaboration which was manifestly so different from the usual classroom experience.

It may be useful to examine these four stressors in greater detail.

Low Self-Efficacy

Low self-efficacy, learners' negative judgments on their capacity to carry out a given learning task, was shown to be an important cause of stress, leading to increased intrinsic cognitive load in engaging in online collaboration and affecting the learners' motivation to complete the task.

In this situation, lack of self-efficacy in reading and writing particularly tended to influence the level of stress. It was therefore suggested that the instructors should take careful account of learners' prior experiences and competencies in both online collaboration and written communication and apply appropriate scaffolding strategies such as introducing instructor-led, appropriately structured discussions at the initial stage and then continue providing encouragement and support while progressively reducing their interventions in the collaborative activities as the learners are found to have gained confidence.

Poor Instructional Design

Poorly designed online collaborative learning environments will also increase extraneous cognitive load on the participants. Our study confirmed the findings of Akgun and Ciarrochi (2003) that inappropriate choice of group tasks, lack of clear expectations of the tasks, lack of timely support by instructors, and unclear evaluation criteria can all lead to stress. How much structure needs to be embedded in an online collaborative task and what kinds and levels of support are necessary need to be determined in the light of learners' readiness for online interactions, their learning styles and cultures, and the nature of and inherent difficulties in the learning tasks.

Lack of Technology Skills

Lack of skills or high anxiety in using technology is another stressor for students engaged in online collaborative learning. In this regard, fears of making technical errors with the tools of online discussion, lack of technical support, and technical problems such as lost connections appear to be the major concerns. This confirms the importance of technological orientation at the initial stage of collaborative learning and just-in-time support at the later stages to eliminate the possibilities of unnecessary extraneous cognitive load attributable to technical matters.

Online Collaboration

The online collaborative process itself is found to cause stress and increase intrinsic cognitive load. The students may very well experience difficulties in building online relationships with the other students, participating in group decision making, and reacting to group pressures. This will particularly be the case if they are much more familiar with teacher-centered classrooms and individual learning, especially as they may have little or no chance of seeing those they are collaborating with, or understanding their circumstances, values, attitudes and prior learning as in asynchronous online learning. These problems may be addressed by using tools such as Skype but generally speaking, this finding stresses the importance of instructors making clear the rules and roles, helping to achieve a sense of social presence, for example by encouraging the learners to exchange photos of themselves and brief biodata, and striking an appropriate balance between group and individual assessments—another bone of contention in such learning which we consider later.

Relationship Between Stress and Cognitive Load in Online Collaboration

Figure 7.1 presents a conceptual map of the relationship between stress and cognitive load as described above. **Based on the aforementioned theories and empirical studies on cognitive load and stress, we can draw some implication for designing and facilitating active online collaboration while minimizing unnecessary cognitive load and stress.**

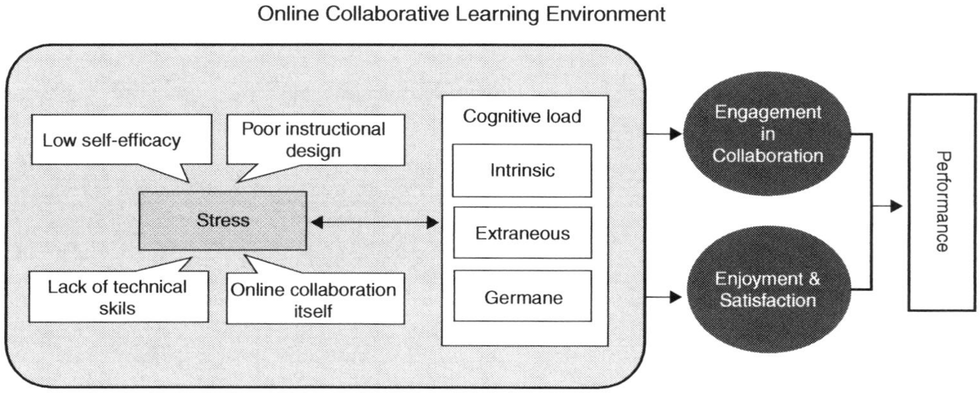

Figure 7.1 Conceptual Map of Relationship Between Cognitive Load and Stress

Strategies to Promote Engagement and Reduce Unnecessary Cognitive Load and Stress

Given the nature of these cognitive and psychological challenges, we suggest some strategies for use in online collaborative learning.

Design Strategies

Heterogeneous Grouping

To help group members collaborate in learning tasks and better manage intrinsic cognitive load, we suggest forming heterogeneous grouping based upon learners' different backgrounds and perspectives so that they can share different ideas and information and develop more diverse insights. While no consistent effect of heterogeneous grouping on online collaboration is found, it is commonly recognized that 'two brains are better than one', and Jung and Suzuki (2013) found that members of heterogeneous groups with different cultural backgrounds participated more equally in the collaborative editing in a wiki-based activity and yielded more diverse findings and ideas in their final reports, even although they felt less comfortable with each other than their counterparts in homogeneous groups formed from more or less the same cultural backgrounds. We therefore suggest:

- Forming heterogeneous groups based on learners' characteristics such as cultural backgrounds, study interests, and/or abilities that are most relevant to the collaborative task in hand.
- Offering opportunities for members of these heterogeneous groups to get to know each other prior to the actual online collaboration in order to minimize stress, uncertainty and conflict and work towards open communication, disclosure and mutually agreed task completion (Palloff & Pratt, 2005).

Task Structure and Task Difficulty

While the difficulty of learning tasks will vary from learner to learner, three factors have been identified as affecting task difficulty by Skehan (1998): code difficulty (e.g., difficulty with language used or language input); cognitive difficulty (e.g., the demands from processing tasks and accessibility to relevant resources); and communicative stress (e.g., time pressure for task completion, group size, and the modality of communication). These factors are also applicable in online collaboration.

Collaborative online learning environments typically require highly developed communication skills (especially when writing and reading in a foreign language), are cognitively complex and highly resource-demanding, and involve more subtasks and people than individual online learning. We therefore suggest the following strategies:

- Providing fewer resource-demanding tasks in the initial stages of online collaboration, tasks that require less writing and reading of postings and simpler cognitive processing.
- Decomposing tasks into several subtasks, especially for learners with low self-efficacy. The advantages of this strategy have been shown by Ho (2010) and others. It maximizes the chance of learners experiencing success in completing tasks, something which is particularly important in the early stages of the collaborative learning.

Worked Examples

The use of worked examples that explain the steps needed to arrive at a correct solution or model answers will help to reduce unnecessary extraneous cognitive load in online collaborative learning. As noted by Sweller (2006), these need to be used with discretion. We suggest:

- Using worked examples with novice learners. Kalyuga, Ayres, Chandler, and Sweller (2003) show that experienced learners are less likely to need these.
- Ensuring that the worked examples are neither too detailed nor too indicative of the intended outcomes as this may hinder creative thinking during online group discussions. Worked examples should be sufficiently detailed to elucidate the problems and suggest ways of addressing these without actually defining in detail the means of working towards, and the form of, the final solution.

Facilitation Strategies

Instructor-Led and Learner-Centered

Learners more used to study in highly structured and instructor-led environments may find it difficult to engage in asynchronous, text-based interactions with fellow students. We therefore suggest:

- Providing initial instructor-led activities that provide clear directions and define the aims and expectations before leaving the students to collaborate in the learning without undue instructor support and guidance.
- Then, as Siemens (2010) suggests, the instructors act as facilitators: amplifying, curating, wayfinding, aggregating, filtering, modeling, and staying present.

Reflection and Dialogue

It is important to allow for both individual reflection and group discourse in online collaborative. Garrison (2006) argues that allowing opportunities for personal reflection before contributing to the group discussion adds a qualitative feature to online collaboration. Such reflection enables links to be made between recent ideas, findings and experiences and earlier ones and commonalities, differences and interrelations to be recognized, all of which lead to higher order learning. In each of the inquiry phases, learners should be allowed to go between the subjective, reflective space, and the group dialogue space. So we suggest:

- Allowing sufficient time for individuals to come to personal terms with the issues under consideration before engaging in group discussions, thereby avoiding cognitive stress.
- Encouraging such activities as individual reading and research to gain new information, periodically sharing personal reflection notes, reviewing the outcome of discussions as well as student–student and instructor–student testing and negotiating of ideas.

Social Presence

The awareness of being connected with others is an important variable influencing learner satisfaction (Gunawardena & Zittle, 1997); the development of a learning community (Rourke, Anderson, Garrison, & Archer, 2001; Rovai, 2002); the level of collaboration (So & Brush, 2008); and the learning outcomes (Richardson & Swan, 2003). It can also reduce stress (Jung et al., 2012). To ensure a sense of social presence in online collaborative learning environments, we suggest:

- Providing virtual spaces for social interactions, personal profile exchanges, ice-breaking, etc.
- Organizing short Skype meetings, optional face-to-face sessions or the use of social media such as Facebook to encourage personal acquaintance and mutual trust and respect.

Metacognitive Scaffolding

Metacognitive scaffolding helps learners take increasing responsibility for planning, monitoring and evaluating their cognitive process and thus contributes to fostering germane cognitive load in online collaboration while lessening stress. We suggest:

- Encouraging learners to record their thinking processes during their engagement in the collaborative learning tasks. As McLoughlin (2002b) suggests, computer-supported cognitive tools such as an electronic notepad, an online journal and other note-taking applications can be used by learners to recognize and regulate their particular cognitive processes.
- Encouraging learners to openly reflect upon their learning, share their thoughts and emotions with, and seek advice on their own progress from, other members of the group.

Assessment Strategies

Individual and Group Assessments

This can be a source of conflict in any kind of collaborative learning. Instructors are challenged to find fair ways of: a) assessing teamwork within a group, b) assessing group project outcomes, and c) assessing individual work within the group. In our stress study (Jung et al., 2012) we found that students feel stressed in online collaboration when they are not sure how fairly their own particular efforts are going to be assessed. To eliminate such worries and possible controversy, we suggest:

- Evaluating the performance and learning achievements of the group as a whole *and* individual performance.
- Adopting peer evaluation as a means of assessing individuals' contributions to group tasks. Each group can be assigned to write a group dialogue journal and assess individual contributions to the group work, as suggested by Barkley et al. (2005).
- Analyzing individual students' log data saved in the computer system in order obtain quantitative information on each individual's contribution to the group discussion (e.g., the number and time of postings and viewings).

Conclusions

To make online collaboration effective and less stressful for the participants, instructors need to ensure that they develop and apply instructional design and facilitation strategies that address the problems of cognitive load and stress. In this chapter, we have suggested some strategies derived from theories and findings in the current literature. We believe that these strategies can be helpful, both to the instructors and to the learners. However, we recognize that further studies need to be conducted for the following purposes:

- To further elaborate and clarify the relationship between cognitive load and stress shown in Figure 7.1, both at the conceptual and empirical levels.
- To apply each of the suggested strategies in a variety of contexts (e.g., asynchronous versus synchronous collaboration, high-context versus low-context cultures, different levels of education institutions, etc.), with different tasks (e.g., tasks with different difficulty levels, tasks requiring different levels of cognitive processing, tasks demanding different resources etc.), and with different learner groups (e.g., learners with different learning styles, experiences or interests, learners at different ages, etc.) and examine its various effects on cognitive load, stress, collaborative processes, and outcomes.

Acknowledgements

This study was partly funded by the 2010–2012 Grant-in-Aid for Scientific Research (Kakenhi) from the Japan Society for the Promotion of Society.

References

Akgun, S., & Ciarrochi, J. (2003). Learned resourcefulness moderates the relationship between academic stress and academic performance. *Journal of Educational Psychology*, 23(3), 287–294.

Allan, J., & Lawless, N. (2003). Stress caused by on-line collaboration in e-learning: A developing model. *Education and Training*, 45(8–9), 564–572.

Atkinson, R. K., Renkl, A., & Merrill, M. M. (2003). Transitioning from studying examples to solving problems: Effects of self-explanation prompts and fading worked-out steps. *Journal of Educational Psychology*, 95(4), 774–783.

Barkley, E. F., Cross, K. P., & Major, C. H. (2005). *Collaborative learning techniques: A handbook for college faculty*. San Francisco, CA: Jossey-Bass.

Benbunan-Fich, R., Hiltz, S. R., & Turoff, M. (2003). A comparative content analysis of face-to-face vs. asynchronous group decision making. *Decision Support Systems*, 34(4), 457–469.

Bernard, R. M., Rojo de Rubalcava, B., & St-Pierre, D. (2000). Collaborative online distance learning: Issues for future practice and research. *Journal of Distance Education*, 21(2), 260–277.

Cacciamani, S. (2010). Towards a knowledge building community: From guided to self-organized inquiry. *Canadian Journal of Learning and Technology*, 36(1). Retrieved from http://cjlt.csj.ualberta.ca/index.php/cjlt/article/view/582/285

Clark, T. (2003). Disadvantages of collaborative online discussion and the advantages of sociability, fun and cliques for online learning. In *Proceedings of the 3.1 and 3.3 Working Groups Conference on International Federation for Information Processing: ICT and the Teacher of the Future* (pp. 23–25). Melbourne, Australia: IFIP. Retrieved from http://portal.acm.org/citation.cfm?id=857104&dl=ACM&coll=GUIDE

Eryilmaz, E., Alrushiedat, N., Kasemvilas, S., Mary, J., & van der Pol, J. (2009). *The effect of anchoring online discussion on collaboration and cognitive load.* Paper presented at The 15th Americas Conference on Information Systems, 6 August, San Francisco, California. Retrieved from http://www.academia.edu/728190/The_Effect_of_Anchoring_Online_Discussion_on_Collaboration_and_Cognitive_Load

Garrison, D. R. (2006). Online collaboration principles. *Journal of Asynchronous Learning Networks*, 10(1), 25–34.

Graham, C. R., & Misanchuk, M. (2004). Computer-mediated learning groups: Benefits and challenges to using group work in online learning environment. In T. S. Roberts (Ed.), *Online collaborative learning: Theory and practice* (pp. 181–202). Hershey: Information Science.

Gunawardena, C. N., & Zittle, F. J. (1997). Social presence as a predictor of satisfaction within a computer-mediated conferencing environment. *American Journal of Distance Education*, 11(3), 8–26.

Ho, H-N. (2010). *The relationship between levels of expertise, task difficulty, perceived self-efficacy, and mental effort investment in task performance.* Unpublished doctoral dissertation, University of Southern California, Los Angeles.

Johnson, D., Johnson, R., & Smith, K. (1991). *Cooperative learning: Increasing college faculty instructional productivity* (ASHE-ERIC Higher Education Report No. 4). Washington, DC: The George Washington University, Graduate School of Education and Human Development.

Jung, I., Choi, S., Lim, C., & Leem, J. (2002). Effects of different types of interaction on learning achievement, satisfaction and participation in Web-based instruction. *Innovations in Education and Teaching International*, 39(2), 153–162.

Jung, I., Kudo, M., & Choi, S. K. (2012). Stress in Japanese learners engaged in online collaborative learning in English. *British Journal of Educational Technology*, 43(6), 1016–1029.

Jung, I. S., & Suzuki, Y. (2013). Scaffolding wiki-based collaboration in a multicultural language learning context. Manuscript in preparation.

Kalyuga, S., Ayres, P., Chandler, P., & Sweller, J. (2003). The expertise reversal effect. *Educational Psychologist*, 38(1), 23–31.

Karatzias, A., Power, K. G., Flemming, J., Lennan, F., & Swanson, V. (2002). The role of demographics, personality variables and school stress on predicting school satisfaction/dissatisfaction: Review of the literature and research findings. *Journal of Educational Technology*, 22(1), 33–50.

Kirschner, F., Paas, F., & Kirschner, P. A. (2009a). Individual and group-based learning from complex cognitive tasks: Effects on retention and transfer efficiency. *Computers in Human Behavior*, 25, 306–314.

Kirschner, F., Paas, F., & Kirschner, P. A. (2009b). A cognitive load approach to collaborative learning: United brains for complex tasks. *Educational Psychology Review*, 21, 31–42.

Kirschner, P. A. (2001). Using integrated electronic environments for collaborative teaching/learning. *Learning and Instruction*, 10(1), 1–9.

Koschmann, T. (2003). CSCL, argumentation, and Deweyan inquiry: Argumentation is learning. In J. Andriessen, M. Baker, & D. Suthers (Eds.), *Arguing to learn: Confronting cognitions in computer supported collaborative learning environments* (pp. 261–269). Boston: Kluwer.

Kudo, M. (2007). Searching for an alternative instructional strategy for remedial EFL online learning: Based on cognitive load theory. *Proceedings of E-learn 2007 conference*, 1663–1668.

Lawless, N., & Allan, J. (2004). Understanding and reducing stress in collaborative e-learning. *Electronic Journal on E-learning*, 2(1), 121–128.

Lazarus, R.S., & Folkman, S. (1984). *Stress, appraisal, and coping.* New York: Springer.

Lepine, J. A., Lepine, M. A., & Jackson, C. L. (2004). Challenge and hindrance stress: relationships with exhaustion, motivation to learn, and learning. *Journal of Applied Psychology*, 89(5), 883–891.

McConnell, D. (2000). *Implementing computer supported cooperative learning.* London: Kogan Page.

McLoughlin, C. (2002a). Computer supported teamwork: An integrative approach to evaluating cooperative learning in an online environment. *Australian Journal of Educational Technology*, 18(2), 227–254.

McLoughlin, C. (2002b). Learner support in distance and networked learning environments: Ten dimensions for successful design. *Distance Education*, 23(2). Retrieved from http://www.c3l.uni-oldenburg.de/cde/media/readings/mcloughlin.pdf

Moreno, R. (2007). Optimising learning from animations by minimising cognitive load: Cognitive and affective consequences of signalling and segmentation methods. *Applied Cognitive Psychology*, 21, 765–781.

Paas, F., & van Merriënboer, J. (1994). Variability of worked examples and transfer of geometrical problem-solving skills: A cognitive-load approach. *Journal of Educational Psychology*, 86(1), 122–133.

Palloff, R. M., & Pratt, K. (2005). *Collaborating online: Learning together in community*. San Francisco: Jossey-Bass.

Pollock, E., Chandler, P., & Sweller, J. (2002). Assimilating complex information. *Learning and Instruction*, 12(1), 61–86.

Retnowati, E., Ayres, P., & Sweller, J. (2010). Worked example effects in individual and group work settings. *Educational Psychology*, 30(3), 349–367.

Richardson, J. C., & Swan, K. (2003). Examining social presence in online courses in relation to students' perceived learning and satisfaction. *Journal of Asynchronous Learning Networks*, 7(1), 68–88.

Rourke, L., Anderson, T., Garrison, D. R., & Archer, W. (2001). Assessing social presence in asynchronous text-based computer conferencing. *Journal of Distance Education*, 14. Retrieved from http://cade.athabascau.ca/vol14.2/rourke_et_al.html

Rovai, A. P. (2002). Building a sense of community at a distance. *International Review of Research in Open and Distance Learning*, 3(1). Retrieved from http://www.irrodl.org/index.php/irrodl/article/view/79/152

Sawyer, R. K. (2006). Analyzing collaborative discourse. In R. K. Sawyer (Ed.), *The Cambridge handbook of the learning sciences* (pp. 187–204). Cambridge: Cambridge University Press.

Schnotz, W., & Kürschner, C. (2007). A reconsideration of cognitive load theory. *Educational Psychology Review*, 19, 469–508.

Siemens, G. (2010). Teaching in social and technological networks. Retrieved from http://learn231.wordpress.com/2011/03/11/the-changing-role-of-teachers-cck11/

Skehan, P. (1998). *A cognitive approach to language learning*. Oxford: Oxford University Press.

So, H.-J. (2008). When groups decide to use asynchronous online discussions: Collaborative learning and social presence under a voluntary participation structure. *Journal of Computer Assisted Learning*, 25(2), 143–160.

So, H-J., & Brush, T. A. (2008) Student perceptions of collaborative learning, social presence and satisfaction in a blended learning environment: Relationships and critical factors. *Computers & Education*, 51(1), 318–336.

Suthers, D. D. (2006). Technology affordances for intersubjective meaning making: A research agenda for CSCL. *International Journal of Computer-Supported Collaborative Learning*, 1, 315–337.

Sweller, J. (2006). The worked example effect and human cognition. *Learning and Instruction*, 16(2), 165–169.

Sweller, J., Ayres, P., & Kalyuga, S. (2011). *Cognitive load theory*. New York: Springer.

Sweller, J., & Chandler, P. (1994). Why some material is difficult to learn. *Cognition and Instruction*, 12(3), 185–233.

Van Bruggen, J., Kirschner, P.A., & Jochems, W. (2002). External representation of argumentation in CSCL and the management of cognitive load. *Learning and Instruction*, 12, 121–138.

van Merriënboer, J., & Ayres, P. (2005). Research on cognitive load theory and its design imprecations for e-learning. *Educational Technology Research and Development*, 53(3), 5–13.

8 Formulating Best Practices and Guidelines for Emerging E-learning Technologies

Robert A. Wisher, Robert C. Brusso, Christina K. Curnow, Josh Hatfield, Arthur Paddock, and Randall D. Spain

The excitement and interest in using new e-learning technologies begs the question of how best to use that technology. Emerging technologies may assert "seductive details" to entertain and stimulate learner interest, but that stimulus may be only tangentially related to the learning topic and irrelevant to the overall learning theme (Harp & Mayer, 1998). With a new technology come new possibilities, along with promise and hype. But until sufficient experimentation has been conducted, documented, and critiqued, and there is a solid baseline of evidence for application, best practices can be proposed but not yet declared. Such is the case for mobile devices, virtual worlds, and video-based game scenarios as training platforms. The good news is that progress is being made in loading the empirical baseline with relevant samples.

This chapter describes a methodology for systematically synthesizing empirical findings and expert opinions in the use and assessment of mobile devices, virtual worlds, and video-based game scenarios for e-learning. Specifically, the focus is on the application of these technologies in adult learning with a special interest on an integration of technologies for a more comprehensive learning environment. *Integrated*, as used here, refers to the use of multiple platforms for training, such as one for initial instruction, a second for assessment, and possibly a third for adaptive instruction tailored to performance. The strategy, then, is to benchmark the present literature, through 2012, and establish whether there is sufficient evidence for pronouncing best practices and guidelines in applying these platforms for adult learning.

Researchers have previously developed a robust and clear set of guidelines based on a large body of evidence in the areas of multimedia usage and instructional strategies (DeRouin, Fritzsche, & Salas, 2004, 2005; O'Neil, 2004; Tynjälä & Häkkinen, 2006). For example, work conducted by the University of Southern California in conjunction with the Center for Research and Evaluation on Standards and Student Testing at UCLA led to a set of 52 guidelines around the distance-learning dimensions of management strategies, learner characteristics, assessment strategies, multimedia strategies, and instructional strategies (O'Neil, 2004). Clearly, a number of these guidelines still apply to the three training platforms of interest here, as well as virtual classrooms in general, particularly those dealing with instructional design. However, practices with these specific technologies and their integration were not directly addressed. Novel applications using new platforms may leave trainers without a firm basis for effective teaching and assessment practices (Herrington, Reeves, & Oliver, 2009).

Research Strategy and Technical Approach

Our first step was to identify exemplars of training and assessments in operational environments using the targeted training platforms and virtual classrooms with distributed learning examples. Of highest relevance were training activities that integrated multiple platforms within a single training effort. Added interest was on any training effort that exemplified a best practice by incorporating assessments that offered multiple levels of feedback. The next step was to review the literature, extract exemplars, organize expert input, and synthesize this information as a benchmark measure from which to seek preliminary guidelines.

Criteria for Exemplars

Exemplars highlighted exceptional examples of integrated training and assessment, providing the information basic to developing key takeaways. These serve as a footing for preliminary guidelines. We developed a set of criteria for determining whether a particular practice should be considered an exemplar. Qualification criteria are outlined in Table 8.1. Our technical approach was to seek full exemplars through literature searches and SME interviews.

Table 8.1 Qualification Criteria for Exemplars

Criterion	*Description*
1. Distributes training via one or more platforms in the following categories: mobile device, virtual worlds, or videogame-based scenarios	Training activities included training across multiple platforms, preferably all three platforms of interest. Highly effective training programs deployed in a single mode are also considered.
2. Includes individual and/or collective assessment of learning progress and/or assessment of one or more learning outcomes	There is a high interest in the methodologies used to generate, deploy and evaluate training and assessments. Attention should also be paid to the level of evaluation (i.e., reactions, learning, behavior, outcomes). Statistical analysis must include at least a within-platform assessment of pre and post learning.
3. Relevance to technology-based instruction and empirical strength	Based on a scoring system with the highest score being 49 points. Points are awarded on the basis of 27 factors.*
4. Is used in an operational setting	Not a "proof-of-concept," test product, or prototype that has not reached an operational stage. There should be individuals currently receiving for-credit training through this effort, preferably in a field setting. Educational programs in classroom settings do not qualify, but may offer exemplary elements.
5. Is something that fits as a "case study"	A discrete training course or closely linked group of courses, set in an authentic environment in which learners are seeking a certification, qualification, or course credit. The report tracked learning outcomes, assessment techniques, delivery platforms etc. Laboratory studies would not qualify.
6. Comes from groups of interest	Adult learning environments from the public and private sector.

* Space limitations preclude a full explanation of these factors.

Literature Review

Literature search. Our literature review included searches of the Education Resources Information Center, EBSCOhost, Google Scholar, Defense Technical Information Center, and various electronic resources including relevant sources from the reference lists of previously flagged sources. Approximately 1,200 sources from our searches were identified as potential candidates for coding and analysis.

Although we initially considered using the qualification criteria for the exemplar list (see Table 1) in determining the inclusionary status for sources, preliminary searches demonstrated that sources could provide valuable information while not suiting fully all attributes of exemplar status. This led to the inclusion of *exemplary elements*. Exemplary elements refer to singular training practices, assessment events, or clever applications judged to be of a high standard in the targeted areas, but not necessarily integrated across the platforms or assessing learner performance over time. Thus, our revised approach was to seek full exemplars while recognizing exemplary elements.

Rater reliability. To assess the reliability of rater coding, the analysis of two sources from a preliminary search served as a reliability check. Reliability was assessed with rater agreement across three raters. For text-based fields, agreement was assessed by demonstrating comparable content, not identical content. The assessment demonstrated that raters had 100 percent agreement across fields.

Interviews

Participants. A total of 22 subject matter experts (SMEs) were interviewed. SMEs consisted of individuals from one of four categories: 1) those having specific knowledge of assessment methods within technology-driven training platforms; 2) leading researchers and academics with a known record of research and publication within the domains of training and assessment; 3) experts with deep knowledge of training implementation across relevant technology-based training platforms; and 4) individuals with knowledge of specific potential exemplars. SMEs were identified and recruited directly through publication productivity, professional standing, and recommendations from other SMEs.

Materials. The format of the interviews was a blend of structured and unstructured inquiry. The intent of this format was to provide both structure on the central questions and flexibility to gather relevant information based on the particular backgrounds and current work of each SME.

Results

We provide key takeaways supported by the exemplars and exemplary elements as they relate to mobile learning, virtual worlds, videogame-based scenarios, simulations, virtual classrooms using distributed learning, and general assessments. The benefits and challenges of using the technology platforms, as noted in the literature, are also reported. We then shift to the findings from the SME interviews, in which their experiences and lessons learned are reflected in the form of "interview insights," organized around several dimensions. We conclude by discussing themes common in both the literature review and interviews. Based on these themes, provisional guidelines are then presented in the Discussion section. This process is illustrated in Figure 8.1.

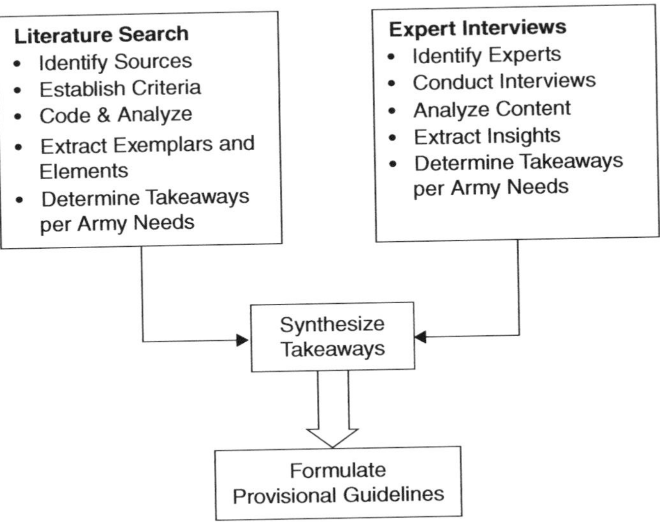

Figure 8.1 Process Model for Guideline Identification

Literature Review

Using a list of relevant search terms and a Boolean search strategy, our first cut from databases, conferences, and miscellaneous documents yielded approximately 1,200 results. Using the exemplar criteria as a guide, a total of 77 literature documents were selected for further review and coding for data analysis. Based on the exemplary criteria, we pinpointed a total of three reports that met the criteria for full exemplar (Chen, Chang, & Wang, 2008; Montijo, Spiker, & Nullmeyer, 2010; Ross & Kobus, 2011). However, we also extracted a total of 23 exemplary elements.

Exemplary Criteria

Slightly more than half (55%) of the reports coded distributed training across one or more of the platforms of interest (criterion 1 from Table 1). Regarding criterion 2, of the 77 reports coded, 64 (83%) assessed either individual and/or team learning progress or outcomes. Out of 49 possible points in our *ad hoc* measure for relevance to adult learning and empirical strength criterion (criterion 3), the maximum score awarded was 19. The percentages for the number of sources that met the remaining criteria (criteria 4 to 6) ranged from 17% to 61%. These frequencies highlight that much of the research, although incorporating assessment strategies and the platforms of interest, is from a nonoperational setting (83%) and is largely academic (57%).

Literature Review Coding Results

The results demonstrate that training research leveraging mobile platforms as a delivery method was limited (n = 14 or 18%), as were reports of training that evaluated trainees with progress tests (n = 22 or 29%) or multiple posttests (n = 13 or 17%). Further, there was a paucity of training that assessed trainees in an adaptive manner, including adaptive testing (n = 1 or $<$ 1%) and adaptive instruction (n = 2 or $<$ 1%).

Additionally, our findings highlight the small number of empirical studies on mobile devices in training (n = 11 or 14%). Finally, our results demonstrate the discrepancy between the number of empirical studies using a virtual classroom platform and those using more innovative platforms; 46% of the sources used virtual classrooms as a training platform whereas 54% of the sources used other platforms (mobile, virtual world, simulation, and videogame combined).

Key Takeaways: Mobile

Research on mobile learning (e.g., Holden & Sykes, 2011) cites a number of potential advantages for using this platform, such as providing learners more flexible access to learning materials, which can increase learning gains. By shifting training devices into the hands of learners, individuals can access performance support information or training information in the same context in which it is applied, which situated cognition theory predicts should be beneficial.

Only 11 of the 77 included sources (14%) were empirical mobile studies. Yet, our results do provide several key takeaways with a mobile focus. First, the challenges to mobile learning often center on usability issues (e.g., using a small form for learning content that is usually displayed in a much larger area). When details are important, this can become a limiting factor. There are also issues with security concerns (e.g., potential theft), signal strength in field settings, and the ability to provide extended text feedback to instructors or content developers. Further, it is simply not yet possible to draw empirically based conclusions about mobile training due to the lack of reported data on learning outcomes, a takeaway supported by previous work (see Tucker, 2010).

Key Takeaways: Virtual Worlds, Videogames, and Simulations

Although the number of innovative virtual and gaming training prototypes continues to increase, there is much less focus on assessing and evaluating training in these environments than in traditional classroom training. A review of the data demonstrates that approximately half of the coded articles that discussed a virtual world, videogame, or virtual simulation attempted any assessment. Further, only 10 out of the 77 (13%) coded articles used formative assessments in virtual worlds, videogames, and simulations combined. Formative assessment is necessary if a truly adaptive training is the goal; without initial and multiple assessments, training content cannot be tailored to an individual trainee's current knowledge or proficiency level. This oversight is a large setback considering that assessment of performance in virtual worlds, gaming, and other virtually simulated environments is required for tailoring instruction, assigning levels of competency or proficiency to trainees, tracking trainee performance, and evaluating overall training system effectiveness.

Key Takeaways: Virtual Classrooms and Distributed Learning

There were 22 (29%) entries in the literature review database that addressed virtual classroom training efforts using distributed learning. In general, the majority of virtual classroom and distributed learning articles incorporated some type of assessment (i.e., pretest, progress test, posttest), although many of these learning efforts included "blended" learning solutions. Numerous sources analyzed social exchanges within virtual classroom environments as a means of assessing trainee collaboration or various learning outcomes, typically via content analysis. These assessments informed instructors and designers on how trainees used the technology or factors that influenced responding through the medium. However, there were also examples of incorporating social exchange assessments into composite training–performance scores.

The literature review also highlighted specific strategies for enhancing learning outcomes through incorporating virtual classroom strategies in a "blended" framework, such as enabling interaction between trainees and mentors via online chats and providing trainees with knowledge progression status. Evidence from the literature review also showed that, under certain conditions, blended strategies incorporating distributed learning can provide results (e.g., trainee pass rate, trainee performance) that are equal or superior to those achieved by traditional in-class delivery.

Use of Assessments Across Platforms

Though the focus of the literature review was to identify useful integrative assessments from the platforms of interest, we saw value in analyzing the general use of assessments. Of interest are the small number of included studies that used adaptive knowledge tests ($n = 1$), utilized adaptive instruction ($n = 2$), and assessed retention ($n = 13$). The number of studies is reduced when examining only the platforms of interest. Further, only 13 (17%) reports concerning the platforms of interest actually used progressive assessment techniques (i.e., assessments during and throughout training). This deficiency is important because the degree to which training can be tailored to meet individual learners' needs is limited by the number of assessments measuring current competency levels. These findings highlight an overall lack of measurement rigor across platforms.

Expert Interviews

We conducted a content analysis of the interview notes to summarize key insights provided by the interviewees. The primary unit of data was termed an *interview insight*. To assist in analyzing interview notes, and to provide additional structure for identifying relevant concepts, we linked interview results to characteristics of the model proposed for developing a learner-centric environment. After interview insights were formulated, we created short key takeaway statements that offered a relevant prescriptive approach that can be inferred from each interview insight. Such statements served as a connective to the analogous takeaways described in the exemplars and exemplary elements from the literature review, allowing us to combine the findings and recommend provisional guidelines. From the 80 interview insights recorded, several categories surfaced, namely: Assessment Models and Strategies, Implementation Frameworks, Customized Examples, and Related Information.

Assessment Models and Strategies

This category was defined by the team as containing those interview insights addressing issues of assessments ($n = 31$). Specifically, comments related to assessment models included those related to overarching methods for assessment within training programs. These insights were relatively general and usually provided global recommendations for the structure and application of assessment. Assessment strategies, on the other hand, were generally representative of issues related to specific and sometimes unique method and implementation activities within assessment practices.

Implementation Frameworks

Interviews yielded valuable information to inform best practice for training design, development and implementation. Interview insights related to the creation of training distributed over the platforms of interest for this study (i.e., mobile, virtual worlds, videogames, and virtual classrooms) were assigned to this category (n = 25).

Customized Examples

Interviews with experts typically involved the identification of exemplary activities that highlighted the practical application of training strategies, particularly those integrating assessment. This category included interview insights by experts on specific and detailed examples (n = 16). Insights and related key takeaways typically offered unique perspectives on issues, such as specific challenges encountered, successful strategies discovered, and practical recommendations linked to specific activities. These examples provided specialized lessons learned and ideas for future training delivery and design.

Related Information

Occasionally, interview insights were extracted that were considered highly relevant to the current research question but did not fit into the categories listed above. Insights and related key takeaways in this category addressed topics such as specific training challenges, general suggestions for training development, and general comments about the state of training capabilities (n = 8).

After the literature review and interview analyses were complete, we extracted themes that were common to both of these methodologies.

Extracted Themes

Information extracted from the exemplars, exemplary elements, and interview insights was synthesized using categorical assignment methodology similar to a q-sort methodology. This process of synthesizing takeaways is represented in Figure 8.1. Common themes extracted from this synthesis are listed below in Table 8.2. Provisional guidelines based on these themes are presented in the Discussion, along with supporting exemplary sources, exemplary elements, and interview insights.

Discussion and Guidelines

Below we present some general considerations regarding the results of the literature review and expert interviews. We then discuss promising themes that span interview insights and literature review findings. From these, we propose a set of Provisional Guidelines. These guidelines are based on expert judgment and supported by empirical work, but they may not yet have been fully verified or widely replicated. At this point, they can be considered as prospective foundations for best practices. Our Provisional Guidelines are presented in the following sections, beginning with five Provisional Guidelines related to assessments, followed by two related to implementation.

Table 8.2 Extracted Themes

Themes
• The importance of planning for training assessment.
• The use of a sole one platform for both training and assessment.
• The importance of adaptive applications.
• The importance of frequent testing.
• The utilization and evaluation of social exchanges.
• The importance of learning sciences' principles.
• The importance of training content availability.
• The development and use of selection strategies and tools for training platform decision recommendations.
• The importance of aligning individual training objectives to the most relevant environment context.
• The importance of understanding the capability of testing technology.

Provisional Guideline 1. A theme that resonated throughout the interviews and reports was the importance of care and consideration when planning training assessments. Although the use of innovative technologies has the potential to change the training arena, the importance of assessments remains high. Just as training design teams must rely on ISD principles to design effective training programs, so must design teams allocate effort to apply guidelines and principles for assessment strategies.

Specifically, it is important to plan the level, scope, detail, and impact of assessments in areas such as: 1) determining the knowledge, skills, and abilities (KSAs) of interest for the assessment, 2) determining the behaviors and performance indicators of these KSAs, and 3) determining what actions would indicate that learning had occurred. As noted from the interviews, if the behaviors indicative of the KSA are unclear, assessment is a moot point. For example, if trainers are interested in assessing leadership emergence but fail to operationally define this competency, or the indicative behaviors, assessing the level of leadership emergence that learners demonstrate would prove problematic.

An assessment map is one way to begin framing an assessment strategy. Event-Based Approaches to Training (EBAT) and Evidence-Centered Design are two examples of assessment mapping techniques (Fowlkes, Dwyer, Oser, & Salas, 1998). Both approaches emphasize determining the linkages between the competencies of interest, the indicators of these competencies within a training environment, and the assessment options and techniques. These decisions are best made by teams of experts in the subject matter of interest as well as in performance assessment.

Another important insight from one of the interviews was the potential for data overload. Technologically innovative platforms supply a mass of data that can become unwieldy to interpret if assessment decisions are not made *a priori*. Thus, careful consideration should be given to training content and technology features when creating an assessment plan to determine what information will be used and how it will be evaluated.

Finally, assessment planning can illuminate differences in assessment that may potentially indicate delivery differences, as opposed to criterion/criteria differences. Specifically, the delivery platform could potentially become an unexpected confound in the assessment process. As an example, comparing speeded test scores on mobile phones to those on a desktop computer may be more indicative of the display and keyboard size differences and less demonstrative of criterion differences. Integrating the previous information, the following provisional guideline is proposed:

Provisional Guideline 2. There was little evidence of assessments being carried out across platforms. We did find examples of using the training platforms for assessing individual learners as they progressed through a training program, rather than the less efficient approach of switching an assessment to other test platforms. For instance, relevant examples assembled from our interviews included using games themselves as an assessment tool, building calculators in simulations to assess performance, making assessments a structural component within a game or simulation, using knowledge checks throughout training and linking the knowledge checks to work actions, streamlining the observation process through mobile devices or electronic checklists, and embedding work samples into a simulation or game and scoring virtually by expert judges. Certain features of some potential test vehicles, however, are not yet sufficiently mature for widespread use, such as speech recognition.

The literature search yielded similar practices, as depicted in building ubiquitous learning into student learning models, monitoring learner states in an intelligent mobile learning system, training higher ordered cognitive skills in flight training, and assessing communications in asynchronous discussions and chat rooms. Overall, it is evident that the practice has been in use in quality research reports; thus, the following Provisional Guideline is proposed:

Provisional Guideline 3. Another theme is the use of adaptive applications in training. Our interviews showed there are many ways assessments can be used in an adaptive manner, such as using assessment results to adapt training *content* to individual learning style or prior knowledge, or using assessment of behavioral performance in a virtual environment to prescribe tailored pedagogical strategies. The use of adaptive testing is another way assessments, themselves, can be used adaptively. For example, assessments can increase or decrease in difficulty or focus on a particular content area based on a learner's response. One limitation to using adaptive testing is that some complex stimuli and constructed responses may not be positioned to take advantage of computer adaptive testing due to the difficulty of calibrating non-multiple-choice items. Further, testing that is truly adaptive requires a rigorous item analysis, which can be costly and time consuming. These drawbacks may be the reason that only one of the 77 sources used adaptive testing. Based on these findings, the following Provisional Guideline is proposed:

Provisional Guideline 4. The third theme concerns testing as a training activity. This has some overlap with the guidance to use the same platform in training and testing, but goes further in the methods of use. Insights from the interviews revealed promising uses of testing-as-training such as: testing as a form of learning; testing in continuous assessments by mobile devices; testing that is invisible to the user as a structured learning component; and testing delivered while engaging in videogame-based learning scenarios

The interviews clearly suggested that, since tests can both train and assess, more testing equates to more training. Similarly, the related evidence gathered in the literature illustrates uses in developing situational awareness skills and in engineering content into an assessment component. Overall, these findings led to the following Provisional Guideline:

Provisional Guideline 5. Technology affords many methods of testing that take advantage of computational power, such as recording structured behaviors while interacting with learning content, conducting after-action reviews within virtual environments, conducting assessments on a frequent basis through mobile devices, mining data based on any user activity in virtual worlds, or applying advances in computational linguistics for scoring essays and short responses. Understanding the congruence between the capabilities of the proposed platform (e.g., virtual world), the training objectives (e.g., improve group communication skills), and assessment strategies is vital to the success of a training. Certain capabilities may be available in some platforms and not others. For example, in videogame simulations, duration, quality and/or quantity of certain gameplay actions may be used as indicators of different competencies. A failure to consider the capabilities of the technology could lead to either an inability to assess learners adequately or the missed opportunity to assess in more innovative or complex ways beyond multiple-choice items.

The provisional guideline proposed here encourages those involved with planning to look beyond the initial layer of what a testing technology can offer and extend that to assess knowledge and skills at a deeper cognitive level or at a more frequent schedule.

Implementation Framework

Beyond the Provisional Guidelines on assessment strategies, two additional provisional guidelines were developed related to the implementation framework.

Provisional Guideline 6. One theme that surfaced from interviews was that best-practice construction and implementation of learning frameworks should be linked to effective application of findings from the learning sciences. For example, our SMEs stated that, regardless of delivery platform, the integration of effective strategies, such as ISD strategies, throughout the training development and implementation process is critical. Several specific practices emerged related to this theme. Interviews also provided specific examples of using decision tools for determining when learning objectives can be addressed by mobile platforms.

Consistent with our theme from the interviews to use decision tools for selecting appropriate training platforms, the literature also provided specific examples of strategies and tools developed for the design of game-based training efforts. The literature review also demonstrated that when the appropriate learning science strategies are followed, training design patterns could be shared between games and between virtual classroom tools. Finally, the literature review also provided supportive evidence for the best practice involving integrating SMEs throughout the training development process. Based upon these findings, Provisional Guideline 6 is proposed:

Provisional Guideline 7. Future learning models will value using peer-based and collaborative learning as a strategy for cultivating a learner-centric environment. Evidence from interviews provided specific examples of how this strategy is currently being implemented across various training efforts. Examples were given, such as developing communities of practice where geographically dispersed individuals can collaborate and establish unstructured learning networks, the development of "wiki" technologies to assist in co-creation of knowledge among peers, and fielding mobile applications that encourage users to modify the application for their own use and to provide specific functional suggestions to training developers to make the content more relevant to peers.

Another specific theme from the interviews was the issue of collecting and using data generated from social exchanges in collaborative environments mediated by technology. A specific topic from one interview was that data from social exchanges should be combined and analyzed across exchange mediums and among all parties participating (i.e., learners, collaborators, instructors) in order to obtain the most informed picture of how peer and collaborative learning is taking place.

The literature review provided specific examples of how social exchange data has been collected and used in specific training platforms. Examples showed mapping of social interactions within virtual worlds and analysis of data from online discussion forums within virtual classrooms. Based upon our findings, we propose our final Provisional Guideline.

Conclusion

Our multisource, multimethod analysis led to the formulation of seven provisional guidelines. These were based on the considerations from an initial set of 77 reports and interviews with 22 experts from the military, government, academia, and industry. We examined the use of new instructional technologies and delivery platforms with integrated assessments across platforms in ways that are relevant to the needs of the future Army learning model. This exploration covered new ground. Accordingly, provisional guidelines were developed on how to approach this integrated challenge based on the current state of research and practice.

There is insufficient evidence to declare a robust set of guidelines for employing mobile devices, virtual worlds, and video-based game scenarios as training platforms at a level of certainty comparable to the What Works series (O'Neil, 2004). Before these guidelines can be fully established and best practices can emerge, there needs to be a stronger foundation of evidence and support offered by both researchers and the practitioners responsible for their implementation. For those pursuing the implementation of training on these platforms, we offer seven provisional guidelines while recognizing that the guidelines concerning design issues promulgated in O'Neil (2004) can also apply to these training platforms.

Acknowledgment

This work is supported by the U.S. Army Research Institute under Contract No. W5J9CQ-11-D-0002–0005 to ICF International "Delivering Training Assessments in a Soldier-Centered Learning Environment." The view, opinions, and/or findings contained in this chapter are those of the authors and should not be construed as an official Department of the Army position, policy, or decision.

References

Chen, G.D., Chang, C.K., & Wang, C.Y. (2008). Ubiquitous learning website: Scaffold learners by mobile devices with information-aware techniques. *Computers & Education, 50*, 77–90.

DeRouin, R.E., Fritzsche, B.A., & Salas, E. (2004). Optimizing e-learning: Research-based guidelines for learner-controlled training. *Human Resource Management, 43*(2–3), 147–162. doi:10.1002/hrm.20012

DeRouin, R.E., Fritzsche, B.A., & Salas, E. (2005). E-learning in organizations. *Journal of Management, 31*(6), 920–940. doi:10.1177/0149206305279815

Fowlkes, J., Dwyer, D.J., Oser, R.L., & Salas, E. (1998). Event-based approach to training (EBAT). *International Journal of Aviation Psychology, 8*(3), 209–221.

Harp, S.F., & Mayer, R.E. (1998). How seductive details do their damage: A theory of cognitive interest in science learning. *Journal of Educational Psychology, 90*, 414–434.

Herrington, J., Reeves, T., & Oliver, R. (2009). *A guide to authentic e-learning*. Hoboken, NJ: Routledge.

Holden, C.L., & Sykes, J.M. (2011). Leveraging mobile games for place-based language learning. *International Journal of Game-Based Learning, 1*(2), 1–18.

Montijo, G.A., Spiker, V.A., & Nullmeyer, R. (2010). Training interventions to reduce predator crew errors. *Proceedings of the Interservice/Industry Training, Simulation, and Education Conference*, USA, pp. 3021–3031.

O'Neil, H. (2004). *What works in distance learning: Guidelines*. Greenwich, CT: Information Age.

Ross, W.A., & Kobus, D.A. (2011). Case-based next generation cognitive training solutions. *Proceedings of the Interservice/Industry Training, Simulation, and Education Conference*, USA, pp. 2858–2864.

Tucker, J.S. (2010). *Mobile learning approaches for U.S. Army training*. Arlington, VA: U.S. Army Research Institute. Retrieved from: http://www.dtic.mil/cgi-bin/GetTRDoc?AD=ADA528742

Tynjälä, P., & Häkkinen, P. (2006). E-learning at work: Theoretical underpinnings and pedagogical challenges. *Journal of Workplace Learning, 17*(5/6), 318–336. doi:10.1108/13665620510606742

9

Revisiting the Need for Strategic Planning for E-learning in Higher Education

Mark Bullen

Introduction

For over a decade higher education institutions and governments have been urged to recognize the growing importance of e-learning and to plan for it more effectively. Bates (2000) has been one of the most consistent advocates of planning for e-learning and of its transformational potential. De Frietas & Oliver (2005) emphasized the critical role of e-learning policy and "the relationship between policy, organizational change and the implementation of e-learning" (p. 81). In a survey of e-learning in higher education published in 2005, the Organization for Economic Cooperation and Development (OECD) called for countries to focus more on developing the "social, organizational and legal contexts in order to foster the further development of e-learning" (p. 18). In 2007, Bullen and Janes argued that higher education institutions were not, for the most part, responding appropriately to the rapidly changing needs of society by planning effectively for e-learning:

> Organizational arrangements, funding, development processes, faculty and learner support and other policies vary widely from institution to institution. Quality is also variable and often unflattering. Long pages of lecture notes, poorly designed Web sites, lack of interaction, and the inadequate use of the rich resources available on the Internet characterize much of the present world of online e-learning.
>
> (p. vii)

Today, this description of the state of e-learning in higher education is still relevant. To be fair, progress has been made and many more institutions have developed and implemented e-learning strategies but the institutional response to e-learning still tends to be reactive rather than proactive. Witness the response to the emergence of Massively Open Online Courses (MOOC). Institutions, fearing they will be left behind, have rushed to jump on this technological bandwagon without serious consideration of how MOOCs fit into their existing e-learning practices or of how they align with their strategic directions (Bogost, 2012; Kim, 2013; Tilsley, 2013; Vaidhyanathan, 2012).

The pace of change has accelerated since 2000 and higher education is facing much more serious challenges as it struggles to deal with declining funding and growing demands for quality, relevance, accountability, efficiency and responsiveness (Bates & Sangrà, 2011). E-learning is not the "magic bullet" but it can play a role in addressing some of these issues if it is dealt with strategically. This means integrating e-learning into the core operations of our higher education institutions, aligning it with institutional strategic plans and developing strategic plans specifically for e-learning. As Haughey (2007) argues, "the place of digital technologies in the entire mission of the university needs to be clarified. Without such a vision, an organization will find it difficult" to make effective use e-learning (p. 30).

In this chapter I discuss the key reasons for developing e-learning strategies and the key components of an effective strategy and I draw on my recent experience developing an institutional e-learning strategy to highlight the key elements of the strategy development process.

Introducing E-learning into Higher Education

Bates (2007) argues that higher education institutions typically move through five stages as they introduce and ultimately integrate e-learning (see Table 9.1). This begins with *lone rangers*, the enthusiastic early adopters who experiment with e-learning without any formal institutional support and culminates with the *sustainability* stage at which e-learning has become a core activity and has been integrated into the institutional planning and budgeting processes. In between these beginning and end points, institutions provide progressively more support to e-learning, moving from what Bates calls *encouragement* to *chaos* and then to the penultimate *planning* stage when senior management finally begins to take e-learning seriously by starting to integrate it into the institutional planning process.

As the use of e-learning continues to grow, it is becoming increasingly important for institutions to focus their efforts on moving from the early stages of e-learning development, which are characterized primarily by the efforts of individual faculty, to the higher levels of planning and sustainability, characterized by institutional support and integration. The critical ingredients are an e-learning strategy and the implementation of the e-learning strategy.

Table 9.1 The Five Stages of eLearning Integration in Higher Education

Stage 1	*Stage 2*	*Stage 3*	*Stage 4*	*Stage 5*
Lone Rangers	*Encouragement*	*Chaos*	*Planning*	*Sustainability*
• Early adopters • Individual initiative • No direct institutional support	• Early adopters supported with small grants or reductions in teaching load	• Increase in use of e-learning • Growing administration concerned about lack of coordination or standards, duplication and costs	• Senior administration begins to address the "chaos" by setting standards, addressing need for faculty support and controlling costs and workload	• Stable e-learning system established that is cost-effective and scalable

Bates, 2007

What Is E-Learning?

One of the problems in trying to motivate institutions to develop e-learning strategies is the ambiguity of the concept; there is no common, broadly accepted understanding of e-learning. It is essential, then, that we clearly explain what e-learning is so that everybody involved in the planning process is talking about the same thing.

Figure 9.1 depicts one conceptualization of e-learning. It situates e-learning on a teaching and learning continuum showing face-to-face teaching *without* the use of information and communication technologies (ICT) at one end and fully online distance learning at the other end.

As we move along the continuum from fully face-to-face teaching, more and more technology is used to replace the face-to-face elements. Initially, this has very little impact on how teaching and learning is organized because the technology is used primarily to enhance the face-to-face teaching. But as we move further along the continuum (from left to right), the nature of teaching and learning and how it is organized is increasingly affected by the use of ICT. Somewhere around the middle of the continuum we have blended learning where significant amounts of the face-to-face elements are replaced by ICT. Fewer class sessions are held as technology is used increasingly to deliver the teaching and to facilitate the learning. Once we reach the right end of the continuum, all face-to-face contact between teacher and learner has been replaced by ICT. According to this framework, e-learning includes all situations in which technology is used to replace at least some of the face-to-face teaching.

Why Should Higher Education Institutions Develop an E-learning Strategy?

There is much skepticism about the value of strategic planning, particularly in public higher education institutions. Birnbaum (2001), for example, argues that higher education has blindly adopted business planning practices that often have already been tried and rejected by business. Bates & Sangrà, (2011) describe planning and decision making as "messy processes . . . driven as much by personalities, departmental priorities, empire building, and plain jealousies, as they are by logic, vision, the desire to improve services, or other lofty goals" (p. 94). Nonetheless, while there may be much to criticize in how planning is actually conducted, there is a consensus that planning is essential to any organization. As de Freitas & Oliver (2005) conclude,

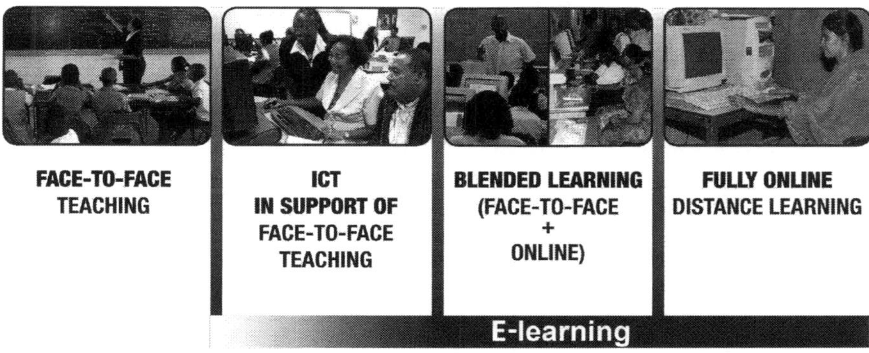

Figure 9.1 The E-learning Continuum

"e-learning policy does drive change. It first leads to organizational redevelopment (whether formally through staffing structures or informally through locally-negotiated changes in staff roles), then this is expressed through the changed pedagogic practices of staff" (p. 94). The focus, however, should be on the strategic *thinking* that goes with the planning. This means dealing with issues such as:

- The learning outcomes that are required in a knowledge-based society and how technology can help develop such outcomes;
- Developing competencies in the use of information and communications technologies within specific areas of study;
- More flexible delivery of programs to accommodate a more heterogeneous student body;
- The redesign of courses and programs to integrate technology better;
- Better services to students;
- Greater efficiencies in both teaching and administration. (Bates & Sangrà, 2011, p. 101)

When it comes to strategic planning for e-learning, there is a range of factors or pressures facing higher education that highlight the need for institutions to develop an e-learning strategy. Social and economic changes have had a profound impact on the way students pursue their post-secondary education and training. Going to college or university is no longer a one-time event with students completing a degree or diploma and entering the workforce. Once in the workforce, graduates will increasingly find they need to return for technical and professional upgrading. To meet this growing demand for continuous learning, higher education institutions are facing increasing pressure to provide flexible access to their programs, and e-learning is seen as a key tool for achieving this goal. This is particularly relevant for higher education institutions in the developing world where there is a need to address a growing demand for skills training in many sectors.

As well, students increasingly expect to access their educational institutions, their services and their instructors online (Dahlstrom, 2012; JISC, 2008) While this is more relevant to institutions in developed countries, particularly in North America, it is increasingly a global expectation of students (Pedro, 2009).

The rationale for e-learning, then, is tied to the need for increased and flexible access to education, to student expectations for quality, convenience, and use of ICT and a desire to enhance and transform our teaching and learning.

E-learning and Institutional Change

Most advocates of e-learning in higher education explicitly or implicitly link e-learning to the need for institutional transformation, through new approaches to teaching and learning and new organizational models (Bates & Sangrà, 2011; de Freitas & Oliver, 2005). This raises the critical of issue of change management and the need to consider how organizational change is conceptualized. De Freitas & Oliver (2005) propose five models of organizational change (Fordist, evolutionary, ecological, community of practice and discourse-oriented) that can help frame the development of e-learning policy and strategy.

The Fordist Model

This model is "rational and corrective" and is a cyclical process that involves establishing a vision and then continuously aligning the organization to that vision. Change is treated as an engineering process and this model has its roots in the concept of "scientific" management.

The Evolutionary Model

In the evolutionary model, change is viewed as more organic and involves a Darwinian process of variation, selection, retention and struggle. Institutional change happens after variations in practice emerge intentionally or by chance, and then survive "natural" selection processes such as the impact of market forces or internal organizational restructuring.

The Ecological Model

The relationships between individuals in an organization are key to this model of change. Unlike other models, in the ecological model social and intellectual capital are not seen as something separate from the organization. An information ecology is "a system of people, practices, values and technologies in a particular environment" (Nardi & O'Day, 1999, p. 49).

The Community of Practice Model

In this model, organizations are viewed as "collections of individuals, rather than as systems or organisms" (de Freitas and Oliver, p. 85). Practice is inherently local and meaning is constructed through mutual interpretation of the individuals in an organization (Wenger, 1998). Practices consist of artefacts, concepts and labels that are developed within specific communities (Wenger, 1998). For practices to be adopted in different communities, they must be made sense of in the new context.

The Discourse-Oriented Model

In a discourse-oriented perspective new forms of work (or change) are legitimated through the negotiation of meaning and practices that occur through the conversations people have with each other. "Within such an analysis, close attention is paid to the naturalization of discourses—the way in which particular perspectives become taken-for-granted and unquestionable" (de Freitas & Oliver, 2005, p. 86).

Strategic Planning for E-learning and Its Components

Strategic planning tends to be functionalist in orientation and informed by Fordist notions of rationality in which organizations are viewed as systems in which change can be "engineered". However, public higher education institutions are not automobile factories and while they are increasingly influenced by managerial perspectives, the collegial organizational culture is still dominant (Bergquist & Pawlak, 2008). As a result, the strategic planning process needs to be adapted to fit the cultural reality of public higher education. This means that it needs to incorporate elements of some of the other models of change described earlier, particularly the community of practice and the ecological perspectives and, to a lesser extent, the evolutionary perspective.

Whatever the underlying philosophy of the process, the end product should be a document that articulates the strategic thinking about how to use e-learning to transform teaching and learning at an institution. It should represent the collective thinking of the key stakeholders, i.e., faculty, staff, students and administrators, and it should provide a road map for implementation.

While e-learning strategies will differ from institution to institution depending on their specific needs, they should include the following components:

- A vision for the use e-learning at the institution;
- A rationale for the use of e-learning at the institution;
- Core principles that frame and guide the e-learning strategy;
- Strategic goals or outcomes;
- Outputs tied to the strategic goals or outcomes; and
- Specific implementation activities that will produce the outputs and achieve the goals.

Rationale

The rationale and vision for e-learning need to be developed concurrently. Unless there is a shared understanding of why e-learning is seen as critical to the institution, it would be difficult to develop a clear, coherent and shared vision. Likewise, developing a rationale without having some preliminary ideas about what the future state of the institution will look like is difficult. A generic rationale for e-learning was described earlier (Why Should Higher Education Institutions Develop an e-learning Strategy?). Institutions may have unique reasons for wanting to develop an e-learning strategy. The following are some of the reasons that higher education implements e-learning on an institution-wide basis:

- to meet the flexible needs of students;
- to increase access to programming;
- to distribute programs across multiple campuses;
- to enhance the quality of teaching and learning;
- to better prepare students for the requirements of business and industry;
- to better accommodate different teaching and learning approaches;
- to improve cost-effectiveness of institutions. (Bates & Sangrà, 2011)

Vision

This is a concrete description of what the organization will look like if and when the e-learning strategic plan is fully implemented. It is often useful to develop a vision by describing specific scenarios related to key areas of the plan. For example, what will it be like to be a student when e-learning is fully implemented? What will it be like to be an instructor, etc.? As mentioned earlier, the vision and rationale should not be developed in isolation.

Administrative departments need to be involved in the process of developing an e-learning vision as well, as e-learning involves both academic and administrative services. Core support departments such as the Registrar's Office, the Library, the Bookstore, and Program Advising need to develop their own visions for e-learning.

Guiding Principles

Establishing some clear guiding principles for the e-learning strategy at the outset can help dispel misconceptions about the potential impact of e-learning and the motivations for pursuing it.

This can help to establish a more positive climate and generate a more productive engagement with faculty and staff. Bates (2007) suggests the following core principles:

- The benefits of using e-learning must be clearly identified before program development begins;
- Faculties and academic departments should make decisions about how e-learning will be used to support their academic goals;
- E-learning will not displace instructors but will strengthen their role in teaching and learning and improve teaching practice;
- Increases in instructor workload will be avoided by following best practices in e-learning. This includes providing support to course and program development through the services of a central learning and teaching centre;
- Faculty development will be given a high priority so that instructors have adequate training in the use of e-learning; and
- Costs of developing e-learning programs will be controlled by using a project management approach and the centralized resources of a learning and teaching centre and the IT department.

Strategic Themes

Strategic themes can be helpful in organizing and framing an e-learning strategy and giving it an appropriate focus. For example, to avoid giving too much emphasis to technical issues and ensure that educational matters are given priority, it can be helpful to identify strategic themes related to educational quality and faculty development.

Goals/Outcomes

Goals or outcomes describe in concrete terms what the institution hopes to achieve by implementing the plan. Achieving the goals entirely would make the vision a reality. The goals of the e-learning strategy should be aligned with the goals of the institutional strategic plan.

Ouputs and Implementation Activities

Outputs and implementation activities are key to achieving the goals. The outputs are the products of the implementation. One or more implementation activities may need to be undertaken to produce the outputs for a specific goal. Table 9.2 provides an example of how the output and implementation activities that support one goal (quality and innovation in the use of e-learning) are related to one strategic theme (educational quality).

An E-learning Strategy Case

The rest of this chapter describes the process followed to develop an e-learning strategy at a Canadian higher education institution, the British Columbia Institute of Technology.

Institutional Context

The British Columbia Institute of Technology (BCIT) is a public technical/vocational institution in the province of British Columbia on Canada's Pacific coast. It offers a broad range of

Table 9.2 The Relationship Among Theme, Outcome Outputs, and Implementation Activities

Strategic Theme	*Goal/Outcome*	*Outputs*	*Implementation Activities*
Educational quality	Quality and innovation in the use of e-learning.	• Quality standards for instructional design, assessment, learner support, teaching and technology. • Applied research focused on e-learning practice at BCIT.	• Research, develop and implement quality standards. • Develop standards for instructor responsibilities and expectations in online courses. • Develop an applied research agenda focused on e-learning practice at BCIT.

technical, professional and vocational programs at the diploma, baccalaureate and master's level to approximately 18,000 full-time and 28,000 part-time students. It has over 2,000 full- and part-time instructors and operates with a budget of approximately $CDN 280 million. It is a face-to-face institution that emphasizes an experiential learning approach and prides itself on developing job-ready graduates who possess high level skills that meet identified labour-market needs. BCIT is also one of the largest providers of online and distance learning in the province of British Columbia and is increasingly using blended delivery approaches to meet the needs of working students.

Background to the Planning Process

Developing an e-learning strategy at BCIT was a long and difficult struggle. The first attempt to develop a strategy was in 2006 shortly after I took over as Associate Dean of the Learning & Teaching Centre (LTC). The LTC is a central department funded out of the institutional operating budget with responsibility for curriculum and instructor development, educational technology, online course development and general instructor support for teaching and learning.

In my first attempt to develop an e-learning strategy, I first sought and gained the support of the Vice-President, Learning & Technology Services, to whom I reported, and then developed a short concept paper with a rationale for an e-learning strategy. The concept paper included a recommendation that it be taken to the institutional leadership team for review and approval so that the development of an e-learning strategy could be undertaken. Unfortunately, shortly after putting this forward, the institution faced a serious financial crisis that resulted in cutbacks and layoffs. It also diverted the attention and energy of the leadership team to dealing with the immediate crisis at the expense of planning for the future. To further complicate matters, there was significant instability at the senior management level with the departure of the President and Vice-President, Education within the space of a year, followed by the departure of the new Vice-President, Education less than six months after taking over the position. It was nearly three years before the senior administration of the institution had been stabilized and there were any serious attempts at institutional planning.

Four years later, in 2010, with the return of organizational and financial stability, the leadership team was able to move away from its focus on day-to-day operational issues and begin to look to the future. A new institutional strategic plan had been implemented the year before and there was increasing talk of the need to look at online learning as way of transforming teaching and as a means to provide for more flexible access. In 2011 the President released a white paper on the future of the institution in which he identified the need to consider online learning and other technology-mediated forms of teaching and learning. The release of the book *The Innovative University* that year also raised the profile and credibility of online learning. In their book, Clayton Christensen and Henry Eyring argued that, in order to survive, higher education needed to look at disruptive strategies such as online learning and to reengineer the university to meet the new demands of the twenty-first century (Christensen & Henry, 2011). This coincided with a financial crisis in the American public higher education system, and suddenly online learning was on the minds of higher education leaders and was increasingly being talked about as a way to not only transform teaching learning but also to address the growing higher education financial crisis and make the system more efficient.

The Planning Process

Against this backdrop of heightened interest and acceptance of online learning institutionally and in higher education generally, the time seemed right to restart the e-learning strategy process. An additional factor that seemed to favor the development of an institutional e-learning strategy was the recent appointment of new Deans in three of the six BCIT schools. These new Deans brought a fresh and progressive view of teaching, learning and technology and began advocating for greater use of e-learning. A final factor was the appointment of a new Chief Information Officer who also appeared to favour the development of an e-learning strategy. The stars, then, seemed to be aligning. In September 2011 I developed a second discussion paper that made a case for why an e-learning strategy was needed. The paper contained a vision and rationale for e-learning and proposed a set of guiding principles and strategic themes.

Guiding Principles

- Strategic
- Quality first
- Pedagogically driven
- Industry-relevant
- Sustainable
- Student-centered
- Need for faculty support

Strategic Themes

- Quality teaching and learning models
- Learner support
- Faculty development
- Use of technology
- Funding models

I presented the discussion paper to the Deans' Council and following that, the Leadership Team, which approved the recommendation to proceed with the development of an institutional e-learning strategy and implementation plan.

A project charter was then developed that included an organizational structure and a timeline for the planning process. The e-learning plan was to be guided by an e-learning Strategy Steering Committee with the following representation:

- Dean of the Learning & Teaching Centre
- Vice-President, Education
- Vice-President, Learning & Technology Services
- Dean, School of Business
- Chief Information Officer

Reporting to this steering committee was an e-learning Strategy Working group chaired by the Dean of the Learning & Teaching Centre and with faculty representatives from three of the six schools and an instructional development consultant from the Learning & Teaching Centre.

The organizational structure was kept deliberately simple and the two committees small to allow for agility and the rapid development of the e-learning strategy. We wanted to avoid the tendency to let the consultation process paralyze decision-making. The representatives on the two committees were explicitly appointed not to represent their particular constituencies but rather to contribute their expertise and to present an institutional perspective. Having the Dean of the Learning & Teaching Centre on the Steering Committee and the Working Group was intended to provide a formal, operational link between the two committees to help facilitate communication between the two groups. A separate consultation process, described below, provided some of the data that the two committees would use to inform their deliberations and, ultimately, the e-learning strategic plan.

The Consultation Process

Consultation and buy-in are critical to the success of any strategic plan but there is a fine line between too much and too little consultation. Public higher education institutions can be extremely cautious, and often consultation becomes a way to delay decision-making. The e-learning Strategy Working Group was conscious of this and also of the reality that there could be resistance to greater use of e-learning and that it would be impossible to please everybody and address all needs. As a result, we decided to expedite the consultation process and ensure that it was completed within four months. We held nine community consultation sessions with faculty and staff at all five of the BCIT campuses. These sessions were designed as interactive workshops in which participants worked in small groups to brainstorm key issues related to the five strategic themes. The discussion was framed according to three perspectives:

- **The Current "learnscape/teachingscape" (Present)**: What are you doing right now in terms of teaching? How? What tools and resources are you using?
- **Vision (Future)**: What does the future look like? What is your vision for e-learning at BCIT?
- **Challenges**: What are the possible challenges that may hinder the attainment of your vision?

In order to make it possible for as many people to participate as possible, we scheduled the consultation sessions at nonteaching times and we publicized them through e-mail notices, flyers, and the institutional website. We continued to schedule sessions until participation started to drop off.

In addition to the community consultation sessions, we hosted an online discussion on the e-learning strategy website which was restricted to the institutional community. The consultation process ran from January to April 2012.

In June 2012 we launched the first of a series of e-learning showcases to allow faculty to share their e-learning expertise with each other by showcasing examples of e-learning use. The decision to organize these events emerged from the community consultation sessions. One of the key themes that emerged was the need for more sharing and collaboration and a sense that faculty were often working isolation without any awareness of what their colleagues were doing with e-learning.

In addition to consulting with faculty staff and students, we also conducted an environmental scan to get a sense of what other postsecondary institutions were doing, and to review other institutional e-learning strategies. In all we reviewed 15 institutional e-learning strategies from colleges and universities in Canada, the United States, Australia and the United Kingdom.

The Plan

Once the consultation process was complete, the e-learning Strategy Working Group met to review the data gathered from the consultations and the environmental scan and to identify key themes and potential strategic priorities. I was tasked with preparing first draft of the e-learning Strategy which was then shared with the Working Group for feedback. After numerous revisions a final draft was completed and taken to the e-learning Strategy Steering Committee for discussion. Based on feedback from this group, further revisions were made and a final draft of "e-learning Strategy" was submitted to the Steering Committee on August 13, 2012. The next steps in the process were to take it to the Deans' Council in September 2012 and then seek formal approval from the senior Leadership Team in October 2012. Implementation of the plan was planned for the 2013/14 fiscal year beginning in April 2013.

Conclusion

Bates and Sangrà (2011) examined the practices in managing ICT in postsecondary education, drawing on empirical studies of over 20 universities and an in-depth study of 11 universities and colleges in Europe and North America. Based on their analysis they proposed six criteria for the successful planning and implementation of e-learning in higher education:

- A flexible institutional strategic plan that recognizes the importance of e-learning is a necessary prerequisite to the successful implementation of e-learning.
- A compelling vision for e-learning is essential and it should be a vision for "radical change directed at new and better learning outcomes, greater flexibility for students, and increased cost-efficiencies" (p. 99).
- Teaching staff must be directly involved in the visioning and strategic thinking processes for e-learning.
- The vision and institutional strategy for e-learning must be shared and supported by all members of the executive and that support needs to extend beyond the terms of the current executive as it will take many years to fully implement an e-learning strategy.

- Developing an institutional e-learning strategy is not a one-time event. Planning for e-learning needs to be an ongoing process to keep up with the rapid pace of technological change.
- Planning for e-learning needs to be integrated with overall educational planning, particularly budget and financial planning.

The draft BCIT institutional e-learning Strategy met most of these criteria. The vision put forward is perhaps not a prescription for radical change but there is a clear transformational imperative underlying the strategy. It will not be clear if the vision is shared by all members of the executive team until it is brought forward for discussion and approval, but certainly the executive fully supported the recommendation to develop an e-learning strategy. Similarly, we will not know if planning for e-learning becomes an ongoing process until the proposed strategy is approved and implemented. However, the notion of continuous planning is already in place for the broader institutional strategic planning at the institute. And finally, one of the recommendations of the proposed strategy is to ensure that planning for e-learning is integrated with the overall educational planning process, and particularly the budget development process.

There is a tendency to see e-learning as a technical issue but it should be about educational transformation and making education more accessible, flexible, relevant and meaningful for learners. Technical solutions are needed to achieve these learning goals, but we need to remind ourselves that the technology is there to support and enhance the learning experience. We also need to remember that how change is viewed and implemented in an organization is critical to the successful implementation of e-learning. The five models of change described by de Freitas and Oliver (2005) provide useful insight into the issue of change management. Perhaps more relevant is their assertion that neither a top-down nor a bottom-up approach to planning alone is sufficient. Instead, they argue, we should consider a combined approach in which policy, strategy and activities interact and inform one another. Finally, planning for e-learning should be integrated into broader institutional planning and it should be an ongoing process that provides for continuous input from the teaching staff.

References

Bates, A. W. (2000). *Managing Technological Change: Strategies for College and University Leader*. San Francisco: Jossey-Bass.

Bates, A. W. (2007). Strategic Planning for eLearning in a Polytechnic. In M. Bullen & D. Janes (Eds.), *Making the Transition to ELearning: Strategies & Issues* (pp. 47–65). Hershey, PA: Information Science.

Bates, A. W., & Sangrà, A. (2011). *Managing Technology in Higher Education: Strategies for Transforming Teaching and Learning*. San Francisco: Jossey-Bass.

Bergquist, W. H., & Pawlak, K. (2008). *Engaging the Six Cultures of the Academy*. San Francisco: Jossey-Bass.

Birnbaum, R. (2001). *Management Fads in Higher Education: Where They Come From, What They Do, Why They Fail*. San Francisco: Jossey-Bass.

Bogost, I. (2012). *MOOCs Are Marketing. The Question Is Can They Be More*? Retrieved January 21, 2013, from http://www.bogost.com/blog/moocs_are_marketing.shtml

Bullen, M., & Janes, D. (2007). Preface. In M. Bullen & D. Janes (Eds.), *Making the Transition to ELearning: Strategies & Issues* (pp. vii-xiv). Hershey, PA: Information Science.

Christensen, C. M., & Eyring, H. (2011). *The Innovative University. Changing the DNA of Higher Education from the Inside Out*. San Francisco: Jossey-Bass.

Dahlstrom, E. (2012, September). *ECAR Study of Undergraduate Students and Information Technology, 2012* (Research Report). Louisville, CO: EDUCAUSE Center for Applied Research. Retrieved July 22, 2013, from: http://www.educause.edu/ecar.

de Freitas, S., & Oliver, M. (2005). Does eLearning policy drive change in higher education? A case study relating models of organizational change to eLearning implementation. *Journal of Higher Education Policy & Management, 27*(1), 81–95.

Haughey, M. (2007). *Organizational Models for Faculty Support: The Response of Canadian Universities.* In M. Bullen & D.P. Janes (Eds.), Making the Transition to E-Learning: Strategies and Issues (pp. 17–32). Hershey, PA: Information Science.

JISC (2008). *Great Expectations of ICT: How Higher Education Institutions Are Measuring Up.* Report of the Joint Information Systems Committee (JISC), UK. Retrieved July 22, 2013, from: http://www.jisc.ac.uk/media/documents/publications/jiscgreatexpectationsfinalreportjune08.pdf

Kim, J. (2013). *MOOCs, Online Learning and the Wrong Conversation.* Retrieved January 21, 2013, from: http://www.insidehighered.com/blogs/technology-and-learning/moocs-onlineLearning-and-wrong-conversation

Nardi, B., & O'Day, V. (1999). *Information Ecologies: Using Technology With Heart.* Cambridge, MA: MIT Press.

OECD (2005). *E-Learning in Tertiary Education: Where Do We Stand?* Paris: OECD.

Pedró, F. (2009). New Millennium Learners in Higher Education: Evidence and Policy Implications. Paris: OECD-CERI.

Tilsley, A. (2013, January 29). Not Rushing Into MOOCs. *Inside Higher Education.* Retrieved from: /01/29/yale-takes-time-reflect-evaluate-jumping-moocs"www.insidehighered.com/news/2013/01/29/yale-takes-time-reflect-evaluate-jumping-moocs

Vaidhyanathan, S. (2012). *What's the Matter with MOOCs?* Retrieved January 21, 2013, from: http://chronicle.com/blogs/innovations/whats-the-matter-with-moocs/33289

Wenger, E. (1998). *Communities of Practice.* Cambridge: Cambridge University Press.

10

E-learning Design—From Instructional Events to Elements

Florence Martin

Introduction

Robert Gagné, in the first edition of his book *The Conditions of Learning* (1965), proposed nine events of instruction that provide a sequence for organizing a lesson. These events remain the foundation of current instructional design practice. They represent desirable conditions for effective learning in an instructional lesson and increase the probability of successful learner achievement. The events serve as a major vehicle for incorporating the conditions of learning into an instructional situation, and serve as a framework for the design of lessons both for the face-to-face classroom and for e-learning. Several authors have conducted further research on the events of instruction that promote student learning from an instructional program (Dick, Carey, & Carey, 2005; Sullivan & Higgins, 1983).

The emphasis on specifying behavioral objectives and providing frequent practice and feedback to enhance the mastery of objectives show that there is a strong behavioral emphasis in these events. However, focusing on the aspects of learning (such as thinking, reflection, memory, and motivation) also brings out the emphasis of cognitive learning psychology. These events of instruction are deliberately arranged external events to support the learning process (Gagné, 1985). This chapter reviews literature on instructional events and provides practical suggestions in the design of e-learning lessons. This is supported by the examples from an e-learning module titled "Know Your Computer" which was designed by the author.

From Instructional Events in the Classroom to Instructional Elements for E-learning

The instructional events that Gagné incorporated into his model have been the subject of a substantial body of research. Figure 10.1 is an adaptation of Gagné's nine events. A tenth event on "review," which is not on Gagné's list, has been included.

1. Attention (Gaining Attention)

This event alerts the learner on reception of stimuli. In order for any learning to take place, the attention of the learner must first be captured. Attention could be gained by the introduction of

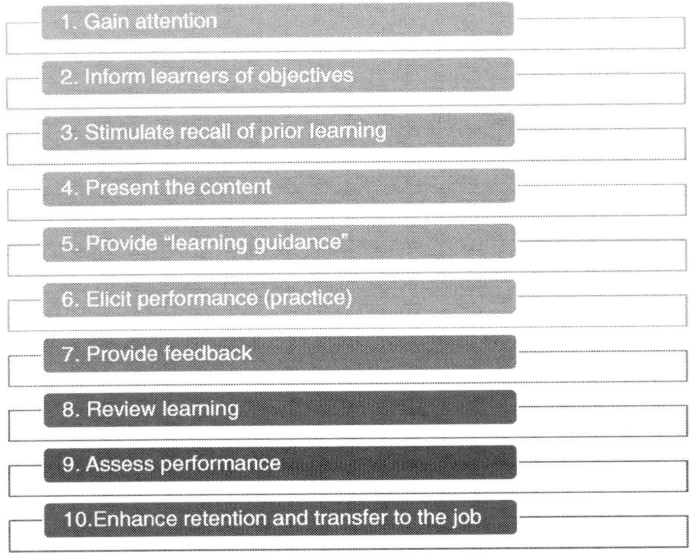

Figure 10.1 Adaptation of Gagné's nine events
Adapted from Gagné & Driscoll, 1988.

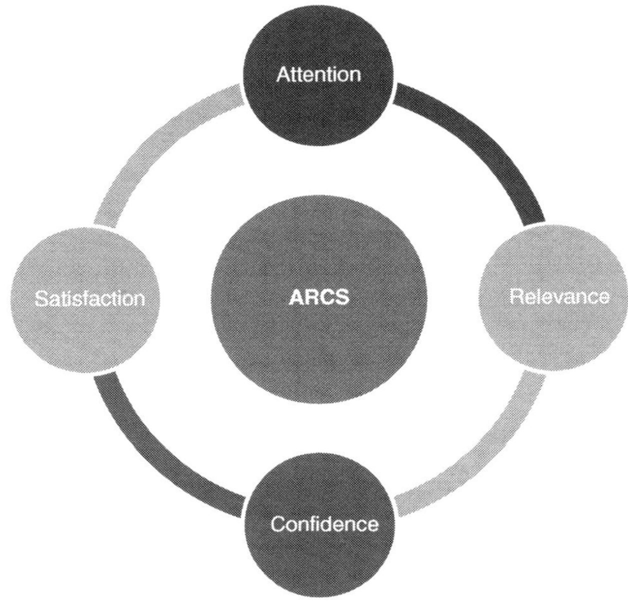

Figure 10.2 Keller's ARCS Model
Reprinted with permission from John M. Keller.

a rapid stimulus change such as change in the room's brightness, a sudden sound, or alteration in the pitch of the teacher's voice (Gagné & Driscoll, 1988).

John Keller's ARCS model explains how an instructor can ensure that the learner is motivated to learn and can gain and sustain the learner's attention.

Keller's strategies (Keller, 1987) for attention include perceptual arousal (creating curiosity), inquiry arousal (increasing curiosity), and variability (maintaining interest). Perceptual arousal is created by the use of novel, surprising, incongruous, or uncertain events in instruction. Inquiry arousal is created by seeking behavior by posing or having the learner generate questions or a problem to solve. Variability is created by varying the elements of instruction (Keller & Suzuki, 1988). According to Keller, it is easier to design for learner motivation in a classroom setting, where teachers can respond to changes as soon as they sense them. However, it is a greater challenge to make self-directed learning environments responsive to the motivational requirements of the learners (Keller, 1999).

Gigliotti (1995) considered a self-assembled slide show featuring novelty and humor to assist the lecturer in gaining attention and help in avoiding the boredom of the audience. A variety of communication techniques, such as discussion questions, help one to capture and maintain the attention of the learners (Catt, Miller, & Schallenkamp, 2007). Rieber (1990) pointed out that gaining attention is one of the major functions of animation. Zhu and Grabowski (2006) compared the effects of web-based animation with static graphics to gain the attention of learners. It is important not only to gain the attention of the learner at the beginning of the module, but also to maintain that attention throughout the module.

In an e-learning course, attention can be gained by

- a thought-provoking question or an interesting fact;
- an animated title screen sequence accompanied by sound effects or music that startles the senses with auditory or visual stimuli;
- engaging learners with interactive screens where they click in response to instruction;
- asking the learner to enter his or her name, and personalizing the module for the learner by referring to him or her by their name;
- stating expectations for the learner;
- providing high-quality multimedia in the form of a video or visual.

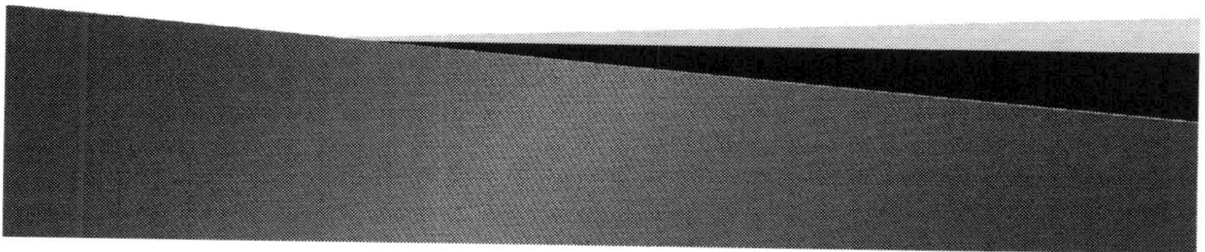

Figure 10.3 Title Screen of the IPSO Module
Surface: Available under Creative Commons license. Some rights reserved by Wilson Hui.

2. Objectives (Informing the Learner of the Objective)

An instructional objective is a statement that describes an intended outcome of instruction (Mager, 1984). Objectives help to activate a mental set that focuses learner attention and directs selective perception of specific lesson content (Gagné, 1985). According to Ausubel (1968), stating an objective at the beginning of instruction will help the individual learners to structure their own learning. Reiser and Dick (1996) state,

> At a fairly early stage, learners should be informed of what it is that they are going to be able to do when they finish the instructional process. By knowing what will be expected of them, learners may be better able to guide themselves through that process.
>
> (p. 48)

Objectives are critical to good design and to effective communication regarding intent. Providing objectives establishes expectancy in the learner and contributes to self-efficacy (Gagné & Driscoll, 1988). Providing objectives gives the learner an overall picture of the course and informs the learner of what is expected of him or her at the end of the lesson. This motivates the learner to complete the lesson. Objectives also form the basis for assessment and evaluation. When clear, concise behavioral objectives are developed, it is easier to evaluate the impact of the program or educational activity (Boone & Boone, 2005). An instructor is able to practically and efficiently evaluate how well learners are progressing toward the achievement of a goal in an online discussion by identifying purposeful online interactions that work toward defined learning goals/objectives (Seo, 2006). Well-written objectives are used to select good assessments, content, and activities, and to point out what's needed for a highly effective course (Shank, 2005). When students are not evaluated against objectives, it does not help us measure if the learners have mastered the skills that they were expected to master from the course.

Objectives are like a road map that tells the learner where he or she is going. Objectives must be stated appropriately in order for them to be useful in instructional planning and assessment of student learning. The two elements that have to be clearly specified when writing an objective are: 1) the description of the expected student performance and 2) the description of conditions for assessing. It is also important to use verbs that indicate observable behavior rather than internal state (Sullivan & Higgins, 1983). Objectives are generally sequenced in a particular order so that each skill can be built upon and the learner feels supported in the instructions (Hannafin & Peck, 1988) and reduces memory load (Nesbit & Hunka, 1987). Hannafin (1987) found that, when computer-based instruction was systematically designed, the presence of objectives did not make a difference, but that it did influence performance in lessons that were not well designed. Research on effectiveness of objectives in computer-based cooperative learning indicated that learners who received instructional objectives performed significantly better on posttest items than learners who received either advance organizers or no orienting activities (Klein & Cavalier, 1999).

In an e-learning course, you can include objectives by

- stating the objectives at the beginning of each section in the e-learning module and listing them again at the end of the module;
- writing a version of the objective for the learner that is different from the three-part objective that you write for the e-learning team. Make it sound exciting and fun;
- starting each section of the e-learning module with a scenario, at the end of which you ask the learner, "do you know what you would do in this situation?", and then provide them in easy words, what they would be able to do at the end of the section;

- approaching it from the learner's perspective and how it will help the learner. For example, as a teacher, you may find it necessary to integrate different technology in various situations. In this module, you will learn how to use the smartnotebook application to create effective smartboard lessons. This will help learners see the value in the e-learning module.

Here is an example of using a scenario to introduce the objectives: http://Elearning-examples.s3.amazonaws.com/emergprep/story.html

3. Prior Knowledge (Stimulating Recall of Prior Learning)

Jonassen and Grabowski (1993) defined prior knowledge as the knowledge, skills, or abilities brought by learners to the learning environment before instruction. Before new learning takes place, previously learned items have to be retrieved (Gagné & Driscoll, 1988). When there are links to personal experience and knowledge, it helps the learners to encode and store information in long-term memory. One simple way to stimulate recall is to ask questions about previous experiences, the understanding of previous concepts, or content learned (Kruse & Kevin, 1999). This process of asking questions helps scaffold student learning. Bransford and Johnson (1972) demonstrated that prior knowledge is an important factor in learning and memory. Ausubel's (1968) assimilation theory considered prior knowledge as the foundation for learning. Prior knowledge enhances human information processing by increasing the accessibility of knowledge and reducing the load on working memory. Prior knowledge is believed to influence the direction of attention, the encoding of information, its processing in working memory, its storage in the long-term memory, and the retrieval of information from long-term memory (Dochy, 1994).

Learning Objectives

At the end of this section, you will be able to:

- Explain input, processing, storage, and output.
- Describe the function associated with the input operation in a computer.
- Describe the function associated with the processing operation in a computer.
- Describe the function associated with the storage operation in a computer.
- Describe the function associated with the output operation in a computer.

Figure 10.4 Previously Presenting Objectives in the IPSO Module

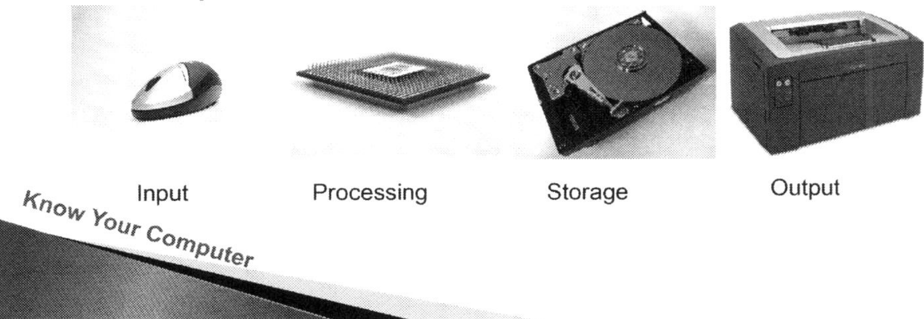

Figure 10.5 Presenting Objectives with a Personal Connection

Mouse: Available under Creative Commons license. Some rights reserved by Trostle. Processor: Available under Creative Commons license. All rights reserved by pdonaghy. Hard disk: Available under Creative Commons license. Some rights reserved by kuert_datenrettung. Printer: Available under Creative Commons license. Some rights reserved by Sir Adavis.

Dochy, Segers, and Buehl (1999) concluded from their research that prior knowledge is strongly associated with learning outcomes. Accurate prior knowledge can aid learners in extracting information from a text; inaccurate prior knowledge can actually interfere with learning (Shapiro, 2004). Hannafin (1997) suggested that individuals who have higher prior knowledge are able to quickly determine their own learning needs, generate their own learning strategies, and assimilate new information into their existing knowledge structure when compared to individuals who have lower prior knowledge. Meyer (2004) found that novice teachers held superficial conceptions of knowledge and prior knowledge, while expert teachers held a complex conception of prior knowledge and made use of their learners' prior knowledge in significant ways during instruction. According to Cook (2006), prior knowledge is critical in determining the impact of visual representation on learners' cognitive structures and processes. For learners with low prior knowledge, higher learning occurs when verbal and visual information are presented simultaneously and they are able to make referential connections between verbal and visual information content and their existing knowledge on their own (Mayer & Anderson, 1992).

In an e-learning course, you can ask the learners to recall their prior knowledge by

- asking them to describe a related personal experience;
- quizzing them on their previous experience;
- prompting them to brainstorm ideas related to the content;
- asking them to identify what they already know and what they don't know about a particular topic.

Figure 10.6 Reminding the Learner of Previous Situations

Hardware: Available under Creative Commons license. Some rights reserved by kniemla.

4. Information (Presenting the Content)

A significant part of the instructional process involves presenting learners with the necessary information for learning (Reiser & Dick, 1996). All models of direct instruction include presenting information to learners. The content presented depends on what is to be learned (Gagné & Driscoll, 1988). When the new content is actually presented to the learner, it should be chunked and organized meaningfully. Distinctive features of what is to be learned should be emphasized or highlighted when the information is presented (Gagné, 1985).

Multimedia computing also provides a variety of information presentation modality combinations (i.e., text, pictures, narration, animation, and video) (Andres & Petersen, 2001). Mayer's (2001) multimedia learning principles have strong implications to the design and development of multimedia content. Mayer's modality effect suggests that multimedia presentations invoke the use of both the verbal and the visual working memory channels, resulting in a reduction of the cognitive load imposed by increased information complexity. This stresses the importance of designing both textual and visual information. Mayer's multimedia principles have strong implications. The spatial contiguity principle states, "Students learn better when corresponding words and pictures are presented near rather than far from each other on the page or screen" (p. 81). The temporal contiguity principle states, "Students learn better when corresponding words and pictures are presented simultaneously rather than successively" (p. 96) The coherence principle states, "Students learn better when extraneous material is excluded rather than included" (p. 113). Students learning to perform a new task normally lack basic information needed to perform the task correctly. It is important to present the necessary information in a clear and concise manner and to present only the information necessary for learning to perform this task. The redundancy principle states, "Students learn better from animation and narration than from animation, narration, and on-screen text" (p. 184). The benefits of the flexibility of information presentation in multimedia educational systems make it necessary for designers to think about linking and timing of what is to be presented to the learner and when (Tong, 2001).

In an e-learning course, you can make the information provided effective by

- applying Mayer's Multimedia Principles such as presenting the information in a variety of modalities (text, pictures, narration, animation, and video);
- organizing and chunking information;
- providing information that is aligned to the objectives and assessment;
- emphasizing the important aspects in the lesson by highlighting or by providing sufficient contrast from the rest of the content;
- creating content as reusable learning objects, which will be beneficial to the designer
- applying text design and graphic design principles.

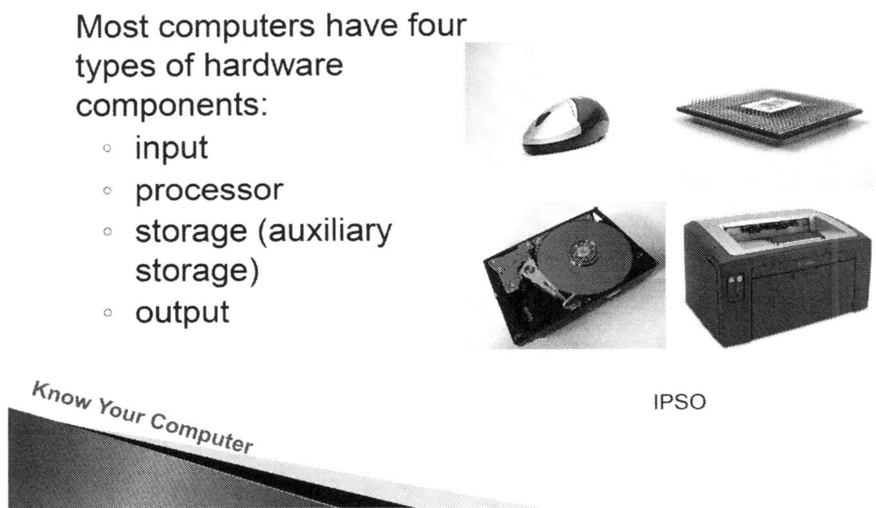

Figure 10.7 Presenting Chunked Information

Mouse: Available under Creative Commons license. Some rights reserved by Trostle. Processor: Available under Creative Commons license. All rights reserved by pdonaghy. Hard disk: Available under Creative Commons license. Some rights reserved by kuert_datenrettung. Printer: Available under Creative Commons license. Some rights reserved by Sir Adavis.

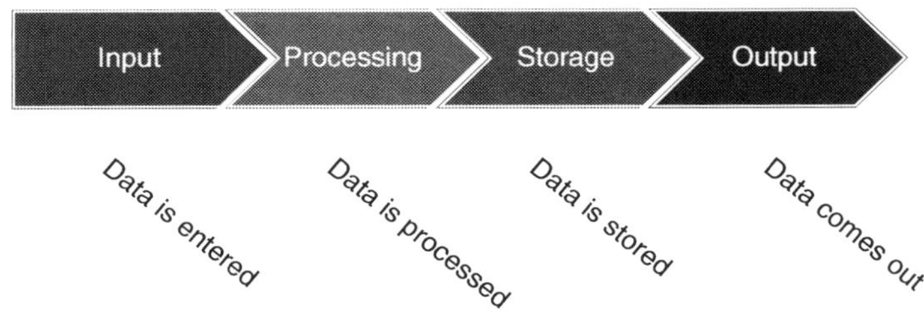

Figure 10.8 Presenting Text and Visuals to Explain the Process

5. Examples (Providing Learning Guidance)

This is the event that brings about meaningful organization (semantic encoding) and helps in the entry of the content learned into the long-term memory (Gagné & Driscoll, 1988). To help learners encode and store information in long-term memory, additional guidance should be provided along with the presentation of new content (information). Guidance is provided by the use of examples, nonexamples, case studies, graphical representation, mnemonics, and analogies that can be used to further clarify new content that is presented (Kruse & Kevin, 1999).

Walczyk and Hall (1989) reported a significant difference for participants who received examples over those who did not in comprehension assessments. Freitag and Sullivan (1995) found that adults who received examples in a training program significantly outperformed those who did not. A considerable amount of research has been conducted recently on the effects of worked examples as an instructional aid (Atkinson & Renkl, 2007; Atkinson, Catrambone, & Merrill, 2003; Atkinson, Renkl, & Merrill, 2003; Renkl, Stark, Gruber, & Mandl, 1998). Crippen and Earl (2007) found that the combination of a worked example with a self-explanation prompt produced improvement in performance, problem-solving skills, and self-efficacy.

In an e-learning course, you can provide examples by

- presenting verbal or graphical information that provides additional clarification of rules or information presented to learners;
- providing worked examples for the learner, especially in mathematical content.

Figure 10.9 Presenting an Example to Teach the Concept

6. Practice (Eliciting Performance)

Practice is defined as the event of instruction provided to learners after they have been given information required to master an objective (Gagné, 1985). This is the event that asks the learner to practice what is to be learned (Gagné & Driscoll, 1988). Eliciting performance provides an opportunity for learners to confirm their correct understanding, and repetition increases the likelihood of retention (Kruse & Kevin, 1999). Unlike questions in a posttest, the exercise within a lesson should be used to help the learners confirm their understanding and not for formal scoring. Practice is effective when it is aligned with the assessment in the form of a posttest and also is aligned with the skills, knowledge, and attitudes reflected in the objectives (Reiser & Dick, 1996). Learners attempt practice activities after they have been presented with the information required to master an objective. Practice provides an opportunity for the learner to confirm his or her understanding of what they have learned. The repetition of the task also helps the learner to retain the information.

Practice provides significant learning experience if learners are provided with an opportunity to perform an identical task to that assessed on the posttest. It is important to reinforce the learners by helping them practice on the exact task stated in the objectives. Researchers have found that practice has a significant effect on performance. Research has found that practice effects were more pronounced for facts than for applications in interactive video (Philips et al., 1988) and in computer-based instruction (Hannafin, Philips, & Tripp, 1986; Hannafin et al., 1987). Philips et al. (1988) found a significant difference favoring practice over no practice in an interactive video in which practice items were embedded questions.

Input Device – Practice

- Identify the peripheral that is used to transfer data from the outside world into a computer system. Select one that applies and click Submit.
  A. Input device
  B. Processing device
  C. Storage device
  D. Output device

Figure 10.10 Providing Practice by a Multiple-Choice Item

Simple practice typically tends to support the learning of factual information, while elaborate practice tends to aid the learning of inferential information (Philips, 1987). Hannafin (1987) confirmed the power of practice in learning of verbal information. Factually explicit practice items have increased learning of verbal information, but have not increased learning in higher-level skills (Hamaker, 1986; Philips et al., 1988). Higher-order questions are more effective than factual questions in helping learners apply what they learn from a lesson (Andre, 1979; Hamaker, 1986). When combined with feedback, practice also enables learners to confirm their correct understandings and identify their incorrect ones. This increases the probability of retention of correct responses and decreases the probability of incorrect responses (Philips et al., 1988; Reiser & Dick, 1996).

In an e-learning course, you can provide practice by

- creating interactive activities such as multiple-choice items, drag-and-drop items;
- creating and facilitating online discussions on a given topic or writing a short answer or an essay using web 2.0 tools;
- providing feedback on the practice items and not using it for formal scoring;
- providing frequent practice;
- creating practice items that are aligned with the objectives and assessment in the module;
- providing an opportunity to solve problems via problem-solving scenarios.

7. Feedback (Providing Feedback)

Feedback is defined as "knowledge of one's performance provided" (Delgado & Prieto, 2003, p. 73). Practice provides an opportunity for feedback that confirms the learner's answer as being correct or indicates that it is incorrect. As learners practice new behavior, specific and immediate feedback on their performance has to be provided (Kruse & Kevin, 1999). The display of performance should be closely tied to informative feedback, so that reinforcement can occur. This informs the learner of the degree of correctness or incorrectness of the performance (Gagné & Driscoll, 1988). Feedback is provided to the learners after they get a chance to practice. A learner needs to know whether the selected option is correct or not. Practice provides an opportunity for feedback that confirms the learner's answer as being correct or indicates that it is incorrect.

Feedback strengthens the probability of correct responses and reduces the probability of subsequent incorrect responses (Philips et al., 1988). Providing feedback in response to written instruction increases the amount of correct information remembered from the target material (Kulhavy, Yekovich, & Dyer, 1979). Feedback facilitates criterion performance as it corrects the inaccurate information obtained during instruction, and has little effect on correct responses where the learner has correct understanding of the text information (Kulhavy & Anderson, 1972). Kulhavy and Stock (1989) describe feedback as information that includes two components: verification and elaboration. Verification is the simple, dichotomous judgment that an initial response was right or wrong, while elaboration consists of all substantive information contained in a feedback message. Pridemore and Klein (1995) found that the level of feedback (elaboration feedback, correct-answer feedback, and no feedback) had a significant effect on achievement and attitudes. Simple forms of feedback are effective when learners answer items correctly and for verbal information types of learning (Kulhavy, White, Topp, Chan, & Adams, 1985). However, more elaborate forms, such as providing and explaining the correct answer and explaining why a wrong answer is incorrect, are helpful when learners answer items incorrectly (Kulhavy, 1977).

Input Device – Practice

- Identify the peripheral that is used to transfer data from the outside world into a computer system. Select one that applies and click Submit.
  A. Input device
  B. Processing device
  C. Storage device
  D. Output device

Input device is the correct answer. This is the device that collects the data from outside and transfers it to the computer.

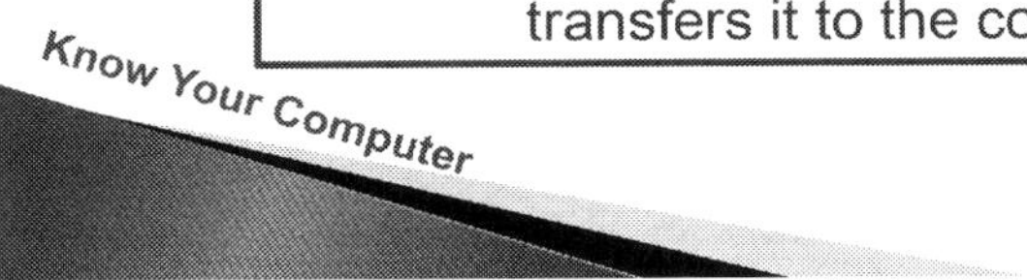

Figure 10.11 Providing Feedback to a Multiple-Choice Practice Item

In an e-learning course, you can deliver feedback by

- providing immediate responses to interactive practice activities such as multiple-choice items;
- further explaining to the learner why other answers are incorrect;
- providing responses via text and audio.

8. Review (Not an Original Event in Gagné's Sequence)

The review process typically provides an outline of the key information that was presented to learners. It is intended to reinforce learning at the end of the instruction, often just before students are tested. Review is used to provide an outline of the key information that was presented to learners. This is an instructional event that is not included in Gagné's nine events of instruction. However, it further reinforces the content learned and it is typically provided between the feedback for practice and the assessment. Mattiske (2001) suggests that holding a review activity immediately after participants have learned something new reassures them that they are learning. Klein and Pridemore (2004) suggest that learners should be given time to reflect and review after new information has been presented to them. Gagné et al. (2005) indicate that spaced reviews should be given to learners to help them retrieve and use newly acquired information. It is good to provide some format of review or summary at the end of the lesson before the students are ready to take their assessment. This helps them remember the content that was taught earlier and also helps them reflect on what was learned in the lesson.

Reiser and Dick (1996) cite the value of reviews to bring closure to instruction and to help reinforce the skills and knowledge students should have acquired. Research has suggested that reviews benefit learning of incidental material because instructional stimuli are introduced after the

Input Device – Review

Keyboard	Sends messages by pressing keys
Mouse	Sends data by clicking
Joystick	A rotary lever and used in computer games
Digitizing tablet	Pointing device that inputs drawings
Touch sensitive screen	Interacts by touching the screen
Light screen	Draws directly on the screen
Digital cameras	Inputs images from camera to computer
Optical mark reader	Inputs numbers or letters
Scanner	Scans photo or text into computer

Figure 10.12 Providing Review in a Table Format

content has been presented and initially processed (Kaplan & Simmons, 1974). The use of reviews to summarize salient information has been shown to enhance learning (Hartley & Davies, 1976). In studies on prose learning, reviews of relevant information yielded significantly better performance than information presented without review (Bruning, 1968). Lee (1980) examined the effects of different types of review questions on transfer skills on seventh-grade math students and found that relatively difficult review questions can effectively facilitate the retention of these skills.

In an e-learning course, you can provide review by

- creating it as a summary page, a table with the outline of the content provided, or a concept map of the lesson;
- providing it right before learners complete the assessment.

9. Assessment (Assessing Performance)

Assessments are used to determine whether and to what extent learners have learned specific knowledge or skills based on the instructional goals and objectives of the lesson. Upon completing the instructional module, learners should be given a posttest or final assessment that helps to measure their learning. This assessment should be completed without additional coaching, feedback, or hints. Mastery of material or certification is granted after learners have achieved a certain score (Kruse & Kevin, 1999). Herman, Aschbacher, and Winters (1992) point out that "learners perform better when they know the goal, see models, know how their performance compares to the standard" (p. 20). Assessments should also be designed in such a way that they are aligned with the objectives and measure the learning of all the objectives in the instructional material.

Assessment helps learners reflect on the course as a whole and consider what they have gained from it. It also provides an opportunity for learners to think about their learning process and what has helped and hindered it. Assessment should be designed such that it helps learners make connections between classroom material and "real life," which is crucial to intellectual growth. In addition, the assignment gives the teacher one final opportunity to offer learners personal feedback, such as study tips based on the learning strengths and weaknesses (Lerner, 2007). Assessment helps assess how well students can perform on each objective. It helps in determining whether the students learned what was intended and how well they learned it. When writing the assessment items, the two things to consider are: 1) Does the assessment item and procedures require the same performance of the student as that specified in the instructional objective? and 2) Does the assessment item provide the same conditions or given as those specified in the instructional objective? Assessment items should be clearly written so that students understand exactly what is required (Sullivan & Higgins, 1983).

In 1956, a group of educational psychologists headed by Benjamin Bloom found that more than 95 percent of test questions required learners merely to recall facts. In response, Bloom developed a classification of intellectual behavior important in learning. These six levels, now revised (Remembering, Understanding, Applying, Analyzing, Evaluating, and Creating), start with recall of facts and move up through increasingly complex and abstract levels to creation.

Along with the traditional assessment, alternate assessments have also become popular. Since the implementation of IDEA (Individuals with Disabilities Education Act), three academic assessment response formats have been used for alternate assessment: portfolios, observations, and performance assessments. With *portfolios*, teachers collect student work samples during the year, usually selected according to some general criteria. With *observations*, teachers are asked to select a behavior that represents a student need and then observe it in a functional environment. *Performance assessments* reflect the kind of measurement most similar to the traditional testing program. Basically, a series of tasks is administered to the student and scored in terms of correctness (Yovanaff & Tindall, 2007).

An assessment rubric delineates the expectations for a task or assignment (Stevens & Levi, 2005). As a result of clearly describing the concept and evidence of its understanding, students and faculty are more likely to recognize it when students perform it. In addition, rubrics facilitate communication among students and provide students, preceptors, and faculty with language to foster both feedback and discussion (Lasater, 2007).

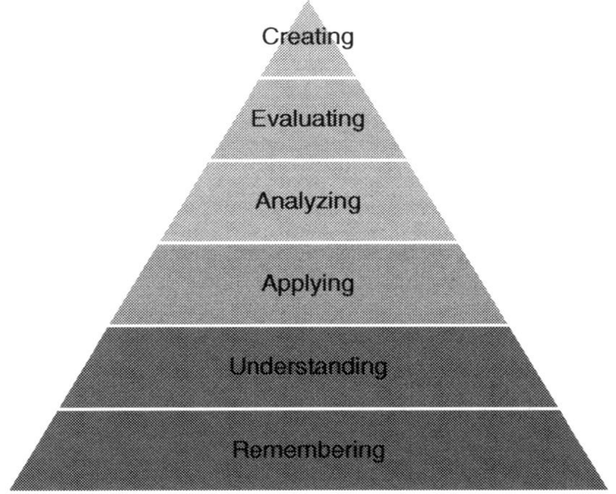

Figure 10.13 Revised Bloom's Taxonomy

Input Device – Assessment

1. Which of the following is called a "point and click" device? Select one that applies and click Submit.

A. Magnetic reader
B. Optical mark reader
C. Mouse
D. Digital camera

Submit

Figure 10.14 Assessing the Learner

In an e-learning course, you can provide assessment by

- creating different types of assessment items, such as short answers, essays, multiple-choice answers, drag-and-drop, and true/false;
- creating assessment as posttest or an alternative assessment, such as a portfolio or project depending on the skill that is taught; and
- grading some of the different test items automatically so that immediate feedback is provided to the student. The disadvantage of these automatic assessments is that students are not seeing the thought behind the answer instruction.

10. Retention and Transfer (Enhancing Retention and Transfer)

The repetition of learned concepts is an effective means of aiding retention (Kruse & Kevin, 1999). Transfer of learning to other fields is made possible by providing a variety of examples and situations. Promotion of transfer of learning is made possible by instruction that provides novel tasks for the learner that are spaced over time and calls for the use of what was learned previously (Gagné & Driscoll, 1988). Retention can be defined as the power of retaining and recalling past experiences and information gained. The underlying rationale for any kind of formal instruction is the assumption that knowledge, skills, and attitudes learned in this setting will be recalled accurately, and will be used in some other context at some time in the future. If we want transfer, then not only do we have to increase learner performance while at school but we also need to teach in ways that actually enhance the probabilities of transfer. Teachers can also better prepare students by giving them predictable real-world tests.

Halpern and Hakel (2003) provide five principles for how one can enhance retention and transfer: 1) Provide practice at retrieval, 2) Vary the conditions under which learning takes place. It makes learning harder for learners but results in better learning, 3) Require learners to take information that is presented in one format and re-represent it in an alternative format, 4) Remember that lectures work well for learning assessed with recognition tests, but work badly for understanding, 5) Bear in mind that the act of remembering influences what learners will and will not remember in the future. These principles can be applied in any adult learning situation, including distance education with online components, learning from texts, laboratory and classroom instruction, and learning in informal settings. Gagné and Driscoll (1988) mention that spaced reviews enhance retention and retrieval of what is learned. Discovery learning activities were found to improve student learning, retention, and transfer (Foster, 1996). The students became more aware of what they were doing and why they were doing it when the teacher asked them leading questions that helped them focus on the task at hand.

In an e-learning course, you can enhance transfer and retention by

- asking questions on how learners will apply the content learned in their workplace or other life situations;
- having learners complete a reflection on the importance of the e-learning module, and whether it would help them on the job.

Conclusion

The instructional events have been very beneficial in the design of lesson plans and continue to be used by teachers. The instructional elements provide a similar structure for the design of e-learning lessons, and when designed appropriately, make the e-learning modules effective. This chapter provided a review of research on instructional events followed by steps in the design of effective e-learning using instructional elements. This chapter has implications for those who are designing and developing e-learning. A number of the instructional elements proposed in this paper should be included in the design of e-learning. This chapter also has implications for those who use e-learning in their online and blended courses.

References

Andre, T. (1979). Does answering higher-level questions while reading facilitate productive learning? *Review of Educational Research, 49*, 280–318.

Andres, H., & Petersen, C. (2001). Presentation media, information complexity, and learning outcomes. *Journal of Educational Technology Systems, 30(3)*, 225–246. doi:10.2190/3TWA-NVA7-0MEW-402J

Atkinson, R.K., Catrambone, R., & Merrill, M.M. (2003). Aiding transfer in statistics: Examining the use of conceptually oriented equations and elaborations during subgoal learning. *Journal of Educational Psychology, 95(4)*, 762–773.

Atkinson, R.K., & Renkl, A. (2007). Interactive example-based learning environments: Using interactive elements to encourage effective processing of worked examples. *Educational Psychology Review, 19(3)*, 375–386.

Atkinson, R.K., Renkl, A., & Merrill, M.M. (2003). Transitioning from studying examples to solving problems: Effects of self-explanation prompts and fading worked-out steps. *Journal of Educational Psychology, 95(4)*, 774–783.

Ausubel, D.P. (1968). *Educational psychology: A cognitive view*. New York, NY: Holt, Rinehart and Winston.

Boone, H.N., & Boone, D.A. (2005). ABC's of behavioral objectives—Putting them to work for evaluation. *Journal of Extension (ASCII Edition), 43(5)*, 1.

Bransford, J.D., & Johnson, M.K. (1972). Contextual prerequisites for understanding: Some investigations of comprehension and recall. *Journal of Verbal Learning and Verbal Behavior, 11*, 717–726.

Bruning, R. H. (1968). Effects of review and test like events within the learning of prose materials. *Journal of Educational Psychology, 59(1)*, 16–19.

Catt, S., Miller, D., & Schallenkamp, K. (2007). You are the key: Communicate for learning effectiveness. *Education (Chula Vista, Calif.), 127(3)*, 369–377.

Cook, M.P. (2006). Visual representations in science education: The influence of prior knowledge and cognitive load theory on instructional design principles. *Science Education, 90(6)*, 1073–1091.
Crippen, K.J., & Earl, B. (2007). The impact of web-based worked examples and self-explanation on performance, problem solving, and self-efficacy. *Computers & Education, 49(3)*, 809–821.
Delgado, A.R., & Prieto, G. (2003). The effect of item feedback on multiple-choice test responses. *British Journal of Psychology, 94*, 73–85.
Dick, W., Carey, L.M., & Carey, J. 0. (2005). *The systematic design of instruction* (6th ed.). Boston, MA: Pearson/Allyn and Bacon.
Dochy, F., Segers, M., & Buehl, M.M. (1999). The relation between assessment practices and outcomes of studies: The case of research on prior knowledge. *Review of Educational Research, 69*, 145–186.
Dochy, F.J.R.C. (1994). Prior knowledge and learning. In T. Husen & T.N. Postlethwaite (Eds.), *International encyclopedia of education* (pp. 4698–4702). New York: Pergamon Press.
Foster, W.T. (1996). A discovery learning activity to improve student learning, retention, and transfer. *The Technology Teacher, 56*, 34.
Freitag, E., & Sullivan, H. (1995). Matching learner preference to amount of instruction: An alternative form of learner control. *Educational Technology Research and Development, 43(2)*, 5–14.
Gagné, R. (1965). *The conditions of learning*. New York: Holt, Rinehart & Winston.
Gagné, R. (1985). *The conditions of learning* (4th ed.). New York: Holt, Rinehart & Winston.
Gagné, R., & Driscoll, M. (1988). *Essentials of learning for instruction* (2nd ed.). Englewood Cliffs, NJ: Prentice-Hall.
Gagne, R. M., Golas, K. C., Keller, J. M., & Wagner, W. W. (2005). *Principles of instructional design*. Belmont, CA: Wadsworth.
Gigliotti, E. (1995). Let me entertain . . . er . . . teach you: Gaining attention through the use of slide shows. *Journal of Continuing Education in Nursing, 26*, 31–34.
Halpern, D.F., & Hakel, M. (2003). Applying the science of learning to the university and beyond: Teaching for long-term retention and transfer. *Change, 35(4)*, 36–41.
Hamaker, C. (1986). The effects of adjunct questions on prose learning. *Review of Educational Research, 56*, 212–242.
Hannafin, M. (1987). The effects of orienting activities, cueing and practice on learning of computer-based instruction. *Journal of Educational Research, 81(1)*, 48–53.
Hannafin, M.J. (1997, October). *Better learning with multimedia? Concepts and results from psychology and education*. Paper presented at the Multimedia und internet-neue perspektiven für die bildung, Gesellschaft für Padagogik und Information (GPI), Munich, Germany.
Hannafin, M.J., & Peck, K.L. (1988). *The design, development, and evaluation of instructional software*. New York, NY: Macmillan.
Hannafin, M., Philips, T., Rieber, T., & Garhart, C. (1987). The effects of orienting activities and cognitive processing time on factual and inferential learning. *Educational Communications and Technology Journal, 35*, 75–84.
Hannafin, M.J., Philips, T.L., & Tripps, S.D. (1986). The effects of orienting, processing, and practice activities on learning from interactive video. *Journal of Computer-Based Instruction, 13*, 134–139.
Hartley, J., & Davies, I. K. (1976). Pre-instructional strategies: The role of pretests, behavioral objectives, overviews, and advance organizers. *Review of Educational Research, 46*, 239–265.
Herman, J. L., Aschbacher, P. R., & Winters, L. (1992). *A practical guide to alternative assessment*. Alexandria, VA: Association for Supervision and Curriculum Development.
Jonassen, D.H., & Grabowski, B.L. (1993). *Handbook of individual differences, learning, and instruction*. Hillsdale, NJ: Erlbaum.
Kaplan, R., & Simmons, F. (1974). Effects of instructional objectives used as orienting stimuli or as summary/review upon prose learning. *Journal of Educational Psychology, 66(4)*, 614–622.
Keller, J.M. (1987). Strategies for stimulating the motivation to learn. *Performance and Instruction, 26(8)*, 1–7.
Keller, J.M. (1999). Using the ARCS motivational process in computer-based instruction and distance education. *New Directions for Teaching and Learning, 78*.
Keller, J.M., & Suzuki, K. (1988). Use of the ARCS motivation model in courseware design. In D.H. Jonassen (Ed.), *Instructional designs for microcomputer courseware*. Hillsdale, NJ: Lawrence Erlbaum.
Klein, J.D., & Cavalier, J.C. (1999). *Using cooperative learning and objectives with computer based instruction*. Paper presented at the Annual Convention of the Association for Educational Communications and Technology. Houston, Texas.
Klein, J.D., & Pridemore, D.R. (1994). Effects of orienting activities and practice on achievement, continuing motivation, and student behaviors in a cooperative learning environment. *Educational Technology Research and Development, 42(4)*, 41–54.

Klein, J.D., & Pridemore, D.R. (1995). Control of practice and level of feedback in computer-based instruction. *Contemporary Educational Psychology, 20*, 444–450.

Kruse, K., & Kevin, J. (1999). *Technology-Based training: The art and science of design, development and delivery.* San Francisco: Jossey-Bass.

Kulhavy, R.W. (1977). Feedback in written instruction. *Review of Educational Research, 47(1)*, 211–232.

Kulhavy, R.W., & Anderson, R.C. (1972). Delay-retention effect with multiple-choice tests. *Journal of Educational Psychology, 63*, 505–512.

Kulhavy, R.W., & Stock, W.A. (1989). Feedback in written instruction: The place of response certitude. *Educational Psychology Review, 1*, 279–308.

Kulhavy, R.W., White, M., Topp, B., Chan, A., & Adams, J. (1985). Feedback complexity and corrective efficiency. *Contemporary Educational Psychology, 10*, 285–291.

Kulhavy, R.W., Yekovich, F.R., & Dyer, J.W. (1979). Feedback and content review in programmed instruction. *Contemporary Educational Psychology, 4*, 91–98.

Lasater, K. (2007). Clinical judgment development: Using simulation to create an assessment rubric. *Journal of Nursing Education, 46(11)*, 496–503.

Lee, H. (1980). The effects of review questions and review passages on transfer skills. *Journal of Education Research, 73(6)*, 330–335.

Lerner, J. E. (2007). Teaching students to learn: Developing metacognitive skills with a learning assessment. *College Teaching, 55(1)*, 40.

Mager, R. F. (1984). *Preparing instructional objectives* (Rev. 2nd ed.). Belmont, CA: Fearon.

Mattiske, C. (2001). *Train for results: Maximize the impact of through review.* Warriewood, Australia: Business and Professional.

Mayer, R.E. (2001). *Multimedia learning.* New York: Cambridge University Press.

Mayer, R.E., & Anderson, R.B. (1992). The instructive animation: Helping students build connections between words and pictures in multimedia learning. *Journal of Educational Psychology, 84(4)*, 444–452.

Meyer, H. (2004). Novice and expert teachers' conceptions of learners' prior knowledge. *Science Education, 88(6)*, 970–983.

Nesbit, J.C., & Hunka, S. (1987). A method for sequencing instructional objectives which minimizes memory load. *Journal of Instructional Science, 16(2)*, 137–150.

Philips, T. L. (1987). *The effects of practice questions, processing task and reading ability on learning from computer-based instruction* (Unpublished doctoral dissertation). Pennsylvania State University, University Park, PA.

Philips, T.L., Hannafin, M., & Tripp, S. (1988). The effects of practice and orienting activities on learning from interactive video. *Educational Communications and Technology Journal, 36(2)*, 93–102.

Reiser, R.A., & Dick, W. (1996). *Instructional planning: A guide for teachers* (2nd ed.). Boston: Allyn and Bacon.

Renkl, A., Stark, R., Gruber, H., & Mandl, H. (1998). Learning from worked-out examples: The effects of example variability and elicited self-explanations. *Contemporary Educational Psychology, 23*, 90–108.

Rieber, L.P. (1990). Animation in a computer-based instruction. *Educational Technology Research and Development, 39(1)*, 77–86.

Seo, K.K. (2006). Coming out of the darkness: Utilizing a systematic approach to evaluate online discussion forums in light of learning objectives. *Educational Technology, 46(6)*, 24–28.

Shank, P. (2005). Writing learning objectives that help you teach and students learn (part 2). *Online Classroom*, 4–8.

Shapiro, A. M. (2004). How including prior knowledge as a subject variable may change outcomes of learning research. *American Educational Research Journal, 41(1)*, 59–89.

Stevens, D.D., & Levi, A.J. (2005). *Introduction to rubrics: An assessment tool to save grading time, convey effective feedback, and promote student learning.* Sterling, VA: Stylus.

Sullivan, H. J., & Higgins, N. (1983). *Teaching for competence.* New York: Teachers College Press.

Tong, A.K.Y. (2001). Linking and timing information presentation in multimedia educational systems. *Journal of Educational Multimedia and Hypermedia 10(2)*, 185–203.

Walczyk, J., & Hall, V. (1989). Effects of examples and embedded questions on the accuracy of comprehension self-assessments. *Journal of Educational Psychology, 81(3)*, 435–437.

Yovanaff, P., & Tindall, G. (2007). Scaling early reading alternate assessments with statewide measures. *Exceptional Children, 73(2)*, 184–201.

Zhu, L., & Grabowski, B. (2006). Web-based animation or static graphics: Is the extra cost of animation worth it? *Journal of Educational Multimedia and Hypermedia, 15(3)*, 329–347.

11

Competences for Teaching and Learning in an E-learning Setting

Guillermo Bautista and Anna Escofet

This chapter deals with the competences that both faculty and students should acquire to carry out learning processes in online and face-to-face settings and take part in them. These competences have been obtained and described in a research and development project (EDU2009-12125), financed by the government of Spain, where the aim was to analyse the so-called digital natives' uses, preferences and attitudes regarding digital technologies in higher education (Prensky, 2001; Trinder, Guiller, Margaryan, Littlejohn, and Nicol, 2008).

Educational institutions should put into practice policies and strategies in order for these competences to be acquired gradually by faculty as much as by students. These policies and strategies must go beyond a mere inclusion of technology in the classrooms. To that effect, new teaching methodologies and new instructional contents should be introduced both at the student—from initial to undergraduate level—and the teacher training level. In this new scenario the role and the tasks that faculty and students fulfil and develop will change and should be re-thought as regards traditional pedagogy.

ICT, University Students and Lecturers

The emergence of information and communication technology (ICT) in our societies has transformed the ways in which most of young people adopt forms of consumption and cultural production, and how they interact, communicate, find information and learn, as shown by several sociological, anthropological, communicational and educational studies and analyses (Turkle, 1995; Postman, 1991; Lankshear and Knobel, 2008). Throughout the last decade, this has generated different forms of identifying and referring to children and young people who have grown up surrounded by digital media. Many of these young people use multiple devices—computers, mobile telephones, digital cameras, game consoles, PDAs, portable audio and video players, etc.—that provide access to the Internet and have the supporting software to create and participate in social networks and other informal activities generally linked to free time.

One of the first references to the generation born into the digital world was made by Tapscott (1999), who named it the *Net Generation*, pointing to the appearance of new skills developed by this digital generation such as their facility for multitasking, the speed with which they carry out these tasks, their personalisation of digital tools and their constant innovation. Another conceptualisation was provided by Prensky (2001), who created the term *digital natives* to refer to this new generation characterised by having lived with digital media since birth and having adopted a new language that facilitates the use of multimedia environments. Later, Tapscott (2009) continued his research in this field along the same lines proposed by Prensky. Other authors such as Oblinger (2006) and Padró (2006) have written studies on the digital generation that are more focused on digital natives in formal educational contexts. Lenhart, Rainie and Lewis (2001) have also conducted research into what they call the *Instant message generation*. These authors argue that digital natives, who have integrated ICT into their everyday lives, tend to possess certain characteristics determined by the use of these technologies such as, for example, greater autonomy, a higher degree of interaction and decision-making and greater collaboration and communication among peers thanks to Web 2.0 tools.

However, recent studies indicate a lack of homogeneity in the use of technology among digital natives, and there is scant empirical evidence that digital natives are highly or very highly competent in the use of these technologies in all contexts. Investigations such as those conducted by Kennedy et al. (2006) question the existence of digital natives and their characteristics. In higher education, for example, it would seem that, although university students are very familiar with the use of digital technologies and tools, very few of them use these to produce content in formal education. In this regard, there is a clear difference between the technologies used in informal contexts and those which students use in their learning processes at university.

A recent study (Gros, García and Escofet, 2012) conducted among Catalan University students indicates that students have frequent and widespread access to ICT. The students consider themselves fairly competent in most areas. They use general technology (computers, mobile telephones and Internet) for rapid communication and good access to services and information. However, when looking beyond these technologies and tools, the patterns of access, use and preference among a wide range of different technologies show considerable variation. In fact, the data do not necessarily reveal that these competences are reflected in the habitual performance of academic tasks.

The outcomes of the above-mentioned study are consistent with other earlier research. The investigation carried out by the UCL-CIBER Group (2008) attempted to identify the knowledge that young university students possess in relation to the use of technology for research purposes. The results highlighted that most of the young people studied used the Internet casually and were capable of carrying out multiple tasks at the same time. These young people used the Internet for leisure and social purposes, but they did not use searches effectively in a formal setting. Therefore, the study concluded that the competences for a more formal use of the Internet in an educational context are not clear. Likewise, Duart, Gil, Pujol and Castaño (2008), in a study on Internet use in the Catalan university system, observed a difference between Internet use inside and outside the classroom. Outside the classroom, both teachers and students consider themselves habitual and expert Internet users for communication, social interaction and searching for information; while within the context of the university classroom they recognise much more restrictive and traditional uses.

Thus, it could be said that there is a large gap between informally used technology and that which is used in university education. As stated by Lorenzo, Oblinger and Dziuban (2006, 4), "Not all students have had the benefit of technology. Higher education comprises a highly diverse student body with a wide variety of information literacy capabilities".

It would seems clear, therefore, that we cannot assume that just because young people in developed countries have habitual access to technology that this means they know how to apply it strategically to optimise their learning in formal contexts.

An important consideration in this argument is the most common type of technology use in education. If we look at this data we find that university virtual campuses and Internet searches for information clearly predominate. However, a more creative use, or one linked to producing online knowledge, is much scarcer. The technological resources most used by teachers are not necessarily those that are most highly rated by students and vice versa. In fact, applications such as PowerPoint, Google Docs and YouTube are very highly rated by students, although the findings of the cited research (Gros, García and Escofet, 2012) reveal that these are rarely used to support academic tasks. Nevertheless, the degree to which some technologies and tools are being used indicates a promising number of opportunities to integrate technology into the university curriculum. The potential of these types of technologies is important and is being widely studied (Downes, 2004; Johnson, Levine, Smith and Stone, 2010) at present.

Universities are facing a great challenge: how to integrate young people's informal learning culture into teaching. In this framework, teachers play an important role in focusing and guiding the appropriate use of communication, sources of academic information and participative and collaborative environments; i.e., developing digital competences.

Digital Competences and University Teaching

Digital competences comprise the knowledge, skills and attitudes that enable the subject to resolve situations in various contexts (work, leisure, learning, social participation, etc.) linked to different forms of ICT use. (Ala-Mutka, 2011; Ferrari, 2012).

The need to acquire digital competences in the educational sphere, with the aim of teaching and learning more efficiently, paints a very different picture to the one we have been used to until now. These competences are linked to communicating; searching, managing and recreating information; and participating and collaborating with others. All while using digital tools and in virtual environments.

Using digital tools and virtual contexts requires adapting the knowledge, tasks and skills that teachers and students must possess and put into practice in face-to-face contexts, but it also calls for other new competences. In fact, it is not a case of replacing existing competences to suit the new context, but rather, of helping these skills to evolve and adding new ones to those that already exist. Face-to-face contexts are gradually becoming mixed environments as they are integrating and using digital environments and tools (chart 1). This variation of the formal setting for interaction between teachers and students in which learning occurs has changed dramatically in recent decades.

The physical classroom demands competences linked to face-to-face interaction, with a teaching plan for synchronous and ephemeral communication, a well-organised physical space and directed teaching activity, with fundamentally oral and gestural communication and clearly defined time fragments in which the teaching and learning action takes place. However, virtual or e-learning environments, which are increasingly converging in the organisational methods and resources that they use, involve other actions and requirements in teaching and learning, which is why they also call for other competences to be brought into play. Virtual learning environments offer a much wider range of possibilities for pedagogical interaction. More and more digital resources are being used in education. These increase the opportunities available to teaching staff and students in e-learning contexts. However, virtual environments do not allow the teacher to take such direct, immediate and hierarchical action in the activities that the students undertake in order to learn. As different authors have pointed out when defining the characteristics of teaching in online environments, the teacher is seen more as a guide or companion, among other diverse functions, than as the conductor of the process (Goodyear, Salmon, Spector, Steeples and Tickner, 2001; Guasch, Álvarez and Espasa, 2010; Bautista, Borges and Forés, 2011).

Competences Related to Communication

Competences related to communication in e-learning contexts are linked to the need to adapt to a basically written language, but also one mediated by screens and with the option of multimedia messages. These characteristics require both the teacher and the students to acquire a very diverse range of skills and strategies for effectively interacting in a way that is different to face-to-face exchanges. For example, in an e-learning environment the teacher must substitute regular physical presence for frequent communicative presence in a digital support and format.

Communication in virtual settings must distinguish among different functions and formats (i.e., videoconference, forum, mail, social networks, etc). For example, both the teaching staff and students have to communicate their messages to different audiences (i.e., individually, to a small group of colleagues, to the whole group/class or globally to a virtual community, etc.). In face-to-face contexts, communication almost always flows from the teacher to the students; however, in an online environment there are different types of communication flows and these can have differing reaches (i.e., virtual classroom, individual e-mails, learning community, etc.) With digital media it is relatively simple to create and maintain a multidirectional communication network (i.e., Facebook, Twitter, forums, distribution lists, etc.).

From the teacher's point of view, communication means frequent interaction and a presence in the e-learning environment. For this reason it is important to know how to plan the communication dynamic in a context of this type. It is vital that teachers be able to capture, understand and express emotions through the environments and devices they use to communicate, often without being able to see the face of their interlocutor, solely through written texts.

The teacher should know how and be able to perceive, use and regulate the affective charge of the communication in an electronic environment, whatever media and form are used. This effective mediated communication should, in an educational context, have a goal related to different aspects of didactic interaction, such as motivation, comprehension, requirement, disappointment, etc. The teacher must also be capable of creating and transmitting a climate of empathy with the students. In this way, the teacher will have the strategies for knowing and being able to understand what is occurring on the other side of the screen. This is a success factor in the teaching–learning process in an e-learning environment and also a mechanism for counteracting the potential loneliness students may feel and which is sometimes attributed to these learning contexts.

Communication in e-learning environments is the way in which teachers can demonstrate their 'presence' in digital settings. This presence should appear on a triple level, as indicated by Garrison, Anderson and Archer (2001): cognitive, socioaffective and didactic and, therefore, teachers' interventions should take into account when and in what form each of these is envisaged.

In the sphere of communication, teachers play an important role as models for students; students who want to learn the correct way to communicate and express themselves in an e-learning environment will probably use them as a reference. This competence will become

Table 11.1 Teachers' Interventions

Teaching presence	*Social presence*	*Cognitive presence*
Design and Organisation • *The instructor clearly communicated important course topics* • *The instructor clearly communicated important course goals* • *The instructor provided clear instructions on how to participate in course learning activities* • *The instructor clearly communicated important due dates/time frames for learning activities*	*Affective expression* • *Getting to know other course participants gave students a sense of belonging in the course* • *Students were able to form distinct impressions of some course participants* • *Online or web-based communication is an excellent medium for social interaction*	*Triggering event* • *Problems posed increased students' interest in course issues* • *Course activities piqued students' curiosity* • *Students felt motivated to explore content-related questions*
Facilitation • *The instructor was helpful in identifying areas of agreement and disagreement on course topics that helped students to learn* • *The instructor was helpful in guiding the class toward understanding course topics in a way that helped clarify students' thinking* • *The instructor helped to keep course participants engaged and participating in productive dialogue* • *The instructor helped keep the course participants on task in a way that helped students to learn* • *The instructor encouraged course participants to explore new concepts in the course* • *Instructor actions reinforced the development of a sense of community among course participants*	*Open communication* • *Students felt comfortable conversing through the online medium* • *Students felt comfortable participating in the course discussions* • *Students felt comfortable interacting with other course participants*	*Exploration* • *Students utilised a variety of information sources to explore problems posed in this course* • *Brainstorming and finding relevant information helped students resolve content-related questions* • *Online discussions were valuable in helping students appreciate different perspectives*
Direct Instruction • *The instructor helped to focus discussion on relevant issues in a way that helped students learn* • *The instructor provided feedback that helped students understand their strengths and weaknesses* • *The instructor provided feedback in a timely fashion*	*Group cohesion* • *Students felt comfortable disagreeing with other course participants while still maintaining a sense of trust* • *Students felt that their point of view was acknowledged by other course participants* • *Online discussions help students to develop a sense of collaboration*	*Integration* • *Combining new information helped students answer questions raised in course activities* • *Learning activities helped students construct explanations/solutions* • *Reflection on course content and discussions helped students understand fundamental concepts in class*

(*Continued*)

Table 11.1 Continued

Teaching presence	*Social presence*	*Cognitive presence*
		Resolution • *Students can describe ways to test and apply the knowledge created in this course* • *Students have developed solutions to course problems that can be applied in practice* • *Students can apply the knowledge created in this course to student work or other non-class-related activities*

Adapted from Garrison, Anderson and Archer, 2001.

increasingly necessary in any future workplace, which is why students will also have to acquire this collection of knowledge, skills and attitudes as part of their basic education and across the full range of knowledge in their degree course.

Communication competence in the field of education is also related to the body of knowledge and skills linked to creating and disseminating information in and with different formats. Nowadays, teachers and students have a wide range of options to choose from when sending messages in different formats, with images, video, sound, animation, mental maps, etc. Furthermore, there are numerous tools and techniques for planning and developing these messages (i.e., Microsoft's Movie Maker, Google.docs, Mind42, etc.). ICT enables educational dialogue and communication to be enriched and that is why it is important for teachers to master the different communication forms and techniques with these new tools.

Competences Related to Information

Mastering these new message forms is also connected with competences related to identifying, localising, managing, evaluating and processing information in digital format and, subsequently, to reprocessing this data as individual information/communication production that reflects knowledge and thought.

The role assigned to the teacher as a guide and companion in the learning process in online contexts makes mastering the most important aspects of searching for and organising digital information a fundamental factor for teaching quality. In e-learning contexts information is presented in a completely different way to face-to-face contexts. Moreover, teachers and students acquiring information competences should bear in mind that digital information comes from innumerable different sources. These varied origins mean that there is a greater need to adopt a critical attitude when using this information and to apply knowledge and skills when selecting the necessary and appropriate information for each learning situation.

Selecting sources of information and having knowledge of the tools for managing it and helping to organise and access it are also indispensable in today's world, given that the quantity of digital information teachers and students has access to is enormous. This need could be related to the awareness and consideration that teachers and students control their information environment very well, which is often linked to the concept of personal learning environments, which we will look at later. Teachers and students must master useful systems for organising and classifying digital information and the concepts linked to them (i.e., how a digital database works, how to use tags, what social bookmarking is and how to use it, what an RSS reader is, etc.). They should be capable of creating and disseminating information clearly and sufficiently in order to transmit the right message for the recipient or possible recipients and this message should fulfil the communication aims it was created for (i.e., iGoogle, RSS, DropBox, Delicious, etc).

Competences Related to Participation and Collaboration

We have reviewed the evolution of the Internet, which has been characterised by the gradual appearance of spaces and applications that allow users to produce information online. Moreover, today's Web 2.0 applications have further increased the possibility of interaction between people connected to the Internet. Web 2.0 is characterised by offering users a space for participation and collaboration. This new setting for multidirectional communication and interaction enables a climate of mutual influence to be generated among people.

People interconnected on the Internet build communities and produce systems and subsystems that, in turn, generate a flow of participation and collaboration in which multiple mutually influencing learning situations among equals undoubtedly take place, all in an informal context. This has been related by some authors to what are known as Personal Learning Environments (PLEs).

A PLE is an environment made up of individuals working in a personal capacity through their participation in social networks and the group of applications they use to connect with all types of agents and various sources of information in online settings. Today there are customisable online environments and applications (e.g., iGoogle) that make it easier for individuals to organise their environment and, as a result, their participation in the networks they belong to, and to access their personal applications and all the information providers they subscribe to. These personal environments are potential resources and tools for autonomous and collaborative learning.

The appearance of these new environments, accessible by any teacher or student, requires competences that enable correct participation and collaboration among peers on the Internet. Delocalised and asynchronous communication, collaboration and participation are developed. Depending on the role we play in these communities or the tool or service we are using to participate, certain knowledge is needed and particular skills, attitudes and strategies for communication and participation must be put into practice. Harnessing the power of these new tools and subenvironments within the Internet sometimes leads, for example, to the teacher acquiring the role of moderator and motivator in a small learning community (the class group) which in turn may interact with another larger community. On other occasions, it may be a student that leads a collaborative learning group in an online setting. Both teachers and students must have the knowledge and judgement to select the right resources, environments, sources of information, etc. There are many situations that occur for different people in these new learning dynamics and the competences that are required also differ from those needed in more traditional teaching and learning processes.

Digital Competences and Digital Environments: Changing the Way We Teach and Learn

Digital competences added to those basic competences that everybody should have, as well as the habits and practices of using new devices and technological resources enable the ways people develop their lives and learn to be substantially modified. In this regard, the figure of the teacher as the only person responsible for the educational process is becoming less and less pronounced. In turn, the role of the student as an active subject in the learning process is becoming increasingly clear. Furthermore, learning environments are gradually becoming more easily adapted to the characteristics, needs and interests of the teacher and in particular of the students. All of this leads us to interpret the need for ICT to be integrated into classrooms, so that its use is as natural as possible, using this term in the sense that technology becomes invisible and is firmly integrated into the curriculum.

Furthermore, the line between learning in a formal setting and in an informal setting is becoming less clearly defined. As we have seen in Chart 1, the walls of the traditional classroom as we know it can be broken down by opportunities to connect with external educational agents. There are more and more possibilities for the formal educational activities carried out in schools, colleges and universities to transcend the physical space and restrictive timetables. The didactic work performed by teaching staff and the learning process followed by students should be adapted to e-learning environments and to online or blended education models, as these are gaining a great deal of recognition on all levels.

In this text we have shown how changes to the teaching and learning environment are already a reality and this new setting leads us toward new contexts and new forms of teaching and learning. For this reason, both universities in their basic teacher training curricula and administrations responsible for continuous professional development for education professionals should seriously consider the need for teachers to develop digital competences in order to teach in e-learning environments. In turn, educational institutions must also ensure that their students are prepared to learn using the new tools and in the new digital contexts. Therefore, it is highly recommended that educational plans and curricula at all levels take into account the need to acquire digital competences across all fields in order to learn.

Teachers should, therefore, consider ICT as another educational resource and integrate it into their teaching work. The ultimate aim is to promote the bond with the digital world that young people intrinsically possess in their lives because of its capacity to motivate them, the opportunities for connection it provides, its proximity, intuitiveness, etc., thereby awarding the necessary importance to digital competences and the possibilities these offer for teaching and learning.

References

Ala-Mutka, K. (2011). *Mapping digital competence: Towards a conceptual understanding. JRC Technical Notes.* European Commission. Retrieved from: ftp.jrc.es/pub/EURdoc/JRC67075_TN.pdf

Bautista, G.; Borges, F. & Forés, A. (2011). *Didáctica universitaria en entornos virtuales de enseñanza y aprendizaje.* Madrid: Narcea.

Downes, S. (2004). "Educational blogging". *Educause Review,* 39(5), 14–26. Retrieved from: http://connect.educause.edu/Library/EDUCAUSE+Review/EducationalBlogging/40493

Duart, J.M.; Gil, M.; Pujol, M. & Castaño, J. (2008). *La universidad en la sociedad red. Usos de Internet en Educación Superior.* Barcelona: Ariel.

Ferrari, A. (2012). *Digital competence in practice: An analysis of frameworks. Joint Research Center Technical Report.* European Commission. Retrieved from: http://ftp.jrc.es/EURdoc/JRC68116.pdf

Garrison, D.R.; Anderson, T. & Archer, W. (2001). "Critical thinking, cognitive presence, and computer conferencing in distance education". *American Journal of Distance Education*, 15(1), 7–23.

Goodyear, P.; Salmon, G.; Spector, M.; Steeples, C. & Tickner, S. (2001). "Competence for online teaching: A special report". *Educational Technological, Research and Development*, 49(1), 65–72.

Gros, B.; Garcia, I. & Escofet, A. (2012). "Beyond the Net Generation debate: A comparison of digital learners in face-to-face and virtual universities". *International Review of Research in Open and Distance Learning*, 13(4), 190–210.

Guasch, P.; Álvarez, I. & Espasa, A. (2010). "University teacher competencies in a virtual teaching/learning environment: Analysis of a teacher training experience". *Teaching and Teacher Education*, 26, 199–206.

Johnson, L.; Levine, A.; Smith, R. & Stone, S. (2010). *The 2010 horizon report*. Austin, Texas: The New Media Consortium.

Kennedy, G.; Krause, K.-L.; Gray, K.; Judd, T.; Bennett, S.; Maton, K.; Dalgarno, B. & Bishop, A. (2006). "Questioning the Net Generation: A collaborative project in Australian higher education". In L. Markauskaite; P. Goodyear & P. Reimann (Eds.), "Who's learning? Whose technology?" *Proceedings of the 23rd Annual Conference of the Australasian Society for Computers in Learning in Tertiary Education* (pp. 413–417). Sydney: Sydney University Press. Retrieved from: http://www.ascilite.org.au/conferences/sydney06/proceeding/pdf_papers/p160.pdf

Lankshear, C. & Knobel, M. (2008). *Nuevos alfabetismos*. Madrid: Morata.

Lenhart, A.; Rainie, L. & Lewis, O. (2001). "Teenage life online: the rise of instant-message generation and the Internet's impact on friendship and family relationships". Washington, DC: Pew Internet & American Life Project. Retrieved from: http://www.pewinternet.org/Reports/2001/Teenage-Life-Online/Summary-of-findings.aspx

Lorenzo, G.; Oblinger, D. & Dziuban, C. (2006). "How choice, co-creation, and culture are changing what it means to be Net savvy". *EDUCAUSE Quarterly*, 30(1). Retrieved from: <http://connect.educause.edu/Library/EDUCAUSE+Quarterly/HowChoiceCoCreationandCul/40008>

Oblinger, D. (2006). "Listening to what we're seeing". *Keynote paper presented at ALT–C*. Retrieved from: http://www.alt.ac.uk/docs/Diana_Oblinger_20060905_25MB_88Mins.mp3

Pedró, F. (2006). *Aprender en el nuevo milenio: un desafío a nuestra visión de las tecnologías y la enseñanza*, OECD-CERI. Retrieved from: http://idbdocs.iadb.org/wsdocs/getdocument.aspx?docnum=848274

Postman, N. (1991). *Divertirse hasta morir*. Barcelona: La Tempestad.

Prensky, M. (2001). "Digital natives, digital immigrants". *On the Horizon*, 9(5). Retrieved from: http://www.marcprensky.com/writing/Prensky%20-%20Digital%20Natives,%20Digital%20Immigrants%20-%20Part1.pdf

Tapscott, D. (1999). "Educating the Net Generation". *Educational Leadership*, 56(5), 6–11. Retrieved from: <http://www.ascd.org/readingroom/edlead/abstracts/feb99.html>

Tapscott, D. (2009). *Growing up digital: How the Net Generation is changing your world*. New York: McGraw-Hill.

Turkle, S. (1995). *La vida en la pantalla. La construcción de la identidad en la era de Internet*. Barcelona: Paidós.

Trinder, K.; Guiller, J.; Margaryan, A.; Littlejohn, A. & Nicol, D. (2008). "Learning from digital natives: bridging formal and informal learning. Research project report". *The Higher Education Academy*. Glasgow Caledonian University. Retrieved from: http://www.academy.gcal.ac.uk/ldn/LDNFinalReport.pdf

UCL-CIBER Group (2008). *Information behavior of the researcher of the future* ('Google Generation' project). University College London CIBER Group. British Library and JISC. Retrieved from: http://www.ucl.ac.uk/infostudies/research/ciber/downloads

12

Creating Online Courses Step-by-Step

Peter S. Cookson

Introduction

Experienced instructors will find the principles of online course design outlined in this chapter similar to those that prevail for face-to-face instruction. In writing this chapter, however, my assumption is that the instructional design principles described by such authors as Dick and Carey (1996) and Merrill (2013) adaptable to both face-to-face and e-learning settings. While face-to-face learning settings are characterized by physical and temporal contiguity of teachers and students, online learning settings are characterized by geographical and/or temporal gaps between instructors and students. Technology must be harnessed to bridge those gaps. The interplay of those gaps and one or more types of technology transforms the teaching/learning environment and hence the way instructional design principles may be applied.

Although converting a face-to-face course into an online course can be a daunting task, flexibility and convenience are key features that can benefit teachers as well as students using e-learning. Professors, as well as students, decide when and from where they will connect to their online courses. Instructors can continue to interact with their students while they attend professional conferences, conduct research, or engage in University or public service. Students can accommodate online course within busy schedules of employment, family duties, recreational activities, and even attendance in other courses. Once instructors have done all of the heavy lifting required to create the online course materials, they can then switch their role from one of a "sage on the stage" to that of a "guide on the side."

During the past decade, while helping university professors develop e-learning courses, I have searched in vain in the distance education literature for practical guidance for writing online course materials. While I found explanations of theoretical frameworks and descriptive accounts of how specific courses were developed, I found few details about how to actually structure and write e-learning courses. Consequently, to meet the need to assist professors from a number of Mexican higher education institutions in developing course-creating competencies, I decided to write such guidelines in Spanish that combined ideas of various authors and presented an outline for faculty instructors elsewhere who, due to sparse or scattered resources, budget limitations, time constraints, academic procedures and policies that may not fully accommodate distance learning, or other reasons outside their control, "find themselves tasked with developing an online course from start to finish with little or no help" (Ralston-Berg and Gordy, 1995) from a formal course development team. Upon my return to English-speaking North America, recognizing that faculty instructors, particularly those who were developing e-learning without support, were looking for more explicit and simpler instructions about how to create e-learning courses, I subsequently prepared more practical guidelines that provided step-by-step instructions for creating hybrid and online courses.

These training materials shared the following common set of steps to develop online courses:

- Build the instructional design
  - Analyze learner attributes
  - Identify and sequence performance
  - Classify recurrent and nonrecurrent tasks
  - Specify procedural information
  - Specify supportive information
  - Formulate learning objectives
- Draft instructional narrative
- Integrate multimedia
- Add learning activities
- Plan assessments
- Pilot and evaluate the course
- Revise the course

These seven steps dissect an e-learning course into its constituent elements: instructional design, instructional narrative, multimedia, learning activities, assessments, piloting and course revision. Each of the steps will now be explained.

Step 1: Create the Instructional Design

While face-to-face instructors can make instructional decisions one or two days prior to a class session or even on the occasion of a class meeting, online instructor/subject matter experts ideally plan and write all components of online courses prior to delivery. Faculty experts writing online courses therefore must get the course "right" before students enroll. Hence the importance of an overall design to guide the myriad of decisions associated with the creation of online courses. Preparation of online course materials before students enroll can free up the instructor to focus on space interacting with students, helping them to fully engage with course content and to resolve any difficulties. Instructional design provides the foundation for the development of the course materials and comprises the following six substeps:

Analyze Target Learner Attributes

The characteristics of those who participate in your course can affect dramatically the effectiveness of the learning activities. Before you begin converting an on-campus course or creating a new online course, you would do well to take into consideration the following characteristics of students likely to enroll in your online course: background, schooling, social roles, previous online learning experience, existing knowledge related to course content, work activities, attitudes, interests and expectations.

Identify and Sequence Terminal Performance Outcomes

Having identified the characteristics of your students that you will take into account, it is important to determine what you intend students to learn to do upon course space completion. This substep calls for you to identify the terminal performances (the integrated competencies of knowledge, skill and sensitivity) that you want students who successfully complete the course to carry out.

Once the learning objectives students will achieve upon completion of the course have been identified, you will have an idea of the learning tasks that will be emphasized in your course. You can now determine the sequence in which competent professionals carry out the different performances.

The cognitive science literature offers clues about how to sequence terminal performances. Cognitive science suggests such strategies as *chunking, structuring* and *organization* as tools that permit grouping of the performances to organize instructional content. West, Farmer and Wolff (1991, p. 39) identify four common kinds of sequencing strategies: spatial strategies, narrative strategies, procedural strategies and logical strategies. Three additional principles to apply to ordering performances are: general to specific, simple to complex, and easy to difficult.

Classify Learning Tasks

Van Merriënboer and Kirschner (2008) offer a number of ways to classify learning tasks: *whole* versus *constituent, terminal* versus *en route* performances and *recurrent* versus *really. Recurrent tasks* are performed "in a highly consistent way from problem situation to problem situation"—for example, skills needed to drive an automobile, cross-country skiing, keyboarding at a computer or adding a list of numbers. At first they are executed consciously but, following sufficient practice, they become habitual. *Nonrecurrent tasks*, on the other hand, require learners to apply reasoning and problem-solving skills, for example, to write an essay, plan a political campaign, diagnose the cause of a diseased plant, conduct a bibliographical search or solve a quadratic equation.

Provide Procedural Information for Recurrent Performances

To enable learners to master routine tasks, van Merriënboer and Kirschner (2008) call for instruction to comprise procedural information, explanation of cognitive rules and assurance that students possess prerequisite knowledge. Depending upon which of these elements are offered in course materials that have already been utilized for on-campus courses, you may need to provide additional procedural information. Correct performance of tasks using just-in-time displays, quick reference guides, demonstrations, critical incidents and corrective feed-back in response to student submitted assignments. Instructional materials may also incorporate on-demand procedural information in the form of a comprehensive table of contents, index, informative diagrams or a section on frequently asked questions.

Provide Supportive Information for Nonrecurrent Performances

For nonrecurrent performances, learner support may vary from high to none. For some tasks initial learner support may be high, only to be reduced gradually via a process of *scaffolding*.

Case studies exemplify *high* learner support because they describe the performance of an integrated set of tasks followed by a series of questions for the learner to explain "the effectiveness of the approach taken, possible alternative approaches, [and] the quality of the final [outcomes]" (van Merriënboer and Kirschner, 2007, p. 18). A type of scaffolding referred to as *intermediate* support asks learners to execute partial performance of certain learning tasks after which they are then queried about how the tasks may be completed. At the other end of the support continuum, conventional tasks require learner to complete the task with *low* or *no* support or guidance. Supportive information may be provided by a textbook, other readings and multimedia materials.

One aim of systematic instructional design is to enable learners to replace their intuitive mental models with conceptual, causal or structural models that you share with them in your course. Cognitive strategies refer to the reasoning and problem solving invoked by proficient task performers as they carry out the skills that you want your students to develop. According to Van Merriënboer and Kirschner (p. 137), mental models "represent how competent task performers perceive the way a domain is organized)". To identify the cognitive strategies and mental models for the domain that corresponds to your course, you may need to examine existing documents or interview proficient task performers.

Formulate Learning Objectives

Building on the outcomes of these four preceding substeps, you are now ready to formulate specific learning objectives that inform the remaining steps. Effective performance objectives comprise:

- An action verb
- Conditions, including the time constraints and access to certain materials or instruments (tools), under which the learner is to perform the action
- Standards or criteria whereby the performance must correspond to a specified level of performance in the real world

More than half a century ago, Bloom et al. (1956) formulated a taxonomy of educational objectives: *cognitive*, intellectual outcomes; *affective*, related to interests, attitudes, appreciation and methods of adjustment (Gronlund, 2000, p. 30); and *psychomotor*, motor skills. In higher education courses, educational outcomes tend to emphasize cognitive objectives that may be classified into the following six categories: knowledge, comprehension, analysis, application, synthesis and evaluation.

Students will experience more meaningful learning of the concepts, principles and practices in your course when you activate higher-order categories of analysis, application, synthesis and evaluation. Whenever possible an effort should be made to enable students to demonstrate learning performance in terms of these "higher-level" cognitive objectives.

Organize Thematic Clusters and Designate Course Modules

Once you have listed the learning objectives and specified their sequence, they can then be organized into different thematic clusters that comprise the content of your course. Taking into account the duration in number of weeks of your course, you can then order these clusters to correspond to the topics to be addressed in course modules. These thematic clusters now permit you to identify the topics to be listed in your course outline.

Step 2: Draft the Instructional Narrative

The instructional design generated by the first step provides the framework on which to build the content, structure and process of your online course. Step 2 calls for you to draft your instructional narrative as a study guide for students enrolled in your course. In addition to course texts or anthologies of readings, the instructional narrative addresses course content and substitutes for the role of the face-to-face instructor. Once the instructional narrative is drafted, it can then be enriched by integrating relevant multimedia (Step 3), adding a variety of learning activities to enable students to practice the performances (Step 4), and preparing different kinds of assessment (Step 5) to determine how well your students can perform the performances that you identified when you completed steps 1.a. through 1.g.

As indicated in Table 12.1, while some elements of the instructional narrative pertain to the course as a whole, others pertain to each module.

Table 12.1 Structural Elements of the Instructional Narrative

Structural elements	*Syllabus/entire course*	*Each module*
• Overview of course content with a list of the modules and sections (themes) within the modules		
• Message of welcome		
• Introduction		
• Calendar or schedule		
• Advance organizer		
• Purpose and learning performance objectives		
• Advance organizer		
• How to proceed		
• Instructional narrative		
• Didactic prose		
• Guided didactic conversation		
• Worked examples		
• Learning practice activities		
• Questions for reflection		
• Topics for discussion		
• Learning resources (essential/ complementary)		
• Rubrics and evaluation criteria		
• Learning assessment		
• Summary of content and processes		
• Student feedback on effectiveness of module		

Step 3: Integrate Multimedia with Instructional Narrative

Step 3 calls for purposeful selection and integration of multimedia with the instructional narrative of online courses to increase the likelihood that students avoid "the Great Wall of Text" (Horton, 2000, p. 447) and experience meaningful learning, defined as

> deep understanding of the material, which includes attending to important aspects of the present material, mentally organizing it into a coherent cognitive structure, and integrating it with relevant existing knowledge. Meaningful learning is reflected in the ability to apply what was taught to new [real world] situations.
>
> (Mayer and Moreno, 2003, p. 44)

The range of media available for integration will depend on the a priori decision about how much of the course will be synchronous or asynchronous and how much will be fully online or both online and face-to-face (blended). Recognizing that when two or more media are combined to transmit online instruction learning results can be superior to those that result when only one medium is used, this step emphasizes integration of media and multimedia to promote *multimedia learning*, defined as learning that results from a combination of text, pictures, graphics to convey information or learning. However, it is vital that e-learning instructors use the multimedia most suitable for the particular learners and the intended learning tasks.

Interaction and E-learning

Two conceptual frameworks may inform selection of suitable multimedia to add to the instructional narrative. The first framework, proposed by Moore (1989, p. 1) emphasized three types of interaction:

> between the learner and the content or subject of study . . . between the learner and the expert who prepared the subject material . . . [and] between one learner and other learners, alone or in group settings, with or without the real-time presence of an instructor.

This typology provides a framework to classify media to consider adding to the instructional narrative of e-learning courses. Table 12.2 illustrates how it may apply to alternative single media; Table 12.3 illustrates how it may apply to alternative multiple media.

Cognitive Theory of Multimedia Learning

While the three types of interaction that characterize distance education enable identification of the different types of media, this step draws on cognitive load theory to inform the selection of multimedia most likely to produce effective, efficient and engaging e-learning.

This theory rests on assumptions that humans possess different channels to process words and images differently. Their capacity to process such information in their working memory is limited. Learning requires substantial cognitive processing in order for information to be integrated with prior knowledge that comprises long-term memory.

Cognitive load theory has produced useful insights about how to increase students' meaningful learning that Mayer and Moreno (2003, p. 43) define as "the understanding of the material, which includes attending to important aspects of the presented material, mentally organizing it into a coherent cognitive structure, and integrating it with relevant existing knowledge."

Table 12.2 Alternative Asynchronous and Synchronous Single Media by Type of Student Interaction

Media	*Asynchronous*	*Interaction with:*			*Synchronous*	*Interaction with:*		
		Content	*Instructor*	*Students*		*Content*	*Instructor*	*Students*
Text	Instructional narrative of modules				Text-based chat			
	Other reading resources							
	PowerPoint presentations							
	E-mail							
	Online discussion forum							
Sound	Audio recording				Audioconferencing			
	Podcasts							
	Audio feedback on assignments							
Graphics	Still photo/ visual representation				White board			
	Chart/figure							
	Concept map							
Video	Screen casting				Application sharing			
Virtual reality (VR)	Animation/ simulation				Animation/ simulation			

Adapted from Tuovinen, 2000

According to Mayer and Moreno (2003, p. 43), "A central challenge facing designers of multimedia instruction is the potential for cognitive overload—in which the learner's available cognitive capacity exceeds the learner's available cognitive capacity." When information is successfully processed, the person's working memory transfers the information to the long-term memory where it becomes part of a schema. The complexity of subjects to be learned may vary according to the level of interactivity of their respective elements. Subjects that require learners to focus on multiple aspects simultaneously are *highly interactive* and require more extensive processing than elements of low interactivity. An example of high interactivity would be the task of solving a quadratic equation. A *low interactive* task would be to add 2 + 2 or to memorize definitions of a list of Spanish verbs. The degree of interactivity determines how much students who seek to learn something will experience *intrinsic* cognitive load.

Learners are better able to process the information when instructors reduce extraneous cognitive load of the material by eliminating unnecessary elements in the material to be learned and increase germane cognitive load by preparing well-organized instruction and "creating an

Table 12.3 Alternative Asynchronous and Synchronous Multimedia by Type of Student Interaction

Multimedia	*Asynchronous*	*Interaction with:*			*Asynchronous*	*Interaction with:*		
		Content	*Instructor*	*Content*		*Students*	*Instructor*	*Students*
Text + sound	Narrated PowerPoint presentation				Narrated PowerPoint presentation			
Graphics + sound	Text + sound				Narrated PowerPoint presentation			
Video + sound	Webcam video				Video chat			
	Video recording/ movie				Webcast/ video streaming			
	Webcast/video streaming							
Virtual reality	Simulation/ animation				Animation/ simulation			

Adapted from Tuovinen, 2000

engaging learning environment in which the narrator uses a conversational style and polite wording" (Mayer, 2009, p. 81). Thus, effective use of multimedia enables learners to transfer intended learning from within the working memory to the long-term memory for construction and automation of schemata (Sweller, van Merriënboer & Paas, 1998).

Mayer (2009) and Moreno (2006) have identified a number of research-based principles that can guide selection of media to incorporate in the instructional narrative. Based on cognitive load theory, Moreno (2006, p. 65) has summarized these principles as follows: learning is enhanced when words are spoken more than printed, graphics and narration are combined, there are multiple forms of visual information, extraneous material is excluded, words and graphics appear together and students have opportunities to reflect on what they are learning.

Adhering to these principles, e-learning instructors decide how to combine text, audio, video, and virtual reality to optimize the cognitive processing of their students. Incorporating multimedia into your instructional narrative can provide alternative ways in which learners can interact with content, instructor and other learners.

Step 4: Integrate Learning Activities with Your Instructional Narrative

To achieve the educational objectives you have set for your course, students will have to do more than merely read about the competencies real-world performers possess. Step 4 calls for you to identify learning activities to incorporate in the instructional narrative of the modules of your online course.

Classification of Learning Activities

Two conceptual schemata provide a basis for classification of learning strategies and thus inform selection of specific learning activities that enable students to gain experience in enacting or simulating performance of competent professionals in the real world. According to the first schema proposed by Horton (2006), an important criterion for selection of learning activities is its intended purpose relative to the instructional program. Three types of learning activities can thus be classified:

- **Activities to absorb.** These activities provide opportunities for students to read, watch and/or listen, thus enabling them to acquire new knowledge, skill, or sensitiveness. (Horton, 2006, p. 38)
- **Activities to do.** These activities provide opportunities for students to gain experience, to practice and to exercise competencies required to achieve the learning performances. (Horton, 2006, p. 38)
- **Activities to connect.** These activities enable learners to link new skills, knowledge and sensitivities to prior learning and guide students to think more deeply about course content. (Horton, 2006, p. 38)

When introducing students to desired terminal performances, you will normally want to introduce activities to absorb. Once learners have been introduced to the *what* they are to learn, activities to practice can be combined with activities to link with prior knowledge and skills. Learning is promoted when new knowledge is integrated into the learner's world, combined with activities to connect to performances they are to perform.

Paulsen's Classification of Methods

Paulsen (2004) proposed a second schema to classify learning activities based on the concepts of method and technique, as defined by Verner (1964), and four teaching methods (one alone, one-to-one, one-to-many, and many-to many) elaborated by Harasim (1989). Horton's concept of intended purpose of learning Table 12.4 presents 68 methods/techniques that instructors can deploy in online courses.

It is amazing how often uninformed individuals express the view that online distance courses merely comprise lectures in print or streaming video via the Internet. Unlike this naive view, the list in Table 12.4 reveals a vast and rich repertoire of learning activities that online instructors may select from in accordance with the following assumptions of "First Principles of Instructional Design" enunciated by Merrill (2002, 2013):

- Problem-centered: Learning is promoted when learners are engaged in solving real-world problems.
- Learning is promoted when existing knowledge is activated as a foundation for new knowledge.
- Learning is promoted when new knowledge is demonstrated to the learner.
- Learning is promoted when new knowledge is applied by the learner.
- Learning is facilitated when new knowledge is integrated into the learner's world.

In deciding which learning activities to use, keep in mind the different purposes different activities can serve: to activate learner engagement, to associate new knowledge with students' existing schemata, to provide opportunities to demonstrate the intended learning performances, and to enable students to apply their learning to real-world or simulated real-world performance.

Table 12.4 Classification of Distance Learning Activities by Purpose and Teaching Method

Learning activities	*Purpose*			*Teaching arrangements*			
	To absorb	*To do*	*To connect*	*One alone*	*One to one*	*One to many*	*Many to many*
Apprenticeships		•	•		•		
Analysis of readings (compare and contrast, classify, outline, evaluate)		•					
Assigned readings	•						
Brainstorming			•			•	
Buzz group			•				•
Case studies for individual or group analysis	•	•	•		•	•	
Chat			•		•		•
Correspondence			•		•		
Debate			•				•
Discussion forum (asynchronous) by entire group			•				•
Discussion forum (asynchronous) by small groups			•				•
Essays			•		•		
Demonstration of a particular operation/ activity	•		•			•	•
Examples provided by students			•			•	•
Exercises that require students to seek and share Internet-based resources pertinent to themes of specific modules	•	•	•		•	•	
Research on how to apply concepts principles and practices studied to settings meaningful for students			•	•			
Explanation of advantages and disadvantages of certain concepts			•	•			

(Continued)

Table 12.4 Continued

Learning activities	*Purpose*			*Teaching arrangements*			
	To absorb	*To do*	*To connect*	*One alone*	*One to one*	*One to many*	*Many to many*
Explanations in the instructional narrative	•		•	•		•	
Discussion forum			•				•
Guided research activities that require students to consult various information sources	•			•			
Individual student presentations	•		•	•		•	
Group presentations	•		•				•
Informal interaction among pairs			•		•		
Instructor-delivered tutorials (via e-mail, online discussion forum, text/voice chat sessions)	•			•			
Internships		•	•		•		
Interviews with real-world expert (performers of competencies that are the focus of the course)	•		•		•		
Learning contract		•	•		•		
Learning journal			•	•			
Learning–teaching teams to prepare and make group presentations	•		•				•
Lecture	•					•	
Nominal group technique			•				•
Observation of demonstration of implementation of target competencies by real-world performers	•					•	
Online database		•	•	•			
Online discussion between classmates as peers and among members of small groups			•				•

(Continued)

Table 12.4 Continued

Learning activities	*Purpose*			*Teaching arrangements*			
	To absorb	*To do*	*To connect*	*One alone*	*One to one*	*One to many*	*Many to many*
Online or face-to-face interviews with experts	•		•	•		•	
Online publication	•		•	•		•	
Online software		•	•	•			•
Podcasts or audio presentations delivered via the Internet	•					•	
Personal account of the instructor and/or other students of experiences			•			•	
PowerPoint presentation	•					•	
Practical projects that call for application of what is learned to real-world settings		•				•	
Preparation and presentation of individual or group reports for critical evaluation by the instructor, classmates or real-world performers			•			•	•
Presentation by individual students			•			•	
Presentation by group of students			•				•
Problem-solving exercise		•	•	•		•	
Processing of documents and procedures typical of real-world settings		•	•	•		•	
Proposal to carry out a real-world project		•	•	•		•	
Questions to stimulate critical thinking in the discussion forum			•			•	
Reading assignments	•			•		•	
Research on how concepts, principles							

(*Continued*)

Table 12.4 Continued

Learning activities	*Purpose*			*Teaching arrangements*			
	To absorb	*To do*	*To connect*	*One alone*	*One to one*	*One to many*	*Many to many*
and practices described in the case study are manifest in real-world settings		•	•	•	•		
Review of student peer assignments		•	•	•			
Rhetorical questions			•		•	•	
Role-play		•	•				•
Seminar	•	•	•			•	
Simulation and games		•	•			•	•
Skit X			•			•	•
Stories by the instructor			•		•	•	
Stories by the students		•	•				•
Summaries of what has been learned			•			•	
Symposium	•					•	
Synchronous chat session			•		•	•	•
Self-assessment			•	•			
Peer assessment			•		•		
Computer-marked assessment (CMA)			•			•	
Instructor-marked assessment (IMA)			•		•	•	
Transcript-based assignments		•	•	•			
Web-based research to identify additional reading resources			•				•

Step 5: Integrate Assessment with Instructional Narrative

Step 5 calls for you to integrate assessment with the instructional narrative to which multimedia and learning activities have been added. Different forms of assessment allow you to document and judge the value and significance of activities performed by students to demonstrate that they have acquired the knowledge, skills and sensitiveness possessed by competent performers in the real world. Assessments may be conducted to diagnose how much content to be learned in an online course is already known, to provide *feedback* on student performance on the learning tasks (referred to as *formative evaluation*), or to *classify* (grade) student performance (referred as summative evaluation).

Forms of Assessment

Assessment can be applied in online courses in different ways:

- **In text questions (ITQs).** In the instructional narrative, questions for reflection may be inserted, spurring students to engage mentally with the content they read.
- **Self-assessment (SA).** This type of assessment may be given at the beginning of either the online course or each course module. Palloff and Pratt (1999, p. 149) suggested, "Evaluation of student assignments in an online course should not be the job of the instructor alone." SAs permit students to know for themselves how effectively they achieve the outcomes intended for the different modules.
- **Peer assessments (PAs).** Collaboration among student peers is a distinctive feature of online distance education. Not only do PAs save time and energy for the instructor, but students who evaluate the work of fellow students also gain valuable insight from their peers' assessments as well as from applying criteria to their peers' assignments.
- **Computer-marked assessments (CMAs).** These include quizzes that can be corrected automatically through the learning management system.
- **Performance-based assessment (PBA).** This type of assessment focuses on performance of tasks that have been learned. PBA allows us to determine if intended outcomes have been achieved. In other words, can students who participate in an educational program apply what they learn in a real-world or simulated setting?
- **Informal feedback.** To assist students in applying the concepts, principles and practices relating to the desired learning performances, informal feedback can be instrumental. Personal notes written on students' essays and verbal comments recorded and returned with assignments or given in one-on-one meetings during virtual office hours can encourage students to persevere despite their discouragement. Personal comments of commendation for particularly insightful postings in discussion forums, essays and term papers signal the instructor's awareness of and concern for students' success.
- **Teacher-marked assessments (TMAs).** This form of assessment involves feedback on student performance on assignments, participation in the online discussion forums, and examinations.

When constructing items for both CMAs and TMAs, it is important to avoid the temptation to ask questions that address only the lower levels of Bloom's taxonomy. As indicated by Inglis, Ling and Joosten (1999, p. 99): "with careful design, computer-score tests are capable of measuring higher-order learning outcomes such as explanation, comparison, analysis, synthesis and hypothesizing."

The Use of Rubrics

To remove the mystery that students often associate with the instructor's assessment criteria and, at the same time, to make the task of judging the academic quality of assignments submitted by students more efficient, I recommend that you refer students to scoring rubrics. Picket and Dodge (2007) point out that students who determine for themselves how their performance meets the standards indicated in the rubric, then

> take more responsibility for their own learning, are empowered by being involved in the teaching/learning process, and have a clearer idea of what is expected in terms of specific

performance. Stakeholders are given clear information about student assessment and instructional objectives. Teachers clarify their goals, expectations, and focus, and even find that their paperwork is reduced because students are a part of the process of assessment development.

Flash (2008) has outlined how to create a grading rubric:

- Determine the important characteristics or criteria that the assignment must have.
- Weight the criteria at each level of performance; e.g., excellent, good, acceptable, deficient.
- Provide a description of the expected student performance for each criterion at each level on the assessment scale.
- Distribute the criteria, their respective weights, and levels of success in a grid or table.

Step 6: Pilot and Evaluate the Course

Once each of the preceding five steps has been completed, the e-learning course is ready to be offered for the first time. To determine areas of strength or that require improvement, this step calls for evaluation of the course during its pilot test to answer the following questions:

- Reaction. How satisfied are students with their learning experience?
- Learning. How well are students able to achieve academically the learning objectives of the course?
- Behavior. How well are students who complete the course able to demonstrate real-world or simulated real-world performance?
- Results. What is the impact of course participation on students, the instructor and the institution? Are students more likely to participate in other online courses? Is the instructor more likely to conduct other online courses? Is the institution more likely to sponsor more online courses? (Kirkpatrick and Kirkpatrick, 2006)

The findings of this evaluation are compiled and reported so that they may illuminate further improvements.

Step 7: Revise the Course

Taking into account the experience of offering the pilot study of the course, the seventh step calls for the e-learning instructor to revise the course materials. Noting parts of the course that may have caused confusion or that fell short of expectations, Step 7 calls for the e-learning instructor to make the appropriate corrections and other changes.

Conclusion

This chapter has presented seven steps that an e-learning instructor can implement to prepare an online course. Although under ideal circumstances e-learning instructors would be able to count on additional support of several course development team members, including a web designer, multimedia specialist, instructional designer, editor and project manager, the seven steps can be implemented by an e-learning instructor who has to enact those multiple roles alone.

By implementing each of the seven steps, even e-learning instructors assuming a Lone Ranger approach will be able to create high quality e-learning instruction.

References

Bloom, B. S. (1956). *Taxonomy of educational objectives. Handbook I: The cognitive domain.* New York: David McKay.

Dick, W., & Carey, L. (1996). *The systematic design of instruction* (4th ed.). New York: HarperCollins.

Flash, P. (2008). Creating grading rubrics for writing assignments. *University of Minnesota Center for Writing.* Retrieved from: http://writing.umn.edu/tww/responding_grading/creating_rubrics.html

Gronlund, N. E. (2000). *How to write and use instructional objectives.* Upper Saddle River, NJ: Merrill.

Harasim, L. (1989). On-line education: A new domain. In R. Mason & A. Kaye (Eds.), *Mindweave: Communications, Computers, and Distance Education* (pp. 50–62). Oxford: Pergamon Press.

Horton, W. (2000). *Designing web-based training: How to teach anyone anything anywhere anytime.* New York: Wiley.

Horton, W. (2006). *E-learning by design.* San Francisco: Pfeiffer.

Inglis, A., Ling, P., & Joosten, V. (1999). *Delivering digitally: Managing the transition to the knowledge media.* London: Kogan Page.

Kirkpatrick, D. L., & Kirkpatrick, J.D. (2006). *Evaluating training programs: The four levels* (3rd ed.). San Francisco, CA: Berrett-Koehler.

Kirschner, P. & van Merriënboer, J.J.G. (2008). "Ten Steps to Complex Learning: A New Approach to Instruction and Instructional Design." In T. L. Good (Ed.), *21st century education: A reference handbook* (pp. 244–253). Thousand Oaks, CA: Sage.

Mayer, R. E. (2009). *Multimedia learning.* Cambridge: Cambridge University Press.

Mayer, R. E., & Moreno, R. (2003). Nine ways to reduce cognitive load in multimedia settings. *Educational psychologist, 3*(1).

Merrill, M. D. (2002). First principles of instruction. *Educational Technology Research and Development, 50*(3), 43–59.

Merrill, M. D. (2013). *First principles of instruction: Identifying and designing effective, efficient and engaging instruction.* San Francisco: Pfeiffer.

Moore, M. G. (1989) Editorial: Three types of interaction. *American Journal of Distance Education, 3*(2), 1–6.

Moreno, R. (2006). Learning in high tech and multimedia environments. *Current Directions in Psychological Science, 15*(2), 63–67.

Palloff, R. M., & Pratt, K. (1999). *Building learning communities in cyberspace.* San Francisco: Jossey-Bass.

Paulsen, M. F. (2004). Teaching and learning activities in higher distance education online. Unpublished module for the University for Peace of the United Nations. (Financed by the Canadian international development agency.)

Pickett, N., & Dodge, B. (2007). *Rubrics for Web lessons.* Retrieved from: http://webquest.sdsu.edu/rubrics/weblessons.htm

Ralston-Berg, P., & Gordy, B. (1995). *Mission impossible: How to design an online course without a team.* Paper presented at the 18th Annual Conference on Distance Teaching and Learning. Retrieved from: http://www.uwex.edu/disted/conference/Resource_library/proceedings/02_W4.pdf

Sweller, J., van Merriënboer, J., & Paas, F. (1998). Cognitive architecture and instructional design. *Educational Psychology Review, 10*, 251–296.

van Merriënboer, J.J.G., & Kirschner, P. A. (2007). *Ten steps to complex learning: A systematic approach to four-component instructional design.* New York: Lawrence Erlbaum.

Verner, C. (1964). Definition of terms. In A. A. Liveright & W. Hallenbeck (Eds.), *Adult education: Outlines of an emerging field of university study* (pp. 27–39). Washington, DC: Adult Education Association.

West, C. K., Farmer, J., & Wolff, M. (1991). *Instructional design: Implications from cognitive science.* Englewood Cliffs, NJ: Prentice Hall.

13

The Role of the Online Learner

A Competential Model for Students When Learning Online

Federico Borges and Anna Forés

Introduction

Learning online requires a combination of general and specific traits and skills: the way students perform in other contexts, such as in a face-to-face setting, will not suffice entirely in a digital setting (Gaiser, 1997; Piskurich, 2004). Therefore online learners need to be aware of which skills, and how and when, are required in order to be competent as online learners, going beyond their former role in the face-to-face classroom to adapt to the online setting (Birch, 2001; Cleveland-Innes et al., 2007). Moreover, the learners' role commonly accepted in traditional higher education is changing to a role which is "more appropriate for continuous learning in an information-based, complex, global society" (Kinsel et al., 2004). Around the world, most onsite, classroom-based higher education includes online teaching and learning or online practice to a certain extent and in many forms. Even so, relevant literature on the online learner shows a lack of a specific theoretical framework which accounts for the online learners' role, that is, for learners' performance when learning online (Borges, n.d.).

Sociological principles in Role Theory provide clues to understand what a role is and its importance in human life: a role is a model of behaviour that human beings may adopt, perform or even discard during his or her lifetime. A role helps to describe oneself, and one's actions, and describe or recognize those of others too (Johnstone and Connick, 2005).

New Roles for Online Settings: The Role of the Online Learner

What Is the Role of the Online Learner?

There is a widespread perception of the learner's performance online as consisting mostly of a number of actions and traits related to the use of computers and digital tools, and so the competences needed to learn at a distance in a digital setting are a matter of "digital literacy" (Zawacki-Richter, 2009). However, as practice shows, learning online entails more than digital literacy or the appropriate use of digital tools. This restricting, limited vision whereby online learners' performance is mostly a matter of instrumental competence can be overcome by a more comprehensive approach, one which aims at an integral model for adequate performance as an online learner. This approach can be shaped as a comprehensive *Role of the Online Learner*, intended to be a valid framework, guide or reference to students' performance online.

The Role of the Online Learner is made up of three statements (Borges, n.d.):

- There is a role which is specific to learners when learning online.
- Online learners adopt this specific role and perform accordingly.
- The Role of the Online Learner can be modelled as the interrelation of four competentional clusters.

First, there is a role specific to learners when they learn online. A digital, online medium of educational delivery affords opportunities for new learning spaces, implying appropriate learning within them, fitting learner behaviour and adequate teaching within those new learning spaces (Visser, 2008). In turn, online students are expected to do certain things in certain ways in order to learn online, as a review of the relevant literature shows (Borges, n.d.).

Second, there exists a combined, intertwined process of role adoption and role performance when learning online (Cleveland-Innes et al., 2007; Kinsel et al., 2004). Novice online learners find a new setting, where there are new requirements and expectations, with particular ways of participating and communicating. As is known, what learners are expected to do in an online setting is not exactly the same as what they are expected in an onsite classroom; what one would do in a face-to-face setting simply does not work well enough in an online one (Gaiser, 1997; Piskurich, 2004). All this makes students realize, implicitly or explicitly, that:

- there is a role to comply to as online learners,
- they have to adopt it by whatever means they can.

Third, the Role of the Online Learner can be explained as the interrelation among these four competentional clusters:

- Operational
- Academic
- Relational
- Metacognitive

The concept of *the learner being competent in a number of explicit clusters of competences when performing online* is fundamental to the Role of the Online Learner. We consider a competence to be the tangible, measurable result of integrating a number of skills, abilities, and personal traits, all of them put in action in order to achieve a goal or carry out a task. Let us note that the requirement should be competent *enough*, that is, being proficient just enough to be able to achieve one's goals by means of these competences and their corresponding outputs.

The Role is a cross-curricular core of four cluster competences – Operational, Academic, Relational, Metacognitive – required irrespectively of the online course, online programme or online studies, as long as the student is logging in and does not coincide physically with other students or with faculty. These competences gather learners' expected actions and expected behaviour when learning online: online students must be proficient in the use of the tools and the setting for their learning, they need to be academically competent online, they will relate to others online when learning and for learning, and a degree of self-regulation and reflection will be required, too.

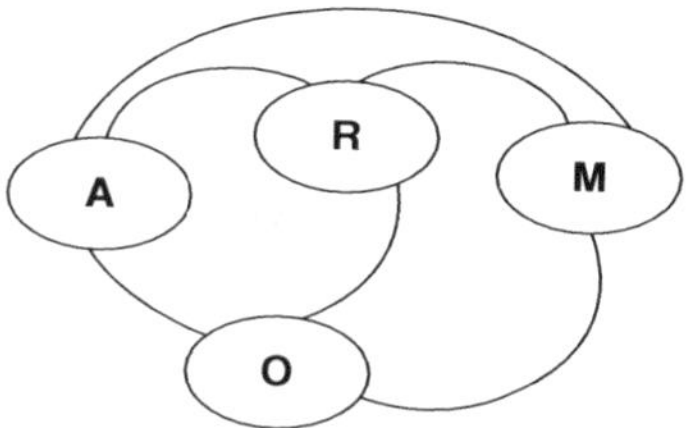

Figure 13.1 Model for the Role of the Online Learner

The outer frame in Figure 13.1 represents that:

- there is no hierarchy among competences,
- competences are all interrelated,
- more than one competence can occur at the same time,
- competences are manifested when needed and as needed.

A Closer Look at the Competences in the Role

A breakdown of the four cluster competences, as in tables 13.1–13.4, shows their nature in various examples, and can help students to be aware of them in order to adopt the Role; although not comprehensive, this breakdown of instances of specific competences and likely outputs may indicate students' competence and proficiency and can be used as a reference.

In the instances of competences and outputs for each of the clusters below it is important to note that they are not merely a list of items, nor a definitive set of elements, and that some competences and outputs can be part of more than one competence.

Operational Cluster Competence

This competence consists of a proficient use of the online setting and ICT tools for learning. Students competent in the instrumental dimension are in a position to apply and develop the rest of the competences in the Role; given that the medium for learning and relating is digital, it is absolutely essential for the learner to be proficient enough in this competence.

Academic Cluster Competence

Naturally, students must be as competent as possible in studying, assimilating course contents, working academically, using learning materials, and obtaining passing grades in their course or programme, and all this is to be done and attained online; in addition, students must acquire the necessary skills, strategies and attitudes to be competent in degree-related issues, on their field of knowledge or course-related issues, and apply them online. Therefore this competence includes the cognitive competence in studying and learning in an online setting, be it asynchronous or real-time.

Table 13.1 Operational Cluster Competence

Competences	*Outputs*
Adequate competence in the use of ICT tools for learning. Adequate expertise in the use of the online setting communication tools and programmes. Satisfactory knowledge of facilities and navigation throughout the online setting. Competence in accessing course info (e.g. course programme or study guide), course materials and resources.	**Participation in course forum/s or spaces.** **Posting mails to fellow students and to faculty.** **Getting to specific places in the online setting, e.g. course resources, computing support, institutional support etc.** **Downloading and reading course information, course materials and resources.**

Table 13.2 Academic Cluster Competence

Competences	*Outputs*
Connect frequently to the course setting. Prepare participation in discussions beforehand. Participate efficiently in online discussions and online assignments. Learn from other students' and instructor's contributions. Study using online resources. Work/share with team/group members online. Know where academic help is available. Know where technical help is available.	**Regularly log on to the course setting.** **Post with quality participation in course discussions and course activities (active participant).** **Read as many contributions to course discussions and course activities as possible (passive participant).** **Offer feedback to others.** **Request feedback.** **Incorporate relevant info and knowledge from all sources: discussions, instructor, resources etc.** **Have course materials readily available: downloading, mobile access, printing etc.** **Look up in course materials, course resources or the Internet on own initiative.** **Contribute to team/group work online.** **Mail asking for help when necessary.**

Relational Cluster Competence

This competence is manifested in any learning setting, and key to an adequate performance as an online learner. There are a number of social, affective and communicative skills which an online learner has to acquire and use for a satisfactory course performance. For an online student it is essential to be competent in communicating and collaborating with fellow students and with their instructor. Being competent in relating in an online learning setting is pointed out as a key competence by researchers and students alike (Borges, n.d.), and these competences may contribute to a satisfactory learning experience.

Table 13.3 Relational Cluster Competence

Competences	*Outputs*
Use communication tool/s in the learning setting. Write and speak efficiently for communication online. Express ideas, opinions, feelings online. Work/share with team/group members. Negotiate meaning and get to agreements. Take into account classmates' and instructor's ideas and criticism. Relate to fellow learners as part of an online community of learning.	**Posting quality contributions to class discussion.** **Participation in communication space/s in the online setting with a relation purpose.** **Mail/s with timely help to classmates or to faculty/instructor.** **Mail/s thanking others for help.**

Metacognitive Cluster Competence

Self-direction and self-management of one's own learning and one's own performance in the online setting are key, given the high degree of autonomy the learner has in online settings. The Metacognitive competence therefore is made up of a set of strategic skills and actions on the part of the online learner. We could say that this is the strategic competence in the Role. What a learner does about self-monitoring and self-appraisal, the amount of reflection put into learning, his or her feelings and emotions, all that is just as important as skills directly applied for learning contents or for using ICT tools and course resources.

In understanding the competence clusters of the Role this is to be noted:

- When needed and as needed, each learner may bring to action a different set of skills, strategies and capabilities in order to be competent in his or her role, according to his or her personal profile, needs and goals and context.
- For a competence, other components may intervene too to a diverse extent for each learner, such as personal experience, motivation and will, intellectual or physical abilities, and this may influence what the learner puts into performing the tasks, and how.
- Competences are put in practice to a different and variable degree to accomplish a learner's goals, according to the performance each student feels is required.
- Students are bound not to be equally competent all the time, since every learner may undergo a varied array of states: there can exist periods of effective learning, spans of time when things do not go right, goals may vary or may be adjusted, other commitments may get in the way, and so on.

It must be stressed that the specificity of the Role does not lie solely on the operational competence, or on advanced digital literacy: it would be erroneous to think that what makes the Role of the Online Learner specific to online learners are operational skills and operational outputs. The Role is specific to the online learner because it goes beyond ICT skills; it requires a number of competences applied online. Although the three nonoperational dimensions are not exclusive of online learning, they are of key importance to online learning, in view of the usual design of online courses with delayed communication among participants or real-time communication from a different location, collaboration and fostering of autonomy, student self-regulation and student-centred academic competences.

Table 13.4 Metacognitive cluster competence

Competences	*Outputs*
Organization and management of one's resources for learning adequately, particularly time.	**Write up own schedule/calendar, taking into account course contents and dates, plus family and work commitments.**
Self-discipline: adhering consistently to one's goals and one's time scheduling.	**Negotiate time and amount of dedication to learning with family (spouse) or at work.**
Flexibility: updating goals and schedule according to developments.	**Mail the instructor to check progress and for advice.**
Self-motivation, and checking on it from time to time.	**Revise own schedule/calendar from time to time.**
Being responsible for one's own learning, which means being autonomous and proactive rather than passive and reactive.	**Say no to unscheduled leisure when study or assignments are due.**
Self-monitoring of one's efforts, actions and progress.	**Enroll in new courses based on own goals, own progress, personal resources and available time.**
Thinking of ways to improve one's organization and management of learning.	**Modify lifestyle or personal timetable if necessary.**
Reflecting on or reminding of one's own goals for self-remotivation.	

Online learning requires that students do a number of things, in certain ways, and at certain moments in time during their performance online, as seen above in tables 13.1–13.4. This unique combination of existing competences is essential for an effective performance on the part of the student in an online setting, and these are part of the Role. As an instance of such 'old' things which are done in a 'new' way, Cleveland-Innes, Garrison and Kinsel (2007) outline the requirements for online learners to adapt to their digital setting, and these could roughly correspond to the competentional dimensions in the Role:

- acceptance of technology and technological skills (this would be part of the Operational competence),
- adapting to a new learning setting in terms of time and space (this could be connected with the Academic competence),
- new modes of communication with faculty, fellow students, and the institution (part of the Relational competence),
- a higher level of self-direction on the part of the student (part of the Metacognitive competence).

The Role should be regarded therefore as a dynamic model that fits a variety of modes of online learning, a model from which all kinds of learners can benefit, which can be adapted to any cultural setting, and which can account for variations in performance due to time, students' expertise or students' preferences.

The representations of the model in Figures 13.2, 13.3 and 13.4 below show how the Role is not immovable, nor static, as it represents the stages that an online learner goes through. Whereas the place and size of the four competence clusters seen in Figure 1 are neuter for the sake of illustrating, in Figure 2 place and size show relative importance of competences in the Role of the Online Learner as online learners begin their course or programme.

Irrespective of whether the online learner is a digital immigrant or a digital native, there is the need to use certain equipment and/or software required at his or her learning, along with knowing his or her way around the learning setting. The student is mostly struggling—or simply checking—to cope with ICT tools and with the technological setting, so the operational competence outweighs the rest for the time being. Also, a learner's operational competence, as with the other three, will largely depend on his or her other skills, experience, attitude, compliance with faculty advice and so on; therefore this competence may be highly relevant to some learners, while perhaps not being that much so for others. While time and effort spent on the rest of the competences does exist, they are not so prominent at that initial stage in comparison; also, the Metacognitive competence appears smaller than the rest because it is not yet as important as it will be in later stages, where it will become more prominent as the learner needs to monitor his or her learning and progress.

Soon into the course learners are competent enough in, or familiar enough with, digital tools and the setting to be able to focus on how to perform online (Academic competence) and on the communication with their faculty or with other students (Relational competence), as shown in the model in Figure 13.3. As students have changing needs during their learning online, so they apply their competence to different tasks at different times, as they need them

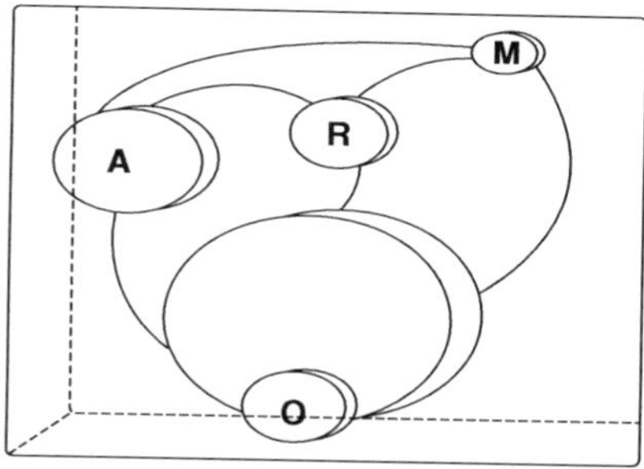

Figure 13.2 The Role of the Online Learner at Early Stages in Performance

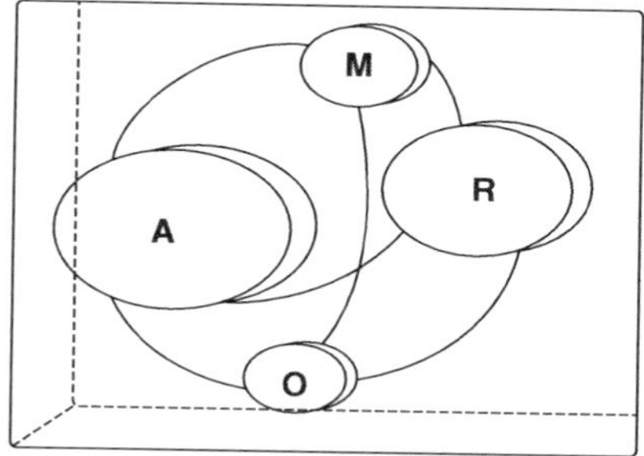

Figure 13.3 Relative Importance of Competences in the Role of the Online Learner in the Course

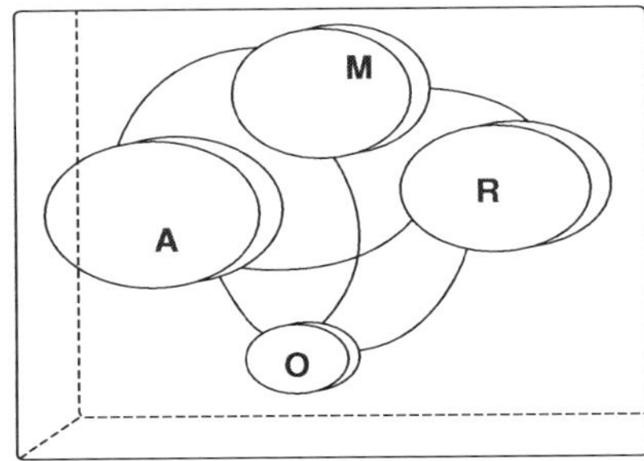

Figure 13.4 Self-Direction, Planning or Self-Management in Action in the Course

and when they need them. Figure 13.3 depicts online learners' competence needs well into the course: Academic and Relational competences become more common and significant than the Operational and Metacognitive at that stage. This is so because during a good deal of the time learners are mostly devoted to studying, communicating, participating, contributing their ideas, submitting assignments and so on; that is, their academic competence and their relational competence are more relevant at that stage than the other two competences. That said, although both Operational and Metacognitive competences are not so much of an issue at that stage, still they are being used and they are important, because studying, communicating, collaborating and so on could not be possible without the use of the Operational competence, and in applying academic and relational competences many elements of the reflection, planning and self-regulation of the Metacognitive competence are present.

A likely stage at which the Metacognitive competence cluster becomes more prominent is when students work on their self-regulation, reflection and planning, or on their time management, in ways that are important, as shown in Figure 13.4. It represents a stage where there is an important activity going on in the academic and relational competences—it may well be that there is some group work being done at that time—and the metacognitive dimension has grown, in comparison with previous stages in the course, when actions of a metacognitive kind were minor or less important.

The Role of the Online Learner Put to Use

By providing a performance model of the Role, a model nonexistent so far, students can be aware of what it takes to learn online and how to go about it in an online setting in order to succeed academically and personally, and have a satisfactory learning experience. The Role made explicit will help students in their role adoption, as "the responsibilities and requirements of working online are not readily apparent to those new to the role" (Cleveland-Innes et al., 2007, p. 4). By knowing about the role, or by being trained, online students can learn what their role is like and they can identify with it, setting themselves to the task of an overall better performance as learners.

Role competences are liable to be developed by means of training (ibstpi, 2010); therefore a number of key issues in online programmes such as orientation, role adjustment (Garrison et al., 2004), quality design and training of both online learners and online faculty can be addressed by means of the Model of the Role put forward above.

More often than not, online learners' role adoption comes through daily experience, by trial and error, by imitation or observance of someone who is more seasoned, in the way of the school of hard knocks, so to speak. It is natural to think that online learners would be willing to add to this 'in-service' role adoption any kind of formal training on what their role is supposed to be. Then, the Model of the Role can be used to train novice—and seasoned—online learners in what it means to learn online, and the way to go about it to perform competently. Although the Role is individual, it is not isolated but connected with other learners' competences, by means of the Relational competence; in addition, relating to other competent learners may contribute to increase the learner's own competences (De la Teja, 2011).

Institutions and faculty should address the need for role awareness in online students by providing their students with orientation or training of what it means to learn online by using the concept of the Role. In devising related training, the following points should be taken into account:

- The Role is also relevant to onsite, face-to-face students whenever they do online a part of their course or programme, or do activities online.
- Full orientation on the four competences is preferable to incomplete orientation which focuses solely on operational and/or administrative issues. The format, be it online training, an online tutorial, an online manual or printed material, is not as important as the depth and extent of the information or training provided on the Role.
- Faculty and instructors can present information on the Role or train their students as specific training or as an element of the course, without having to leave it necessarily to the institution, as a sort of 'on the go' orientation; for want of a more comprehensive training, this kind of orientation on the role would address the issue and would be adapted to performing competently in the corresponding course.

In putting to use the Role of the Online Learner it must be noted that faculty are key in contributing to students becoming aware of their role and adopting it. The Role of the Online Learner cannot stand alone without including the performance of the online instructor or online faculty: there can be no Role of the Online Learner without a Role of the Online Faculty that facilitates it. The literature about faculty and their competences shows how the teaching role and its competences has been present in distance education literature (Harasim, 1995; Berge, 2000; Mishra, 2005), or examined in handbooks or manuals for online instructors (O'Rourke, 2003). The two roles are so directly related that one of the competences in the Role of the Online Faculty would be that of developing competent online learners—what without an explicit learner's role has been referred to as "facilitating learners to develop their learning skills" (O'Rourke, 2003, p. 62). Both roles, the online learner's role and the online instructor's role, are related in such a way that one cannot be adequately and fully developed without the other. The way a course or programme has been designed and the way online teaching is carried out will shape the extent to which online learners can take up their role and perform online to the best of their potential; conversely, online learners' performance sets the boundaries of the online instructor's or online faculty's teaching role.

Conclusions

Students adopt a specific role as online learners when they learn online. The Role of the Online Learner as put forward, a combination of four cluster competences, Instrumental, Academic,

Relational and Metacognitive, is a comprehensive framework which can be a model to help students to adopt their role, beyond daily trial and error, when learning online. The Role competences are manifested in recognizable outputs, and these can be shared with students when faculty and institutions explain what the Role is when providing orientation or training on the essentials of learning online. Training students on the Role of the Online Learner can contribute to quality design of online courses and programmes, to a satisfactory learning experience online, to an ability to keep abreast of emerging new ways of learning, and to cater for the transformation of roles in Education.

References

Berge, Z. (2000). *New roles for learners and teachers in online higher education*. Retrieved 18 July 2005 from <http://www.whirligig.com.au/globaleducator/articles/BergeZane2000.pdf>

Birch, D. (2001). *E-learner competencies*. Retrieved 6 June 2005 from <http://www.brightways.net/Articles/wp01_elc.pdf>

Borges, F. (n.d.). The role of the online learner. A model for students' performance in online learning. (Unpublished).

Cleveland-Innes, M., Garrison, D.R., & Kinsel, E. (2007). Role adjustment for learners in an online Community of Inquiry: Identifying the challenges of incoming online learners. *International Journal of Web-Based Learning and Teaching Technologies, 2*(1).

De la Teja, I. (2011). Competències per a la docència en línia, International Workshop, Universitat de Barcelona—eLearn Center, UOC—Barcelona, Spain, 7 September 2011.

Gaiser, T.J. (1997). Conducting on-line focus groups. A methodological discussion. *Social Science Computer Review, 15*(2), 135–144.

Garrison, D. R., Cleveland-Innes, M., & Fung, T. (2004). Student role adjustment in online Communities of Inquiry: Model and instrument validation. *Journal of Asynchronous Learning Networks, 8*(2), 61–74.

Harasim, L., Hiltz, S.R., Teles, L., & Turoff, M. (1995). *A field guide to teaching and learning online* (1997 ed.). Cambridge, MA: The MIT Press.

ibstpi. (2010). *Competencies*. Retrieved 6 March 2010 from http://www.ibstpi.org/competencies.htm

Johnstone, S.M., & Connick, G.P. (Eds.). (2005). *The distance learner's guide* (2nd ed.). Upper Saddle River, NJ: Pearson.

Kinsel, E., Cleveland-Innes, M., & Garrison, D.R. (2004). *Student role adjustment in online environments: From the mouths of online babes*. Retrieved 18 October 2005 from <http://www.uwex.edu/disted/conference/Resource_library/proceedings/04_1228.pdf>

Mishra, S. (2005). Roles and competencies of academic counsellors in distance education. *Open Learning, 20*(2), 147–159.

O'Rourke, J. (2003). *Tutoring in open and distance learning: a handbook for tutors*. Retrieved 14 May 2010 from <http://www.col.org/PublicationDocuments/pub_odltutoringHB.pdf>

Piskurich, G.M. (Ed.) (2004). *Getting the most from online learning*. San Francisco: Pfeiffer.

Visser, J. (2008). Constructive interaction with change: Implications for learners and the environment in which they learn. In J. Visser & M. Visser-Valfrey (Eds.), *Learners in a changing learning landscape. Reflections from a dialogue on new roles and expectations* (pp. 11–35). Boston, MA: Springer.

Zawacki-Richter, O. (2009). Research areas in distance education: A Delphi study. *International Review of Research in Open and Distance Learning, 10*(3).

14

Collaborative Design Models for Blended, Online, and Traditional Courses

Five Approaches That Empower Students and Educators in the Twenty-first Century

Craig Perrier

P21 identifies collaboration as a priority in one of their four student outcomes, *Learning and Innovation Skills*. Linking global competencies with education, P21's emphasis is on shared responsibility, flexibility, and the "ability to work effectively and respectfully with diverse teams . . . to accomplish a common goal." (http://www.p21.org/storage/documents/P21_Framework_Definitions.pdf) Similarly, one of the key features of the Common Core Standards, "Speaking and Listening", associates collaboration with literacy and information skills:

> Students must learn to work together, express and listen carefully to ideas, integrate information from oral, visual, quantitative, and media sources, evaluate what they hear, use media and visual displays strategically to help achieve communicative purposes, and adapt speech to context and task.
>
> (http://www.corestandards.org/ELA-Literacy/introduction/how-to-read-the-standards , para. 8)

Finally, the U.S. Department of Education notes in their 2010 executive summary on twenty-first-century education that the convergence between student technological realities and the educational possibilities should be embraced.

> Many students' lives today are filled with technology that gives them mobile access to information and resources 24/7, enables them to create multimedia content and share it with the world, and allows them to participate in online social networks where people from all over the world share ideas, collaborate, and learn new things.
>
> (http://www.ed.gov/sites/default/files/netp2010.pdf , p. 10)

As an instructional practice, student collaboration, using a range of educational technology, can be implemented beyond classroom walls. Integrating technology with collaborative learning experiences facilitates exchange, expands cohorts, exposes a range of perspectives, and offers personalized, student-centered instruction and learning.

This chapter explores five approaches which foster student collaboration through educational technology. It is important to note that utilizing technology in the classroom is most effective when educators integrate and normalize it. Classroom structures, instruction, content, and assessment can be integrated with technology on a regular basis. This frames technology not as an add-on, but as part of the daily practices associated with teaching and learning. To do so, a teacher need not be a master of all technology. Instead, educators' opportunities to become familiar with a variety of tools and practices used to complement their curriculum should be provided and nurtured by school administrations. Educator Meg Ormitson reminds us that "just as learning often succeeds best when it is collaborative, so too will the ideal classroom become a reality if all of the school stakeholders are involved." (Ormitson, 2011, p. 32) The objective of this chapter is to provide models of technology-based student collaboration which are adaptive and inspire teachers to utilize these approaches throughout the school year.

Students presently enrolled in school have grown up with technology and social media around them. This reality has created the generational sobriquet *digital natives* while those born before have been identified as *digital immigrants*. These distinctions, however, do not equate to students' proficiency with educational technology. Creating effective, positive, and successful collaborative learning environments, therefore, remains the purview of teachers. In fact,

> the active-learning classroom today is an environment in which technology is integral. A significant amount of active learning also is likely to be collaborative . . . and the learning activities may continue outside of the classroom using Web 2.0 tools.
>
> (Moeller and Reitzes, 2011, p. 9)

The five models of collaboration outlined below describe successful practices I have utilized in my classrooms. Each can be modified to fit your needs, experiences, and instructional goals.

Model 1—Learning Management Systems: Adding Dimension to a Flat Classroom

Learning Management Systems (LMS) are platforms that facilitate online learning. Schools typically purchase district-wide LMS contracts for schools to utilize. Common platforms include Blackboard and Desire2Learn. However, in the absence of these large-scale purchases, departments and teachers may also select from a growing number of LMS which are free to users. Popular free educational LMS include Moodle, Haiku, CourseSites, Canvas, and BrainHoney.

Typical features of LMS include a menu of management tools, assessment items, lesson and module features, communication tools (both synchronous and asynchronous), student features, and collaborative interfaces. Utilizing an LMS in your classes provides an online learning area that supports student collaboration through interactive technology, allows for self-paced learning, and empowers students to engage course content anytime and anywhere. It is important to remember, however, that the main factor driving a successful online learning experience for students is the same factor impacting a traditional classroom: good teaching. Regardless of the LMS platform you use or the subject you teach, there are some core beliefs and best practices to consider when engaging students in technology-drive collaboration. To these ends, Lepi (2012) notes that "online education shouldn't be a solitary endeavor. Students may be working remotely . . . but they should never feel like they're alone in the online learning process. Support from instructors and other students is critical for success" ("Online learning may be remote, but it shouldn't be solitary").

Model 2—Wikis

In the past, teachers were forced to utilize class time around "group work" so students could organize and interact with each other in person. Both Web 2.0 tools and social media render this scenario antiquated. A basic feature of online collaboration is the elimination of time and space barriers to student social learning experiences. Simply put, online collaboration allows students to work anytime, anywhere, with multiple collaborators from a cohort larger than their class enrollment.

Demystifying educational technology around the concept of *collaboration* often alleviates teachers' hesitation and anxiety about using technology. To these ends, *wikis* are perfect introductory tools for newcomers. Most LMS come with a wiki option. A wiki is an online space for groups of students to generate, modify, comment, and delete content, depending on the wiki's settings. Student contributions are tracked and are easily updated. What's more, teachers, depending on the tool and platform, can assess progress and final products around collaboration in more detail, and with greater frequency and reliability, than in face-to-face settings. All that is needed is a teacher-designed learning experience with essential question, practices, and outcomes.

The case study outlined below was designed by two philosophy teachers from schools located in different states. Their instructional design targeted the upper four thinking skills in Bloom's Revised/Digital Taxonomy: Applying, Analyzing, Evaluating, and Creating (see www.usi.edu/distance/bloom%20pyramid.jpg). Demonstrating these skills was done through individual posting, commentary, and then student synthesis of knowledge. Using the wiki tool Campus Pack, the project centers around student-generated knowledge based on a common topic explored in their respective classes—the nature and manifestation of evil.

Case Study: Inter-Class Collaboration Project—Wiki on "The Concept of Evil"

Philosophy I is an honors-level course open to students in grades 10, 11, and 12. During the spring semester, school A had 23 students and school B had 20 students enrolled in their respective classes. Both school's catalog descriptions of "Philosophy 1" note that students

> will be challenged to think critically on (their) own, but always taking into consideration what others say . . . Philosophy enhances the improvement of the analysis of personal convictions, the understanding of the diversity of arguments of others and the awareness of the limited character of our knowledge . . . As a participant in this philosophy course you will be challenged to think critically and learn to think with the ideas and points of view of past and contemporary philosophers.
>
> (https://my.vhslearning.org/PublicCourseDescription.aspx?c=170 , paras. 1-3)

The explicit references to collaboration in the course overview made Philosophy I an ideal course for the collaborative wiki project.

The methodology for Philosophy's inter-class project focused on the delivering differentiated content sources in each school. School A addressed the concept of evil from the understanding of philosopher Friedrich Nietzsche. School B engaged Hannah Arendt's ideas concerning the banality of evil. The "content expert specialization" approach establishes two distinct bodies of knowledge around a shared course topic. Furthermore, this approach inherently draws on the visions of collaboration outlined by P21, CCSSI, and the Department of Education.

Students from separate schools collaborated in a shared wiki featuring a shared landing page and group student pages organized by school. Students matched up with groups from the other school (for example group 1 from school A worked with group 1 from school B). Students engaged with guiding questions that facilitated students' teaching the partner school on what they had learned in their own classrooms. The wiki allowed for revisions to initial posts and for comments to be made by students in either section over a two-day timeframe. Student ownership of the content individualized students in a collaborative context. The project's final product was a reflective "This I Believe . . ." statement (modeled after the National Public Radio program. See http://www.npr.org/series/4538138/this-i-believe) which synthesized the knowledge they had learned at their school with what was learned in the online wiki.

Postscript

The differentiated, content specialist model of this project has clear potential across content areas. Likewise, the length and outcome of the collaborative project is flexible to the needs of the participants and instructional design used. Also, the collaborative project recognized that temporal and geographic boundaries are no longer insurmountable obstacles due to educational technology and social media.

Model 3—Infographics

A picture may be worth a thousand words, but a collaboratively generated infographic is priceless. Infographics are student-generated research products combining text and graphics—typically specialized maps, charts, and illustrations—in one creative and specially designed medium. In the past, infographics were called collages or posters. Today, an infographic's focus on research, collaboration, and technology distinguishes them from previous iterations. In addition, their educational appeal has grown with the advent of "media literacy" and "information literacy" as twenty-first-century skills related to college and career readiness and the adoption of the Common Core State Standards.

David Considine, a media specialist, notes:

> While more young people have access to the internet and other media than any generation in history, they do not necessarily possess the ethics, the intellectual skills, or the predisposition to critically analyze and evaluate their relationship with these technologies or the information they encounter.
>
> (Jacobs, 2010, p. 139)

Teaching Media Literacy empowers students to locate, manipulate, connect, and manage information. Once a plan is set, students can use infographics to demonstrate their knowledge. Attaining competency in media literacy can be reached through three guiding steps:

1. Know the message you want to convey.
2. Information is accurate. Cite your sources.
3. Determine your layout.

Present Web 2.0 tools that will help students create infographics include:

- https://venngage.com/
- http://vizualize.me/
- http://piktochart.com/
- http://www.easel.ly/
- http://create.visual.ly/
- http://www.photostatsapp.com/
- http://www.icharts.net/

These tools allow students to collaborate anywhere. Once a tool is selected, students can use a three-step approach to complete their project: Research-> Design-> Publish.

This online component, similar to the wiki example above, extends learning beyond the class through online collaboration, which, Ormitson reminds us, "engages students with one another in the pursuit of content knowledge and understanding." (Ormitson, 2011, p. 82)

Model 4—Interactive Timelines

Creating meaningful learning events for students which address the multitude of demands on educators requires a creative, synthetic approach to classroom teaching. Teachers willing to utilize online learning tools engage students in the development of meaningful skills, and provide options for students to demonstrate their understanding while integrating technology. One Web 2.0 tool that has gained wide appeal is interactive, online timelines. A selection of web-based interactive timelines includes:

- http://timeglider.com/
- http://www.timetoast.com/
- http://www.tiki-toki.com/
- http://www.capzles.com/
- http://www.xtimeline.com/index.aspx
- http://www.dipity.com/
- http://www.preceden.com/
- http://timerime.com/
- http://www.preceden.com/
- http://whenintime.com/

Sample Activity Plan: World History

Objective

Demonstrate your understanding of historical narrative through the creation of a timeline addressing a theme in World History 1945–Present. Remember, there is not one, true master narrative about your selected theme. However your narrative timeline must be coherent and each item related to the others or interconnected through a larger theme. This is fleshed out in your description below.

Use our class materials/resources as main sources. You may certainly use your own research, but be sure your resources are valid.

Due Dates

By end of the week—6 items added to your timeline
By next week—12 items added to your timeline

Each Timeline Entry Must Include

- Title (this should be designed to your selected theme from week 1).
- Date (either a specific date or range).
- Description: This write-up explains how you see this event, group, idea, system, individual in relation to you theme. By including this event in your timeline, you have given it higher value in your understanding. It also includes your reasons for selecting the link and image. This is the main writing part of this assignment.
- Link to a video, podcast, or website that adds content and further explanation to your choice.
- Add a relevant image with a caption.

Assessment

- Students will publish their timeline.
- Examine 2–3 timelines that have been created in our class. Select 4 items that are on each that demonstrate/represent the development of globalization. Write an essay addressing using those items to address a global issue.
  - In your introduction, explain the issue.
  - In your body paragraphs, explain how the 4 items you selected from the timeline relate to each other and are indicative of your understanding of globalization.
  - In your conclusion, suggest a plan that addresses the issue in an attempt to improve or resolve the issue.

Interactive timelines promote students' creativity and personalize their own learning. Their use is an effective way to address the question posed by Wilmarth: "Are students improving their ability to think critically, to express themselves, and to develop usable literacies by participating in Web 2.0 tools?" (Jacobs, 2010, p. 101) What's more, these timelines can be shared, continuously modified, and embedded in social media for mass consumption.

Model 5—Online Discussion Boards

Online discussion boards provide opportunities for student–student and student–teacher interaction. The ideas generated in discussion boards are, if responding to higher-order prompts and questions, one of the purest forms of social knowledge construction available in education. In turn, online discussion boards, whether text based, audio, or visual, should be embraced by educators as an opportunity to extend their classrooms experiences beyond their physical walls.

Teachers can enrich the online experience for students by planning, customizing, and using the discussion board as a pedagogical enhancement in their classes. At its best, the result is a dynamic forum that democratizes knowledge through collaboration, involves peer and teacher review, and builds on media literacy essential for the twenty-first century.

A primary purpose, and advantage, of discussion boards is the ability to establish a level of collegiality which is at times not fostered in traditional classrooms among classmates. By moving individual students, groups, or entire classes out of isolation and into a collaborative environment, participants experience a community which can positively impact motivation, self-confidence, and skill acquisition. Moreover, discussion boards provide an opportunity for students to take advantage of an extended global network, encourage students to become reflective learners, and enhance students' twenty-first-century literacy skills by helping them learn to communicate effectively in a virtual environment. Finally, discussion boards are best when they engage students with provocative questions and meaningful prompts which relate to the course content and knowledge construction. These prompts challenge students to both apply and question their knowledge in a dynamic setting.

To these ends, discussion boards function best with open-ended questions and subjective prompts inviting interpretation and multiple perspectives. They should invite students to explore, apply, connect, and reflect on course content and personal experience. It is important to note, therefore, that discussion boards should not be a place to post homework, essays, or any other assignment.

Discussion questions and prompts should not address limited or restrictive answers or permit students the opportunity to copy something off the internet and drop it into a class discussion. Teachers should craft questions and prompts that are engaging and relevant, and that embrace a multiplicity of responses. Some samples of open-ended prompts are provided below.

- "Are you more in favor of or more opposed to (course issue/theme etc)? Explain in a paragraph why."
- "Suggest an alternative method, process, or perspective regarding (course issue/theme etc)."
- "Make two comments on this week's reading which relate to previous concepts in the course."
- "To what extent do you agree with this quote? Provide support for your rationale."
- "Explain 3–4 ways in which your understanding was impacted by (class source). Quote or give examples from the piece to support your claims."

These sample prompts are easily modified and can be used across disciplines. When facilitators establish clear expectations and offer open-ended prompts, class discussions have a greater possibility of being marked by robust contributions which open doors to student inquiry and insight. Being skilled in facilitating those exchanges is as important to the experience as crafting the inspiring discussion prompt. Also, to structure the discussion board, establish clear expectations for students' responses including the number of original posts per week, length of posts, and quality of responses. Providing a sample post is a very effective way to illustrate requirements. Likewise, a "Do and Do Not" list is an easy reference and reminder for students to access.

A successful discussion board facilitator uses the opportunity provided by open-ended discussion questions and prompts to engage, expand, and assess student knowledge and understanding. Too often, facilitators will remain silent and view forums as a student-only area of interaction. Imagine using this approach in a face-to-face classroom! Claims that teachers are inactive to avoid "poisoning the well" of student thought don't hold up when confronted with the spectrum of roles teachers can assume in online discussions.

To fully utilize the online forum, teachers, simply put, need to be involved. Failing to comment is characteristic of a disinterested teacher who may not even be reading students' posts. This inaction threatens the fidelity of the discussion board itself and relegates it to "busywork".

Both the "sage on the stage" and the "guide on the side" are roles too limiting for effective discussion board facilitation. Instead, teachers who explicitly detail their roles to students and assign varying roles to students have a larger repertoire to pull from. Some effective facilitation roles and actions to utilize in online courses include:

1. *The Clarifier:* Correct misconceptions or errors about content that is covered in a discussion.
2. *Devil's Advocate:* Offer dissenting opinions that ask students to consider other possibilities.
3. *Give Me More:* Ask students to be more explicit in their posts. For example, you could copy and paste their ideas in their post and then ask them to elaborate on the ambiguous part.
4. *Adding to the Menu:* Bring in an outside source, additional point, or hypothetical situation in order to stir the pot. Injecting another source, anecdote, or reference can open a perceived closed discussion.
5. *Citation Police:* You can require students to cite the week's reading in their posts as evidence or support for their claims. This would connect two aspects of the class and have them practice with citations.
6. *The Questioner:* In order to further the discussion, you should end your post with a question or ask for clarification.
7. *Avoid Absolutes:* Construct your contributions as suggestions: "It seems to me . . .", "I think. . . ." Absolute, definite statements like "It is obvious that . . .", "Clearly . . .", "We all know . . ." are difficult to substantiate and may inhibit contributions from others. Avoid *all, everyone, none*, and *never*.
8. *The Inviter:* Change the subject line of your post to invite the class to read and respond to your prompt. For example, you could write "EVERYONE SHOULD READ" or "FOR THE ENTIRE CLASS" in the subject line.

Teacher comments are effective models of what their students should be writing and be more than simple phrases of praise like "good job" or "nice work." That's the virtual equivalent of putting a check on every piece of paper passed in. Moreover, these comments are seen as "full stop" posts that do not push the discussion further. Dead-end forums can be overcome by requiring students to end their posts with a question or hypothetical situation for classmates to consider.

An advantage to the online discussion is that students have time to contemplate and work things out on their own for a day or two. You don't have to instantly jump into the middle of every exchange between students. Synthesizing quality and quantity in your post is a skill to be developed. Also, effective communication in online discussions involves being moderate in your contributions. Lengthy posts are self-defeating as students will not read them. Present your ideas in digestible screen-sized chunks. Last, it is okay if all questions aren't answered during that specific discussion week. In fact, returning to discussion posts can be a powerful instructional tool. Deciding how your discussion boards are utilized is best determined prior to students' posting their first idea.

Conclusion

What can we do to make sure our students experience a relevant, collaborative, and skill-based education? As educators, we must commit to a dynamism in our profession which reframes teachers from knowledge hubs to facilitators, contextualizers, and promoters of student-centered learning. It is imperative that contemporary education move the classroom from a formal learning space to a networked activity center focused on information management, knowledge creation, collaboration, and personalized learning. "There is ample evidence that the informal learning gained from social interactions and peer-mediated learning is substantial. And the more diverse, global, and heterogeneous a set of networks that one participates in, the more learning that occurs." (Boyd and Ellison, 2007, p. 221)

Once students are collaborating with peers beyond your classroom, teachers can empower their twenty-first-century classroom by placing student work in the public sphere. What is meant by the "public sphere"? Simply put, the public sphere is anything beyond the teacher's eyes only. The idea of students writing a paper for a teacher's eyes only is an anachronism. Placing students in the public sphere is easy to do with social media. One suggestion is to do this in a secure course in your school's LMS. Moreover, students accept greater responsibility and are more invested in their work. Consider the list below a continuum moving from "narrow" to "broad" public spheres. Next to each dimension are a few suggested ways student work can interact beyond teacher-eyes-only models.

What Is Meant by the Public Sphere in Education?

a) **classroom**: gallery walks, class discussion of student work
b) **department:** peer editing from other sections, presenting to other classes, discipline web site highlighting student work
c) **school:** display tables at lunch, displays in hallways, newspapers, library archives, part of parent nights
d) **community:** student work in civic buildings, displays, local newspapers
e) **nation:** engage in projects like National History Day, collaborate with schools, and colleges, engage in contests
f) **international**: establish sister schools, link with nonprofits, video conferencing
g) **cyber space:** present at online conferences, post work on web sites, establish a learnist board, comment on blogs, utilize Web 2.0 tools

Who is calling for students to generate knowledge and publish it for public consumption? It is argued that

> As pressures mount for society to equip today's youth with both the global and digital understandings necessary to confront the challenges of the 21st century, a more thorough analysis must be undertaken to examine the role of technology on student learning.
>
> (Maguth, 2012, p. 177)

Likewise,

> youth are active participants, producers, and distributors of new media. The digital production of youth includes over 38% of designing personal websites, 23% constructing online videos and slideshows, and 8% launching digital causes campaigns . . . The internet has allowed youth new opportunities in fostering global awareness of civic, humanitarian, political, economic, and environmental causes.
>
> (Maguth, 2012, p. 3)

Publications come in a variety of forms. Overall, this is a very exciting part of education that should be part of any collaborative classroom in the twenty-first century.

Below is a partial list of concrete suggestions.

Publish What?

Writing (all types)	Visuals/mind-maps	Blogs/Wikis	Infographics
Presentation	Video/Audio/Media posts	Comments to established web pages	

Ultimately, twenty-first-century educators must reflect on their profession and decide where, when, and how they can advance their practice. A central question to explore is: *Can we change our traditional culture of teaching and learning so that students are empowered to take more responsibility for making important contributions to their own learning and to their learning community?* The answer must be yes. Getting there can happen in a variety of ways, but a common element to success is embracing educational technology that supports student collaboration. Doing so, some skeptics may argue, is unnecessarily reinventing the wheel of learning. The reality is that education has fully changed because of the students we are teaching; the reasons that schools and teachers exist have changed. It is time to reinvent the wheel.

References

Boyd, D., & Ellison, N. (2007). Social network sites: Definition, history, and scholarship. *Journal of Computer Mediated Communication, 13*(1), 210–230. Retrieved from www.corestandards.org www.ed.gov/technology

Jacobs, H. (2010). *Curriculum 21: Essential education for a changing world*. Alexandria, VA: ASCD.

Lepi, K. (2012, October 5). 20+ tips from the most effective online teachers. *Gilfus Education Group*. Retrieved from www.gilfuseducationgroup.com/20-tips-from-the-most-effective-online-teachers

Maguth, B. (2012). *New directions in social education research: The influence of technology and globalization on the lives of students*. Charlotte, NC: Information Age.

Moeller, B., & Reitzes, T. (2011). *Integrating technology with student-centered learning*. Quincy, MA: Nellie Mae Education Foundation.

Ormiston, M. (2011). *Creating a digital-rich classroom: Teaching and learning in a Web 2.0 world*. Bloomington, IN: Solution Tree. Retrieved from www.p21.org www.thevhscollaborative.org

15

Learner Interaction in E-learning

Cynthia D. Cummings, Diane R. Mason, Sheryl R. Abshire, and Daryl Ann Borel

Learner Interaction in E-learning

Web-based environments have significantly impacted how, when, and where students learn (Sher, 2009). Bacow, Bowen, Guthrie, Lack, and Long (2012) reported that e-learning is being offered at almost every college or university. Enrollments in online courses continue to grow at a faster rate than overall higher education enrollments in the United States (Allen & Seaman, 2010). According to a survey of 4,523 United States higher education institutions conducted by the Babson Survey Research Group, data from 2,512 respondents revealed over 6.1 million students took at least one online course in 2010 and there was an additional reported increase of 560,000 in 2011 (Allen & Seaman, 2011). Furthermore, 31 percent of the students in higher education reported having taken at least one online course, and 65 percent of the responding higher education administrators reported that the continued online learning upswing created more need for building long-term strategies to address e-learning (Allen & Seaman, 2011). In 2009, Ambient Insight Research released a forecast study predicting there will be 27.34 million higher education students in the United States by 2014. The study predicts a 2 percent increase in total higher education students planning to take higher education classes by 2014. Moreover, they estimate 3.55 million (12.8 percent) will complete all of their coursework online, 18.65 million (68.2 percent) will take some online courses, and 5.14 million (19 percent) will participate in face-to-face courses.

In spite of the exponential growth of online learning, critics are still concerned about the lack of effective and efficient interaction among students and professors (Arbaugh, 2000). The massive growth of online learning opportunities accessible to students through public, private, for-profit, and free resources brings to light the need for ongoing discussions and research regarding overall learner effectiveness (Allen & Seaman, 2011; Ambient Insight Research, 2009). Garrison (2000) contended that in order to silence the critics, distance educators need to provide a theoretical framework for interaction. Because interaction is at the core of learner effectiveness in online/distance learning, the seminal work of Moore's transactional distance theory was the most promising and appealing. This chapter is devoted to Lamar University's application of interaction in an online master's program.

Contextual Framework

The regional southeast Texas university, located in the United States, offers a wide array of fully online courses with a total enrollment of 6,205 students (Distance Education Committee, October, 2012). The online course deliveries extend from high school dual credit courses in varied content areas, to undergraduate and master's degrees in a number of disciplines, and a doctoral degree in educational leadership. Increasing numbers of online students in multiple programs created a need for university online program decision-makers to engage in dialogues and research conversations about effective learner interaction strategies. The conversations with higher education administrators, instructors, students, and community stakeholders led to the implementation of online learning institutional dispositions.

The institutional dispositions forming the contextual framework for online learning experiences at the university are founded upon three key resources: the Five Pillars of the Sloan Consortium (SLOAN-C) Quality Online Framework, The Quality Scorecard for the Administration of Online Programs, and the Quality Matters Rubric (MarylandOnline, 2010; Sloan Consortium, 2012a; Sloan Consortium, 2012b). Each specific resource provides anchoring concepts for the planning, design, and implementation of learner interactions in the online environment.

The Sloan Five Pillar framework includes five important components: Learner Effectiveness, Scale (Cost Effectiveness and Commitment), Access, Faculty Satisfaction, and Student Satisfaction (Bourne & Moore, 2002; Sloan Consortium, 2012a). Each of the components is assessed and progress is reported annually to online learning stakeholders.

The Quality Scorecard for the Administration of Online Programs serves as a tool for measuring quality within the total higher education online program by offering 70 indicators as benchmarks for program quality (Sloan Consortium, 2012b; Shelton, 2010). The Quality Scorecard provides opportunities for online program administrators and faculty to identify areas of weaknesses and components of strength for strategic and continuous improvement planning (Sloan Consortium, 2012b). The areas acknowledged as needing improvement become the focal point for strategic planning and faculty development, which includes using the Quality Matters Rubric to assess specific online course content and development.

The Quality Matters (QM) Rubric was developed by MarylandOnline and consists of a series of 70 quality indicators used in a faculty peer-review process to assess the quality of online or blended courses (MarylandOnline, 2010). The QM Rubric consists of three features: a written set of indicators, a peer review process, and professional development. The university uses the QM Rubric as a key guideline for the development of online coursework. Subsequent peer reviews of coursework provide the framework to determine faculty professional development needs and next steps needed to successfully create, modify, or maintain online courses.

Theory and Application

Moore first coined the idea of transactional distance when referring to a separation of space between the teacher and learner in independent studies or distance learning (Boyd & Apps, 1980). In the transactional theory, Moore (1997) posited that in a distance learning environment the distance between instructor and student could lead to gaps in communication and possible misunderstanding between the two (Moore & Kearsley, 1996). Moore (1997) identified three factors that were needed for transaction between instructor and students. These three factors were dialogue, structure, and learner autonomy. Dialogue is about more than just how often it takes place, including the quality and how well it is used to solve problems the learner may encounter. Structure refers to the course's rigidity or flexibility in meeting the needs of the learner. Autonomy refers to the learner's perception of his or her independence and interdependence in the course.

To ensure clarity in the meaning of Moore's transactional distance theory (1993), Moore proposed three types of communication in distance education: learner to content, learner to instructor, and learner to learner. In addition, Hillman, Willis, and Gunawardena (1994) expanded Moore's seminal work to include learner to interface interaction. In a dissertation study, Kuo, Walker, and Schroder (2010) found learner to instructor and learner to content interactions greatly contributed to student satisfaction in a fully online learning situation.

The importance of interaction is reinforced by Laurillard (2000), who argues that a university education must go far beyond access to information or content and include "engagement with others in the gradual development of their personal understanding" (p. 137). This engagement is developed through interaction between teachers and students and among students, and forms the basis of Laurillard's (2000) approach to teaching and learning. Garrison (2011) defined all forms of education, including distance education, as interactions among instructors, students, and content. Thus, both human and nonhuman interactions are integral and reciprocal components of a quality online experience.

A number of researchers agree that one key element contributing to student learning success and satisfaction in online coursework is related to learner interactions (Cho, 2011; Hillman et al., 1994; Keegan, 1990; Moore & Kearsley, 2005). Learner effectiveness, particularly as it pertains to student success, satisfaction, and engagement, is of significant interest to higher education administrators, instructors, students, and community stakeholders (Lim & Park, 2010; Advisory Committee on Student Financial Assistance, 2012).

As part of the university's commitment to student success in online education, learner interaction was the priority for building an exceptional online program. All courses at Lamar University were designed and peer reviewed using the Quality Matters Rubric to ensure high quality interactions for learner to content, learner to instructor, learner to learner, and learner to interface.

Learner to content. According to Swan (2004), interaction with content refers "to the learners' interactions with the knowledge, skills and attitudes being studied" (p. 64). This has to do with the learners' interaction with the course materials. The interaction between the learner and the content is the process of changing the learner's understanding and view of the content. It is a critical element to learning new concepts (Moore, 1989).

In the Lamar University online master's program in Educational Leadership and Educational Technology Leadership, Blackboard™ serves as the primary learning management system (LMS). Additionally, students are required to interact with content delivered through a variety of online resources, which includes open source applications, social media, and electronic portfolios. Content is organized into five separate weekly modules that include content-related readings, reflection upon and response to a variety of contextual probes through discussion boards and electronic portfolios, videos lectures, and course-related assignments.

Learner to instructor. Moore (1993) suggested that designers of online courses identify instructional goals related to the instructor's own interaction with the student in order to initiate and maintain student interest and engagement in the online course. Interaction with instructors includes strategies used to teach, guide, support, and provide ongoing feedback to their students (Moore, 1989). This interaction can be either synchronous (in real time) or asynchronous (not in real time) communication. At Lamar University, master's candidates participate in several learning opportunities with course instructors such as virtual office hours and weekly Adobe

Connect™ web conferences, which often include polling used to gather feedback, chat, texting, phone conferencing, Skype™, and assignment feedback.

Branon and Essex (2001) examined practices of online instructors and concluded that virtual office hours help to enhance learner to instructor interactions. Contemporary literature has drawn attention to examining learning and teaching through the use of web conferencing (Keir & Elizondo, 2010; Premchaiswadi & Tungkasthan, 2007; Suggs, Myers, & Dennen, 2010). Some studies extend this to recommend pedagogical strategies for learning and teaching in web conferencing environments, including self-assessment questionnaires and polls (Abourbih & Witham, 2007), techniques for facilitating turn-taking (Suggs et al., 2010), and teacher-guided collaborative problem-solving approaches (Bower, 2011). Thurairajah, Williams, and McAdam (2011) found that learner experience in an online environment was enhanced using web conferencing.

Learner to learner. Moore (1993) stated that learner to learner interaction is advantageous for building cognitive processes and developing motivational support, and is based on social theories of learning. Interaction among peers includes the interactions among learners or among learners working in small groups, which can take many forms.

Collaborative interaction occurs when learners discuss issues that are related to their learning on discussion boards or solve problems collaboratively (Dabbagh & Bannan-Ritland, 2005; Moller, 1998). Even though this type of interaction is encouraged in a task-oriented learning situation, it also has a social dimension. Interpersonal or social interaction occurs when learners receive social feedback from their peers through personal encouragement and motivational assistance (Ingirige & Goulding, 2009).

Master's candidates at Lamar University are provided opportunities to interact with their peers in the form of collaborative grouping, project-based learning activities, which includes scenario-based problem solving; sharing of ideas, practices, and concepts through interactive web conferencing; peer-review of electronic portfolio and assignment activities; and social media environments. Lamar master's candidates critically reflect upon their own learning and provide feedback to peers through review of electronic portfolios, group projects, and discussion board postings within the context of online professional learning communities (PLC).

In a recent study by Mason and Cummings (2013, February), quantitative data from the Online Teamwork Satisfaction Scale (Tseng, Ku, Wang, & Sun, 2009) indicate that the majority of the Lamar Educational Technology Leadership online master's candidates reported a high level of satisfaction with teamwork and learner to learner interaction in EDLD 5364, Teaching with Technology. Survey responses indicated 92% of candidates selected *agree* or *strongly agree* on the satisfaction scale range in response to the statement *My team members share knowledge during the teamwork processes*, and 69.4% made those selections in response to the statement *Working with my team produced better project quality than working individually.* This study supports Moore's value of learner to learner interaction.

Learner to interface. With the growth of technology in distance education, Hillman et al. (1994) added learner to interface interaction, acknowledging the fact that the learner in a distance education environment has to interact with the technology. They reported that for technology novices, the interface may be a barrier to learning. According to Ross (1996), one of the barriers for novice users is that the learner becomes more engaged with the technology and not the content of interaction. As students became more comfortable with the technology, their interaction was enhanced (Tsui & Ki, 1996).

According to Anderson (2002), learner to interface interaction focuses on the access to content delivery, skills necessary to adequately interact with the delivery system, and a positive mindset necessary for successful learning. Learner to interface interaction is a compilation of a variety of interaction types. Becoming proficient in communication and the technical skills required to be successful are often overlooked by students entering an e-learning environment.

One of the five pillars of Sloan C is quality access. As part of the quality access, Lamar candidates are provided with tutorial and orientation videos on accessing and navigating the LMS. Furthermore, students are presented with the characteristics of successful online learners and tips for becoming a successful e-learner. The university help desk support for the LMS and other technical questions and concerns is readily available for all online students. Another embedded level of support to assist students who may be struggling with the technology and maneuvering in an online environment is the use of small-group facilitators. These facilitators, referred to as Instructional Associates (IA), provide content and technology support for groups of 25 students.

Challenges to Effective Interaction

Muirhead (2004) affirmed that instructors were charged with designing learning communities that fostered effective interaction between learner to instructor, learner to learner, learner to content, and learner to interface. However, challenges existed in creating this interaction in online learning environments. A review of the literature identified common challenges such as technology issues, lack of academic readiness, time commitment, and quality course structure (Arabasz, Pirani, & Fawcett, 2003; Haugen, LaBarre, & Melrose, 2001; Kop, 2011; Murphy & Coleman, 2004; Yang & Cornelius, 2005; York & Richardson, 2012).

Success in delivering and participating in online learning rests on the fact that both instructor and learner have the technology skills and access needed (Arabasz et al., 2003; Murphy & Coleman, 2004). Arabasz et al. (2003) identified technology challenges for learners and instructors. Instructors are challenged to design high-quality courses utilizing current technology trends, overcome their lack of technology skills and confidence to use technology, support different platforms and software, and work through network and learning management system issues, often without adequate training.

Technology issues for learners included lack of network access, inability to keep up with the technology demands, lack of basic technology skills, and inability to navigate learning management systems. Even if learners do have computer literacy, there is no assurance that these learners have the academic readiness skills, such as reading; writing; researching; and the ability to find, evaluate, and use information effectively (Chen & Yang, 2005). Since the majority of course content is delivered through written content and instruction, reading and writing skills are requirements for online learners (Haugen et al., 2001).

According to Arabasz et al. (2003), the amount of time required by instructors to develop and maintain quality online courses proved to be one of the most challenging issues for instructors. Disorganized learners struggled with submitting assignments in a timely manner and procrastinating when it came to participating in course requirements. Both instructor and learner need good time management skills to ensure success in the online learning environment.

Course structure, identified as a critical factor influencing interaction, posed challenges for instructors developing online courses (Northrup, 2002). These challenges included designing relevant and rigorous assignments that replaced seat time with meaningful interaction, providing tutorials and support, structuring assessments for the online environment, providing timely feedback, providing social interaction for learners, and the instructor being active in the course (Arabasz et al., 2003; Haugen et al., 2001; Northrup, 2002; Shea, Swan, Li, & Pickett, 1994; Smith & Winking-Diaz, 2004).

Conclusion

Creating a community of learners where the quantity and quality of interactions with peers and faculty foster student engagement is an essential factor for a successful online educational experience (Grandzol & Grandzol, 2006; Meyers, 2008; Ozden, 2011). Astin (1993) found that the quality and quantity of interactions with peers and faculty in both academic and social activities were the most important factors fostering student engagement, a powerful predictor of student success. Furthermore, research indicates that there is value in working in small group collaborations where online learners utilize a variety of tools, such as Web 2.0, e-portfolio, and video (Mason, Abernathy, Abshire, Cummings, & Liu, 2012). Therefore, it is essential that online courses be developed intentionally to allow student-to-student interaction and student-to-faculty interaction on both the academic and the social levels (Astin, 1993). Additionally, students enrolled in online courses prefer a structured and comfortable classroom environment that provides opportunities for participation in the learning activities (Young, 2006). According to Caliskan (2009), one of the most important online course components is interaction, especially learner to learner interaction. The review of Schullo et al. (2005) confirms that there is considerable evidence in the literature that interaction is important for effective distance learning teaching and that interaction, whether instructor to learner or learner to learner, improves student attitude, depth of learning, and student retention. The bottom line is that students should "feel a personal and emotional connection to the subject, their professor, and their peers" (Grandzol & Grandzol, 2006, p. 7).

Although there are many challenges for both online learners and instructors, Lamar University's Department of Educational Leadership has taken steps to address and minimize the barriers related to technology issues, lack of academic readiness, time commitment, and quality course structure. Ongoing professional learning opportunities provide instructors with the technology competencies that are needed to teach in the learning management system, create and conduct effective synchronous web conferences, promote collaborative learning, and develop learning communities within an online learning environment. To ensure quality courses, the university uses the Quality Matters Rubric as a key guideline for the development of online coursework. The rubric consists of a series of 70 quality indicators used in a faculty peer-review process to assess the quality of online or blended courses (MarylandOnline, 2010). The subsequent peer reviews of coursework provide the framework to determine faculty professional development needs and next steps needed to successfully create, modify, or maintain quality online courses. To assist with learner challenges in the Lamar program, students are provided with support that includes technical assistance for the LMS, course content assistance from instructional associates and course professors, video and written tutorials, and collaborative opportunities with course instructors such as virtual office hours and weekly Adobe Connect™ web conferences. Lamar's faculty continues to view interaction and student engagement as central to the students' learning experiences and crucial in the success of online learners.

References

Arabasz, P., Pirani, J., & Fawcett, D. (2003). Supporting e-learning in higher education. Research report 3, 1–91. Boulder, CO: EDUCAUSE Center for Applied Research. Retrieved from http://www.educause.edu/ir/library/pdf/ers0303/rs/ers0303w.pdf

Abourbih, J., & Witham, R. (2007). Using web-based conferencing and presentation software to improve teaching effectiveness and the learning environment. In T. Bastiaens & S. Carliner (Eds.), *Proceedings of the*

World Conference on E-Learning in Corporate, Government, Healthcare, and Higher Education (pp. 4180–4185). Chesapeake, VA: AACE. Retrieved from http://www.editlib.org

Advisory Committee on Student Financial Assistance. (2012, February). *Pathways to success: Integrating learning with life and work to increase national college completion*. Report to the U.S. Congress and Secretary of Education. Retrieved from http://www2.ed.gov/about/bdscomm/list/acsfa/ptsreport2.pdf

Allen, E., & Seaman, J. (2010). *Class difference: Online education in the United States*. Babson Survey Research Group and the Sloan Consortium. Retrieved from http://sloanconsortium.org/publications/survey/class_differences

Allen, E., & Seaman, J. (2011). *Going the distance: Online education in the United States in 2011*. Babson Survey Research Group and Quahog Research Group, LLC. Retrieved from http://sloanconsortium.org/publications/survey/going_distance_2011

Ambient Insight Research. (2009). *The U.S. market for self-paced elearning products and services: 2010–2015 forecast and analysis*. Retrieved from http://www.ambientinsight.com/Resources/Documents/AmbientInsight_2006_US_eLearning_Market_Snapshot.pdf

Anderson, T. (2002). The hidden curriculum of distance education. *Change Magazine, 33*(6), 28–35.

Arbaugh, J.B. (2000). Virtual classroom characteristics and student satisfaction with internet-based MBA courses. *Journal of Management Education, 24*, 32–54.

Astin, A.W. (1993). *What matters in college: Four critical years revisited*. New York: Macmillan.

Bacow, L., Bowen, W., Guthrie, K., Lack, K., & Long, M. (2012, May 1). *Barriers to adoption of online learning systems in U.S. higher education*. Retrieved from http://www.sr.ithaka.org/research-publications/barriers-adoption-online-learning-systems-us-higher-education

Bourne, J., & Moore, J. (Eds.). (2002). *Elements of quality in online education* (Vol. 3). Needham, MA: Sloan-C.

Bower, M. (2011). Synchronous collaboration competencies in web conferencing environment—Their impact on the learning process. *Distance Education, 32*(1), 63–83. doi:10.1080/01587919.2011.565502

Boyd, R., & Apps, J. (1980). *Redefining the discipline of adult education*. San Francisco: Jossey-Bass.

Branon, R., & Essex, C. (2001). Synchronous and asynchronous communication tools in distance education: A survey of instructors. *TechTrends, 45*(1), 36, 42.

Caliskan, H. (2009). Facilitators' perception of interactions in an online learning program. *Turkish Online Journal of Distance Education, 10*(3), 193–203. Retrieved from https://tojde.anadolu.edu.tr/tojde35/pdf/article_13.pdf

Chen, E., & Yang, B. (2005). Teaching information literacy in higher education: What can we learn from faculty? *Journal of Educational Computing, Design and Online Learning, 6*. Retrieved from www.uni.edu/chenhaa/research/informationalliteracy.pd

Cho, T. (2011). The impact of types of interaction on student satisfaction in online courses. *International Journal on E-Learning, 10*(2), 109–125. Chesapeake, VA: AACE.

Dabbagh, N., & Bannan-Ritland, B. (2005). *Online learning: Concepts, strategies, and application*. Upper Saddle River, NJ: Merrill Education, Prentice Hall.

Distance Education Committee. (2012, October 17). *Meeting on distance education and academic partnerships*. Paula Nichols, Ed. D., Chair. Lamar University, Beaumont, TX.

Garrison, D.R. (2011). *E-learning in the 21st century: A framework for research and practice* (2nd ed.). London: Routledge/Falmer.

Garrison, R. (2000). Theoretical challenges for distance education in the 21st century: A shift from structural to transactional issues. *International Review of Research in Open and Distance Learning, 1*(1), 1–17. Retrieved from http://www.irrodl.org/index.php/irrodl/article/viewFile/2/22

Grandzol, J., & Grandzol, C. (2006). Best practices for online business education. *International Review of Research in Open and Distance Learning, 7*(1), 1–18. Retrieved from http://www.irrodl.org/

Haugen, S., LaBarre, J., & Melrose, J. (2001). Online course delivery: Issues and challenges. *Issues in Information Systems, 2*, 127–131. Retrieved from http://iacis.org/iis/2001/Haugen127.pdf

Hillman, D., Willis, D., & Gunawardena, C. (1994). Learner-interface interaction in distance education: An extension of contemporary models and strategies for practitioners, *American Journal of Distance Education, 8*(2), 30–42.

Ingirige, B., & Goulding, J. (2009). Maximizing social interactions and effectiveness within distance learning courses. *Journal for Education in the Built Environment, 4*(1), 75–99. Retrieved from http://usir.salford.ac.uk/2225/1/BingunathIngirige4(1)-JEBE.pdf

Keegan, D. (1990). *Course creation issues in distance education. Foundations of distance education*. New York: Routledge.

Keir, S., & Elizondo, J. (2010). Utilizing Elluminate to provide professional development for school staff in the Pacific Region. In D. Gibson & B. Dodge (Eds.), *Proceedings of Society for Information Technology & Teacher Education International Conference* (pp. 2748–2753). Chesapeake, VA: AACE. Retrieved from http://www.editlib.org

Kop, R. (2011). The challenges to connectivist learning on open online networks: Learning experiences during a massive open online course. *International Review of Research in Open and Distance Learning, Special Issue, 12*(3), 19–38. Retrieved from http://www.irrodl.org/index.php/irrodl/issue/view/44

Kuo, Y. C., Walker, A., & Schroder, K.E.E. (2010). *Interaction and other variables as predictors of student satisfaction in online learning environments.* Paper presented at the Annual Meeting of the Society for Information Technology & Teacher Education (SITE), San Diego, CA, March 29–April 2, 2010.

Laurillard, D. (2000). New technologies and curriculum. In P. Scott (Ed.), *Higher education re-formed* (pp. 133–153). London: Falmer Press.

Lim, J., & Park, S. (2010). Learner Created Learning Contents (LCLC) as an instructional strategy: Tools and practices in online learning. In D. Gibson & B. Dodge (Eds.), *Proceedings of Society for Information Technology and Teacher Education International Conference 2010* (pp. 633–641). Chesapeake, VA: AACE. Retrieved from http://www.editlib.org/p/33415

MarylandOnline. (2010). *Quality matters rubric.* Retrieved from http://www.qmprogram.org/

Mason, D., Abernathy, K., Abshire, S., Cummings, C., & Liu, X. (2012). Evaluation of an online technology leadership master's program. In J. Tareilo & B. Bizzell (Eds.), *NCPEA handbook of virtual/online instruction and programs in educational leadership* (pp. 183–207). Ypsilanti, MI: NCPEA Press.

Mason, D., & Cummings, C. (2013, February). *Online teamwork satisfaction in a master's course.* Paper presented at the meeting of Southwest Educational Research Association (SERA), San Antonio, TX.

Meyers, S. (2008). Using transformative pedagogy when teaching online. *College Teaching, 56*(4), 219–224.

Moller, L. (1998) Designing communities of learners for asynchronous distance education. *Educational Technology Research and Development, 46*(4), 115–122.

Moore, M. (1989). Three types of interaction. *American Journal of Distance Education, 3*(2), 1–6.

Moore, M. (1993). Three types of interaction. In K. Harry, M. John, & D. Keegan (Eds.), *Distance education: New perspectives* (pp. 12–24). London: Routledge.

Moore, M. (1997). Theory of transactional distance. In D. Keegan (Ed.), *Theoretical principles of distance education* (pp. 22-38). New York: Routledge.

Moore, M., & Kearsley, G. (1996). *Distance education: A systems review.* Belmont: Wadsworth.

Moore, M., & Kearsley, G. (2005). *Distance education: A systems view* (2nd ed.). Belmont, CA: Thomson Wadsworth.

Muirhead, B. (2004). Encouraging interaction in online classes. *International Journal of Instructional Technology and Distance Learning, 1*(6), 45–50. Retrieved from http://www.itdl.org/journal/jun_04/article07.htm

Murphy, E., & Coleman, E. (2004). Graduate students' experiences of challenges in online asynchronous discussions. *Canadian Journal of Learning and Technology, 30*(2). Retrieved from http://cjlt.csj.ualberta.ca/index.php/cjlt/article/view/128/122

Northrup, P. (2002). Framework for designing interactivity into web-based instruction. In A. Rossett (Ed.), *The ASTD e-learning handbook: Best practices, strategies, and case studies for an emerging field* (pp. 127–138). New York, NY: McGraw-Hill.

Ozden, S. (2011). *Adult learners' perception of using web-conferencing in hybrid classes.* Paper presented at the International Society of Technology in Education Conference, Philadelphia, PA. Retrieved from http://www.isteconference.org/conferences/ISTE/2011/handout_uploads/KEY_60810541/YilmazOzden_Iste_SYilmazOzden_RP.pdf

Premchaiswadi, W., & Tungkasthan, A. (2007). An implementation of an interactive virtual classroom on Internet. In C. Montgomerie & J. Seale (Eds.), *Proceedings of World Conference on Educational Multimedia, Hypermedia and Telecommunications* (pp. 1299–1304). Chesapeake, VA: AACE. Retrieved from http://www.editlib.org

Ross, A. 1996. The influence of computer communication skills on participation in a computer conferencing course. *Journal of Educational Computing Research, 15*(1), 37-32.

Schullo, S., Barron, A., Kromrey, J., Venable, M., Hilbelink, A., Hohlfeld, T., & Hogarty, K. (2005, April). *Enhancing online courses with synchronous software: An analysis of strategies and interactions.* Paper presented at the Annual Meeting of the American Educational Research Association, Montreal, Canada. Retrieved from http://coedu.usf.edu/cream/paper/AERA_STARS_final_paper_v5.pdf

Shea, P., Swan, K., Li, C., & Pickett, A. (1994). Developing learning community in online asynchronous college courses: The role of teaching presence. *Journal of Asynchronous Learning Networks, 9*(4), 59–82. Retrieved from http://sloanconsortium.org/publications/jaln_main?field_jaln_author_value=&field_jaln_keywords_value=&field_jaln_volume_value=9&field_jaln_issue_value=4

Shelton, K. (2010). *A quality scorecard for the administration of online education programs: A Delphi* (Doctoral dissertation, University of Nebraska). Retrieved from http://digitalcommons.unl.edu/cgi/viewcontent.cgi?article=1039&context=cehsedaddiss

Sher, A. (2009). Assessing the relationship of student-instructor and student-student interaction to student learning and satisfaction in web-based online learning environment. *Journal of Interactive Online Learning, 8*(2), 102–120. Retrieved from www.ncolr.org/jiol

Sloan Consortium. (2012a). *The Sloan Consortium: The 5 pillars*. Retrieved from http://www.sloan-c.org/5pillars

Sloan Consortium. (2012b). *The Sloan Consortium: A quality scorecard for the administration of online programs*. Retrieved from http://sloanconsortium.org/quality_scoreboard_online_program

Smith, M., & Winking-Diaz, A. (2004). Increasing students' interactivity in an online course. *Journal of Interactive Online Learning, 2*(3), 1–25. Retrieved from http://www.ncolr.org/issues/jiol/v2/n3

Suggs, C., Myers, J., & Dennen, V. (2010). Raise your hand if you wanna speak: Navigating turn-taking in a WebEx course. In J. Sanchex & K. Zhang (Eds.), *Proceedings of World Conference on E-Learning in Corporate, Government, Healthcare, and Higher Education* (pp. 2212–2219). Chesapeake, VA: AACE. Retrieved from http://www.editlib.org

Swan, K. (2004). Learning online: Current research on issues of interface, teaching presence and learner characteristics. In J. Bourne & J.C. Moore (Eds.), *Elements of quality online education, practice and direction* (pp. 63–779). Needham, MA: Sloan Center for Online Education.

Thurairajah, N., Williams, A., & McAdam, B. (2011, July). *Using synchronous web conferencing to enhance situated distance learner experience in a built environment context.* Paper presented at the Education in a Changing Environment (ECE) 6th International Conference: Creativity and Engagement in Higher Education, Greater Manchester, UK. Retrieved from http://usir.salford.ac.uk/17019/1/paper_146.pdf

Tseng, H., Ku, H., Wang, C., & Ling, S. (2009). Key factors in online collaboration and their relationship to teamwork satisfaction. *Quarterly Review of Distance Education, 10*(2), 195–206.

Tsui, A., & Ki, W. (1996). An analysis of conference interactions on Telenex: A computer network for ESL teachers. *Educational Technology Research and Development, 44*(4), 23–44.

Yang, Y., & Cornelius, L. (2005). Preparing instructors for quality online instruction. *Online Journal of Distance Learning Administration, 8*(1), 1–16. Retrieved from http://www.westga.edu/~distance/ojdla/spring81/yang81.htm

York, C., & Richardson, J. (2012). Interpersonal interaction in online learning: Experienced online instructors' perceptions of influencing factors. *Journal of Asynchronous Learning Networks, 16*(4), 83–98. Retrieved from http://sloanconsortium.org/jaln/v16n4/interpersonal-interaction-online-learning-experienced-online-instructors-perceptions-infl

Young, S. (2006). Student views of effective online teaching in higher education. *American Journal of Distance Education, 20*(2), 65–77.

16

VISCAL

A Practical Guide for Adapting Face-to-Face Course Materials for Effective Online Delivery

Emily A. Moore

Introduction

Although successful online instruction differs significantly from successful face-to-face instruction, requiring new methods of course design, interaction among course participants, and instructor preparation and support (Crawford-Ferre & Wiest, 2012, p. 12), in my four-plus years' experience as an instructional designer in higher education (both university and community college) I have noted that the recognition and significance of skills required to move a class online are vastly and consistently underreported.

In essence, faculty are being asked to take on the role of digital author, editor, and publisher; software interface designer; graphic designer; and video postproduction editor—with little to no training, release time, remuneration, or instructional (or technical) support. At the institutions for which I've worked, dedicated instructional design support has been made available to faculty, but the amount of support varies widely depending on staffing and workload.

And while there has been a proliferation of models and rubrics in recent years aimed at helping guide effective online course development, as Andrews and Goodson (1980) pointed out, "educators are often confused about which model to use because of the bewildering array reported and because of the omission of some basic component of the literature that describes the model or reports on how the model has been used" (p. 2).

Even in those cases where an institution does decides to adopt a particular model or rubric, faculty are still left trying to decide how to translate and implement such vague standards as "Learning activities provide opportunities for interaction that support active learning" (Quality Matters Program, 2011, p. 1). A few guides exist that do attempt to provide step-by-step instructions, but these are often anecdotal, leaving faculty to figure out how to adapt the suggestions given to their own unique situations. Or they assume that online classes are being built from the ground up, which is rarely the case—thereby forcing faculty to extricate the online-specific strategies that they need from among the standard pedagogical strategies that they've already addressed.

It is little wonder, then, that despite studies beginning to emerge that claim efficacy of some online learning approaches in some content areas for some students, a significant concern persists among students (Jaggars, 2013, p. 9), instructors (Allen & Seaman, 2013, p. 27), and administrators

(Allen & Seaman, 2013, p. 24) regarding the overall effectiveness of online learning, in terms of both student outcomes (Singh, Rylander, & Mims, 2012, p. 94) and retention (Gleason, 2004, p. 395).

I developed VISCAL for two reasons: to address quality concerns from the beginning of the online course/design development cycle, and to reduce the time it takes to produce a high-quality online course.

In my professional experience, faculty have little time to devote to the online course design and development process, and even less time or inclination to educate themselves about the specifics of how best to present information in a digital format. Yet in my initial years of working with faculty as an instructional designer, I often experienced "pushback" that slowed the design process. For example, some instructors demanded to know why uploading their PowerPoint slides wasn't the end of the conversation—after all, wasn't a PowerPoint lecture the sum total of what face-to-face students were receiving in the classroom? Other instructors were resistant to the idea of creating short self-introduction videos and graded course-orientation activities. All instructors' eyes glazed over when I tried to explain how and where those PowerPoint files, self-introduction videos, and course-orientation activities fit into the overall course design using ambiguous rubric criteria such as "developed media must support your course learning objectives" (Quality Matters, 2011, p. 1).

I needed a common language—a practical guide that would translate theoretical models into actionable items; that would bridge what all successful face-to-face instructors already understand about teaching and learning to the specific techniques by which those strategies can be implemented in an online course.

I couldn't find such a practical guide, so I developed one: VISCAL.

VISCAL provides a new, intuitive way of looking at an existing face-to-face course—as a collection of six critical elements that "break" when the course is moved online. The VISCAL model also provides commonsense suggestions for rebuilding and optimizing each "broken" element for effective online delivery via a learning management system.

Face-to-Face Course

In my experience (strongly corroborated by anecdotal evidence from colleagues), the first assumption face-to-face faculty tend make when asked to move a course online is that development of the online version of their course should begin with the uploading of their existing PowerPoint slides and handouts.

But focusing on specific artifacts designed for a face-to-face course isn't useful in the beginning design stages of an online course; in fact, doing so tends to hamstring the course redesign phase, because framing the conversation as "PowerPoint slides" necessarily restricts the instructor to providing PowerPoint slides. Expanding and redefining the conversation as "visual communication," however, is much more useful because it makes explicit the need not just to include PowerPoint slides, but also to identify and adapt the additional visual communication the instructor is providing in the classroom (such as drawing on a whiteboard or grading representative essays on an overhead projector).

The suggestions of many well-known theoretical models and rubrics can be synthesized and reorganized so that virtually every aspect of a course—whether delivered face-to-face or online—falls into one of the following six categories: visual communication, interactivity, structure, collaboration, assessments, and learner-centric focus (see Table 16.1).

I have found that identifying each of these six elements (visual communication, interactivity, structure, collaboration, assessments, and learner-centric focus) for a successful face-to-face

Table 16.1 VISCAL Categories

VISCAL	*Chickering's 7 Principles for Good Practice in Undergraduate Education* Chickering and Gamson (1996, p. 3)	*Quality Matters Rubric* Quality Matters Program (2011, p. 1)	*Blackboard Exemplary Course Program Rubric* Blackboard Exemplary Course Program Rubric (2012, pp. 2–7)	*iNACOL's Teaching and Learning Standards* National Standards for Quality Online Courses, Version 2 (2011, pp. 7–16)
V = Visual	Encourages active learning	Instructional Materials	Content Presentation	Curriculum and Course Design
I = Interactivity	Encourages contact between students and faculty; encourages active learning; gives prompt feedback	Learner Interaction and Engagement	Learner Engagement; Feedback	Curriculum and Course Design
S = Structure	Emphasizes time on task; communicates high expectations	Course Overview and Introduction; Learning Objectives; Learner Support; Course Technology	Goals and Objectives; Content Presentation; Interaction Logistics; Orientation to Course and LMS; Supportive Software (Plug-ins); Instructor Role and Information; Course/Institutional Policies & Support	Curriculum and Course Design; Support Standards (Students); Guidance Services
C = Collaboration	Develops reciprocity and cooperation among students	Learner Interaction and Engagement	Communication Strategies; Development of Learning Community;	Curriculum and Course Design
A = Assessments	Respects diverse talents and ways of learning; communicates high expectations	Assessment and Measurement	Expectations; Assessment Design; Self-assessment	Assessment of Student Performance
L = Learner-centric focus	Respects diverse talents and ways of learning	Accessibility	Technical Accessibility Issues; Accommodations for Disabilities	Curriculum and Course Design

course and then rebuilding each element specifically for online delivery is the quickest way to move a face-to-face course online. In addition, feedback from instructors and students from online courses developed using this approach—while not codified into a formal research study—encourages me to believe that applying the VISCAL practical model positively affects the quality of the resulting online course. I have successfully applied VISCAL to courses from computer science to art appreciation, business management, American literature, and composition.

Visual Communication

Question for Instructor: "If I Were a Student in Your Classroom, What Would I See?"

Virtually all classroom instructors communicate visually. Many do stick with PowerPoint slides; others supplement their PowerPoint lectures by drawing pictures and diagrams. Others simply stand in front of the class and lecture from memory, using their hands as props. For asynchronous online delivery, all of these visual communications must be recreated digitally—either as still images, or as moving images.

- Still images include drawings and photographs. Three options for obtaining images to use in an online course are listed below.
  - Sourcing images from a textbook publisher. Many textbook publishers (such as Pearson) offer digital versions of the illustrations and figures their textbooks contain. Others may grant permission for the *ad hoc* scanning and uploading of textbook artwork, as long as the materials are presented in an enrollment-only online classroom setting. This is a good approach for instructors who rely heavily on a specific textbook.
  - Creating images from scratch. The easiest approach is to scan in hand-drawn images and photos; but instructors can also use software to create and edit basic images. Obviously, proprietary software packages designed specifically for image creation and manipulation (such as Adobe Photoshop) exist, but their cost and steep learning curves tend to be prohibitive for casual users (i.e., anyone who is neither a graphic artist nor a dedicated, well-funded instructional designer). More affordable and easy-to-use options include Microsoft Paint, PowerPoint, and Word. Freely downloadable software that can be used to create and edit images includes the Windows-only Paint.net (www.getpaint.net) and the cross-platform GIMP (www.gimp.org).
  - Searching online. Instructors can search sites such as CreativeCommons.org and Google Images for images that support their course content. Note, however, that while this option may appear to be the quickest approach to locating supporting images, it rarely is (unless the image you're looking for is extremely common, like a shot of the Eiffel Tower or the Mona Lisa). Because most repositories neither screen for quality and fitness of purpose nor provide detailed search capability, instructors can waste hours searching for a specific image that they might be able to create themselves in minutes.

However instructors obtain images, the same best practices apply to their use in an online course as described below.

- Use images generously to illustrate examples, both good and bad.
- Add callouts, labels, and captions to draw students' attention to specific areas of an image. Doing so reduces confusion and quickly allows students to make meaning of any accompanying text or audio narration.

   - Make sure every image pulls its own weight. All images included in a course should directly support course content. Using them as "eye candy" (solely to break up long passages of text) is a waste of precious development time.
- Moving images. It's useful to distinguish between two different types of moving images based on the way each type is created. *Narrated animations* are created using presentation and/or screen capture software; *videos* are created using a video camera.
   - Narrated animations are series of still images displayed sequentially—such as slideshows or PowerPoint presentations—accompanied by spoken audio. Faculty without access to a dedicated instructional designer or media center have two options for obtaining narrated animations to use in an online course.
      - Creating from scratch. Creating animations is typically more effective than providing a handful of links to resources on third-party sites and can be as easy as adapting and narrating a PowerPoint presentation used in in the face-to-face classroom. Using software such as the cross-platform Camtasia (www.techsmith.com/camtasia.html), instructors can add callouts and embed interactive quizzes directly into their animations. Free options include Jing (www.techsmith.com/jing.html) and Microsoft's Photo Story.
      - Searching online. Textbook publishers frequently offer narrated animations that support individual textbooks. Other sites, such as TED's Educational Channel (ed.ted.com), the Khan Academy (www.khanacademy.org), and the Federal Resources for Educational Excellence (http://free.ed.gov/index.cfm), offer animations applicable to multiple disciplines.

When creating animations:

- Be generous with images and movement. This doesn't mean flipping through images at a frenetic pace; rather, it means changing something on the screen about every four seconds—if only to add a callout or a label for emphasis.
- Limit text (or leave it out entirely). If content demands the presentation of text, use it sparingly—and time the text to appear with the narration. Don't present a lot of text, and avoid presenting text that differs from the narration.
- Add your voice. Unless you're extremely skilled at conveying information visually, narrated animations are more effective than nonnarrated animations. Aim for clearly articulated, well-modulated speech paced slower than for a face-to-face audience.
- Always create a script to match your presentation and rehearse it prior to recording the voiceover narration; don't just "wing it." (If you do wing it, plan to spend extra time in postproduction fixing your goofs.) In a face-to-face lecture, occasional "ums," "ahs," false starts, and lengthy digressions are acceptable; in an online animated presentation, that same spontaneity comes across as ill-preparedness, which can negatively impact learning.
- Keep animation length to about five minutes. Students either skip or "tune out" longer clips.

The following best practices apply to all animations, whether homegrown or sourced.

- Use only animations that directly support student learning objectives. Animations included solely because they're entertaining or because the instructor believes that online learning "should" include animated clips tend to be ineffective.

    - Use animations to drive the achievement of learning objectives actively. Simple strategies include embedding multiple-choice questions in the video, and presenting students with questions or concepts to look for before they watch a video and then administering a brief assessment (such as a multiple choice quiz or reaction paper) after.
- Video clips are audiovisual recordings of live action events such as demonstrations, performances, events, discussions, or lectures. Setting up a video camera and recording a typical 50-minute face-to-face lecture is rarely the most effective approach to adapting lecture materials for the online environment, because the result is typically too long and the lecture typically isn't concise enough or visually interesting enough to "play well" online. However, video can be employed effectively in an online course.
    - Incorporating at least some videotaped face-to-face lectures "puts a face" on the course, which may help boost student engagement. It also gives online students the chance to hear in-class student questions (and answers) in a natural way.
    - Demonstrating physical processes—a chemistry experiment, a surgical procedure, the steps required to tune a guitar—is best done using video.
    - Adapting, condensing, scripting, and splitting up face-to-face lectures into logically coherent segments before videotaping lets instructors organize the resulting material as a collection of short, independently accessible clips, each of which is ideally around 5 minutes in length.

To Create Videos:
Many institutions offer video creation and postproduction as part of the media services available to faculty. However, instructors can also use low-cost webcams to tape short demonstrations themselves—and then use low-cost video editing software such as Camtasia or ScreenFlow (www.telestream.net/screenflow/overview.htm) to trim too-lengthy clips and add captions and callouts.

To Find Suitable Videos on the Web:
In addition to the resources listed under "Narrated animations," good places to look for educational videos online include Educreations (www.educreations.com), NBC Learn's Chemistry Now (http://www.nbclearn.com/portal/site/learn/chemistry-now/), and the American Museum of Natural History's Web site (http://www.amnh.org/content/search/%28offset%29/10?SearchText=documentary). Finding a suitable video on YouTube (http://www.youtube.com) or TeacherTube (http://www.teachertube.com) is possible, though often time consuming. Note: Safeshare.tv provides a way to "scrub" YouTube links so that students are exposed only to the YouTube video you want them to view (vs. sending them directly to the YouTube interface, which may display inappropriate or distracting material).

Best Practices for Incorporating Videos in an Online Course:
The following best practices should be applied to all videos, whether instructor-created or outsourced:

- Make sure the video is relevant to student learning objectives. Instructors should include only those videos they believe will help students meet one or more previously identified student learning objectives.
- Avoid recordings of one person talking for minutes at a time alone on the screen. The "talking head" approach is perfectly natural in real life; on a screen, it's ineffective.

Whenever possible, break up videotaped lectures with multiple camera angles and cutaways to drawings, lists, vocabulary terms, or other postproduction "add-ons" that make the resulting video more attractive, help students focus on what's being said, and emphasize key points.

- Let students know up front what they should be getting out of watching the video. Precede the embedded or linked video with a brief statement or two that poses questions the video answers, or lists key points that watching the video should explain.

Note: Instructors who create their own original visuals, or provide links to others' works, are automatically in compliance with copyright guidelines. Incorporating third-party works in any other way, however, falls under Fair Use guidelines, which limit the amount of material you can use even for educational purposes (U.S. Copyright Office, 2012).

Interactivity

Question for Instructor: "What Kinds of Things Do You Do in the Classroom to Get Students to Engage with the Content, with You, or With Each Other?"

Anything that drives active student participation and provides feedback in real time is an example of interactivity. Common examples include asking students to read aloud or participate in guided discussions, calling for a show of hands, and asking students physically to demonstrate their understanding of a process or concept. All of these classroom activities must be adapted if they are to be delivered online.

Strategies for adapting classroom activities include the following:

- Asking students to read aloud. The purpose of having students read aloud in class is twofold: To require them to interact with course material, and to provide them with feedback—either on their reading facility, on their ability to understand and apply the concepts just read, or both. Providing real-time feedback to weak readers is difficult online. Following are several approaches for accomplishing the second, more common goal of getting students to engage with the course material.
  - Embedding multiple-choice and T/F quizzes in animations. Using Camtasia or Captivate, instructors can "stop the action" midway through an animated presentation and administer a quiz before allowing students to continue the presentation.
  - Requiring each student (or small group) to master and present one chapter of a textbook to the entire class. Students can make their "jigsaw" presentations synchronously, using a product such as the free Google Hangouts (www.google.com/+/learnmore/hangouts/) or for-fee GoToMeeting (www.gotomeeting.com), or asynchronously by constructing their reports as wikis, blog entries, or multimedia presentations.
  - Assigning graded peer reviews. Instructors can structure graded assignments in two parts: Students submit their work via discussion board (or via a Web-based multimedia discussion board such as VoiceThread), and then review at least two other students' submissions.
  - Encouraging active watching (or reading). Instructors can present students with questions that students must watch a video or animation (or read a text) to answer.
- Asking students to participate in guided discussions. The purpose of this technique is to help students think through material and deepen their understanding of it through exploring, defending, and adapting their understanding of a topic and—ideally—applying

their newly constructed knowledge to novel situations. Class discussions are supported in virtually every learning management system, or LMS, using built-in discussion boards or forums. Best practices for managing discussions online include the following:

- Set ground rules. Spell out issues of netiquette and what constitutes a "post" in the course syllabus; also consider providing a rubric for post elements such as substance, clarity, and extension of the original poster's ideas.
- Seed discussion boards. Present thought-provoking, open-ended questions that require students to research, think critically, and defend their positions.
- Model appropriate behavior. Write clearly and respectfully. Quote judiciously and succinctly, refer to students by name, and use meaningful subject lines.
- Monitor boards frequently. Check discussion boards at least twice a day throughout the discussion period.
- Actively guide discussions. Praise, prod, and ask for clarification. Require students to back up their assertions with reasons or references.

- Calling for a show of hands. The purpose of this technique is to get a feel for what students think about a particular statement or concept so that you can correct misperceptions and determine which concepts need more of your attention. Virtually all LMSs allow instructors to conduct polls; so does the free service SurveyMonkey (www.surveymonkey.com).
- Demonstrating understanding of a process or concept. Following are four strategies for implementing this approach online.
  - Assign students roles, present them with a situation, and have them "act out" the situation on a discussion board.
  - Assign one student a position to challenge, and another to defend.
  - Require students to describe the process or concept via written report or multimedia presentation.
  - For physical processes (such as biology lab assignments), consider having students take and submit digital photos or phone videos of the process at predetermined steps.

Where to find activities online:

To be effective, activities must be customized to match a course's content, instructor, and students. However, the availability of third-party activities is growing. In addition to the materials textbook publishers are increasingly providing, the following sites are good places to look for supplementary activities:

- Web Adventures (online role-playing games set in microbiology and forensic science contexts available at http://webadventures.rice.edu/).
- iCivics (WebQuest activities related to political science and government available at http://www.icivics.org/teachers).
- Interact Math (a mix of interactive math exercises based on—but that don't require access to—Pearson mathematics textbooks; available at http://www.interactmath.com).

Best practices for incorporating activities into an online course:

- Aim for making the online adaptations match the in-person activities. If an instructor interrupts lectures to administer quizzes or breakout sessions, for example, mimic that activity online: Embed quizzes in narrated presentations and direct students to participate in break-out discussions between viewing presentation clips.

- Provide a mix of online activities. Ideally, some activities should require students to interact with course materials; some, with the instructor; and some, with each other.

Structure

Question for Instructor: "How Do Students in Your Face-to-Face Class Know What They Need to Do to Be Successful, When They Have to Do It, and Whom to Call if They Run into Problems?"

In a face-to-face classroom, students learn what to do and how to do it naturally. When an instructor goes over the syllabus in class, for example, her or his tone—and the amount of time the instructor spends explaining certain items—communicates to the student implicitly what is important and what can safely be ignored. A student also learns how to act in class by observing and listening to those around her or him.

None of this is the case online. Learning online is, by its very nature, isolating. To adjust for this, a well-designed online course must describe precisely what students must do to be successful, how they should do it, and what to do if they have questions or problems doing it.

Four ways to provide this structure in an online course include using:

- The course calendar. Understanding what assignments are due and when is important to all students—but especially to online students, who cannot rely on in-class reminders such as "Text Next Friday" scrawled on a whiteboard. Printable calendars that tie learning modules to specific dates allow students to see, in one place, all activities and deadlines.
- The course syllabus. An online course syllabus must be more explicit than one for a traditional course; it must also address several online-only concerns. An effective online syllabus:
  - Explicitly informs students that the course is fully online.
  - Presents clearly defined, measurable learning objectives tied to each module or week.
  - Clearly states expectations for success by stating the number of hours students can expect to spend on projects (and the course as a whole), by providing rubrics and examples of exemplary work, and by listing the software and software-related skills students must possess prior to the class start date.
  - Clearly states instructor office hours and policies as well as contact information. In a friendly, informal tone, the syllabus should explicitly encourage students to contact the instructor with course-related questions and let them know how soon they can expect responses to their e-mails and discussion postings (ideally 24 hours or less, barring holidays and emergencies).
  - Clearly describes student-to-student interaction guidelines. With respect to discussion board postings, for example, instructors should present guidelines that prohibit flaming and direct students to reply to a discussion post's content instead of its author. Also useful to state are minimum participation requirements (such as a certain number of substantive posts per student per topic).
  - Clearly describes the individuals or departments students can contact to get help with technical problems and emphasizes that it is their (the students') responsibility to get help as soon as they encounter a problem.
  - Explains how assignments will be graded. Include rubrics whenever possible and emphasize that students should reference rubrics before and during the completion of their assignments.

- Includes a feedback policy so students know how soon to expect feedback on assignments and assessments and how to access their grades.
- Includes a definition and examples of plagiarism and describes the penalty for plagiarism.
- Includes concise, explicit instructions for accessing materials and completing assignments. Strongly consider using ordered lists and check-off forms when appropriate, and highlight important information by bolding it.
- Includes proctoring procedures, if applicable, such as proctoring locations and contact information.

- Interactive orientation activities. Online course materials should include three orientation activities to be completed by all online students during the first week of class:
  - A narrated "meet your instructor" video in which the instructor provides a few personal details, including contact information. Because your online students will likely never see or hear you, this visual introduction can be crucial in boosting their comfort level and, therefore, participation level.
  - A narrated video that "walks" students through the course visually, explaining how the course is set up and showing students how to access materials, turn in assignments, take tests, and contact both the instructor and fellow students.
  - A graded activity that requires students to read the course syllabus and exercise all of the LMS functions they will be expected to use throughout the course (such as posting to an "Introduce Yourself" forum and submitting the answers to a syllabus quiz).
- Course layout based on sound usability principles. Although LMS capabilities vary slightly, all support the following best practices.
  - Clearly and meaningfully label all course materials. Examples of effective file descriptions include "Video lecture for Unit 1—The Persuasive Essay (3:12)" and "Chapter 6 Online Quiz—Mitosis and Meiosis." Ineffective descriptions include "click here" and "watch."
  - Organize course materials logically, efficiently, and consistently. Materials and activities should be listed in the order in which you expect students to access them and follow a clear pattern (such as weekly readings followed by a discussion session followed by an assessment).
  - Make course materials as easy as possible for students to locate and access. Modules—whether week-by-week or based on units or chapters—should be clearly delineated. Assignments and quizzes shouldn't be "hidden" within readings or other resources; instead, all activities for which students are to be held responsible should be presented sequentially in a single, clearly marked area.
  - Provide repeated instructions at the point of contact. For example, include key test and assignment specifics so that they appear when a student clicks a test or assignment link (in addition to appearing in the syllabus).

Collaboration

Question for Instructor: "What Kinds of Things Do You Do in Your Classroom to Require Students to Work Together? If You Don't Do Anything Now, What Kinds of Things Could You Do?"

Collaboration is a specialized form of interaction. It merits its own category in the VISCAL practical guide because studies including Berge's (2002, p. 184) suggest that student-to-student collaboration is especially critical in an online course. Collaboration can help reduce the isolation online students often feel and, therefore, may improve retention.

The following strategies add meaningful collaboration to an online course:

- Assign a beginning-of-semester icebreaker project. For example, require students to interview at least two classmates and report their findings to the entire class via discussion board.
- Adapt face-to-face group projects for the online environment. Having students collaboratively research, write, and/or create and deliver reports or multimedia presentations can be a good fit for online projects. Instructors may allow group members to work together synchronously through Web conferencing software such as Google Hangouts, or through e-mail. Students can collaborate on documents using (for example) the free document creation and distribution services Google Docs, DropBox, or Blogger.
- Have students peer-review each other's assignments and post their comments on a discussion board so the entire class can benefit. As with any collaborative effort, make sure the course syllabus covers expectations; also be sure to include a rubric.
- Conduct discussions (via discussion board) that require students to argue different points of view and build consensus. For example, for each topic—on a rotating basis—an instructor might assign one student to challenge a given statement, another to defend it, a third to point out a possible common ground, and so on.
- Set up one discussion group just for informal student-to-student assistance. Studies suggest the effectiveness of a virtual "student lounge" varies: Some instructors (and some students) find them useful, and others don't. Because setting one up in a LMS typically takes less than a minute, however—and because the discussion group won't need to be monitored after the semester is underway—it's worth doing, just in case.

Assessments

Question for Instructor: "What Do You Do in a Classroom to Measure How Well Your Students Are Meeting Their Student Learning Objectives?"

Just as all face-to-face assessments should align with one or more specific, measurable learning objectives, all online assessments should align with one or more specific, measurable learning objectives. But online assessments must also take into account the increased opportunities for cheating, plagiarism, and identity theft that learning online makes possible. In addition, effective online assessments should take advantage of the unique opportunities for instant, rich, targeted feedback and self-checking that learning online provides.

Strategies for adapting face-to-face assessments for effective online delivery include the following.

- Randomize test questions. One way to make cheating more difficult is to use a test bank and randomize questions to create different tests for each online course section and semester (and even to create a unique question order for each student). Most LMSs provide a way to randomize test questions easily.
- Structure assessments as timed, "open book" tests. This approach assumes students will consult third-party material, and test question difficulty takes this into account.
- Require exams to be proctored. Onsite proctors can enforce traditional classroom controls, such as verifying student identification and banning notes, in multiple ways convenient for students.
- Embed assessments in coursework (such as day-to-day participation in online discussions and essays or other work products that can be revised incrementally for grades) helps make cheating irrelevant.

- Require students to submit their essays to a plagiarism detection service such as TurnItIn (www.turnitin.com) before submitting them for grading.
- Provide detailed instructions for assessments, including when and how long they're available, how students should access them, and what students should do if their computers crash mid-test.
- Create online assessments, such as multiple-choice quizzes, that provide students with rich, instant feedback. Providing not just the correct answer but also a description of the correct answer and a link to where the topic is covered in-depth in the course material allows students to use ungraded assessments as study aids.
- Providing a mix of assessments: for example, solo and group, work product, short answer, and so on.
- Requiring students to scan and submit assessments written longhand, such as math proofs. Another option for assessments that require handwriting (or drawing) is to make SmartPens (http://www.livescribe.com/en-us/smartpen/) available to students. SmartPens capture pen strokes and audio narration; the resulting videos can then be viewed by the instructor.
- Requiring students to submit performance-based assessments such as reports and presentations in real time using Google Hangouts or some other Web conferencing software. The pressure of performing "live" may increase student effort—and presenting students can take advantage of immediate group feedback.

Learner-Centric Focus

Question for Instructor: "What Do You Typically Do in the Classroom to Accommodate Student Differences (Such as Disabilities or Different Learning Styles or Preferences)?"

Learner-centric focus in this context means providing ways of accessing materials and demonstrating competencies that make sense for each learner. While accessibility is beyond the scope of this chapter, supporting multiple learning preferences in an online course can be accomplished by providing course materials in multiple formats as described below.

- Provide closed captioning in instructor-created animations. Doing so helps hearing-impaired students as well as those experiencing temporary audio difficulties (and those accessing the animations in a noisy environment). Captivate (www.adobe.com/products/captivate.html) and Camtasia make adding closed captioning to an animation or video relatively easy.
- Provide printable text versions of course materials. This helps students who like to make notes on texts—as well as students who prefer to (or who must) study away from their computer screens.
- Provide audio (mp3) versions of lecture materials. This approach helps time-strapped students as well as students who prefer listening to reading.

Conclusion

The VISCAL practical guide presents a straightforward approach to adapting and optimizing face-to-face courses for online delivery that is easy for faculty (and those supporting them) to understand and quick for them to implement (see Appendix I). In addition, VISCAL represents a practical way to evaluate implemented courses.

Institutions that already have mature, high-quality online course offerings and dedicated instructional design teams in place to assist faculty in adapting face-to-face courses for online delivery may not benefit much from VISCAL, because they are likely to have implemented a similar adaptation process in-house (whether formally or informally).

However, VISCAL is likely to be of use in institutions in which faculty must bear the burden of adapting their own courses; in which budgets for instructional designers are shrinking; and in which the quality of online courses and/or the time it takes to move courses online is of concern.

Appendices

Appendix I: VISCAL Course Materials Development Worksheet

Viscal

V = Visual Communication

Some courses aren't visual at all (think Research Fundamentals). Others, like a course in art appreciation, may be extremely dependent on visuals such as photographs, images, drawings, performances, demonstrations, and audiovisual clips.

How much does your face-to-face course rely on visual material?

If you currently . . .	*Consider . . .*	*Remember . . .*	*Your visual plan*
Use photos, charts, illustrations, or drawings in your classroom	Scanning them in or creating them yourself using graphic design software such as Microsoft Paint (typically preinstalled on PCs), GIMP (free download that works on both PCs and Macs), or a specialty program such as Adobe Fireworks. For simple illustrations, the drawing tools in Microsoft Word and PowerPoint may be all you need. You can also hand-draw figures and scan them.	You must obtain explicit permission to use any visuals you didn't create yourself. That typically means contacting your textbook publisher (if you'd like to scan illustrations and figures from your required text) or e-mailing the author of anything you find online to ensure you have permission to use it in your course materials. Use labels and callouts to draw students' attention to specific parts of an illustration or drawing.	
Use examples to explain concepts or processes	Create narrated animations that "walk" students through examples using callouts, labels (or captions), and your voice.	Anything you find yourself describing on a whiteboard (or on the back of a napkin during office hours) is	

(Continued)

If you currently . . .	*Consider . . .*	*Remember . . .*	*Your visual plan*
	The simplest way to create your own animations is to create a visual-based PowerPoint and record it (along with your voice narration) in a software program such as Camtasia or the freely downloadable Jing or Brainshark. (More advanced animations may require higher-end capture or postproduction software such as Adobe Captivate.) If you're a math teacher, you might want to look into SmartPens, which capture pen strokes and audio in an interactive PDF file (useful for writing out proofs that students can replay and listen to step-by-step, for example). Videotape yourself performing a demonstration.	a good candidate for a narrated animation. Handouts that describe step-by-step processes are also good candidates for narrated animations. Ideally, animations are primarily visual, with voiceover narration and minimal text (for callouts and labels). "Winging" the narration rarely results in a high-quality result. Always type out a script so that you can condense and edit it before you record your narrated animation; your presentation will serve as a storyboard. (Bonus: You can provide that text script as a valuable extra for students to download and print.)	
Rely on in-class demonstrations	Videotape demonstrations yourself, or with the help of your institution's media services staff. If it's appropriate, you may also want to supplement your course materials with video demonstrations you've found on the Web.	Consider breaking a single demonstration into conceptual "chunks" so learners can replay (or so that you can assess) specific chunks independently.	

I = Interactivity

While it's technically possible to create an online course that features little to no student-to-student or student-teacher interaction, it's not a good idea. Student isolation is a big problem in online courses, affecting both student participation and retention. To be effective, an online course must include as much interactivity as possible.

S = Structure

Many students need the predictability of showing up to the same classroom at the same time twice a week. These students benefit greatly from being told face-to-face about important upcoming events (such as tests and assignment deadlines) and from being given instructions, assignments, and tests in a natural, easy-to-use form. (Online, just figuring out when a test

What kind of interactions do you already include in your face-to-face course?

If you currently . . .	*Consider . . .*	*Remember . . .*	*Your interactivity plan*
Conduct in-class activities such as having students read aloud or work problems on a whiteboard in front of the class	Have students post their work to a discussion board and peer-review it. Have students research individual topics and then report their results to each other (via presentation or online discussion). Set up synchronous meetings and have students present to each other in real time.	Because the relative anonymity of an online course can decrease polite interactions, provide explicit instructions for student critiques.	
Quiz students informally during class (for example, by requesting a "show of hands" at key points during a lecture)	Build in to your course materials ungraded quizzes that give rich, specific feedback. Conduct frequent polls. Provide points for correctly answering the "question of the week" or a fellow classmate's question via discussion board.	Polls can be delivered via most LMSs in addition to a free service such as SurveyMonkey.com. You may also be able to set up a discussion forum in your LMS earmarked for polls.	
Rely on class discussions as a way to help students explore or work through concepts.	Create assignments that require students to work together.	Discussion boards and *wikis* (document construction tools that track authors and versions) help you track evidence of student participation.	
Provide real-time performance feedback (for example, critiquing a music student playing an assigned piece or a nursing student inserting an IV)	Structure the course as a hybrid. Require students to come to campus for the performance components and complete the balance of the course (such as required readings or reports) online.		
Provide little student-to-student interaction	Require student-to-student interaction online by using one or more of the suggestions above.	Even if you don't focus on interaction in your face-to-face course, you'll need to focus on it online. Without it, students easily become discouraged and disoriented, which can lead to their dropping the course.	

You will need to . . .	*Strongly consider . . .*	*Your structure plan*
Provide a syllabus that:	Presents clearly defined, measurable learning objectives tied to each unit (or chapter, or however you chose to organize your course schedule). Includes a personal "About the Instructor" introduction in the form of a document with a photo or (better) a brief video clip. Clearly states expectations for classroom success by stating the number of hours students can expect to spend on projects (and the course as a whole) and providing rubrics and examples of exemplary work. Clearly states your office hours and policies as well as your contact information and explicitly encourages students to contact you during the course. Clearly describes student-to-student interaction guidelines (netiquette, discussion post length, etc.) Clearly describes what students can do to get help with technical problems and emphasizes that it's their responsibility to get help as soon as they experience a problem. Explains how assignments will be graded and includes rubrics whenever possible. Describes how students can access grades and how long after submitting work they can expect to access them. Includes a definition and examples of plagiarism, and clearly describes the penalty for plagiarism. Explains what a proctored exam is and how to schedule one (if appropriate). Include proctoring hours, locations, and contact information. Includes concise, explicit instructions (image/text or video clips) for accessing materials and completing assignments.	
Provide a calendar that:	Ties the units, chapters, or lessons presented in your syllabus to specific dates so that students know exactly what's due when. Lists due dates not just for assignments, quizzes, and tests, but also for graded project milestones when appropriate (for example, 1/4 completed, 1/2 completed, etc.).	
Provide course materials in an LMS that:	Are meaningfully labeled. Are organized logically. Are as easy as possible for students to locate and access. Tie back directly to the measurable learning objectives described in your syllabus. Include a "getting started" assignment that requires students to read your course syllabus, identify important course elements, and access all necessary course materials. For example, ask students to post a self-introduction to a discussion board, answer questions about course testing and grading policies, and submit their answers using the assignment submitting process.	

will be given—let alone what to click on to take it or what to do if a power outage occurs midtest—can be problematic for some students.)

Although much of the structure an effective online course can provide must be delivered while the course is live, as much structure as possible must be built in during course delivery.

C = Collaborative

Collaboration can be an effective learning strategy, online or off. But studies suggest that **collaboration isn't an option in an online class; it's essential to effective online learning and student retention**.

If you currently . . .	*Consider . . .*	*Remember . . .*	*Your interactivity plan*
Incorporate group projects	Adapt projects for the online environment by setting up ways for students to "meet" online (via dedicated discussion board, e-mail, or web conference) and assigning project products that can be delivered online (such as multimedia presentations or wiki reports). Require groups to provide feedback on other groups' projects. Provide grades both for individual and group effort.	Provide rubrics. Provide examples of exemplary work (from prior semesters, for example) that students can access online. Stage the grading of large projects into two or more milestones to help students keep on schedule.	
	Assign a beginning-of-semester icebreaker project. For example, require students to interview at least two other students and report their findings to the entire class.		
	Have students peer-review each other's assignments.		
	Conduct discussions (via discussion board) that require students to argue different points of view and build consensus.	Expect to spend a significant amount of time guiding the discussions. Contact nonparticipating students privately and invite them to join in the discussion.	
	Set up one discussion group just for informal student-to-student assistance.		

A = Assessments

As in a face-to-face course, all online assessments must match one or more of the specific, measurable learning objectives you've identified and listed in the course syllabus. But the assessments you devise must take into account the increased opportunities for cheating that learning online affords (as well as the improved ability to provide rich, targeted feedback on a per-question basis).

What kinds of assessments do you currently use?

If you currently . . .	*Consider . . .*	*Remember . . .*	*Your interactivity plan*
Use multiple-choice, T/F, essay, or short-answer assessments	Recreate them online either as graded or ungraded (self-check) assessments. For T/F and multiple-choice quizzes, provide precise, informative feedback for correct and incorrect responses. Vary the order in which questions are presented to circumvent cheating.	Assessments must always match specific, measurable learning objectives. Ideally, assessments are meaningful. If one learning objective is to write a two-page persuasive paper, for example, a meaningful assessment would be to ask students to write a two-page persuasive paper. (Asking students to choose the elements of a persuasive paper via multiple-choice is an example of a non-meaningful assessment.) Set up assessments to tell students not only which questions they got wrong, but why. For each wrong answer, provide a description of the correct answer as well as a link to where the topic is treated more in-depth online.	
Use performance assessments such as reports and presentations	Have students deliver their work in real time using Google Hangouts, GoToMeeting, or some other Web conferencing software. Alternatively, have them post their work and peer-review their fellow students' efforts.		
Require students to handwrite answers	Have students handwrite their exams, scan them in, and send you the scanned file.		
Need to ensure students don't take tests for each other	Require proctored exams.		
Need to assess student competencies face-to-face	Structure your course as a hybrid course.		

Consider providing . . .	*Remember . . .*	*Your learner-centric plan*
Closed captioning in videos	Camtasia and Adobe Captivate make closed captioning easy. It's easier if you use a script when you record your animation or video, but you can add it after the fact, too.	
Printable text versions of video lecture materials	Some students need to print materials out and take notes. If you've developed a scripted animation, the script can serve as the printed version.	
Audio versions of text and video materials	Not all video-based materials make sense in audio-only format, but some do.	

L = Learner-Centered

Providing materials in multiple formats can assist students who prefer one format over the other as well as those students who, due to a disability or hardware malfunction, are limited in terms of the formats they can use.

References

Allen, I.E., & Seaman, J. (2013). Changing Course: Ten Years of Tracking Online Education in the United States. *Sloan Consortium*. Retrieved from http://www.onlinelearningsurvey.com/reports/changingcourse.pdf

Andrews, D.H., & Goodson, L.A. (1980). A Comparative Analysis of Models of Instructional Design. *Journal of Instructional Development, 3*(4), 2–16.

Berge, Z. L. (2002). Active, Interactive, and Reflective Elearning. *Quarterly Review of Distance Education, 3*(2), 181–190.

Blackboard Exemplary Course Program Rubric. (2012). 1–8. Retrieved from http://www.blackboard.com/getdoc/7deaf501-4674-41b9-b2f2-554441ba099b/2012-Blackboard-Exemplary-Course-Rubric.aspx

Chickering, A., & Gamson, Z. (1996). Seven Principles for Good Practice in Undergraduate Education. *AAHE Bulletin, March 1987*, 3–7. Retrieved from http://www.lonestar.edu/multimedia/SevenPrinciples.pdf

Crawford-Ferre, H. G., & Wiest, L. R. (2012). Effective Online Instruction in Higher Education. *Quarterly Review of Distance Education, 13*(1), 11–14.

Gleason, B. J. (2004). *Retention Issues in Online Programs: A Review of the Literature*. Paper presented at the Second AIMS International Conference on Management, December 28–31, 395–398.

iNACOL (International Association for K-12 Online Learning). (2011). *National Standards for Quality Online Courses, Version 2*. Retrieved from http://www.inacol.org/resources/publications/national-quality-standards/

Jaggars, S. (2013). *Choosing Between Online and Face-to-Face Courses: Community College Student Voices*. CCRC Working Paper No. 58. Retrieved from http://ccrc.tc.columbia.edu/publications/online-demand-student-voices.html

Quality Matters Program. (2011). *Quality Matters Rubric Standards 2011–2013 edition with Assigned Point Values*. Retrieved from http://www.elo.iastate.edu/files/2014/03/Quality_Matters_Rubric.pdf

Singh, S., Rylander, D. H., & Mims, T. C. (2012.) Efficiency of Online vs. Offline Learning: A Comparison of Inputs and Outcomes. *International Journal of Business, Humanities and Technology*, *2*(1), 93–98.

U.S. Copyright Office website. (2012). "How much of someone else's work can I use without getting permission?" Retrieved from US Copyright Office, http://www.copyright.gov/help/faq/faq-fairuse.html#howmuch

17

Practical Strategies for Motivating and Retaining E-learners

Andrea Henne

Introduction

Student retention in e-learning is a broad topic with numerous components, including student readiness, student motivation for learning, faculty preparation, institutional resources, and instructional strategies. In this chapter, we will examine the major factors that impact student motivation and retention in e-learning and present a variety of best practices that have been shown to increase course completion rates. Each section in the chapter begins by asking a key question. The responses to the key question provide effective practical strategies that can be adapted to meet the varying needs and characteristics of higher education e-learning programs.

Leaders of successful e-learning programs look closely at their data on student retention and examine the trends, underlying causes, and factors that have positive and negative impacts on rates of retention. The focus on student retention in e-learning is significant because of the persistent gap between the retention and success rates of online students when compared with traditional oncampus students. Students enrolled in an online course (e-learning) typically have a lower rate of retention than students enrolled in a traditional oncampus course. Student success rates, which are determined by course grades of A, B, or C, are also typically lower for students enrolled in online courses (California Community Colleges Chancellor's Office, 2011). The same holds true for students enrolled in MOOCs (Massive Open Online Courses), as recent data show (Hill, 2013).

Retention rates are calculated based on enrollments several weeks into the start of the semester, and therefore do not usually record the number of students who drop within the first several days or first week of the course. Taking these early dropouts into account, an online course that begins on the first day with 30 students may see as few as half persisting through the end of the course. Some students who enroll do not even log in and begin the course—these "no shows" as they are called, are also an issue worth examining.

In the following pages, we will take a closer look at the issues, examine what we've learned from practitioners and researchers in the field, and provide solutions for e-learning leaders to explore in their own institutions.

Key Question No 1: What Are Some of the Most Frequently Reported *Student Factors* that Impact Online Student Retention?

Student Retention Factors

The degree to which a student has the following abilities, skills, motivation, and knowledge will determine whether the student is likely to be successful in e-learning. Based on a review of the information published over the past several years as well as personal experience as an online instructor in both graduate and undergraduate programs, the following have emerged as the most important attributes that a student needs to be successful in online learning:

- Ability to communicate in writing. Since the majority of coursework involves written communication through online discussions, wikis, blogs, journals, e-mails, the student must be able to demonstrate clarity and accuracy through correct spelling, grammar, and punctuation.
- Ability to work independently. Students who are used to relying on face-to-face instruction in a classroom setting often report a sense of isolation and a need for more individual and immediate personal contact and have a difficult time adjusting to a learning environment that depends upon their ability to work by themselves and seek help when needed (Schaeffer & Konetes, 2010).
- Availability of time. Students often enroll in e-learning courses because their obligations to family and their work schedule prevent them from attending oncampus courses. They view e-learning as more convenient and a way to fit coursework into their busy schedules. Yet, the most frequently reported reasons for dropping an e-learning course are precisely the same reasons for enrolling—personal circumstances and work schedule (Innovations in Online Retention Webcast, 2009).
- Clear expectations. Students who fully understand the requirements for e-learning and the specific demands of each course in which they are planning to enroll are more prepared for success (Heyman, 2010).
- Onscreen reading rate and recall. The facility with which an e-learning student is able to read and comprehend the course material directly impacts his/her learning outcomes and ability to demonstrate learning in tests and assessments. It is impractical to print out all the onscreen material throughout the course; therefore, a successful online student is able to adapt to digital learning.
- Persistence. Students who work steadily toward completing their coursework week by week and who do not permit outside obstacles or personal challenges to deter them from completing the course, and then return to enroll in more courses each semester, demonstrate the persistence that will lead to success.
- Plan for graduation or completion goal. Successful students focus on the rewards that will come with completion of the requirements for certification or a degree. Students who follow an individual education plan and who have a clear path toward graduation are more likely to resist the impediments and obstacles along the way ("Improving Retention,", 2009, p. 1).
- Self-discipline. With the competing demands in their busy lives, online students are particularly vulnerable to distractions and obligations outside of the course. A strong work ethic and belief in their individual strengths provides a successful online learner with a buffer to overcome the potential pitfalls.

- Self-motivation. The e-learning environment requires that students have the drive to succeed. A combination of internal and external motivational forces is necessary to stay focused and on track. Successful e-learners need to be motivated self-learners (Hartnett, St. George, & Dron, 2011).
- Skill in using a computer, laptop, or mobile device. Although it is not necessary to be an expert with computers, e-learners must have basic skills and competencies and be able to adapt to a variety of digital tasks. Configuring the computer for e-learning and understanding the Internet connectivity requirements and peripherals such as webcams, browser plug-ins, and external storage devices or cloud storage are foundational requirements that must be in place right from the start.
- Speed and reliability of computer and Internet connection. E-learning courses are comprised of onscreen materials, streaming video and audio, files that need to be downloaded, assignments and exams that need to be submitted. Without a fast and reliable computer and a dependable connection to the Internet, a student's ability to meet the course requirements will be in jeopardy.
- Time-management skills. Students often enroll in e-learning courses because they have a busy schedule. Survey responses to a study of distance education retention in the California Community Colleges in 2009 included comments such as: "My work schedule is heavy and a distance education course is more convenient" as one of the most frequently reported reasons for enrolling. And one of the top reasons for dropping an e-learning course was the same—a busy schedule (WCET Webcast, 2009). Students who are unable to handle the study and work requirements often find themselves falling behind and unable to catch up. Managing time for online learning requires that students have the ability to schedule not only login time to view the e-learning course content, but also study time, and time to work on the assignments and projects. Overcoming the urge to procrastinate and knowing how to manage time are critical factors in student retention.

The bulleted list of student retention factors discussed above is arranged in alphabetical order; however, it must be noted that personal traits such as self-motivation, persistence, and self-discipline are probably the most critical and yet are the most difficult to *teach*. This reality is particularly true for students who are enrolled at the higher education level. Since these personal traits are so important for being successful in e-learning, institutions must offer the student support services and implement instructional strategies that are discussed later in this chapter.

Student characteristics such as the ability to communicate in writing, the ability to work independently, onscreen reading rate and recall, and technology skills are predictable and can be measured before the class begins; and ideally before the student registers and enrolls. In fact, early intervention is highly recommended as a retention strategy. Learning readiness indicators such as SmarterMeasure™ (www.readi.info) identify these types of skills and personal traits that are necessary for online learning success. Once the individual student's readiness for e-learning has been assessed, then the remediation and supportive attention can be provided. Each student can focus on his/her own areas that need improvement as part of a personal development plan that would need to be completed prior to enrolling in an e-learning course.

Identification of factors that put students at risk for persisting in e-learning was the focus of the community colleges in the SUNY (State University of New York) and led to their creation of a database of risk factors with tips and advice. They recommended that these risk factors be addressed, as described below, prior to starting any e-learning course or program of study ("Lessons from SUNY," 2010, pp. 4, 7).

- Academic Advising. Before registration can be completed, an advisor who has been trained in understanding e-learning requirements and student risk factors must review the student's education plan and approve it.
- Developmental needs. When two or more of the retention risk factors are present and the student's academic record shows a below-average grade point average and/or the student received a low score on an e-learning readiness assessment, enrollment in an online course should be contingent upon improvement.
- Technical factors. For first-time e-learning students, providing an orientation that focuses on the technical aspects of e-learning, including practicing navigating a sample course, using the course tools such as discussions, messaging, and quizzes is an important factor in promoting student retention. The orientation could include information about being a successful e-learning student. Ideally, this orientation would be available as part of the preregistration and advisement process or at least be part of the first activities once the course begins. Online student orientations can be delivered as an on-demand tutorial that students can complete at their own pace, which is more practical than scheduling face-to-face sessions. Conducting live webinar orientations is another method for providing new e-learning students with the information that will help them to be successful. These orientations could be repeated during the first or second week of the semester so that students can ask questions or brush up on some of the pointers that they may have missed.
- Time of registration—SUNY recommends that registration in online sections be blocked after the course start date. Research has shown that students who register late are less likely to be successful (Moltz, 2011). After the official start of classes, a student's registration should require that an advisor or the instructor give permission.

Once the course is underway, social, financial, and personal issues often arise that impact student retention. Students need to have access to support services such as counseling, advising, and peer mentoring that they can turn to for help with these personal challenges. Results from a Fall 2012 survey of e-learning students revealed that, of the reasons for dropping an online course, personal reasons such as health, family, or finances were a major factor (SDCCD, 2013).

Other research studies point to personal problems accounting for as much as 43 percent of the reasons for dropping. These barriers to online course completion are situational in the context of the individual's social, economic or personal environment (Darrow, 2011).

The next section in this chapter will consider what practical strategies an institution might implement to support students with personal challenges and also what strategies have proven effective for retaining e-learners in general.

Key Question No 2: What *Institutional Factors* Influence Online Student Retention and Success?

Institutional Resources and Support Factors

While many of the individual student factors that impact retention are out of the control of e-learning leaders, institutions that offer e-learning do have control over the support that they provide and the ways in which they address the barriers that hamper student retention ("Persistence in Online Education", 2009, p. 2). In order for e-learning to be a successful method of educating students, the institution must strategically plan and budget for institutional resources and support. The role of e-learning in the mission and goals of the institution must be clearly defined and well grounded in a theoretical framework. The institutional parameters for online operations must be established. It is necessary that the institution be prepared and equipped to offer student services to current and prospective e-learners equivalent to the range of services offered to traditional oncampus students and available beyond traditional business hours. Student services that are essential for supporting and retaining e-learners are: Admissions, Counseling/Advising, Financial Aid, Tutoring, Library, and Technical Support ("Understanding Attrition," November, 2009). Personnel trained and dedicated to providing e-learning support need to be present.

Once the mission and goals have been established and the e-learning program is operating under a coherent theoretical framework, the institution needs to ensure that the following areas that impact the retention of e-learners are being addressed:

- Administrative Support. Policies and procedures that clarify the role of e-learning, with designated leadership to implement, monitor, and manage the program are necessary to ensure that the e-learning students, faculty, and the staff have clear pathways and structure to be successful. Processes and institutional expectations for all aspects of e-learning should be transparent to students before they enroll.
- Technical Infrastructure. A robust system of hosting, managing, and delivering the e-learning courses as well as securely authenticating the user accounts is undoubtedly necessary to prevent student frustration that can lead to dropping out of e-learning courses. In fact, Meyer and Barefield (2013) found that when the technical issues caused the system to be unreliable and unstable or when there was a lack of assistance in working through student technical issues with the course, students' e-learning success was negatively affected.
- Curriculum Development. The quality of the course curriculum in meeting student goals—whether to attain a degree, transfer from a two-year to a four-year institution, or prepare for a career—must be high if e-learning students are to be motivated and retained. Although the learning outcomes for e-learning and traditional oncampus instruction are equivalent, curriculum development for e-learning requires adaptations in the types of content, organization, resource materials, and assessment methods that comprise the course. Faculty who are responsible for developing, reviewing, and approving the curriculum for e-learning should have firsthand experience with teaching online in order to make informed decisions about the curriculum that comprises the courses and programs that are approved for distance education delivery.
- Instructional Support and Training. As we will see in the next section of this chapter, high-quality instructional methods used by faculty are essential for motivating and retaining e-learners. Therefore, a critical component of an institution's e-learning program is providing faculty with the tools and techniques for teaching online. This support needs to begin prior to being given an assignment to teach an e-learning course. Individualized and customized assistance in designing the course, training in best practices for teaching online, and ongoing assistance with managing the e-learning environment and all aspects of student learning are vital to ensure that student retention and success strategies are being implemented.

- Learning Communities. Just as oncampus students have places set aside on campus where students can join clubs, meet to study, and socialize, the e-learning environment can provide the same opportunities through social networking tools that are either built into the course delivery platform or are part of an institutional portal. Students can form study groups online, connect with other students who are pursuing the same career and educational goals, or just create contacts to be in their networks. Learning communities build a sense of connection to the institution that foster retention, persistence, and perhaps even loyalty after graduation as alumni. We will discuss the importance of learning communities within the course itself later in this chapter in the section on instructional strategies for retaining e-learners.
- Early Alert Systems. Technology systems such as Starfish (http://www.starfishsolutions.com) that gather student data to identify students at risk for withdrawing from class are becoming more prevalent as an e-learning retention strategy. Students who have not been logging into the e-learning courses and submitting assignments, students who are earning low grades, or students who are exhibiting other low-performance indicators will trigger an alert that can be addressed. These types of student success analytics promise to help an institution improve the rates of student retention and persistence.

The final section in this chapter will consider the instructor's role and impact on online student motivation and retention.

Key Question No. 3: What Can the *Instructor* Do to Improve Online Student Motivation and Retention?

Effective Practices That Make a Difference

Up to this point, the e-learning motivation and retention strategies in this chapter have focused on the student and institutional factors for success. While the characteristics of successful e-learners and the institutional support policies and practices are most often beyond the purview of the faculty, in this next section, we will examine the critical impact that individual instructors have on the motivation and retention of their students.

It has been well established that the instructor plays a vital role in the online learning process. While it has often been said that the instructor in an e-learning course is the "guide on the side" rather than the "sage on the stage," we believe that this notion that the instructor merely facilitates the course and primarily is there to answer questions from students when needed lacks a clear understanding of the importance and effectiveness of the instructor role.

While most students are initially attracted to an online program because of the convenience, what keeps them enrolled is the instructional quality of the program and the nature of the relationships with the online faculty.

Satisfaction with the experience of being an e-learner is directly related to these factors:

- Instructor attitude toward online learning and online learners.
- Instructor understanding of the pedagogy of online student motivation and retention.

A study by Sun, Tsai, Finger, Chen, and Yeh (2008) found that the attitudes of instructors toward online learning had an impact on students. Students were more motivated when their instructors were enthusiastic and exhibited a positive attitude about the subject matter and the students' ability to succeed. When the instructor is engaged and involved with the students as they perform the learning activities, students were more likely to be satisfied.

Faculty who are selected to teach online need to be well trained and prepared to meet the challenges of teaching online. Rapid changes in technology require that faculty keep up to date with the e-learning field through continual professional development. In addition to being trained to use the course delivery system, whether open source or proprietary, the course management tools, the digital media creation and other technologies, faculty need to have training in the pedagogy or andragogy of online learning and then receive support as they develop, teach, and manage their courses.

The classic work on instructional strategies to encourage and motivate students that has stood the test of time and is still relevant today is that of Chickering and Gamson (1987). Their "Seven Principles for Good Practice" provide an excellent foundation for e-learning instructors because they directly address the techniques that foster success in the e-learning environment, regardless of the technology, tools, or whether the course is offered as a MOOC or other form of competency-based course or as a regular online course.

- Encourage contact between students and faculty—right from the start.
- Develop reciprocity and cooperation among students. Create a community of learners.
- Encourage active learning and student engagement. Offer frequent opportunities to participate.
- Give prompt feedback. Personalize the feedback for each learner. Use rubrics to streamline grading.
- Emphasize time on task. Time plus energy equals learning.
- Communicate high expectations. Recognize accomplishments and foster a sense of achievement and progress.
- Respect diverse talents and ways of learning. Vary the activities and method of delivering content. (Chickering & Gamson, 1987)

Online student motivation is positively impacted when the course material is relevant, varied, interesting, challenging, and presented in a learning environment that encourages students to do their best.

An interesting piece by faculty at Park University took an in-depth look at online student motivation. In their paper they provided a chart to guide instructors with strategies to implement throughout the course, starting with the week before it starts through the final week of the course (Dennis, Bunkowski, & Eskey, 2007).

For example, Dennis et al. (2007) propose that, in the week prior to opening day, instructors establish a preview week where students can log in and view the syllabus and introductory materials with clear instructions about how the course will be conducted. If contacting students before the class is not feasible, then instructors can send students a welcome e-mail with start-up instructions early on the first day.

Strategic Steps by the Instructor Prior to Opening Day could include the following:

- Post his/her photo and a friendly introduction.
- Create a thread to post weekly Teacher's Tips & Tricks and invite students to share their best tips.

- Create a virtual lounge—an ungraded area for students only.
- Ask students to self-assess their readiness for e-learning, their knowledge of the subject matter, their goals, and areas where they would like to improve their learning skills.

Day 1 of the Course:

- Vividly describe the course's value and relevance.
- Log in 2–3 times; be responsive and genuinely enthusiastic.
- Clarify expectations; Let students know the turnaround time they can expect for responding to e-mails and for receiving their graded assignments and exams.
- Summarize self-assessments and improvement goals; urge peers to support one another to create a community of learners.
- Recognize every student in some manner.
- Internalize caring and show sincere interest.
- Provide rubrics that clarify the grading standards for assignments, and for activities such as discussions.
- Clarify policies such as whether you will accept work turned in after the deadline.

End of Week 1:

- Urge students to form peer learning support teams.
- Continue to log in regularly and respond to students promptly.
- Demonstrate and promote deep learning versus superficial thinking.
- Clarify course expectations, performance, and grading.
- Have instructor ask: What effect am I having upon my students' motivation to learn?

Weekly Strategies:

- Promote critical thinking via good questioning.
- Encourage linkages between the course and life experiences and current events.
- Illustrate standards of expected performance.
- Praise and otherwise reinforce quality efforts.
- Give personalized feedback to each student.
- Correct privately and respectfully.

At Midterm:

- Summarize course journey to date.
- Post and praise evidence of student learning improvement.
- Ask the students for feedback on what is/isn't working well in the course.
- Continue using a psychological lens to view each student's attitude, effort, and performance and adjust yours accordingly.

Strategies for the Final Week of the Course

- Summarize and reinforce the Core Learning Outcomes within the context of the students' career aspirations and their responsibility to the global society.

- Urge students to explore the more complex issues and their implications on a broader scale.
- Reflect upon the lessons learned while teaching this course for future use, and ask yourself, "How can I use these experiences to improve my own teaching and learning?" (Dennis et al., 2007)

E-learning instructors need to have their own "Online Retention Toolkit"—selecting, experimenting, and creating what works for their subject matter, their style of teaching, and the learning styles of their students. Instructional techniques that impact student satisfaction and motivation to complete their course and enroll in future e-learning courses are based on these proven best practices in the pedagogy of online retention.

Conclusion

Strategies for motivating and retaining e-learners have been researched, discussed, and analyzed for the past 15 years in literature, in webinars, in blogs, and at professional conferences. From our review, it is clear that e-learning can and should be redesigned to ensure that students are well prepared in advance of enrollment; that the critical institutional support structures, resources, policies, and procedures are in place; and that instructors be provided with thorough training and support throughout the course design, and development, and on an ongoing basis. The unique requirements of successful e-learning programs and the special needs of online students and faculty must continue to be recognized and addressed if we are to continue to make progress and have e-learning be recognized without hesitation as an effective method of learning.

References

California Community Colleges Chancellor's Office. (2011, April). *Distance education report*. Retrieved from http://californiacommunitycolleges.cccco.edu/Portals/0/reportsTB/DistanceEducation2011_final.pdf

Chickering, A. W., & Gamson, F. (1987). Seven principles for good practice in undergraduate education. *AAHE Bulletin, 39*(7), 3–7.

Darrow, R. (2011, May 13). Research: Online learning part 2. *Calfornia Dreamin' Blogpost*. Retrieved from http://robdarrow.wordpress.com/2011/05/13/research-online-learning-part-2.

Dennis, K., Bunkowski, L., & Eskey, M. (2007). The little engine that could—How to start the motor? Motivating the online student. *InSight Journal of Scholarly Teaching, 2*. Retrieved from http://www.insightjournal.net/Volume2/The%20Little%20Engine%20That%20Could-%20How%20to%20Start%20the%20Motor-%20Motivating%20the%20Online%20Student.pdf

Hartnett, M., St. George, A., & Dron, J. (2011, October). Examining motivation in online distance learning environments: Complex, multifaceted, and situation-dependent. *International Review of Research in Open and Distance Learning, 12*(6). Retrieved from http://www.irrodl.org/index.php/irrodl/article/view/1030/1954

Heyman, E. (2010). Overcoming student retention issues in higher education online programs. *Online Journal of Distance Learning Administration, 8*(4). Retrieved from http://www.westga.edu/%7Edistance/ojdla/spring61/miller61.htm

Hill, P. (2013, February 26). The most thorough summary (to date) of MOOC completion rates. *E-Literate*. Retrieved from http://mfeldstein.com/the-most-thorough-summary-to-date-of-mooc-completion-rates/

Improving retention. (2009, October 15). *Distance Education Report, 13*(20), 1–2, 7.

Lessons from SUNY. (2010, August 1). *Distance Education Report, 14*(15), 4, 7.

Meyer, J., & Barefield, A. (2013, Summer). Infrastructure and administrative support for online programs. *Online Journal of Distance Learning Administration, 16*(2). Retrieved from http://www.westga.edu/~distance/ojdla/Fall133/

Moltz, D. (2011, March 11). Ending the late option. *Inside Higher Education*. Retrieved from https://www.insidehighered.com/news/2011/03/11/texas_community_college_bans_late_registration

Persistence in online education. (2009, October 15). *Distance Education Report, 13*(20), 2.

Schaeffer, C. E., & Konetes, G. D. (2010, May). Impact of learner engagement on attrition rates and student success in online learning. *International Journal of Instructional Technology & Distance Learning,* 7(5). Retrieved from http://www.itdl.org/Journal/May_10/index.htm

SDCCD Office of Institutional Research. (2013, January). *All colleges online course student satisfaction survey report*. Retrieved from http://research.sdccd.edu/docs/Research%20Reports/Surveys/Online%20Course%20Satisfaction/2012/Online%20Report_All%20Colleges_Fall%202012.pdf

Sun, P.C., Tsai, R. J., Finger, G., Chen, Y. Y., & Yeh, D. (2008). What drives a successful e-learning? An empirical investigation of the critical factors influencing learner satisfaction. *Computers & Education, 50*(4), 1183–1202.

Understanding attrition. (2009, November 1). *Distance Education Report, 13*(21), 1–2, 7.

WCET. (2009, April). *Innovations in online retention Webcast*. Retrieved from http://wcet.wiche.edu/advance/resources#retention

18

Accessibility and Instructional Design in E-learning

Cindy Poore-Pariseau

Note: Although the statistics cited are based on U.S. postsecondary education student populations, the ideas outlined herein can be applied beyond the U.S., as the needs of disabled students are universal (Poore-Pariseau, 2010).

Introduction

The percentage of disabled students participating in postsecondary education increased from 6% in 1996 (National Center for Education Statistics, 2000) to 10.8 % in 2008 (Snyder, Dillow, & Hoffman, 2010). Along with this increase, Fichten et al. (2009) note that the demand to secure course accessibility, including accessibility in online environments, is steadily increasing. In terms of online learning and the World Wide Web, accessibility means that "people with disabilities can perceive, understand, navigate, and interact with the Web, and that they can contribute to the Web" (World Wide Web Consortium, 2005, para 1). The following chapter is a discussion of the importance of intentionally designing online courses with accessibility in mind.

Designing Effective Online Instruction

Designing courses for online learning takes a specialized set of skills that are different, in many ways, from those skills necessary for designing on-ground courses (Yang & Cornelious, 2005). For example, traditional face-to-face education is often designed in a teacher-centered model, whereas the format for online learning lends itself more to student-centered learning (Yang & Cornelious, 2005). The necessary skill set in this instance is for the designer (who may also be the instructor) to take the focus off of him or herself as the authority who imparts knowledge and to place the focus on the students, while acting as a guide for the students as they move through the process of meeting the course goals through the use of technology.

In the traditional, face-to-face role, Yang and Cornelious (2005) observed, faculty members are often lecturers who disseminate information for students to reflect upon, whereas online instruction often involves allowing, if not encouraging, students to become a community of learners who "collaborate with each other in order to develop personal understanding of course content" (p. 4). If collaboration is important in the learning process, then designers must know how to effectively set up their courses in a way that encourages this process among a diverse group of students. Additional challenges faced when designing online instruction include understanding how to effectively utilize appropriate technology and to be able to guide students through the process of learning to utilize the technology in a way that promotes learning (or have access to resources that can provide students with such assistance).

Changing from synchronous to asynchronous classroom discussions is one significant difference between on-line and face-to-face learning. In their study of 116 students enrolled in hybrid courses, Wu and Hiltz (2004) found that online discussions improved perceived student learning outcomes. However, as noted by Yang and Cornelius (2005), facilitating discussion in face-to-face classrooms is different from doing so online. Online environments allow all students to participate in discussions, whereas student discussions in a face-to-face setting may be limited by factors such as time constraints and students who monopolize discussion. However, an abundance of information, as well as the change of format from synchronous to asynchronous, may lead to information overload for students, necessitating assistance from the online instructor in discovering what is important as well as how to navigate this new mode of learning. Students may also need assistance from their instructors in discovering how to move an asynchronous discussion forward in a scholarly fashion, and overall assistance regarding how to adjust to the technology and a new mode (and model) of learning.

In a study conducted by Cleveland-Innes, Garrison, and Kinsel (2007) about the adjustments online learners must make from the traditional on-ground classroom learning model, the researchers note that the adjustments are not merely a matter of students feeling comfortable in the new environment; online learning has "significant learning implications as well" (p. 12) that require competence from instructors that extends beyond the subject area in which they are instructing. Students no longer have a passive role in learning and must receive guidance from their instructors regarding how to make this adjustment in a way that will move their learning processes forward and will keep them motivated to continue to make necessary adjustments to their new roles (Yang & Cornelious, 2005).

Accessibility

In very broad terms, accessibility involves one's ability to obtain or utilize something. In terms of online learning environments, Vanderheiden, Harkins, and Barnicle (as quoted by Schwartz, 2004) write that accessibility

> involves the ability to use online content without vision, without hearing, without pointing or manipulation, and without speech, by persons with cognitive limitations, with language disabilities, with low vision and limited or no hearing, and with alternative languages.
>
> (p. 1)

In other words, when designed properly, online courses should be accessible to almost all students with any one of a number of differences (or combination of differences) without the need for individual accommodations.

Creating and maintaining accessible online learning environments is necessary from at least two standpoints. First, in the United States as well as in many other countries, there are a number of laws that mandate that course materials be accessible to all students, regardless of the mode of delivery (Crow, 2008). Moore and Kearsley (2005) and Lin (2007) add that making learning environments accessible is, ethically speaking, the right thing to do from a social standpoint.

As more learning opportunities move on-line, a lack of accessibility will significantly impact learning opportunities and will, in turn, become a societal issue as is exemplified in the following passage:

> When this population [disabled students] is not supported through policies that enhance its chances for success in college and professional employment, the cost to the nation is likely to be higher. This is so because of the supplemental and/or dependent support they may require from others . . . for individuals who do not obtain a degree in a postsecondary education program, prospects for finding meaningful and remunerative employment are increasingly limited.
>
> (Frieden, 2003, para. 19)

Lin (2007) also argues for the importance of accessibility to education by pointing out a connection among education, employment and income level. The overarching ideal is that providing accessibility to education is not only the law; it is also the right thing to do, not just for those who are disabled, but for society as a whole.

Accessibility and Instructional Design

Creating an accessible online learning environment is not the same as creating accessibility in on-ground classrooms. Stone, Jarrett, Woodroffe, and Minocha (2005) note that designing accessible instruction online requires an understanding of related ethical and legal issues as well as knowledge of the technological and pedagogical issues associated with educating diverse bodies of students. While formal programs in instructional design include courses that teach this information, evidence suggests that faculty members who design their own courses do not receive this knowledge in a formalized manner (Chodock & Dolinger, 2009), which often results in faculty members' being unprepared or underprepared to develop and teach courses online that are fully accessible (Grabinger, Aplin, & Ponnappa-Brenner, 2008). When accessibility is not considered and implemented, some students will be left with the task of having to search out or, in some cases, develop their own accessibility adaptations.

Difficulties accessing learning environments are not new for disabled students. In 2002, Rose and Meyer expressed the importance of accessibility when they discussed the significance of student interaction to educational success. "Barriers to learning," they tell readers, "occur in the interaction with the curriculum—they are not solely in the capacity of the learner. Thus, when education fails, the curriculum, not the learner, should take responsibility for adaptation" (p. 20). Although this issue remains, to some extent, efforts are being made to overcome such obstacles. One such approach that is used to proactively incorporate learning strategies that are beneficial to many students, including those with disabilities, is universal design for learning (UDL), which grew out of the concept of universal design.

Universal Design for Learning

Universal design is a term developed by architect Ron Mace in the 1970s to describe "the design of products and environments to be usable by all people, to the greatest extent possible, without

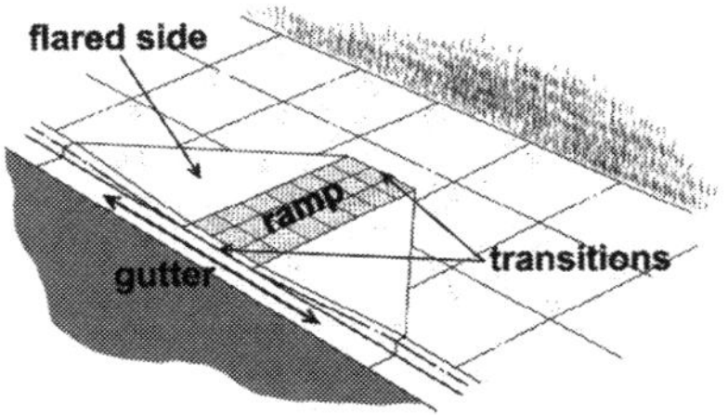

Figure 18.1 Curb Cuts

U.S. Department of Justice. (2010). Images. In *Flared ramp*. Retrieved February 28, 2010, from www.ada.gov/images/flaredramp1.jpg

the need for adaptation or specialized design" (Center for Applied Special Technology, 2008, para 2). An example of the universal design concept is curb cuts (Figure 18.1), which were initially designed to allow complete street and sidewalk access to people who use wheelchairs. Today, however, curb cuts are used to allow the same access to those who use bicycles, strollers, roller blades, and other equipment that make full curbing difficult to negotiate (Poore-Pariseau, 2010).

The concept of universal design was then extended into the educational environment and the term *learning* was added, transforming universal design to universal design for learning (UDL) (Center for Applied Special Technology, 2008). According to the Center for Applied Special Technology (2008), UDL is a system for providing a variety of means (e.g. seeing, hearing, touching, reading/writing) for students to access and engage with course material, and demonstrate their knowledge of the curriculum. This approach to teaching and learning allows individuals to draw upon and utilize their particular learning strengths, while acknowledging that not all students learn in the same manner. The following statement from Learning Opportunities Task Force (2003) emphasizes the wide-ranging benefits of UDL:

> A core concept of Universal Design is that by anticipating and planning for the diverse needs of potential users during the design process, the resulting product or outcome will better suit the needs of all users. . . . When applying the concept of Universal Design to instruction, the benefits are much the same. Anticipating and planning for the diverse needs of students, including but not limited to students with disabilities, results in a better learning experience for all students.
>
> (p. 1)

Accessibility: Design Expectations

At one time the expectation for course design was that all students received the same material from which to learn, regardless of their individual learning needs (Grabinger, Aplin, & Ponnappa-Brenner, 2008). In such instances, neither adaptations nor accommodations were provided. Later, recognition was given to the need for different types of instruction for students with varying abilities; in such instances, students were given specialized material that often did not equal the curriculum of the nondisabled student and therefore did not prepare the students to move on to the next grade (Sapp, 2009). However, as classrooms became more diverse and disability-related laws were put into place, and as technology began to permeate all areas of life, the expectations regarding how material can and should be presented to students began to evolve. Jane Seale, author *of E-Learning and Disability in Higher Education* (2006), makes this point when she states that

> one of the key consequences of the growing numbers of disabled students that are entering higher education is that it has influenced those working within these sectors to address the extent to which they understand the learning needs of disabled students and can provide support that adequately addresses those learning needs.
>
> (p. 10)

While many learning management systems profess to be developed in an accessible manner, the content placed on the platforms by faculty members may not be, unless there is a conscious effort on the part of the instructor or the institution to ensure that accessibility issues are addressed (Poore-Pariseau, 2010). The significance of a student's ability to effectively access course material is revealed, in part, by Moore and Kearsley's (2005) statement that "a well-designed course will provide the instructor with many opportunities to engage students in discussion, criticism, and constructing knowledge" (p. 136).

Crow (2008) suggests that the first step toward providing accessible online content is an institutional commitment to the accessibility of all technologies, including online instruction. When an institutional commitment to providing resources (such as training for faculty) that promote accessible online learning is not made and course material is not accessible, the impact can be tremendous (Seale, 2006). For example, if a course has not been designed to meet accessibility standards and guidelines such as section 508 or Web Accessibility Content guidelines (WCAG), students may be excluded from effectively engaging in discussions and other interactions that are so vital to the educational process, leaving not only these students at a disadvantage, but also the class as a whole, as they will not be able to benefit from the contributions of all students. An example, in the words of a student, of how learning may be hindered by inaccessible content can be found at http://webaim.org/articles/visual/blind. In this video, a student who is blind tells listeners about his experience:

> Now days the classes are moving more and more towards the internet. You're able to take entire courses online. And I have tried to stay away from those because I am 90% sure that as a blind individual I will run into problems accessing those sites. I will be using the JAWS screen reader in connection with the Internet. JAWS stands for Job Access with Speech. . . . screen readers are very helpful, but if the Web site is written in a manner that the screen reader cannot access that Web site it does me no good. One of the bad experiences I've had trying to navigate the Internet.

A second step toward providing accessible content is understanding that people learn and process information in different ways (Center for Applied Special Technology, 2008). Given the view that individuals do not all learn in the same manner, and, as noted by Sims and Stork (2007), they espouse a variety of cultural/situational/social norms, the challenge becomes how to design instruction in a way that allows all to take advantage of their learning strengths. As a way to manage this challenge, Sims and Stork propose that, because it is nearly impossible to gather a full spectrum of data about a cohort of students in online environments, designers should steer away from designing for particular populations but instead, design in a way that allows "students to integrate their individuality, experience and culture into the teaching and learning dynamic" (para 1). Similarly, Sprenger (2008) suggests that giving students a choice about how (i.e., the medium in which) they learn material can facilitate the learning process. Because they allow for individual choices, these concepts are similar to the Center for Applied Special Technology's (2008) suggested use of UDL.

The term *Universal Design* is often used interchangeably with the terms *accessibility* and *usability*, but each holds a different meaning. While accessibility is a legal term that is measured, for the most part, in objective legal terms, usability is more subjective, based on individual learning characteristics and how well individuals are able to perform particular tasks or functions, from their individual perspectives (Iwarsson & Stahl, 2003). While one may argue that a universally designed learning management system is, by default, accessible, an important note is that content loaded onto the universally designed learning management system may not be accessible, particularly if the designer (faculty members, for example) is not familiar with accessibility standards as they apply to technologically mediated instruction. Another important distinction to make is that not everything that is accessible to all is (effectively) usable by all.

One difficult piece in the UDL model is how to offer alternatives that will support the learning needs of every student; Sims and Stork (2007) argue against this, given the difficulty of knowing the particulars of every student, especially in a distance learning environment. For this reason, when a UDL model is used as a proactive way of providing accessibility to students, occasional accommodations may still need to be inserted in order for full accessibility to be obtained (Burgstahler, 2007). For example,

> due to the extensive process of turning material into Braille as well as the expense, Brailed material may be best produced as a retrofit, on a case by case basis. Although Braille may not be a preference in most cases, there are some instances, such as in the case of math and music, when Braille may be necessary for access. The cost to turn text into Braille can range from $3 per page (for words) to $17 per page for music (Braille Inc., 2008). Therefore, this may be an instance when it is more efficient to make this accommodation on an as needed basis rather than as a universal design for learning process.
>
> (Poore-Pariseau, 2011, p. 61)

However, UDL was never meant to solve all accessibility issues. According to the Center for Applied Special Technology (2008), UDL

> provides a blueprint for creating flexible goals, methods, materials, and assessments that accommodate learner differences. . . . Universal does not imply a single optimal solution for everyone. Instead, it is meant to underscore the need for multiple approaches to meet the learning needs of diverse students . . . UDL uses technology's power and flexibility to make education more inclusive and effective for all.
>
> (p. 25)

The proactive use of UDL can alleviate some practical and legal accessibility-related concerns, but not all, thus necessitating occasional accommodations (Rose & Meyer, 2002).

Although it cannot make all learning accessible at every turn, UDL can be a means to change the approach for giving students access to the curriculum from reactive only (i.e., accommodations) to a proactive UDL approach, in addition to, when necessary, adding accommodations (Burgstahler, 2007). For example, in a UDL online environment, reading material may be made available for students to: a) read from their computer screen (by the students or by assistive technology), b) download when they wish to print the material, and c) listen to audio for those whose learning is enhanced when they can hear text. Although audio may not be practical in some cases, there exists technology that can make the process manageable, when the designer deems this step practical and, of course, not in violation of copyright laws.

How to Support Faculty

Faculty members who design their own online learning courses face many challenges that extend beyond knowing and teaching their subject matter. With the move to online environments, faculty members must now "master, design and delivery strategies, techniques and methods for teaching on-line courses" (Yang & Cornelious, 2005, p. 12). Although faculty members who teach in institutions of postsecondary education have a foundation of knowledge within their discipline, they often do not have a fund of knowledge from which to draw when it comes to course design (Chodock & Dolinger, 2009; Hinson & LaPrairie, 2005). A lack of knowledge regarding instructional design can be exacerbated by a lack of understanding of online pedagogy, necessitating support to gain the knowledge and understanding needed to be effective (Sims, 2006).

> For faculty teaching online the type of pedagogy used may differ significantly from face-to-face classes. The growth of on-line courses and programs has increased the need for faculty to become comfortable with online teaching and gain the necessary skills to make online courses a success.
>
> (Allen & Seaman, 2009, p. 3)

Because of the increasingly diverse makeup of online students, this support and training should include elements necessary to design pedagogically sound instruction that increases accessibility.

One place to begin this type of training is to assess what tools and knowledge the faculty members possess and what they are lacking. While formal programs in instructional design at institutions such as Capella University (2010), George Mason University (2010) and Syracuse University (2010) include courses that teach formal instructional design models such as the ADDIE model (Analysis, Design, Development, Implement, Evaluate), evidence suggests that faculty members who design their own courses do not receive this knowledge in a formalized manner (Chodock & Dolinger, 2009)

In their study of 271 college level faculty members and teaching assistants, Izzo, Murray, and Novak (2008) found that

> Faculty wanted more professional development training on UDL, and they wanted to access training on an as-needed basis . . . that would be specific enough to offer basic guidance when a student discloses a disability before asking Disability Services to intervene.
>
> (p. 65)

This study signals awareness among faculty members that they lack some of the tools (including UDL knowledge) necessary to design inclusive and accessible courses.

Conclusion

Research regarding the intersection of online learning and accessibility has focused on technological rather than learning aspects of the course development process in regard to faculty development (Hutchins, 2003; Kochhar-Bryant, Basset, & Webb, 2009; Roh & So, 2005). This technological foundation is not sufficient for faculty members to create accessible online courses (Telg et al., 2005) because the student, and all that the student brings, must be constantly considered as an integral part of the designing equation (McCombs & Vakili, 2005).

In considering how to design in a way that accounts for important factors such as accessibility, one can look to Sims' (2009) Proactive Design for Learning and Sprenger's (2008) discussion about student choice and universal design for learning (Center for Applied Special Technology, 2008), which each view instruction from the standpoint that students have individual learning needs that cannot be met with a one size fits all model. Thus, those charged with teaching as well as designing online instruction have an enormous task before them. Not only must they have a mastery of their subject matter, but they must also understand the legal and technical issues involved in designing accessible courses, which may involve developing knowledge about learning theories as well as instructional design theories and processes.

Online instructors are being asked to make the shift from the instructor-centered teaching model often used in the traditional face-to-face setting to a student centered-model, where they are now facilitators rather than disseminators of knowledge. In order to design effective, accessible online instruction, instructors must accomplish what is nearly impossible in online learning environments: to "discover students' learning preferences, integrate technology tools, apply appropriate instructional techniques, put them all into practice and generate the most suitable method [of learning] for individuals" (Yang & Cornelious, 2005, p. 6). One approach that has been proposed to accomplish the above-cited challenges is to implement the principles of universal design for learning (Center for Applied Special Technology, 2008).

One of many examples of steps that may be taken to implement a universal design model is outlined in the University of Iowa's "Universal Access Project":

- Step 1: Identify the course and describe the essential goals, objectives, and content.
- Step 2: Define the universe by describing who will potentially take the course, their demographics, educational plans, and instructional needs. Remember to keep *all* potential students in mind.
- Step 3: Involve students by finding ways to involve students in the course development For example, ask a group of students who have taken the course to critique these three areas: content, environment, presentation.
- Step 4: Adopt instructional strategies and identify particular pedagogical methods appropriate to subject and conventions of the field. Be sensitive to student needs and find creative ways to satisfy the requirements of the field by offering a rich array of potential means of engaging students, including varying presentation methods, refining one's delivery and classroom/lab presence, and potentially adjusting assessment style. CAST.org is an excellent resource to accomplish this.
- Step 5: Apply instructional strategies and try implementing the selected strategies. A match between the characteristics of the target audience from step 2 is vital to integrating the methods identified in step 4. The test of the efficacy of the course will be in this interaction. How will the strategies be evaluated?
- Step 6: Build in accommodations. Assume the need for evaluating usability and plan scaffolds for accessible physical spaces, access, time, durations, and methods of instruction in order to meet the course objectives vis-à-vis every student's needs and characteristics.

- Step 7: Evaluate by building in evaluation of the course environment, presentation, and products at all levels and points. Ask students to describe what they learned, whether the way in which it was learned was useful and meaningful (relevant), and what work they had to do to move closer to the center of the field's community of practice.

(University of Iowa, 2010)

Moving forward, institutions of higher education must address this growing need for accessibility for ethical as well as legal reasons and can do so by implementing regular faculty training about the principles of UDL. In taking this step, educational institutions will be playing their role as called upon by Jan Svato ,Vice-Rector for Student Welfare and Lifelong Learning of Masaryk University, Czechoslovakia, when he issued the following challenge at the 2011 Universal Design for Learning conference: "Making university education accessible is the responsibility of the whole academic world!" (Cooper, 2011, para. 3).

References

Allen, I.E., & Seaman, J. (2009). *Staying on course: On-line education in the United States, 2009*. Needham, MA: The Sloan Consortium.

Burgstahler, S. (2007). Accessibility training for distance learning personnel. In *Postsecondary education and disabled students*. Retrieved August 3, 2009, from http://www.athenpro.org/node/56

Capella University. (2010). *Overview*. Retrieved February 14, 2010, from http://www.capella.edu/online-degrees/masters-instructional-design-online-learning/

Center for Applied Special Technology. (2008). Research and development. In *UDL guidelines*. Retrieved April 20, 2009 from http://www.CAST.org/research/index.html

Chodock, T., & Dolinger, E. (2009). Applying Universal Design to information literacy: Teaching students who learn differently at Landmark College. *Reference & User Services Quarterly, 49*(1), 24–32. Retrieved from Academic Search Premier database.

Cleveland-Innes, M., Garrison, D. R., & Kinsel, E. (2007). Role adjustment for learners in an on-line community of inquiry: Identifying the challenges of incoming on-line learners. *International Journal of Web-Based Learning and Teaching Technologies, 2*(1), 1–16.

Cooper, M. (2011, February 9). *Near live blog from Universal Learning Design 2011 Conference*. Retrieved May 8, 2011, from http://martyncooper.wordpress.com/2011/02/09/near-live-blog-from-the-universal-learning-design-2011-conference/

Crow, K. (2008). The legal environment of accessible postsecondary on-line learning. *Quarterly Review of Distance Education, 9*(2), 169–179. Retrieved from Academic Search Premier database.

Fichten, C., Ferraro, V., Asuncion, J., Chwojka, C., Barile, M., Nguyen, M., et al. (2009). Disabilities and e-learning problems and solutions: An exploratory study. *Journal of Educational Technology & Society, 12*(4), 241–256. Retrieved from Academic Search Premier database.

Frieden, L. (2003). *People with disabilities and postsecondary education*. [Position Paper]. Retrieved December 3, 2009, from http://www.ncd.gov/newsroom/publications/2003/education.htm

George Mason University. (2010). *College of education and human development*. Retrieved February 14, 2010, from http://learntech.gmu.edu/learning-technologies-schools/

Grabinger, R., Aplin, C., & Ponnappa-Brenner, G. (2008, January). Supporting students with cognitive impairments in on-line environments. *TechTrends: Linking Research & Practice to Improve Learning, 52*(1), 63–69. Retrieved September 22, 2009. doi:10.1007/s11528–008–0114–4

Hinson, J. M., & LaPrairie, K. N. (2005). Learning to teach online: Promoting success through professional development. *Community College Journal of Research and Practice, 29*, 483-493.

Hutchins, H.M. (2003). Instructional immediacy and the seven principles: Strategies for facilitating on-line courses. *On-line Journal of Distance Learning Administration, 6*(3), 1–13.

Iwarsson, S., & Stahl, A. (2003, January 21). Accessibility, usability and universal design—Positioning and definition of concepts describing person-environment relationships. *Disability & Rehabilitation, 25*(2), 57–66. Retrieved August 31, 2009, from Academic Search Premier database.

Izzo, M., Murray, A., & Novak, J. (2008). The faculty perspective on Universal Design for Learning. *Journal of Postsecondary Education and Disability Journal, 21*(2), 60–72. Retrieved August 31, 2009, from Academic Search Premier database.

Kochhar-Bryant, C., Bassett, D., & Webb, K. (2009). *Transition to postsecondary education for disabled students.* CA: Corwin Press.

Lin, H. (2007). The ethics of instructional technology: Issues and coping strategies experienced by professional technologists in design and training situations in higher education. *Educational Technology Research & Development, 55*(5), 411–437. doi:10.1007/s11423–006–9029-y

McCombs, B., & Vakili, D. (2005). A learner-centered framework for e-learning. *Teachers College Record, 107*(8), 1582–1600.

Meyer, A., & Rose, D. (1998). *Learning to read in the computer age.* Cambridge, MA: Brooline Books.

Moore, M., & Kearsley, G. (2005). *Distance education: A systems view* (2nd ed.). Belmont: Wadsworth.

National Center for Education Statistics. (2000). *Postsecondary students with disabilities* (NCES 2000–092). Retrieved April 24, 2009, from Stats in brief: http://nces.ed.gov/pubs2000/2000092.pdf

Newman, L., Wagner, M., Cameto, R., & Knokey, A.M. (2009). *The post-high school outcomes of youth with disabilities up to 4 years after high school.* A report from the National Longitudinal Transition Study-2 (NLTS2) (NCSER 2009–3017). Menlo Park, CA: SRI International.

Poore-Pariseau, C. (2010). Online learning: Designing for all users. *Journal of Usability Studies, 5*(4), 147–156.

Poore-Pariseau, C. (2011). *Principles of Universal Design for Learning: What is the value of UDL training on accessible pedagogy?* Retrieved May 20, 2013, from ProQuest database.

Roh, S. Z., & So, H.J. (2005). Designing accessible Web-based instruction for all students. *19th Annual Conference on Distance Teaching and Learning*, 1–6. Retrieved May 20, 2013, from http://www.uwex.edu/disted/conference/Resource_library/proceedings/03_78.pdf

Rose, D., & Meyer, M. (2002). *Teaching every child in the digital age.* Alexandria, VA: Association for Supervision & Curriculum Development.

Sapp, W. (2009). Universal Design: On-line educational media for disabled students. *Journal of Visual Impairment & Blindness, 103*(8), 495–500. Retrieved from Academic Search Premier database.

Schwartz, L. (2004). Using Internet audio to enhance on-line accessibility. *International Review of Research in Open and Distance Learning, 5*(2), 1–7.

Seale, J. (2006). *E-learning and disability in higher education.* New York: Routledge.

Sims, R. (2006). Beyond instructional design: Making learning design a reality. *Journal of Learning Design, 1*(2), 1–8. [Keynote Paper]. Retrieved May 20, 2013, from http://www.jld.qut.edu.au/publications/vol1no2/documents/beyond%20instructional%20design.pdf

Sims, R. (2009). From three-phase design to learning design: Creating effective teaching and learning environments. In J.W. Willis (Ed.), *Constructivist instructional design (C-ID): Foundations, models, and examples* (pp. 379–392). North Carolina: Information Age.

Sims, R., & Stork, E. (2007). Design for contextual learning: Web-based environments that engage diverse students. *AusWeb: The Thirteenth Australasian World Wide Web Conference.* Retrieved August 2, 2009, from http://ausweb.scu.edu.au/aw07/papers/refereed/sims/paper.html

Snyder, T., Dillow, S., & Hoffman, C. (2010). *Digest of education statistics 2008.* Washington, DC: U.S. Department of Education, National Center for Education Statistics. Retrieved April 20, 2010, from http://nces.ed.gov/pubs2010/

Sprenger, M. (2008). *Differentiation through learning styles and memory.* Thousand Oaks, CA: Corwin.

Stone, D., Jarrett, C., Woodroffe, M., & Minocha, S. (2005). *User interface design and evaluation.* San Francisco: Morgan Kaufmann.

Syracuse University. (2010). *Instructional design, development, and evaluation.* Retrieved February 14, 2010, from http://soeweb.syr.edu/academic/Instructional_Design_Development_and_Evaluation/default.aspx

Telg, R., Lundy, L., Irani, T., Bielema, C., Dooley, K., Anderson, E., et al. (2005, Winter). Distance education training for distance education trainers. *Quarterly Review of Distance Education, 6*(4), 331–342. Retrieved September 12, 2009, from Academic Search Premier database.

University of Iowa. (2010). *How UDL will improve your courses.* Retrieved May 20, 2013, from http://research.education.uiowa.edu/universalaccess/udl/how-to-implement-udl

U.S. Department of Justice. (2010). Images. In *Flared ramp.* Retrieved February 28, 2010, from www.ada.gov/images/flaredramp1.jpg

World Wide Web Consortium (W3C). (2005). Introduction to web accessibility. In *What is web accessibility?* Retrieved February 24, 2010, from http://www.w3.org/WAI/intro/accessibility

Wu, D., & Hiltz, S.R. (2004). Predicting learning from asynchronous on-line discussions. *Journal of Asynchronous Learning Networks, 8*(2), 139–152.

Yang, Y., & Cornelious, L. (2005, Spring). Preparing instructors for quality on-line instruction. *On-line Journal of Distance Learning Administration, 8*(1), 1–17.

19
An Overview of Accessible E-learning

Aina G. Irbe and Jonathan Avila

An Overview of Accessible E-learning

E-learning offers many benefits and challenges for people with disabilities; access is provided without many of the physical, social, and transportation barriers of the traditional learning environment. However, the electronic presentation, collaboration, and content may present barriers when they are not accessible. According to Jaeger (2008):

> Accessibility is the equal access to information and communication technologies (ICTs) for individuals with disabilities. . . Accessibility allows individuals with disabilities, regardless of the types of disabilities they have, to use ICTs, such as Web sites, in a manner that is equal to the use enjoyed by others.
>
> (p. 24)

There are many different types of disabilities, of which the core categories include people who are blind, vision impaired, deaf, hard of hearing, and people who have motor disabilities, speech/communication, neurological, and cognitive or learning disabilities (Web Accessibility Initiative (W3C), 2005). Due to incongruous means of measurement and data collection, global statistics on disability may be incomplete. Rates of disability by country range from 1% to 20% of the population (Mont, 2007). In the United States (U.S.) alone, according to the 2010 U.S. Census, 18.7% of the total U.S. population (56.7 million people in the civilian noninstitutionalized population) have a disability (Brault, 2012).

As use of technology and the Internet grows exponentially each year, people with disabilities turn to Assistive Technology (AT) to assist and allow them to use the plethora of available information and communication tools and options. AT is an umbrella term used to describe a variety of devices used by persons with disabilities to help accomplish tasks that would be difficult or otherwise not possible. These devices can be anything from a mobility aid, to an augmentative and alternative communication device, to a computer program that uses text-to-speech to announce information on a computer screen. When used with computers, assistive technologies are sometimes referred to as *adaptive technology* that may be software or hardware.

Examples include screen readers, screen magnification software, speech recognition software, onscreen keyboards, and captions. In the context of e-learning, AT refers to computer programs, hardware, or tools used in the access of ICT.

Global Perspectives

Internationally, a common method of defining disability is a social model that does not focus on the functional limitations of people, but focuses on the social interactions of a person with their environment, culture, and policy (Hughes & Paterson, 1997; Shakespeare & Watson, 1997). This is the model used by the International Classification of Functioning, Disability and Health (ICF) developed by the World Health Organization (WHO) (WHO, 2013). Furthermore, the United Nations Convention on the Rights of Persons with Disabilities (UNCRPD) and its optional protocol, a comprehensive human rights treaty that focuses on the rights of people with disabilities, were adopted in 2006. Since then many nations have signed and ratified the treaty. Specifically, article 24 of the treaty addresses the need for governments to ensure equal access to the education system at all levels (United Nations Enable, 2013).

To actualize the models and treaties, international and country-specific standards, guidelines, and laws have emerged. The Web Content Accessibility Guidelines (WCAG) version 2.0 were developed by the Web Accessibility Initiative (WAI) of the World Wide Web Consortium (W3C) as the basis for international guidelines used to harmonize accessibility requirements for technology-neutral web content (Web Accessibility Initiative, 2012a). The WCAG guidelines are not an international law, but rather the basis for national and regional disability laws. WCAG consists of four main principles: perceivable, operable, understandable, and robust, under which success criteria are established. Success criteria are indicated at three different levels, Level A, Level AA, and Level AAA; level A is the minimum level of conformance (Web Accessibility Initiative, 2012b). Sufficient techniques to meet each success criteria are identified for a number of web technologies in nonnormative documents. The guidelines address accessibility for a wide range of disabilities in a testable and repeatable manner. Furthermore, conformance to the guidelines must be determined based on five factors, including support for assistive technology.

There are three primary types of disability civil rights laws and policies related to accessible use of ICT. These include laws or policies dealing with the accessibility of government websites, laws that apply to government procurement of accessible ICT, and disability discrimination laws. In the United States, a set of standards mandated under Section 508 of the Rehabilitation Act requires accessibility of government websites. Additionally, Section 508 of the Rehabilitation Act in the United States applies to the government's use, procurement, and maintenance of ICT. Although individual states within the United States are not bound by the Section 508 law, many have adopted legislation similar to Section 508 requiring the procurement of accessible ICT at the state level. Similarly, in Canada, the province of Ontario requires that government sites adhere to WCAG 2 levels A and AA under the Accessibility for Ontarians with Disabilities Act (AODA).

In the European Union (EU), a draft set of procurement requirements has been created under mandate 376. Disability discrimination laws such as the Americans with Disabilities Act (ADA) in the United States, the AODA in the province of Ontario, Canada, and the Equality Act in the United Kingdom also address access information and communication in public accommodation and education. Disability discrimination laws in many countries address discrimination in employment, transportation, and other areas, such as public sector services. In the US, the Department of Justice issued an advanced notice of proposed rulemaking indicating its intent to apply WCAG levels A and AA to websites of public accommodation under Titles II and III of the ADA (U.S. Department of Justice, 2010).

The UNCRPD and many national disability-related and equality laws cover equal access to education. Accessibility standards and guidelines exist to assist in meeting these laws. Spinello (2006) wrote that part of core human good within ethical principles is autonomy, which "includes those goods that we need to complete our projects (ability, security, knowledge, freedom, opportunity, reason)" (p. 4). Such goods also include education and training as part of knowledge, including the development of equally accessible e-learning programs, which imply that "the holder of this right be provided with whatever one needs to pursue this right" (Spinello, p. 12). To this end, the principles of Universal Design for Learning (UDL) arose out of Universal Design (UD), a concept conceived to make "everything we design and produce usable by everyone to the greatest extent possible, without the need for adaptation or specialized design" (McGuire, Scott, & Shaw, 2006, p. 167). Universal Design is intended to address all aspects of life, from architecture, to means of transportation and the use of everyday items, in order to afford access to as many people as possible.

The Center for Applied Special Technology (CAST) created the concept of Universal Design for Learning (UDL) to focus specifically on educational environments (CAST, n.d.; McGuire, Scott, & Shaw, 2006). CAST described UDL as "an approach to planning and developing curricula in ways that promote access, participation, and progress in the general curriculum for all learners" (McGuire et al., p. 169). Rose and Meyer (2002) raised the issue of applying the principles of UDL to both the instructional design and the technology of learning, accentuating the importance of providing not only physical access to learning, but also access to learning itself for all learners. Larger and broader audiences can be reached by incorporating the principles of Universal Design for Learning (UDL) (Burgstaher, 2001), by holistically combining technical and educational design approaches.

Accessibility and E-learning

E-learning Background

The Internet has brought great promise for education through a myriad of delivery choices and multimedia features. More people than ever are now able to learn online through e-learning programs; the audience for any e-learning program subsequently becomes more diverse.

As opposed to the traditional classroom, the online learning environment provides a multitude of options for delivery of learning. E-learning may be synchronous, asynchronous, instructor-led, self-paced and instructor-less, or a combination of online and classroom environments, better known as blended or hybrid learning. In the e-learning environment, learners can access learning anywhere and anytime (Kumar, 2006, p. 1274). The online classroom reaches geographically and globally across cultures, languages, age, physical or cognitive disabilities, and those who might not have had access to learning in the traditional setting.

Both in the academic setting and in the workplace, new information and knowledge quickly multiply, fostering organizations to seek more return on investment (ROI) from training programs to remain competitive in the marketplace (Ionescu, 2012, Jokić, Pardanjac, Eleven, & Djurin, 2012; Penicina, 2011). To achieve this goal, more organizations are increasingly turning to e-learning solutions (American Society for Training and Development (ASTD), 2011; Lim, 2012). Thus, training programs today must also consider the online and corporate environments and be designed for audiences that "constantly learn new skills and adapt to new work conditions in shorter times" (Cheong, Wettasinghe, & Murphy, p. 201), and who are increasingly diverse.

E-learning Potential

Education delivered through e-learning provides many benefits. For people with disabilities, accessing education through the Internet increases opportunities in education. E-learning eliminates geographical and physical barriers to those who might not be able to access a physical classroom. E-learning is available to diverse communities and people around the world but also provides a community for people with disabilities who may be isolated or socially shunned due to social or political attitudes toward people with disabilities. The e-learning environment may also provide anonymity—an online learner may have the choice to disclose whether he or she has a disability, especially if the e-learning course is accessible.

In addition to people with disabilities, people with different learning styles and people from different cultures and age groups are served by accessible e-learning. For example, auditory learning approaches are not appropriate for users who are deaf or hard of hearing. Visual learning styles are not effective approaches for the blind but auditory or tactile (hands-on) are, depending on the specific needs of the learner. Other users such as those with low vision may have a visual learner preference—content that is accessible in combination with assistive technology, such as screen magnification software, can provide this visual learning experience to users with low vision. Learners with cognitive and learning disabilities may find auditory or visual styles better than the other delivery means—or use one to support the other. A learner with a print disability, such as dyslexia, may find an uncluttered presentation of text with a custom-chosen font face with synchronized text-to-speech software the best option for reading. Similar potential and challenges exist for older learners.

Curran and Robinson (2007) explored the growing need for web accessibility for this older generation. They highlighted figures showing that more and more senior citizens are using the Internet "to improve their quality of life" (p. 337), including expanding their education. But as individuals age, disabilities, and thus barriers to Internet access, increase. Curran and Robinson further noted that by the year 2030, 20% of the U.S. population alone will be senior citizens, increasing the number of online consumers and learners with a variety of disabilities (p. 337). Moreover, developing website and e-learning to meet accessibility standards opens more possibilities to various learner types. For example, a visual learner will be able to view or print a synchronized transcript and gain more information by reading the transcript than by just listening to a lecture (Sims & Stork, 2007).

In the list of benefits for using accessibility features, the W3C explains that while accessibility focuses on people with disabilities, it also "overlaps with other best practices such as mobile web design, device independence, multi-modal interaction, usability, design for older users, and search engine optimization (SEO)" (Web Accessibility Initiative (WAI), 2012a, para. 7).

Accessibility Challenges

To best take advantage of the benefits of e-learning, designers and developers of e-learning must recognize there are still both technical and pedagogical challenges to a truly accessible e-learning experience. Rose and Meyer (2002) described that "barriers to learning are not . . . inherent in the capacities of the learner, but arise in learners' interactions with inflexible educational materials" (p. iv). The importance of UDL lies in the fact that UDL draws on "the versatility of digital media and its capacity to be transformed and networked . . . In this manner it empowers us to teach every student, not just some" (p. 84).

The technical and functional aspects of e-learning can be a barrier to people with disabilities in the access, use, and manipulation of the ICT. Access to mainstream ICT, including electronic books and rich internet content, by people with disabilities has increased but still lags behind the equal access to and acquisition of knowledge afforded by many e-learning environments. Often this is due not to the lack of a technological solution but rather to a failure in the policy, design, or development process. Accessible e-learning does not require building assistive technology into e-learning content, but rather e-learning environments should be designed to allow for the greatest use and interoperability with users' needs and assistive technology without building-in all possible requirements for all disabilities. Despite great improvements in assistive technology, mainstream and e-learning technology is always advancing, and assistive technology and the methods it uses to communicate with ICT must constantly be updated.

In order for most assistive technologies to be effective tools, e-learning must produce accessible content. The use and application of accessibility features in a variety of rapid e-learning development tools is not standardized. Thus, any given e-learning development team might not have all the details or a set process necessary to fully meet the needs of its users with disabilities.

For example, the many formats of e-learning also make it complicated for a school, learning institute, or organization to detail and follow implementation of accessibility goals for each online environment. Accessibility guidelines and checklists do not provide definite technical solutions; many gray areas exist regarding how to include what is acceptable as accessible. Curran and Robinson (2007) quoted the Irish National Disability Authority, which said, "It is not enough to just have guidelines and policy. To create accessible services within time and . . . budgets, developers need to follow an effective and efficient development process" (p. 334). However, as Stewart and Waight (2008) found, instructional design team size, talent, audience characteristics, and even technology choices affect how an e-learning development team creates e-learning courses. If this is the case, then the combination of the various e-learning delivery environments and the myriad of e-learning development tools with the nuances of accessibility implementation would hinder any consistency in development or delivery of accessible e-learning. In addition to the technical side and the e-learning development tools, the design of the e-learning also has to be accessible; neither AT nor development tools completely compensate for inaccessible design of e-learning. Process and attention to accessibility in the instructional design process itself is key.

Reigeluth (1999, 2011) explained that the existing traditional paradigm of training and education was designed to sort workers, rather than encourage them to learn at higher levels and maximize learning. He further explained that because every learner has an individual learning style and different needs, current standardized training or learning approaches do not effectively meet the needs of any learner, and in turn, the learners that are employees will not receive the level of training for the required workplace skills. Furthermore, as each individual has a unique means to learn and process information, the traditional approach of one-size-fits-all can no longer be applied to education, specifically in the online environment (McGuire, Scott, & Shaw, 2006; Sims & Stork, 2007). Reigeluth believed the design of training needs to be reconsidered, stating, "This transformation will require advances in both instructional theory and instructional technology" (p. 1).

Following Reigeluth's (2011) conclusion that the current training paradigm is based on pre-industrial era tenets, the sequential and systematic instructional design used to develop training for in-class delivery may no longer be appropriate for the online environment. Using a "cookie-cutter" top-down instructional design approach will not incorporate all learners or adequately measure the success of an individual or the success of the training courses as a whole. Both Reigeluth (1999) and Lim (2012) explained that a teacher-centered model does not fit into the new world of technological advances, nor does it take into consideration the instructional possibilities of technology. Thus, the traditional instructional design approach for classroom-based, teacher-centered learning is not the solution in designing online learning (Lim), especially accessible online learning.

Designing Accessible E-learning

In order to allow the pursuit of education for individual autonomy through e-learning programs, it seems logical that the development of any e-learning program would incorporate accessibility principles suggested by the World Wide Web (W3C) (Stone, Jarrett, Woodroffe, & Minocha, 2005, p. 178). In order to meet the needs and address individual differences for online learners, instructional designers and developers cannot focus only on the learner, but must revisit the entire approach to the technical aspects as well as the instructional design for the e-learning environment.

Developing for accessibility, if planned from the onset of a project, adds little to minimal time for the instructional design or development process; however, trying to retrofit in accessibility features is both time consuming and costly. McDaniel and McGrew (1999) strongly believed it to be an ethical obligation for the web developer to design the website to be accessible, but do not believe the developers have enough information. Thus, if developers and instructional designers have the correct knowledge, it is easy and possible to provide distance learning courses and websites for the benefit of a greater audience. The biggest challenge to the world of e-learning development thus becomes dissemination of knowledge of and best practices for accessibility implementation.

Application of Accessible Instructional Design

As McDaniel and McGrew (1999) suggested, the instructional designer must be informed of accessibility standards, guidelines, laws, challenges, and options, both technical and educational. Rapid e-learning design tools may save budget in the creation of the content, however, if the chosen tool does not generate accessible content the project goal cannot be met. Some projects attempt to use tools that generate inaccessible content and then provide an alternative for people with disabilities. Providing an alternative version of e-learning content rarely provides an equivalent experience for learners with disabilities and often limits the types of learners that can use that content. For example, creating a text-only page alternative to an interactive course does not provide the interaction or feedback to users of the alternative. Similarly, low vision users who may rely on structural information in the interactive course such as visual headings, lists, and visual learning aids cannot benefit from these when only a text-only alternative is provided. A self-assessment based file without fillable assessment questions is likely not equivalent to an interactive online assessment. Alternative forms of content can be offered as learning options to users but should not be the sole method of providing access to learners with disabilities.

In following the Analyze, Design, Develop, Implement, and Evaluate (ADDIE) instructional design framework (Molenda, 2003), knowledge and planning are critical. In the analyze phase, the entire design plan should investigate and include:

- Applicable accessibility standards, guidelines, and laws
- Budget
- A well designed schedule that takes into account review and testing
- Delivery environment
- Required e-learning development tools or programming languages
- Accessibility testing approach and script
- Pedagogical approach
- Writing guidelines
- Interactivity options (UDL principles)
- Testing and assessment plan

During the design phase, the storyboards should provide the blueprint for the technical and educational approach in detail. Many accessibility principles must be considered in the design phase. For example, decisions such as the use and contrast of color must be addressed in this phase. Use of color can aid many learners including learners with cognitive disabilities, however, use of colors alone to convey meaning will prevent other users, such as those with color deficiencies or those who are blind, from acquiring the information conveyed by color alone. Storyboards should include:

- The content, including goals and objectives
- Content flow
- Accessibility approach, such as creating alternative text for graphics
- Specific programming details
- Clear directions to team members such as graphic designers and developers
- A review of the content for accessible information and pedagogy

After the design plan and storyboards have been used as the blueprint to develop a part or the entire course, testing for editorial and accessibility will commence. Accessibility testing should include:

- Automated and manual testing for the accessibility principles of perceivable, operable, understandable, and robustness. Sufficient techniques to meet each of the identified success criteria must be present. Additionally, other requirements such as the interoperability with assistive technology, access by users with disabilities, and accessibility of the system as a whole must also be evaluated.
- Use of Assistive Technology
- Live testers, with and without disabilities
- A review of the usability of the product
- A review of the cognitive presentation and flow of the content

The Implementation and Evaluation phases of the ADDIE framework (Molenda) should include any final updates and collection of feedback on how all users experienced the course.

Conclusion

Although e-learning offers both benefits and challenges for people with disabilities; a rise in international awareness of accessibility, technological advances, and a new vision for instructional design for e-learning are working together to eliminate many accessibility challenges. Accessibility **must be considered both from the technical and pedagogical perspective in any e-learning project from the onset. The e-learning environment provides a tremendous opportunity to extend learning opportunities to many people with and without disabilities across the globe.** If developers and designers have the correct knowledge about accessibility, it is practical and possible to provide e-learning courses for the benefit of a greater audience. The biggest challenge to the world of e-learning development thus becomes dissemination of knowledge about and best practices for accessibility implementation, not accessibility itself.

References

American Society for Training and Development (ASTD). (2011). *ASTD's annual review of workplace learning and development data.* State of the industry report, 2011. Alexandria, VA: ASTD.

Brault, P. (2012). Americans with disabilities: 2010. *Household Economic Studies.* U.S. Census Bureau. Retrieved from http://www.census.gov/prod/2012pubs/p70–131.pdf

Burgstahler, P. (2005). Universal design of instruction: Definition, principles, and examples. Smith College Web Site. Retrieved from http://www.smith.edu/deanoffaculty/Burgstahler.pdf

Center for Applied Special Technology (CAST). (n.d.). What is Universal Design for Learning? Retrieved from: http://www.cast.org/research/udl/index.html

Cheong, E., Wettasinghe, M., & Murphy, J. (2006). Professional development of instructional designers: A proposed framework based on a Singapore study. *International Journal on E-Learning, 5*(2), 197–219. Retrieved from http://search.proquest.com/docview/210368099?accountid=27965

Curran, K., & Robinson, D. (2007). An investigation into web content accessibility guideline conformance for an aging population. *International Journal on E-Learning, 6*(3), 333–349. Retrieved from http://www.editlib.org/p/21021

Hughes, B., & Paterson, K. (1997). The social model of disability and the disappearing body: Towards a sociology of impairment. *Disability & Society, 12*(3), 325–340.

Ionescu, A. (2012). E-learning, as a strategic tool for competences development process. *Metalurgia International, 17*(8), 118–121.

Jaeger, P. (2008). User-centered policy evaluations of Section 508 of the Rehabilitation Act: Evaluating e-government web sites for accessibility for persons with disabilities. *Journal of Disability Policy Studies, 19*(1), 24–33. Retrieved from Academic Search Premier database.

Jokić, S., Pardanjac, M., Eleven, E., & Djurin, S. (2012). Training and development of employees through e-learning. *Metalurgia International, 17*(4), 149–153.

Kumar, P. (2006). Using Universal Design principles for e-learning. In T. Reeves & S. Yamashita (Eds.), *Proceedings of world conference on e-learning in corporate, government, healthcare, and higher education 2006* (pp. 1274–1277). Retrieved from http://www.editlib.org/p/23885

Lim, D. H. (2012). A comprehensive approach of e-learning design for effective learning transfer. *International Journal on E-Learning, 11*(1), 55–71. Chesapeake, VA: AACE. Retrieved from http://www.editlib.org/p/33292

McDaniel, W., & McGrew, P. (1999). Ethical considerations in web-site design: Developing a graphical metric. In *Proceedings of WebNet World Conference on the WWW and Internet 1999* (pp. 729–733). Retrieved from http://www.editlib.org/p/7448

McGuire, J.M., Scott, S.S., & Shaw, S.F. (2006). Universal Design and its applications in educational environments. *Remedial & Special Education, 27*(3), 166–175. Retrieved from ProQuest Psychology Journals.

Molenda, M. (2003). In search of the elusive ADDIE model. *Performance Improvement, 42*(5), 34–37. doi:10.1002/pfi.4930420508

Mont, D. (2007). Measuring disability prevalence. *World Bank Disability and Development Team HDNSP social protection discussion paper,* 0706. Retrieved from http://siteresources.worldbank.org/DISABILITY/Resources/Data/MontPrevalence.pdf

Penicina, L. (2011). Towards E-Learning Capability Maturity Model. *Computer Science (1407–7493),* 4688–4691.

Reigeluth, C. (Ed.) (1999). *Instructional-design theories and models: A new paradigm of instructional design.* Mahwah, NJ: Erlbaum.

Reigeluth, C. (2011). An instructional theory for the post-industrial age. *Educational Technology, 51*(5), 25–29.

Rose, D., & Meyer, A. (2002). *Teaching every student: Universal design for learning.* Alexandria, VA: Association for Supervision and Curriculum Development.

Shakespeare, T., & Watson, N. (1997). Defending the social model. *Disability & Society, 12*(2), 293–300.

Sims, R., & Stork, E. (2007). *Design for contextual learning: Web-based environments that engage diverse learners.* Paper presented at the 13th Annual Australasian World Wide Web Conference AusWeb, Coffs Harbor, Australia. Retrieved July 13, 2009, from http://ausweb.scu.edu.au/aw07/papers/refereed/sims/paper.html

Spinello, R.A. (2006). *Cyberethics: Morality and law in cyberspace* (3rd ed.). Boston, MA: Jones & Bartlett.

Stewart, B., & Waight, C. (2008). E-learning teams and their adult learning efforts in corporate settings: A cross analysis of four case studies. *International Journal on E-Learning,* 7(2), 293–309. Retrieved from http://www.editlib.org/p/23506

Stone, D., Jarrett, C., Woodroffe, M., & Minocha, S. (2005). *User interface design and evaluation.* San Francisco: Morgan Kaufmann.

United Nations Enable. (2013). *Article 24: Education.* Retrieved from http://www.un.org/disabilities/default.asp?id=284

U.S. Department of Justice. (2010). *Fact sheet: Advanced notice of proposed rulemaking on accessibility of* web *information and services.* Retrieved from http://www.ada.gov/anprm2010/factsht_web_anrpm_2010.htm

Web Accessibility Initiative (WAI). (2005). *What is* web *accessibility.* Retrieved from http://www.w3.org/WAI/intro/accessibility.php

Web Accessibility Initiative (WAI). (2012a). *Financial factors in developing a Web accessibility business case for your organization.* Retrieved January 26, 2015 from http://www.w3.org/WAI/bcase/fin.html

Web Accessibility Initiative (WAI). (2012b). *Web content accessibility guidelines (WCAG) overview.* Retrieved from http://www.w3.org/WAI/intro/wcag.php

World Health Organization (WHO). (2013). *Classifications: International classification of functioning, disability and health (ICF).* Retrieved from http://www.who.int/classifications/icf/en/

20
E-learning Evaluation

John G. Hedberg and Thomas C. Reeves

E-learning Evaluation

Bonk (2009) proclaimed, "The World Is Open" as far as access to e-learning is concerned. However, for many commentators, researchers, and especially practitioners, e-learning continues to be long on promise and short on results, especially with respect to the quality of its design, implementation, and outcomes (Jung & Latchem, 2012). More than 10 years ago, Greenagel (2002) suggested, "E-learning has not kept pace with the development of increasingly rich IP-based delivery platforms because the e-learning experience is far too often puerile, boring, and of unknown or doubtful effectiveness" (para. 1). There is little evidence that e-learning experiences for students or learning outcomes have been sufficiently enhanced over the last decade despite major advances in e-learning infrastructure (Garrison, 2011).

Although institutions around the world will inevitably continue to spend enormous sums on e-learning initiatives, few people involved in these initiatives can honestly claim that e-learning has fulfilled their own expectations, much less that e-learning has reached the enormous potential predicted for it in commercial as well as scholarly publications. We contend that one of the most important reasons that e-learning has not reached its potential is that it has not been adequately evaluated during its design, development, and implementation. This chapter addresses the importance and methods of e-learning evaluation.

The Rationale for E-learning Evaluation

When it comes to e-learning design, there has long been a debate about whether it is best viewed as a form of science or craft. Those who believe that e-learning design should be more scientific base their design work on books such as *E-Learning and the Science of Instruction: Proven Guidelines for Consumers and Designers of Multimedia Learning* by Ruth C. Clark and Richard E. Mayer (2011) or *First Principles of Instruction* by M. David Merrill (2012). Those who view e-learning design as more akin to a craft are inspired by books such as *The Power of E-Learning: The Essential Guide for Teaching in the Digital Age* by Shirley Waterhouse (2005) or *Simulations and the Future of Learning: An Innovative (and Perhaps Revolutionary) Approach to E-Learning* by Clark Aldrich

(2004). While Clark and Mayer (2011) prescribe cognitive psychology and educational research as the foundations of e-learning design, Waterhouse (2005) cautions that most research findings have limited applicability and recommends that e-learning should be designed based upon the common-sense strategies that experienced teachers have developed over years of practice.

Regardless of whether you view e-learning design as a science, a craft, or some blend of the two orientations (see Herrington, Reeves, & Oliver, 2010 for a blended design model), evaluation has a critical role to play (Reeves & Hedberg, 2003). Further, we concur with Phillips, McNaught, and Kennedy (2012) who wrote, "e-learning evaluation should focus on holistically evaluating learning environments, rather than just evaluating the technologies which contribute to the environment" (p. 8). Although e-learning technologies are important, pedagogical design principles and instructional methods are much more important with respect to influencing learning directly (Clark, 2012).

One of the greatest challenges in e-learning appears to be how far designers and their collaborators (e.g., subject matter experts and instructors) can move their design efforts beyond slavish replication of classroom practices, and often the translation is less effective as a pedagogical strategy. Most of the commercial platforms used to drive e-learning label their major features with common classroom terminology such as lectures, discussions, and quizzes, all of which are about technologies fashioned to fit existing practice. Salmon (2011) described innovative approaches required to teach and learn effectively online as managing the interactions to achieve engagement and higher-order conceptual activities, but most e-learning experiences are marked by a paucity of active interactions and a reliance on rather simplistic behaviorist pedagogy.

The current enthusiasm for Massive Open Online Courses (MOOCs) highlights the continuing triumph of technology over pedagogy and instructional design (Chronicle of Higher Education, 2012). Coursera co-founder Daphne Koller proclaimed, "The progress of Coursera, and the MOOC adoption more broadly, has greatly exceeded my wildest expectations" (Cassidy, 2013, para. 18). However, an expert analysis by Bates (2012) of the MOOCs emerging from Coursera revealed overreliance on traditional *transmissionist* (teaching by telling) pedagogy. Bates (2012) also concluded that these courses are being designed by trial and error rather than through painstaking instructional design guided by rigorous formative evaluation. The widely reported collapse of a Coursera MOOC focused on Online Learning Design in early 2013 highlighted the lack of sound instructional design and evaluation being applied to some MOOCs before they are launched (Jaschik, 2013). For example, given that MOOCs are still developing, it seems they could go in, at least, two possible design directions: (1) course-centric transmission of content; or (2) learner-led design where interactions and collaboration changes the way the courses are designed. This might involve a design model where learners have much more control over e-learning course structures—in effect something like a crowd-sourced course, where learner input is one of the key elements in the evaluation while the product is still being developed.

Evaluation Within the Learning Design Process: A Multistage Approach

Evaluation is essentially about collecting evidence to support decisions that need to be made about the design, operation, and implementation of e-learning. Evaluation is critical if practitioners seek to ensure that the planned design supports the learning activities of the learners. The affordances of e-learning design include simple access to video, interactive resources, and readings, support for discussion forums, personal or shared construction of knowledge representations (e.g., blogs or wikis), and the completion of authentic tasks (Herrington et al., 2010).

In reviewing what was being offered as web-based learning on four university campuses in Australia, Preston et al. (2010) found that the complexity of learning activities was limited and there was little creative pedagogy in most courses. In fact they found that the introduction of new e-learning technology in these four universities failed to act as the catalyst for fundamental change. Among the findings reported by Preston et al. (2010) were:

- 43.2% of staff respondents had not changed their lecturing style;
- 36.7% had not changed what they do in their lectures; and
- 74.9% had not changed the structure of their course.

This limited approach to e-learning pedagogy is the reason critics can often claim justifiably that the nearly ubiquitous provision of digital technologies on campus has not sufficiently improved the learning experience for students or enhanced achievement (Bauerlein, 2008; Cuban, 2001).

Traditional instructional design has adopted models that organize the learning experience using a variety of systematic functions. One of the most often used instructional design approaches is the Analysis, Design, Development, Implementation and Evaluation (ADDIE) model (Branch, 2008). ADDIE in practice often results in a sequence of processes or activities (e.g., prototyping) in which each process happens without being sufficiently informed by the kinds of evidence yielded by sound evaluation (Reeves & Hedberg, 2003). The placement of evaluation at the end of the ADDIE acronym is unfortunate because all too often evaluation is not done at all or is carried out too late in an instructional design project to have any meaningful impact (Allen & Sites, 2012). Reeves and Hedberg (2003) proposed a responsive evaluation model that is a more dynamic interplay between design/development functions and informing evidence from evaluation functions (Figure 20.1).

We suggest that as the tools and technologies have rapidly shifted over the past decade, the Reeves and Hedberg (2003) conceptualization can be extended, and that is one of the goals of

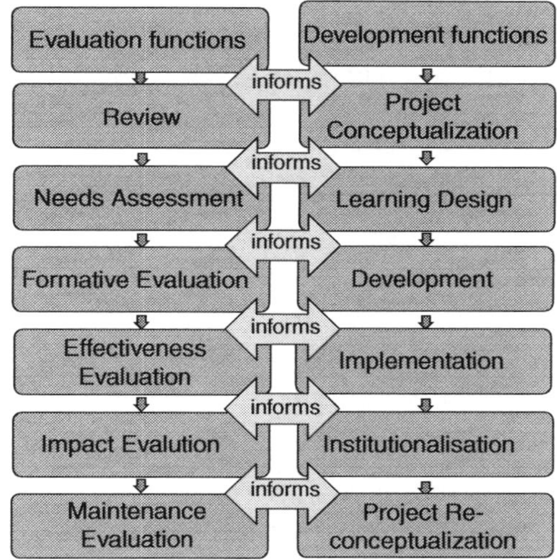

Figure 20.1 Evaluation Informing Design and Development

this chapter. The pace of technology adoption in learning contexts has accelerated as schools rush to bring mobile smart devices into classrooms and universities jump on the online learning bandwagon. Increasingly, even individual students and teachers frequently grab the latest technological tools and press them into serving their own needs and desires without much concern for the interplay between design and evidence. Many new tools can be instantly employed in personal creation of shared artifacts or demonstrations of learning strategies. For example, in a recent study on the implementation of tablets in schools, the teachers were amazed at the ability of grade 1 students to describe how they created their solutions and solved mathematical problems (Howe & McCredie, 2012). While student-centered solutions to standard mathematical problems hold some value, such innovation would be much more effective if adoption decisions were informed by evaluation results and if teachers became more effective evaluators of their own teaching and learning designs. If evaluation activities are to be utilized by teachers and designers and to provide useful guidance, evaluation processes applied to e-learning must be streamlined as described below.

E-learning Evaluation Stages

We propose four stages in the design and implementation of e-learning when evaluation should be undertaken. These are:

1. Review and Needs Assessment
2. Formative Evaluation
3. Effectiveness Evaluation, Impact Evaluation, and Return on Investment
4. Maintenance Evaluation

Stage 1 Evaluation Prior to Design—Review and Needs Assessment

To be effective, instructional design should begin with thoughtful consideration of the alignment among the essential components of any learning environment, regardless of whether digital enhancement is involved (Reeves, 2006). Alignment within any learning environment concerns the degree to which various components of the environment are synchronized with one another. According to Reeves (2006), the eight components or factors within any learning environment that should be carefully aligned are:

1. objectives
2. content
3. model of instruction (or learning design)
4. nature of learner activities
5. allocation of time
6. roles of teacher(s)
7. roles of technology tools
8. assessment

There isn't space for detailed explication of these components (see Reeves & Reeves, 2012 for more information). But we wish to stress the role of needs assessment and review as critical evaluation processes that can inform the processes of making decisions about how these components will be instantiated and aligned within an e-learning environment. Consider number 7,

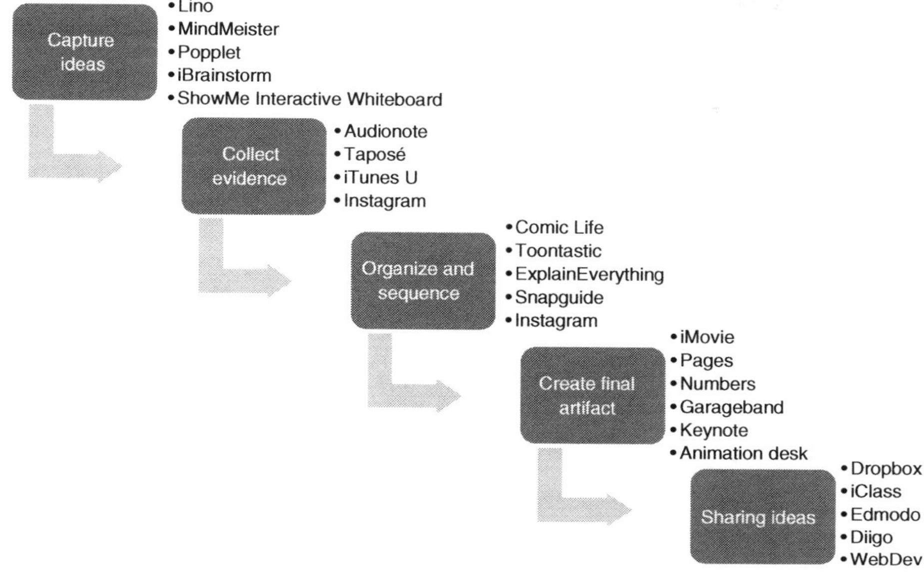

Figure 20.2 Learning Processes that iOS Apps Support (this is a very easily extended list)

the roles of technology tools. Review is the evaluative process of carefully examining whatever tools already exist to reveal best technology integration practices and preclude reinventing the wheel. Choosing the right tools involves finding the tools that best support the intended learning interactions. Given that individual apps come and go, and improved or newly released versions are often provided at no or limited cost, focusing on the potential learning benefits of the tools is critical. Figure 20.2 illustrates an evaluative process that can be used to review and choose apps that support the learning processes or tasks that might be incorporated into the e-learning environment.

Tools such as note-taking apps can support effective learning, but adopters must be aware of the limitations each tool will impose on the pedagogy. Rigorous review and needs assessment enables designers and developers as well as practitioners to scrutinize the alignment between the pedagogical dimensions and the affordances of different technology tools such as apps. This focus on apps can help to ensure that learners will be able to present their ideas and constructions in a range of media forms and be less constrained by the few tools available in most large e-learning management systems.

Stage 2 Evaluation During Design and Implementation—Formative Evaluation

If resources are limited, formative evaluation is the function that has the biggest payoff in our experience. For example, once the implementation of an e-learning program, such as a MOOC, begins, formative evaluation will reveal how well students are:

- Enjoying the program (and if they spend time interacting with the resources and learning tasks).

- Understanding the learning activities, comprehending sequences (and how the Learning Management System organizes resources and represents them to the learner).
- Achieving the intended learning outcomes and verifying that each critical activity has been completed by each student.
- Providing interactions with other students to assist peer assessment and support of group tasks.
- Understanding the ideas and how they are being represented results in no misconceptions by virtue of the choice of representation.
- Exploring how collaborative activities work with or without tutor support.

Formative evaluation has a long history (Flagg, 1990; Scriven, 1967). Many formative evaluation strategies and tools specifically designed for e-learning can be found in books such as those by Phillips et al. (2012), Khan (2005), and Reeves and Hedberg (2003).

Stage 3 Evaluation After Implementation Commences—Effectiveness Evaluation, Impact Evaluation, and Return-On-Investment (ROI)

Demonstrating the effectiveness, impact, and value of an e-learning design is a complex process that focuses on providing evidence to estimate the costs, usage, and relevance of e-learning strategies. For instance:

- We might also include the growing area of learning analytics to provide a "picture" of the learning strategy of the students and where they are finding difficulties or other issues with the learning tasks. This also includes the links between different information sources that until now were not used to monitor students' use of resources and efficiencies in their learning strategies.
- Explore the challenge in different costing models between adding an e-learning component to a face-to-face course versus creating an online course from scratch. There are many forms of blending of components and the strategy chosen might use quick, expedient ways of recording content presentation or managing learner interactions with other learners or tutors.
- Explore the cost model of how the elements are going to be deployed across the local class groups and whole institution, and ensure that students who have time pressure to study and work, can access what they need and when it is conveniently available.
- Explore the open resource model of access to information and how it is used and structured. Increasingly, much academic publication is being required to be available on open access when the funding was provided by public research granting bodies.

It is beyond the scope of this chapter to provide a complete overview of methods for effectiveness, impact, and return-on-investment evaluations. Additional information can be found in books by Phillips et al. (2012), Khan (2005), Patton (2008), and Reeves and Hedberg (2003).

Stage 4 Evaluation During Continuous Use—Maintenance Evaluation

Although earlier stages of evaluation may provide evidence of an e-learning program's effectiveness, impact, and value, it is not sufficient to warrant the continued use of the program without further evaluation. Although periodic accreditation of instructional programs and educational institutions is related to maintenance evaluation, traditional accreditation has limitations (Jung & Latchem, 2012). Maintenance evaluation involves addressing questions such as:

- Is the curriculum still relevant?
- Are enrollments being maintained or has the world moved on to new e-learning environments?
- Are the tools still the most appropriate for the learning tasks?
- What is happening in terms of future trends?

Aligning Evaluation Decisions, Questions, and Methods

It is essential to align decisions, questions, and methods within the context of e-learning evaluation (Reeves & Hedberg, 2003). The degree of alignment among these three major parts of an evaluation plan (i.e., decisions, questions, and methods) is critical because if the most appropriate methods are not selected to provide the information needed to answer the evaluation questions, and the questions are not designed to inform decision making, the whole evaluation enterprise can be fruitless. After all, evaluation is not an end in itself, but a means to providing the evidence that e-learning designers, managers, and practitioners need to make sound decisions on a continuing basis.

Case Studies of Successful E-learning Evaluations

Three case studies of successful e-learning evaluations are offered in this chapter. The first involves a formative evaluation within the context of a MOOC. The second involves another formative evaluation, this one focused on an e-learning program developed for professional certification purposes. The third also exemplifies formative evaluation, in this instance of a learning design that involved students collecting data in the field and sharing it as part of an environmental education course. The authors of this chapter played direct or supervisory roles in these three evaluations.

Case 1: Formative Evaluation of a MOOC

In the summer of 2012, planning began for the provision of a MOOC focused on development of open educational resources (OERs) to be offered by a Western higher education institution with a long history of and excellent reputation for distance education. A cadre of leaders in the field of open education and online learning were recruited to lead various weeks of the nine-week MOOC, which was offered during the first quarter of 2013. By October 2012, several of the early weeks of the MOOC had been fleshed out to the point that they were ready to be reviewed for formal formative evaluation. Formative evaluation as first conceived by Scriven (1967) focuses on improving whatever is being evaluated in contrast with summative evaluation, which is focused on determining the effectiveness, impact, and value of the program, product, or project being evaluated.

Whenever we evaluate a course or a unit of instruction, we begin by constructing a matrix that describes the learning objectives (or expected outcomes), the activities in which learners will be engaged that will allow them to accomplish the stated objectives, the assessment strategies that will be used to indicate to both the instructor and the learners that the objectives have been accomplished, and the time allocated for these activities (see Figure 20.3). We try to

Week	Objectives	Activities	Assessment	Time
1	• Explore a variety of definitions of learning design • Define learning design, as a field of research and a practice. • Identify some of the challenges of using a learning design approach for developing OERs • Identify specific topics of interest for OER development • Initiate own learning design projectwith at least two other learners	• View course overview video • View Week 1 introduction video • Read "OER Design" whitepaper • Brainstorm OER topics with two or more learners using Skype, Google Hangout, etc. • Review and select tools for collaboration	• Learning design projects identified • Teams formed • Design wikis created • Week 1 learning blog posted	4–6 hours
2	•	•	•	

Figure 20.3 Course Alignment Matrix

construct the matrix based on the same information that learners will be given regarding the course to ensure that the syllabus and other materials communicate the nature of the course to the learners as clearly as possible. We carefully look for aspects of the e-learning design where a lack of alignment might be evident.

In analyzing the design of a course using the matrix illustrated in Figure 20.3, we try to answer these types of questions:

1. How clear are the objectives within any given period of time (e.g., a week)?
2. To what extent are the objectives within each week actually learning objectives or enabling objectives? (The former describes a learning outcome whereas the latter describes a learning activity.)
3. To what extent do the objectives from one week to another build on each other systematically in a manner that enables the accomplishment of the overall goals of the course (e.g., to become a skilled designer of OERs)?
4. How well do the various activities in each week provide adequate opportunities to accomplish the objectives for that week?
5. How well do the various activities from week to week relate to each other systematically so that learners perceive they are engaged in meaningful activities and making progress toward the ultimate accomplishment of the course goals?
6. To what extent do the assessment strategies for each week provide evidence that the learning objectives for that week were accomplished?
7. To what extent are the assessment strategies across the whole course building a portfolio of evidence that the ultimate course goals have been accomplished?
8. What accommodation, if any, is made for learners who fall behind or fail to demonstrate adequate progress in the course?

Formative Evaluation Log

Week1 – Learning DesignMOOC	Reeves	24 Oct12
Component Reviewed	(Reviewer)	(Date)

Section	Comments and Suggestions	Actions Taken
Intro	The week one video has excellent content, but the audio levels change from time to time. We tried it on three browsers and this was a problem each time, especially 35 seconds into the video.	
Design Outcomes and Learning Outcomes	This week has both Design Outcomes and Learning Outcomes. None of the other weeks have stated "Design Outcomes." It would be valuable to add "Design Outcomes" to the other weeks. Alternatively or in addition, you could include a list of "deliverables" for each week.	

Figure 20.4 Formative Evaluation Log Example

In addition to the Course Alignment Matrix, we usually use a Formative Evaluation Log instrument to record and communicate the results of this type of formative review of a course or unit. Figure 20.4 illustrates the types of information that can be captured and shared with a Formative Evaluation Log. Of course, an actual log would be much longer.

Carrying out this type of formative review enabled the MOOC design team to make improvements in the e-learning environment before the initial week began. Additional formative reviews were carried out throughout the implementation of the MOOC, resulting in additional improvements to the e-learning experience for participants.

Case 2: Formative Evaluation of an E-learning Simulation

In the first quarter of 2011, a formative evaluation was conducted of an e-learning simulation designed to help prepare breast cancer surgeons for their Maintenance of Certification (MOC) exams. Specifically, this evaluation was designed to address the following questions:

1. How do members of the target audience for the MOC program, specifically general surgeons with a range of experience with Breast Cancer Surgery, interact with the MOC program?
2. How do members of the target audience for the MOC program evaluate their experience with the MOC program?
3. What ideas do members of the target audience for the MOC program have for enhancing the MOC program?

Thirty breast cancer surgeons completed the MOC simulation related to breast cancer diagnosis and treatment decisions. All participants completed an online questionnaire seeking information about their reactions to the program and their ideas for enhancing it. In addition, six participants were interviewed by telephone. Data collection began in early January 2011 and

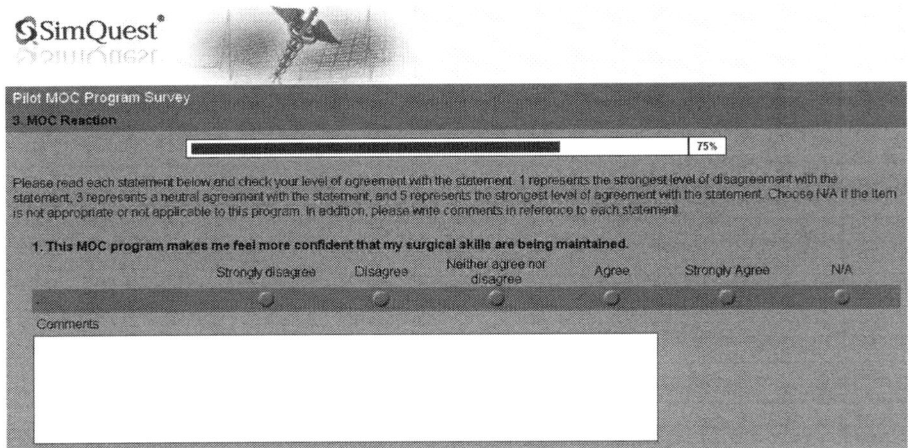

Figure 20.5 One Item from an Online Survey that Included 18 Items
Reprinted with permission from SimQuest.

ended in late February 2011. Surgeons were recruited via e-mail and phone calls through various medical schools, hospitals, and military medical centers using snowball sampling whereby early participants recommend other participants. Participants were paid an honorarium of $500 for their evaluation of the program. The survey was distributed using SurveyMonkey, a popular web-based survey software program. Figure 20.5 shows one item from the online survey.

Results of this formative evaluation were quite positive with 85% of the surgeons expressing positive attitudes toward the capacity of the MOC simulation program to enhance their breast cancer diagnosis and treatment decision-making skills and to prepare them for the MOC exams. The results of the telephone interviews with six of surgeons were also quite positive with the unanimous opinion that the program provided surgeons with important and valuable opportunities to keep up with the latest developments in an area as dynamic as breast cancer treatment.

The following recommendations were made based on the results of this formative evaluation:

1. Continue to develop the MOC program with more cases.
2. Enhance the feedback provided at the end of the case scenarios. This feedback should acknowledge other ways in which each case may have been effectively managed. Perhaps instead of presenting one ideal path, the program could offer:
   a. a description of how the case was actually handled;
   b. expert narrative commentary on the case management from both the surgeon who originally handled the case and two other expert surgeons; and
   c. an opportunity for surgeons to enter their own comments and questions concerning the case.
3. Support the case management decisions with the best available research literature and other data, ideally from clinical trials. At a minimum this should include references to specific studies along with an abstract.
4. Consider modifying the MOC program interface so that more complex interactive responses can be made, involving factors such as multiple tests, consultation with other specialists such as radiologists and plastic surgeons, and the like. However, any modifications

to the current interface should be accompanied by ongoing usability evaluation to make sure that the current strengths of the interface are not lost during the modification of the program.

5. The program developers should scrutinize the detailed recommendations from the online survey and interviews to correct errors in the program, such as misspellings of certain medical terms.

Significant modifications were made in the design of the MOC simulation program based on the results of this formative evaluation. Figures 20.6 and 20.7 show before- and after-screen design improvements that were made based on the results of this formative evaluation.

Case 3: Formative Evaluation of Mobile Learning Field Data Collection

In a large Australian city, 90 students from middle year classes across a comprehensive high school and its local primary schools were combined in mixed groups to work collaboratively to assess the health of their local environment. The rationale for the wider project (of which field work formed a component) was to create links between schools to focus on the design and implementation of an integrated, inquiry-based unit of work focusing on sustainability. The schools involved in the project were located in northern beachside suburbs, with two classes of 60 students from the final year in the primary school combining in smaller groups with a class of 30 first-year high school mentors.

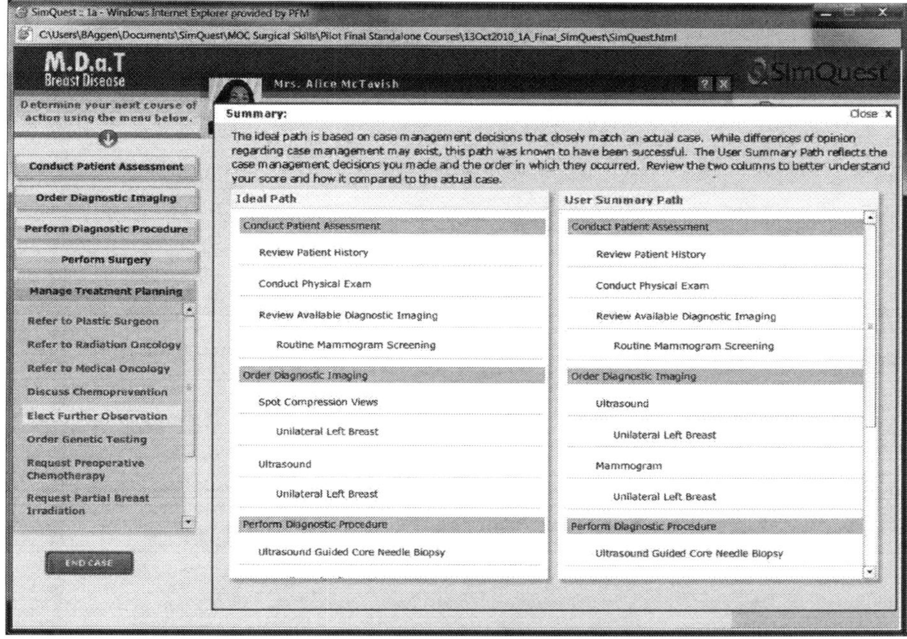

Figure 20.6 Case Management Feedback Screen before Formative Evaluation
Reprinted with permission from SimQuest.

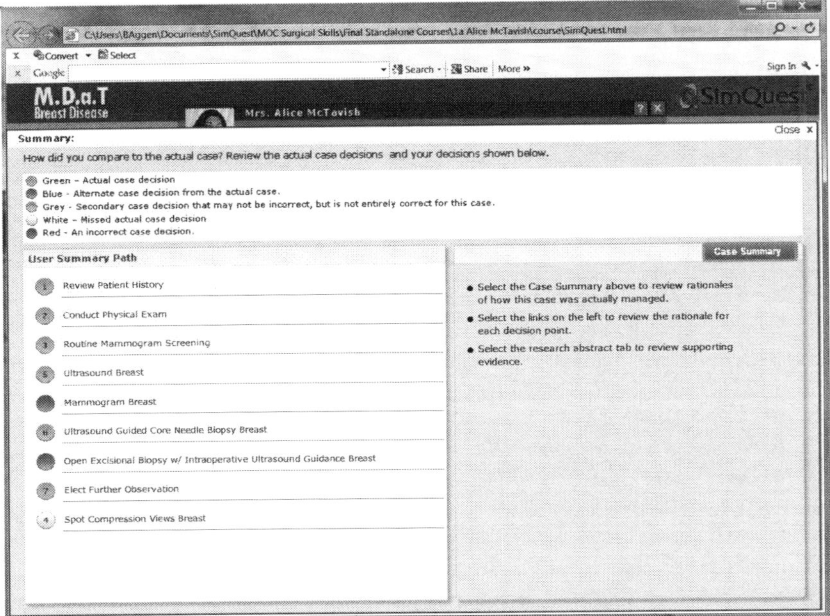

Figure 20.7 Case Management Feedback Screen after Formative Evaluation
Reprinted with permission from SimQuest.

The project was supported by ICT expertise and mobile tablet devices. Closely linked to the project schools was the local environmental education center, which provided expertise and access to information about local ecosystems. These ICT specialists and community environmental educators worked with student groups in the field to use project technologies to capture and record information about the biodiversity of the local area.

The devices used in the project included tablet computers with word-processing, imaging, and drawing software. A wiki was used as a tool to support a range of collaborative activities including support of a discussion forum between teachers, between teachers and students, and between the students themselves. The wiki also served as a site for each group of students to record, store and access their fieldwork data from a number of sites including their school, their homes, and the field.

The fieldwork activities were located in the skill-building phase of the inquiry-based course. In this early stage of the teaching sequence, students were engaged in building their knowledge and skills in a range of areas, including: understanding local environmental and sustainability content, expertise in use of the project technologies, teamwork and collaboration, mentoring, thinking and organizational skills. These understandings and skills could be assessed by the project before students moved on to demonstrating their understandings by creating a group presentation around their interpretation of human impact on the local environment.

Before the commencement of the project, teachers attended the ICT center for professional development in the use of the project devices and the project wiki. After the commencement of the project, staff from the ICT center visited the high school to train the secondary students in the use of the handheld computer and its accompanying data loggers as well as the digital camera. These students then trained the primary student members of their team in the use of this technology during the two fieldwork events associated with the project.

The evaluation questions associated with this project were:

1. To what extent can the students mentor the younger students and work with them to collect data from the field?
2. To what extent can the data be captured, stored and retrieved easily?
3. To what extent can the students compile their evidence for groups to use in responding to the challenges of sustainability and present a reasoned explanation?

Data collected in the field were transferred from the mobile tablets into a project web site. Typically students were involved in a set of monitoring activities, each one resulting in a digital product. These products were then transferred from the device onto the host computer system and then into a wiki. Figure 20.8 is an example of a resulting group wiki entry. This wiki entry is a permanent, high-quality record of the day's activities. This project involved the collection of data by the requirements of the learning task, so by the end of the day if a team did not collect data and use the tablet device correctly, no data would be recorded on the main system.

This project used the data collected and stored with the apps in the tablet device. Carefully selecting apps made it possible to record spatial data so that each photograph and data point had a positional reference. This meant that if students were not careful with their field notes, that was a second source of information. As a result, no data were lost after the training session. The devices were considered simple enough for each of the high school mentors to effectively support their teams to collect their field data and notes. When the study began, smartphones were used; but initial evaluations demonstrated that it was difficult for multiple users to view the screen, and hence team decision making was hampered. By using tablets, this was avoided although working in sunlight could still make it difficult to read the screen data.

The following findings were reported based of the results of this formative evaluation:

1. The use of the same equipment for collection, note taking and sharing was seen as a strength of the choice of technology and software.
2. Given that students were novice data collectors and were not used to working with real data, the strength of the choice of tools and software was important to help the students understand the source of the data, its location, its storage, and its aggregation into an argued presentation.
3. The students understood the links between location and the data that described it. The use of a light tablet in the field worked to support data capture and the students could return to the captured data in order to explain the process of their thinking.
4. The choice of technology was such that it reduced the effort required to link data to place yet maintained authenticity of the learning task.

Recommendations and Steps Forward

In the rush to develop e-learning programs with the latest technological tools, instructional designers often treat evaluation in the same way that people treat exercise and diet

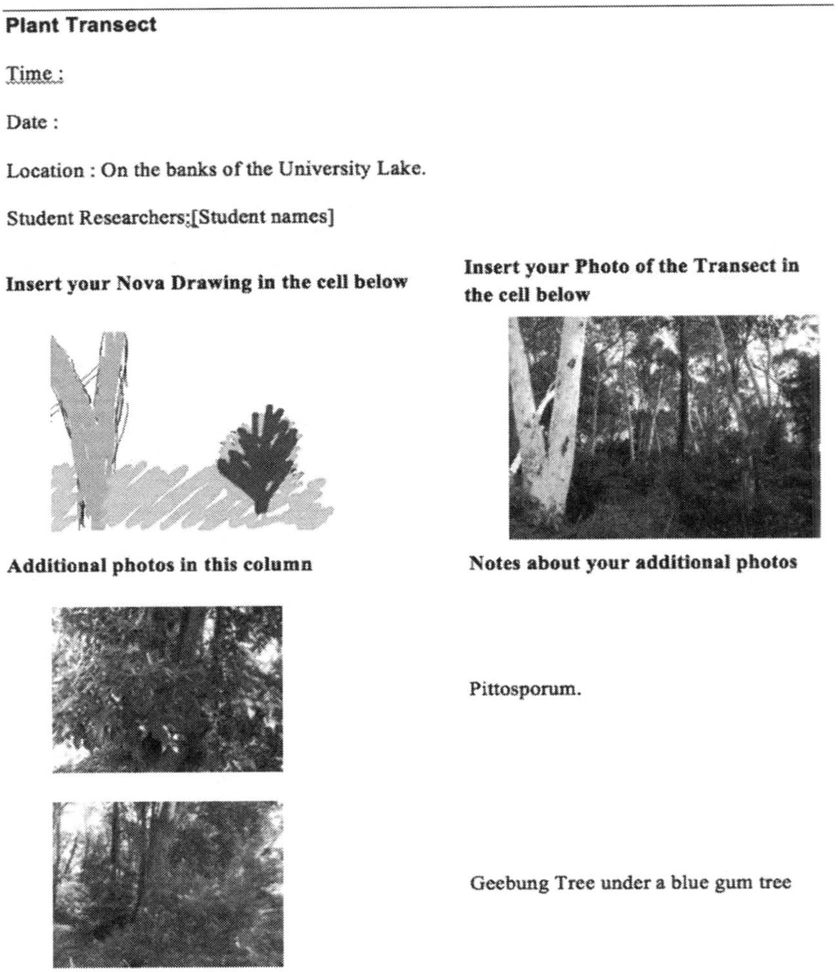

Plant Transect

Time :

Date :

Location : On the banks of the University Lake.

Student Researchers:[Student names]

Insert your Nova Drawing in the cell below	**Insert your Photo of the Transect in the cell below**
Additional photos in this column	**Notes about your additional photos**
	Pittosporum.
	Geebung Tree under a blue gum tree

Figure 20.8 Wiki Record Produced by Student Group

in everyday life. That is, we have the best of intentions, including such beliefs that we really wanted to go to the gym today, we did not really mean to eat a donut during the staff meeting this morning, and we swear we'll do better tomorrow. Designers really meant to allow budget and time for rigorous formative evaluation, but the deadline for delivery of the e-learning program slipped and those 3D animations ended up costing more to produce than anyone predicted. So evaluation, like exercise and diet, is put off or cancelled altogether. We recognize that this often happens, but we urge instructional designers and others involved in the development of e-learning to incorporate sound evaluation practices (especially formative ones) into their work. Unless this is done, e-learning will not begin to provide the learning opportunities and performance enhancement around the world it is capable of providing.

Author Note

Correspondence concerning this chapter should be addressed to:

Professor John G. Hedberg PhD
Millennium Innovations Chair of ICT and Education
School of Education
Faculty of Human Sciences
Macquarie University NSW 2109
Australia
Email john.hedberg@mq.edu au
Phone +61–2–9850 9894

References

Aldrich, C. (2004). *Simulations and the future of learning: An innovative (and perhaps revolutionary) approach to e-learning*. San Francisco: Pfeiffer.

Allen, M.W., & Sites, R. (2012). *Leaving ADDIE for SAM: An agile model for developing the best learning experiences*. Alexandria, VA: American Society for Training and Development.

Bates, T. (2012). *What's right and what's wrong about Coursera-style MOOCs?* Retrieved January 26, 2015 from http://www.tonybates.ca/2012/08/05/whats-right-and-whats-wrong-about-coursera-style-moocs/

Bauerlein, M. (2008). *The dumbest generation: How the digital age stupefies young Americans and jeopardizes our future (or, don't trust anyone under 30)*. New York: Penguin.

Bonk, C.J. (2009). *The world is open: How web technology is revolutionizing education*. San Francisco, CA: Jossey-Bass.

Branch, R.M. (2008). *Instructional design: The ADDIE approach*. New York: Springer.

Cassidy, M. (2013). *Coursera class offers peek into determination of student body*. Retrieved March 3, 2013, from http://www.mercurynews.com/mike-cassidy/ci_22696060/cassidy-coursera-class-offers-peek-into-determination-student

Chronicle of Higher Education. (2012, October 1). *Online learning supplement: MOOC madness*. Retrieved January 26, 2015 from http://chronicle.com/section/Online-Learning/623/

Clark, R.C., & Mayer, R.E. (2011). *E-learning and the science of instruction: Proven guidelines for consumers and designers of multimedia learning*. San Francisco: Pfeiffer.

Clark, R.E. (Ed.). (2012). *Learning from media: Arguments, analysis, and evidence* (2nd ed.). Charlotte, NC: Information Age.

Cuban, L. (2001). *Oversold and underused: Computers in the classroom*. Cambridge, MA: Harvard University Press.

Flagg, B.N. (1990). *Formative evaluation for educational technologies*. Hillsdale, NJ: Lawrence Erlbaum.

Garrison, D.R. (2011). *E-learning in the 21st century*. London: Routledge.

Greenagel, F.L. (2002). *The illusion of e-learning: Why we are missing out on the promise of technology*. Retrieved February 25, 2013, from http://www.league.org/publication/whitepapers/index.html

Herrington, J., Reeves, T.C., & Oliver, R. (2010). *A guide to authentic e-learning*. New York: Routledge.

Howe, C., & McCredie, N. (2012). *iPads in the classroom: Year 1 maths*. Retrieved March 3, 2013, from http://macict.webfactional.com/wp-content/uploads/iPads-Final-Report-.pdf

Jaschik, S. (2013, February 4). *MOOC mess*. Retrieved March 3, 2013, from http://www.insidehighered.com/news/2013/02/04/coursera-forced-call-mooc-amid-complaints-about-course

Jung, I., & Latchem, C. (2012). *Quality assurance and accreditation in distance education and e-learning: Models, policies and research*. New York and London: Routledge.

Khan, B.H. (2005). *Managing e-learning: Design, delivery, implementation and evaluation*. Hershey, PA: Idea Group.

Merrill, M.D. (2012). *First principles of instruction*. San Francisco: Pfeiffer.

Patton, M.Q. (2008). *Utilization-focused evaluation* (4th ed.). Thousand Oaks, CA: Sage.

Phillips, R., McNaught, C., & Kennedy, G. (2012). *Evaluating e-learning: Guiding research and practice. Connecting with e-learning*. London: Routledge.

Preston, G., Phillips, R., Gosper, M., McNeill, M., Woo, K., & Green, D. (2010). Web-based lecture technologies: Highlighting the changing nature of teaching and learning. *Australasian Journal of Educational Technology, 26*(6), 717–728. Retrieved April 7, 2013, from http://www.ascilite.org.au/ajet/ajet26/preston.html

Reeves, T.C. (2006). How do you know they are learning?: The importance of alignment in higher education. *International Journal of Learning Technology, 2*(4), 294–309.

Reeves, T.C., & Hedberg, J.G. (2003). *Interactive learning systems evaluation*. Englewood Cliffs, NJ: Educational Technology.

Reeves, T.C., & Reeves, P.M. (2012). Designing online and blended learning. In L. Hunt & D. Chalmers (Eds.), *University teaching in focus: A learning-centred approach* (pp. 112–127). Camberwell, VIC, Australia: ACER Press.

Salmon, G. (2011). *E-Moderating: The key to online teaching and learning* (3rd ed.). London: Routledge.

Scriven, M. (1967). The methodology of evaluation. In R. Tyler, R. Gagne, & M. Scriven (Eds.), *Perspectives on curriculum evaluation* (pp. 39-83). Chicago: Rand McNally.

Waterhouse, S. (2005). *The power of e-learning: The essential guide for teaching in the digital age*. Boston: Pearson.

21

Designing and Evaluating E-learning Interactions

João Mattar

Introduction

Although Godwin, Thorpe, and Richardson (2008) found no evidence of the impact of interaction on distance learning students' performance, completion and pass rates, grades, perceptions of the quality of their courses, or approaches to studying, several other studies point to key effects of interactions in e-learning. Thurmond (2003) concluded that interaction activities that occur in a Web-based environment have a great impact on students' satisfaction and likelihood of enrolling in other online courses. Zhao, Lei, Yan, Lai, and Tan's (2005) meta-analysis found that interaction is a key component in deciding the effectiveness of distance learning compared to face-to-face instruction. Evans and Gibbons (2007) observed that students using an interactive system outperformed those using a noninteractive system in a problem-solving test and needed less time to complete both memory and problem-solving tests. Bernard et al.'s (2009) review concluded that designing and arranging conditions or environments to promote interaction in distance education courses positively affects student learning.

1. Interaction and Interactivity

Wagner (1994, 1997) attempted to differentiate the terms *interaction* and *interactivity*: Interaction involves behaviors where individuals and groups influence one another in the cases of reciprocal events requiring two objects and two actions, while interactivity involves the attributes of technology used in distance learning that allow real-time connections. However, this distinction is not pervasive in the literature, and other authors use the words interchangeably.

This conceptual debate has been recently revived in the Portuguese language. Silva (2012), on one hand, argues that the concept of interactivity represents the spirit of a new era and a revolution in communication. Interactivity points to the unpredictable, being a broader concept than interaction. Primo (2007), on the other hand, says he does not know what interactivity is and rejects the concept, considering only interaction. The mere interaction with machines does not interest him, only interactions between and among humans, mediated or not by computers. Tori (2010), adding a third perspective, validates both concepts and defines interaction as shared work or activity where there are reciprocal influences and exchanges, while interactivity would be the potential of a system to generate interaction, in a sense similar to the way we use the words *radiation* and *radioactivity*.

One can however say, as did Rose (1999), that in instructional technology, the concept of *interactivity* is fragmented and inconsistent, deconstructing itself easily when closely examined. It is not the goal of this chapter to solve this conceptual debate, so we use the word *interaction* focusing on the design of e-learning activities, indicating when necessary whether we are talking about human–human or human–machine interactions and keep the word *interactivity* when it is used by cited authors.

2. Types of Interaction

Moore (1989) started a taxonomy of types of interaction in distance education with his classical article on learner–instructor, learner–learner, and learner–content interactions, later enriched by: learner–interface (Hillman, Willis, & Gunawardena, 1994); learner–environment (Burnham & Walden, 1997); instructor–instructor, instructor–content, and content–content (Anderson & Garrison, 1998); learner–self (Soo & Bonk, 1998); learner–context (Gibson, 1998); learner–designer (Sims, 1999); vicarious interaction (Sutton, 2001); and learner–tool (Hirumi, 2002). This section reviews the types of interaction most discussed in the literature.

Learner–Content

"The first type of interaction is interaction between the learner and the content or subject of study" (Moore, 1989, p. 2). Berge (2002) argues that interaction *with* content is a problematic formulation because "content cannot interact, hold a dialogue, or answer back" (p. 185); what really happens is interaction *about* content inside the students' heads. Zimmerman (2012) concluded that learners who spent more time interacting with course content achieved higher grades than those who spent less time. Sabry and Baldwin (2003) prefer the broader notion of *learner–information interaction*, including information that is not specific to course material. Their study demonstrated that learner–information interaction has the highest score in terms of frequency of use and perception of its usefulness when compared with other types of interaction.

Learner–Instructor

Thurmond (2003) found that the most significant predictor of student outcomes was students' perceptions regarding their interaction with instructors. Yacci (2000) emphasizes the importance of instructor feedback: Without an interactive loop, interactivity does not happen. An instructor question answered by a student, though, cannot be considered interactive because there was no feedback. Likewise, delayed feedback from instructors may cause negative effects; generally, students will no longer be interested in reading what the instructor wrote because there is a right or maximum timing for the response, after which the original purpose of the message might already have been forgotten by the learner and the interactive loop does not complete.

Learner–Learner

Learner–learner or interpersonal interactions (Berge, 1999) may happen synchronously and/or asynchronously, fostering cooperative and collaborative learning, creating a feeling of belonging to a community, and decreasing the sense of isolation of learning at a distance.

Learner–Self

Called *learner–self interaction* (Soo & Bonk, 1998), *intrapersonal interaction* (Berge, 1999), and *internal learner interaction* (Hirumi, 2011), self-interaction emphasizes the importance of the internal dialogue that students have with themselves during engagement with the content of learning. It includes therefore students' reflections on the content and on their own process of learning, that is to say, cognitive and metacognitive processes.

Vicarious Interaction

According to Sutton (2001), vicarious interaction takes place when a student actively observes, absorbs, and processes interactions between other students and instructors. In the same sense, we can speak of a vicarious interactor and a vicarious learning process.

Learner–Others

Learner–others covers all the interactions a learner might have with people outside the course. Ally (2008) uses the expression *learner–expert interaction*, and Xenia and Christos (2012) use *community–student interaction*; Rhode (2008) proposes *learner–network interaction* to cover informal learning; Gilbert and Moore (1998) talk about social interactivity involving the social context. The context beyond the classroom, according to Gibson (1998), may include family, coworkers, friends, and institutions, that is to say, interactions with culture in a broad sense. Ally (2008) conceives context as an opportunity for applying and transferring knowledge: "There should be strategies to promote learner–context interaction, to allow learners to apply what they learn in real life so that they can contextualize the information" (p. 33).

Stoerger (2013) examined the use of social media beyond the formal boundaries of an online course. Students were instructed to follow and make connections to individuals affiliated with the topics covered by the course. Most of the students who followed blogs were enthusiastic about the information they acquired, and the majority of the students stated that the activity led to a greater understanding of the course topic. Extending the proportion of learner–others interactions, Miyakita, Murai, Tomine, and Okawa (2013) proposed a unique learning infrastructure of performing arts education allowing communication with a global audience in synchronized time.

Learner–Environment

Burnham and Walden (1997) define *learner–environment interaction* as "a reciprocal action or mutual influence between a learner and the learner's surroundings that either assists or hinders learning" (Findings section, para. 2). These interactions occur when learners visit locations or work with resources outside the virtual computer environment (Hirumi, 2011).

Learner–Designer

According to Sims (1999), if you conceptualize the learner as actor using elements of performance and theatre and you integrate elements of conversational and communication theory, a form of learner-designer communication can be established, transcending the learner–computer interface and the learner–computer(content) communication. Hedberg and Sims (2001) argued that interaction between the designer and the learner must be taken into consideration by design as an indirect discourse for designing "encounters".

Learner–Interface

Hillman et al. (1994) added a fourth category to the three originally proposed by Moore: the interaction between the learner and the interface, unique to distance education. It includes the interactions between the student and the technology used to deliver instruction, as the student must use technology to interact with the content, the teacher, and other students.

Learner–Tools

Hirumi (2011) proposes *learner–tool interactions* to represent the interactions of the learner with tools both within and outside of the learning management system (LMS), such as telecommunication tools (e.g., electronic mail, discussion forums, and chats), productivity tools (e.g., word processors, spreadsheets, and graphic applications), external tools (e.g., microscope), and content generators tools (e.g., video cameras and other recording devices), all of which enrich the e-learning experience.

Instructor–Content, Instructor–Instructor, and Content–Content

Anderson and Garrison (1998) stressed the tendency of teachers to act as authors and instructional designers (*teacher–content interaction*), due to authoring and delivery tools having become more user-friendly. They also introduced the idea of *teacher–teacher interaction* through communities and social networks and *content–content interaction* covering a range of elements from RSS feeds to complex programs and the semantic web.

3. Other Taxonomies

It is a common criticism that these models often emphasize the *who* of the interaction, leaving aside the *what;* that is to say, these approaches focus on the agents that interact instead of defining the nature of the interactions. Therefore, alternative models have emerged seeking to classify goals, learning outcomes, levels, activities, tools, and other characteristic elements of interaction.

Northrup (2001, 2002) identified four major purposes for interaction: to interact with content, to collaborate and converse, to help monitor and regulate learning, and to support performance. Wagner (1997) identified different goals for interaction: participation, development of communication, reception of feedback, elaboration and retention, learner control and self-regulation, increase in motivation, negotiation of understanding, discovery, exploration, clarification of understanding, and closure.

Sims (1997) reviewed the theories of levels of interactivity from more reactive to more proactive. Considering however that these theories still represent a behaviorist approach, he proposed concepts to evaluate the production of multimedia material for education: object interactivity, linear interactivity, support interactivity, update interactivity, construct interactivity, reflective interactivity, simulation interactivity, hyperlinked interactivity, nonimmersive contextual interactivity, immersive virtual interactivity, and characteristic of virtual worlds. In another article, Sims (2006) proposed metrics to assess how interactions can help achieve the learning outcomes of a course: learning style, course completion, cognitive activity, roles, audio/visual effects, feedback, and design for learning.

Bonk and King (1998) discussed how interaction is linked to different tools, such as electronic messaging devices, delayed collaboration tools, real-time brainstorming and conversational tools, synchronous text collaborative writing tools, and collaborative multimedia and hypermedia tools.

4. Model for Designing and Evaluating E-learning Interactions

Several authors developed models and frameworks for designing e-learning interactions.

Berge (2002) presented an e-learning design model focusing on three types of interaction: learner–content, learner–learner, and learner–instructor. According to him, "the secret to designing successful learning is to align three elements: learning goals, learning activities, and feedback and evaluation" (p. 182). He also stressed the importance of infrastructure, support services, and a learning environment for the learning process.

Chou (2003) proposed a technical framework for including nine interactive dimensions and thirty-six interactive functions in learning Web systems, linked to the three types of interaction suggested by Berge (2002) plus learner–interface.

Strijbos, Martens, and Jochems (2004) proposed a process-oriented framework for designing computer-supported group-based learning settings focusing on the elicitation of expected interaction processes. They identified five critical elements that affect the emergence of interactions grouped into three dimensions (learning objectives, task type, and level of pre-structuring) and two discrete categories (group size and computer support).

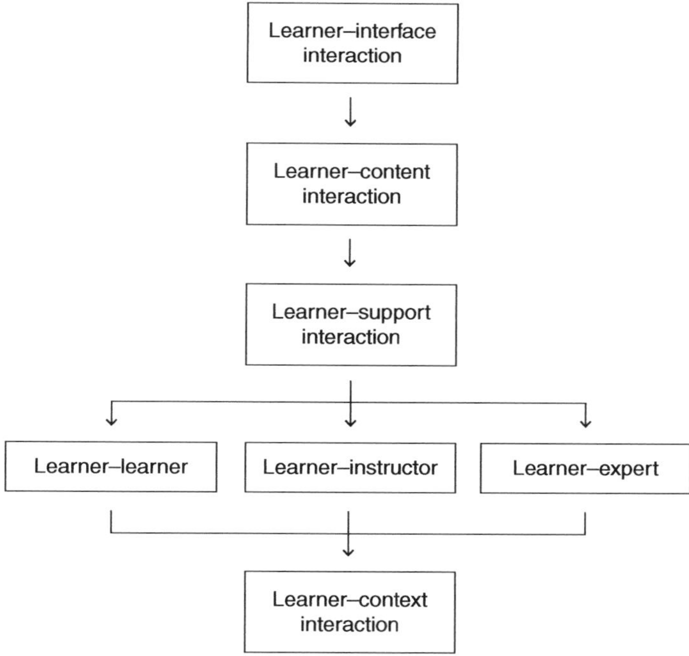

Figure 21.1 Levels of Interaction in Online Learning (Ally, 2008, p. 32)
Reprinted with permission from Athabasca University Press.

Ally (2008) proposed a model for designing and developing effective online materials and instruction. Initially, he outlined different kinds of interactions and interactive strategies to promote learning at varied levels, as illustrated in Figure 21.1. Then he proposed a model for learning components that should be used when designing online materials, represented in Figure 21.2.

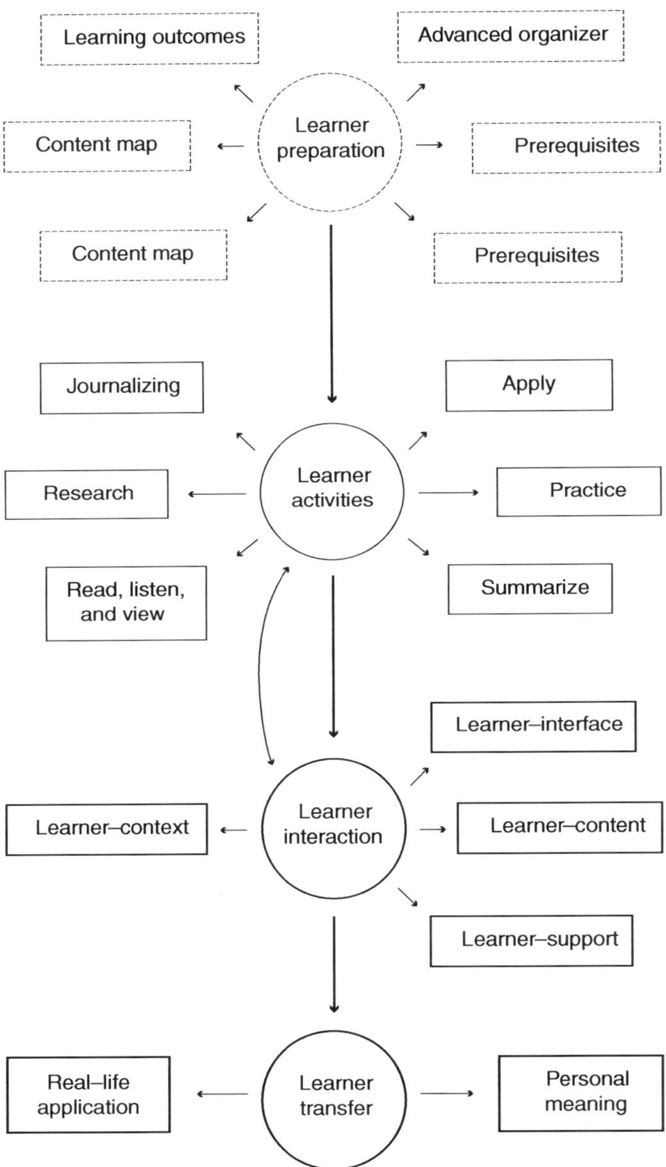

Figure 21.2 Components of Effective Online Learning (Ally, 2008, p. 37)
Reprinted with permission from Athabasca University Press.

Hirumi (2002, 2006, 2011) has been developing a comprehensive framework for designing and sequencing e-learning interactions with three levels of planned e-learning interactions: internal learner (level 1); human (learner–instructor, learner–learner, and learner–other) and nonhuman interactions (learner–content, learner–tool, and learner–environment), with learner–interface interaction positioned under all of them (level 2); and learner–instruction (level 3).

Hirumi (2011) argues that although available taxonomies reveal a plethora of e-learning interactions, existing research and literature do not provide systematic and practical guidelines for designing and sequencing interactions for e-learning.

This section initially presents a micro-model for designing and analyzing types of student-centered e-learning interactions based on the review of the previously discussed taxonomies. A macro-model (encompassing this micro-model) is then proposed and justified based on the review of these models and frameworks, providing guidelines for designing and evaluating student-centered activities and interactions.

Types of Interaction

We consider that instructor–instructor, instructor–content, content–content, and learner–designer are not interactions to be designed for learners, which is our focus. We also consider learner–support, in the sense of contacts with staff members or electronic interactive characters, and FAQs, online help on content, and user guidance on system (CHOU, 2003) as continuous interactions that are not elaborated as intentional activities by a designer or instructor. So they are not included in our model.

Although Hirumi (2011) argues that his grounded approach neither subscribes to, nor advocates any particular epistemology, his decision of distinguishing internal learner interactions from all the others as one of the three fundamental levels within his framework seems indeed to privilege a specific type of learning in an era where connectivism claims that learning should no longer be considered an internal and individualistic activity (Siemens, 2004; Anderson & Dron, 2010, 2012). Anyway, we consider learner–self interactions, in the sense of self-perception, self-regulation, and metacognition (Hirumi, 2011) as a continuous exercise parallel to learning, not a separate type of interaction. So, we included learner–self interaction in our model specifically for the cases where a designer or instructor proposes a reflection activity for the learner.

Although recognizing interface as a key element in e-learning, in many online courses or sections the student might not have any contact with a course interface, as in activities held outside an LMS such as social networks, other tools, or even the real world. It seems, however, more adequate to consider interaction with the environment in a broader sense, including interface as part of that interaction. Besides that, we consider learning–interface a continuous interaction, a medium for other interactions. As Hillman et al. (1994) state, "It is important to make the distinction between the perception of interface as an independent, fourth mode of interaction, and the use of an interface as a mediating element in all interaction" (p. 34). In our model, the interface as a mediating element of other interactions is not included, but we use learner–interface interaction for activities in which the learner is intentionally asked to navigate through the course and understand its layout.

The same can be said about learner–tool interactions, as almost everything might be considered a tool. Tools are also mediating elements in other interactions, but some activities might include meta-interaction with a tool, such as tutorials on how to use it. Although this could be considered part of the learner–content interaction, it is a special category. In our model, it represents the activities where the student is asked to learn how to work with a specific tool.

Figure 21.3 illustrates our model.

Learner–interface and learner–tools interactions are grouped on the upper part to symbolize that they are mediating elements of other interactions and are usually proposed as activities in the beginning of a course. They are aligned with learner–content interactions because we consider them variations of the latter.

Learner–content is grouped with learner–self interaction because they flow together. We consider vicarious interaction part of other interactions in the same sense that learner–self, when not designed as an activity, is not listed in the model.

Strijbos et al. (2004) stressed that group size is one of the critical elements that affect the emergence of interaction. In our model, we exploded learner–learner interactions into three subtypes: learner–learner one (one-to-one interaction as in a peer-to-peer individual assessment), learner–learner group (interactions in groups created, for example, by the instructor in an LMS), and learner–learner course (for example, all the students of the course interacting in a general forum). This distinction is needed because each of these types of interaction involves clearly different and unique design and assessment strategies. Learner-learner is positioned in the middle of learner-content and learner-self interactions, indicating that these types of interaction might happen simultaneously and are correlated.

Learner–context interactions cover learner–expert and learner–context interactions (Ally, 2008), informal learning, social interactivity, social context, culture, community–student, and learner–others interactions. Learner–context and learner–environment interactions are grouped

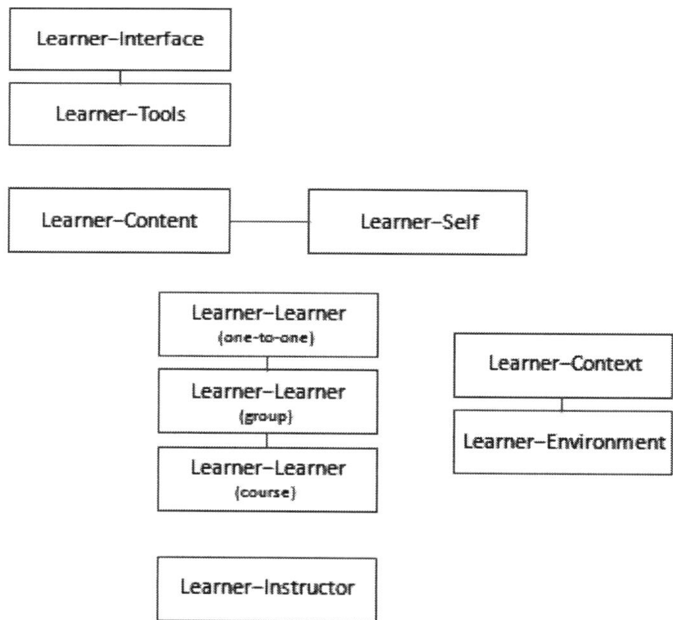

Figure 21.3 Model for Designing and Analyzing Student-Centered Interactions

because they intertwine: When interacting in environments outside the LMS, the student will usually also interact with people.

Model

Building on this previous micro-model of types of interaction, we propose a macro-model for designing and evaluating student-centered e-learning activities and interactions. We presuppose that a previous context and learner analysis was conducted, general learning objectives were formulated, and a virtual learning environment was defined. We consider, as Hirumi (2011) himself does, that his level III is a meta-level that transcends and is used to guide the design of other interactions; it is then what our model proposes: The model should not be inside itself. We view learning style, prestructuring support, and infrastructure as preparation or continuous processes that precede the design of activities and interactions in e-learning or flow parallel to them, so they are not included in our model. And we envisage Ally's (2008) learner preparation broken into learner–content and learner–self interactions.

Besides the types of interactions presented in our micro-model, our macro-model includes the three elements proposed by Berge (2002) as the secret of successfully designing learning: learning goals, learning activities, and feedback and evaluation (what we call assessment). Ally's (2008) link between learner activities and learning interactions is critical in our model.

The elements proposed by Strijbos et al. (2004) deserve a closer evaluation. Learning objectives are part of our model; task type is actually a mix of what we call objectives, activities, and level/structure; level of prestructuring might be considered our level/structure; group size is part of what we consider a previous phase of design but also guided our proposal for three kinds of learner–learner interactions; and computer support is also part of previous design, although also involving what we call tools.

Our model includes eight key elements:

- Objectives
- Activities
- Types
- Level/Structure
- Resources
- Media
- Tools
- Assessment

and two discrete choices:

- Synchronous/Asynchronous
- Duration

The model has similarities with some steps Hirumi (2011) suggests for design—objectives, events, type of interactions, and tools—but includes more variables and does not follow a linear sequence. Figure 21.4 illustrates the main components of the model.

Strijbos et al. (2004) suggested that learning objectives be depicted on a continuum ranging from open skills to closed skills. Wagner (1997), Northrup (2001, 2002), and Berge (2002) also list different goals and purposes for interactions and activities.

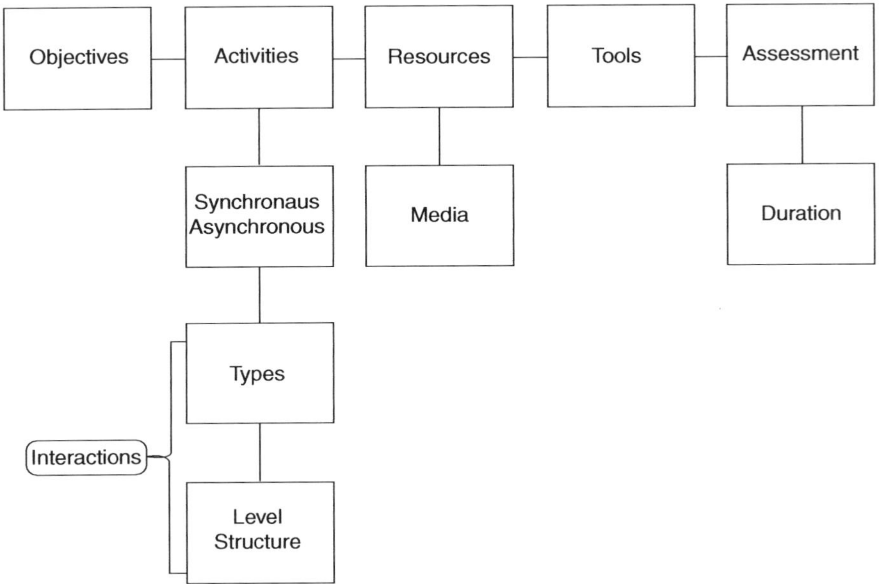

Figure 21.4 Model for Designing and Evaluating Student-Centered E-learning Activities and Interactions

Berge (2002) considered learning activities one of the three basic components of e-learning. Chou (2003) cited several types of activities (what he called interactive functions), such as exploring links and multimedia materials, search, self-evaluation, surveys, learners contributing to learning materials, and chats. Bonk and Dennen (2003) made valuable compilations of online pedagogical activities and ideas, such as case studies, icebreakers and closing activities, scavenger hunt, interactive peer commenting, peer feedback roles, team work, discussion forums, role play, round-robin activities, Web publishing of student work, symposia, brainstorming, guest experts, and online portfolios. Planning rich and varied activities and linking them to the other elements of the proposed model might be considered the key to making e-learning interactive.

On level/structure of the interactions we classify the learner's involvement, from more reactive to proactive. Strijbos et al. (2004) argued that task types are linked to interaction processes on a continuum ranging from well-structured to ill-structured tasks. Their discussion of interaction prestructuring, as well as some of Chou's (2003) interactivity dimensions and Sims' (1997) concepts might also be classified here. It is notable that level/structure of the interaction is not part of Hirumi's (2002) framework.

We consider that resources and media (such as text, sound, graphics, videos, animation, and games) used in activities and interactions are also critical elements and should be treated as separate categories in the design.

We also propose, as do other authors, that choosing the appropriate tools, social media, and technologies for delivering e-learning and for students' productivity deserves a specific place in a design model.

Several authors consider assessment a key element in designing e-learning activities and interactions. Berge (2002) stated, "Feedback, including evaluation, is another aspect of interaction" (p. 185). Chou (2003) includes online quizzes for self-evaluation and individualized test/

quizzes as interactive functions. Wagner (1997), Yacci (2000), and Sims (2006) also stressed the importance of feedback. Assessment might include instructor-to-student, student-to-student and self-interactions, both formative and summative. Instructors giving feedback on students' works, peer-to-peer paper commenting based on rubrics, collectively grading forum posts, and self-evaluation based on eportfolios are examples of the use of interactive assessment strategies in e-learning. Armenteros, Benítez, and Curca (2013) presented the design of an interactive trivia game, used as an online educational resource for football and assistant referees, which focuses on assessment and uses 1,500 multiple-choice questions. It is notable that assessment is not part of Hirumi's (2011) framework.

The literature does not stress the importance of including the previewed duration of the activity and interaction in the design, but we consider it a key element for properly communicating with the students.

Finally, we propose, contrary to Hirumi (2011), that the design can start from different points because in some cases the learning objectives, resources, content, and/or lessons plans might have already been defined. As Strijbos et al. (2004) argued, the learning objectives and the expected interactions should be determined simultaneously, as their design focuses "on interaction processes rather than static learning outcomes" (p. 417). Our macro-model, though, doesn't have arrows indicating order and direction, but lines connecting its elements.

Conclusion

The proposed model, based on established theories and practices, can assist designers and instructors both in designing new courses and in evaluating existing courses with focus on activities and interactions. Experimental studies are needed to evaluate its effect on design and learners, although it is not simple to measure how interaction affects learning. As Clark and Mayer (2011) argued, high levels of behavioral activity (such as pressing a button or choosing from a list) might not be enough to stimulate the psychological engagement essential for learning. On the other side of the continuum, there is the risk of cognitive overload. There is also a need to discuss whether design can encompass unplanned and unexpected interactions. We hope that this chapter inspires the development of research on interactions in e-learning.

References

Ally, M. (2008). Foundations of educational theory for online learning. In T. Anderson (Ed.), *The theory and practice of online learning* (2nd ed., pp. 15–44). Edmonton, AB: AU Press. (1st ed. 2004)

Anderson, T., & Dron, J. (2010). Three generations of distance education pedagogy. *International Review of Research in Open and Distance Learning*, 12(3), 80–97.

Anderson, T., & Dron, J. (2012). Learning technology through three generations of technology enhanced distance education pedagogy. *European Journal of Open, Distance and E-Learning*, 2012/2.

Anderson, T., & Garrison, D.R. (1998). Learning in a networked world: New roles and responsibilities. In C.C. Gibson (Ed.), *Distance learners in higher education* (pp. 97–112). Madison, WI: Atwood.

Armenteros, M., Benítez, A.J., & Curca, D. (2013). Interactive trivia of laws of the game as a resource for training FIFA football referees. In H. Yang & S. Wang (Eds.), *Cases on formal and informal e-learning environments: Opportunities and practices* (pp. 200–214). Hershey, PA: IGI Global.

Berge, Z.L. (1999). Interaction in post-secondary web-based learning. *Educational Technology*, 39(1), 5–11.

Berge, Z.L. (2002). Active, interactive, and reflective learning. *Quarterly Review of Distance Education*, 3(2), 181–190.

Bernard, R.M., Abrami, P.C., Borokhovski, E., Wade, C.A., Tamim, R.M., Surkes, M.A., & Bethel, E.C. (2009). A meta-analysis of three types of interaction treatments in distance education. *Review of Educational Research*, 79(3), 1243–1289.

Bonk, C.J., & Dennen, V. (2003). Frameworks for research, design, benchmarks, training, and pedagogy in web-based distance education. In M.G. Moore & W.G. Anderson (Eds.), *Handbook of distance education* (pp. 331–348). Mahwah, NJ: Lawrence Erlbaum.

Bonk, C.J., & King, K. (1998). Computer conferencing and collaborative writing tools: Starting a dialogue about student dialogue. In C.J. Bonk & K. King (Eds.), *Electronic collaborators: Learner-centered technologies for literacy, apprenticeship, and discourse* (pp. 3–23). Mahwah, NJ: Lawrence Erlbaum.

Burnham, B.R., & Walden, B. (1997). *Interactions in distance education: A report from the other side*. Paper presented at the 1997 Adult Education Research Conference. Stillwater, Oklahoma.

Chou, C. (2003). Interactivity and interactive functions in web-based learning systems: A technical framework for designers. *British Journal of Educational Technology*, 34(3), 265–279.

Clark, R.C., & Mayer, R.E. (2011). *E-learning and the science of instruction: Proven guidelines for consumers and designers of multimedia learning* (3rd ed.). San Francisco: Pfeiffer.

Evans, C., & Gibbons, N.J. (2007). The interactivity effect in multimedia learning. *Computers & Education*, 49(4), 1147–1160.

Gibson, C.C. (1998). Social context and the collegiate distance learner. In C.C. Gibson (Ed.), *Distance learners in higher education: Institutional responses for quality outcomes* (pp. 113–126). Madison, WI: Atwood.

Gilbert, L., & Moore, D.R. (1998). Building interactivity into Web courses: Tools for social and instructional interaction. *Educational Technology*, 38(3), 29–35.

Godwin, S.J., Thorpe, M.S., & Richardson, J.T.E. (2008). The impact of computer-mediated interaction on distance learning. *British Journal of Educational Technology*, 39(1), 52–70.

Hedberg, J., & Sims, R. (2001). Speculations on design team interactions. *Journal of Interactive Learning Research*, 12(2), 189–214.

Hillman, D.C., Willis, D.J., & Gunawardena, C.N. (1994). Learner-interface interaction in distance education: An extension of contemporary models and strategies for practitioners. *American Journal of Distance Education*, 8(2), 30–42.

Hirumi, A. (2002). A framework for analyzing, designing, and sequencing planned elearning interactions. *Quarterly Review of Distance Education*, 3(2), 141–160.

Hirumi, A. (2006). Analysing and designing e-learning interactions. In C. Juwah (Ed.), *Interactions in online education: Implications for theory and practice* (pp. 46–71). New York, NY: Routledge.

Hirumi, A. (2011). Applying grounded strategies to design and sequence e-learning interactions. Manuscript submitted for publication.

Miyakita, G., Murai, Y., Tomine, T., & Okawa, K. (2013). Designing a new performing arts education through constructing a global theatre. In H. Yang & S. Wang (Eds.), *Cases on formal and informal e-learning environments: Opportunities and practices* (pp. 314–336). Hershey, PA: IGI Global.

Moore, M.G. (1989). Editorial: Three types of interaction. *American Journal of Distance Education*, 3(2), 1–6.

Northrup, P. (2001). A framework for designing interactivity into web-based instruction. *Educational Technology*, 41(2), 31–39.

Northrup, P.T. (2002). Online learners' preferences for interaction. *Quarterly Review of Distance Education*, 3(2), 219–226.

Primo, A. (2007). *Interação mediada por computador: comunicação—cibercultura—cognição*. Porto Alegre, Brazil: Sulina.

Rhode, J.F. (2008). *Interaction equivalency in self-paced online learning environments: An exploration of learner preferences* (Doctoral dissertation). Retrieved from http://gradworks.umi.com/3291462.pdf

Rose, E. (1999). Deconstructing interactivity in educational computing. *Educational Technology*, 39(1), 43–49.

Sabry, K., & Baldwin, L. (2003). Web-based learning interaction and learning styles. *British Journal of Educational Technology*, 34(4), 443–454.

Siemens, G. (2004). *A learning theory for the digital age*. Retrieved from http://www.elearnspace.org/Articles/connectivism.htm

Silva, M. (2012). *Sala de aula interativa: Educação, comunicação, mídia clássica . . .* (6th ed.). São Paulo, Brazil: Loyola.

Sims, R. (1997). *Interactivity: a forgotten art?* Retrieved from http://www2.gsu.edu/~wwwitr/docs/interact/

Sims, R. (1999). Interactivity on stage: Strategies for learner-designer communication. *Australian Journal of Educational Technology*, 15(3), 257–272.

Sims, R. (2006). Beyond instructional design: Making learning design a reality. *Journal of Learning Design*, 1(2), 1–7.

Soo, K., Bonk, C.J. (1998). *Interaction: What does it mean in online distance education?* Paper presented at the ED/MEDIA/ED-TELECOM 98 World Conference on Educational Multimedia and Hypermedia & World Conference on Educational Telecommunications, Freiburg, Germany, 1998.
Stoerger, S. (2013). Making connections: How students use social media to create personal learning networks. In H. Yang & S. Wang (Eds.), *Cases on formal and informal e-learning environments: Opportunities and practices* (pp. 1–18). Hershey, PA: IGI Global.
Strijbos, J.W., Martens, R.L., & Jochems, W.M.G. (2004). Designing for interaction: Six steps to designing computer-supported group-based learning. *Computers & Education*, 42(4), 403–424.
Sutton, L.A. (2001). The principle of vicarious interaction in computer-mediated communications. *International Journal of Educational Telecommunications*, 7(3), 223–242.
Thurmond, V.A. (2003). *Examination of interaction variables as predictors of students' satisfaction and willingness to enroll in future web-based courses while controlling for student characteristics* (Doctoral dissertation). Kansas City, KS. Retrieved from http://www.bookpump.com/dps/pdf-b/1121814b.pdf
Tori, R. (2010). *Educação sem distância: As tecnologias interativas na redução de distâncias em ensino e aprendizagem.* São Paulo, Brazil: Editora Senac São Paulo.
Wagner, E.D. (1994). In support of a functional definition of interaction. *American Journal of Distance Education*, 8(2), 6–29.
Wagner, E.D. (1997). Interactivity: From agents to outcomes. *New Directions for Teaching and Learning*, 71, 19–26.
Xenia, Z., & Christos, G. (2012). Open source computer-mediated collaborative community learning. *International Journal of Computer and Information Technology*, 01(01), 67–76.
Yacci, M. (2000). Interactivity demystified: A structural definition for online learning and intelligent CBT. *Educational Technology*, 40(4), 5–16.
Zhao, Y., Lei, J., Yan, B., Lai, C., & Tan, H.S. (2005). What makes the difference? A practical analysis of research on the effectiveness of distance education. *Teachers College Record*, 107(8), 1836–1884.
Zimmerman, T. (2012). Exploring learner to content interaction as a success factor in online courses. *The International Review of Research in Open and Distance Learning*, 13(4), 152–165.

22
A Theory of Mobile Learning

Helen Crompton

A Theory of Mobile Learning

Mobile devices are quickly becoming ubiquitous throughout today's society. Educators are extending the boundaries of traditional pedagogies with mobile learning (m-learning) that provides new affordances to the learner, such as learning that is personalized, contextualized, and unrestricted by temporal and spatial constraints. While m-learning uses digital technologies, there are many differences when a comparison is made between m-learning and conventional tethered electronic learning (e-learning). The unique attributes of mobile learning provide a new approach to learning, which requires a new theory.

In this chapter, the first section explicates the necessity for m-learning to have its own theory and how it is different from conventional tethered electronic learning and traditional learning. The next section summarizes the criteria, identified in the literature, of what should be included in an m-learning theory. This is followed by a review of the proposed theoretical models for m-learning, while considering the existing theories used to underpin the new m-learning theories. In the final section of this chapter, the themes emerging from the m-learning literature are revealed to state that *context, connectivity, time*, and *personalization* are the underpinning components of m-learning.

Definition and Electronic Devices

In order to consider a theoretical approach to m-learning, it is imperative to establish what m-learning is and to review how it is defined in the literature. As the field of m-learning is still emerging, it is prone to many changes and refinements. Therefore, the scholarly definitions provided are often quickly dated as new mobile technologies become available that further extend the boundaries of traditional pedagogies.

Scholars (viz., Brown, 2005; Sharples, Taylor, & Vavoula, 2007; Traxler, 2009a) debate what key components should be included in a definition of m-learning. The four reoccurring themes appear to be: (1) technological devices, (2) social interactions, (3) learning pedagogies, and

(4) context.[1] Therefore, the definition selected for this chapter encompasses those four constructs to say that m-learning is "learning across multiple contexts, through social and content interactions, using personal electronic devices" (Crompton, 2013, p. 4).

In a parallel dilemma, as electronic devices are constantly being updated, a concomitant discussion has centered on the types of devices that should be included within the category of m-learning (Caudill, 2007; Traxler, 2009a). Specifically naming types of devices to be included in a definition of m-learning can be highly problematic as these lists can quickly become dated. For example, Traxler (2009a) listed PDAs, palmtop, handhelds, and smartphones as mobile devices. He then went on to say that he questioned if tablets should be included within this category as they were not as portable as their smaller mobile counterparts. In addition, he described how tablets have a longer start-up time than handhelds and were therefore not as readily available for action as other handheld devices that took seconds to start.

A few months after Traxler's (2009a) explication of which electronic devices should be included in the category of m-learning, tablets, such as the iPad, were made commercially available. These new tablets are much more portable than their predecessors and as quick to start as a smartphone from standby mode. Traxler's choice of mobile devices had quickly become incorrect and dated. Therefore, it is best not to specifically list devices that can or cannot be included, but instead to describe general attributes of the devices. One should consider m-learning as the utilization of those electronic devices that are easily transported and used at any time and in any place (Crompton, 2013b).

A New Theory

In this section, an argument is made for why electronic learning (e-learning) is different from m-learning. Commonalities are identified between the two while revealing why an autonomous theory of m-learning is warranted. While the meaning of the terms m-learning and e-learning may seem intuitively obvious, the way the two differentiate from each other is not as clear. Tavangarian, Leypold, Nolting, and Voigt (2004) posited e-learning to be "*all forms of electronic supported learning and teaching* . . . Information and communication systems, whether networked or not, serve as specific media to implement the learning process" (Tavangarian et al., 2004, p. 274). Thus, m-learning is included in this definition as the process of learning utilizing electronic technologies.

M-learning has always tacitly meant mobile e-learning (Traxler, 2009b); nonetheless, m-learning is set apart in Figure 22.1 as an autonomous component of e-learning. While all forms of e-learning use various types of electronic technologies, the attributes of mobile technologies can yield a different learning experience from learning via *conventional* e-learning technologies. Conventional e-learning is tethered. In other words, the electronic technology, such as a desktop PC, is connected for the majority of the time to an electrical outlet via a cord. As a result, students are unable to move about freely as they learn. In addition, large technologies, such as desktop PCs are not very portable.

To use these tethered electronic devices, students usually have to designate a time to be situated at these electronic technologies. Furthermore, students often sit facing these technologies, and social and environmental interactions can often be incidental to learning. Learning partners need to also be seated in front of these technologies to view the screens. What makes m-learning different from the conventional tethered e-learning is the lack of those spatial and temporal constraints; learning has portability (Laurillard, 2007; Sharples, 2006), ubiquitous access (Melhuish & Falloon, 2010), and social connectivity (Koole, 2009).

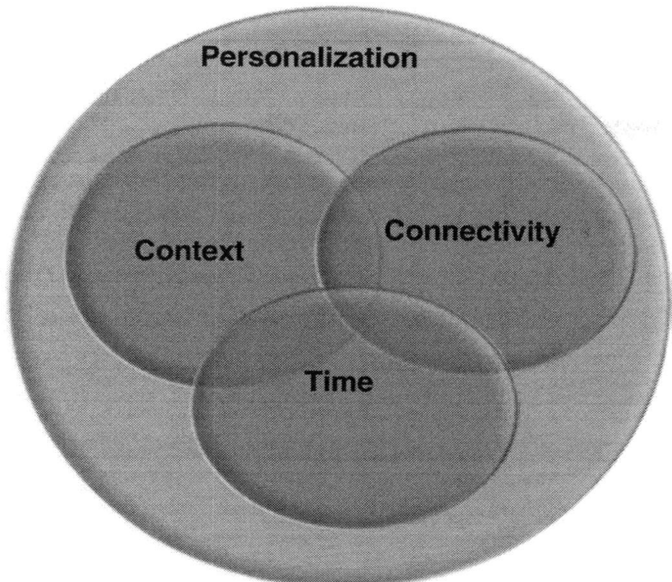

Figure 22.1 Overview of the Emerging Themes Surrounding M-learning

Adapted from "Mobile Learning: New approach, new theory," by H. Crompton, 2013, in *Handbook of Mobile Learning* by Z. L. Berge & L. Y. Muilenburg (Eds.). Copyright 2013 Routledge.

To highlight the difference between the two learning theories of e-learning and m-learning, academics have analyzed the nomenclature characterizing conventional tethered e-learning and m-learning. Traxler (2009c) compiled a list of repeating terms from m-learning conference proceedings. His work uncovered the terms *personal, spontaneous, opportunistic, informal, pervasive, situated, private, context-aware, bite-sized,* and *portable.* For conventional e-learning, Traxler searched the literature and found words such as *structured, media-rich, interactive, intelligent,* and *broadband.* Laouris and Eteokleous (2005) posited that nomenclature for the field of m-learning should include the terms *connected, spontaneous, situated, intimate, informal,* and *personal.* For conventional e-learning, Laouris and Eteokleous selected the terms *computer, multimedia, interactive, hyperlinked,* and *media-rich environment.*

Traxler's and Laouris and Eteokleous's lists both have identical or synonymous terms for m-learning and conventional e-learning. Through a form of folksonomy, the attributes have determined the nomenclature for each particular field. In other words, the users of both m-learning and e-learning in society have highlighted the different affordances for conventional e-learning and m-learning. To provide further clarity on how m-learning is different from conventional tethered e-learning, Table 22.1 includes examples of how traditional learning, conventional e-learning, and m-learning compare when those particular attributes are considered within pedagogical practice.

For each attribute in the far left column, a familiar continuation can be found in each of the other columns. This chart illustrates that more and more affordances appear as you move from

Table 22.1 Comparing Traditional Learning, E-Learning and M-Learning with Various Learning Attributes

	Traditional Learning	*Conventional tethered e-learning*	*m-learning*
Time	Often constrained by formal school hours.	Constrained to time sitting in front of a computer, but can occur at any time of the day.	No time constraints. Learning can take place anywhere you can carry and use a mobile device and at any time of the day.
Personalized	Limited in all aspects of differentiation and concepts taught.	Some personalization with a choice of programs and concepts to be taught, but computers are typically shared and nonpersonalized.	Personalization through applications, concepts, and often the ownership of devices personalized for the user.
Private learning	Not private	Typically private	Private
Context	Highly limited to a set location and framework.	Various locations, although still tied to specific locations and milieu.	Learning can take place in numerous environmental and social settings where wireless access can be obtained.
Formal/Informal	Formal	Formal and informal	Informal and can also be formal.
Socio-connectivity	Connections made to those in direct environment.	Virtual connectivity to the networked world.	Connections made to those in the direct environment and those networked.
Spontaneity	Not spontaneous	Partially spontaneous	Highly spontaneous

Note. For particular attributes such as private learning and spontaneity, these describe opportunities available to that form of learning. It is not to propose that m-learning is always private and highly spontaneous, but that opportunities are available for it to be so. Adapted from "Mobile Learning: New approach, new theory," by H. Crompton, 2013, in *Handbook of Mobile Learning* by Z.L. Berge & L.Y. Muilenburg (Eds.). Copyright 2013 Routledge.

the traditional learning column to the conventional tethered e-learning column, and then onto the m-learning column. For example, time for traditional learning is constrained by formal school hours. E-learning extended that boundary by allowing the learner to study at any time the learner could be in front of a conventional tethered electronic technology, such as a PC. M-learning removes time limitation by allowing the learner to study anywhere he or she can carry and use a mobile device. These pedagogical differences could be due to the technologies used, or result from the way the technologies mediate and facilitate the learning experience (Peters, 2009).

This section has explicated the interconnected nature of conventional tethered e-learning and m-learning. An argument has been provided separating the two fields in terms of the attributes and learner experiences, thus determining that there is a need for m-learning to have a theory of its own. The next section of this chapter provides a description of the criteria necessary for incorporation within a theory of m-learning.

Criteria for a Theory of M-learning

Sharples et al. (2007) specifically defined four criteria necessary for considering a theory of m-learning. The first step is to determine what distinguishes m-learning from other learning activities—a belief also held by Traxler (2009c), who pointed out the differences concerning the underlying learning experience. This difference was discussed in the previous section of this chapter. The second consideration posited by Sharples et al. (2007) is to consider the location in which the learning takes place. Sharples, Sánchez, Milrad, and Vavoula (2009) suggested that this second consideration be split into various components to highlight how learning can dynamically change dependent on the learner's location, personal interests or commitments.

The third criterion for a theory of m-learning (Sharples et al., 2007) is that the learning must use pedagogies already considered effective practices. For example, the socioconstructivist approach is considered a successful learning pedagogy (Sullivan Palincsar, 1998; Vygotsky, 1978), promoting higher-order thinking skills, collaboration, and reflection (Collison, Elbaum, Haavind, & Tinker, 2000). The final consideration posited by Sharples et al. is that the fundamental properties of the various ubiquitous mobile technologies be considered.

Laouris and Eteokleous (2005) listed a number of similar considerations. However, they made the crucial point that each of the factors needs to be taken into account, as do the way the factors interact and influence one another. To do this, Laouris and Eteokleous proposed the mathematical formula mLearn $= f\{t, s, LE, C, IT, MM, M\}$, to emphasize that m-learning is a function of each parameter: t = time, s = space, LE = environment, C = content, IT = technology, MM = learner's mental capabilities, and m = method of delivery and interaction with content. This section identified criteria that one must consider when constructing a theory for m-learning. The following section provides a summary of the m-learning theories presented in the literature thus far, and the approaches used to develop a new theory.

The Theories Proposed

In the last section of this chapter, the confounding variables were described that one must remain cognizant of when proposing a new theory for m-learning. Despite this difficulty, Koole (2009), Laurillard (2007), Naismith, Lonsdale, Vavoula, and Sharples (2004), and Sharples et al. (2007) have created models to describe various aspects of m-learning. These models appear to directly connect with an existing theory or theories. Conversation theory is one such theory used, which is a cybernetic and dialectic framework developed by Pask in 1975.

Laurillard (2007) used conversation theory to create a framework for new technologies to be assessed according to how the technology supports the learning process. Laurillard (2007) posited that conversations are common to all forms of learning. Conversations are available through digitally facilitated location-specific activities. Sharples et al. (2009) used Pask's conversational theory and the writings of Dewey (1916) to propose a theory of m-learning: Students learn using conversation and exploration as mobile devices act as a system in which knowledge can be created and shared.

Activity theory is another theory used to develop a theory of m-learning. Activity theory is a theoretical framework for analyzing people's practices as developmental processes, while considering individual and social influences as interlinked (Kuutti, 1996). Koole (2009), Uden (2007), and Zurita and Nussbaum (2007) all used activity theory to create conceptual frameworks for various aspects of m-learning. Koole designed the Framework for the Rational Analysis of Mobile Education (FRAME), which is based on activity theory as it pertains to Vygotsky's (1978) work on mediation and the zone of proximal development.

Zurita and Nussbaum (2007) used activity theory to develop a model for analyzing the tasks, needs, and outcomes when designing m-learning activities. They used Engeström's (1987) expanded activity theory, which was an extended version of Vygotsky's (1978) conceptualization of the mediated relationship between the learner and the object/mobile device.

Uden (2007) used activity theory to develop a frame for designing applications for m-learning. Connecting with the tenets of activity theory articulated by Engeström (1987), Uden described how m-learning is fundamentally situated and socially mediated. Sharples et al. (2007) also utilized Engeström's 1987 expanded activity theory to describe tool-mediated activity. Sharples et al. dichotomized the framework into two layers: the semiotic layer, with learning as a semiotic system, in which the learner's object-oriented actions are mediated by cultural tools and signs; and the technological layer, in which technologies function as active agents in learning.

There are scholars (viz., Naismith et al., 2004; Keskin & Metcalf, 2011) who developed an m-learning theory using multiple theories. Keskin and Metcalf cited 15 different preexisting theories: constructivism, collaborative learning, situated learning, problem-based learning, context awareness learning, socio-cultural theory, behaviorism, cognitivism, conversational learning, lifelong learning, informal learning, activity theory, and the more recent theories of connectivism, location-based learning, and navigationalism. Naismith et al. (2004) used six existing theories: situated, constructivist, collaborative, behaviorist, informal and lifelong, and learning and teaching support. Thus, the argument has been made that m-learning is somewhat different from other technological learning approaches, and the emerging theories have been explicated. This next section reveals the overarching themes that emerge from both the criteria for developing an m-learning theory and the proposed theories.

The Essence of M-learning

M-learning has been unpacked to reveal the attributes that make m-learning different from conventional tethered e-learning. A pattern of themes emerged from the socially determined nomenclature, the criteria for consideration, and the proposed theories. These themes are context, connectivity, time, and personalization, which are the very essence of m-learning. This next section will provide examples of how the four themes emerged from the literature.

Context

"Mobile learning is a noisy phenomenon where context is everything" (Traxler, 2007, p. 5). Context can refer to the surrounding environment and also the frame of reference in regard to the subject the student is learning. In addition, what makes m-learning unique are the different milieus that are created with the changeable sociocultural and technological structures (Cook, Pachler, & Bachmair, 2011). The portability of the mobile devices breaks through the boundaries of traditional pedagogies to enable learning in a context that corresponds with the learning materials (Jeng, Wu, Huang, Tan, & Yang, 2010).

Koole (2009) affirmed that mobile devices actively support learners in the comprehension and the transfer of information by the way the device allows accessibility to content in multiple formats, emphasizing the contexts and uses of the information. Traxler (2011) described the role of context in m-learning as "context in the wider context" (p. 1), referring to the way in which context becomes progressively richer as it interweaves the context in relation to personalized or location-based services with the social and informal experience that m-learning is.

Connectivity

Connectivity describes two types of interactions. It is the social connections (face-to-face or virtual), or connections with content that are available through the many networks provided. For example, those networks can connect learners to information available on the World Wide Web, or to a learning partner via e-mail. With this strong link to connectivity, it is not surprising that scholars (viz., Laurillard, 2007; Sharples et al., 2009) used Pask's (1975) conversation theory as the underpinning theory behind m-learning. Sharples et al. (2009) in particular emphasized the importance of connectivity, stating, "It is not the learners, nor their technology, but the communicative interaction between these to advance knowing" (p. 4).

Unlike conventional tethered e-learning, connectivity is not hindered by spatial restraints. Learners are evolving both practices and meanings in their interactions that are found inside and outside of formal learning systems (Pachler, Bachmair, & Cook, 2010).

Time

A significant difference between m-learning and other learning approaches is the erosion of formal learning times. The irrelevance of time is a significant shift in the learning paradigm. This shift began with the distance learning and e-learning epoch, as students were able to learn at times beyond the typical academic schedule. Nonetheless, for e-learning the learner is still restricted to times of the day when the learner could sit in front of a computer. With the emergence of m-learning, learning happens whenever the student wishes to learn (Melhuish & Falloon, 2010). Sharples et al. (2009) described m-learning as "learning dispersed in time" (p. 3) as learning can be distributed across different points in time.

Personalization

Personalization is an overarching theme that encompasses context, connectivity, and time as it affords learners the choice of what, where, when, and how they learn. Figure 22.1 provides a simplified overview of the complex field of m-learning as the visual displays the interconnected and nested attributes. There are many attributes embedded within each theme discussed in this section. Some of those attributes overlap within each theme, although personalization is overarching in that it develops as a result of context, connectivity, and time.

To provide an example of this interconnectivity, consider a student who is personalizing her learning as she *chooses* to conduct her mathematics homework outside of traditional school hours and setting. It is 9 p.m. (*time*) and this student is learning while traveling on a bus (*context*) home from an evening with friends. She uses her mobile device to connect with the mathematics (*context*) class website (*connectivity*) and download the homework file to her device. As the student reads over the homework, she realizes that she cannot remember the formula to solve the first problem and chooses to text a friend (*connectivity*) for help. This friend promptly responds and the student is able to complete the work before arriving home at 10 p.m.

Conclusion

Throughout this chapter, the argument is made that m-learning has a number of tangible differences from conventional tethered e-learning. Due to these differences, m-learning requires a separate theory of its own that highlights the unique attributes that are available with this form of learning. Several early theories have been proposed for this relatively new field that tie to theories already in existence. To support the further development of a cogent m-learning theory, the scholarly literature is unpacked to reveal reoccurring themes. Those recurring themes are context, connectivity, time, and personalization.

Note

1 The numbered list does not connote an ordinal position of importance.

References

Brown, H.T. (2005). Towards a model for m-learning in Africa. *International Journal on E-Learning, 4*(3), 299–315.

Caudill, J.G. (2007). The growth of m-learning and the growth of mobile computing: Parallel developments. *International Review of Research in Open and Distance Learning, 8*(2), 1–13.

Collison, G., Elbaum, B., Haavind, S., & Tinker, R. (2000). *Facilitating online learning: Effective strategies for moderators*. Madison, WI: Atwood.

Cook, J., Pachler, N., & Bachmair, B. (2011). Ubiquitous mobility with mobile phones: A cultural ecology for mobile learning. *E-Learning and Digital Media, 8*(3), 181–195.

Crompton, H. (2013a). A historical overview of mobile learning: Toward learner-centered education. In Z.L. Berge & L.Y. Muilenburg (Eds.), *Handbook of mobile learning* (pp. 3–14). Florence, KY: Routledge.

Crompton, H. (2013b). Mobile learning: New approach, new theory. In Z.L. Berge & L.Y. Muilenburg (Eds.), *Handbook of mobile learning* (pp. 47–57). Florence, KY: Routledge.

Dewey, J. (1916). *Democracy and education*. New York: Free Press.

Engeström, Y. (1987). *Learning by expanding: An activity-theoretical approach to development research*. Helsinki, Finland: Orienta-Konsultit.

Jeng, Y.L., Wu, T.T., Huang, T.M., Tan, Q., & Yang, S.J.H. (2010). The add-on impact of mobile applications in learning strategies: A review study. *Educational Technology & Society, 13*(3), 3–11.

Keskin, N. O., & Metcalf, D. (2011). The current perspectives, theories, and practices of mobile learning. *Turkish Online Journal of Educational Technology, 10*(2), 202–208.

Koole, M.L. (2009). A model for framing mobile learning. In M. Ally (Ed.), *Mobile learning: Transforming the delivery of education and training* (pp. 25–50). Edmonton, Canada: Athabasca University Press.

Kuutti, K. (1996). Activity theory as a potential framework for human-computer interaction research. In B.A. Nardi (Ed.), *Context and consciousness: Activity theory and human-computer interaction* (pp. 17–44). Cambridge, MA: MIT.

Laouris, Y., & Eteokleous, N. (2005, Oct 25–28). *We need an educationally relevant definition of mobile learning*. Paper presented at the 4th World Conference on mLearning, Cape Town, South Africa.

Laurillard, D. (2007). Pedagogical forms for mobile learning: Framing research questions. In N. Pachler (Ed.), *Mobile learning: Towards a research agenda* (pp. 153–175). London: WLE Centre.

Melhuish, K., & Falloon, G. (2010). Looking to the future: M-learning with the iPad. *Computers in New Zealand Schools: Learning, Leading, Technology, 22*(3), 1–15.

Naismith, L., Lonsdale, P., Vavoula, G., & Sharples, M. (2004). Literature review in mobile technologies and learning. In *NESTA Futurelab Literature review series* (Report 11). Retrieved November 5, 2011, from Futurelab http://archive.futurelab.org.uk/resources/publications-reports-articles/literature-reviews/Literature-Review203

Pachler, N., Bachmair, B., & Cook, J. (2010). *Mobile learning: Structures, agency, practices*. New York: Springer.

Pask, G. (1975). Minds in media in education and entertainment: Some theoretical comments illustrated by the design and operation of a system for exteriorizing and manipulating individual theses. In R. Trappl & G. Pask (Eds.), *Progress in cybernetics and systems research* (pp. 38–50). London: Hemisphere.

Peters, K. (2009). M-learning: Positioning educators for a mobile connected future. In M. Ally (Ed.), *Mobile learning: Transforming the delivery of education and training* (pp. 113–134). Vancouver, Canada: Athabasca University Press.

Sharples, M. (Ed.). (2006). *Big issues in mobile learning* (Report of a workshop by the Kaleidoscope Network of Excellence Mobile Learning Initiative, pp. 14–19). Nottingham, England: Learning Sciences Research Institute.

Sharples, M., Sánchez, I., A., Milrad., M., & Vavoula, G. (2009). Mobile learning: Small devices, big issues. In N. Balacheff, S. Ludvigsen, T. de Jong, A. Lazonder, & S. Barnes (Eds.), *Technology-enhanced learning: Principles and products* (pp. 223–251). Berlin, Germany: Springer-Verlag.

Sharples, M., Taylor, J., & Vavoula, G. (2007). A theory of learning for the mobile age. In R. Andrews & C. Haythornthwaite (Eds.), *The Sage handbook of e-learning Research* (pp. 221–247). London: Sage.

Sullivan Palincsar, A. (1998). Social constructivist perspectives on teaching and learning. *Annual Review of Psychology, 49*, 345–375.

Tavangarian, D., Leypold, M.E., Nolting, K., & Voigt, D. (2004). Is e-learning the solution for individual learning? *Electronic Journal of E-learning, 2*(2), 273–280.

Traxler, J. (2007). Defining, discussing, and evaluating mobile learning: The moving finger writes and having writ. *International Review of Research in Open and Distance Learning, 8*(2), 1–12.

Traxler, J. (2009a). Learning in a mobile age. *International Journal of Mobile and Blended Learning, 1*(1), 1–12.

Traxler, J. (2009b). The evolution of mobile learning. In R. Guy (Ed.), *The evolution of mobile teaching and learning* (pp. 1–14). Santa Rosa, California: Informing Science Press.

Traxler, J. (2009c). Current state of mobile learning. In M. Ally (Ed.), *Mobile learning: Transforming the delivery of education and training* (pp. 9–24). Edmonton, Canada: Athabasca University Press.

Traxler, J. (2011). Context in a wider context. *Medienpädagogik, 19 Mobile Learning in Widening Contexts.* Retrieved November 8, 2011, from Medienpädagogik Zeitschrift für Theorie und Praxis der Medienbildung http://www.medienpaed.com/zs/content/blogcategory/45/82/

Uden, L. (2007). Activity theory for designing mobile learning. *International Journal of Mobile Learning and Organization, 1*(1), 81–102.

Vygotsky, L.S. (1978). *Mind in society: The development of higher psychological processes.* Cambridge, England: Harvard University Press.

Zurita, G., & Nussbaum, M. (2007). A conceptual framework based on activity theory for mobile CSCL. *British Journal of Educational Technology, 38*(2), 211–235.

23

Developing Instructional Materials and Assessments for Mobile Learning

Jack A. Hyman

Designing Instructional Materials and Assessments for Mobile Learning

Institutions of learning have had to adapt to many changes because of innovations in educational technology. While many institutions have invested a significant amount of time and money in developing sound e-learning systems, few have taken the same measures to identify, create, and deploy solutions for mobile devices. Many learners own one or more mobile devices; yet, most instructional units offered in traditional e-learning settings cannot be viewed on a mobile device anytime, anywhere. Herrington and Herrington (2008) discussed at length the reality that while mobile devices are widespread in use throughout educational institutions for social purposes, little use is made of mobile computing in the learning context. The application of mobile technology in a learning environment lacks theoretical significance.

Learners assume that instructional content and assessments are readily available for mobile delivery. Mobile devices afford the learner the same functions as a computer, while being lightweight. The problem is that the platform, delivery methodology, and methods for disseminating quality instructional content and assessments must be understood in relation to other resources and tools. Mobile devices are not a replacement for personal computers, printed textbooks, or pen and paper solutions (Kukulska-Hulme, 2010). Instructional delivery using mobile technologies is seldom the only platform for learner usage and information consumption. Rather, mobile technologies tend to be utilized as instructional aids for traditional electronic platforms.

This paper will accomplish three objectives. First, it will briefly identify mobile platforms for instructional consumption. Second, it will discuss the best way to deliver instructional content on a mobile device, with emphasis on mobile applications and mobile websites. Finally, the paper will provide a framework for instructional designers and courseware developers to follow, with emphasis on quality dimensions (information quality, system quality, and service quality) for developing sound instruction and assessments for mobile usage.

Mobile Learning

There are many definitions associated with mobile learning (m-learning). Some of these definitions extend e-learning, while others are independent and focus on the use and application of educational theory to define the learning context. Early adapters focused on technology and defined m-learning as the delivery of training by means of mobile devices, such as mobile phones, PDAs, digital audio players, digital cameras, voice recorders, and pen scanners (Keskin & Metcalf, 2011). MoLoNET (2007) defines m-learning as "the exploitation of ubiquitous handheld technologies, together with wireless and mobile phone networks, to facilitate support, enhance and extend the reach of teaching and learning." Other views, including those of Keegen (2005), imply that m-learning should be restricted to learning on small and portable devices. The focus is on "anytime, anywhere" knowledge consumption.

Laouris and Eteokleous (2005) provide several definitions, including that of Quinn (2000), stating that m-learning is "simply learning that takes place with the help of mobile devices" (p. 2). Traxler (2005, p. 2) defined m-learning as "any educational provision where the sole or dominant technologies are handheld or palmtop devices." Sharples (2005, p. 2) stated that m-learning is "a process of coming to know, by which learners in cooperation with their peers and teachers, construct transiently stable interpretations of their world." Fotouhi-Ghazvini, Earnshaw, Moeini, Robison, and Excell (2012) explained that m-learning is not bound by time and space. Rather, it can enhance the process of learning, especially in an academic environment. Learning can occur anywhere. Students can manage data regardless of the learning context. M-learning can apply one or more learning theories, including "Behaviorism, Cognitivism, Constructivism, Situated Learning, Problem-Based Learning, Context Awareness Learning, Socio-Cultural Theory, Collaborative Learning, Conversational Learning, Lifelong Learning, Informal Learning, Activity Theory, Connectivism, Navigationism, and Location-based learning" (Keskin & Metcalf, 2011, p. 202). In this paper, the author assumes that m-learning has limited context awareness; the learner uses a mobile device to acquire instructional materials to increase his or her knowledge, given limits set forth by a course facilitator and based on the target mobile device, mode of delivery, and content quality necessary to achieve skill mastery.

Mobile Device Form Factor

M-learning content and assessments can be viewed on one of four device form factors: smartphone, tablet, feature phone, and e-reader. Each device type can access the Internet to view mobile-oriented content. Device form factors offer some common characteristics such as screen size, portability, interactivity, multimedia presentation, and location-awareness/contextualizing functionality. Table 23.1 outlines four mobile device form factors, as described by the Association of Magazine Media (2011).

Each of the mobile device form factors can augment traditional curricula to varying degrees. Edutopia (2012) noted that, unlike traditional classrooms, where the student is often a passive participant, the mobile classroom requires the student to play an active role in learning, rapidly respond to feedback, and engage in task-based activities. The learner must connect with the content through constructive engagement. Table 23.2 presents an overview of when each form factor is appropriate in the mobile context.

The first question an instructional designer and courseware developer should consider is: What is the instructional outcome and how is the learner supposed to interact with the content? Trifonova and Ronchetti (2003) explain that there are a few considerations: the output (i.e., the

Table 23.1 Types of Mobile Devices That Can Deliver Mobile Content

Type of Device	*Description of Mobile Device Form Factor*
Smartphone	A smartphone is a handheld device that integrates mobile phone capabilities with several features found on a handheld computer or PDA. Smartphones allow users to store information, e-mail, and install programs, along with having a mobile phone in one device.
Tablet	Tablets are devices with touch screen interfaces, screen sizes ranging from 5 inches to 12 inches, color displays, Wi-Fi or 3G Internet connectivity, and advanced mobile operating systems such as Apple iOS, Google Android, Windows 7, or Blackberry.
Feature Phone	A feature phone is a cell phone that contains a fixed set of functions besides voice calling. Feature phones may offer Web browsing, but they cannot download and install applications from an online marketplace. Messaging functionality is limited.
E-reader	An e-reader is a portable electronic device that is designed primarily for reading digital books and periodicals. E-readers use e-ink technology to display content. Some e-readers can access the Internet, download and play Java-based apps, and listen to music.

Table 23.2 Uses for Mobile Devices in the Context of M-learning

Type of Device	*Device Uses in the Context of M-learning*
Feature Phone	• Group discussions via text messaging • Response tool for option-based assessments • Used for photography projects • Voice recorder • Basic Internet surfing
E-Reader	• Reading books in a digital format • Storing paper-based documents • Can replace paper-based library content for digital versions • Source for accessing references (dictionary, thesaurus) • Basic information-seeking tool (only if there is Internet access available)
Smartphone	All the features of feature phones and e-readers plus: • Send e-mail • Send plain and multimedia-based text messages • Review documents created using word processing, spreadsheet, and presentation software • Render multimedia and animation type files that mix sound and audio • Run applications and device-scaled software • View most types of websites • Telephonic services • Synchronous video communication (presence)
Tablet Computer	All the features of feature phones, e-readers, and smartphones plus: • Download multifunctional apps • Act as a computer replacement • Replicate full Internet functionality • Watch and make movies and audio recordings • Take photographs in high resolution • Complete transactional activities that can mimic traditional e-learning platforms.

screen size and resolution capabilities, etc.), the input (i.e., keypad, touch screen, voice input), processing power and memory, and supported applications and media types to be exposed to the learner. The challenge to the instructional designer and courseware developer is to take the e-learning paradigm and shift it to the mobile setting. Cao, Tin, McGreal, Ally, and Coffey (2006) recommend that when developing an m-learning based solution, the content be separated from the device format, as there is no optimal display solution for the various mobile operating systems and web browsers available. A lack of standards in current mobile technologies, which include operating systems and web browsers, creates a challenge for the m-learning developer due to limited capability, flexibility, and ability to render functionality across all device form factors.

Mobile Applications and Mobile Websites

M-learning content can be distributed through one of two channels, a mobile application or a mobile website. Raman (2011) explained that mobile applications are downloaded to the mobile device by the end-user. The application could be offered for free, come at a premium by accessing the phone vendor's application store, or be downloaded from a mobile-ready website. An application is capable of handling complex graphics, can present a more unified user experience, and can make use of a device's native capabilities. An application can use the device's context and sensor technology to personalize the user experience without any configuration. However, mobile websites afford the learner the ability to view much of the same content that appears on a traditional e-learning website. The only real difference between an m-learning and an e-learning website may be that the content may be organized differently so that users can view it on smaller screens. One significant difference that schools consider is the cost of developing a mobile-based solution. If affordability and being technologically agnostic are essential attributes for m-learning implementation, a mobile website is the delivery platform a school should consider.

While mobile applications only operate on a specific operating system (OS), mobile websites are hardware, or OS independent. Mobile websites have evolved as mobile web-browsing, the programmatic markup language, and advances in devices have evolved. With the evolution of mobile phones, the delivery of web content has come a long way. Users of feature phones who review websites on a mobile device have found the experience to be relatively primitive. The OS, along with the device form factor (screen size, input mechanisms, network connectivity, and limited operability between the traditional web and the mobile web browser), led to the development of various alternative solutions for mobile users to view content. Regardless of whether the user has a mobile phone that optimizes the content displayed by creating a separate version of a website, the website version does not change from the Internet version and its mobile counterpart. However, when a website is transcoded to a mobile format without the use of a markup language, usage barriers exist for both the consumer and the content producer.

Smartphone and tablet devices running on OSs such as the Apple iOS, Google Android, Research in Motion Blackberry, or Windows Mobile OS have helped remove several barriers of entry. Each mobile platform provides the user with larger screens that allow for mobility to be maintained, enable haptic interfacing, support high-capacity network connectivity (3G+), and allow for the consumption of not only a mobile website, but also traditional website mediums. Hong and Kim (2011) noted that enjoying full-sized mobile websites that are not WAP- or WML-based still presents problems to mobile users. Nielsen (2010) pointed out that, despite growth in the ability to deliver mobile-ready sites, a site that applies the appropriate parameters in its design receives poor scores on a usability scale.

Buettner and Simmons (2011) compared the differences between mobile applications and mobile websites. The advantage of mobile applications is that they can run offline if no new data needs to be fetched. The mobile application user experience is more consistent and pleasing to the end user. Additionally, a mobile application can take advantage of the device's integrated hardware features. Downloading a mobile application also allows for user-based personalization. These features are not available using the mobile web.

Mobile websites also have several advantages. Mobile websites can be cross-platform compatible. Like mobile applications, a mobile website can access a subset of the device sensors and hardware interfaces to present relevant, timely content. Mobile websites are often able to detect phone orientation, location, and device form factors to cache personal preferences for future usage. Mobile websites use cross-platform web-based markup languages to present relevant information and transactional content. Educational institutions can promote mobile website content with search tools. On the other hand, search is not optimized for mobile applications. Mobile websites can be viewed through a standard mobile web browser. A mobile application requires a separate mobile interface. Distribution, approval, and display of mobile web content does not require approval prior to publishing. Content can also be updated in real time on a mobile website, which is often not the case with mobile applications.

Buettner and Simmons (2011) also indicated that there are several drawbacks with mobile applications and mobile websites. Mobile applications are not cross-platform compatible. Once developed, they are no longer managed by courseware developers, but by the OS marketplace. Developing a mobile application also restricts the number of potential users that can reach a platform.

There are also several drawbacks to using mobile websites. Mobile websites have limited access to geo-location functionality on the device when content is presented through a web browser. A mobile website's user experience is often inconsistent between form factors, as content is rendered using end-user personal preferences. Network connectivity determines a mobile website's availability and performance. Security limitations set by the end user can potentially limit the mobile user experience. Finally, the mobile website user experience is limited because most native mobile browsers are unable to display highly interactive graphical content or utilize built-in phone functionality.

Determining the Mobile Platform

The choice between developing a native application and a mobile website varies significantly. Each of these platforms should include a distinct but strong navigational topology and meaningful user experience, and should present a structured way to submit queries and retrieve results for a targeted audience. The criteria presented are a requisite for m-learning platforms regardless of delivery format or form factor. There are additional considerations that are specific to m-learning because of the need for agnostic user design, widespread availability, and cost to reach the educational marketplace. Table 23.3 addresses key differentiators relevant to m-learning, as adapted by Summerfield (2012) and Hyman (2012).

A Framework for Developing M-learning Instruction and Assessments

Classic information systems success and marketing measurement literature pertaining to quality dimensions and satisfaction measurement are relevant to the development of a framework for m-learning instruction and assessment. The constructs of information quality (IQ), system

Table 23.3 M-learning Selection Criteria for Mobile Websites vs. Mobile Applications

Consideration	*M-Learning Approach*
Immediacy: Instantly accessible across all mobile device form factors through a standard web browser.	Mobile Website
Compatibility: Can be made accessible across multiple device form factors using same instructional design platform. Applications require standalone development for each operating system.	Mobile Website
Upgradability: Applications require a mobile consumer to download a new version for each revision. Mobile OS vendor app store may require approval of content each time new versions are deployed. Upgrades to mobile website content are instantaneous across all form factors. Delivery and presentation are also flexible.	Mobile Website
Findability: Finding m-learning instruction is not dependent on a single authoritative source. Content can be found using search platforms or third-party sources without restrictions.	Mobile Website
Sharing: Sharing content between users is more plausible. Content publishers can easily distribute content in a systematic, streamlined manner across all form factors.	Mobile Website
Lifecycle: The overall time an application is deemed usable is short (i.e. the duration of a course). A mobile website can evolve over time and be versioned for repeat use, making mobile websites less cost prohibitive.	Mobile Website
Supportability: Developers and instructional designers need to support a single platform with a mobile website. Multiple platforms must be supported for native applications.	Mobile Website
Interactivity/Gaming: Highly graphical, multimodal design that does not stream over the Internet is best using a native application. Mobile websites are focused on transactions and content whereas an application is more visual and has a specific purpose.	Native Applications
Personalization: If targeting user-specific data and storing such personalization to ensure user retention, native applications are more appropriate than mobile websites.	Native Applications
Complex Analytical Requirements: If complex calculations, charts, report generation, or graphics must be rendered, a native application is a more appropriate approach for mobile learning.	Native Applications
Connectivity: If the platform requires limited to no use of Internet connectivity post download, the native application approach is recommended.	Native Applications

quality (SQ), and service quality (SERVQUAL) are regarded as elements of user satisfaction (DeLone & McLean, 2003, 2004; Wang & Liao, 2007). Each of these constructs consists of dimensions that are determinants of positive or negative influence in user satisfaction. Learners who are satisfied with the mobile user experience are more likely to adapt mobile instruction and participate in a mobile-based assessment (Wang, Wu, & Wang, 2008).

This section presents a framework, as depicted in Figure 23.1, that the author has derived based the creation of various m-learning based units for smartphone and tablet consumption.

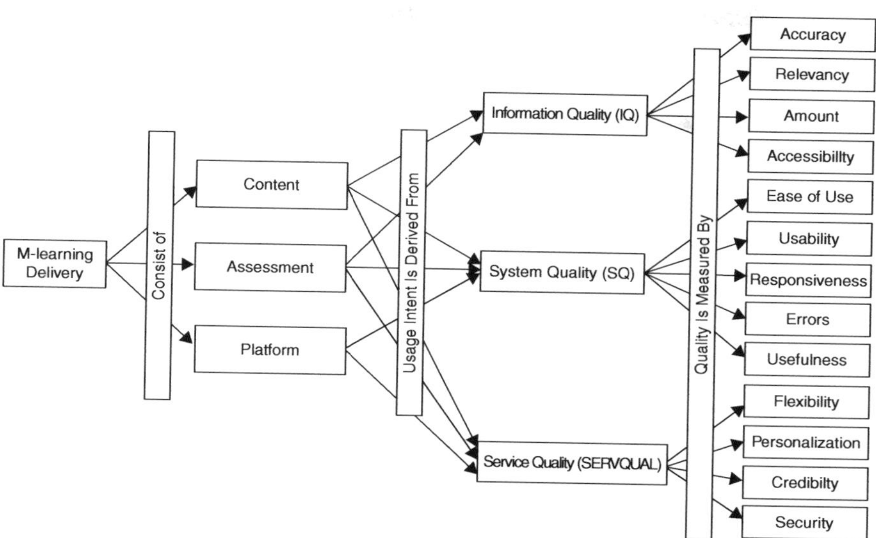

Figure 23.1 Proposed M-learning Delivery Adoption Framework

The framework identifies the essential elements required for the delivery of instruction and assessments using a mobile device, given specific content design, assessment preparation, and platform parameters. To define these three attributes requires a detailed evaluation of the usage intent quality attributes (information, system, and service) that lead to learner adoption and retention. For each quality dimension, there are specific attributes associated with learner acceptance.

Mobile Learning Delivery Satisfaction

Mobile learning delivery satisfaction (MLDS) can be achieved when a learner's need is met given the delivery of content and assessments for one or more mobile platforms. M-learning satisfaction can be measured based on the information consumed by the user (IQ), the physical and emotional qualities presented by the system (SQ), and the intangibles that make the learning experience unique and service oriented (SERVQUAL). Based on the framework proposed in Figure 23.1, m-learning delivery satisfaction as part of the instructional system design (ISD) life cycle consists of three elements: (i) content, (ii) assessment, and (iii) platform. Usage intent is positively or negatively correlated with quality dimensions. Each quality dimension has related attributes that require consideration during the m-learning ISD process.

Well-designed instructional content drives solid assessment creation and enhanced learning experience. The platform synthesizes the content and assessment as a unified solution for learner consumption. Content can be formatted as text, graphics, video, audio, or a combination of formats. Kwon and Lee (2010) indicated that content ubiquity can be achieved assuming the instructional designer and courseware developer adhere to four principles: (i) apply learning activities as part of the content structure, (ii) contextualize learning given a situation, (iii) design the content based on the mobile display, and (iv) present content layouts across platforms. Baird and Whitear (2006) focused on content chunking of instructional content in order to avoid overcrowding of content when using a mobile display. Coursaris and Kim (2006) refer to this in their contextual usability framework as *task-orientation*. Developing content as m-learning objects (MLO) is the approach described by Pierre and Diamantini (2009). An MLO is a succinct module presented in a mobile format not to exceed an amount of time, that integrates text and audio. All three studies provide user-based evidence that the learner preferred the MLO content-based learning experience because ease of use could be achieved on the mobile device; the learning experience was deemed useful because the learning occurred given a context of use, and the use of the mobile device was engaging rather than laborious. Challenges presented by instructional designers and courseware developers through all three studies included mobile form factor size, usability limitations, and unified content design. All three authors agreed with Martin, Pastore, and Snider's (2012) assertion that to develop the appropriate mobile platform, it is essential to address accessibility, functionality, and development practices.

Assessment in traditional learning systems coincides with the completion of a formal learning unit. In the traditional learning setting, a summative assessment, such as a quiz or an exam, is used to assess a learner's proficiency at the end of a given unit. An assessment is a type of learning instrument used to help the learner and the instructor understand strengths and weaknesses. Corrective measures can be made easily due to a symbiosis between instructor and learner. There is often two-way communication, even if the dialogue is applied in an asynchronous e-learning setting. Summative assessments provide a constant feedback loop, are concise in presentation, focus on small chunks of learning, and are more effective for learner efficacy. Woodill (2012) implied that using formative assessments is a better approach for m-learning. Formative evaluations should be integrated into the instructional content so that as learners are engaged in the unit, they gain valuable ongoing, constructive feedback. M-learning-based mobile assessment should act more as integrative guidance or scaffolding so that the learner can move to the next step in the learning process. Formative assessment is often integrated into the instructional unit as part of the overall unit messaging. Summative instruction and assessment enables the instructor to attain the necessary standalone real-time metrics to increase learner intellectual capacity. While Quillen (2011) felt that most mobile apps do not allow teachers to monitor qualitative-oriented student progress or measure student data in the same way as can established classroom or e-learning settings, the learning experience can be evaluated through the use of metrics based on the learner's context of use, as well as through self-tracking analytics mechanisms. Mobile-assisted feedback, such as confirmation queues, instant feedback (sound or visual oriented), or dialogues can be presented just in time to provide the learner and the instructor assurances on information, system, and service quality.

Quality Dimensions

In the proposed framework, content, assessment, and platform usage, intent is highly linked with quality dimensions such as IQ, SQ, and SERVQUAL. When instruction and mobile assessments are poorly suited for mobile devices, users may abandon the use of their mobile device (Zhang, 2007). Designing the optimal m-learning platforms presents harder challenges than traditional software design because of technical barriers and end-user resistance to the use of m-learning tools (Holtzblatt, 2005). Traditional information systems literature relates the satisfaction of a system in terms of how end users perceive usability and usage intent to quality constructs such as IQ, SQ, and SERVQUAL (Aladwani & Palvia, 2002; Bailey & Pearson, 1983; Barnes & Vidgen, 2003; DeLone & McLean, 1992, 2003; Doll & Torkzadeh, 1988; Ives, Olson, & Baroudi,

1983; Kettinger & Lee, 1994; Kettinger, Lee, & Lee, 1995; Seddon, 1997; McKinney, Yoon, & Zahedi, 2002; Parasuraman, Zeithaml, & Berry, 1985; Wang, Tang, & Tang, 2001; Wang & Tang, 2003; Zmud, 1979). While DeLone and McLean (2003) asserted that user satisfaction can be ascertained by using the variables of IQ, SQ, and SERVQUAL, the context and the dimensions identified in traditional information systems literature are not applicable to m-learning. Typical m-learning environments depart significantly from previous e-learning and traditional information systems due to physical limitations, which include the m-learning platform on which instruction is disseminated.

IQ is both a product and a service in the m-learning setting. The content delivery platform, be it instruction or assessment, is relevant to the information quality dimension. Information quality in the m-learning context also includes the input and output of information into the system and how it impacts learning effectiveness. Characteristics associated with IQ include the amount of information presented in both the content delivery and structure of an assessment, content accuracy, relevancy of information based on instruction objectives, and accessibility of instruction across device platforms.

How systems work and the way in which a user interacts with the learning environment impacts performance outcomes. SQ is a determinant of usage, success, and satisfaction. In the mobile learning context, SQ is a way of evaluating the user experience, the quality of the mobile platform, and the value of the delivery format.

SERVQUAL is often deemed intangible, as a service cannot be counted, measured, inventoried, tested, and verified as absolute until the end user begins using the information system. In the mobile learning context, SERVQUAL faces the same challenges. For an instructional designer and courseware developer to achieve a measurable experience, SERVQUAL can be defined as the ability for the learner to feel confident with the environment in which he or she is engaging; learning results from: (a) institutional and content credibility, (b) appropriate levels of security, (c) reliability of the product and services being presented, and (d) learner-driven personalization.

Conclusion

If the instructional designer or courseware developer is to be successful in the delivery of m-learning content and assessments, varying degrees of IQ, SQ, and SERVQUAL should be integrated into the platform of choice, be it a native application or mobile website. Given the criteria presented for selecting the appropriate delivery format and device form factor, the instructional designer and courseware developer can create content and assessments that lead to learner engagement regardless of mobile context. In designing the unit, the m-learning experience should be user friendly, efficient in the presentation of content, effective in delivering specific learning objectives, and error free to avoid learner abandonment.

Structured yet concise design, accompanied by one or more summative assessments, is appropriate and the most accepted approach for formal m-learning settings. If learning is informal or contains a variety of multimodal instructional techniques delivered through the mobile platform, formative rather than summative assessments are recommended. Formative assessments reduce learner abandonment because fatigue may result if the end user becomes overwhelmed by the learning platform.

M-learning satisfaction can be achieved by creating formative-based short, target-oriented units that are user friendly, content rich, and provide ample feedback. The content delivered should lack substantive interactivity so that SQ and SERVQUAL can be strong. Following such an approach will result in broad learner acceptance. In order to achieve broad appeal, the characteristics associated with the quality dimensions should be applied to the creation of instruction and assessments based on the formality of the learning objectives, the target audience, the delivery format chosen, the target delivery devices used to present the instructional unit, and user interaction principles for the instructional context of use.

References

Aladwani, A.M., & Palvia, P.C. (2002). Developing and validating an instrument for measuring user-perceived web quality. *Information & Management, 39*(6), 467–476. doi:10.1016/S0378–7206(01)00113–6

Association of Magazine Media. (2011). *Persona, mobile devices: Tablets, e-readers, and smartphones* [White paper]. Retrieved from Magazine Publishers of America website: http://www.magazine.org/

Bailey, J.E., & Pearson, S.W. (1983). Development of a tool for measuring and analyzing computer user satisfaction. *Management Science, 29*(5), 530–545. doi:10.1287/mnsc.29.5.530

Baird, P., & Whitear, C. (2006). *Mobile charting with Flash Lite 2: Designing for the mobile device interface.* Retrieved from Adobe, Mobile and Devices Developer Center website: http://www.adobe.com/devnet/devices.html

Barnes, S.J., & Vidgen, R. (2003). Measuring website quality improvements: A case study of the forum on strategic management knowledge exchange. *Industrial Management & Data Systems, 103*, 297–306. doi:10.1108/02635570310477352

Buettner, K., & Simmons, A. M. (2011). Mobile web and native apps: How one team found the happy medium. *Lecture Notes in Computer Science, 6769*, 549–554. doi:10.1007/978–3–642–21675–6_63

Cao, Y., Tin, T., McGreal, R., Ally, M., & Coffey, S. (2006, July). The Athabasca University mobile library project: Increasing the boundaries of anytime and anywhere learning for students. *Proceedings of the 2006 International Conference on Wireless Communications and Mobile Computing* (pp. 1289–1294). doi:10.1145/1143549.1143808

Coursaris, C.K., & Kim, D. (2006, August). A qualitative review of empirical mobile usability studies. In G. Rodriguez-Abitia & I. Ania (Eds.), *Proceedings of the 2006 Americas Conference on Information Systems* (pp. 1–14). Acapulco, Mexico: Association for Information Systems.

DeLone, W.H., & McLean, E.R. (1992). Information system success: The quest for the dependent variable. *Information Systems Research, 3*(1), 60–95. Retrieved from isr.journal.informs.org/

DeLone, W.H., & McLean, E.R. (2003). The DeLone and McLean model of information systems success: A ten-year update. *Journal of Management Information Systems, 19*(4), 9–30. Retrieved from http://www.jmis-web.org/

DeLone, W.H., & McLean, E.R. (2004). Measuring e-Commerce success: Applying the DeLone and McLean information systems success model. *International Journal of Electronic Commerce, 9*(1), 31–48. Retrieved from http://www.ijec-web.org/

Doll, W.J., & Torkzadeh, G. (1988). The measurement of end-user computing satisfaction. *MIS Quarterly, 12*(2), 259–274. doi:10.2307/248851

Edutopia. (2012). *Mobile devices for learning: What you need to know.* Retrieved from http://www.edutopia.org/files/existing/pdfs/guides/edutopia-mobile-learning-guide.pdf

Fotouhi-Ghazvini, F., Earnshaw, R., Moeini, A., Robison, D., & Excell, P. (2011). From e-learning to m-Learning–The use of mixed reality games as a new educational paradigm. *International Journal of Interactive Mobile Technologies, 5*(2), 17–25. doi:10.3991/ijim.v5.i2.1463

Herrington, A.J., & Herrington, J.A. (2008). Authentic mobile learning in higher education. In P. Jeffrey (Ed.), *Proceedings of the Australian Association for Research in Education (AARE) International Educational Research Conference* (pp. 1–9). Australia: AARE.

Holtzblatt, K. (2005). Designing for the mobile device: Experiences, challenges, and methods. *Communications of the ACM, 48*(7), 33–35. Retrieved from http://cacm.acm.org/

Hong, S., & Kim, S.C. (2011). Mobile website usability: Developing guidelines for mobile web via smart phones. In A. Marcus (Ed.), *1st International Conference on Design, User Experience, and Usability. Theory, methods, tools and practices* (pp. 564–572). Orlando, FL: Human-Computer International.

Hyman, J.A. (2012). *Towards an understanding of mobile website contextual usability and its impact on mobile commerce* (Doctoral dissertation). Available from ProQuest Dissertation and Theses database. (UMI No. 3523972)

Ives, B., Olson, M.H., & Baroudi, J.J. (1983). The measure of user information satisfaction. *Communications of the ACM, 30*(5), 586–603. Retrieved from http://cacm.acm.org/

Keegen, D. (2005, October). The incorporation of mobile learning into mainstream education and training. *Proceedings of mLearn 2005–4th World Conference on m-Learning*. Retrieved from http://www.mlearn.org.za/CD/papers/keegan1.pdf

Keskin, N.O., & Metcalf, D. (2011). The current perspectives, theories and practices of mobile learning. *Turkish Online Journal of Educational Technology, 10*(2), 202–208. Retrieved from http://www.tojet.net/articles/v10i2/10220.pdf

Kettinger, W.J., & Lee, C.C. (1994). Perceived service quality and user satisfaction with the information services function. *Decision Sciences, 25*, 737–766. doi:10.1111/j.1540-5915.1994.tb01868.x

Kettinger, W.J., Lee, C.C., & Lee, S. (1995). Global measures of information service quality: A cross-national study. *Decision Sciences, 26*(5), 559–588. doi:10.1111/j.1540-5915.1995.tb01441.x

Kukulska-Hulme, A. (2010). Mobile learning as a catalyst for change. *Open Learning, 25*(3), 181–185. doi: 10.1080/02680513.2010.511945

Kwon, S., & Lee, J.E. (2010). Design principles of m-learning for ESL. *Procedia-Social and Behavioral Sciences, 2*, 1884–1889. Retrieved from http://www.journals.elsevier.com/procedia-social-and-behavioral-sciences/

Laouris, Y., & Eteokleous, N. (2005, October). We need an educationally relevant definition of mobile learning. *Proceedings of mLearn 2005–4th World Conference on m-Learning*. Retrieved from http://www.mlearn.org.za/CD/papers/Laouris%20&%20Eteokleous.pdf

Martin, F., Pastore, R., & Snider, J. (2012). Developing mobile based instruction. *TechTrends, 56*(5), 46–51. doi:10.1007/s11528-012-0598-9

McKinney, V., Yoon, K., & Zahedi, F. (2002). The measurement of web-customer satisfaction: An expectation and disconfirmation approach. *Information Systems Research, 13*(3), 296–315. doi:10.1287/isre.13.3.296.76

MoLoNET. (2007). *What is the mobile learning?* Retrieved from http://www.molenet.org.uk/

Nielsen, J. (2010). iPhone Apps Need Low Starting Hurdle. Retrieved from http://www.nngroup.com/articles/mobile-apps-initial-use/

Parasuraman, A., Zeithaml, V.A., & Berry, L. L (1985). A conceptual model of service quality and its implications for future research. *Journal of Marketing, 49*(4), 41–51. Retrieved from http://www.marketingpower.com/

Pierre, M., & Diamantini, D. (2009). From e-learning to mobile learning: New opportunities. In M. Ally (Ed.), *Mobile learning: Transforming the delivery of education and training* (pp. 247–264). Edmonton, Canada: AU Press.

Quillen, I. (2011). Mobile apps for education evolving. *Education Week, 4*(2), 16–17. Retrieved from http://www.edweek.org

Raman, S. (2011, October 7). Mobile web vs. mobile apps: Which strategy is best? *Fierce Mobile*. Retrieved from http://www.fiercemobilecontent.com/special-reports/mobile-web-vs-mobile-apps-which-should-i-choose

Seddon, P.B. (1997). A respecification and extension of the DeLone and McLean model of IS success. *Information Systems Research, 8*(3), 240–253. doi:10.1287/isre.8.3.240

Sharples, M. (2005, April). Learning as conversation: Transforming education in the mobile age. *Proceedings of Conference on Seeing, Understanding, Learning in the Mobile Age* (pp. 147–152). Retrieved from http://www.socialscience.t-mobile.hu/2005/Sharples_final.pdf

Summerfield, J. (2012). Mobile website vs. mobile application (Application): Which is best for your organization? *Human Service Solutions*. Retrieved from http://www.hswsolutions.com/services/mobile-web-development/mobile-website-vs-apps/

Traxler, J. (2005). Learning in a mobile age. *International Journal of Mobile and Blended Learning, 1*(1), 1–12. Retrieved from http://www.academia.edu/171500/Learning_in_a_Mobile_Age

Trifonova, A., & Ronchetti, M. (2003). Where is mobile learning going? *Proceedings of the World Conference on E-Learning in Corporate, Government, Healthcare, and Higher Education, 2003*(1), 1794–1801. Retrieved from http://www.aace.org/conf/elearn/

Wang, Y.S., & Liao, Y.W. (2007). The conceptualization and measurement of m-commerce user satisfaction. *Computers in Human Behavior, 23*(1), 381–398. doi:10.1016/j.chb.2004.10.017

Wang, Y.S., & Tang, T.I. (2003). Assessing customer perceptions of websites service quality in digital marketing environments. *Journal of End User Computing, 15*(3), 14–31. doi:10.4018/joeuc.2003070102

Wang, Y.S., Tang, T.I., & Tang, J.T. (2001). An instrument for measuring customer satisfaction toward websites that market digital products and services. *Journal of Electronic Commerce Research, 2*(3), 89–102. Retrieved from http://www.csulb.edu/journals/jecr/

Wang, Y.S., Wu, M.C., & Wang, H.Y. (2008). Investigating the determinants and age and gender differences in the acceptance of mobile learning. *British Journal of Educational Technology, 40*(1), 92–118. doi:10.1111/j.1467–8535.2007.00809.x

Woodill, G. (2012, July 6). Mobile tracking and assessment of informal learning: Part of a revolution? [Blog post]. Retrieved from http://floatlearning.com/2012/07/mobile-tracking-and-assessment-of-informal-learning-part-of-a-revolution/

Zhang, D. (2007). Web content adaptation for mobile handheld devices. *Communications of the ACM, 50*(2), 75–80. Retrieved from http://cacm.acm.org/

Zmud, R.W. (1979). Individual differences and MIS success: A review of the empirical literature. *Management Science, 25*, 966–979. doi:10.1287/mnsc.25.10.966

24

Emerging Learning Ecologies as a New Challenge and Essence for E-learning

Antonella Esposito, Albert Sangrà and Marcelo Fabián Maina

Introduction

This chapter discusses the perspectives of 'ecology' and 'learning ecology' as lenses to consider e-learning (Andrews & Haythornthwaite, 2011; Ellis & Goodyear, 2009) in the age of the "social Web" (Boulos & Wheleer, 2007). The metaphor of 'ecology' has variously been adopted to shed light on the entangled facets of sociocultural activities and educational contexts. Drawn from studies on ecosystems, the notion of ecology refers to the dynamic relationships between individual organisms and their environment (as a whole identified as an 'ecosystem'), characterized by interactions with other living or nonliving organisms.

Key attributes of ecology such as 'ecology' such as 'complex', 'self-organized' and 'adaptive', as applied to digital ecosystems (Louviere, 2012) lead to consideration of the range of conditions underlying the self-organization of learners exchanging information and knowledge in the open Web. The notion of ecology refers to the activities occurring among learners and digital tools and is concerned with the endless cycle of technology change to which users and educational institutions are subject and have to respond. Ecological perspectives

> may offer a new 'language' to conceptualise change and stasis in a variety of environments, contexts and spaces of activity, which exist in linked scales or levels, ranging from the global to the local, from the micro to the macro.
>
> (Hodgson & Spours, 2009, p. 9)

The ecology metaphor is differently inflected according to sociotechnical approaches, focusing on the mutual influence of people and technologies (Andrews & Haythornthwaite, 2011; Nardi & O'Day, 1999) or to sociocultural approaches, privileging the exploration of the relationships between the learners and the intricacies of the local environment (Barron, 2006; Luckin, 2010; Pachler, Cook, & Bachmair, 2010). Properly indicated as 'learning ecology', it is adopted to explore learning contexts and processes of communities of learners and individual learners; and it is thought of as *hybrid* when physical and virtual configurations are considered as competing or blurring.

As applied to e-learning, learning ecologies suggest the need to identify continuities and discontinuities in the adoption of technology-mediated learning practices as an informed basis for the design in any empirical settings of e-learning interventions (Ellis & Goodyear, 2009). It helps to gain a holistic view on the components of the e-learning enterprise (Andrews & Haythornthwaite, 2011) and on the needs and interests of higher education learners promoting a collaboration culture via digital networks (Mitchell, 2002).

Moreover, the notion of learning ecologies is functional for accounting phenomena related to the informalisation of education (Sangrà & Wheleer, 2013) and finds valid allies in ICTs (Information and Communication Technologies) and online learning. In fact, learning ecologies provide a frame to interpret the manifold learning opportunities enabled by the current complex digital landscape, in which issues such as the integration of formal, informal and non-formal opportunities and needs for personalization are at work to improve lifelong learning and professional development (Sangrà et al., 2011). Furthermore, this notion highlights the *distributing potential* (Brown, 2012) of the Web 2.0 tools across more or less resilient contexts, rather than underlying claims on general, celebrated affordances of emerging digital media. On the other hand, just the versatility of the ecological metaphor and the variety of ways in which it is adopted in literature constitutes both the strength and the weakness of this construct.

This chapter briefly outlines the ways 'ecology' and 'learning ecology' are adopted to interpret digitally mediated educational contexts, account for e-learning in higher education and refer to emergent forms of networked environments and related learning practices. Moreover, the chapter sketches a discussion on the extent to which an ecological approach and the notion of learning ecologies are applied to a research case focusing on the investigation of PhD students adopting social media in their doctoral journey.

Learning Ecology and Digital Ecosystems

A review of literature discussing ecological approaches concerned with teaching and learning issues in a digital age returns a range of terms and conceptual definitions. For instance, these definitions show a more or less strong legacy from studies on biological ecosystems, variously treat the Web as a new kind of learning environment or as a component in a more complex entanglement among individuals and tools, and focus on sociocultural contexts or on the metaphorical power of specific ecological concepts. This flexibility implies opportunities and challenges for the researcher, who has to define her analytical focus in order to better orient her choice.

Like other theoretical frames such as activity system and actor–network theory, ecological views draw attention to the "cyclical and emergent nature of human activity" (Andrews & Haythornthwaite, 2011, p. 159), including learning, as related to broader social and cultural processes (Lave & Wenger, 1991). In the last decade of twentieth century the advent of the Web is often examined through the lens of 'learning ecology', in order to explore the extended learning possibilities enabled by the Web and to examine learning environments in a more systematic way.

Seely Brown (2000, p. 20) views the Web as a learning medium enabling a "new, self-catalytic system", namely a 'learning ecology', to emerge. This 'self-catalytic system' is characterized by a dense fabric of intellectual interactions occurring everywhere and among diverse subjects, and producing and expanding the core competencies of a local context. Seely Brown (1999) focuses on *knowledge ecologies*, defined as "an open system, dynamic and interdependent, diverse, partially self-organizing and adaptive" (p. 3), and highlights affordances of twenty-first-century modes of knowledge building an educational system should take into account.

Unlike most ecological theory, especially focusing on populations rather than on individuals, Looi (2001) defines Internet as an ecology in which anyone can become an author and contributes content. It is "the first mass media that is becoming product of its audience" (p. 19). The Internet fosters "the growth and richness of learning ecologies" (p. 19) by conveying multiple media formats, providing diversity of participation and information access, enabling new forms of learning communities and supporting links among people, information, tools and artifacts.

Authors such as Davenport (1997) and Nardi and O'Day (1999) draw attention to the ecology approach applied to information technology. Nardi and O'Day develop their seminal conceptualization of *information ecologies*, defined as the interconnected system of "tools, people, values and practices in a particular local environment" (1999, p. 49). In such systems *keystone species* are organisms playing a crucial role in the functioning of the ecology, even if their work is invisible and peripheral: they preserve the key functions within the ecosystem, ensuring sustainability and "balance found in motion, not stillness" (p. 53). The concept of *keystone species* was introduced by Robert Paine's (1966) studies on biological ecosystem, where keystone species are said to have a disproportionately large effect on the species assemblage despite the fact that they are low in number of exemplars. The role of a keystone species is analogous to the architectural function of a keystone in an arch and includes organisms which "(I) control potential dominants, (II) act as mutualists, (III) provide critical resources, and (IV) modify the environment" (Payton, Fenner & Lee, 2002, p. 5). Applying this concept to scholarly community, Nardi and O'Day attribute to librarians a role as keystone species: in fact, they preserve modes of knowledge distribution while introducing new technology-mediated practices, enabling innovative ways to access, create and distribute materials. The interplay of individuals and technologies is interpreted according to the key concept of 'locality', that is related to participants in specific settings who "construct the identities of their technologies through the rhythms and patterns of their use" (Nardi & O'Day, 1999, p. 55). In fact, a technological application, for instance a group page curated in Facebook, is located in a network of relationships comprised of people using it and other kinds of related applications and devices.

Focusing on school-based education, Zaho and Frank (2003) develop a relevant analytical framework aiming to integrate the diverse factors affecting the adoption of ICT in the classroom. These factors are often examined in an isolated manner, leading to ill-defined explanations of what the introduction of technology implies in educational settings. Zaho and Frank describe classrooms as ecosystems in which teachers belong to a 'keystone species' and technological innovations are seen as "invasions of exotic species" (p. 9). Interestingly, they liken technologies to living species, said to have a similar evolution. Reaching interdependence (a state of internal equilibrium) among the different factors and living and nonliving species plays a key role in the acceptance and adoption of ICT. This view is aligned to a conception of the digitally permeated classroom as a 'digital ecosystem', in which the interplay between control and chaos is analyzed through the open exchange of information occurring in person-to-person and digital activities (Louviere, 2012).

Within a sociocultural approach, Barron defines the notion of learning ecology as the "set of contexts found in physical or virtual spaces that provide opportunities for learning" (2006, p. 195) which may include formal, informal and nonformal settings. She pursues a research interest in fostering 'technological fluency' in her students and in exploring "synergies between participation in technologically mediated informal learning activities and more formal educational environments" (p. 198). She aims at highlighting the conditions enabling boundary-crossing activities and examining the characteristics of diverse learning spaces, intended as specific contexts showing a "unique configuration of activities, material resources, relationships, and the interactions that emerge from them" (p. 198).

Barab et al. (1999) suggest context is fundamental in the ecological approach to learning and focuses on the learner's participation in a community of practice. In their perspective the learner (self) is coupled within the learning context (non-self) and "the individual, the task, the intention, practices, meanings and environmental particulars exist as parts of an interrelated system, not as isolated components" (p. 354). A more radical view of context and ecological learning is taken by Frielick (2004), who builds on an emergent ecological philosophy. He suggests the interweaving of individual and universal mind, and on stances attendant to fluid identities in networked environments. He sees teaching and learning as "an ecosystemic process of transforming information into knowledge, in which teacher, subject and student relationships are embedded or situated in a context where complex interacting influences shape the quality of learning outcomes" (Frielick, 2004, p. 328).

Normak, Pata, and Kaipainen (2012) set out to provide a universal theoretical framework to structure and enable design of self-directed learning opportunities. To this end they propose an ecological approach to learning processes in which spatial concepts are particularly valued. In their model, a learner develops a learning path within a niche (or between niches) in a learning space, moving from a progressive series of steps toward a final target, whilst absorbing suggestions from the learning community.

Within the interdisciplinary fields of information systems and media studies, the spontaneous combinations of technologies and mixed forms of physical and virtual are named as 'digital ecologies' (Girard & Stark, 2007). Crabtree and Rodden (2008) are interested in the socially organized ways a technology-enhanced environment affords collaboration. They discuss the concept of 'hybrid ecologies' as a subsystem of digital ecologies, characterized by new kinds of environments merging physical and digital interaction and providing the user with a new fragmented interaction experience.

Given this brief review of terms and approaches, our choice is directed toward a sociocultural perspective on 'learning ecology', in which the transitions of the individuals across a range of contexts providing diverse learning opportunities (Barron, 2006) can improve the understanding of the interdependence of the institutional and the personal level in an educational use of emerging ICTs.

Ecological Approaches to E-learning

The ecology metaphor is used to better analyze the entanglement between technology and higher education: from the 'microsystem' level, considering the factors influencing the individual's immediate environment to 'macrosystem' level, focusing on the interplay of settings in the wider society (Bronfenbrenner, 1979). Taking an ecological approach to student experience of e-learning in higher education provides a perspective for thinking of the 'new' and the 'traditional' technological means and related learning and sociocultural practices in educational contexts as a place "in which new and old entities find ways of coexisting" (Ellis & Goodyear, 2009, p. 17). This approach stresses cooperation, relationships and interdependence rather than competition and polarisations. Reaching balance and sustainability becomes crucial for embedding innovations, against approaches focusing on technology as a 'challenger' and a driver of disrupting change in the pre-existing educational system. Ellis and Goodyear (2009) elaborate on an ecological framework in which learning enfolds the key functions of teaching and learning, research and service in higher education. This ecological approach fosters the self-awareness of the diverse parts against the whole among stakeholders, a systematic collection of feedback about the effectiveness of specific interventions and a recursive self-correction in the effort to respond to rapid change. An ecological approach suggests a participatory nature of e-learning design, policy and research processes. In fact, it is being applied to reconsider quality and assessment practices in learning with Web 2.0 tools (e.g. Ehlers, 2010; Manion & Selfe, 2012).

The ecology-grounded concept of 'resilience' is the ability to learn and adapt, smooth risks and find effective solutions preserving one's own identity and key functions (Walker et al., 2004). This concept gained an increasing importance in discourses related to the relationships between technology and higher education, challenged by socioeconomic disruption (Attwell, 2010; Downes, 2010; Jones, Selby, & Sterling, 2010).

Hall and Winn (2010) discuss this concept as applied to university educational systems and to open education practices enabled by digital networks. They endorse a critical view of technology used in higher education, aiming to promote through open education a deeper engagement of all stakeholders in identifying reliable solutions in times of crisis. Open forms of higher education are said to be crucial "in framing spaces for personal and communal resilience" (p. 6), prefiguring more complex learning futures. In their view, despite the range of tensions within universities, technology plays a key role in enabling open curricula for resilience. It improves students' agency; provides diversity of approaches and modes of communication and production; and facilitates effective feedback and as a consequence enables students to recognize the impact of their actions.

Unlike ecology approaches endorsing overall perspectives, Andrews and Haythornthwaite (2011) consider a 'personal' ecological view on e-learning, resonating the current "on-the-ground experiences of teachers and students" (2011, p. 157), in order to better understand expectations and responses to new technologies demands. They refer to 'personal ecologies' as a new way to think about e-learning, since pervasiveness of social media and ownership of personal devices are challenging the conventional view of e-learning as an institution-bounded set of technology-mediated learning practices. They build on Nardi and O'Day's (1999) information ecologies and focus on university students seen as individual actors co-evolving with the academic environment and emerging as new 'species' of e-learners, previously playing a 'peripheral' role. The sociotechnical combinations of offline and online communication tools are said to be increasingly complex and to prefigure "cyber-local e-learning classes" (Andrews & Haythornthwaite, 2011, p. 152) in which learners strive to manage control about potentially competing ecologies, in order to design their own learning context (Luckin, 2008). This approach of 'personal ecologies' can be coupled to an ecological view of agency (Priestly, Edwards, & Priestly, 2012), in which the capacity of the individual is entangled with contextual factors and can be understood spatially and temporally.

With an aim to design technology-rich learning activities, Rose Luckin (2008, 2010) devises the learner-centric framework of 'ecology of resources'. Focusing on the individual learner in their ecosystem, it "considers the resources with which an individual interacts as potential forms of assistance that can help that individual to learn" (Luckin, 2010, p. 159). The goal is to identify the components (people, technologies, frames) supporting the educational experience of learners and any related adjustment providing learners with the appropriate scaffolding. The learner's intentionality is the axis from which the context can be interpreted as unified lived experience, making sense of the multiple interactions between people, and activities and resources. A context is always "local to a learner", since it consists of an individual's subjective experience of the world, that is always spatially and historically situated (2010, p. 18). In this view, technology plays a mediation role helping "to make these connections in an operational sense" (p. 18). Emerging technologies have a peculiar role as mediational tools: they foster the production of "learner-generated contexts" (Luckin et al., 2010, p. 74) and provide students with the opportunity to achieve "greater agency" (p. 74) in defining goals and boundaries of their learning contexts. This model provides an individual perspective to look at learning ecologies and considers static and dynamic representations of the interactions occurring between the learner and "potential forms of assistance" (Luckin, 2010, p. 111).

Emerging Learning Ecologies

The ecological metaphor is specifically used to suggest (Siemens, 2003) and explain the nature of the Web 2.0 phenomenon as "an artifact evolving with the shifting user engagement" (Brown, 2012, p. 50) and enabling open participatory learning ecosystems (Seely Brown & Adler, 2008).

Williams, Karousou, and Mackness (2011, p. 39) point to "learning ecologies in Web 2.0" (*sic*) as *loci* in which new kinds of learners are developing their self-directed learning practices. They refer to these pioneer-learners as "*silent experts* in how, where and by whom they want to be educated" (p. 41). These "silent experts" strive to balance "emergent and prescriptive learning" by coping with "openness and constraint" (p. 55) provided by the open Web and by institution-led educational opportunities.

Likewise, Pata and Laanpere (2011) focus on competing formal and informal digitally mediated modes of learning in higher education. They provide a vision of learning ecologies as biological systems rather than as metaphors. In their assumption networked learning environments actually function like ecosystems. They build on the construct of "hybrid learning ecosystems" (slide 5) to highlight the tensions between formal educational assets and "open learning ecosystems" (para. 1) where digitally literate learners are dwelling in the social Web. Their view stresses the key issues related to the opportunities for learners arising from the open Web and the commitment required to the educational institutions to shape and channel these opportunities.

Finally, working on the emergence of learning with mobile devices, Pachler, Cook, and Bachmair (2010) develop a sociocultural perspective on learning ecology. Learning is meant to be a meaning-making process. They view mobile learning as "an educational response to complex cultural changes in socialization" (p. 155), with a special reference to individualised mass communication. Their ecological perspective considers mobile learning in its interplay with changing sociocultural and pedagogical contexts. They devise an analytical framework interweaving the dimensions of 'agency' (the capacity of individuals to appropriate mobile devices according to personal relevance), technical and institutional 'structures' and 'cultural practices', linked to the uptake of digital tools for everyday life communication and for educational uses, inside and outside institutions.

It is worth noting that in Web 2.0 literature a sense of 'ecology' is usually cited (but it is sometimes tacit) along with the conceptualizations of the PLE (Personal Learning Environment) which is "related to the use of technology for learning focusing on the appropriation of tools and resources by the learner" (Buchem, Attwell, & Torres, 2011, p. 1). However, in order to gain insights on the individual learner's moves across learning ecologies in formal and informal settings, it seems to be more useful to consider the theoretical stances attendant to the role of the 'social presence' in e-learning settings (Dron & Anderson, 2007; Garrison & Anderson, 2003). In fact, social presence assumes a pivotal role in not only setting the educational climate but also in supporting discourse and creating the educational experience (Garrison & Anderson, 2003). This key role can gradually evolve, according to three different levels of learners aggregation, from Group to Network to Collective. These three levels are characterized by different group-minds enabled by the social software tools: "aggregated groups may move amongst the three models as their collective needs are modified over time and context" (Dron & Anderson, 2007, p. 4). In this view, it can be advanced that 'social presence' could variously affect student agency of, as an example, individual doctoral researchers striving to tentatively adopt social software in order to build new forms of academic socialization.

An Ecological Approach in the Study on Doctoral E-researchers

Given the illustrated review of ecological approaches and concepts, this section sketches a possible application of some ecological stances to a specific case study. This chapter stems from ongoing research focusing on how the doctoral journey is changing from the impact of new digitally mediated practices. It makes the case for 'personal ecologies' (Andrews & Haythornthwaite, 2011) of Italian doctoral researchers, dealing with the learning opportunities provided by their formal research training setting and by the open Web. It is designed to illustrate how alternative or complementary learning spaces and temporal configurations are being utilized and co-constructed by a niche group of PhD candidates—named as 'doctoral e-researchers'—as they are absorbing conventional practices and tacit norms from a defined research department. In an early definition, doctoral e-researchers are PhD scholars using social media to carry out activities such as preliminarily exploring new topics, searching for updated research materials, disseminating early findings, experiencing networking in digital spaces, improving their own personal development, critically discussing relevant issues and collecting and organizing inquiry data and the research project as a whole. The exploratory approach of the study is directed to reveal any tensions occurring between institution-led prescribed learning practices and these self-organised digitally mediated practices undertaken by the doctoral researchers. Personal ecologies of doctoral researchers are thought of as a possible element of discontinuity in academic contexts where digitally mediated practices are enacted but actually not yet thematized to be an integral part of the formation of future researchers.

An ecological view of agency and the concepts of 'resilience' and 'keystone species' are considered useful to frame the case of doctoral researchers working in academic contexts comprised of hybrid (physical/digital) spaces that influence each other (Kazmer, 2005).

This study focuses on individual learners rather than on doctoral students as 'population': the suggested perspective on analysis is therefore to be developed at a micro level (Bronfenbrenner, 1979), by examining the contextual factors surrounding and to a degree shaping individual's behaviours. Individual learner is viewed situated in a specific institution-bounded ecosystem and coping at the same time with institution-led and self-organized learning ecologies (Barron, 2006). The doctoral e-researchers strive to develop their own set of interactions (e.g. with supervisors and peers) and "negotiated forms of agency" (McAlpine & Amundsen, 2011, p. 18), dwelling on the opportunities for research training and apprenticeship of their local context, and on a range of knowledge production and exchange practices they found and imitate in the social Web. For instance, some PhD students might use the open Web for an early exploration of a research topic, whereas one mines the library databases to subsequently refine the literature search; in other cases, they might follow the formal channels of the peer-reviewed research journals for the required publications, and in parallel practice academic writing by running a group blog, sharing views and methodological issues with peers. Institutional and self-directed learning ecologies are seen as filtered by the intentionality, motivations and evolving learning needs of individual doctoral students producing unique learning contexts. The attention is therefore directed to an ecological view of agency (Priestly et al., 2012), in which the individual student's ability to adopt social Web for research purposes is seen as grounded in a specific academic context, shaped by different subject-bounded modes of working and ICTs appropriation (Fry & Talja, 2007) and located in the diverse phases of the doctoral journey (Zaman, 2010).

Thus, a doctoral researcher working in a humanistic subject area, where an individualistic mode of ICTs appropriation is common (Fry & Talja, 2007), is likely to show different digital practices with respect to a doctoral researcher working in a technoscientific area, where the prevalent mode of working is team-based and the technology uses are usually collectively organized. Likewise, a PhD student at the beginning of her doctoral journey is likely to much more rely on well-established academic conventions than a colleague in her final phase, when there are growing concerns about personal development and visibility of one's own academic profile in multiple digital venues.

Considering such a variety, the model of 'ecology of resources' (Luckin, 2010) provides the researcher with a heuristic tool to map out the range of 'forms of assistance' available to doctoral e-researchers in institutional and self-directed learning ecologies. In other words, this tool allows us to draw contextual factors shaping the doctoral experience of the PhD students and to ask questions about their motivations. In fact, as a learner-centric model, the ecology of resources provides a perspective to think of learning context as a product and as a process related to a learner and therefore linked to her effort to 'internalize' selected resources and interactions. In this view, the doctoral e-researcher draws 'trajectories' of combinations of people, resources and relationships that give evidence of the boundary-crossing activities between formal and informal learning ecologies (Barron, 2006). The capacity of the individual learner to develop original intersections of formal and informal learning ecologies might return the emergent profile of a doctoral e-researcher striving to build personal academic identity beyond the models and conventions provided by the local research training setting. The implied question is the extent to which doctoral e-researchers are able to develop resilience in their own research context. Among the observed examples of resilience there are: an individual PhD student able to search in the open Web and harness the opportunities for additional research training to supplement the flaws of her or his local context; or a group of doctoral students challenging a conservative context by organizing a PhD scholars-led seminar, using a Facebook group page in order to amplify the dissemination of their contributions.

Moreover, the study sets out to reveal if the observed events denoting resilience can support the consideration of doctoral e-researchers as a new 'keystone species' in the scholarly community—in other words, able to create "niches of co-evolution" (Nardi & O'Day, 1999, p. 51) both as digital learners and as prospective e-researchers. Thus, to a degree doctoral e-researchers are considered as change agents whose action is likely to have an indirect impact (a "loose coupling effect", according to Andrews & Haythornthwaite, 2011, p. 172) on the related ecosystem, represented by their local research training context. Otherwise, one might wonder if the innovative digital practices of a few individuals are emergent phenomena that remain isolated at a personal level, not shared with other 'species' (e.g. supervisors, senior researchers) and as a consequence not valued.

This leads us to consider 'social presence' (Garrison & Anderson, 2003) as a catalytic element to foster student agency in a social media age. Focusing on the strand of the 'networking' activites in the doctoral experience, the PhD researcher might move across different kinds of aggregation: from a behaviour coupled to the model of Group to Network and to Collective (Dron & Anderson, 2007). This would include in-person meetings with peers combined with the use of a password-protected mailing list, to the adoption of a Networking groupmind, through the use of an open and research-based digital network in which they can build academic reputation, finally moving toward a Collective groupmind, in which practices such as updating new publications and disseminating one's own work go beyond the academic boundaries in favour of the open knowledge exchange. The question is the extent to which the moves across these different groupminds can be spontaneously and tentatively undertaken by isolated PhD researchers or if these pioneers need to be critically supported by research contexts enabling new forms of academic socialization.

In this inquiry underway, the analysis of learner experience and student agency aims to suggest the interpretation that both prescribed and emergent learning need to be part of an integrated learning ecology (Williams et al., 2011), in a perspective leading beyond the ecological approach as a metaphor, toward a study of local ecologies as a frame for developing resilience and change (Hall & Winn, 2010; Hodgson & Spours, 2009).

Conclusions

This chapter presents an overview of the range of ways in which notions of 'ecology' and 'learning ecology' are applied to approach the impact of the Web on knowledge exchange and to frame different forms of e-learning at institutional and individual levels.

As a whole, an ecological approach to e-learning is evolving as a way to think of technological innovations in educational settings as recursive attempts to find balance and sustainability among complementary alternatives, rather than replacing old means and practices with new ones. Furthermore, an ecological perspective resonates with participatory approaches in design and implementations of new digitally mediated forms of education, combining critical thinking on technology and action to harness its potential. The ecological approach enables a focus on individualised forms of appropriation of technologies for specific needs, paying attention to the relationships between peripheral and central modes of ICTs adoption in a local context.

Given this repertoire of opportunities opened up by ecological approaches and concepts, the chapter briefly discusses a research case of Italian doctoral students adopting Web 2.0 tools along with institutional facilities to conduct research activities in their own doctoral journey. Thinking of individual doctoral students using social Web tools for academic purposes in ecological terms helps in considering the adoption of ICTs as a component in an ecology of resources and as a response to changing needs to learn and adapt their behaviour in the academic ecosystem.

However, there are limitations and risks in the adoption of the lens of learning ecology which the researcher should be aware of. First, it is easy to misunderstand findings, for instance attributing a general value to phenomena related to a local context. Second, it is rarely clarified what level of human ecology is being investigated, in a continuum from a micro to a macro level (Hodgson & Spours, 2009). Third, it is noted (Frielick, 2004) that often the analytical uses of 'learning ecology' are loosely defined and the adherence to a specific ecological view is not made explicit. This leads to the danger of being unaware of one's own epistemological assumptions. For instance, in the instance under investigation, focus on personal ecologies and on student agency underlies a constructivist view of human ecology, in which the individual's capacity, although shaped by environmental factors, is a key to act upon the situated context and create forms of resilience.

References

Andrews, R.L., & Haythornthwaite, C. (2011). E-learning ecologies. In R.L. Andrews & C. Haythornthwaite (eds.), *E-learning. Theory and practice* (pp. 144–160). London: SAGE.

Attwell, G. (2010, August 2). Notes on open education and critical pedagogy [Blog post]. Retrieved from http://bit.ly/d3a2kK

Barab, S., Cherkes-Julkowski, M., Swenson, R., Garrett, S., Shaw, R., & Young, M. (1999). Principles of self-organization: Learning as participation in autocatakinetic systems. *Journal of the Learning Sciences, 8*(3/4), 349–390.

Barron, B. (2006). Interest and self-sustained learning as catalysts of development: A learning ecology perspective. *Human Development, 49*, 193–224. doi:10.1159/000094368

Boulos, M., & Wheleer, S. (2007). The emerging Web 2.0 social software: An enabling suite of sociable technologies in health and health care education. *Health Information and Libraries Journal, 24*(1), 2–23.

Bronfenbrenner, U. (1979). *The ecology of human development: Experiments by nature and design*. Cambridge, MA: Harvard University Press.

Brown, S.A. (2012). Seeing Web 2.0 in context: A study of academic perceptions. *Internet and Higher Education, 15*(1), 50–57. doi:10.1016/j.iheduc.2011.04.003

Buchem, I., Attwell, G., & Torres, R. (2011, July). *Understanding Personal Learning Environments: Literature review and synthesis through the activity theory lens*. Paper presented at The PLE Conference 2011, Southampton, UK. Retrieved from http://www.scribd.com/doc/62828883/Understanding-Personal-Learning-Environments-Literature-review-and-synthesis-through-the-Activity-Theory-lens

Crabtree, A., & Rodden, T. (2008). Hybrid ecologies: Understanding cooperative interaction in emerging physical-digital environments. *Personal and Ubiquitous Computing, 12*(7), 481–493. doi:10.1007/s00779–007–0142–7"10.1007/s00779–007–0142–7

Davenport, T.H. (1997). *Information ecology: Mastering the information and knowledge environment*. New York: Oxford University Press.

Downes, S. (2010, April 12). Collaboration and cooperation [Blog post]. Retrieved from http://www.downes.ca/post/53303

Dron, J., & Anderson, T. (2007). Collectives, networks and groups in social software for e-Learning. In G. Richards (Ed.), *Proceedings of World Conference on E-Learning in Corporate, Government, Healthcare, and Higher Education* (pp. 2460–2467). Chesapeake, VA: AACE.

Ehlers, U.-D. (2010). Innovation and Quality for New Learning Cultures. In U.-D., Ehlers, & D. Schneckenberg, (Eds.), *Changing Cultures in Higher Education: Moving ahead to future learning* (pp. 417–432). Berlin: Springer-Verlag.

Ellis, R.A., & Goodyear, P. (2009). Thinking ecologically about e-learning. In R.A. Ellis & P. Goodyear (Eds.), *Students' experiences of e-learning in higher education: The ecology of sustainable innovation* (pp. 16–38). London: Routledge.

Frielick, S. (2004). Beyond constructivism: An ecological approach to e-learning. In R. Atkinson, C. McBeath, D. Jonas-Dwyer, & R. Phillips (Eds.), *Proceedings of the 21st ASCILITE Conference* (pp. 328–332). Perth, Australia: ASCILITE. Retrieved from http://www.ascilite.org.au/conferences/perth04/procs/frielick.html

Fry, J., & Talja, S. (2007). The intellectual and social organization of academic fields and the shaping of digital resources. *Journal of Information Science, 33*(2), 115–33. doi:10.1177/0165551506068153

Garrison, D.R., & Anderson, T. (2003). *E-learning in the 21st century: A framework for research and practice*. London: Routledge Falmer.

Girard, M., & Stark, D. (2007). Socio-technologies of assembly: Sense-making and demonstration in rebuilding lower Manhattan. In V. Mayer-Schonberger & D. Lazer (Eds.), *Governance and information technology: From electronic government to information government* (pp. 145–176). Cambridge, MA: MIT Press.

Hall, R., & Winn, J. (2010). The relationships between technology and open education in the development of a resilient higher education. *Proceedings of Open ED 2010*, Barcelona; UOC, OU, BYU. Retrieved from http://hdl.handle.net/10609/4867

Hodgson, A., & Spours, K. (2009). *Collaborative local learning ecologies: Reflections on the governance of lifelong learning in England* (IFLL Sector Paper 6). Leicester: National Institute of Adult Continuing Education. Retrieved from http://www.niace.org.uk/lifelonglearninginquiry/docs/IFLL-Sector-Paper6.pdf

Jones, P., Selby, D., & Sterling, S. (2010). *Sustainability education. Perspectives and practice across Higher Education*. London: Earthscan.

Kazmer, M.M. (2005). Cats in the classroom: Online learning in hybrid space. *First Monday, 10*(9). Retrieved from http://firstmonday.org/ojs/index.php/fm/article/view/1278/1198

Lave, J., & Wenger, E. (1991). *Situated learning: Legitimate peripheral participation*. Cambridge, UK: Cambridge University Press.

Looi, C. K. (2001). Enhancing learning ecology on the internet. *Journal of Computer Assisted Learning, 17*, 13–20. doi:10.1111/j.1365-2729.2001.00155.x

Louviere, G. (2012). Ecosystems in the learning environment. *Educational Facility Planner, 45*(1/2), 10–13. Retrieved from www.cefpi.org

Luckin, R. (2008). The learner-centric ecology of resources: A framework for using technology to scaffold learning. *Computers in Education, 50*(2), 449–462. doi:10.1016/j.compedu.2007.09.018

Luckin, R. (2010). *Re-designing learning contexts: Technology-rich, learner-centred ecologies*. London, UK: Routledge.

Luckin, R., Clark, W., Garnett, F., Whitworth, A., Akass, J., Cook, J., et al. (2010). Learner-Generated contexts: A framework to support the effective use of technology for learning. In M. Lee & C. McLoughlin (Eds.), *Web 2.0-Based e-learning: Applying social informatics for tertiary teaching* (pp. 70–84). Hershey, PA: Information Science Reference. doi:10.4018/978-1-60566-294-7.ch004

Manion, C.E., & Selfe, R.D. (2012). Sharing an assessment ecology: Digital media, wikis, and the social work of knowledge. *Technical Communication Quarterly, 21*(1), 25–45. doi:10.1080/10572252.2012.626756

McAlpine, L., & Amundsen, C. (2011). Making meaning of diverse experiences: Constructing an identity through time. In L. McAlpine & C. Amundsen (Eds.), *Doctoral education: Research-based strategies for doctoral students, supervisors and administrators* (pp. 173–183). Netherlands: Springer.

Mitchell, A. (2002, October). *New learning ecologies. Promoting learning in the digital age—A holistic perspective.* Paper presented at the RIBA HEDQF Conference: New Learning Environments, London. Retrieved from www.m-learning.org/docs/Learning%20ecologies%2024%20Oct%2002.pdf

Nardi, B., & O'Day, V. (1999). *Information ecologies: Using technology with heart*. Cambridge, MA: MIT Press.

Normak, P., Pata, K., & Kaipainen, M. (2012). An ecological approach to learning dynamics. *Educational Technology & Society, 15*(3), 262–274.

Pachler, N., Cook, J., & Bachmair, B. (2010). Whither a socio-cultural ecology of learning with mobile devices. In *Mobile learning. Structures, agency, practices* (pp. 155–171). London: Springer. doi:10.1007/978-1-4419-0585-7

Paine, R.T. (1966). Food web complexity and species diversity. *American Naturalist, 100*(910), 65–75.

Pata, K., & Laanpere, M. (2011, September). *An ecological meta-design framework for open learning ecosystems*. Paper presented at the ECER 2011 Conference, Berlin, Germany: European Educational Research Association. Draft retrieved from http://tihane.wordpress.com/2011/04/

Payton, I.J., Fenner, M., & Lee, W.G. (2002). Keystone species: The concept and its relevance for conservation management in New Zealand. *Science for Conservation, 203*. Wellington, New Zealand: Department for Conservation. Retrieved from http://csl.doc.govt.nz/Documents/science-and-technical/SFC203.pdf

Priestly, M., Edwards, R., & Priestly, A. (2012). Teacher agency in curriculum making: Agents of change and spaces for maneouvre. *Curriculum Inquiry, 42*(2), 191–214. doi:10.1111/j.1467-873X.2012.00588.x

Sangrà, A., Guitert, M., Pérez-Mateo, M., & Ernest, P. (2011, June). *Lifelong learning ecologies and teacher's professional development: A roadmap for research.* Paper presented at EDEN 2011 Conference. Dublin: EDEN. Retrieved from http://www.eden-online.org/system/files/Annual_2011_Dublin_BOA_0.pdf

Sangrà, A., & Wheleer, S. (2013). New informal ways of learning: Or are we formalising the informal? *RUSC—Revista de Universidad y Sociedad del Conocimiento, 10*(1), 286–293. Retrieved from http://rusc.uoc.edu/ojs//index.php/rusc/

Seely Brown, J. (1999). Sustaining an ecology of knowledge. *Leader to Leader, 12*(1). doi:10.1002/ltl.40619991207

Seely Brown, J. (2000). Growing up digital: How the web changes work, education and the ways people learn. *Change: The Magazine of Higher Learning, 32*(2), 11–20. doi:10.1080/00091380009601719

Seely Brown, J., & Adler, R.P. (2008). Minds on fire: Open education, the long tail, and learning 2.0. *Educause Review, 43*(1), 16–32.

Siemens, G. (2003, October 17). Learning ecology, communities, and networks. Extending the classroom [Blog post]. Retrieved from http://www.elearnspace.org/Articles/learning_communities.htm

Walker, B. H., Holling, C. S., Carpenter, S. R., & Kinzig, A. (2004). Resilience, adaptability and transformability in social–ecological systems. *Ecology and Society, 9*(2), 5. Retrieved from http://www.ecologyandsociety.org/vol9/iss2/art5

Williams, R., Karousou, R., & Mackness, J. (2011). Emergent learning and learning ecologies in Web 2.0. *International Review of Research in Open and Distance Learning, 12*(3).

Zaman, M. (2010). Doctoral programs in the age of research 2.0. In M. Anandarajan & A. Anandarajan (Eds.), *E-research collaboration. Theory, techniques and challenges* (pp. 233–246). Berlin: Springer Verlag. doi:10.1007/978-3-642-12257-6

Zhao, Y., & Frank, K. A. (2003). Factors affecting technology use in schools: An ecological perspective. *American Educational Research Journal, 40*(4), 807–840. doi:10.3102/00028312040004807

25

The Leadership Imperative for Higher Education in the Twenty-first Century

Narimane Hadj-Hamou

Introduction

The new leadership imperative in the context of a knowledge-based economy emphasises the long-lasting impact that is generated through applying servant and transformational thinking in leadership, as opposed to institutional-based leadership that has traditionally been geared toward steering- and performance-based outcomes. Indeed, it is increasingly the case that institutions of higher learning are expected to proactively be engaged in social change, for instance. The role of leaders in this sense is to look at higher education institutions as part and parcel of the wider system that involves different stakeholders and that is at the heart of the communities that they wish to serve. Whilst technology as a critical enabler for revamping the provision of learning opportunities is perhaps the new and most profound development, there are however softer changes in the social structure around universities that need to be taken into account. The question therefore is no longer whether the leadership in higher education needs to do what is necessary to support radical change and the dynamic developments surrounding that change, but more importantly how higher education institutions need to change themselves in order to be inclusive and an integral component of the broader system.

The new leadership imperative causing higher education institutions to propel themselves into the future using technology-enhanced learning as the means for supporting the growth and development of learning opportunities in various aspects of society is based on the following elements:

- Leadership that has a new mindset compatible with the requirements of a modern society and is able to respond to the needs of a digitally based economy.
- Acceptance of the notion that higher education institutions are the engine for delivering learning opportunities in a tangible, meaningful and impactful manner at all levels within society.
- The provision of continuing learning and lifelong learning opportunities by widening access and creating opportunities for all.
- Acceptance of the reality that institutions of higher education are no longer ivory towers and cannot be insular in their practices but have to change to operate as open systems.

- Adoption of the academic enterprise mentality where governance is a concept that can apply to higher education institutions in the same way as to other sectors of the economy.
- Appreciation that social change has consequentially redefined the need for learning and stakeholders' needs from institutions of higher learning. This therefore means structured learning, casual learning and social learning are phenomena that are taking place in the wider society and that universities and institutions of higher learning need to get to grips with.
- Investment in developing solutions which are technology driven for making learning viable, useful, accessible and enjoyable.
- The need for positive engagement on a wider basis for making learning not for its own sake but rather as a means to an end. In this sense, using the academic enterprise mindset, leaders of academic institutions will need to revisit the value of academic programmes and courses on offer. The acceptance of commoditisation in learning as much as communisation is accepted as the norm in other sectors of the economy.
- The display of exemplary leadership by providing value and impacting positively on raising standards and also providing the capacity for other sectors of the economy to function and deliver a competitive advantage.

Within the realm of higher education, the leadership imperative for the twenty-first century is not necessarily associated just with maintaining the status quo and modernising through incrementalism; it also includes taking charge at the core level of what higher education institutions do, reinventing and recreating the universities of the future that will be capable of engaging, partnering and impacting on a wider basis.

The Need for Transformational Thinking in Higher Education

Transformational leadership is one of the most prevalent leadership theories and is considered to be an emerging concept in higher education. It is in a sense a practice of leadership that is aimed at stimulating and inspiring others and is intended to create involvement, engagement, passion and the delivery of sustainable outcomes. Furthermore it has been used to create leadership capacity by inspiring and developing new generations of leaders and followers.

The real value of transformational leadership in higher education in the context of e-learning implementation is that it can act as a catalyst for the following factors:

- **The positive engagement and involvement of individuals**—These are strategies for dealing with the resistance to change and facilitating the acceptance of e-learning as a viable option for steering universities in the future.
- **Intellectual stimulation**—Transformational leadership through the broadening, the participation and the engagement of individuals will also allow for individuals to look at technology-enhanced learning as an opportunity for intellectual stimulation and therefore as a development tool for their own needs and requirements.
- **Inspirational motivation**—Transformational leadership is about selling change and creating enthusiasm for technology as an option for dealing with inherent problems and solving chronic problems that traditional universities tend to suffer from.
- **Fostering the acceptance of teamwork and group based goals**—Transformational leadership is about rallying people around similar goals and dealing with conflict by

building synergy levels and inspiring people with positive messages and using technology as a key for change, eliminating negativity and opening new doors and avenues that will help the institutions concerned in addition to directly and indirectly providing benefits for individuals.

- **A precursor for recognising and rewarding**—Transformational leaders place a lot of emphasis on recognising and acknowledging contributions and rewarding accomplishments as a means for getting people to remain motivated and to rely on their trust and commitment to further the implementation of new change initiatives such as e-learning.

Transformational leadership can perhaps be analysed through a set of imperatives that are expected to be tackled in order to modernise, re-engineer and implement e-learning and steer higher education institutions to become universities of the future. The twenty-first century presents challenges for all sectors of the economy and the education sector is included in this challenge. The global change phenomenon has shifted to focus more on knowledge as a currency for managing businesses and building value. Human capital is also considered to be the main asset as opposed to traditionally based methods of evaluating the wealth of nations through physical assets. Technological development is seen as the driver for establishing new types of competitive advantages, and the wider changes which are socially related have also put citizens, customers and other stakeholders in the driver's seat. It is more the case that society at large has become enlightened; people are technologically savvy, and the needs and expectations have changed significantly where more and more demands for new innovations and the need for consumerism are also real things to deal with. Higher education institutions and the modern transformational thinking of leadership have to tackle the following *Strategic Challenges* (SC) to enable universities to be relevant and viable in the long term.

- Creating a new mindset where universities can operate as an open system by removing barriers and developing the enterprise thinking mindset.
- Creating value propositions based on blending learning opportunities and establishing value-oriented programmes that will serve the purpose of customers, users and other stakeholders in the wider context.
- Encouraging the development of entrepreneurial thinking and in particular as it is related to technology. By making universities less obsessed with the notion of brick and mortar principles and making them exploit technology and the internet in particular, universities will be propelled to move positively forward and will allow a new type of growth which is not hindered by the confines of physical space and where resources can be smartly exploited and used for providing value to learners and society at large.
- Creating an environment for learners where they can thrive, prosper and especially collaborate and co-create. This means that the world of the internet is the best means for inducing excellence in student experiences and creating connectivity for stimulation, knowledge transfer, and inspiration and and for raising standards.
- Emphasising the need for lifelong learning. By absorbing the concept of commoditisation in knowledge and developing learning opportunities as opposed to preserving rigid standards and sticking to redundant course material, institutions of higher education will focus more on replenishment and enhancing learning capabilities in a progressive manner.

- Investing in technologically savvy and competent individuals. The human capital involved in facilitating the growth and development of learning opportunities and in making learning experiences unique, relevant and delightful is perhaps at the core of the new leadership imperative. Having capabilities in modern teaching and learning approaches such as the use of synchronous, asynchronous and core media as new methods for providing learning will allow for a major leap forward relevant to the new requirements of the twenty-first century.
- Collaborating and building strategic alliances. Doing so will enable institutions of higher learning to grow and develop through knowledge transfer, leveraging and rendering value on a sustainable basis.
- Incorporating learning technologies into strategic thinking. It is important for the new leadership imperative to get away from the traditional mindset of preserving the status quo, being absorbed with all legacies and using insular mentalities that make universities drift away from society at large. Technology is a key enabler for ensuring modernity and relevance and more importantly is the means by which universities can change, modernise and provide value on a sustainable basis.
- Measuring learning quality. It is important in the modern learning environment to put students in the driver's seat and ensure that learning experiences are evaluated from a wider basis using positive feedback and encouraging the involvement of consumer (i.e. learner) assessment, review and change. Universities will therefore need to get away from the notion of managing learning outcomes from their own internal perspectives only as this is no longer a valid option.
- Achieving a competitive advantage for institutions in higher education. The use of enterprise thinking and getting universities to operate on an open system will soon make leaders realise that modern competitiveness is possible and can be achieved only by treating students as customers and providing value that is differentiated from that of the competition and developing a value proposition that is distinctive based on core capabilities and institutionalising quality for consistency, reliability and being student and customer centric.
- Transforming bureaucracy, culture and assumptions. Real change means change at the core and that means getting rid of the old baggage: to stop being obsessed with old legacies and welcome the opportunity that technology-enhanced learning brings to higher education institutions. A culture that lives in the past will miss the present and certainly will not plan well for the future, and leadership that emphasises the preservation of old standards will certainly not be progressive enough in terms of achieving the levels of ambitions put on paper. The new change order, which is driven by technology in all aspects of creating the University of the Future, is real and is the main challenge that the new leaders of higher education institutions must become aware of, building competencies in driving it and establishing the new legacy levels which are technology oriented.

The transformational aspects of modern leadership that can drive e-learning effectively are well described in an article by D. E. Hanna (Hanna, 2003, p.25–34). In this paper the aforementioned 11 strategic challenges are well covered and the paper does present a useful template for creating the transformation from an old traditional mindset to the new mindset of an emerging institutional culture that can be ready to drive e-learning in a positive and effective manner.

The illustration demonstrates that transformational leadership is about creating a cohesive, totally aligned, committed and passionate family of professionals who welcome change and accept that a modern academic environment is one that focuses on creating value and being student centric.

Table 25.1 Evolving College/University Culture

The Traditional Academic Culture	The Continum	The Emerging Academic Culture
Leader and staff abide by time-honored rules, policies, procedures, and protocols.	⟺	Leaders and staff draw on their knowledge and expreience but take risks, often without a pre-tested methodology.
Formal academic programs drive departmental decision-making	⟺	Learner's needs drive departmental decision-making; academic programs are responsive to the needs of the individual learner.
Tenured faculty are primary academic decision-makers.	⟺	Faculty share academic decision-making with key customers/stakeholders.
Administrative and academic structures support the delivery of programs and courses.	⟺	Academic support structures are tailored to the needs of the learner.
People who can work within given structures are most important.	⟺	People who can anticipate market shifts are most important.
Key message is "Don't rock the boat."	⟺	Key message is "seize the day."
Communication strategies are -internal -vertical, -formal.	⟺	Communication strategies are -external and internal, -horizontal, -informal.
Emphasis is on system and resources "in hand."	⟺	Emphasis is on systems and resources "in waiting."
Strategic partnerships go unrecognized and untapped.	⟺	Strategic alliances and partnerships are sought out and implemented.
Segmented, specialized organizational structures are prevalent.	⟺	Integrated, cross-functional organizational structures are reinforced.
Budgets are stable and committed to existing programs; deficit financing is avoided.	⟺	Budgets are fluid and opportunity-seekings; deficit financing is common.
New acadmic programs complement existing programs.	⟺	New program create openings for new markets.
New programs must fit with existing structures.	⟺	The best structure is determined for each new program.
Actions tend to be evolutionary.	⟺	Actions tend to be revolutionary.
Risk-adverse behavior seeks to minimize competition with others through regulation.	⟺	Risk-seeking behavior seek to exploit competitive advantage over others.
Stewardship and preservation are the critical elements of leadership.	⟺	Vision and strategy are the critical elements of leadership.
Stewardship and preservation focus on assessing the impact of new activities on exiting undertakings.	⟺	Strategies gravitate toward new market niches.
Change efforts focus on improving programs and activities deemed valid by competitors.	⟺	Change efforts focus on being first to develop a new program or activity.
Staff tend to work to their own agendas and act independently of their colleagues.	⟺	Staff often collaborate with each other and disciplines in pursuit of organizational goals.
Appraisal, reward, and recognition are based primarily on individual scholarly perfermance.	⟺	Appraisal, reward, and recognition are based on individual and group scholarly and enterpreneurial performance.
Organizational recognition comes from interaction with, and recognition by, peers in other institutions and in terms of contribution to the discipline	⟺	Organizational recognition may also from interaction with, and recognition by, immediate colleagues and terms of contribution to the organization.

More importantly, the new e-learning-based mindset for academic leadership is also about accepting the notion of risk in driving ambitious strategies and prioritising on the basis of value creation and creating a sustainable impact. Last, as Table 25.1 illustrates, the emerging e-learning-based academic environment is one where institutional growth and development is enabled significantly through a revolutionary basis inspired and supported by technological developments.

The New E-learning Revolution

A newly published report looks at the changes taking place in the university sector and proposes some scenarios for the future. It is clear that e-learning is going to be the central driving force for revolutionising learning and education for the future and will provide solutions to inherent problems but will also reshape the way in which learning and education are provided and how the experience of learning in the future is going to take place. The basis of the research conducted by Ernst and Young (2012) is that there are several drivers that will change the future of higher education (Figure 25.1).

As Figure 25.1 illustrates, the key components of these drivers of change for the future of higher education are mainly the continuous introduction and availability of new technology, the introduction of digital technologies for changing and developing learning delivery methods and wider forces including, for instance, global mobility, the need to integrate with industry and the need for universities to adopt an enterprise thinking mindset. It is now acknowledged that the democratisation of knowledge and the widening of access are going to drive the global education revolution on an unprecedented scale. This shift will create new opportunities but also will act as a source of competition. It is widely accepted now at a leadership level in higher education that teaching methods and the approach adopted in providing education have to change radically. It is no longer sufficient to focus on delivering content but is more about customisation, contextualisation and using new ways of thinking that are purely developmental and which will provide a tangible and measureable learning experience. As far as democratisation of knowledge is concerned, the traditional ways of perceiving universities as the hubs for knowledge generation and knowledge development and delivery through physical environments and the brick and mortar principle is no longer valid as a concept. Whether it be the libraries, or

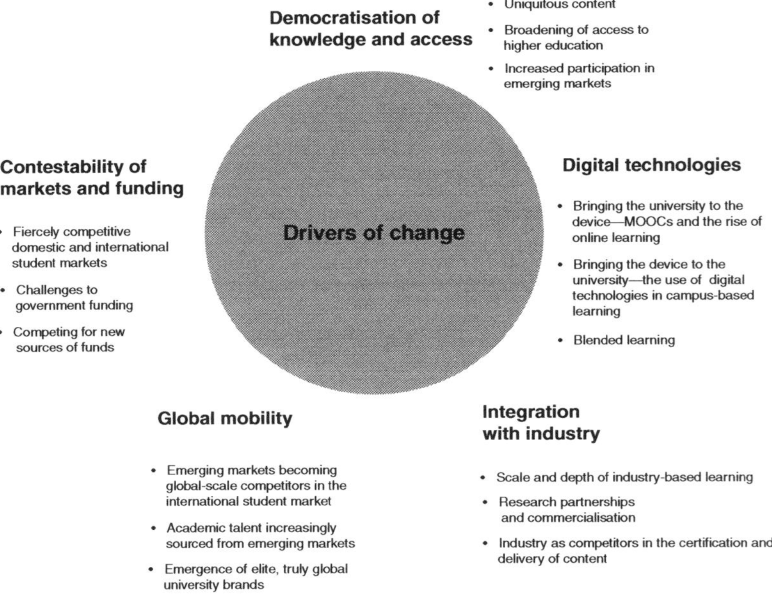

Figure 25.1 Drivers of Change

faculty expertise or the research that institutions carry out, this is no longer the core domain of a privileged base. Knowledge is widely accessible, expertise is also widely available and resources are abundant on the internet.

As one of the higher education leaders quoted in the 2012 Ernst and Young report said, "our major competitor in ten years time will be Google . . . if we are still alive!" (p. 9). Digital technologies are the innovation of the future and they will continue to disrupt the way we think, the way we operate and the way our various sectors of the economy are interconnected. Online education for instance is still progressing, albeit slowly, but it is disrupting the ways in which conventional universities are operating. It has to be accepted that digital technologies in the form of e-learning are not going to cause the total disappearance of campus-based or brick and mortar-based delivery of teaching and learning. However they are gradually transforming the ways in which education is provided experiences are considered. Furthermore e-learning through digital technologies is providing the opportunity to reshape the academic value chain by making sure that content generation, content aggregation, mass distribution, certification and commercialisation are value driven and focussed on customised needs and requirements. Collaboration is also a new facet introduced by digital technologies for the continuing progression of e-learning. At the present time massive open online courses (MOOCs) are gradually emerging as new models for providing knowledge as a consumable and as a commodity product.

The report concludes by stating that the traditional university model is the analogue of the print newspaper. In 15 years' time the new and radical revolution will be felt throughout the whole higher education sector. It is the case that universities in the next 15 years or so will have to undergo the following radical transformations:

- Joining a new learner business model as competition. This is going to increase and the war for talent will accelerate. This will also be exacerbated by students and learners choosing and switching and also the shrinking pool of funding.
- Operating as enterprises providing value whilst maintaining the freedom for enquiry and academic rigour.
- Taking advantage of the opportunity that has been demonstrated by private institutions in exploiting professional market niches and positioning themselves through fast tracking and by focussing on creating value.
- Introducing change and becoming relevant in terms of operating in a knowledge-based economy by being integrate into the wider economic sector, driven by the adoption of a wider perspective by policy makers regarding free education for citizens.
- Considering their levels of offerings across different disciplines and with mass customisation in mind, along with building their capability for replenishing and shrinking the life cycle of knowledge product development.
- Offering experiences and targeting potential students as customers by better understanding their specific needs and preferences and therefore segmenting the market and rationalising their offerings so that products are made to suit specific needs.
- Creating new channels to the market by making e-learning the key driving force as a digital channel for engaging potential students and managing their experiences through a life cycle perspective with e-learning support.
- Looking at the support basis through the lens of value creation and quality offerings and ensuring that institutions of higher learning have got the right infrastructure to support the growth and development of e-learning provision and in an uninhibited manner.

The Leadership Challenges for the Implementation of E-learning

The implementation of e-learning does not necessarily just depend on dealing with technology-based issues or the provision of learner experiences that are useful and meaningful, or on sorting out and modernising the existing infrastructure or on the development of new attractive programmes. Academic leaders will need to look at the widely reported challenges that significantly impact the effective implementation and benefits of e-learning. Several reported issues make e-learning implementation both a challenge and incompatible with the existing academic mindset. These range from dealing with e-learning as a separate issue from the core teaching and learning aspect, for instance the subcategorisation of e-learning as a support function and not as a core academic concern and the ability to seek ways and means to integrate e-learning at the core of educational development activities such as new programmes in order to customise, avoid duplication and be leaner centric. Additional reported challenges include staff considering e-learning as a task separate from the core learning and teaching and therefore not making any effort to absorb the advantages of e-learning and seeing it as a viable alternative to traditional methods. Furthermore there are issues associated with the lack of recognition for educational development work that is pioneering in terms of introducing e-learning technologies, new pedagogies and innovative thinking for content development etc.

As far as academic leadership is concerned, these are the type of issues that need to be taken into account prior to developing a comprehensive and meaningful e-learning strategy and its implementation. The following areas are critical in considering the implementation of effective e-learning strategies:

- Ensuring that there is enough capacity of academic staff who are directly involved in e-learning innovation and development.
- Ensuring that staff and in particular faculty are well prepared with current information and advice on e-learning methods and new developments so that they see the benefits of e-learning and do not consider that it will threaten the ways in which they deliver teaching and learning from a traditional standpoint.
- Facilitating close working relationships between individuals who are specialists in pedagogy and e-learning and academic staff responsible for programme development.
- Creating multidisciplinary mindsets, building bridges and encouraging synergy and cooperation from the point of view of pedagogy, e-learning expertise, staff expertise and student and learner needs and requirements.
- Ensuring that academic staff who are expected to absorb and endorse e-learning are also brought up to speed with the new pedagogies that will make e-learning more effective.
- Considering, for leaders of academic institutions contemplating the implementation of e-learning, the development of a proper learning and technology strategy at policy and governance levels which incorporates e-learning from an integrated perspective across the board.
- Learning as leaders how to lead e-learning initiatives by visiting institutions that are pioneers with e-learning and by finding best practice examples for successful applications in order to promote the virtues of e-learning as a viable alternative in a meaningful manner.
- Looking at e-learning as an integrated mindset-driven approach as opposed to a technology-enabled initiative. In this regard leaders need to look at e-learning pedagogies on a wider basis by incorporating, for instance, collaborative learning, individualised learning and social learning as some of the new forms and preferred options for learning.

- Looking at learning resource support on a wider basis and redefining, for example, the role of a library in supporting learning experiences in a digitally based environment.
- Encouraging educational innovation and evaluation of options through support for experimentation, academic staff engagement and team-based work for looking at the viability, optionality and effectiveness of making e-learning work in a specific academic institution.
- Engaging external stakeholders in the creation of an e-learning-based strategy and in particular to define the characteristics of an effective learning experience and look at provision arrangements on a wider basis. Streamlining the higher education institutions structures and management systems to allow the focus to be more on value creation, learner experiences and managing the delivery engine from a quality and value perspective.
- Creating dialogue and open debate while dealing with cultural resistance and alleviating fears so that e-learning is perceived as a liberating force and a catalyst for tackling inherent problems and enabling the institutions concerned to prosper, grow and remain effective in delivering learning and education opportunities.
- Creating a new learning environment where students are supported in autonomous learning, self-study, the effective use of resources and access to library content, competence in using e-learning applications, the focus on a lifelong learning portfolio which is customised, access to online support for specific needs and requirements, and flexibility in study patterns for both on-campus and distance-based students.
- Dividing modularized courses into sections so that learning is consumed in blocks and assessing skills on an ongoing basis as they are being developed in acknowledgment of the increasing commoditization of the provision of academic programmes. Creating horizontal means whereby students can engage with their peer groups and encouraging collaborative learning and lateral and horizontal exchanges to assess soft skills.
- Developing a holistic integrated quality assurance system that tracks the consumption of learning as a process but also evaluates the experience that each individual student goes through. Measuring resource consumption as well as the impact generated from e-learning as a viable alternative to conventional teaching and learning, classroom-based methods.
- Modernising institutional infrastructure by having the right learning platforms, tools, services, authentication and ways by which emerging technologies and supporting services can be explored and evaluated on a consistent basis. Extending the value chain by widening access and downstreaming the innovative means by which assessment can be e-based, thereby encouraging and allowing students to move toward the completion of their learning experience journey.

Characteristics of E-learning Leaders

There are eight possible characteristics that transformational leaders who can re-engineer and create institutions of higher learning for the future need to possess. These are different from the leadership characteristics that are required for managing conventional, traditional, brick and mortar-based institutions of learning (Figure 25.2).

- **Visionary**
  Leaders of e-learning institutions have to be visionary due to the fact that the levels of disruption caused by ongoing technological development will remain relentless. It is important for transformational leaders to continue to propel their institutions by evaluating,

Figure 25.2 Characteristics of E-learning Leaders

adopting and impacting with new generations of technologies and by exploring potential that exists in a digitally oriented society, thereby helping to co-create the future.

- **Passionate Learner**
  Leaders in the twenty-first century have to be totally literate with technology and they therefore have to manage the need to absorb new developments in technology and to manage through learning. Knowledge-based work environments require knowledgeable leaders; otherwise the decision-making process will be useless and the organisations concerned will not be able to achieve any of their ambitious goals and objectives. In the context of leadership for e-learning, education it is not learning for learning's sake but learning in order to understand, accept and implement with passion by influencing others, to create buy-in and to ensure that the organisations concerned can reap the benefits of evolving and modern e-learning approaches.
- **Inspired by Change**
  An organisation that operates as an open system is akin to a house that has open windows to allow fresh air to flow in. Change therefore brings ideas, fertilises existing practices and injects the right mindset. It is the role of leaders to make sure that anything associated with e-learning and its growth and development is pervasive and can permeate their institution's work climate to allow their staff to be refreshed and inspired.

- **Flexible and Adaptable**
  With the rapid development of new technologies and the changing dynamics of markets and also the impositions coming from consumers and learners with higher expectations, leaders for e-learning have to be flexible and adaptable. Therefore their institutions of higher learning have to be managed with fluidity and dynamism. Getting prepared with this mindset will allow higher education institutions to keep from falling behind and always to be at the forefront with development and with delivery capability.
- **Innovator**
  It goes without saying that the pace of technological development means that the potential for innovating in so many different areas is immense. Leaders can more or less re-create their entire institutions of higher learning through e-learning and technology-based learning opportunities. It means on the soft side that a new climate can be recreated, skills and competencies of a new nature can be added and developed and approaches and methods for delivery can be significantly enhanced or newly created.
- **Entrepreneur**
  The face of higher education in the future will be akin to that of business enterprises, and therefore academic leaders can no longer be the custodians of rigid and old-fashioned academic standards and the preservers of all legacies. It is mandatory for leaders of e-learning institutions to adopt the mindset of creating value, customer orientation and competitiveness based on differentiation and brand-building power. Leaders must think like entrepreneurs not only in terms of acquiring technologies and securing customer bases but also in terms of securing funding for development and sustaining the future of their institutions.
- **People Oriented**
  Excellent leaders are those who can attract high-calibre professionals and can provide the right climate for their growth and development, inspiring and motivating them to remain and sustain their loyalty to their institutions. Furthermore in the context of e-learning, the war for talent is going to accelerate and high-quality leaders will be those who can capitalise on the human capital available to them and secure their share of skills and expertise needed.
- **Results Driven**
  The jury is out on e-learning and it is therefore important for leaders of e-learning institutions to constantly evaluate the return on investment in terms of e-learning being a viable alternative to traditional, classroom-based teaching and learning methods. The new type of leader also needs to focus on other aspects of being results driven, including intangible aspects of creating a dynamic, flexible and fast-growing institution of learning in a virtual world.

As Figure 25.2 illustrates, these eight characteristics are ones that modern leaders of e-learning institutions are expected to have, and they are very similar to characteristics that exist in other sectors of the economy; but more importantly, they are characteristics that reflect the requirements of a modern business environment and of a knowledge-based era where technology is prevalent and its impact is going to continue to grow at a significant level.

Leading the Effective Implementation of E-learning—A Proposed Road Map

As Figure 25.3 illustrates, e-learning implementation cannot be based simply on finding the right technological solutions; nor can it be based on providing the right portfolio of learning

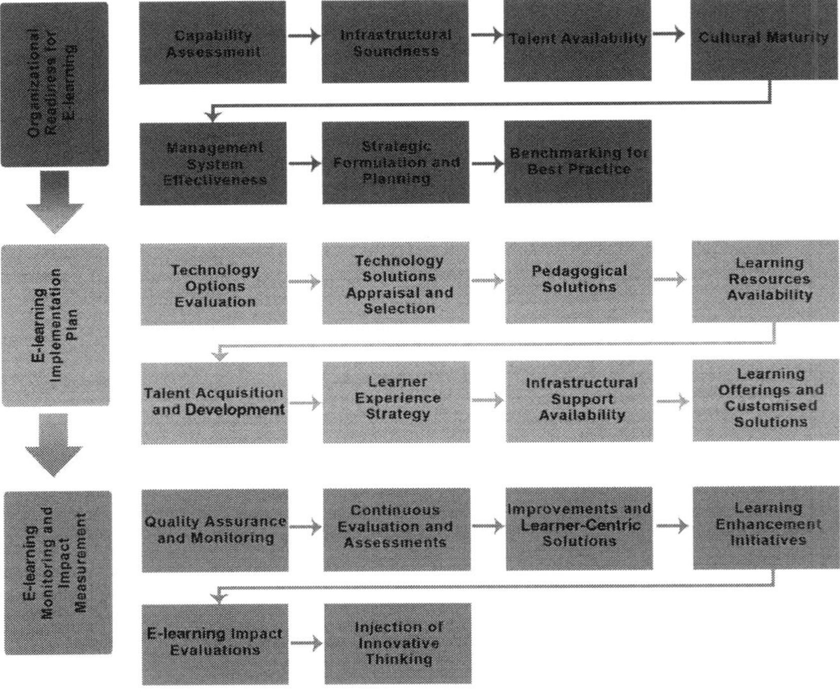

Figure 25.3 Proposed Road Map

opportunities. The proposed road map therefore looks at a holistic, integrated lifecycle perspective for the leading and implementing of effective e-learning strategies.

There are three levels to the proposed road map that characterise different challenges for leaders building e-learning capability in their higher education institutions:

- **Organisational Readiness for E-learning**
  The starting point for any organisation is to look at where it wants to go, what capabilities it has and what needs to be done for it to get there. Similarly the creation of an e-learning institution does require specific and systematic steps of evaluation and consideration before any decision is made on moving forward with e-learning. At the start it is important for any organisation to assess its internal capabilities and to identify its core strengths and competitiveness, as well as where the major weaknesses are. In the context of e-learning and in order to make sure that this is not technology oriented, it is additionally important to look at the wider perspective, including the soundness and the robustness of the existing infrastructure and more importantly the talent pool that will be expected to absorb, work with and drive the growth of e-learning in the academic work environment. There are of course additional factors related to the culture of the institutions concerned, the level of resistance that may be available and the degree of maturity demonstrated in absorbing change and exploiting a new technology. There are cases where e-learning has failed to be implemented because the environment in which it was being implemented is rigid, using bureaucratic management systems and operating in a silo mentality mindset.

One more step to pay attention to is the inspirational elements that need to be present prior to building a blueprint for e-learning implementation. Leaders are therefore expected to conduct benchmarking on a wide scale and to look at best practices available to them in order to choose the right options that can be tailored to their institutions. Last in this context will be the task of preparing the blueprint through strategic formulation and planning.

- **E-learning Implementation Plan**
In order to ensure that technology is only an enabler and the core aspects of e-learning provision are going to be based on the learning experience itself, a set of activities must be integrated that will include the careful exploration and evaluation of technology options available, the suitability and the careful appraisal and selection of the most viable options and in this context to look at the right way of offering technology-enhanced education or technology-supported education through pedagogical solutions. This is only one side of the challenge. In addition, leaders will have to look at the core aspects of making learner experiences unique: the academic talent available and the need to acquire suitable expertise for technology-based learning in the form of e-learning. The learning experience strategy is perhaps the main pillar in the e-learning implementation plan, and this will mean that highly customised options are made possible together with the constant requirement for putting the learners at the centre of all endeavours and supporting them through the availability of learning resources and ensuring that the infrastructure for horizontal and vertical learning modes is taken care of. Within that context, the development of academic programmes and learning opportunities will have its meaningful place if all the other factors are considered carefully and through an integrated perspective.
- **E-learning Monitoring and Impact Measurement**
Leaders of e-learning institutions will have to ensure that the implementation strategies of e-learning are going to succeed through careful preparation, comprehensive planning and execution and the adherence to quality assurance and monitoring as a mindset through a multilevel perspective. Not only should evaluation and assessment focus on learners and their learning experiences with the closed loop perspective on enhancement, improvement and rectifying deficiencies in the services or the learning experience itself, but also it will be about the injection of best practice thinking and the enhancement of learning from a quality perspective.

Last, the overall evaluation of e-learning and its impact has to be made at an institutional level together with a reconsideration of innovation so that e-learning continues to remain viable and can continue to propel the institutions concerned toward world-class status and having a significant impact.

References

Ernst & Young, Australia. (2012). *University of the future: A thousand year old industry on the cusp of profound change.* (R. Srivastava, M. Narayanan, J. Singh, M. Gendy, & Y. Arun, Eds.). Retrieved March 03, 2013, from Ernst & Young Publication: http://www.ey.com/Publication/vwLUAssets/University_of_the_future/$FILE/University_of_the_future_2012.pdf

Hanna, D. E. (2003). Building a leadership vision: Eleven strategic challenges for higher education. *Educause*, July–August, 25–34.

26

Leadership Challenges in Online Distance Education

John Nworie

Introduction

Online distance education continues to expand in higher education and other educational settings. Distance education (DE) has gained acceptance in dual-mode institutions, maintains a conspicuous place, and is positioned for continued growth (Allen & Seaman, 2010; Davies, Howell, & Petrie, 2010). For-profit and nonprofit colleges and universities have invested time and resources to make distance learning one of their key initiatives. According to Rovai and Downey (2010), some institutions have achieved significant levels of success in their DE programs. The factors that helped fuel their growth included the desire to increase enrollment, developments in information technology (Allen & Seaman, 2010), the need to support the growing interest of adult learners to continue their education, and various economic factors (Cornford & Pollock, 2003; Folkers, 2005; Milligan & Buckenmeyer, 2008; Rovai & Downey, 2010; Williams, Paprock, & Covington, 1999). The 2012 Sloan Consortium (Sloan-C) study of distance education in the United States found an increase in online enrollment to 6.7 million students.

The growth and expansion of online DE programs and enrollment continues to demonstrate that it is a viable alternative to conventional face-to-face instruction. While that growth continues, Saba (2005) and Garrison (2000) observed that the field of distance education is replete with confusion, which they attributed, in part, to its rapid growth and the evolution of new terms. As institutions widely embrace DE, and as the practice grows, it has come to be associated with different names, practices, and terminologies. The introduction and use of new terminologies in describing distance education can create confusion. For example, DE is variously referred to as virtual, open, web-based, distributed education, and online learning or e-learning. Some programs offer courses identified as correspondence courses, telecourses, videoconferencing, and other names. The terms often reflect the delivery system instead of the field of practice or the conventional name of distance education.

Adding to the naming confusion is the constant and rapid emergence of new technologies, innovative course designs and instructional approaches, evolving and increasing program demands, varying learning styles, new communication and interaction patterns among students, new audiences, vendors touting tools and technologies they offer as panaceas for learning difficulties, and a wide array of commercially competitive for-profit and nonprofit DE providers. DE programs deal with several of these issues that may not be familiar to senior institutional administrators in conventional colleges and universities. The growth and nature of the DE environment have contributed to complicating the task of traditional educational administrators who must manage DE, identify DE leaders, and define their roles.

The unabated growth of online distance education programs and its expanding complexities presents the need for educational administrators to find leaders to effectively guide the DE programs. Institutional attempts to meet this demand have often followed the pattern of filling any other higher education administrative position. Institutions search for DE leaders, most of whom are found through a regional or national search process or internal promotion (Nworie, Haughton, & Oprandi, 2012). In the search process, distinction has not been sufficiently made between the uniqueness and qualities of DE leadership and those of other administrative positions.

The need to effectively manage the DE programs poses challenges for senior institutional administrators as they strive to cope with DE operations in their institutions. DE leaders equally face different challenges in managing the DE programs. Bower and Hardy (2004) identified some of the challenges that DE leaders face: stakeholders not fully supporting distance education, management of required changes in teaching at a distance, provision of required innovations in student support services, acquisition of necessary technology skills by faculty members, and full utilization of the potential of DE to alter the culture of conventional educational institutions.

The educational alternatives and opportunities DE offers provide an unprecedented opportunity for institutional and DE leaders to identify and promote practices that meet this wide range of emerging educational challenges, pursue growing opportunities to expand audiences beyond their institutions, and provide diverse and rewarding experiences for both educators and learners. DE leaders can have a profound influence on the success of higher education DE programs despite the challenges they face in an environment of constant and pervasive change, competition from outside vendors, confusion with terminology, adoption of emerging technologies, and changes to teaching and learning requirements.

The purpose of this chapter is to examine the challenges encountered by DE leaders in higher education and offer suggestions for successful navigation of those challenges in order to meet the needs of institutions and students. While the focal point is higher education, the issues discussed can be applied to other educational settings. Similarly, this chapter focuses on online DE mediated by computers and other digital devices; however, the ideas shared here can be applied to other delivery methods such as correspondence, radio, television, computers, and videoconferencing.

For the purpose of this chapter, the term *distance education leader* has been used to describe the DE leader who oversees the DE operation in an institution, irrespective of the title of the position and name of the DE program. The DE leadership role is assumed by a person who is responsible for the day-to-day operations; short and long-term strategic planning; direction of all institutional DE programs and activities, including curricula and/or degree programs; and motivating others to achieve the desired results within their areas of authority. The leader may hold the title of Coordinator, Director, Dean, or Assistant/Associate Vice President or Assistant Provost for Distance Education, E-learning, or Online Learning or similar position titles.

Leadership in Distance Education

Good leadership is central to the success of any organization (Brown & McLenighan, 2005; Covey, 1990; Zekeri, 2004). Successful leaders set the tone of the organization as they influence organizational cultures and lead in organization development (Davis, 2007; Covey, 1990;

Sharma & Dakhane, 1998). DE in higher education and other educational settings is not different. Leadership has been variously defined and discussed. For example, Yukl (1989) defines a leader as one who will "influence processes involving determination of the group's or organization's objectives, motivating task behavior in pursuit of these objectives, and influencing group maintenance and culture" (p. 5). Bass (1990) describes leadership as a *universal phenomenon* and "an interaction between two or more members of a group that often involves a structuring or restructuring of the situation and the perception and expectations of the members" (p. 19). Lussier and Achua (2010) define leadership as "the influencing process of leaders and followers to achieve organizational objectives through change" (p. 6). And Beaudoin (2003b) notes that leaders possess "a set of attitudes and behaviors that create conditions for innovative change, that enable individuals and organizations to share a vision and move in its direction, and that contribute to the management and operationalization of ideas" (p. 519). Many more definitions and literature on leadership abound. In discussions about leadership, there is a general agreement about the need for good leadership for the success of organizations and institutions and the notion that the dynamics of leadership vary in different contexts. Discussions on leadership include the different leadership styles, some of which will be valuable for DE leaders. Knowledge of an assortment of leadership styles and qualities can provide direction on how a leader operates in a variety of situations and how to navigate when in different levels of authority (Northouse, 2007) and equips the leader with the behavioral, philosophical, theoretical, and operational models from which to operate to reach her or his goals (Bolman & Deal, 2003).

Leadership qualities that have worked in other organizational environment can be adapted for the DE contexts (Beaudoin, 2004; Nworie, 2012; Portugal, 2006). Leadership is examined here as it affects DE in educational settings and particularly within higher education institutions. There are possible differences in the administration of DE in single-mode and dual-mode institutions, two-year community colleges, and corporate educational settings as leadership in these organizations have some similarities and differences. The differences may require the right qualities to operate in those educational contexts. DE leadership challenges are generally discussed and the challenges will affect the various organizational settings in varying ways. The DE environment with its peculiarities and the emergence of the DE leadership position within conventional educational contexts that have deep traditions and practices results in challenges that need the right leadership style or a blend of styles in managing.

DE leadership is an area that needs more focus. Despite the sustained interest in DE, the corresponding increase in DE leadership positions, and the major role that DE leadership plays in managing DE programs, the subject of DE leadership has not attracted the attention of many researchers (Beaudoin, 2003a; Harry, 1999; Marcus, 2004; Satyanarayana & Meduri, 2007; Schrenk, 2011), resulting in the paucity of research and literature. This includes work in defining the DE leadership position, identifying core competences and roles, and research into the right kinds of leadership styles and traits. On the contrary, other areas in DE in have generated a large body of extant literature on DE (Beaudoin, 2003a; Chang, 1998; Irlbeck, 2002; Lape & Hart, 1997), of which a limited number focus on DE leadership (Beaudoin, 2002). Beaudoin's extensive survey of literature on various aspects of DE (which included major national and international distance education journals, conference proceedings, and other publications) found that about 70% of the literature focused on other aspects of DE and only a small percentage was devoted to distance education leadership. In their discussion of DE research topics, Lee, Driscoll and Nelson (2007) stated that between 1997 and 2005, only 9% of the research in the field was directed to the topic of management, while 36% focused on theory and research and 21% on topics related to design (p. 34). In their study of articles on distance education published between

2000 and 2008, Zawacki-Richter, Backer, and Vogt (2009), found that only 18 of 695 (2.6%) published articles were directed toward issues of DE management and organization. There is the lack of a robust body of work on the appropriate distance education leadership styles and competencies. Without well-defined competencies, roles, and responsibilities, there is bound to be leadership ambiguity. This suggests that, as DE programs grow, more focus is needed on leadership issues. DE leadership is a relatively new position in higher education that faces the problems of definition and assimilation, the difficulties of placement, issues of competition and acceptance, and the tensions of working in a dynamic environment.

The diversified functions of DE leaders are performed with much expectation and in unconventional contexts. The roles and responsibilities of the DE leader in higher education have been identified as many and necessary to help institutions realize their goals for DE (Moore, 1994; Nworie et al., 2012; Schrenk, 2011). DE leaders are assuming increasingly complex roles and responsibilities as they work with multiple internal and external constituencies, operate in a field that must function within the traditional educational system, and manage emerging technologies (Beaudoin, 2003a; McKenzie, Ozkan, & Layton, 2005; Nworie et al., 2012; Otte & Benke, 2006; Schrenk, 2011; Simonson, Smaldino, Albright, & Zvacek, 2011). These roles are performed in complex educational settings as many DE programs operate alongside conventional learning environments resulting in dual-mode environments, and some leadership aspects of the two areas tend to vary. Understanding the unique DE environment and the nature of its leadership, as well as determining the qualities that would enable DE leaders to thrive and surmount opposing challenges, would be advantageous. The leadership qualities of DE leaders have implications for institutional outcomes, program functions and success, sustainability of DE, and the vision and future direction of their institution. The DE leaders' knowledge base, the effectiveness of their plans, the efficiency of their staff, and the satisfaction of their stakeholders can contribute to the success of their programs and the impact they have as leaders (Schrenk, 2011). The success of DE programs depends on effective DE leadership and not on how large the programs are or on the latest and most impressive technology (Beaudoin, 2003a; Irlbeck, 2002; Marcus, 2004; McKenzie, Mims, & Bennett, 2003; McKenzie et al., 2005; Moore, 1994; Nworie et al. 2012; Nworie 2012). As DE continues to evolve, new roles will emerge, requiring DE leaders to guide institutions through the stages of development and challenges resulting from the growth.

Online DE has contributed to the complexity of leading in higher education. The increasing influence of online distance education is prompting administrators in colleges and universities to rethink the best approaches to manage, staff, evaluate, administer, and lead distance education programs to be successful and to meet institutional needs. In such a context, Cohen and Brawer (2008) suggest that because "colleges have grown larger and more complex, administrators, faculty members, and trustees all have had to adjust" and the "adjustments will have to be made with increasing frequency" (p. 155). DE programs need to be guided, nurtured, and structured well by institutional administrators; available resources must be efficiently managed and utilized; technologies must be adopted and utilized effectively; and a vision of the future of DE for the institution must be articulated and communicated to the entire institution. The support of institutional administrators will in turn enable the DE leaders to manage the constant challenges they face in their DE environment.

Challenges

The administration of DE has been fraught with challenges. As higher education institutions continue to embrace the implementation of online distance education, DE leaders in a dual-mode institution face unique challenges as they straddle the duality of their context; ensure innovative course design and delivery for the DE environment; monitor the effective use of technology for the delivery of instruction; prepare faculty to be successful online learning facilitators; and develop, implement, and plan viable online DE programs. In addition, DE leaders face the challenges of establishing quality instruction, preventing misuse of technology, and maintaining cost effectiveness (McFarlane, 2011). The challenges may be more pronounced in dual-mode campus-based conventional institutions than in the single-mode institutions that are dedicated to teaching at a distance and in the online learning environments in corporate settings. The following discussion describes such challenges.

The New Learning Environment

Higher education DE programs introduce a learning environment to administrators who may not be familiar with the DE learning context, including the new delivery systems needed as a result of the separation of instructors and learners; adjustments needed to identify and use appropriate pedagogical styles; changes in the duration of a semester, as some DE programs now offer courses that last 5–6 weeks instead of the traditional 15 weeks; the need to adjust to the rapid and constant change in technologies; the emerging quality assurance processes; and a learning environment that must assimilate and adapt to new information. DE leaders and senior institutional administrators face these changes and emerging trends.

There is a perception that distance education leadership is different from leadership in other areas of higher education (Beaudoin, 2003a; McKenzie et al., 2005; Simonson et al., 2011). This notion is based on the DE program practices, activities, and operational methods that are evidence of a postindustrial society and economy, which differs from the traditional higher education context that still bears the relics of the industrial age and operates in the old economy (Beaudoin, 2003a). Prior to the '80s, earlier forms of DE operated on the periphery in conventional higher education institutions. In contemporary contexts, DE operates in an instructional environment that is designed to meet the educational needs of traditional-age students, adult learners, and a global community of students who are geographically dispersed and more culturally diverse with cutting-edge technologies. Successful DE programs use innovative pedagogical approaches that depend extensively on constantly changing technologies for course delivery; flexible instruction that can be offered as fully online distance learning, hybrid, or web-based programs and delivered either synchronously or asynchronously; a shift in the role of the instructor to that of a facilitator; and a diverse student body whose members take a more active role in their learning while at the same time expecting quality instruction that meets their academic, professional, and cultural needs.

DE leaders work with a diverse population of internal and external constituents, including faculty, students, administrators, parents, accrediting organizations, and professional associations, within an environment in which DE and traditional instruction share the same context (Beaudoin, 2003a; McKenzie et al., 2005; Nworie et al., 2012; Otte & Benke, 2006; Simonson et al., 2011). The traditional environment tends to encourage dependent and passive learning in contrast to DE courses that use instructional strategies that encourage students to take ownership of their learning (Holmberg, 2005; Moore & Kearsley, 2005). In addition to its support of instruction delivery, DE relies on technology to facilitate communication between instructors and students and among the students themselves, and to provide interaction with course materials. This is a dynamic environment that challenges the DE leaders to be well grounded in current instructional technologies and teaching strategies in order to be effective.

Leadership Criteria

Identifying the right leadership for DE programs is a challenge as there is no clearly defined leadership path and preparation. A review of position announcements and the qualities sought by higher education institutions reveals diverse qualifications (Nworie et al., 2012), and different institutions emphasize different qualities. The path that DE leaders often follow is that of faculty from conventional institutions and different academic disciplines who take up DE positions following their careers in teaching and research. According to Schrenk (2011), there is about a 50% chance that DE leaders were hired because of previous experience in distance education and a 40% chance that they were hired from educational settings not related to DE. Transitioning from the classroom to the DE leadership position may mean that they will learn about the field of distance education—its peculiar concerns, the leadership challenges, and the required skills, competencies, roles and responsibilities—on the job, as these are extensive (Nworie et al., 2012; Schrenk, 2011). With its relatively short history in higher education, online DE does not have the long experience of traditional academic departments. Without an established career path across many institutions for DE administrators, a prospective DE leader could accept such a position with minimal experience in DE (Schrenk).

Lack of Appropriate Precedents

In a typical dual-mode institution, there is no historical precedent for online distance education and how it fits into an academic community that operates mostly from a traditional face-to-face format. While many senior administrators in higher education are generally familiar with DE and would like their institutions to embrace it, they are unsure about how to manage this new enterprise. They hope that whoever is selected to manage the DE program will get it right. But, successful management can be problematic without precedents to rely on, and with no institutional DE goals or policies and a lack of adequate resources. This challenge is more pronounced when there are no patrons who can champion the cause of DE and when an institution adopts DE just to be competitive with other institutions. Without precedents and generally accepted norms, institutions must determine their own criteria for what DE leadership should be.

Inadequate Institutional Support and Limited Power

There is the problem of insufficient support and diminished authority. Distance education leadership is one of the areas in higher education where the incumbent often has position and responsibilities, but limited authority. That lack of authority may be a reflection of the importance and value placed on DE by the institution or the level of control that top administrators exert over DE leaders. When a leader hired to manage a DE program does not receive adequate support and power, that leader's effectiveness is diminished. It is difficult to operate when a leader has to justify having an appropriate title; receives insufficient funding, which hinders budgeting and advance planning; is not equitably compensated; lacks the authority to contribute in the selection of the courses that will be scheduled online or who will teach them because these decisions are made by departmental chairs; cannot hire needed staff; and lacks authority to manage DE support services, which are overseen by student affairs directors. Some power struggles may result from lack of authority to manage technology issues that relate to the delivery of instruction, as these are often the responsibility of the chief information officer (CIO).

DE leaders deal with the reality that DE decisions are often made without their involvement or approval. This can be common when the DE program is decentralized, or when an influential academic program on campus sets up an eccentric DE program (without intending to be adversarial; or perhaps not knowing what else is available on campus). The DE leader of the departmental program may not be aware of university DE policies or of extant DE leadership. Alternatively, maverick programs may be the result of senior institutional administrators' deciding on broad DE policy without giving thought to the practicalities of such a program, without consulting the DE leader, and without considering what already exists. In some instances, administrators are embracing new DE ideas to cope with competitive image, such as jumping in to establish a MOOC (massive open online course), without adequate consultation or planning.

Distance education to some extent shares in the plight of academic support units that work under pressure to justify their existence and demonstrate their benefits to the institutions. Academic technology, faculty development, and media services, for example, seem to operate in environments that lack power and recognition. The discharge of the responsibilities of leaders of such units is influenced by the decisions of administrators who may not be familiar with their role (Wunsch, 2000). Wunsch (2000) observed that senior administrators who are unfamiliar with technology or do not realize the value of technology in the delivery of instruction are not likely to be supportive of investments in technology; technology-related initiatives; or units that provide technology services, including leadership positions for those services. Duderstadt, Atkins, and van Houweling (2002) suggest that many top-level institutional leaders are unaware of the threats of not fully embracing technology or of the potential benefits of deploying information technology, and they argue that institutions benefit from information technology when leaders at the executive level support its use. Institutional leaders who have the authority to hire DE leaders benefit from understanding the unique nature of the DE context and the leadership traits required for DE leaders who will be successful in leading their institutions in times of unprecedented change and of rapid technological evolution.

Campus Politics

According to Roche (2001), leaders have the ability to effect change when they have political power within their institutions. Politics exists in higher education and those who operate from positions that lack or have limited power are at a disadvantage. When the position title of a DE leader is not on a par with that of other unit administrators, that DE leader will lack political power and resources. DE administrators cannot lead effectively when they are not empowered to make the necessary decisions about their programs or report to an appropriate institutional leader. For instance, DE programs are expected to offer high-quality courses and degree programs that meet regional and programmatic accreditation standards, but academic administrators who have traditionally selected the courses their departments will offer and the faculty members who will teach them are often not interested in receiving directives from DE leaders on such matters. To be successful in the political and competitive educational environment, DE leaders will need to have the authority that comes with elevated position, political power, and the ability to negotiate.

Staffing Issues

DE leaders face challenges in the hiring and development of personnel in their programs. There is competition by various interested parties for faculty, trainers, instructional designers, instructional technologists, and content developers. The challenges of finding people with the right skills or losing effective staff members to competitors can adversely affect a DE program. This may not have the same effect on a traditional academic department. Insufficient funding can be a deterrent to hiring the right caliber of support staff and required number. Managing technical and creative people who are needed to develop courses can be equally challenging. There is also the challenge of identifying and preparing faculty to teach DE courses. Teaching at a distance requires a unique professional experience and qualities that are different from teaching in a face-to-face environment, making it necessary for faculty members to be prepared to teach online DE courses.

Operational Policies and Structure

DE leaders are often expected to manage programs in an institutional setting where there are no DE polices or plans and no structure is present. This is typical of institutions where the DE program started with innovative individual faculty members who ventured into online DE on their own. Over time, other faculty members began teaching online and the institution generated multiple online courses, and thereafter became a DE institution without any institutional plan or policies for DE in place. In a climate devoid of structure, policies, and procedures for an inclusive DE effort, there are usually no institutional mechanisms in place for DE curriculum and course design and development, no established assessment plans, no quality measurement processes, and no efforts to fit DE into the institutions' accreditation processes. In such environments faculty members continue to develop and teach courses without the benefit of instructional designers, assessment specialists, and others in the course development effort. Such haphazard arrangements can result in DE's not being included in the institution's missions, strategic plans, funding, or processes and priorities.

Delivery of Quality Instruction

Questions frequently surface about whether DE programs measure up to the quality of traditional face-to-face instruction. Even when the program is poorly funded and the position of the DE leader is reduced to that of a technical support person, the expectations for quality instruction are still there. DE leaders are under pressure to certify that their programs maintain high standards. Davies et al. (2010) noted that there is a "deep-rooted insecurity within the distance learning community, a fear that distance education is regarded as a somewhat substandard and less valued educational practice" (p. 44). In addition to meeting applicable institutional requirements, DE leaders are expected to administer programs that satisfy the conditions and requirements of regional, state, and professional accreditation agencies. The institutional stakeholders expect the DE leader to put in place measures that ensure quality in the design, development, and delivery of courses.

Student Support

DE leaders face the task of ensuring that students are recruited, retained, and supported in the online learning environment in the same way they were supported in the traditional campus environment. Institutions expect their DE programs to provide enriching learning experiences and to make efforts to ensure that students are given opportunities to succeed. To avoid high attrition rates, DE leaders are challenged to develop student retention strategies. While many institutions provide DE courses, students tend to enroll at institutions and programs that meet their needs and expectations. The challenge for institutions is to provide DE programs and befitting student support services that can attract and keep students.

Adopt and Adapt to Change

The DE environment is one that is replete with change. Because DE is mostly driven by technology, DE leaders face the challenge of constantly monitoring emerging technologies, ensuring that they are suitable and cost effective, adopting applicable technologies, and managing resulting change. A cursory look at the history of DE reveals an evolutionary pattern with constant changes in technology, pedagogy, communication, interaction, and operational practices. In the DE environment, educational institutions must continually update technologies, processes, tools, and tasks and assimilate new practices into existing structures. The rapid pace of development of technologies used in DE requires DE leaders to manage change and to understand the adoption and diffusion of innovation process. DE leaders are also expected to follow patterns of changing student characteristics, including demographic and generational shifts; manage cultural sensitivity in course designs; and seek improved and appropriate instructional approaches. As DE programs seek to attract traditional-age students, adult learners, and students from other countries, DE leaders, course designers, and instructors are expected to adapt course materials to be culturally sensitive. The process of introducing change or adopting innovations involves gaining buy-in from institutional constituencies. These challenges present opportunities and occasions to respond, adapt, and embrace changes. As a result of the changes, new hierarchies, functions, roles, positions, and activities emerge. The evolving environment challenges distance education programs, DE leaders, institutional administrators, and faculty to develop appropriate policies, procedures, and practices as they adjust to change (Cornford & Pollock, 2003; Portugal, 2006).

Decision Points

Another challenge facing DE leaders is not having a major decision-point for academic institutions considering or implementing DE. Despite having information provided by related professional associations, DE leaders face perplexing situations with a variety of decisions as they chart the course in the evolving DE environment. For example, there is perplexity regarding what to do with the new state authorization laws that require institutions to obtain authorization from any state in which they plan to serve DE students. These regulations vary from state to state. Some states require nothing and others demand filings, authorization, and fees. There is also the question of whether to partner with external organizations to provide competencies that the institution does not possess such as marketing, online student retention and support, information technology support, course design, and so on. Institutions must decide whether to outsource the entire DE operation or part of it. The DE leaders face the challenge of making wise decisions regarding whether to enter into contracts to manage aspects of the operation, or to build internal capacity to manage the resources and relationship while protecting the academic integrity and reputation of the institution.

Managing the Challenges

Addressing the institutional challenges that DE leaders face requires colleges and universities that hope to have successful DE programs to provide a conducive and enabling environment in which DE programs thrive and DE leaders are effective. Managing the challenges requires institutional support, shared leadership, empowerment of the DE leader, appropriate funding, provision of opportunities for continuous learning, and steps taken to prepare future leaders. Some suggestions are provided to address the identified challenges.

Institutional Support

For DE leaders to be most effective, colleges and universities must provide an environment that is favorable for DE programs. This is best done by providing needed resources and adequate funding, empowering DE leaders by positioning DE within academic affairs, providing the mechanisms necessary for student support, and ensuring access and equitable learning opportunities for all students. In order to fulfill their educational mission and institutional goals and remain relevant in today's DE environment, institutions need to commit to continuous improvement; consistent evaluation of programs; and ongoing updating, refining, and transforming of their teaching and learning practices. Institutional policies and procedures for DE programs must be in place. Proactive leadership at the senior institutional leadership levels can act to dispel DE leaders' concerns.

Having an Institutional Sponsor

When a top institutional or organizational administrator takes an interest in the DE program and nurtures it, the program is bound to be successful. In that top administrator, the DE leader finds an ally, mentor, or benefactor who will ensure that the DE program is funded and that it does not fail. When the DE leader is not in a position to authorize change, the top administrator can step in.

A retrospective view of the evolution of distance education and those who popularized the concept suggests that it is possible for a senior administrators or a leader with keen interest in DE to sponsor a successful DE operation without being a specialist in DE. For example, the founding Vice Chancellor of the British Open University, Water Perry, and the Governor of the State of Utah, who promoted the Western Governors University, were not DE experts; but they sanctioned, articulated, and promoted the ideals of DE, leading to successful DE institutions. DE programs and leadership need such patrons in their settings.

Empowering the DE Leader

The importance that an institution places on DE can be assessed by the support the DE program receives, the place of DE in the institutional strategic plan, the type of leadership it puts in place to manage the DE program, and the financial commitment to the program's work. Empowering the DE leader will necessitate giving that leader a position title that enables her or him to relate with key administrators and grants the authority to make critical decisions and fully direct the DE programs, imbuing her or him with the authority to manage change and offering commensurate compensation to DE leaders and support staff. The level of the position that the DE leader holds can define the type of leadership style needed to succeed (Nworie et al., 2012; Schrenk, 2011). DE leaders should play key roles and have corresponding power and influence within their institutions and be empowered to assess and react to national trends (Schrenk). Beaudoin (2004) suggests that senior institutional leaders can ensure effective DE leadership by authorizing resources and establishing plans and policies that would enable DE programs to succeed in their institutions. Albright and Nworie (2008) made recommendations regarding position titles and responsibilities of academic technology leaders in higher education that would empower them in their contexts, and that could apply to DE leaders.

Rewarding the DE leader and support staff adequately can be a good motivator. One of the difficult issues that confront senior institutional administrators is establishing an equitable reward system for faculty and staff who engage in DE, especially in dual-mode institutions.

Shared Leadership

Involving others in the leadership process relieves the DE leader of involvement in every detail, frees up time for other activities, and gives others an opportunity to be part of the process. By delegating work to subordinates, leaders give those stakeholders a sense of ownership in the process. Forming committees to work on specific projects, establishing an advisory committee, or involving faculty members in the process of adopting new technologies or in other relevant areas can be seen as collegial, enabling others to participate and gaining their support. Shared leadership can be effective in prioritizing and in utilizing opportunities as they occur.

The role of DE leaders requires them to collaborate and cooperate with stakeholders within and outside the institution. These include their staff, faculty, administrators, curriculum developers, student support offices, assessment and accreditation staff, outside vendors, professional colleagues, and the public. With this level of interaction, DE leaders need to be skillful in building relationships with the various constituencies and to maintain good communication in their interactions with others (Martin, 2006). Involving administrative superiors in major decisions affecting the institution can be recognized as a savvy leadership move and evidence of being a team player.

Program Structure

The organizational structure and reporting lines for the DE program and leader are important to the success of the program. Moore and Kearsley (2005) posit that distance education requires special organizational and administrative arrangements to enable practitioners function in the DE environment. As an institution creates a new or manages an existing DE program, it must include DE in the institutional mission and plan, determine the division within which DE will be located, and establish suitable reporting lines of the DE leader. DE programs have been found to be variously located in higher education, including in administration, academic affairs, facilities, and information technology departments (Nworie et al., 2012; Schrenk, 2011). DE has not always been in the mainstream of higher education; therefore, care should be taken to know where to place DE programs and their administrators. An academic affairs division is the most suitable location for DE and the DE leader reports to the Chief Academic Officer. Schrenk (2011) found instances of DE leaders reporting to nonacademic divisions and explained that when DE leaders report to the Chief Information Officer (CIO), for example, their role gravitates toward creating and maintaining technical infrastructure. Since the position title and reporting line of a DE leader reflect the importance that the institution attaches to the position, its level of authority, and the political power that individual can exert, the position title has to be appropriate (Albright & Nworie, 2008; Bates, 2000; Nworie et al., 2012). The location of the DE program and the reporting line is crucial in relating to faculty members. Lokken, Womer, and Mullins (2010) report that when DE leaders are located in departments other than academic affairs they do not report to the same administrators as the faculty, and this can create confusion about the role of the DE program.

Structuring the DE program to be a centralized unit minimizes the problems arising from alternative maverick programs and eliminates confusion for students and faculty members. When institutions adopt a centralized approach for their DE programs, internal and external constituencies benefit from having a single point of contact and one place to go on matters relating to DE.

Systemic Approach

Systems thinking, a holistic and expansionist view of the world (Banathy, 1996), examines the interrelationships and interconnectedness of often disparate parts that make up a whole. Being able to view institutions and the DE programs from a systems perspective can help DE leaders manage change as new technologies and processes are introduced. Any interventions, changes, or introduction of new ideas and technologies will likely affect other parts of the institution because of existing relationships, which can lead to unintended as well as intended consequences. By applying systems thinking, institutions can implement change in a manner that places people, practices, units, ideals, priorities, and goals in proper perspective, effecting change that is transformative and sustainable without adverse consequences (Nworie & Haughton, 2008; Roche, 2001).

Senge (1990) suggests that introducing systems thinking into an organizational context provides the type of discipline and tools necessary to see the interrelationships and patterns of change as a whole, and helps in understanding the complexities and dynamics of systems. Applying systemic and using a systematic approach enables the DE leaders to recognize how change in one area affects other parts that constitute the institution as a whole (Gustafson & Branch, 2002). Systems thinking would help DE leaders plan effectively for the introduction of technologies and processes, and perceive how system-wide change would impact the DE programs.

Identifying Leadership Styles and Competencies

Scholars have examined different leadership styles that will suit the dynamic, evolutionary, and complex nature of DE leadership, and transformational leadership is one of the favored styles for DE leaders (Beaudoin, 2003b, 2004; Irlbeck, 2000; McKenzie et al., 2005; Portugal, 2006; Tipple, 2010). Burns (1978) introduced the concept of transformational leadership, which is built on the idea that leaders and followers can work together to reach high levels of success and moral uprightness. Bass (1985) further developed and expanded the concept. Transformational leaders articulate a vision of the future for their organizations and elevate followers to new heights of motivation and morality as the actions of the leaders are perceived to be based on moral, ethical, and equitable consideration of everyone within an organization (Kezar & Eckel, 2008; Kouzes & Posner, 2002; Northouse, 2007). Transformational leaders may or may not be charismatic, but they are motivational and intellectual, and they show consideration for their followers and exhibit other qualities such as honesty, self-confidence, and integrity (Bass & Steidelmeier, 1998). Lussier and Achua (2010) suggest that transformational leaders know the value of developing trust in their followers and channel their charisma in inspiring others. Transformational leaders are visionaries and have the drive to effect change that is born of their vision and genuine interest in the good of all. They thrive in contexts where change is necessary, communicate well with others, and seek the betterment of their followers and others, and they are able to lead in an environment of ambiguity.

The diverse and worthy qualities of vision, inspiration, trust, care, passion, and commitment make the transformational leadership style amenable to DE leaders (Tipple, 2010). Portugal (2006) suggests that DE leaders must be transformational leaders and innovative visionaries who have the drive to motivate, energize, inspire, and encourage followers as they seek to meet a shared and competitive distance learning plan. Bennis and Nanus (1985) recommend transformational leadership as a worthy model for leaders as they seek to assist institutional stakeholders, including administrators, faculty and staff, students, and other constituencies. Tipple (2010) suggests that situational leadership can be a good fit as DE faces major changes in different areas. Beaudoin (2003b) argues that no one particular leadership style is commonly acceptable, but suggests that transformative and situational leadership styles might be a suitable DE leadership models. Nworie (2012) examined the inherent qualities of various leadership styles and reported that transformational, situational, and complexity leadership theories might be suitable for DE leadership.

Management Roles and Responsibilities

Knowledge of the management needs of the institutions they serve can help DE leaders address administrative issues such as developing strategic plans, establishing purpose, working with colleagues, supervising staff, funding projects, managing budgets, utilizing technology, developing policies, managing teaching and learning processes, and developing quality standards. Distinct lines of accountability in DE and within the institution should be established. Williams (2003) identified these essential skills for the successful DE leader: leadership, interpersonal communication, managerial, budgeting, marketing, strategic planning, and academic policy-making skills. Others are change-agent abilities and knowledge of education theory. According to Williams, 13 distinct functions support the implementation of distance education programs; among them are instructional designer, instructor/facilitator, technology expert, graphic designer, media publisher/editor, trainer, librarian, evaluation specialist, and support staff. DE leaders are more likely to be successful when they employ a team approach in the design of course materials and select knowledgeable staff to manage the support functions.

Beyond visioning and planning, the DE leader is charged with the managerial aspects of the daily operation of the program. The role of supporting faculty and staff, supervising and providing professional development opportunities for their staff, and providing needed support to students rests with the DE leader. The DE leader plans for this, realizing that there are still pockets of resistance, tension, and insecurity toward DE among faculty for various reasons. Setting up administrative infrastructure and providing incentives might help.

Recruiting, Retaining, and Supporting Students

DE leaders are expected to participate in efforts to attract students to enroll in DE. Competition for students with for-profit and nonprofit institutions compels DE leaders to work with their marketing teams to attract students and to make contributions to marketing and recruitment strategies. Assisting in identifying the target audiences for DE programs enables the marketing team to reach an audience with the greatest potential for success. DE leaders must be able to manage support services that will allow their institutions to be competitive in the DE marketplace.

Managing Competing Priorities and Utilizing of Opportunities

DE operates as an area with seemingly unlimited potentials; however, competing issues, projects, opportunities, and administrative functions place demands on the time, attention, and limited resources of the DE leader (Nworie et al., 2012). Opportunities must be prioritized and seized by the DE leader who, given staffing or budget constraints, must make necessary adjustments while weighing the cost of attending to one need over another; the greater the budgetary constraints, the greater the need to prioritize. While going after new opportunities might seem like a distraction from routine and daily administrative tasks, setting priorities can lead to better planning and resource management, to the advantage of the DE program and the institution.

Utilizing Opportunities

The realities of rapid change require DE leaders to take advantage of opportunities as they arise. New opportunities can enhance the program and institutional goals when leaders look beyond their routine practices, comfort zones, and perceived efficiencies to envision how the new opportunities can transform their context. While change may seem to present a challenge as it disrupts existing conditions, practices, processes, and the stability of an established DE program, it can also bring about improvements, forge new alliances, and eliminate waste, redundancies, and unproductive procedures.

Preparation of DE Leaders

Distance education will continue to grow in higher education and other educational settings. Trends that support this conclusion include the growing global demand for higher education, especially from popular institutions; adult learners' need for continuing education; increasing educational needs of developing countries; continuous development in technology; the ubiquitous, affordable, flexible, and reliable nature of technology; the growing interest of students in DE; the engagement in DE by many institutions and organizations; the flexibility it offers to students to determine when and where they learn; and the opportunities and benefits it offers institutions (Williams et al., 1999). Consequently, the need for institutions to hire DE leaders will continue to grow.

Given this anticipated continued growth, deliberate efforts in the preparation of future DE leaders will yield dividends. There are indications that institutions seek to hire DE leaders from the disciplines of educational technology and higher education administration (Nworie et al., 2012; Schrenk, 2011). This suggests greater focus by these academic disciplines on programs that include DE leadership preparation in their academic work. DE professional associations and those in related fields can engage current and future DE leaders in professional development activities designed to equip them with the skills and competencies necessary to become successful administrators.

Leadership in Related Fields

The field of distance education can benefit from discussions about leadership, literature, and practices in other related fields such as academic technology, adult education, and information technology. Beaudoin (2003b) argued that in discussions of DE leadership it is appropriate to look at other areas of educational theory and practice, including adult and continuing education, which are closely related to DE. Bates (2000) identified the need for top administrators in academic technology areas to provide an appropriate platform for leaders, granting them with necessary authority, enabling them to manage change, and placing them in a position to work with other administrators. Albright and Nworie (2008) argued for good leadership in academic technology and discussed competencies for academic technology leaders. Beaudoin cited Simerly (1987), who developed strategies that are deemed crucial to effective continuing education leadership and which could be applicable to distance education, as the body of work on distance education leadership has not been fully developed. They include:

- Analyzing systems and conduct environmental scans.
- Being aware of power. Manage both conflict and agreement and reach consensus.
- Understanding the impact of institutional culture.
- Functioning with ambiguity, complexity, and decentralization.
- Utilizing tactical and strategic planning.
- Demonstrating the value of the educational organization to multiple constituencies.

Conclusion

DE is a growing area of education, with its uniqueness requiring different approaches in course delivery, student interaction and learning, and leadership. It provides an alternative educational environment. Given that DE is a fast evolving and technology-driven operation within and outside conventional learning environments, DE programs and its leadership face various challenges. The challenges may be more pronounced in dual-mode conventional campus-based institutions than in the single-mode institutions that are dedicated to distance teaching. The challenges faced by DE leaders or administrators can be met by educational institutions doing their part to support DE and its administrators. DE leaders have some parts to play. Institutions already play a major role in DE as they invest in technologies and human capital. They also need to invest in DE leadership that is appropriately located in the academic environment and equipped with necessary resources. DE leaders are expected to understand the context of distance education in higher education, function successfully in that environment, and operate successful DE programs in their institutions.

References

Albright, M.J., & Nworie, J. (2008). Rethinking academic technology leadership in an era of change. *Educause Quarterly, 31*(1), 14–23.

Allen, I.E., & Seaman, J. (2010). *Learning on demand: Online education in the United States*. Retrieved from http://www.sloan-c.org/publications/survey/pdf/learningondemand.pdf

Banathy, B.H. (1996). Systems inquiry and its application in education. In D. Jonassen (Ed.), *Handbook of research for educational communications and technology* (pp. 74–92). New York, NY: Simon & Schuster/Macmillan.

Bass, B.M. (1985). *Leadership and performance beyond expectation*. New York, NY: Free Press.

Bass, B.M. (1990). *Handbook of leadership: Theory, research and managerial applications* (3rd ed.). New York: Free Press.

Bass, B., & Steidelmeier, P. (1998). *Ethics, character, and authentic transformational leadership*. Center for Leadership Studies. Binghamton, NY: Binghamton University. [Electronic version, http://cls.binghamton.edu/BassSteid.html]

Bates, A.W. (2000). *Managing technological change: Strategies for college and university leaders*. San Francisco, CA: Jossey-Bass.

Beaudoin, M.F. (2002). Distance education leadership: An essential role for the new century. *Journal of Leadership Studies, 8*(3), 131–145.

Beaudoin, M.F. (2003a). Distance education leadership for the new century. *Online Journal of Distance Learning Administration, 6*(2). Retrieved from http://www.westga.edu/~distance/ojdla/summer62/beaudoin62.html

Beaudoin, M. F. (2003b). Distance education leadership: An appraisal of research and practice. In M.G. Moore & W.G. Anderson (Eds.), *Handbook of distance education* (pp. 519–530). Mahwah, NJ: Lawrence Erlbaum.

Beaudoin, M.F. (2004). Distance education leadership: Appraising theory and advancing practice. In *Reflections on research, faculty and leadership in distance education* (ASF Series, Vol. 8, pp. 91–101). Oldenburg, Germany: Oldenburg University Press.

Bennis, W., & Nanus, B. (1985). *Leaders: The strategies for taking charge*. New York, NY: Harper & Row.

Bolman, L., & Deal, T. (2003). *Reframing organizations: Artistry, choice and leadership* (3rd ed.). San Francisco, CA: Jossey-Bass.

Bower, B. L., & Hardy, K.P. (Eds.). (2004). *From distance education to e-learning: Lessons along the way*. San Francisco: Jossey-Bass.

Brown, B., & McLenighan, H. (2005, June). Only the extraordinary for next generation's leaders. *The School Administrator*. Available from http://www. aasa.org/

Burns, J.M. (1978). *Leadership*. New York, NY: Harper Torch Books.

Chang, V. (1998). *Policy development for distance education* (ECO-JC-98–13). Los Angeles, CA: ERIC.

Cohen, A.M., & Brawer, F.B. (2008). *The American community college* (5th ed.). San Francisco, CA: Jossey-Bass.

Cornford, J., & Pollock, N. (2003). *Putting the university online: Information, technology, and organizational change*. Buckingham, England: The Society for Research into Higher Education & Open University Press.

Covey, S.R. (1990). *The 7 habits of highly effective people*. New York, NY: Foreside.

Davies, R.S., Howell, S.L., & Petrie, J.A. (2010). A review of trends in distance education scholarship at research universities in North America, 1998–2007. *International Review of Research in Open and Distance Learning, 11*(3), 42–56.

Davis, A.L. (2007). *A study of the leadership skills needs of businesses in a community college leadership development curriculum* (Doctoral dissertation, Capella University, 2007). Dissertations & Theses: Full Text database. (Publication No. AAT 3251342)

Duderstadt, J., Atkins, D., & van Houweling, D. (2002). *Higher education in the digital age*. Westport, CT: Praeger.

Folkers, D.A. (2005). Competing in the marketspace: Incorporating online education into higher education: An organizational perspective. *Information Resources Management Journal, 18*(1), 61–78.

Garrison, R. (2000). Theoretical challenges for distance education in the 21st century: A shift from structural to transactional issues. *International Review of Research in Open and Distance Learning, 1*(1), 1–17. Available at http://www.irrodl.org/index.php/irrodl/article/viewFile/2/22

Gustafson, K.L., & Branch, R.M. (2002). What is instructional design? In R.A. Reiser & J.V. Dempsey (Eds.), *Trends and issues in instructional design and technology*. Upper Saddle River, NJ: Pearson Education.

Harry, K. (1999). *Higher Education Through Open and Distance Learning: World review of distance education and open learning (Vol. 1)*. London: Routledge/Commonwealth of Learning.

Holmberg, B. (2005). *The evolution, principles and practices of distance education*. Oldenburg, Germany: Bibliotheks-und Informationssystem der Universitat Oldenburg.

Irlbeck, S.A. (2002). Leadership and distance education in higher education: A U.S. perspective. *International Review of Research in Open and Distance Learning, 3*(2). Retrieved from http://www.irrodl.org/index.php/irrodl/article/viewArticle/91/170

Irlbeck, S.A., & Pucel, D.J. (2000). Dimensions of leadership in higher education distance education. In *Proceedings of international workshop on advanced learning technology* (Vol. 2000, pp. 63–64). Palmerston North, New Zealand.

Kezar, A., & Eckel, P. (2008). Advancing diversity agendas on campus: Examining transactional and transformational presidential leadership styles. *International Journal of Leadership in Education, 11*(4), 379–405. doi:10.1080/13603120802317891

Kouzes, J., & Posner, B. (2002). *The leadership challenge* (3rd ed.). San Francisco, CA: Jossey-Bass.

Lape, D.H., & Hart, P.K. (1997). Changing the way we teach by changing the college: Leading the way together. *New Directions for Community Colleges, 99*, 15–22.

Lee, Y., Driscoll, M.P., & Nelson, D.W. (2007). Trends in research: A content analysis of major journals. In M.G. Moore (Ed.), *Handbook of distance education* (pp. 31–41). Mahwah, NJ: Lawrence Erlbaum.

Lokken, F., Womer, L., & Mullins, C. (2010). *2009 distance education survey results: Tracking the impact of e-learning at community colleges*. Washington, DC: Instructional Technology Council.

Lussier, R., & Achua, C. (2010). *Leadership: Theory, application, skill development* (4th ed.). Mason, OH: South-Western Cengage Learning.

Marcus, S. (2004). Leadership in distance education: Is it a unique type of leadership? A literature review. *Online Journal of Distance Learning Administration,* 7(1). Retrieved from http://www.westga.edu/~distance/ojdla/spring71 /marcus71.html

Martin, A. (2006). What is effective leadership today? *Chief Executive, July/August* (219), 24.
McFarlane, D.A. (2011). The leadership roles of distance learning administrators (DLAs) in increasing educational value and quality perceptions. *Online Journal of Distance Learning Administration, 4*(1).
McKenzie, B., Mims, N.G., & Bennett, E. (2003). Successful online assessment, evaluation, and interaction techniques. *Technology and Teacher Education Annual Meeting* (pp. 426–431). Albuquerque, NM: Association for Advancement of Computing in Education.
McKenzie, B., Ozkan, B., & Layton, K. (2005). Distance leadership practices: What works in higher education. In G. Richards (Ed.), *Proceedings of world conference on e-learning in corporate, government, healthcare, and higher education 2005* (pp. 926–931). Chesapeake, VA: AACE. Available at http://www.editlib.org/p/21298
Milligan, A.T., & Buckenmeyer, J.A. (2008). Assessing students for online learning. *International Journal on E-Learning, 7*(3), 449–461.
Moore, M., & Kearsley, G. (2005). *Distance education: A systems view*. Belmont, CA: Thomson-Wadsworth.
Moore, M.G. (1994). Administrative barriers to adoption of distance education. *American Journal of Distance Education, 8*(3), 1–4.
Northouse, P.G. (2007). *Leadership: Theory and practice* (4th ed.). Thousand Oaks, CA: Sage.
Nworie, J. (2012). Applying leadership theories to distance education leadership. *Online Journal of Distance Learning Administration, 15*(4).
Nworie, J., Haughton, N., & Oprandi, S. (2012). Leadership in distance education: Qualities and qualifications sought by higher education institutions. *American Journal of Distance Education, 26*(3), 180–199.
Nworie, J., & Haughton, N. (2008). Good intentions and unanticipated effects: The unintended consequences of the application of technology in teaching and learning environments. *TechTrends, 52*, 52–57.
Otte, G., & Benke, M. (2006). Online learning: New models for leadership and organization in higher education. *Journal of Asynchronous Learning Networks, 10*(2), 23–31.
Portugal, L.M. (2006). Emerging leadership roles in distance education: Current state of affairs and forecasting future trends. *Online Journal of Distance Learning Administration, IX*(III).
Rovai, A.P., & Downey, J.R. (2010). Why some distance education programs fail while others succeed in a global environment. *Internet and Higher Education, 13*, 141–147.
Saba, F. (2005). Critical issues in distance education: A report from the United States. *Distance Education, 26*(2), 255–272.
Satyanarayana, P., & Meduri, E.D.K. (2007). The qualities of leadership required in distance education. *Asian Journal of Distance Education, 5*(1), 4–7.
Schrenk, R.R. (2011). *Comparison of distance education leadership styles and future investment in two-year colleges* (Doctoral dissertation). The University of Montana, Missoula. ProQuest, UMI Dissertation Publishing, 2012-07-17. Available at http://etd.lib.umt.edu/theses/available/etd-08052011-090348/unrestricted/Schrenk_umt_0136D_10147.pdf
Senge, P. (1990). *The fifth discipline. The art and practice of the learning organization*. New York, NY: Doubleday.
Roche, V. (2001). Professional development models and transformative change: A case study of indicators of effective practice in higher education. *International Journal for Academic Development 6*(2), 121–129.
Sharma, S.K., & Dakhane, S. (1998). Effective leadership: The key to success. *Employment News, 23*(10), 1–2.
Simerly, R.G. (1987). *Strategic planning and leadership in continuing education*. San Francisco, CA: Jossey-Bass.
Simonson, M.R., Smaldino, S., Albright, M., & Zvacek, S. (2011). *Teaching and learning at a distance: Foundations of distance education* (4th ed.). Boston, MA: Pearson Education.
Tipple, R. (2010). Effective leadership of online adjunct faculty. *Online Journal of Distance Learning Administration, 13*(1). Retrieved from http://www.westga.edu/~distance/ojdla/spring131/tipple131.html
Williams, M.L., Paprock, K., & Covington, B. (1999). *Distance learning: The essential guide*. Thousand Oaks, CA: Sage.
Williams, P.E. (2003). Roles and competencies for distance education programs in higher education institutions. *American Journal of Distance Education, 17*(1), 45–57.
Wunsch, M.A. (2000). Killing the old myths: Positioning an instructional technology center for a new era in higher education. *College and University Media Review, 7*(1), 51–71.
Yukl, G.A. (1989). *Leadership in organizations* (2nd ed.). Englewood Cliffs, NJ: Prentice Hall.
Zawacki-Richter, O., Backer, E.M., & Vogt, S. (2009). Review of distance education research (2000 to 2008): Analysis of research areas, methods, and authorship patterns. *International Review of Research in Open and Distance Learning, 10*(6).
Zekeri, A.A. (2004). College curriculum competencies and skills former students found essential to their careers. *College Student Journal, 38*(3), 412–422.

27

Beyond E-learning

Rethinking Purpose and Design

Yoany Beldarrain

Beyond E-learning: Rethinking Purpose and Design

Since its early beginnings in the form of correspondence schools, e-learning has generally sought to provide flexibility and high quality education. While these are indeed noble intentions, the reality of today's connected world demands that such programs focus on a different purpose. As the main purpose of e-learning shifts, so must the design approaches.

Rethinking e-learning requires open-mindedness on the part of academics, designers, cyber educators, legislators, IT and administrators, but also the learners themselves. All who are involved in or impacted by e-learning programs must speak up and finally share their perspectives, but who will be listening? The key to rethinking e-learning lies in the ability of the stakeholders to listen to each other and make decisions which are in the best interest of the learner.

This chapter will propose a new purpose for e-learning and explore promising possibilities for learner-centered design. The future of e-learning can be shaped by the decisions made today, but before any decisions can be made, one must acknowledge e-learning's successes as well as its shortcomings. The purpose of this chapter is to encourage those who are impacted by e-learning to think about the future.

Introduction

In order to identify e-learning's achievements and limitations, or rethink design or purpose, it is important to study the phenomenon from multiple perspectives. The most commonly known instructional design (ID) models such as Dick and Carey, ADDIE, Morrison, Ross and Kemp, and ARCS among others, have for years guided designers in creating e-learning that strives to accommodate learners' needs while utilizing the best technology tools of the day. While some of the ID models available are more linear than others, they all recognize the need to create engaging content and somehow integrate student feedback. But is this enough? The effectiveness of e-learning is made up of many ingredients, not just which particular ID model was used for design.

There are many questions associated with the effectiveness of e-learning. Common questions include: Is it effective? How do we know it is effective? What pedagogical approach is best?

What theories or frameworks are more effective? How does culture impact design? How much flexibility and control should be provided to the learner? How should an e-learning program be evaluated? How should instructors be trained? What resources or infrastructure are needed? The questions are insurmountable and despite all these years of experience with Web-based education and training, no one really has the right answers. Part of the frustration may be the fact that there are as many opinions as there are options and possible answers; and many research studies either lack transferability or are inconclusive.

A review of the literature shows that although many academics talk about the success of e-learning as compared to traditional methods, there is less discussion about the drawbacks of particular ID models, frameworks, taxonomies, theories or methodologies. Furthermore, the literature is mostly devoid of honest discussions about challenges associated with the practical side of e-learning, how to develop a program, how to implement it and how to evaluate it. None of these questions can be addressed unless the issue of evaluation and assessment of e-learning programs is taken seriously.

What Everyone Knows but Is Afraid to Admit

There are many difficulties surrounding Web-based education and training. Some of the challenges that plague the development, adaptation and implementation of e-learning programs can be summarized into several broad topics: 1) lack of proper funding, 2) lack of real training and time to develop the course, 3) lack of technical support or proper resources to develop the course, 4) lack of organizational infrastructure or expertise to support the new program efforts, and most certainly 5) a lack of evaluation ad assessment of e-learning initiatives. Only after cyber educators admit and understand these challenges will they be able to align learning outcomes and real world applications, and reinforce skills and attitudes needed in the workplace. These are essential steps in rethinking the purpose of e-learning.

The real challenges often get pushed to the background because organizations are so eager to jump on the proverbial e-learning bandwagon. Most of the issues stem from the fact that many organizations, especially those in the education sector, do not always have adequate funding to develop and implement quality programs. It is also a fallacy that everyone believes in e-learning; the reality is that in many areas of the world e-learning is still misunderstood, and thus it negatively influences attitudes. Many educators still hold on to traditional methods they believe are superior to anything technology could possibly contribute. Somehow those excited about updating teaching practices too often miscalculate the real challenges behind the process.

It is now a political expectation that educational organizations use e-learning in one way or another to empower their students and move the organizations into the future. E-learning has become an added source of competitiveness. In the US and other countries such as Australia and Canada, higher education and corporations were quick to recognize the benefits of e-learning and pushed ahead. In other countries around the globe however, the situation is different. Some countries, like Germany have been slower to accept e-learning as a valid educational method, while poorer nations continue to struggle with development and implementation even if they have the best intentions and occasional special funding.

According to a trend analysis (Goertz, 2010) Germany will experience growth in the application of digital learning in the coming years, especially as more organizations are expected to create their own learning content. This however, is not indicative of all higher educational institutions, which for the most part still follow very strict and traditional teaching and learning methods. Although the Education Ministry offers e-learning training and creates partnerships with private industry as with the recent Europe-wide contest for MOOC production grants, the majority of educators wish to stay within their comfort zone.

In the case of developing nations, the World Bank has over the years provided funding for special educational initiatives, including distance learning, in order to combat poverty (Foley, 2003). A review of multiple case studies and sources reveals that developing nations experience similar challenges as developed nations when it comes to the issues listed at the beginning of this section (Andersson, 2008; Anuwar Ali, 2004; Bollag & Oberland, 2001; Heeks, 2002; Rajesh, 2003, UNESCO, 2011). The reality is that local educators must make the most of the situation by doing their best to transform attitudes, provide support with limited expert knowledge and resources, and yet create a course or program that will somehow have a positive impact. According to the sources cited above, developing nations face other unique challenges such as language barriers and scalability; but this section will explore only the main issues in common with developed countries.

It is often true that those asked to develop a course, whether for higher education or corporate training, are asked to do so with a limited budget. A limited budget translates into limited access to expert knowledge and resources. This is the case regardless of nation. A common scenario is an instructional designer who wears multiple hats, or an instructor who is left at the mercy of his or her own ingenuity and resources. When this happens, frustration sets in, and the quality of the program is inconsistent with intended outcomes. The worst that could happen is that inferior programs negatively impact student motivation and achievement, waste the organization's money, and undermine the credibility of the organization in the eyes of stakeholders.

Lack of proper training and time to develop materials are common culprits of inferior programs, especially in higher education. Even the most experienced and successful instructor will encounter a learning curve when switching to online. Organizations must understand that aside from the learning curve, there is also an adaptation curve that affects all stakeholders, and that reactions to the new initiative may range from those who want to be cutting edge all the way to those who avoid using the new technology (Arabasz, Pirani, & Fawcett, 2003).

After several years of mentoring instructors new to e-learning, the author concludes that without a sincere and robust training effort, organizations are setting their new instructors and their learners up for failure. The training plan must include sufficient time for the instructor not only to absorb the new information, but also to develop good materials and connect all content and interactions to a suitable theoretical base.

When the instructor new to e-learning does not have a solid theoretical base, there is a domino effect that impacts the level of customization to students' interests, the course is less learner centered, relevance of materials and content may be limited, and best practices for educational technology may not be implemented. Furthermore, the lack of knowledge will prevent the new online instructor from effectively promoting student interaction, providing constructive feedback, creating a safe learning environment, and creating and nourishing a learning community. The more the online instructor possesses content knowledge, is technically savvy and has a strong theoretical foundation, the more real-world applicability the course will have.

No one may want to admit that it is easier to just recreate the traditional course by posting files online than to spend time creating multimedia and other support materials. Even when the new online instructor wishes to be creative however, this vision may soon stifled by the fact that he or she may not have enough technical support or proper resources to develop the course, and there is no other option but to upload PDF files and PowerPoint presentations. The learner on the other hand, may have low technological proficiency to navigate content, or in the case of areas with limited bandwidth, access is limited. This is true especially in developing nations.

Technical support comes in many forms including access to authoring software and training on how to use it, access to experts such as Flash developers and instructional designers, and help in troubleshooting platform issues. While this is mainly from the instructor's perspective, one must not forget to say that the learners must also have adequate technical support, as unresolved or recurring technical difficulties cause frustration and potentially negatively influence the learners' attitudes toward e-learning.

When the instructor lacks support, he or she will be more likely to create a course that relies on rote memory and repetition just like ineffective traditional methods, one that lacks a solid theoretical or pedagogical approach, or is not guided by any particular framework. The learner experiences this in many ways, especially when the instructor is not able to provide adequate learning support during the course. This challenge is compounded when there is a lack of organizational infrastructure or expertise to support the new program efforts.

This is evident in many programs that emerge out of a sudden realization that the organization is falling behind the times. The organization may not have made any prior strategic decisions about implementing e-learning, yet it expects that a program will be developed overnight; a quality program that is. In such scenarios the initiative is put on the shoulders of those who show some kind of competency level, but do not necessarily have the skills required to handle such a paramount task. In this scenario the organization's infrastructure does not yet support the initiative; thus the potential for failure is enhanced. The chances of success depend not only on the level of support and infrastructure, but also on the overall organizational belief that e-learning brings various benefits.

Another undeniable challenge is certainly the lack of thorough and consistent evaluation and assessment of e-learning initiatives. An unabashed review of sources reveals that while there is a consensus regarding the importance of assessing and evaluating e-learning programs, the current research base is definitely not adequate (Attwell, 2006). According to Attwell (2006), experts around the globe agree that there has been too much emphasis on, or even obsession with, evaluating software and platforms instead of focusing on pedagogy and learning that would in turn shape the future of e-learning policy as well as practice. For example, this happens in adult education, where focus on andragogy seems limited in connection with the success of academic or training programs.

The lack of systematic evaluation was also cited as an undisputable weakness in the development and implementation of e-learning programs in Europe (Attwell, 2006); therefore it is crucial that there be a global effort in dealing with this issue. After compiling and analyzing worldwide literature on the subject, Attwell and his counterparts asserted that there is a language discrepancy between the use of the terms *assessment* and *evaluation* in different countries, not enough guidance for using available evaluation tools, and too many case studies and not enough true ROI evaluation reports to demonstrate the real impact of the e-learning program. Furthermore, Attwell (2005) points out that there is no real attempt to evaluate pedagogic approaches of e-learning, that there is a lack of benchmarking models that are based on multiple variables associated with the learning environment or with forward-thinking pedagogies, and that too many meta-studies available are mostly based on US literature. All in all, there is much to be explored.

The challenges of e-learning as discussed in this section, are many. Understanding these challenges will help cyber educators tie learning outcomes to real-world applications and reinforce skills and attitudes needed in the workplace. Once the alignment is accomplished, the real purpose for e-learning becomes evident.

Rethinking the Purpose of E-learning Programs

Sound design, when supported by a good theoretical framework, ensures that there are no discrepancies between content, methods, learning environment, delivery and assessment, but also the intended outcomes. Stakeholders should realize that technology is really nothing more than another avenue for delivering high quality instruction. The purpose for delivering high quality instruction should be the same for face-to-face as for Web-based programs: to equip the individual with skills, knowledge and attitudes that are up-to-date, and are relevant to the job market. This should be a clear intended outcome of the program, the big idea. Whether the e-learning program is geared toward children or adults, this purpose does not necessarily change. Education and training should help the learner develop his/her capacities in order to be a successful and productive global citizen.

This perspective of purpose is not a radical idea. The words may be uttered or the same thoughts expressed in informal settings, but many academics get caught up in the daily routine, try to incorporate buzzwords into their vocabulary, or simply forget the role of technology in education and training. The danger of losing sight of the real purpose becomes inevitable when descriptors such as *convenient, flexible* and *economical* are used to describe e-learning programs.

While it is obviously true that these are some of the added values of e-learning, the focus should be on how technology can deliver instruction in the most effective, efficient and learner-centric way. This may cause the organization to also rethink its mission and strategic goals, and to prioritize investment of resources.

Aligning the goals of academic e-learning program to skills, knowledge and attitudes needed in the marketplace can be achieved first of all, by collaborating and building partnerships with businesses. Second, educational organizations can use these partnerships to create a stronger connection between theory and practice, and create programs where these new skills, knowledge and attitudes seamlessly transfer to the workplace. The result would be a highly skilled workforce that can contribute to the businesses and help the economy move forward.

For corporate training, an in-depth needs assessment would be essential for getting to know the needs of the stakeholders, but also what skills, knowledge and attitudes employees need in order to get the job done. While seamless transfer of new skills, knowledge and attitudes is as paramount as in academic settings, the corporate world is intent on making sure that this all translated into increased profits.

What do employers really want? Businesses, regardless of size, seek to hire highly competent employees whom they can trust with implementing the company's mission and vision, thus helping the company achieve its goals. So what then is the role of educational institutions? As stated previously, educational institutions are in a position to serve those needs by preparing learners of all ages to be self-reliant and enter the workforce. This creates a win-win for the learner, the educational organization, businesses, and finally—society at large.

When restructuring current e-learning programs, those responsible should look for quality indicators. Quality indicators focus on outcomes and should therefore be measurable. While there are some basic indicators such as learner success and satisfaction, academics and practitioners generally agree that organizations should also seek measures of internal quality and develop a sensible yet comprehensive evaluation plan (Buck, 2001; Chapman, 2006; Cleary, 2001; Dirr, 2003; Hansen, 2003; Lorenzo & Moore, 2002; Pond, 2002).

When rethinking and planning e-learning programs there must also be institutional accountability in regards to the time and money invested by the learner. Academic organizations should be transparent in communicating how much their degree programs are really worth. If the content of the degree program is not aligned with what employers want, then the degree is worthless to the learner. The same holds true for training endeavors. Part of setting up an e-learning program for success is getting trainee buy-in. This could be achieved by demonstrating what added value this training has for the individual and not just the company itself. Too often the focus is on what the company desires versus what is good for the employee; but a positive organizational culture is created when employees feel valued, and where management invests in developing human capital.

In the business world, gaining a competitive edge usually means the *us against them* mentality. In academia it is no different, as evidenced by intense competition among colleagues and departments and by organization against organization; everyone wants to be number one. Rethinking e-learning programs however, forces stakeholders to look beyond their own capabilities and resources, and forge partnerships with those whom they would otherwise compete against. Powerful partnerships can provide both sides with much-needed expert knowledge and resources that would otherwise not be accessible. As the saying goes, there is power in numbers. While creating partnerships is beneficial in corporate as well as academic e-learning, it does not mean that a partnership should compromise the organization's strategic goals. At the end of the day, everyone is working toward the same purpose: to equip the individual with skills, knowledge and attitudes that are up-to-date, and are relevant to the job market.

Removing communication barriers among stakeholders and providing transparency will help organizations rethink the purpose of e-learning. The shared goal of education and training should be to develop human capital so individuals can be productive citizens of a globally connected world.

Rethinking Design

When it comes to e-learning design, there are a myriad of suggested approaches and theoretical inclinations. Regardless of interpretation or opinion, researchers and practitioners tend to agree that when it comes to e-learning, there are cognitive and learning factors at play that can be either enhanced or diminished depending on approach used (Hannafin et al., 2003). The key to rethinking design is to first understand what the intended outcomes of the program are, and weigh them against the new purpose of e-learning programs.

Authentic learning is one favored approach for creating learner-centric design. Lombardi (2007, p. 2) defines it as learning that "typically focuses on real-world, complex problems and their solutions, using role-playing exercises, problem-based activities, case studies, and participation in virtual communities of practice." The reason it is considered highly effective is that it allows learners to be highly engaged with the content while discovering new perspectives through interaction with peers; all of which is supported by constructivist as well as activity theory.

Authentic learning facilitates a design that is more customizable than are traditional instructional approaches, allowing flexibility to use cutting-edge instructional and delivery methods and to select authentic assessment options. The validity of authentic learning environments has been established by various researchers, including Herrington and Oliver (2000), who suggest certain criteria be used to add authenticity: (a) a situated learning model, (b) authentic context, (c) authentic activity, (d) multiple perspectives, (e) expert performances, (f) collaboration, (g) reflection articulation, (h) coaching, and (i) scaffolding authentic assessment.

The proposed purpose of e-learning is directly supported by further research from Herrington, Oliver, and Reeves (2006) who after considering authentic learning, situated learning, problem-based learning, and anchored instruction methods, concluded that activities and content should be relevant and applicable to specific professions, provide multidimensional project-based problems that encourage multiple perspectives explored over a period of time, be collaborative, reflective, interdisciplinary, and be integrated with assessment that mirrors the real world. These points are critical in designing e-learning that is directly connected to the overall intended outcomes of the program and the organization's goals, in addition to preparing learners to join the workforce.

Providing choice and flexibility centered on the learner's abilities, learning styles and interests is also a good way to enhance learner-centric environments and add authenticity (Baggio & Beldarrain, 2011). This means that the instructor may have to give up some control over content and assessment to the learners, who can then create, share, and reflect, skills all deemed necessary for today's professionals. This shift helps create a connected and collaborative learning community.

The real learning community emerges as a natural product of an engaging learning environment that promotes critical thinking and encourages learners to consider multiple perspectives. When rethinking design, cyber educators should take into account where the everyday person goes for knowledge. Today, everyone relies on the Web to get information, whether through surfing the Web, receiving RSS feeds, or going to forums to ask other community members for advice. This means that today's learners are more into "do-it-yourself" education than any other previous generation. For this reason, many do not see the point of paying for formal education unless it has an added value.

Cyber educators must also recognize the difference between researching topics out of pure interest and researching topics because they are told to do so as part of a course. An honest look at the two scenarios would indicate that individuals are more likely to be motivated to research a topic in which they are interested. What is the lesson to be learned? Re-design of e-learning programs must leverage student interest and present and deliver content in engaging ways that pique such interest.

As the digital immigrants get older and more digital natives enter higher education and the workforce, more emphasis will have to be placed on designing e-learning that is relevant. Digital natives are known for their uncanny ability to network, create digital content and use technology without fear. Because they are in essence wired differently than previous generations, e-learning design should take into consideration how they access content, process information and use technology. Prensky (2009) suggests that technology has the power to enhance individuals, thus helping them make wiser decisions; he calls it digital wisdom.

This sobering suggestion would be enough to justify rethinking e-learning, and reconsidering old priorities and perspectives on what learning should look like, or how it should be delivered. In the process, cyber educators struggle to stay a step ahead of the digital natives, keep up with technology and plan for applicability and sustainability of their programs.

Rethinking e-learning design requires open-mindedness to try new tools and methods to deliver content and promote collaboration and interaction. Some current options involve creating networked collaborative environments (NCVEs) that connect learners in real time, immersive virtual environments (IVEs) that use the senses to immerse the learner in a simulated world, or even collaborative virtual environments (CVEs) where the learner can take on the identity of an avatar and virtually interact and collaborate with peers.

These options however, are mainly used in games and are seldom applied in education or corporate training. There are many proponents of using new approaches such as digital game-based learning (DGBL), and the literature on the subject continues to flourish. Unfortunately, there is still much discussion about the pedagogy behind DGBL, along with too many unanswered questions. Certain professions such as doctors, pilots and of course, the military, do rely heavily on simulations, while more content developers are creating shorter versions of digital games geared toward education.

One could assume that virtual environments are not broadly used in e-learning yet due to some of the challenges mentioned earlier in this chapter. While small-scale simulations are slowly making their way into small-budget e-learning programs, their potential is still untapped. Forward-thinking cyber educators recognize the potential behind using simulations and immersive environments, but also avatars. The possibilities are endless; for example, avatars could be created to match the learner's preferences, while invisible consultants can be deployed to provide additional help for learners when they are having difficulty with the content, or the flow, amount and type of information can be customized to each learner (Bailenson et al., 2008).

There are many pedagogical applications as well as implications when using new technology tools. The role of the instructor constantly changes and evolves, which may be difficult for some to accept. Interactions also change, not only interaction with the interface, the content, the instructor, but also with peers. The anonymity inherent in the technology has implications of its own, meaning some learners may behave differently when using an avatar for example, than without one; hence the social dynamics within the learning environment and social awareness are altered.

Rethinking design will enable cyber educators to create e-learning programs that are centered on the needs of the learner, provide authentic activities and assessments that are directly connected to real world applications, and take into consideration how learners learn, and how technology can be leveraged to deliver content in the best possible way. A well-designed e-learning program should be directly tied to its intended outcomes and to the overarching purpose for education and training.

Conclusion

E-learning is coming of age yet its potential has not been fully tapped. Stakeholders must openly discuss their own struggles and challenges in developing, adapting and implementing e-learning programs. Acknowledging those challenges, whether they are due to lack of funding, expert knowledge, infrastructure or support, among other reasons, is the first step toward being able to see the real purpose of e-learning and toward creating a highly efficient and effective program.

The purpose for e-learning should be the same as the purpose for any face-to-face program, that is to help the learner develop his/her capacities in order to be a successful and productive global citizen. With this in mind, educational organizations and businesses are able to build stronger partnerships that in turn benefit all stakeholders and eventually, society at large.

There are many difficulties and challenges in regards to Web-based education and training; therefore commitment to research is needed in order to answer the many questions that remained unexplored. Cyber educators need more comprehensive knowledge about assessing and evaluating e-learning programs so continuous improvement may be achieved.

Learner-centered design offers promising possibilities for providing learners with the skills, knowledge and attitudes they will need in the workplace. Authentic learning for example, may include a variety of approaches that provide the learner with more flexibility and control, personalize the learning experience, use cutting-edge technology to immerse the learner in real-world scenarios that may or may not include avatars, leverage collaboration and interaction and promote problem-solving. Cyber educators can further learn how to engage and motivate learners through game-based learning and other emerging options that promote real-world skills.

The future of e-learning will be determined by the ability of stakeholders to recognize successes as well as shortcomings, and their willingness to create an open dialogue to discuss how to best overcome those shortcomings. If the learner is placed at the center of each decision, then e-learning programs will contribute to the overarching purpose of education and training.

References

Andersson, A. (2008). Seven major challenges for e-learning in developing countries: Case study eBIT, Sri Lanka. *International Journal of Education and Development using Information and Communication Technology* (IJEDICT), *4*(3), pp. 45–62.

Anuwar Ali, T. D. (2004). *Issues & challenges in implementing e-learning in Malaysia.* Open University Terbuka. Retrieved January 31, 2013, from http://asiapacific-odl2.oum.edu.my/C33/F80.pdf

Arabasz, P., Pirani, J.A., & Fawcett, D. (2003). Impact and challenges of e-learning. In *Supporting e-learning in higher education* (Vol. 3, pp. 39–48). EDUCAUSE Center for Applied Research. Retrieved January 28, 2013, from http://net.educause.edu/ir/library/pdf/ers0303/rs/ers0303w.pdf

Attwell, G. (2006). Evaluating e-learning, a guide to the evaluation of e-learning. *Evaluate Europe Handbook Series,* vol. 2. Retrieved January 28, 2013, from http://www.pontydysgu.org/wp-content/uploads/2007/11/eva_europe_vol2_prefinal.pdf

Baggio, B., & Beldarrain, Y. (2011). What was good for the goose is no longer good for the goslings. *Anonymity and learning in digitally mediated communications: Authenticity and trust in cyber education.* Hershey, PA: IGI Global. doi:10.4018/978-1-60960-543-8-8.ch009

Bailenson, J.N., Yee, N., Blascovich, J., Beall, A.C., Lundblad, N., & Jin, M. (2008). The use of immersive virtual reality in the learning sciences: Digital transformations of teachers, students and social context. *Journal of the Learning Sciences, 17*(1), 102–141. doi:10.1080/10508400701793141

Bollag, B., & Oberland, M.A. (2001). Developing countries turn to distance education. *Chronicle of Higher Education, 47*(40), 22–29.

Buck, J. (2001). Assuring quality in distance education. *Higher Education in Europe, 26*(4).

Chapman, D. (2006). Building an evaluation plan for fully online degree programs. *Online Journal of Distance Learning Administration, 9*(1).

Cleary, T.S. (2001). Indicators of quality. *Planning for Higher Education, 29*(3), 19–28.

Dirr, P.J. (2003). Distance education policy issues: Towards 2010. In M. G. Moore & W. G. Anderson (Eds.), *Handbook of distance education* (461–479). Mahwah, NJ: Lawrence Erlbaum.

Foley, M. (2003). The global development learning network: A World Bank initiative in distance learning for development. In M. G. Moore & W. G. Anderson, (Eds.), *Handbook of distance education* (pp. 829–843). Mahwah, NJ: Lawrence Erlbaum.

Goertz,. L. (2010). E-learning made in Germany—Market and trends. Study presented at eLBA Conference, Rostock, Germany July 1, 2010. Presentation notes retrieved January 12, 2013, from http://mmb-institut.de/download/vortraege/MMB_Pres_E-Learning_Germany_market_trends.pdf

Hannafin, M., Oliver, K., Hill, J.R., Glazer, E., & Sharma, P. (2003). Cognitive and learning factors in Web-based distance learning environments. In M.G. Moore & W.G. Anderson (Eds.), *Handbook of distance education* (pp. 245–260). Mahwah, NJ: Lawrence Erlbaum.

Hansen, K. (2003). How to assess, demonstrate quality in distance ed. *Distance Education Report, 7*, 18.

Heeks, R. (2002). Information systems and developing countries: Failure, success and local improvisations. *The Information Society, 18*(2), 101–112.

Herrington J., & Oliver, R. (2000). An instructional design framework for authentic learning environments. *Educational Technology Research and Development, 48*(3), 23–48. doi:10.1007/BF02319856

Herrington J., Oliver, R., & Reeves, T. (2006). Authentic tasks online: A synergy among learner, task and technology. *Distance Education, 27*(2), 233–248. doi:10.1080/01587910600789639

Lombardi, M.M. (2007). *Authentic learning for the 21st century: An overview.* ELI Paper Educause. Retrieved January 31, 2013, from http://net.educause.edu/ir/library/pdf/eli3009.pdf

Lorenzo, G., & Moore, J. (2002). *The Sloan Consortium report to the nation: Five pillars of quality online education.* Retrieved January 31, 2013, from http://sloanconsortium.org/publications/books/pillarreport1.pdf

Pond, W.K. (2002). Distributed education in the 21st century: Implications for quality assurance. *Online Journal of Distance Learning Administration, 5*(2). Retrieved January 31, 2013, from http://www.westga.edu/~distance/ojdla/summer52/pond52.html

Prensky, M. (2009). H. Sapiens digital: From digital immigrants and digital natives to digital wisdom. *Innovate, 5*(3). Retrieved January 27, 2013, from http://www.innovateonline.info/pdf/vol5_issue3/h._sapiens_digital-__from_digital_immigrants_and_digital_natives_to_digital_wisdom.pdf

Rajesh, M. (2003). A study of the problems associated with ICT adaptability in developing countries in the context of distance education. *Turkish Online Journal of Distance Education, 4*(2). Retrieved January 12, 2013, from http://tojde.anadolu.edu.tr/tojde10/articles/Rajesh.htm

Unesco, (2011). *ICT for higher education: Case studies from Asia and the Pacific.* Retrieved January 7, 2013, from http://www.icde.org

Glossary

AT—Assistive Technology
EU—European Union
ICT—Information and Communication Technology
UD—Universal Design
UDL—Universal Design for Learning
UNCRPD—United Nations Convention on the Rights of Persons with Disabilities
W3C—The World Wide Web Consortium
WAI—Web Accessibility Imitative
WCAG—Web Content Accessibility Guidelines

Accessibility: Accessibility is the equal access to information and communication technologies (ICTs) for individuals with disabilities.

Accessibility standards: Standards or requirements intended to provide access to a product, service, or environment—particularly by people with disabilities. The requirement of accessibility may be mandated in law or policy, and specified by international or national regulations, standards, or codes.

Accommodation: In postsecondary education, academic adjustments that level the playing field for disabled students but do not fundamentally alter the nature of the course (U.S. Department of Justice, 2005).

Adaptive technologies: See Assistive Technology.

Assessment: An assessment is a type of learning instrument used to help the learner and instructor understand strengths and weaknesses.

Assistive technology: A variety of devices used by persons with disabilities to help accomplish tasks that would be difficult or otherwise not possible. When applied to computers, assistive technology is sometimes referred to as adaptive technology or adaptive software or hardware. According to section 508 of the Tech Act (U.S Department of Justice, 2005), assistive technology is an aid (mechanical or technical) that assists disabled individuals to complete or perform a task that is difficult or impossible due to an individual's impairment.

Asynchronous method: A student-centered teaching approach that uses online learning resources to facilitate information sharing outside the constraints of time and place among a network of people.

Authentic learning: An approach for creating learner-centric learning environments, it includes the use of scenarios, role-playing, collaboration, simulations, and problem-based approaches among others.

Blooms Taxonomy: A classification of learning objectives.

Cognitive learning: "An explanation of how people learn based on the idea of dual channels (information is processed in visual and auditory channels), limited capacity (only a small amount of information can be processed in each channel at one time), and active learning (meaningful learning occurs when learners pay attention to relevant information, organize it into a coherent structure, and integrate it with what they already know)" (Clark & Mayer, 2008, pp. 429–430). Clark, R. C. & Mayer, R. E. (2008). *E-learning and the science of instruction: Proven guidelines for consumers and designers of multimedia learning*. San Francisco: John Wiley & Sons.

Cognitive load theory: Taking into account that working memory can process a limited amount of mental resource. This theory provides guidelines for applications of multimedia learning (Sweller, 2011; Clark & Mayer, 2008, p. 430). Sweller, J. (2011). *Artificial intelligence in Education*. Berlin: Springer.

Clark, R. C. & Mayer, R. E. (2008). *E-learning and the science of instruction: Proven guidelines for consumers and designers of multimedia learning.* San Francisco: John Wiley & Sons

Conventional tethered electronic learning: Learning using a device that is connected via an electric cord.

CVE: Collaborative virtual environment; may use avatars.

Cyber educators: Anyone involved in creating distance education.

DGBL: Digital game-based learning.

Digital competences: Digital competences comprise the knowledge, skills, and attitudes that enable the subject to resolve situations in various contexts linked to different forms of ICT use.

Digital immigrant: Someone who was born before the existence of digital technologies and adopted it to some extent later in life.

Digital literacy: Ability to effectively and critically navigate, evaluate, and create information using a range of digital technologies

Digital native: A person who was born during or after the general introduction of digital technologies and through interacting with digital technology from an early age, has a greater understanding of its concepts.

Disability: The traditional medical model of disability indicates the person has a functional limitation as the basis for disability, whereas the social model of disability defines disability as the concept that a person has a disability because his/her environment is not accessible.

Disabled students: While "person first" language has been popularized in recent years, many professionals argue that, although a person may possess a particular characteristic such as blindness, the label of "disabled" is socially constructed and has been imposed by society (Bowker & Tuffin, 2007). For the purpose of this study, the term "disabled student" will be utilized to signify that the lack of accessibility has caused the learning barrier rather than the impairment itself. Bowker, N., & Tuffin, K. (2007, July). Understanding positive subjectivities made possible on-line for disabled people. *New Zealand Journal of Psychology, 36*(2), 63–71. Retrieved August 28, 2009, from Academic Search Premier database.

Distance Education Leader: Distance education leader refers to the administrator who oversees the DE operation in an institution and who is responsible for the day-to-day operations; short and long-term strategic planning; direction of all institutional DE programs and activities; and motivating others to achieve the desired results within the institution, irrespective of the title of the position and name of the DE program. The leader may hold the title of Coordinator, Director, Dean, or Assistant/Associate Vice President or Assistant Provost for Distance Education, E-Learning, or Online Learning or similar position titles.

Dual mode: Dual mode institutions, which are also referred to as bimodal institutions, are colleges and universities that provide teaching, learning, and administrative systems that support two instructional modes that include the campus-based conventional face-to-face classroom environment and the distance education environment.

Electronic learning (e-learning): Learning using an electronic device. The use of electronic media and information, communication technologies, and social networking tools to enhance content, instruction, and assessment in teaching and learning. The use of electronic media and information, communication technologies, and social networking tools to enhance content, instruction, and assessment in teaching and learning.

Formative assessment: A type of evaluations that is integrated into the instructional content so that as the learner is engaged in the unit and gains valuable ongoing constructive feedback.

Gagne's Events of Instruction: A nine-step instructional design model used in the design of lessons and includes internal and external events.

Information quality (IQ): IQ is both a product and a service in the m-learning setting. The content delivery platform, be it instruction or assessment, is relevant to the IQ dimension. IQ quality in the m-learning context also includes the input and output of information into the system and how it impacts learning effectiveness.

Instructional design: The science and art employed in the design, development, and delivery of instruction. (Reigeluth, 1983 and Rita, Klein, & Tracey, 2011, p. 2)

Instructional narrative: This term refers to the e-learning instructor-prepared digital text and multimedia materials that relate to the content, learning activities, discussion forums, and assessments of an online course.

Instructional objective: Statement that describes an intended outcome of instruction.

Instructional strategies: Determine the approach a teacher may take to achieve learning objectives.

Interaction: Activities involving interface, tools, learners, instructor, content, environment, and/or other elements in which there is mutual influence.

Interactivity: The attributes of technology used in e-learning that allow interaction.

IVE: Immersive learning environment; relies on the senses to immerse the learner in a simulated world ILE

Keller's ARCs Model: A motivational model that includes a four-step process: Attention, Relevance, Confidence, Satisfaction.

Learner-centric: Centered on the learner's needs.

Learning management system (LMS): A software application for the administration, documentation, tracking, reporting, and delivery of education courses or training programs. Examples of popular learning management systems include Moodle, Blackboard, and Desire2Learn.

Mental models: Mental representations of how certain things work and specific ways to achieve some end.

Mobile learning (m-learning): "Learning across multiple contexts, through social and content interactions, using personal electronic devices" (Crompton, 2013, p. 4). Learning that is supported and/or facilitated by the use of ubiquitous handheld technologies (i.e., smartphones) along with wireless and mobile phone networks. Crompton, H. (2013a). A historical overview of mobile learning: Toward learner-centered education. In Z. L. Berge & L. Y. Muilenburg (Eds.), *Handbook of Mobile Learning* (pp. 3–14). Florence, KY: Routledge.

Mobile learning delivery satisfaction (MLDS): A satisfaction measure that is achieved when a learner's need is met given the delivery of content and assessments for one or more mobile platform. M-learning satisfaction can be measured based on the information consumed by the user (IQ), the physical and emotional qualities presented by the system (SQ), and the intangibles that make the learning experience unique and service-oriented (SERVQUAL).

Mobile learning object (MLO): A succinct module, presented in a mobile format not to exceed an amount of time, which integrates text and audio.

Multimedia learning: Learning that results from a combination of verbal messages (e.g., verbal presentations and printed lessons) and pictures (Mayer, 2009). For e-learning words and pictures may be presented via a combination of digital and/or printed formats. Mayer, R.E. (2009). Multimedia learning. Cambridge: Cambridge University Press.

NCVE: A networked collaborative virtual environment; connects the learners in real time.

Nonrecurrent tasks: These are "... (novel, effortful) constituent skills [for which] the desired exit behavior varies from problem to problem situation, and is guided by cognitive schemata that steer problem-solving behavior (cognitive strategies) and allow for reasoning about the domain (mental models)." (van Merriënboer, Clark, & Croock, 2002, p. 42) van Merriënboer, J. J. G., Clark, R. E., and de Croock, M. B. M. (2002). Blueprint for complex learning: The 4C/ID-model. *Educational Technology, Research & Development* 50(2), 39–64.

On-line learning: Any course component for which a student must utilize the Internet. This could be 1% of the student's coursework or 100% on-line (or online) learning.

Performance objectives: Statements that describe the behaviors that students will perform to demonstrate what and how well they have learned upon program completion.

Personal learning environment: Systems that help learners take control of and manage their own learning. This includes providing support for learners to set their own learning goals; manage their learning, both content and process; and communicate with others in the process of learning.

Prior knowledge: Knowledge, skills, or abilities brought by learners to the learning environment before instruction.

Quality matters: A faculty-centered, peer review process that is designed to certify the quality of online and blended courses.

Recurrent tasks: Recurrent tasks are tasks that are performed the same way every time. As described by van Merriënboer, Clark and Croock, 2002, p. 42, "For recurrent (routine) constituent skills the desired exit behavior is highly similar from problem to problem situation, and is driven by rules that link particular characteristics of the problem situation to particular actions."

Service quality (SERVQUAL): SERVQUAL is the ability for a learner to feel confident with the environment he or she is engaging in to learn as a result of: (a) institutional and content credibility, (b) appropriate levels of security, (c) reliability of the product and services being presented, and (d) learner-driven personalization.

Single mode: Single mode institutions are institutions where teaching, learning, and administrative structures are created and devoted entirely to provide distance education.

Sloan Consortium (SLOAN-C): An institutional and professional leadership organization dedicated to integrating online education into mainstream higher education.

Summative assessment: A form of assessment such as a quiz or an exam that is used to assess a learner's proficiency at the end of a given unit.

synchronous methods: A learning environment in which everyone takes part at the same time.

System quality (SQ): SQ is a determinant of usage, success, and satisfaction. In the mobile learning context, SQ is a way of evaluating the user experience, the quality of the mobile platform, and the value of the delivery format.

Traditional learning: Learning within an educational establishment without the use of electronic learning supports, such as a computer.

Training: A systematic set of processes implemented with the goal of helping individuals and groups acquire the skills, rules, concepts, and attitudes that result in improved performance in another environment.

Universal Design: An approach intended to address all aspects of life, from architecture, to means of transportation and the use of everyday items in order to accommodate as many people as possible.

Universal Design for Learning: An "approach to planning and developing curricula in ways that promote access, participation, and progress in the general curriculum for all learners" (McGuire, Scott, & Shaw, p. 169).

Universal Design for Learning: Public law 110–315—AUG. 14, 2008, of the Higher Education Opportunity Act, defines Universal Design for Learning as a "scientifically valid framework" for guiding educational practice that—

> (A) provides flexibility in the ways information is presented, in the ways students respond or demonstrate knowledge and skills, and in the ways students are engaged; and (B) reduces barriers in instruction, provides appropriate accommodations, supports, and challenges, and maintains high achievement expectations for all students, including disabled students and students who are limited English proficient. (p. 11)

To take this a step further, the Center for Applied Special Technology suggests that UDL should give students, regardless of their learning styles, abilities, and backgrounds, the choice of how they (a) access information, (b) engage with course material, and (c) express what they have learned (Center for Applied Special Technology, 2008).

Videogame: A medium that, when used for training, immerses users in a virtual environment (ranging in realism and fidelity) in order to engage users in multiple decision-making exercises, with learning as a primary goal. Center for Applied Special Technology. (1994, March). Project EASI. *Change*, 26(2), 45.

Virtual world: A three dimensional virtual environment, usually with a social networking focus, where users interact with one another through the uses of avatars (virtual characters created by the user); also known as multi-user virtual environments (MUVEs).

VISCAL (visuals, interactivity, structure, collaboration, assessment, and learner-centric focus): A model for adapting face-to-face courses for effective online delivery.

Web accessibility: The degree to which persons with disabilities can perceive, understand, and interact with web content and applications. Web accessibility has additional benefits such as improved access by older people and people using mobile browsers. Web accessibility applies to people with varied types of disability in their access to the web, including visual, auditory, speech, physical, cognitive, and neurological disabilities.

Web 2.0: Web 2.0 tools allow users to interact and collaborate with each other in a social media dialogue as creators of user-generated content in a virtual community.

Wiki: A website that allows its users to add, modify, or delete its content.

Index

Note: Page numbers followed by *f* indicate a figure on the corresponding page. Page numbers followed by *t* indicate a table on the corresponding page.

academic advising 250
academic cluster competence 199, 200*t*
accessibility and instructional design: accessibility, defined 258–9; conclusion 263–5; design expectations 260–3; effective design of 257–8; introduction 257; overview 259; support of faculty in 263; universal design for learning 259–63, 260*f*
Accessibility for Ontarians with Disabilities Act (AODA) 270
accessible e-learning: background 271–2; challenges 272–4; conclusions 276; design of 274–5; global perspectives 270–1; overview 269–70; potential of 272
access to resources 66–7
activation principle 80
activity theory 313–14, 320, 380
adaptive applications 135
adaptive technology (AT) 269–70, 273
administration of learning environment 18
administrative support 251
Adobe Connect conferences 219–20
Advanced Distributed Learning (ADL) 2
affective objectives in online learning 184
AFL–CIO 44
Agricultural Satellite Network 44
AIM Project 42
Aldrich, Clark 279–80
a-learning (anytime, anyplace, anywhere learning) 2
Ambient Insight Research 217
American Association of University Professors (AAUP) 95
American Bar Association 44
American Hospital Association 44
American Journal of Distance Education 48
American Law Institute 44
American Rehabilitation Educational Network (AREN) 44
American School of the Air 41
American Society for Training and Development (ASTD) 271
Americans with Disabilities Act (ADA) 270–1
America Online 47
Analysis, Design, Development, Implement, Evaluate (ADDIE) model 263, 275, 281
analysis stages of e-learning 20, 30*t*–31*t*
animations in course materials 231–2
Appalachian Community Service Network 42
Apple Computer 54
Apple iOS 322
application principle 80
a priori assessment decisions 134
ARPANET 55
Articulated Instructional Media Project (AIM) 42, 43
assessments: expert interviews 132; face-to-face (f2f) course materials guide 237–8; implementation framework 136; in instructional events 165–7, 166*f*, 167*f*; integration in online course creation 193–5; language discrepancy 378; learning objectives 237, 328; literature review 132; performance-based assessment 194, 284; Provisional Guidelines 133–6; rating 28; self-assessment 194, 220, 254, 274; strategies 122–3; for student learning 88–9
Assistive Technology (AT) 269
Association for the Study of Higher Education 97
asynchronous and synchronous multimedia 188*t*
Athabasca University 103
ATS-6 satellite 43
attainment-based *vs.* time-based progress instruction 82–3
attainment options 88
audio-conferencing 43
audio graphics 45
Australia 281

authentic learning 380–1
authentic tasks 88
autonomous learning 351
autonomy: defined 72; of digital natives 172; education for 274; ethical principles and 271; in online settings 201, 218–19; recognition of 74–6; in Semantic Principle 71; social conditions and 96

Banathy, B.H. 4
behaviorism 314, 320
beyond e-learning: conclusions 382–3; difficulties surrounding 376–8; introduction 375–6; purpose and design 375; rethinking e-learning design 380–2; rethinking e-learning programs 379–80
BITNET ("Because It's Time Network") 45
Blackboard platform 208
Black College Satellite Network (BCSN) 44
blended learning 15, 23, 46, 131, 141
Bonk, Curt 69
British Columbia Institute of Technology (BCIT) 145–50
broadcasting 41–2
Brown, Seely 332

cable television (CATV) 42
California Virtual University 47
Camplese, Cole 68
Campus Pack tool 209
Camtasia cross-platform 231
Capella University 46, 263
Catalan University 172
Center for Applied Special Technology (CAST) 260–2, 271
Center for Research and Evaluation on Standards and Student Testing 127
Cerf, Vinton 62
chaos stage of e-learning 140
characteristic of virtual worlds 298
Chasen, Michael 54
chat rooms 53, 135
Chen, Steve 57
Chicago TV College 41
Chris Anderson Sapling Foundation 57
Christensen, Clayton 147
chunking strategy 183
Cisco Systems 52
City University of New York (CUNY) 45
Clark, Ruth C. 279
Clarke College in Iowa 3
Coastline Community College 42
cognitive difficulty 120–1
cognitive disabilities 269
cognitive load in online collaborative learning 117–18, 119–20, 120*f*
cognitive objectives in online learning 184
cognitive science 183
cognitive theory of multimedia learning 186–7
cognitivism 314, 320
collaboration competencies 177
collaborative design models for courses: conclusions 214–16; infographics 210–11; interactive timelines 211–12; learning management systems 208–9; online discussion boards 212–14; overview 207–8; wiki options 209–10
collaborative instruction 83, 95
collaborative virtual environments (CVEs) 381
commoditisation in learning 344, 345
Common Core Standards 207, 210
communication competencies 174–6, 175*t*–176*t*
Community College Satellite Network 44
community of practice model of e-learning 143
competencies: academic cluster competence 199, 200*t*; collaboration competencies 177; communication and 174–6, 175*t*–176*t*; digital competencies/environments 178; in distance education 368–9; face-to-face (f2f) classroom 173, 176; ICT and 171–3, 199, 201, 203; information 176–7; metacognitive cluster competence 201–4, 202*t*, 203*f*, 204*f*; operational cluster competence 199, 200*t*; overview 171; participation and collaboration 177; relational cluster competence 200, 201*t*; Role of the Online Learner 199–204, 200*t*, 201*t*, 202*t*, 203*f*, 204*f*; university teaching 173–7
competitive advantage for institutions 344–6
computer-based training (CBT) 53
computer-marked assessments (CMAs) 194
The Conditions of Learning (Gagné) 153
conferencing tools: audio-conferencing 43, 54; introduction 6; teleconferencing 41, 44, 53; video conferencing 45, 56, 215; web conferencing 56–8, 220, 237–8
connectivism 69–70, 72, 301, 314, 320
Considine, David 210
construct interactivity 298
constructivism/constructivist pedagogy: doing *vs.* teacher presenting 82; of human ecology 339; instructional theory 85; mobile learning 320; overview 72; peer interaction 380; socioconstructivist approach 313; team-based learning 83
content–content interaction 296, 298, 301
content implementation in e-learning 15, 16*f*, 17, 18–20
content preparation 16–18, 16*f*
context analysis 16
context awareness learning 320
context importance 100–1
Control Data Corporation (CDC) 53

conversational learning 314, 320
conversation theory 313, 315
Cormier, Dave 72
Cornell University 46
Corporation for Public Broadcasting (CPB) 42
Course Alignment Matrix, 285–7, 286*f*
courses/course concerns: accessibility 22; animations in course materials 231–2; curriculum development 104, 251, 367; defined 67–8; images in course materials 230–3; multimedia integration in online courses 186–8, 187*t*, 188*t*; time availability for 248; *see also* assessments; collaborative design models for courses; face-to-face (f2f) course materials guide; Massive Open Online Course; online course creation
Crane, Daniel 54–5
CreativeCommons.org 230
creative thinking 115, 121
criterion-referenced *vs.* norm-referenced testing 83
Cross, Jay 52
curriculum development 104, 251, 367
customized *vs.* standardized instruction 83
cyber-local e-learning classes 335
CYCLOPS system 53

dead-end forums 214
demonstration principle 66, 80
designing and evaluating e-learning: conclusion 305; interaction and interactivity 295–6; interaction types 296–8, 301–5, 302*f*, 304*f*; introduction 295; model for 299–301, 299*f*, 300*f*; MOOC 70–1; other taxonomies 298–9
design stage of e-learning 17, 31*t*–36*t*
Desire2Learn 208
developmental needs of students 250
development stage in e-learning 17
digital ecosystems 331, 332–4
digital game-based learning (DGBL) 61, 136, 381
digital immigrants 203, 208, 381
digital literacy 61, 75, 197, 201
digital media 171–2, 174, 253, 273, 332
digital natives 56, 171–2, 208, 381
discourse-oriented model of e-learning 143
distance education (DE): campus politics and 363; challenges 360–91; changes in 365; competition for students 369; criteria for 362; decision points 365; empowerment of 366–7; inadequate institutional support 362–3; institutional sponsor 366; institutional support 366; introduction 357–8; lack of appropriate precedents 362; managing challenges 365–70; new learning environment 361; operational polices and structure 364; opportunities and 369–70; overview 358–60; preparation of 370–1; program structure 367–8; quality instruction and 364; shared leadership 367; staffing issues 363–4; student support 364–5; styles and competencies 368–9; systemic approach 368
Distance Education Online Symposium (DEOS) 48
Distance Learning, Online Learning (OL) 2
distributed leadership 97, 99–103, 109–11
Distributed Learning (DL): introduction 2–3, 4, 4*f*, 6; learner engagement in 111; in literature review 131–2; MOOCs and 37–8; need for 104; training and assessment in 128; virtual classrooms 129, 131–2; web-based education and 46
distributing potential 332
diversity, defined 72
doctoral e-researchers 337–9
DropBox 237
Duke University 45
dynamism 214, 353

Early Alert Systems 252
eArmyU 46
ecological model of e-learning 143
educational context: corporate educational settings 359; digital natives in 172; interpretation of 332; of leadership 102–4; mediated communication in 174; of online collaboration 115; societal pressure and 110; sociocultural activities and 331, 334
eight dimensions of e-learning environment 23–5, 24*t*, 52
e-learning: components and features of 5–6, 6*f*, 7*t*–10*t*; content implementation 17, 18–20; content preparation 16–18, 16*f*; current day 58–9; defined 2–3, 51–2, 141; design stage 31*t*–36*t*; factors of e-learning environment 25*t*–27*t*; foundations of 41–7; future of 59–62, 60*t*; global framework for 23–4, 23*f*; higher education 140, 140*t*; history of 53–62; interaction and 186; introduction 51–2; issues of 27; m-learning *vs.* 310–12, 311*f*, 312*t*; 1980s 53–4; 1990s 54–6; open and distributed learning 3, 3*f*; overview 1–2; People-Process-Product Continuum 11–15, 11*f*, 12*t*–14*t*, 15*f*, 21*f*; product 20–3, 21*f*; review of with framework 27–30; revolution in 348–9, 348*f*; theory and scholarship 47–8; traditional instruction 4; 2000s 56–8; *see also* beyond e-learning; designing and evaluating e-learning; higher education and e-learning; learning ecologies; motivational strategies for e-learners
E-Learning and Disability in Higher Education (Seale) 261

E-Learning and the Science of Instruction: Proven Guidelines for Consumers and Designers of Multimedia Learning (Clark, Mayer) 279
e-learning evaluation: after implementation commences 284; aligning decisions, questions, and methods 285; case studies 285–91; during continuous use 284–5; during design and implementation 283–4; e-learning simulation 287–9, 288*f*; learning design process 280–2, 281*f*; learning field data collection 289–91, 289*f*, 290*f*; MOOC and 285–7, 286*f*, 287*f*; overview 279; rationale for 279–80; recommendations and steps forward 291–2, 292*f*; review and needs assessment 282–3, 283*f*; stages of 282–5, 283*f*; *see also* designing and evaluating e-learning
electronic devices 309–10
Electronic Information Exchange system 47
Electronic Performance Support Systems (EPSS) 37
Electronic University Network 42, 45
element interactivity 117
emerging e-learning technologies: conclusions 137; development and teaching 93; exemplars for 128–9, 128*t*; expert interviews 132–3; extracted themes 133–6, 134*t*; literature review 130–2; overview 127; role as mediational tools 335
Empire State College 42
encouragement stage of e-learning 140
Encyclopedia Britannica online 54
enjoyable *vs.* unpleasant instruction 83
ERIC Clearinghouse document 48
European Union (EU) 270
evaluation 17–18, 195, 284; *see also* designing and evaluating e-learning; e-learning evaluation; formative evaluation
Event-Based Approaches to Training (EBAT) 134
Evidence-Centered Design 134
evolutionary model of e-learning 143
exemplars for emerging e-learning technologies 128–9, 128*t*
expert interviews 132–3
extracted themes 133–6, 134*t*
extraneous cognitive load 117
Eyring, Henry 147

face-to-face (f2f) classroom: classroom competencies 173; conversion to e-learning 2; dissemination of information 257; information competencies 176; instructional decisions 182; online courses 181; online discussion boards 213; purpose of 379; teaching in groups 115; without ICT 141
face-to-face (f2f) course materials guide: assessments 237–8, 244–5; categories 229*t*; collaboration 236–7, 243; conclusions 238–9; development worksheet 239–45; interactivity 233–5, 240; introduction 227–8; learner-centric focus 238, 245; overview 228–30; structure of 235–6, 240–3; visual communication 230–3, 239–40
faculty role change 94–7
faculty views on pedagogical development 104–8
far-term adoption horizon 61–2
Federal Communications Commission (FCC) 42
Federal Resources for Educational Excellence 231
feedback in instructional events 163–4, 164*f*, 193
First American Symposium on Research in Distance Education 48
First Principles of Instruction (Merrill) 279
flexibility in learning 1, 3, 46
flexible/adaptable characteristic 353
folksonomy 311
Fordist model of e-learning 142
formative evaluation: e-learning simulation 287–9, 288*f*; learning field data collection 289–91, 289*f*, 290*f*; Massive Open Online Course 285–7, 286*f*, 287*f*
Formative Evaluation Log 287, 287*f*
formative feedback 88, 90
Foucault's concept of power 99
four device form factors 320–2, 321*t*
A Framework for E-learning (Khan) 51–2
Framework for the Rational Analysis of Mobile Education (FRAME) 313
Freeman, Greydon 45
Fuchs, Ira 45

Gagné, Robert (Gagné's nine events) 153, 154*f*
game-based learning *see* digital game-based learning
George Mason University 263
germane cognitive load 117–18
gesture-based computing 61–2
GIMP cross-platform 230
global framework for e-learning 23–4, 23*f*
Global Industry Analysts, Inc. 1
Global Pacific University 44
Goddard College 42
Goldberg, Murray 54–5
Google Android 322
Google Docs 173, 237
Google Hangouts 233
Google Images 230
GoToMeeting program 233
gratis, defined 66
Great Britain's Open University 42, 53
Gronn's initial taxonomy of distributed leadership 99–100
group assessments 122–3
guiding principles for e-learning 144–5

Health Education Network 44
heterogeneous grouping strategies 120
Hewlett-Packard 53
higher education and e-learning: conclusions 149–50; consultation process 148–9; e-learning defined 141; five stages of 140, 140*t*; institutional change 142–3; introduction 139–40; reasons for strategy development 141–2, 141*f*; strategic planning and 143–8
higher-order thinking skills 313
high school mentors 291
HTML coding 55
Human Resources (HR) 19
Hurley, Chad 57
hyperlinked interactivity 298

IDEA (Individuals with Disabilities Education Act) 166
images in course materials 230–3
immersive virtual interactivity 298
implementation framework 136, 145, 355
independent work skills 248
individual assessments 85–6, 122–3
infographics 210–11
informal feedback 194
informal learning: integration into teaching 173; learner–context interaction 302; learner–network interaction 297; m-learning theory and 314, 320; participation in 333; shift to 59, 338; from social interactions 215; task-focused outcome in 70
information and communication technologies (ICT): access to 273; appropriation 338–9; classroom adoption of 333; competencies and 171–3, 199, 201, 203; digital competencies/environments 178; face-to-face without 141; learning field data collection 290; managing in postsecondary education 149
information competencies 176–7
information ecologies 333, 335
information in instructional events 159–60, 160*f*
information quality (IQ) 323, 325–7
informative feedback 163
The Innovative University (Christensen, Eyring) 147
innovator characteristic 59, 353
inspirational motivation 344
Instant messaging 53, 89, 172
institutional support in online education 366
instructional delivery 102, 104, 319
instructional design (ID) 182–5, 375; *see also* accessibility and instructional design
instructional events: assessments 165–7, 166*f*, 167*f*; attention 153–5; feedback in 163–4, 164*f*, 193; information in 159–60, 160*f*; introduction 153; objectives in 156–7; practice in 162–3, 162*f*; prior knowledge in 157–8, 157*f*, 158*f*; retention and transfer in 167–8; review in 164–5, 165*f*; verification in 163
instructional narrative 182, 185–8, 185*t*, 193–5
instructional strategies: in distance education 361; e-learning guidelines 127; implementation of 249, 264; introduction 247; overview 89, 252–3; postindustrial instruction 80; for reducing cognitive load 117; selection of 86; storyboard 20; task-centered instructional strategy 80–1
Instructional Television Fixed Services (ITFS) 42
instructional theory: conclusions 89–90; for instructional space 86; introduction 6; overview 79–80; situational methods of 81–2; task-based instruction 83–4; for task space 86; universal methods of 80, 81; *see also* postindustrial paradigm
intended purpose of learning 190*t*–193*t*
interaction/interactivity: audio technologies 43; defined 73, 295–6; e-learning and 186, 299–301, 299*f*, 300*f*; features of e-learning 6; timelines 211–12; types of 296–8, 301–5, 302*f*, 304*f*
Interactive Satellite Education Network 44
International Classification of Functioning, Disability and Health (ICF) 270
International University Consortium 42
Internet-Based Training (IBT) 2
internet communication technologies (ICT) 102–3
Internet connection/reliability needs 249
Internet 2 consortium 46
intersubjective meaning making 115
in text questions (ITQs) 194
intrapersonal interaction 297
intrinsic cognitive load 117, 187
IP-based delivery platforms 279
IPSO Module 155*f*, 160*f*
Irish National Disability Authority 273

Job Access with Speech (JAWS) 261
Johns Hopkins University 41

Karin, Jawed 57
Keller's ARCS model 154–5, 154*f*
keystone species 333
Khan, Badrul 46, 55
Khan Academy 231
knowledge, skills, and abilities (KSAs) 134
knowledge management (KM) site 22
Kodak Corporation 44
Koller, Daphne 280

Lamar University 217, 219–20, 222
leadership imperative for higher education: characteristics of 351–3, 352*f*; e-learning revolution 348–9, 348*f*; implementation

challenges 350–1; introduction 343–4; proposed road map for 353–5, 354*f*; transformational thinking needed 344–7, 347*t*
leadership in online education *see* distance education
learner attributes 182
learner-centered strategies 82, 121, 238, 338
learner–content interaction 219, 296, 299, 301–3
learner–designer interaction 296, 297–8, 301
learner–environment interaction 296, 297, 301, 302
learner–expert interaction 297, 302
learner–instructor interaction 27, 219–20, 296, 299, 301
learner–interface interaction 220–1, 296, 298, 299, 301–2
learner–learner interaction 220, 296–7, 299, 301–3
learner–network interaction 297
learner of previous situations 159*f*
learner–self interaction 296, 297, 301, 302, 303
learner–tools interaction 298, 301–2
learner to others interaction 297
learning activities in online course creation 188–93, 190*t*–193*t*
learning by doing *vs.* teacher presenting instruction 82
learning design process 280–2, 281*f*
learning disabilities 269, 272
learning ecologies: conclusions 339; digital ecosystems and 332–4; doctoral e-researchers 337–9; e-learning approaches 334–6; emergence of 336–7; introduction 331–2
learning-focused *vs.* sorting-focused instruction 82
learning guidance 161, 161*f*
Learning Management Systems (LCMSs): collaborative design models for courses 208–9; course accessibility 22; e-learning evaluation and 284; interaction types 301; introduction 18; learner to content interaction 219
learning materials 21–2
learning objectives: achievement of 195, 232; assessments 237, 328; evaluation and 285; formulation of 182–3, 184; introduction 16–17, 157*f*; learner analysis of 303, 305; as measurable 235, 244; media support for 228, 231, 232; in m-learning 327; mobile platforms and 136; teacher effectiveness and 95
Learning Opportunities Task Force 260
Learning & Teaching Centre (LTC) 146, 148
learning times in m-Learning 315
libre, defined 66
lifelong learning 314, 320, 345
linear interactivity 298
literacy skills 75, 213
literature search 128, 129, 135, 337
location-based learning 314, 320
lone rangers in e-learning 140
low interactivity 187
Luckin, Rose 335

Mace, Ron 259
MADLat 71
Maintenance of Certification (MOC) 287–9
maintenance of learning environment 18
marketing of learning environment 18
Masie, Elliot 52
massive, defined 65–6
Massive Open Online Course (MOOC): current enthusiasm for 280; defined 65–8; education and training market 19; emergence of 139, 349; formative evaluation of 285–7, 286*f*, 287*f*; framework applicable to 37–8, 37*f*; instructional strategies with 253; introduction 2; leadership and 363; measuring success of 73–6; motivational strategies for e-learners 247; overview 59, 65; production grants for 377; purpose of 68–70; success factors 70–3; as web-based learning 46
materials in interviews 129
Mayer, Richard E. 279–80
media selection analysis 16
mediation work 249, 313, 335
MERLOT project 74
Merrill, M. David 279
metacognitive cluster competence 201–4, 202*t*, 203*f*, 204*f*
metacognitive scaffolding 122
Mexican higher education institutions 181–2
Microsoft 54
Midlands Consortium 44
mid-term adoption horizon 61
Mind Extension University 42
m-learning objects (MLO) 326
Mobile Learning (m-Learning): conclusions 315–16; connectivity 315; context of 314; criteria for 313; defined 309–10, 320; e-learning *vs.* 310–12, 311*f*, 312*t*; essence of 314; introduction 2; learning times 315; in literature review 131; personalization 315; theory of 309–16, 311*f*, 312*t*
Mobile Learning (m-Learning), materials and assessments: applications and websites 322–3; conclusion 327–8; four device form factors 320–2, 321*t*; framework for 323–7, 324*t*, 325*f*; overview 319–23, 321*t*
mobile learning delivery satisfaction (MLDS) 325–6
MoLoNET 320
monitoring and impact management for e-learning 355
MOOC *see* Massive Open Online Course

Moore, Michael G. 45, 47
Moore's transactional distance theory 217
motivational strategies for e-learners: conclusions 255; institutional factors 250–2; instructional factors 252–5; introduction 247; student retention factors 248–50
MPEG audio and video compression 55
multimedia integration in online courses 186–8, 187*t*, 188*t*
multimedia presentations 159, 233, 234, 237, 320
multimedia usage strategies 127
Multi-Object Oriented MUDs (MOOs) 47
multitasking 171–2
Multi-Users Domains (MUDs) 47

narrated animations 231
National Aeronautics and Space Administration (NASA) 47
National Broadcasting Company (NBC) 41
National Center for Education Statistics 56
National Education Association 44
National Technological University (NTU) 43–4
National University Telecommunications Network (NUTN) 43
navigationalism 314, 320
near-term adoption horizon 60–1
Net Generation 171–2
networked collaborative environments (NCVEs) 381
New Media Consortium (NMC) Horizon Report 59–62, 60*t*
newsgroups 6
New York Institute of Technology 46
New York Times 59
New York University 46
Nomadic Learning, Remote Learning 2
nonimmersive contextual interactivity 298
note-taking apps 283
Nova Southeastern University 42
NTT Software Corporation 47

object interactivity 298
objectives in instructional events 156–7
Offsite Learning 2
Ohio School of the Air 41
Oklahoma State University 43
Oklahoma Telecommunications Network 44
online, defined 67
online activities in course materials 234–5
online collaborative learning: assessment strategies 122–3; challenges to 116–17; cognitive load in 117–18, 119–20, 120*f*; conclusions 123; design strategies 120–1; facilitation strategies 121–2; introduction 115–16; metacognitive scaffolding 122; mobile learning and 320, 350; poor instruction design 119; self-efficacy 118–19; stress/stressors in 118, 119; technology skills, lack 119; *see also* distance education
online course creation: assessment integration 193–5; instructional design 182–5; instructional narrative 185–6, 185*t*; introduction 181–2; learner attributes 182; learning activities 188–93, 190*t*–193*t*; learning objectives 184; learning tasks 183; multimedia integration 186–8, 187*t*, 188*t*; pilot and evaluation 195; procedural information 183; revision of 195; supportive information 183–4; terminal performance outcomes 183; thematic clusters 184–5
online discussion boards 212–14
Online Learning Design 280
Online Teamwork Satisfaction Scale 220
onscreen reading rates/recall 248
open, defined 66–7
openness, defined 73, 76
open philosophy of education 1, 3
operating system (OS) 322
operational cluster competence 199, 200*t*
organisational readiness for e-learning 354–5
Organization for Economic Cooperation and Development (OECD) 139
Ormitson, Meg 208, 211

Paine, Robert 333
Pan-Pacific Education and Communications Experiments by Satellite (PEACESAT) 43
Park University 253
participation competencies 177
passionate learner characteristic 352
pedagogical development: background information 94–104; conclusions 111; context importance 100–1; defining leadership 98–9; discussion over 108–10; distributed leadership 99–100; educational context of leadership 102–4; educational leadership theory 97; faculty role and 94–7, 107–8; faculty views 104–8; future research 110–11; institutional contraints 104–5; introduction 93–4; leadership strategies 97
peer assessments (PAs) 194
peer-mediated learning 215
peer-to-peer (P2) individual assessment 302
peer-to-peer (P2) Internet file sharing 57
Pennarama Network 42
Pennsylvania State University 42, 43, 45, 48, 54
people oriented characteristic 353
People-Process-Product Continuum 11–15, 11*f*, 12*t*–14*t*, 15*f*, 21*f*
performance-based assessment (PBA) 194, 284
personalization in m-Learning 315
Personalized Integrated Educational System (PIES) 89

Personal Learning Environments (PLEs) 177, 336
Pittinsky, Matthew 54
planning stage in e-learning 17, 20, 30*t*–31*t*, 140
PLATO (Programmed Logic for Automated Teaching Operations) 53
positive engagement 344
postindustrial paradigm of instruction 82–3, 85–6; core ideas 82–3; key roles 86–9; task and industrial spaces 85; team and individual assessment 85–6; vision of 85–6
The Power of E-Learning: The Essential Guide for Teaching in the Digital Age (Waterhouse) 279
PowerPoint 6, 173, 228, 377
practice in instructional events 162–3, 162*f*
Prewitt, Vana 98
prior knowledge in instructional events 157–8, 157*f*, 158*f*
Proactive Design for Learning 264
problem-based learning 57, 81, 83, 314, 320, 380
procedural information 182, 183
project plan 20
project support site (PSS) 22
Province of New Brunswick (TeleEducation NB) 54
Provisional Guidelines 133–6
psychomotor objectives in online learning 184
Public Service Satellite Consortium 44
public sphere in education 215

Quality Assurance Criteria items (QACs) 28
Quality Matters (QM) Rubric 218, 219, 222
Quality Scorecard for the Administration of Online Programs 218
Quantum Computer Service 47

rater reliability 129
rationale for e-learning 144
RCA Educational Hour 41
real world-like working environments 116
record keeping for student learning 87–8
reflection and dialogue strategies 121–2
reflective interactivity 298
Regents College of New York 43
registration time requirements 250
relational cluster competence 200, 201*t*
Research in Motion Blackberry 322
resilience concept 335, 337
results driven characteristic 353
results of interviews 129, 130*f*
retention and transfer in instructional events 167–8
return-on-investment (ROI) 5, 18, 284
review in instructional events 164–5, 165*f*
revised course materials 22
role change, defined 96
Role of the Online Learner: competencies in 199–204, 200*t*, 201*t*, 202*t*, 203*f*, 204*f*; conclusions 205–6; introduction 197; overview 197–8, 199*f*; putting to use 204–5
Role Theory principle 197
RSS software 57, 177
rubrics use 194–5

Satellite Communications for Learning consortium 44
satellite programs in K-12 schools 44–5
scaffolding: application of 119, 157, 335; collaboration and 116; evaluation of 264; learning to develop 87, 380; metacognitive scaffolding 118, 122; in m-learning 326; process of 183–4
school-based education 333
Seale, Jane 261
self-assessment (SA) 194, 220, 254, 274
self-discipline skills 248, 249
self-efficacy 118–19
self-motivation skills 87, 249
self-organized inquiry 116
service quality (SERVQUAL) 324–8
Siemens, George 66, 69
silent experts 336
simulation interactivity 131, 298
Simulations and the Future of Learning: An Innovative (and Perhaps Revolutionary) Approach to E-Learning (Aldrich) 279
situated learning 314, 320, 380
Sloan Consortium (SLOAN-C) Quality Online Framework 218, 221
social media: assessment with 212; benefits 122; doctoral students 332, 337, 338; e-learning and 58, 208, 210, 304; group work and 209; instruction and 19, 102; learner to content 219; learner to others 297; peer interaction 220; pervasiveness of 335
social presence 119, 122, 336–8
sociocultural theory 314, 320
Stack Overflow 70
Starfish system 252
Star Schools Program Assistance Act 44–5
State University of New York (SUNY) 249–50
strategic alliances in learning 346
Strategic Challenges (SC) 345–6
strategic themes for e-learning 145
Strategy Steering Committee 149
structuring strategy 183
student-centered e-learning activities 303–5, 304*f*
students/student learning: assessment for 88–9; instruction for 88; new roles for 87; performance considerations 193; planning for 88; record keeping for 87–8; retention factors 248–50

subcategorisation of e-learning 350
subject matter experts (SMEs) 12, 15–16, 129, 135, 182
support interactivity 298
supportive information 183–4
SurveyMonkey 234
sustainability stage of e-learning 140
Svato, Jan 265
synchronous communication features of e-learning 6
Syracuse University 43, 263
system quality (SQ) 319, 323–8

talent management 19
task analysis 16
task-based instruction (TBI) 80, 82, 83–4
task-centered principle 80–1, 89
task structure/difficulty strategies 120–1
Taylor, Janis 3
teacher–content interaction 298
teacher-marked assessments (TMAs) 194
teachers/teaching: faculty views on pedagogical development 104–8; instructional support and training 251; interventions 175*t*–176*t*; motivational factors from 252–5; new roles for 86–7; online teaching 96; *see also* competencies; pedagogical development
Teachers Toolbox 54
teacher–teacher interaction 298
Teaching Media Literacy 210
team assessment 85–6
teamwork and group-based goals 344–5
technical factors in learning 250
technical infrastructure of administration 251
technology: audio technologies 43; emerging technology 93; new roles for 87–8; online collaborative learning 119; *see also* emerging e-learning technologies; information and communication technologies
technology-based institutions 42–3
technology-mediated learning practices 335
TED Talks 57
teleconferencing methods 41, 44, 53
Temple University 46
terminal performance outcomes 183, 189
thematic clusters 184–5
Thomas Edison College 43, 45
3D animations 292
time availability for courses 248
time-management skills 204, 221, 249
Tomlinson, Ray 55–6
tool-mediated activity 314
traditional instruction/learning 4, 312, 312*t*
transformational leadership 346–7
two-way video conferencing 45

UCL-CIBER Group 172
UK Open University 42, 45, 48, 118
United Nations Convention on the Rights of Persons with Disabilities (UNCRPD) 270, 274
Universal Design for Learning (UDL) 259–63, 260*f*, 271, 272–3
universal methods of instruction 80
University of Alaska 43
University of British Columbia 54
University of Hawaii 43
University of Iowa 264–5
University of Kentucky 42
University of Maryland University College 48
University of Mid-America (UMA) 43
University of Oldenburg in Germany 48
University of Phoenix Online 46
University of the Future 346
University of Wisconsin 42, 43, 45, 53
update interactivity 298
U.S. Chamber of Commerce 44
U.S. Department of Education 61, 207
U.S. Department of Justice 270–1

variability in instruction 155
verification in instructional events 163
Vest, Charles 71
vicarious interaction 297
video clips in course materials 232–3
video conferencing 45, 56, 215
videogames 131
virtual classrooms 131–2, 173
Virtual European School Project 47
virtual reality (VR) 47
Virtual Reality Multi-User Dungeon (VRMUD) 47
Virtual Temple 46
Virtual University 46
virtual worlds: e-learning and 353; guidelines 127, 129, 131, 133, 135–7; interactivity 62, 298; origin 58; popularity 57
VISCAL *see* face-to-face (f2f) course materials guide
visionary characteristic 351–2
vision for e-learning 144, 148
Voice Over Internet Protocol (VoIP) 57

Waterhouse, Shirley 279–80
Web 2.0: assessment practices with 335; in classroom 208, 209, 215, 222; collaboration competencies 177; distributing potential of 332; with doctoral studies 339; infographics creation 211; nature of 336; peer-to-peer communication 172; usable literacies in 212
Web Accessibility Content Guidelines (WCAG) 261, 270

Web Accessibility Initiative (WAI) 261
web-based education 46–7, 379
Web-Based Instruction (WBI) 2, 51
Web-Based Learning (WBL) 2, 53
Web-Based Training (WBT) 2
web conferencing 56–8, 220, 237–8
Web Course Tools (WebCT) 54
Web 2.0 tools 211, 332
Wedemeyer, Charles 42, 47
Western Governors University 46
What Works series 137
Wi-Fi (Wireless Fidelity) 57
wiki options 209–10, 290, 292*f*
Windows Mobile OS 322
worked examples strategies 121
working memory 117, 158–9, 186–8
World Bank 22, 377
World Health Organization (WHO) 270
World Wide Web Consortium (W3C) 270

Xerox Alto computer 53–4

YouTube 57, 173

zone of proximal development 313